ASIAN AMERICAN PSYCHOLOGY:

CURRENT PERSPECTIVES

ASIAN AMERICAN PSYCHOLOGY:

CURRENT PERSPECTIVES

EDITED BY

NITA TEWARI & ALVIN N. ALVAREZ

Ψ Psychology Press
Taylor & Francis Group

New York   London

Psychology Press
Taylor & Francis Group
711 Third Avenue
New York, NY 10016

Psychology Press
Taylor & Francis Group
27 Church Road, Hove,
East Sussex, BN32FA

© 2009 by Taylor & Francis Group, LLC
Psychology Press is an imprint of Taylor & Francis Group, an Informa business

International Standard Book Number-13: 978-0-8058-6008-5 (Softcover)

Library of Congress Cataloging-in-Publication Data

Tewari, Nita.
   Asian American psychology : current perspectives / Nita Tewari, Alvin Alvarez.
       p. cm.
   Includes bibliographical references.
   ISBN 978-1-84169-769-7 -- ISBN 978-0-8058-6008-5
     1. Asian Americans--Psychology. 2. Asian Americans--Race identity. 3. Asian Americans--Ethnic identity. 4. Asian Americans--Social conditions. 5. United States--Race relations--Psychological aspects. 6. United States--Ethnic relations--Psychological aspects. I. Alvarez, Alvin. II. Title.

E184.A75T49 2009
155.8′495073--dc22   2008008170

Visit the Taylor & Francis Web site at
http://www.taylorandfrancis.com

and the LEA and Routledge Web site at
http://www.routledge.com

We dedicate this book, *Asian American Psychology: Current Perspectives*, to our Asian American ancestors, parents, families, and mentors who have forged the roads and paths we have traveled as Asian American individuals. As the first book of its kind, this book is dedicated to those of Asian American heritage. Our roads have been forged by the cultural experiences of our past, the present, and soon, our future. The current generation must now create new roads to build upon the future of Asian American psychology.

Contents

Foreword

Asian Americans have had a history in the United States that spans over 200 years. Yet it is amazing and unfortunate that public knowledge and perceptions of Asian Americans have been confined to stereotypes and superficial images. A national survey and focus group interviews sponsored by the Committee of 100 (2001) have revealed limited and often inaccurate impressions of Asian Americans.

What can be done to educate others about Asian Americans? In recent years, there have been public broadcasts and other media programs that help audiences to gain more realistic knowledge of Asian Americans, and with the rapidly growing population of Asian Americans, people have a greater opportunity to work and socialize with members of this minority group. Because higher education generates and transmits knowledge through research and teaching, our colleges and universities should play a vital role in helping others acquire knowledge of Asian Americans. Such knowledge is essential because we live and interact in a multicultural world that involves different societies and diverse groups within societies.

University courses on Asian Americans have had a 40-or-so-year history. The courses have typically focused on Asian American history, literature, gender, political activism, and law. It is only relatively recently that attention has been paid to psychological issues and approaches that involve Asian Americans. Psychologically-oriented Asian American courses, taught in ethnic studies programs or psychology departments, have grown throughout the United States. They have been extremely popular among students, perhaps because students can apply much of the contents (e.g., race relations, stereotypes, identity, etc.) to their own lives. Having regularly taught such courses at the University of California, Davis, UCLA, and the University of Washington, I see that student enrollments are high. At Davis, up to 600 students each year enroll in our Asian American psychology courses.

Some important Asian American books have been written or edited. However, these books have been more technical, narrowly focused on particular psychological issues (e.g., mental health), or have failed to utilize textbook features for undergraduate and graduate level students. What is needed is a textbook on Asian American issues that has depth and breadth and that can appeal to students. The field now has such a book.

In many ways, *Asian American Psychology: Current Perspectives*, edited by Nita Tewari and Alvin Alvarez, is a milestone. This book is about who Asian Americans are. What are the differences among different Asian American groups? How do Asian Americans develop identities as bicultural Americans? What are the physical and mental health problems encountered by Asian Americans? Are stereotypes valid, and what effects do they have? What kinds of strengths exist in Asian American families? Are Asian Americans overachievers in education? What are gender issues faced by Asian American men and women? What factors are involved in interracial dating? These are but a few of the questions addressed in the book. No single or simple answer is given to these questions despite the fact that public stereotypes convey simple and overgeneralized images of who Asian Americans are. The complexities are reflected in the diverse topics covered, such as the analysis of different Asian Americans groups (e.g., South Asians, Filipinos, etc.), family and culture, identity, religion, acculturation, career, physical health, policy formulations, multiracial individuals, mental health, gender, gays/lesbians, acculturation, research methods to study Asian Americans, etc. Several of the chapter contributors are counseling and clinical experts who address the questions of why Asian Americans tend to underutilize mental health services, how services can be made more culturally competent, and what kind of benefits can come from counseling. The depth in the analysis of issues has not been sacrificed for the breadth of topics. The chapters are written by some of the most distinguished Asian American scholars, young and old, in the nation. After reading the book, one cannot help but regard this book as a multifaceted eye-opener of the psychological experiences of Asian Americans.

Although grounded in psychological experiences, the book is interdisciplinary and multi-disciplinary. That is, to understand Asian Americans, one must appreciate the context of Asian American experiences that cut across disciplinary orientations. Many of the contributors to the book include historical, political, anthropological, and postmodern perspectives. Furthermore, the book can easily serve as a major textbook in Asian American studies or psychology. Although chapters are written by different authors, they follow a similar format that is intended to stimulate thinking among students. Case examples, discussion questions, definitions of key terms, and suggested readings and sources are included in each chapter. The book can be assigned to undergraduate students, but the ideas and original insights about who Asian Americans are make this book appealing to graduate students, professionals, and the general public.

I know it is unusual for a chapter coauthor to write the Foreword to an edited book. However, being among the first to teach Asian American psychology courses (starting in 1972), I am in the position to see the changes in knowledge, student interests, number of courses taught, enrollments in these courses, and, most importantly, the textbooks that are available. *Asian American Psychology: Current Perspectives* is a major and unparalleled contribution to the field and to the education of students.

Stanley Sue
July 2007

Reference

Committee of 100 (2001). *American attitudes toward Chinese Americans and Asian Americans. Report of the Committee of 100*. New York: Committee of 100.

Preface

With this book, we come full circle. As undergraduates at the University of California at Irvine, we sat in our respective Asian American psychology and African American psychology courses and found courses that awakened us to ourselves and eventually to our profession. More than a class, our ethnic psychology courses were experiences that resonated with us, not just as students, but as individuals, as Asian Americans, as people of color, as members of larger racial, ethnic, and cultural communities. These courses spoke to what our families had experienced as immigrants and racial and ethnic minorities living in the United States. Here was a history with faces that looked like us. Here were films that had people who sounded like our aunts and uncles. Here were theories that actually wrestled with what happened to us at home, at school, at our temples and churches, in our student organizations. Here was a course that spoke to *us* and was about *us*! In retrospect, these courses were the catalysts that led to fulfilling careers that encouraged us to integrate our personal and professional selves. So, the crafting of this book brings us full circle. As we join with all of our contributors, we offer this book as a way of giving back to our communities, our mentors, and, most importantly, as an invitation—an invitation to a discipline and an invitation to look in the mirror to see yourselves, your families, your friends, as well as your students and future clients within these pages!

This book has been a culmination of many years of teaching Asian American psychology across the country by graduate students and professors alike. Each year at institutions across the United States the course is taught in psychology departments, Asian American studies programs, ethnic studies departments, social sciences programs, and many other programs and departments. Every time the course is taught, the instructor thinks about "What articles should I include? What materials should I use? How should I teach this broad area of psychology?" Most of the time our colleagues and friends dive into their literature searches, compile readings, create mountainous course packets, and use a variety of supplemental materials such as narrative books, handbooks, videos, media articles, clinical case studies, and so on. Although the creativity needed to prepare for such courses can be exciting and fulfilling, the process always led to the inevitable question, and perhaps frustration, of *"What book do I use this time?"*

In the absence of similar texts, it is our hope that *Asian American Psychology: Current Perspectives* provides an answer to this question. Most books on Asian American psychology are primarily targeted at graduate students, scholars, and practitioners with the intent of providing a theoretical and empirical overview of the field of Asian American psychology. As a result, the current literature may be inaccessible and/or irrelevant to undergraduate students and those with minimal exposure to Asian American psychology. In our experience of teaching such courses, a primary strength of the course is the ability to relate the theoretical and empirical literature to a student's personal development as an Asian American. Unlike other psychology courses, issues explored in Asian American psychology courses are often personally meaningful and transformative rather than intellectual abstractions. Thus, one of the book's key objectives is to bridge the gap between scholarship (theoretical and empirical work) and personal development. To achieve this objective and to engage readers, all chapters in the book include activities, discussion questions, practice exercises, clinical case studies, and resources for continued learning through the Internet, literature, film, and community agencies. Hence, the chapters invite you to move beyond the retention of concept and theories—they invite readers to make the abstract come to life and to see how these ideas and concepts relate to their everyday lives. Moreover, the foundation of the text includes current perspectives and key findings from the psychological literature on Asian Americans in addition to content from Asian American studies and related disciplines (history, literature, film, popular media, etc.). It is our belief that psychology is only a single lens through which to view Asian Americans' experiences and that the inclusion of additional disciplines adds both nuance and complexity to our understanding. Last, contributors to the text consist of leading experts, practitioners, and emerging scholars in their respective areas—most of whom have also taught Asian American psychology. Hence, the book draws upon our contributors' expertise as scholars, practitioners, and teachers. In short, we hoped to create a book that brought together the key scholars of Asian American psychology to present their areas of expertise while challenging readers to apply and reflect upon its personal relevance.

To achieve these goals, the book consists of 30 chapters divided into 6 parts. In crafting a book of such a scope, it was our hope to provide instructors with the flexibility to create syllabi that reflect their creativity and expertise. Although there are clear overlaps in some of the chapters, each chapter is self-contained, thereby allowing instructors to pick and choose the topics that they regard as most salient to their audience. The book begins with "Part I: Foundation and Roots of Asian American Psychology," as our authors address the cornerstones of the discipline. In Chapter 1, the section begins with Liu, Murakami, Eap, and Hall's concise overview of the history of Asian Americans in the United States with the intent of situating our communities within a clear historical and sociopolitical context. This overview is followed in Chapter 2 by Leong and Gupta's historical account of the emergence of Asian American psychology as a discipline that was an extension of the social and cultural press brought upon by the Civil Rights movement. The section segues into Chapter 3 and Saw and Okazaki's overview of the research foundations and scientific methods that serve as the basis of the literature on Asian American psychology. In Chapter 4, Lee, Wong, and Alvarez provide a sociohistorical overview and critique of the model minority stereotype—a perception of our communities that is infused into our collective psychological experience. Last, the section concludes with Chapter 5 and Uba's invitation to a postmodernist psychology and a call for a willingness to critique and recognize the existing limitations of Asian American psychology's paradigms.

In "Part II: Balancing Multiple Worlds," our authors address a key aspect of Asian Americans' psychological experience—the negotiation of the various cultural worlds to which one is exposed and its implications for one's psychological well-being. As one of the older theoretical perspectives on Asian Americans' experiences, Chapter 6 opens with Kim's examination of the literature on acculturation and enculturation as it relates to Asian Americans' cultural adaptation to life in the United States. The section then segues into Chapter 7 and Chang and Kwan's investigation of racial and ethnic identity theories to address the developmental process by which individuals identify themselves as members of their respective ethnic groups (e.g., Chinese, Sri Lankan, Thai), as well as the larger racial group (e.g., Asian American). Ano, Mathew, and Fukuyama's Chapter 8 follows with an examination of the nature, prevalence, and implications of spirituality and religion on Asian Americans' daily lives. In Chapter 9, Nadal explores the transgenerational impact of colonialism and how historical and political events in our countries of origin may still have psychological resonance. Last, in Chapter 10, the section concludes with Chen's examination of how Asian Americans integrate and negotiate the multiple aspects of their identity.

The authors in "Part III: Gender and Intimate Relationships" examine the psychological experiences of Asian Americans through the lens of gender and its influence on ourselves as well as our relationships. In Chapter 11, Hall opens the section with a brief history of Asian American women that serves as the context for understanding the impact of gender roles, stereotypes, and the double oppression of racism and sexism that confronts Asian American women. To complement the prior chapter, Iwamoto and Liu explore Asian American masculinity in Chapter 12 and propose that men's identities are shaped by the convergence of gender, race, racism, and sexuality. In Chapter 13, Chung and Singh provide an overview of Asian American lesbian, gay, bisexual, and transgender communities and situate LGBT communities within both Asia and America while also addressing the influence of oppression, religion, and dual identity development. As a central aspect of relationships, Chen and Cho Kim address the role of sexuality in Chapter 14 and its multiple facets from sexual identity to sexual practices to sexual assault. Ahluwalia, Suzuki, and Mir explore the dating, partnering, and marriage practices of Asian Americans in Chapter 15 with particular attention to the historical context and contemporary stressors that influence our relationships. The section concludes as Yee, Su, Kim, and Yancura's Chapter 16 examines the heterogeneity of Asian American families and the developmental challenges they face throughout their lives.

"Part IV: Next Generation" acknowledges the rapid evolution of Asian America and explores emerging experiences and communities that are drawing the attention of Asian American psychologists. In Chapter 17, Hayashino and Chopra survey the broad range of issues and challenges that Asian American parents face in raising children in America—from cultural values to role reversals to racism. Relatedly, as our notions of Asian American families evolve, Lee and Miller's overview of Asian American adoptees in Chapter 18 provides readers with a timely introduction to a sociopolitical history of international adoption and the various factors that contribute to the psychological well-being of adoptees as they negotiate the various communities in which they may be immersed. Similarly, Tsong and Liu's Chapter 19 explores how current patterns of immigration have led to the emergence of parachute kids and astronaut families and introduces readers to the implications of these new family patterns on socioemotional development and parent-child relationships. Last, in Chapter 20, Suyemoto and Tawa challenge the monoracial focus of Asian American psychology and provide an overview of the experiences of multiracial Asian Americans with a particular focus on the multidimensional nature of racial and ethnic identities and their implications for mental health.

"Part V: Social and Life Issues" consists of chapters that address salient life experiences that shape the psychological well-being of Asian Americans. The section begins with Chapter 21 as Alvarez introduces readers to psychological perspectives on racism and the research on the prevalence of racism, its consequences, and how Asian Americans cope with discrimination. As a specific example of racism, the section turns to Chapter 22 and Aoki and Mio's exploration of how Asian Americans have been misrepresented in the media through both historical and contemporary stereotypes. In Chapter 23, Wong, Kinzie, and Kinzie focus their attention on the trauma, stressors, and psychological impact that resulted from the upheaval and resettlement of Southeast Asian refugees. The section then shifts to Lowe's examination in Chapter 24 of the social and cultural factors that influence how Asian Americans negotiate the path of developing their academic and career paths. Last, the section concludes with Chapter 25 as Chen and Philip invite readers to consider activism and advocacy as avenues for addressing social, educational, and political concerns at a systemic level.

The text concludes with "Part VI: Health and Well-Being" as our authors examine various aspects of physical and psychological well-being and their implications for our health. The section begins as Ladhani and Lee contend in Chapter 26 that physical and psychological well-being are fundamentally interrelated as they provide an overview of the major medical concerns facing Asian Americans. To complement this chapter, Meyer, Dhindsa, Gabriel, and Sue survey the mental health status of Asian Americans in Chapter 27 and address the cultural issues, protective factors, and prevalence of psychological disorders. As an intersection of both the physical and psychological, Kawamura and Rice's Chapter 28 addresses body image dissatisfaction, the factors that contribute to dissatisfaction, and strategies for promoting a healthy body image. The section then segues into treatment and healing as Yeh and Kwong expose readers in Chapter 29 to indigenous healing practices and indigenous healers and culture-bound syndromes, as well as the fundamental cultural assumptions around healing. The textbook concludes with Chapter 30 as Tewari demystifies the process of counseling and psychotherapy and introduces readers to the range of mental health providers and the foundations of culturally competent mental health services.

As we review the scope of this book, we have been humbled by this experience. For despite its breadth and scope, a great deal remains unwritten in these pages. To capture the experience of being Asian American, psychology offers but a single lens. To add depth and complexity to one's understanding of our communities, we invite our readers to explore other disciplines such as history, literature, and sociology. Indeed, even within our own discipline, we believe that this text is merely an introduction to the field of Asian American psychology—a lengthy and thorough introduction but an introduction nonetheless. So, it is our hope that this experience has been a catalyst and an invitation to continue exploring the depth of what Asian American psychology has to offer—in journals, in books, in dissertations, and yes, perhaps even in a career.

Nita Tewari
Alvin N. Alvarez

Acknowledgments

We would like to first thank our mentors collectively—Drs. Joe White, Janet Helms, Gene Awakuni, Mary Ann Takemoto, and Thomas Parham. Each of you has inspired us, opened doors for us, and shown us the way to find our passions in life and in psychology.

Second, we would like to thank our students, who have been our best teachers; and our colleagues, whose principles, integrity, and friendship have served as guides to navigate professional waters. To our friends, each of you has played an invaluable role in sustaining our personal and professional growth and development—you all know who you are in our lives.

Third, and perhaps most important, we would like to thank our spouses Debu Tewari and Grace Chen, and our children, Jaya and Sanjay Tewari, for their endless patience and love in the hours spent toward the completion of this book. Without their support, humor, and wisdom, this book would not have been possible.

We would also like to give special thanks to our editors Lori Handelman and Rebecca Larsen at Lawrence Erlbaum Associates (LEA) who began this book journey with us. During our book journey, Taylor & Francis acquired LEA, and a new editorial team began working with us. Therefore, we would also like to acknowledge their time and efforts in working on *Asian American Psychology: Current Perspectives*.

Last, but not least, we would like to thank our parents, Vishwanath and Shashi Tiwari, and Rizalina and Telesforo Alvarez, and in-laws Drs. Krishna and Sujata Tewari for being the foundation of who we are and for teaching us what it means to be Asian American.

Nita Tewari
Alvin N. Alvarez

Editors

Nita Tewari is a second-generation Indian American whose parents emigrated from India about 40 years ago. She was born in Los Angeles County, and was raised and resides in Orange County, California. She completed her bachelor's in psychology from the University of California, Irvine, (UCI), and her doctoral internship at the University of California, Los Angeles Student Psychological Services. She earned her master's in psychology and doctorate in counseling psychology from Southern Illinois University at Carbondale. She has served in the positions of research psychologist at California State University, Long Beach, clinical researcher at UCI's department of psychiatry and human behavior, and staff psychologist in the UCI counseling center and adjunct faculty in the School of Social Sciences and Asian American Studies at UCI. She has taught Asian American Psychology at UCI,

has provided clinical services to university students, and has published in multicultural psychology on Indian/South Asian American and Asian American mental health. In 2002, she cofounded the South Asian Psychological Networking Association (SAPNA), a Listserv and Web site dedicated to connecting individuals interested in South Asian American mental health concerns. Dr. Tewari has also served as the past cochair of the Division on Women for the Asian American Psychological Association and served as a writer for *Audrey Magazine*. Dr. Tewari will be serving as the next vice president of the Asian American Psychological Association for the 2008–2009 term and continues to focus on Asian American mental health issues while being married and raising her two children.

Alvin N. Alvarez immigrated to the United States from Cebu, Philippines, when he was 5 years old, and was raised in Long Beach, California. He completed his undergraduate degree at the University of California, Irvine (UCI) in biological sciences and psychology. An Asian American psychology course sparked his passion in Asian American issues, so he dropped his plans for medical school and earned his doctorate in counseling psychology from the University of Maryland at College Park. Currently, he is a professor and coordinator of the College Counseling Program at San Francisco State University, where he trains master's-level students to be college counselors and student affairs practitioners. His personal and professional interests focus on Asian Americans, racial identity, and the psychological impact of racism. Dr. Alvarez is currently conducting community-based studies funded by the National Institute of Mental Health to examine how Chinese Americans, Filipino Americans, and Vietnamese Americans perceive and cope with racism. In the long term, Dr. Alvarez aims to develop community-based interventions to help Asian Americans cope with racism in constructive ways. Dr. Alvarez served as the president of the Asian American Psychological Association and has been involved in national-level projects and initiatives, advocating for all oppressed groups. He received the Early Career Award for Distinguished Contributions from the Asian American Psychological Association and the Tanaka Memorial Dissertation Award from the American Psychological Association. Consistent with his belief that psychologists serve the communities they came from, Dr. Alvarez is currently a member of the board of directors of the community mental health center, Richmond Area Multi-Services (RAMS) in San Francisco.

Authors

Muninder K. Ahluwalia is an associate professor in the department of counseling, human development and educational leadership at Montclair State University. Dr. Ahluwalia received her PhD in counseling psychology from New York University in 2002. Her research interests are in the area of multicultural counseling, including intersecting identities, assessment, counseling training, and qualitative research methods. Dr. Ahluwalia serves on committees for the American Psychological Association and is on the board of the Asian American Psychological Association.

Gene G. Ano earned his PhD in clinical psychology from Bowling Green State University, Ohio, in 2005. He currently works as a professor in the psychology department at Mount San Antonio College in Walnut, California. Dr. Ano has received numerous accolades, is a member of several professional organizations, and has published various book chapters and empirical research articles in peer-reviewed journals, such as the *Journal of Clinical Psychology, Southern Medical Journal,* and *Journal of Psychology and Christianity,* to name a few. Dr. Ano's clinical and research interests include multicultural competence, couple's counseling, spiritually integrated therapy, Asian American psychology, religious coping, and spiritual struggles.

Guy Aoki was born and raised in Hilo, Hawaii, and attended Occidental College in Los Angeles and the University of Hawaii at Manoa, graduating from Occidental as a psychology major in 1985. He worked as a *Los Angeles Times* reporter, researcher, and mixing producer for Casey Kasem's "American Top 40," and wrote various syndicated radio shows including "Countdown America with Dick Clark" (named "Best Adult Contemporary Radio Show" by *Billboard Magazine* in 1991) and "Dick Clark's U.S. Music Survey." In 1992, he cofounded Media Action Network for Asian Americans (MANAA). The all-volunteer, nonprofit organization is the only group solely dedicated to monitoring the mass media and advocating balanced, sensitive, and positive depiction and coverage of Asian Americans. During Aoki's presidency, MANAA received awards from the L.A. Mayor's Asian Pacific American Heritage Committee, Asian Pacific American Women's Network, and Chinese American Civil Rights Organization. Since 1999, Aoki, along with organizations like the NAACP, has been involved in meetings with the top four television networks to add more people of color to their writing, producing, directing, and acting ranks. And in 2001, Aoki confronted comedian Sarah Silverman on "Politically Incorrect with Bill Maher" after she used a racial slur against Chinese people on "Late Night with Conan O'Brien."

Tai Chang received his PhD in clinical/community psychology from the University of Illinois, Urbana–Champaign, in 1999. He is an associate professor at the California School of Professional Psychology at Alliant International University. His research examines Asian American identity and acculturation, particularly as they relate to adjustment and mental health services utilization and help-seeking. His other interests involve the interface of counseling and the Internet, including online support, mutual help, and self-help.

Grace A. Chen is a licensed psychologist in California and is on staff at Counseling and Psychological Services at California State University, East Bay. She received her doctoral degree in counseling psychology at the University of Texas at Austin in 2005. Dr. Chen's scholarly interests include racial identity of Asian Americans, intersections of multiple social identities, and multicultural issues. Her clinical interests include identity development, stress and coping, interpersonal relationships, acculturation, and multicultural issues (especially regarding international students and students of color). Dr. Chen served as a directorate member (2006–2008) of the Commission for Counseling and Psychological Services, a division of ACPA College Student Educators International.

Karen Y. Chen is currently serving as an AAAS (American Association for the Advancement of Science) Science and Technology Policy Fellow within the Strategic Planning and External Affairs Office (SEA) of the Bureau of Democracy, Human Rights, and Labor (DRL), U.S. Department of State. She supports the SEA director on the bureau's performance planning activities, including developing and updating the Bureau Strategic Plan, Congressional Budget Justification, and other planning and performance documents for OMB and the director of Foreign Assistance. She also works closely with DRL's programming unit to develop and implement a program evaluation protocol for DRL-funded grants to measure performance of DRL grants, and to help grantees improve their program evaluation capabilities and reporting. Prior to this position, Dr. Chen was the James Marshall Public Policy Scholar at the American Psychological Association, integrating scientific research of psychosocial and mental health issues, including HIV/AIDS, immigrant health, and other social justice issues, into policy-relevant work. Trained as a social and cultural psychologist, Dr. Chen received her master's and doctorate from the University of Michigan, Ann Arbor. Her primary research interests included prejudice and discrimination, and understanding cultural differences, with a specific focus on the Asian and Asian American community.

Sapna Batra Chopra completed her doctorate degree in counseling psychology at the University of Maryland, College Park, in 2000. She is a licensed psychologist and full-time lecturer in the counseling department at California State University, Fullerton. Her clinical interests include issues related to parenting, acculturation, counseling South Asian Americans, and women's issues. She also enjoys spending time with her son Armaan, daughter Anya, and husband Palak.

Y. Barry Chung received his PhD in counseling psychology from the University of Illinois at Urbana-Champaign in 1996. He is associate professor and training director of the counseling psychology doctoral program at Georgia State University. Dr. Chung's professional interests include career development, multicultural counseling, and lesbian, gay, and bisexual issues. He has published more than 40 journal articles and book chapters on these topics, and has served on seven journal editorial boards. Dr. Chung was president of the National Career Development Association (2006–2007). He currently serves on the American Psychological Association board of educational affairs and as vice president for education and training in the Society of Counseling Psychology. He is a fellow of the American Psychological Association (Division 17) and the National Career Development Association.

Manveen Dhindsa is a doctoral student at the University of California, Davis, and a research assistant at the Asian American Center on Disparities Research. Manveen obtained her bachelor's degree in psychology from San Jose State University and a master's of arts in social psychology from San Francisco State University. Her research focuses on intimate partner violence across cultures. Her current work seeks to examine cultural factors, such as honor, as they may moderate the relationship between anger and aggression.

Sopagna Eap is a doctoral student in clinical psychology at the University of Oregon. Her research interests include the influence of culture on psychopathology assessment and treatment, community interventions, and parenting.

Mary A. Fukuyama received her PhD from Washington State University in 1981 and has worked at the University of Florida counseling center for the past 25 years as a counseling psychologist, supervisor, and trainer. She is a clinical professor and teaches courses on spiritual issues in multicultural counseling. She is an active member of the University of Florida's Center for Spirituality and Health and her research interests include a qualitative study on "multicultural expressions" of spirituality. She co-authored with Todd Sevig the book *Integrating Spirituality into Multicultural Counseling* with Sage Publications, and she also published a book with Woodrow M. Parker titled *Consciousness Raising: A Primer for Multicultural Counseling* (3rd Edition) with Charles C. Thomas, Publisher. Another area of interest is "navigating multiple social identities." She recently collaborated with Brent Beam in producing a DVD titled *At the Corner of Me and Myself: Voices of Multiple Social Identities*, available through MicroTraining and Multicultural Development. She is a fellow in Division 17 (Counseling Psychology) of the American Psychological Association.

Carmel Gabriel is currently a doctoral student at the Asian American Center on Disparities Research within the social psychology program at the University of California, Davis. She received her bachelor's degree in psychology from the University of California, Santa Barbara, in 2005. Broadly, Carmel's research involves examining the bicultural experience of Asian Americans. Specifically, she is interested in the psychological processes involved in cultural frame switching, acculturation, and stereotype threat as well as factors that contribute to economic disparities within ethnic minority populations.

Arpana Gupta is a doctoral student in the counseling psychology program at the University of Tennessee, Knoxville (UTK). She received an MEd in counseling from Wake Forest University in 2003. Her primary research interests include quantitative research methods such as meta-analysis, structural equation modeling, and factor analysis; and Asian American (AA) psychology, with a specific focus on the following: acculturation, racial identity, stereotype threat, suicide, health disparities, career, and public policy issues related to the Asian population. She is an active member of the profession and currently holds the following leadership positions: American Psychological Association (APA) Div 45 (Society for Ethnic and Minority Psychology), Student Representative; American Psychological Association Grade Students–Committee

on Ethnic and Minority Affairs (APAGS–CEMA), Regional Diversity Coordinator—Central Region; and Asian American Psychological Association (AAPA), board member and student representative. Her hobbies include working out, cooking, dancing, traveling, and painting.

Christine C. Iijima Hall received her PhD in social psychology from UCLA in 1980. Currently, she is the district director of employment and recruitment (VP level) for the Maricopa Community College District, the largest community college system in the United States. Prior to this position, she was the senior associate dean of instruction at Glendale Community College (1998–2000). From 1989–1996, Dr. Hall was the associate vice provost of academic affairs at Arizona State University West. From 1987–1989, she was the director of ethnic minority affairs for the American Psychological Association in Washington, D.C. Dr. Hall was the first female president of the Asian American Psychological Association from 1995–1997. She is a licensed psychologist in Arizona and California. Dr. Hall has authored numerous books chapters and journal articles on multiracial

identity, ethnic women and body image, and the need for psychology to diversify its profession in teaching, research, and practice. She appears on television, radio, and in magazines on the topic of diversity.

Gordon C. Nagayama Hall is professor of psychology at the University of Oregon. His research interests are in the cultural context of psychopathology, particularly sexual aggression. Dr. Hall is currently investigating the effectiveness with Asian Americans of treatments that are empirically supported for other groups. He is also interested in behavioral genomics approaches to genetic and cultural factors implicated in antisocial behavior. He was previously president of the American Psychological Association Society for the Psychological Study of Ethnic Minority Issues and received the Distinguished Contribution Award from the Asian American Psychological Association. Dr. Hall is currently editor of *Cultural Diversity and Ethnic Minority Psychology*, as well as associate editor of the *Journal of Consulting and Clinical Psychology*.

Diane S. Hayashino received her doctoral degree in counseling psychology from the University of Oregon in 2003. She is currently a licensed staff psychologist at Counseling and Psychological Services at California State University, Long Beach. She is also a lecturer in the graduate program in Educational Psychology, Administration & Counseling at CSU Long Beach. She teaches classes in cross-cultural counseling and Asian American psychology. Her clinical and research interests include multicultural counseling competency and supervision, Asian American mental health issues, women's issues, parenting stress among immigrant refugee families, and mentoring. In her free time, Diane enjoys spending time with her family that includes her daughter, Emi, and her partner, Kevin.

Derek Kenji Iwamoto is assistant professor of clinical psychology at the California School of Professional Psychology at Alliant International University, Los Angeles. He received his PhD in 2007 from the University of Nebraska, Lincoln, counseling psychology program. Derek has published numerous articles examining gender role and masculinity formation among Asian American men, integrating hip hop/rap music in counseling, and on racial and ethnic identity development among Asian Americans. Other clinical and research interests entail examining the risk and protective factors of substance use, positive well-being and depression among Asian Americans, and developing hip hop music and other novel group counseling intervention programs in the Los Angeles community. He currently serves as an ad hoc reviewer for the *Journal of Black Psychology.*

Kathleen Kawamura obtained her PhD in clinical psychology in 2001 from the University of Massachusetts, Amherst. She completed her predoctoral internship at the Long Beach Veterans Affairs Healthcare System and her postdoctoral fellowship at Harvard Medical School's Cambridge Healthcare Alliance specializing in behavioral medicine, cognitive behavioral therapies, and the treatment of anxiety disorders. She also has an interest in multicultural issues and has published articles on the topics of perfectionism, parenting styles, and body image in Asian American populations. She is a staff psychologist at the University of California, Irvine, counseling center and also has a private practice in Mission Viejo, California.

Bryan S. K. Kim is associate professor in the department of psychology at the University of Hawaii, Hilo. Dr. Kim received a PhD in counseling/clinical/school psychology, with an emphasis in counseling psychology, from the University of California, Santa Barbara, in 2000. Previously, he was an associate professor at the University of California, Santa Barbara, and an assistant professor at the University of Maryland, College Park. Dr. Kim's research focuses on multicultural counseling process and outcome, the measurement of cultural constructs, and counselor education and supervision. He currently is an associate editor of *Cultural Diversity and Ethnic Minority Psychology* and *The Counseling Psychologist* and a consulting editor for the *Journal of Counseling Psychology, Psychotherapy Theory, Research, Practice, and Training, Measurement and Evaluation in Counseling and Development*, and *Educational Researcher.* In 2003, he received the Early Career Award for Distinguished Contributions from the Asian American Psychological Association. In 2005, he received the ACA Research Award from the American Counseling Association and the *MECD* (*Measurement and Evaluation in Counseling and Development*) Editor's Award from the Association for Assessment in Counseling and Education. Most recently in 2006, Dr. Kim received the Fritz and Linn Kuder Early Career Scientist/Practitioner Award from the Society of Counseling Psychology (Division 17) of the American Psychological Association.

Sara Cho Kim is a doctoral candidate in counseling psychology at the University of Wisconsin, Madison, and is currently completing her internship at University of Maryland, College Park's counseling center. She received her undergraduate and master's degrees from the University of Pennsylvania. She has presented and published on topics related to cultural identity formation, psychosocial factors impacting educational outcomes and well-being. Her major research interests are in examining health disparities in ethnic minority populations and contextual factors influencing adjustment and well-being in Asian Americans. She served as student representative in Division 17's Section on Racial and Ethnic Diversity (SERD) from 2003–2005 and is currently the treasurer in the Division on Women (DoW) for the Asian American Psychological Association (AAPA). Currently, she is the student representative for the section on Positive Psychology in Division 17.

Su Yeong Kim received a PhD in human development from the University of California, Davis, in 2003. She is currently is an assistant professor in the department of human ecology, division of human development and family sciences, at the University of Texas, Austin. She studies the development of adolescents in ethnic minority and immigrant families by examining the intersection of family and cultural contexts in shaping adolescent development. She is the recipient of the Tanaka Dissertation Award from the American Psychological Association for the most outstanding research on ethnic minority psychological issues and concerns. She is currently examining the role of language brokering and its impact on family relationships and developmental outcomes in children of Asian and Latino immigrant families.

J. David Kinzie is professor of psychiatry at Oregon Health & Science University and originated the Intercultural Psychiatric Program in 1977. He is still active in the program, and his caseload includes Cambodian (some of which he has treated for 25 years), Somalian, and Latin American patients. After medical school at the University of Washington he was a general physician in Vietnam and Malaysia, and after residency, also at the University of Washington, taught psychiatry at the University of Malaya School of Medicine. He also was a Transcultural Fellow at the University of Hawaii affiliated program and later taught 5 years in the department of psychiatry at the University of Hawaii Medical School. He has directed the Torture Treatment Center of Oregon and the Child Traumatic Stress Center of Oregon. Dr.

Kinzie has published over 115 articles and book chapters in the fields of transcultural psychiatry, refugee mental health, and post-traumatic stress disorder. He is a Distinguished Life Fellow of the American Psychiatric Association and fellow of the American College of Psychiatrists. He serves on the steering committee of the Transcultural Section of the World Psychiatric Association. He received the 2007 Kun-Po Soo Award, an award that recognizes an individual who has made significant contributions toward understanding the impact of Asian cultural heritage in areas relevant to psychiatry.

J. Mark Kinzie is an assistant professor of psychiatry at Oregon Health and Science University in Portland. He is director of the Torture Treatment Center of Oregon and is a staff psychiatrist in the Intercultural Psychiatric Program at OHSU. He is also associate training director of the Adult Psychiatry Residency Program. Dr. Kinzie received his medical and graduate training at OHSU. He is a graduate of the psychiatry training program at the Neuropsychiatric Institute at UCLA. He has also been a psychiatrist with the Program for Torture Victims in Los Angeles, California.

Kwong-Liem Karl Kwan is a faculty member in the Department of Counseling at San Francisco State University. He earned his PhD in 1996 from the Counseling Psychology program at the University of Nebraska at Lincoln. He was a tenured faculty in the Department of Educational Studies at Purdue University (1996–2005) and at the University of Missouri at Columbia (2005–2008). During his doctoral years in Nebraska, he was a research assistant at the Buros Institute of Mental Measurements. Prior to pursuing his psychology studies in the United States, he worked as a research interviewer at the Psychiatric Epidemiology Research Unit in the Department of Psychiatry at the Chinese University of Hong Kong. His research focuses on the development and assessment of counseling constructs specific to Asians and Asian Americans. He serves on the editorial boards of the *Journal of Counseling Psychology, Asian Journal of Counselling*, and as editor of the International Forum of *The Counseling Psychologist*. Dr. Kwan is a proud member of the Asian American Psychological Association (AAPA). He was a past program co-chair and conference co-chair of AAPA's annual conferences, and he continues to serve as a mentor to student members.

Agnes Kwong is the practicum program coordinator and psychology postdoctoral fellow at Counseling and Psychological Services at University of California, Davis. She received her PhD in counseling psychology from New York University in 2007. Her clinical and research interests and experience include Asian American mental health, biculturalism, cultural adjustment, coping, resilience, and psychological training and supervision.

Shamin Ladhani received her doctorate in clinical psychology from Nova Southeastern University in Fort Lauderdale, Florida, in 2005. She currently works as a clinical health psychologist in the Comprehensive Pain Management Center of Wheaton Franciscan Healthcare in Southeastern Wisconsin. She has previously worked in medical centers in Milwaukee, Newark, and Miami, addressing the biopsychosocial aspects of coping with chronic medical illness. Her interests are in culturally sensitive health care and she actively participates in the training of staff at the medical center. She has also researched and presented on issues that affect the South Asian community and participates in outreach in her local community. Upon graduation from NSU, Dr. Ladhani received the Robert Weitz Award granted to a promising graduating student whose energy, spirit, and enthusiasm represent a

dedication to the profession of psychology and the people it serves. Her clinical interests involve working with underserved medical populations, specifically adults and older adults. She has also been active in governance for the American Psychological Association.

Richard M. Lee is an associate professor of psychology and Asian American studies at the University of Minnesota. He received his PhD in psychology at Virginia Commonwealth University in 1996 and previously taught at the University of Texas, Austin. Dr. Lee conducts research on Asian American development, family, and mental health with a focus on cultural socialization, ethnic identity development, perceived discrimination, and acculturation conflicts. His current work is funded by the National Institute of Mental Health and focuses on the cultural socialization and mental health of Korean children adopted internationally. Dr. Lee has published over 45 journal articles and book chapters and has received state and national early career awards for his scholarship. He is a fellow of Division 17 (Society for Counseling Psychology) in the American Psychological Association and a member and past board member of the Asian American Psychological Association.

Stacey J. Lee received her PhD in 1991 from the University of Pennsylvania. She is professor of educational policy studies at the University of Wisconsin, Madison. Lee is the author of *Unraveling the Model Minority Stereotype: Listening to Asian American Youth* and *Up Against Whiteness: Race, School & Immigrant Youth* both published by Teachers College Press.

Szu-Hui Lee received her PhD from The Ohio State University in 2006. She is a licensed psychologist at the Massachusetts General Hospital/McLean Hospital's Obsessive Compulsive Disorder Institute, a residential treatment facility for patients with severe and refractory OCD. As a clinical instructor at Harvard Medical School, Dr. Lee participates in the psychology training program at McLean Hospital supervising interns and postdoctoral fellows. Dr. Lee also provides clinical services at South Cove Community Health Center, New England's premier primary and preventive health center for individuals of Asian descent. Her clinical and research interests include multidisciplinary mental health treatment and service delivery as well as education/prevention and training within the cross-cultural context. Currently, Dr. Lee is a co-investigator of a federally funded research focusing on the effectiveness of culturally sensitive collaborative treatment of depressed Asians and Asian Americans. She is actively involved with the Asian American Psychological Association, American Psychological Association, and Association for Behavioral and Cognitive Therapies.

Frederick T. L. Leong is a professor of psychology (industrial/organizational and clinical psychology programs) and director of the Center for Multicultural Psychology Research at Michigan State University. He has authored or co-authored over 110 articles in various psychology journals, 70 book chapters, and also edited or coedited 10 books. He is editor-in-chief of the *Encyclopedia of Counseling* (Sage Publications, in preparation). Dr. Leong is a fellow of the APA (Divisions 1, 2, 12, 17, 45, 52), Association for Psychological Science, Asian American Psychological Association and the International Academy for Intercultural Research. His major research interests center around culture and mental health, cross-cultural psychotherapy (especially with Asians and Asian Americans), cultural and personality factors related to career choice and work
adjustment. He is past president of APA's Division 45 (Society for the Psychological Study of Ethnic Minority Issues), the Asian American Psychological Association, and the Division of Counseling Psychology in the International Association of Applied Psychologists. He is currently serving on the APA Board of Scientific Affairs, the Minority Fellowship Program Advisory Committee and the Commission on Ethnic Minority Recruitment, Retention, and Training (CEMRRAT2) Task Force. He is the 2007 co-recipient of the APA Award for Distinguished Contributions to the International Advancement of Psychology.

Cindy H. Liu is a psychology intern at Harvard Medical School/McLean Hospital and sixth-year clinical psychology doctoral student at the University of Oregon. She received her master's degree in psychology from the University of Oregon in 2003 and BS in child psychology and physiology from the University in Minnesota in 2001. Cindy is a recipient of the American Psychological Association Minority Fellowship and Ruth L. Kirschstein National Research Service Award from the National Institutes of Child and Human Development. Currently, she serves as the Ethnic and Racial Issues student representative for the Society for Research of Child Development. Her research focuses on emotion development and clinical intervention among ethnic minority
children and families. Specifically, she is interested in the emotion socialization process among Chinese American and European American mother-child dyads and ethnic differences in emotion expression, regulation, and externalizing and internalizing symptomatology as rated by multiple reporters. Currently, she is involved in prevention research with at-risk youth in the Boston public middle schools. Because ideals of emotional experience and behavior can be construed very differently across cultures, she hopes her research program will inform intervention development for different cultural groups.

William Ming Liu is an associate professor and training director of the counseling psychology program at the University of Iowa. He is the coeditor of the *Handbook for Multicultural Competencies in Counseling and Psychology* (Sage, 2003). He is also associate editor of *Psychology of Men and Masculinity* and serves on the editorial boards of *Cultural Diversity, Ethnic Minority Psychology,* and *The Counseling Psychologist*. His research interests are in social class and classism, men and masculinity, and multicultural competencies.

Yuli Liu is a staff psychologist at the University of California, Irvine, counseling center. She received her PhD in counseling psychology from the University of Southern California in 2003. Her research and clinical interests include multicultural counseling and training, Asian American mental health, career development, acculturation and identity development, immigrant communities, diversity education, and gender issues. She received the Donald E. Super Fellowship from American Psychological Association's Division 17 (Society of Counseling Psychology) for her dissertation research on career development in Asian American college students. In 2003, she was awarded the Paul Bloland Scholar-Practitioner Scholarship from the University of Southern California. She is a member of the American Psychological Association and the Asian American Psychological Association (and of its Division on Women).

Susana M. Lowe received a PhD from the University of California, Santa Barbara. She is currently an associate professor in graduate psychology at the American School of Professional Psychology at Argosy University, Hawaii. Prior to joining the faculty at Argosy University, she was a staff psychologist at University of California, Berkeley, had a small private practice, and served as adjunct faculty at San Francisco State University. Dr. Lowe has also conducted research for the Asian Pacific Islander American Health Forum, and was an assistant professor in the counseling psychology program at Boston College. She has been active in the Asian American Psychological Association, most recently as cochair of the Division on Women. She serves as a consulting editor of *Training & Education in Profession Psychology*.  In all of her roles she has maintained a focus on giving voice to marginalized identities, striving for competency in working with diverse clientele/students, and social justice. Dr. Lowe's passion is to help people discover and articulate meaning in their lives, to assist in fostering understanding of the self-in-context, and to facilitate developing skills to accomplish personal, social, academic, career, community, and political goals. She has great love for food, music, family, friends, and her dog. She tends to care deeply about students, clients, and colleagues. She is especially appreciative of people who mean well and do their best to act accordingly, as well as people who, at times, can laugh heartily about life.

Elizabeth S. Mathew received her PhD in counseling psychology from Texas Woman's University in Denton, Texas, in August 2005. She completed her pre-doctoral internship at the University of Florida's counseling center in Gainesville, Florida. She completed a postdoctoral fellowship in pediatric psychology at the Texas Scottish Rite Hospital for Children in Dallas, Texas. Elizabeth is currently a licensed psychologist at Texas Christian University's Counseling, Testing, and Mental Health Center in Fort Worth, Texas.

Oanh Meyer is currently a doctoral student at the Asian American Center on Disparities Research within the social psychology program at the University of California, Davis. She received her bachelor's degree in psychology and human development from UC Davis, and obtained her master's degree in 2005 from California State University, Sacramento. Her current research is focused on examining ethnic match in psychotherapy from a social psychological perspective. Her research will test for possible mediators for ethnic match's effect on client outcomes.

Matthew J. Miller received a PhD from Loyola University, Chicago, in 2005. He is currently an assistant professor in counseling psychology at the University of Albany, State University of New York.

Dr. Miller conducts research that examines the multiple ways in which race, ethnicity, and culture impact behavior across a number of life domains for Asian Americans. Dr. Miller is currently on the editorial board of the *Journal of Counseling Psychology* and is on the board of directors of the Asian American Psychological Association.

Jeffery Scott Mio is a professor in the psychology and sociology department at California State Polytechnic University, Pomona, where he also serves as the director of the MS in psychology program. He received his PhD from the University of Illinois, Chicago, in 1984. He taught at California State University, Fullerton, in the counseling department from 1984–1986, then taught at Washington State University in the department of psychology from 1986–1994, before accepting his current position at Cal Poly Pomona. His interests are in the teaching of multicultural issues, the development of allies, and how metaphors are used in political persuasion.

Madeeha Mir earned a BA in psychology (2000) and an MA in counseling psychology (2007) from the University of West Florida. Currently, she is a third-year doctoral student in the counseling psychology PhD program at New York University and is a psychology extern at Bellevue Hospital. Her research interests include acculturation and psychological well-being among South Asian and Muslim communities, ethnic identity and multicultural counseling. She co-presented a poster at APA entitled "Young, Muslim and American: A Mixed Methods Exploration," participated in a structured discussion at the Diversity Challenge at Boston College entitled "Muslim Youth 101: A Research Agenda," and was a reviewer for *Applied Developmental Science*. While at UWF, she received the Outstanding Graduate Student Award and the Monroe Stein Memorial Scholarship and the President's Service Award for Volunteerism at NYU.

Jessica Murakami is pursuing her doctorate in clinical psychology at the University of Oregon, where she received her master's degree in clinical psychology in 2004. Prior to moving to Eugene, she graduated from the University of Pennsylvania and worked as a research coordinator at the Depression Clinical and Research Program in Boston, Massachusetts and as a live-in counselor at Wellmet Project, Inc. in Cambridge, Massachusetts. She is receiving funding through the American Psychological Association's Minority Fellowship Program, and is currently working on research projects that attempt to understand factors that influence the development of depression, treatment-seeking, and treatment-outcome in Asian Americans. Her research interests include treatment outcome research for depression, Asian American mental health, and suicide prevention.

Kevin L. Nadal received his PhD in counseling psychology at Teachers College, Columbia University, in 2008. With research focusing primarily on Filipino American identity and experience, his Filipino American Identity Development Model (2004) and other works have encouraged the field to understand the unique sociocultural and psychological experience of Filipino Americans in the United States. As a psychologist, activist, college lecturer, and performance artist, he has delivered many keynote speeches, workshops, and trainings around the country focusing on Filipino American identity, LGBTQ issues, and the impact of racial microaggressions.

Sumie Okazaki is associate professor of psychology at the University of Illinois at Urbana–Champaign. She received her PhD in clinical psychology from the University of California, Los Angeles, in 1994 and completed her clinical internship at UCLA's Neuropsychiatric Institute. She was on the faculty at the University of Wisconsin–Madison in psychology and Asian American studies from 1995–1999. She is the recipient of the Early Career Award for Distinguished Contribution from the Asian American Psychological Association, the Emerging Professional Award from the Society for the Psychological Study of Ethnic Minority Issues, and the Early Career Award from the American Psychological Association Minority Fellowship Program. She is currently serving as an associate editor of the journal *Cultural Diversity and Ethnic Minority Psychology*. In her research, she studies  the role of immigration, community contexts, individual differences, and racial minority status on the mental health of Asian American individuals and families.

Cheri L. Philip received her doctorate in personality psychology from the University of Michigan in 2005. Her dissertation, which explored Asian American racial and ethnic identity was recently added as a scholarly monograph to the Asian Studies collection and published as a book by Cambria Press. Dr. Philip's other research interests include intergroup relations (with a focus on intergroup attitudes among minority group members) and special issues related to immigrant populations. She has more recently become interested in racial and ethnic disparities in health, and is beginning a postdoctoral fellowship working with an interdisciplinary team in this area at the Medical University of South Carolina.

Tiffany Rice received her PhD in counseling psychology in 2006 from Arizona State University. She is currently an assistant professor of psychology at East Los Angeles College. She is co-authoring a book chapter on sexual orientation and multiple heritage identities. Dr. Rice was also an editorial contributor to the American Psychological Association's *Guidelines on Multicultural Education, Training, Research, Practice, and Organizational Change for Psychologists.* Her interests include Asian American mental health, multiracial identity, LGBT issues, cultural competency in teaching, and the intersection of multiple identities.

Anne Saw is a doctoral candidate at the University of Illinois, Urbana–Champaign, and completed her undergraduate degree at the University of California, Berkeley. Her research focuses in the structural and cultural factors that influence the mental health of Asian Americans and other ethnic minorities. She has a special interest in the effects of racialization and immigration on individual, family, and community identities, and narratives.

Anneliese A. Singh is an assistant professor in the department of counseling and human development services at the University of Georgia. She received her doctorate in counseling psychology from Georgia State University in 2007. Her clinical, research, and advocacy interests include Asian American/Pacific Islander psychology, multicultural counseling and social justice, qualitative methodology with historically marginalized groups (e.g., people of color, LGBTQI, immigrants), feminist theory and practice, and empowerment interventions with survivors of trauma. Dr. Singh is the current president-elect of the Association of Lesbian, Gay, Bisexual, and Transgender Issues (ALGBTIC) and is the secretary for the Division of Women in the Asian American Psychological Association. She is the recipient of the 2007 Ramesh and Vijaya Bakshi Community Change Award for her organizing work to end child sexual abuse in South Asian communities and to increase visibility of South Asian LGBTQI people.

Jenny Su is a doctoral candidate in the department of psychology at the University of Minnesota, Twin Cities. Her research focuses on cultural aspects of emotion regulation and other self-regulation processes such as coping. She also conducts research on the influence of culture on human emotion, self-evaluation, interpersonal perceptions, and well-being.

Stanley Sue is distinguished professor of psychology and Asian American studies at the University of California, Davis. He received a BS degree from the University of Oregon (1966) and the PhD degree in psychology from UCLA (1971). From 1981–1996, he was a professor of psychology at UCLA, where he was also associate dean of the Graduate Division. Prior to his faculty appointment at UCLA, he was assistant and associate professor of psychology from 1971–1981 at the University of Washington. His research has been devoted to ethnicity and mental health and the delivery of mental health services to culturally diverse groups.

Karen L. Suyemoto received her PhD from the University of Massachusetts, Amherst, in 1994 and is now an associate professor in psychology and Asian American studies at the University of Massachusetts, Boston. Her teaching and scholarship focus on multidisciplinary understandings of intersections and effects of race, culture, gender, and other systems of social oppression and their relation to mental health practice/training and social justice with particular emphasis on Asian Americans. Recent publications include *Women in Psychotherapy: Exploring Diverse Contexts and Identities* (Guilford Press, 2005) coedited with Marsha Mirkin and Barbara Okun. Current research projects explore ethnic and racial identities in multiracial and Asian American individuals, and how community and education interventions affect racial and ethnic identities, mental health, and empowerment and activism in Asian American youth and college students. Other areas of scholarship are related to mentoring graduate students, who focus on topics such as Korean transracial transnational adoptees identities; Asian American youth and peer relations with diverse racial groups; interracial intimate relationships; intergenerational trauma transmission in Cambodian American refugee families; and race relations between Black and Asian American individuals and communities.

Lisa A. Suzuki is an associate professor in the department of applied psychology at New York University. Prior to this she served as a faculty member in counseling psychology at Fordham University and the University of Oregon. She obtained her PhD from the University of Nebraska, Lincoln in 1992. Suzuki received the Distinguished Contribution Award from the Asian American Psychological Association in 2006. She is senior editor of the *Handbook of Multicultural Assessment,* now in its third edition (Suzuki & Ponterotto, 2008). Suzuki is currently working with coeditors on the latest edition of the *Handbook of Multicultural Counseling* (Ponterotto, Casas, Suzuki, & Alexander). Her research interests are in the areas of multicultural assessment and qualitative research methods.

John Tawa is currently a fourth-year graduate student in the clinical psychology program at the University of Massachusetts, Boston, where he works under the mentorship of Dr. Karen L. Suyemoto. He is currently developing a dissertation project on positive interactions between Black and Asian individuals and communities. This research falls within a broader social justice aim of fostering greater collaboration and solidarity between racial minority groups. Other current and past research foci include understanding how people conceptualize race and ethnicity, how perceiving racism affects mental health, and the meanings and processes of self-construal for bicultural Asian Americans. Clinically, he is currently running psychotherapy groups with primarily Black and Latino youth negotiating contexts of community violence. Within these groups he attends strongly

to the meaning of being an Asian American clinician working with Black and Latino youth, emphasizing our cross-minority alliances as positive contexts for fostering empowerment and promoting systems-level change (e.g., through community violence reduction initiatives).

Yuying Tsong received her PhD in counseling psychology from the University of Southern California in 2004. She is currently a full-time faculty member at Pepperdine University, Graduate School of Education and Psychology. Prior to joining Pepperdine University in 2008, she was the program chair of the MA and EdD programs in counseling psychology at Argosy University, Orange County Campus. She is also a lecturer of the Asian American Psychology class for the cognitive science department at the University of California, Irvine, and has been a research and statistical consultant since 2001. She was the recipient of the Paul Bloland Practitioner-Scholar Award. Her dissertation received the USC Counseling Psychology Program Dissertation of Merit Award and Honorable Mention Award from AAPIC (Association of Psychology Postdoctoral and Internship Centers). Dr. Tsong's research and clinical interests include multicultural counseling/supervision, Asian American mental health, ethnic identity development, eating disorder/body image issues, and learning disability assessment. Dr. Tsong is bilingual in Mandarin and English and has worked in a variety of clinical settings, including urban community mental health services, university counseling centers, and college disability services.

Laura Uba received her PhD in psychology from the University of Colorado, Boulder, in 1979. As a part-time lecturer in California State University Northridge's (CSUN) Asian American Studies Department, she teaches classes ranging from Asian American history to Asian American psychology, including a class on Race & Critical Thinking. Largely on the basis of her three books as well as her empirical studies, policy analyses, and articles and chapters addressing research methodology and pedagogy in Asian American studies and psychology, she was awarded CSUN's 2007 award for Preeminent Scholarly Publications.

Eunice C. Wong received her doctorate in clinical psychology from the University of California, Santa Barbara, in 2003. Dr. Wong is currently an associate behavioral scientist at the RAND Corporation, where she is conducting research on treatment access and service utilization among trauma-exposed populations, new immigrants, and ethnic minority communities. She has research expertise in mental health and substance abuse in racial and ethnic minority populations. Dr. Wong has published on the role of cultural influences on psychological assessment, treatment process, and distress. She has also conducted work on acculturation and substance abuse, racial and ethnic disparities in health, and cultural influences on substance abuse treatment outcomes.

Nga-Wing Anjela Wong is a PhD candidate (ABD) in the department of educational policy studies at the University of Wisconsin–Madison. She received her MA in educational policy studies from UW–Madison in Summer 2005 and BA in Asian American studies and anthropology from San Francisco State University in Fall 2002. Her research interests include race, gender, and class; community-based research; urban and multicultural education; youth, families, and community studies; educational policy studies; and qualitative research methods. She has been involved with various community organizations since her junior year in high school. She truly believes in activism in educational settings and is committed to include and amplify (Diniz-Pereira, 2006) the voices that are unheard, marginalized, and ignored by the system.

Loriena Yancura is an assistant professor in the department of family and consumer sciences, College of Tropical Agriculture and Human Resources at the University of Hawaii, Manoa. She received her PhD in 2004 from the University of California, Davis, in human development, with emphasis on the socioemotional aspects of aging. She is interested in the influences of culture and family roles on health in older adults. One of her current research projects examines cultural differences the perceptions of family duties in grandparents raising grandchildren. Dr. Yancura is a member of the American Psychological Association and the Gerontological Society of America.

Barbara W. K. Yee is a professor and chair of the department of family and consumer sciences, College of Tropical Agriculture and Human Resources at the University of Hawaii, Manoa. She obtained her PhD in developmental psychology from the University of Denver in 1982. Since the fall of Saigon in 1975, she has been interested in how immigrant families, especially middle-aged and elderly Southeast Asians, adapt to the loss of homeland and culture. Her current research examines how gender, health literacy, and acculturation influence chronic disease health beliefs and lifestyle practices across three generations of Vietnamese, Asian Americans, and Pacific Islanders living in the United States. Her latest research adventure examines the impact of health literacy on breast and cervical cancer health beliefs and lifestyle factors among immigrant women. Dr. Yee has served on the editorial boards of the *Journals of Gerontology: Psychological Sciences, Psychology and Aging, Topics of Geriatric Rehabilitation*, and served as guest editor for a 1995 special issue of *Health Psychology* entitled "Behavioral and Sociocultural Perspectives on Ethnicity and Health." She was lead editor for "Developing Cultural Competence in Asian-American and Pacific Islander Communities: Opportunities in Primary Health Care and Substance Abuse Prevention" from the Bureau of Primary Health Care, Center for Substance Abuse Prevention, and Office of Minority Health. Dr. Yee is a fellow of the American Psychological Association and the Gerontological Society of America. In 1999, she was honored for her work in ethnogerontology as the Joseph C. Valley Gerontological Professional of the Year from the University of Texas Houston Health Science Center, Center on Aging and the Okura Community Leadership Award in 2004 from the Asian American Psychological Association, Okura Mental Health Leadership Foundation, for outstanding community leadership that benefits the Asian American community. Dr. Yee serves on the National Institutes of Health Advisory Committee on Research on Women's Health until 2010. She serves on the steering committee for the Bright Futures for Women's Health and Wellness, Health Resources Services Administration, Department of Health and Human Services since 2001 and has served on the Expert Panel of Minority Women's Health, PHS from 1998–2007. She was elected and served on the Committee on Women and Committee on Aging and Minority Fellowship Committee of the American Psychological Association, Minority Taskforce of the Gerontological Society of America, and the Association for Gerontology in Higher Education.

Christine J. Yeh received a PhD from Stanford University in 1996. She is currently an associate professor in the Counseling Psychology department at the University of San Francisco. Her research investigates cross-cultural issues within the field of counseling psychology, including Asian American mental health, Asian immigrant cultural adjustment, issues impacting school counselors, and multicultural modes of coping. Her research applies a broad range of theories such as cultural conceptions of self, interdependence, and ecological perspectives.

1
Who Are Asian Americans?
An Overview of History, Immigration, and Communities

CINDY H. LIU, JESSICA MURAKAMI, SOPAGNA EAP,
and GORDON C. NAGAYAMA HALL

OUTLINE OF CHAPTER

Introduction
Background
History and Immigration
Socioeconomic Status
The "Model Minority"?
References

Gannen-mono. Paper son. *Manong. Pau hana. Gum sahn.* Mountain of Gold. Tengoku. Illegals. Labor contract. *Kanyaku-imin.* Ticket dance. Runaway. Picture bride. Chinese Exclusion Act. Executive Order 9066. "I am Chinese." Flips. *Juk Sing.* "...fight to prove our loyalty." F.O.B. No-No Boy. Manzanar. The Golden Spike. "...your slanty-eyed, Korean ass..." Citizenship. Chinatown. Assimilation. Heritage. Homeland. Gooks. Boat People. "Success Story: Outwhiting the Whites." Hmong quilt. The "Community." Ancestors. Vincent Chin. Homeland. Hawaii Calls. HR 442. haiku. Panoum. *Cababayan.* Green-grocer. Cleaners. Dogeaters. Diploma. Diaspora. Asian American. Song, Encarnacion, Shahid Ali. *Ai. Aiieeeee! The Woman Warrior.* Bruce Lee. Immigration attorney. Kearny Street. International Hotel. Berkeley quota. Wharton School. Chancellor. Tenure. One-and-a-half. Mainland. Homeland...

Introduction

The passage above contains most of the word-cloud by Japanese American poet Garrett Hongo in his introduction to *The Open Boat: Poems from Asian America,* a collection of poems by Asian Americans. Hongo continues, "For the thirty writers here emerge out of more than a hundred years of immigration, sojourning, settlement, misconception, stereotyping, and soul-searching" (Hongo, 1993, pp. xviii–xix). Indeed, the history of Asian Americans in the United States is rich, varied, and often troubling. In this introductory chapter, we provide a brief overview of the history of Asian Americans from the first wave of Asian immigration until the "model minority" image of today. Who are Asian Americans? What does it mean to be Asian American? The focus of this chapter is on the first question, which is much more straightforward than the latter. For now, let us note that what it means to be Asian American varies from person to person, and that the experiences of Asian Americans living in the United States are incredibly diverse, influenced by a number of factors, such as the level of acculturation, country of origin, socioeconomic status, and geographic location.

Background

> When I was a kid back in the 1940s, I was always asked, "Are you Chinese or Japanese?" as if there could be no other options. There are over sixty different Asian groups in the United States today, from origins as diverse as Cambodia, China, India, Indonesia, Japan, Korea, Laos, Myanmar, Pakistan, the Philippines, Thailand, and Vietnam, as well as the islands of Polynesia—each with its own history, language, and culture. Some segments have been in the United States since the 1850s; others arrived only last week.

> –Elaine H. Kim (2003)

Asian Americans are descendents of immigrants from any part of Asia, or are themselves immigrants from Asia to the United States. Countries of origin include East Asian countries (China, Japan, and Korea), Southeast Asian countries (e.g., Cambodia, the Philippines, Thailand, Vietnam, and Indonesia), and South Asian countries (India, Nepal, and Pakistan). Consisting of more than 17 million square miles, Asia is the largest continent on earth, and makes up approximately one-third of the earth's land. More than 60% of the world's population resides in Asia, while approximately 5% of the world's population can be found in the United States.

Within the United States, Asian Americans are the fastest-growing minority group (U.S. Census Bureau, 2000). According to the 2000 Census, Asian Americans number 11,070,913 individuals (3.9% of the U.S. population). This is a sharp increase from the results of the 1990 Census, when Asian Americans numbered 6,908,638 (2.8% of the U.S. population). Chinese Americans make up the largest Asian group in the United States at 0.9% of the country's population, followed by Filipino Americans (0.7%), Asian Indians (0.6%), Korean Americans (0.4%), and Japanese Americans (0.3%). Table 1.1 displays the populations of each Asian ethnic group in the United States. Interestingly, 3,916,204 Asian Americans (1.4% of the U.S. population) identified themselves as "other Asian," which includes other Asian groups and/or mixed heritage. A relatively high percentage of Asian Americans marry outside of their ethnicity. Intermarriage rates among Asian Americans from the 2000 Census indicate that 12% of Asian men and 23% of Asian women are currently married to non-Asians. It has become increasingly common to see (and be a part of) an interracial couple. More and more often, Asian American men and women are marrying outside of their particular Asian group to other Asians (e.g., a Chinese American man marrying a Filipino American woman) and non-Asians (e.g., European Americans, African Americans, and Native Hawaiians).

Until the 2000 U.S. Census, Pacific Islanders were grouped together with Asian Americans. Pacific Islanders are immigrants or descendents of immigrants from one of the Pacific Islands to the United States, including Hawaii, Samoa, Fiji, Guam, and the islands of Micronesia. The term *Asian American* often assumes the inclusion of Pacific Islanders, although more recently the term *Asian American and Pacific Islanders* (AA/PI) has been adopted to explicitly acknowledge the grouping of American Pacific Islanders with Asian Americans. Approximately 0.1% of the American population self-identifies as Pacific Islanders (U.S. Census Bureau, 2000).

According to a census taken in March 2002, 12.5 million Americans identify themselves as AA/PI (4.4% of the population; Reeves & Bennett, 2003). In general, AA/PIs are younger than non-Hispanic Whites. Twenty-six percent of AA/PIs in March 2002 were under the age of 18, while it is estimated that the number of AA/PI youth will increase to 74% by 2015 (Snyder & Sickmund, 1999). Depending on where you grew up, these numbers may be surprising. In cities

Table 1.1 Population of Asian Ethnic Groups

Ethnic group	Asian alone	Two Asian ethnicities	Asian and at least one other race	Total population alone or in any combination
Chinese	2,314,537	130,826	289,478	2,734,841
Filipino	1,850,314	57,811	456,690	2,364,815
Asian Indian	1,678,765	40,013	180,821	1,899,599
Korean	1,076,872	22,550	129,005	1,228,427
Vietnamese	1,122,528	47,144	54,064	1,223,736
Japanese	769,700	55,537	296,695	1,148,932
Native Hawaiian and other Pacific Islanders				874,414
Cambodian	171,937	11,832	22,283	206,052
Pakistani	153,533	11,095	39,681	204,309
Laotian	168,707	10,396	19,100	198,203
Hmong	169,428	5,284	11,598	186,310
Thai	112,989	7,929	29,365	150,293
Taiwanese	118,048	14,096	12,651	144,795
Indonesian	39,757	4,429	18,887	63,073
Bangladeshi	41,280	5,625	10,507	57,412

Source: U.S. Census Bureau. (2000). *Census 2000.* Washington, DC.

such as Honolulu, Asian Americans made up 61.8% of the population in 2000. According to the census taken in March 2002, over half of the AA/PI population resides in the West (51%), 19% in the South, and 12% in the Midwest, while the remaining 19% lives in the Northeast. Ninety-five percent of AA/PIs reside in metropolitan areas, compared to 78% of the non-Hispanic Caucasian population.

Whereas a large percentage of AA/PIs were born in the United States, approximately 69% of Asian Americans (not including Pacific Islanders) are foreign born (U.S. Census Bureau, 2000). As with many other characteristics (e.g., average years of education and income levels), this percentage varies dramatically depending on what particular Asian group is being considered. For example, 40% of Japanese Americans versus approximately 75% of Korean Americans are foreign born. About one-quarter of the foreign-born population in the United States was born in Asia. Of these 7.2 million people, the majority immigrated after 1980, following previous generations of Asian immigrants and adding to the diverse cultural landscape of a growing country.

History and Immigration

The study of Asian Americans often begins with a study of their immigration history. Alongside Europeans, hundreds of thousands of Chinese, Japanese, South Asians, Koreans, Filipinos, Southeast Asians, and Pacific Islanders arrived in the United States in the 19th and 20th centuries. The reasons behind the immigration for each Asian group across the generations differed based on the political and economic landscapes of the United States and of the Asian country from which they came. Alongside the laws created to affect their immigration (see Table 1.2),

Table 1.2 Major Congressional Acts and Judicial Rulings on Asian American Immigration and Naturalization

1882	Chinese Exclusion Law suspends immigration of Chinese American laborers for 10 years
1898	*Wong Kim Ark v. U.S.* decides that Chinese born in the U.S. cannot be stripped of their citizenship
1917	Asiatic Barred Zone Act defines a geographic "barred zone" (including India); immigration from Asia ceases
1922	*Takao Ozawa v. U.S.* declares Japanese ineligible for naturalized citizenship
1923	*U.S. v. Bhagat Singh Thind* declares Asian Indians ineligible for naturalized citizenship, after ruling Indians as being Asian and non-White
1943	Magnuson Act repeals all Chinese exclusion laws, grants right of naturalization and a small immigration quota to Chinese
1946	Luce–Celler Bill grants right of naturalization and small immigration quotas to Asian Indians and Filipinos, allowing a quota of 100 Indians and 100 Filipinos to immigrate to the United States
1965	Immigration and Nationality Services (INS) Act of 1965 abolishes "national origins" as a basis for allocating immigration quotas to various countries—Asian countries now on equal footing

Source: Chan, S. (1991). *Asian Americans: An interpretive history.* CT: Twayne Publishers.

the reactions of the European American majority played a role in the reception of Asian immigrants. These circumstances colored the immigrants' prospects of being American and their experiences in American culture.

Chinese Americans

The Chinese were among the earliest wave of East Asian immigrants to arrive. By the mid-1800s, high taxes, peasant rebellions, and family feuds led to poverty and starvation in China, which prompted thousands of Chinese to flee to countries around the world (Loo, 1998; Hoobler & Hoobler, 1994). This period of strife coincided with the onset of the California gold rush. Dreams of wealth led to the immigration of young Chinese men to the American West, encouraged by stories they heard about America. One young man wrote about America to his brother:

> Oh! Very rich country. . . . They find gold very quickly so I hear. . . . I feel as if I should like to go there very much. I think I shall go to California next summer. (Takaki, 1998, p. 34)

As **sojourners**, these men planned to return to China after earning enough money to support their families (Kitano & Daniels, 1995). These early Chinese Americans emigrated to escape the suffering endured in China, only to encounter it again in America. The hardships, however, were of a different quality. Although the government and public in California initially welcomed the Chinese, White American miners began to feel threatened by their presence (Hing, 1993; Takaki, 1998). Within 6 months of the initial welcome, the California government claimed that the customs, language, and education of the Asiatic races "threatened the well-being of the mining districts" (Takaki, 1998, p. 81). The government then imposed the foreign miners' license tax, the first of many taxes to discourage Chinese immigration (Hing, 1993).

Chinese Americans in the late 1800s often filled the void of low-paying jobs in the growing industries of America. They used their knowledge of agriculture to cultivate farms in the West, and they labored in mining and land development. Approximately 15,000 Chinese Americans played a notable, yet often uncelebrated, role as railroad workers who created the first transcontinental railroad in America (e.g., Loo, 1998; Takaki, 1998; Hoobler & Hoobler, 1994).

During the 1870s, working-class European Americans, incited by an Irish immigrant, Denis Kearney, rallied against the Chinese Americans. Their anti-Chinese movement exploited the Chinese Americans as scapegoats for the economic hardship at that time, and demanded "The Chinese Must GO" (Hoobler & Hoobler, 1994). Not everyone shared the anti-Chinese senti-ment, but the movement still grew, and ultimately led to the Chinese Exclusion Act in 1882, which remained in effect until 1943. This law legally barred Chinese without family already in the United States from entering the country. To enforce this law, Angel Island Immigration Station, billed as the "Ellis Island of the West," was built in 1910 near the city of San Francisco. Immigrants arriving at Angel Island did not receive the same open reception as the Europeans who arrived at Ellis Island. Whereas Ellis Island processed and released immigrants within hours, Angel Island served as a long-term detention center that controlled Asian immigration. As such, Angel Island was often referred to as the "Guardian of the Western Gate" (Chang, 2003). U.S. immigration officials at Angel Island interrogated, received, or refused Asian immi-grants. Many were detained in Angel Island for up to three years (Hoobler & Hoobler, 1994). The frustration and sadness of those detained prompted poetic expression. To this day, the barrack walls display their words:

> Imprisoned in the wooden building day after day,
> My freedom withheld, how can I bear to talk about it?
> . . . My sad mood, even so, is not dispelled. (Hom, 1992, p. 74)

The San Francisco earthquake and fires of 1906 were an inadvertent but auspicious turning point for Chinese who desired to immigrate to the United States. According to the Chinese Exclusion Act of 1882, the United States only allowed family members of Chinese Americans already residing in the United States to immigrate. With immigration documentation and birth records destroyed in these disasters, many Chinese entered the United States as **paper sons**. Pretending to be relatives of Chinese Americans, thousands of paper sons immigrated into the United States. Doing so was not without complication; entrance into the United States required processing at Angel Island so that the U.S. government could confirm their legitimacy. A paper son was often required to provide detailed information regarding the individual whose identity he had taken on (Chang, 2003; Hoobler & Hoobler, 1994).

A dramatic change in American sentiment regarding the Chinese in America occurred shortly before and during World War II. America began to see the Chinese Americans as hard-working and respectful—an idealized image that literature and films of the time helped to pro-mote. Moreover, the Japanese bombing of Pearl Harbor, and the U.S. alliance with the Chinese leader, Chiang Kai-shek, prompted Americans to question the standard idea of what it meant to be American (Kitano & Daniels, 1995). In 1943, the United States repealed the Chinese Exclu-sion Act (Loo, 1998). However, the repeal was primarily a foreign policy matter, aimed at reflect-ing benevolence toward China as an ally. Despite the repeal, the United States operated on a quota system for the next two decades, which allowed only 105 Chinese immigrants to enter the United States each year ("This Month in Immigration History," 2006). What appeared as an overall attitude change toward the Chinese during World War II did not erase racism toward Chinese Americans nor welcome Chinese immigrants to the United States (Kitano & Daniels, 1995).

The Immigration Act of 1965 served as a crucial turning point in immigration for Asian Americans. In fact, your family or other people you know may have immigrated to the United States under this act. Rather than adhering to a quota system, individuals allowed to immi-grate included those with close kin in America and those with specialized entrepreneurial and technical skills (Hing, 1993). The Chinese Americans who initially came during this wave were primarily professionals such as engineers and doctors (Takaki, 1995). Immigration changes in the 1990s that expanded the immigration of educated professionals have led to Chinese Americans pursuing MBAs and law degrees (Kwong & Miscevic, 2005).

Since the 1960s, Asian Americans have been dubbed model minorities, a term that alludes to Asian American achievements (Kitano & Daniels, 1995). Coined during the height of the civil rights movement by mainstream America, the term *model minority* pitted minorities against one another by suggesting that, unlike other minorities, Asian Americans had a work ethic that led to their success as Americans (Zia, 2000). Although seemingly flattering, the term overlooks the adverse experiences among the different Chinese American subgroups, in addition to the persistent discrimination faced by Chinese Americans as a whole. Newly arrived Chinese immigrants, and Chinese Americans who have lived in the United States for generations, continue to struggle with the experience of immigration and negotiation between the perception of mainstream America and their personal development as Americans.

Japanese Americans

The Japanese entered the United States during the 1800s. Alert to the wealth in a booming American economy, these farmers embraced the opportunity to leave for America as contracted farm laborers in Hawaii (Hing, 1993). As one Japanese immigrant expressed it:

Huge dreams of fortune,
Go with me to foreign lands, across the ocean. (Hom, 1992, p. 146)

Following the annexation of Hawaii by the United States, the Japanese began to immigrate to the U.S. mainland. The mainland was attractive to the Japanese, with American wages over and beyond those earned in Japan. In the 1890s, young Japanese American men labored as migrant farm workers and railroad workers (Hoobler & Hoobler, 1995). Although they received

Sadaki Nishimoto emigrated from Kumamoto on the island of Kyushu, Japan to Hawaii in 1911 at the age of 19 to meet his parents, who had been working in the coffee plantations of Hawaii since he was an infant. He worked on the railroad and in construction as a powder man.

low pay, these men were not as destitute as the Chinese Americans who had arrived earlier; the Japanese government selected and monitored Japanese American migrants, who arrived to the United States with money, to ensure that the men were good representatives of Japan (Kitano & Daniels, 1995).

However, like the Chinese Americans, the Japanese Americans faced racism early on. In 1906, the San Francisco School Board forced Japanese American children along with Korean American children to attend a segregated school for Chinese (Takaki, 1998). The incident escalated such that President Theodore Roosevelt agreed to reverse the school board decision, and established the Gentlemen's Agreement of 1908, which halted further immigration of the Japanese to the United States (Takaki, 1998). Specifically, this required that the Japanese government restrict emigration from Japan by stopping the issuing of passports for Japanese to immigrate as "laborers" (Kitano & Daniels, 1995). This did not preclude Japanese Americans from bringing over their family members. What was once a male-dominated Japanese American population transformed into a community with a proportionate number of males and females (Hing, 1993). However, additional immigration laws, such as the Immigration Law in 1924, sought to block Japanese from entering the United States (Hoobler & Hoobler, 1995). As well, the 1922 *Takao Ozawa v. United States* case rejected the citizenship application of a Japanese immigrant who classified himself as Caucasian. The Supreme Court ruled that Ozawa was not White but Mongoloid ("The House We Live In," 2003).

The Japanese American population grew even with the restrictions on Japanese immigration. With the arrival of **picture brides**, or shashin kekkon (literally, "photo marriage"), Japanese women married Japanese American men, whom they would not see until they arrived to the United States. As Riyo Orite, a picture bride, described it: "All agreed to our marriage, but

Akira Kawakami's passport, dated June 28, 1923.

Sadaki Nishimoto, age 31, and Akira Kawakami, age 20, were wed on June 28, 1923—the same day that Akira Kawakami arrived on the shores of Hawaii and met Sadaki Nishimoto for the first time.

I didn't get married immediately. I was engaged at the age of 16 and didn't meet Orite until I was almost 18. I had seen him only in a picture, first" (Takaki, 1998, p. 47).

The increased number of American-born children of Japanese ancestry during that time reflected the impact of the picture brides. According to Hing (1993), there were approximately 4,500 of these children in 1910, 30,000 in 1920, and 68,000 by 1930.

Akira and Sadaki Nishimoto pose for a family portrait with their first daughter, Kashiko Nishimoto.

A second family portrait taken years later. Sadaki (middle) and Akira Nishimoto (far right) pose for a family portrait. Years earlier, Akira arrived in Hawaii from Kumamoto, Kyushu, Japan as a picture bride at the age of 20 in search of a better life. She met and married Sadaki Nishimoto, age 31, on the day that she arrived on the shores of Hawaii. Their five daughters are (from left to right) Kashiko, Namiko, Evelyn Shizuko, Mildred Shizuyo, and Grace Akiko. Both Kashiko and Namiko adopted the American names of Dorothy and Marilyn, respectively, for themselves while growing up. Both Sadaki and Akira Nishimoto lived into their 90s and remained together.

The 1930s saw a Japanese American community with two generations, the Issei, who were the immigrant generation, and their American-born children, the Nisei (Takaki, 1998).

Table 1.3 shows the generational group names of Japanese Americans. The Issei established Japanese American organizations that allowed the Japanese government to exert control in issuing documents the Japanese needed in order to bring their family members into the United States. At the same time, these organizations encouraged Japanese Americans to acculturate and to obtain a good education in the United States (Kitano & Daniels, 1995). The Nisei formed organizations modeled after mainstream American social clubs and church groups (Kitano & Daniels, 1995). Unlike the Chinese Americans whose population had dwindled because of the Chinese Exclusion Act, the Japanese American community acculturated faster to mainstream American culture by creating organizations to promote patriotic values that distanced themselves from the Issei. Even with the attempt to become "more American," these younger Japanese Americans did not integrate with the mainstream American community (Hoobler & Hoobler, 1995). European Americans during this time still had difficulty accepting any Asians as equals to their race (Takaki, 1998).

Table 1.3 Generations of Japanese Americans in the United States

Group	Generation	Nativity
Issei	First	Immigrants from Japan
Nisei	Second	Born in U.S., parents born in Japan
Sansei	Third	Born in U.S., grandparents born in Japan
Yonsei	Fourth	Born in U.S., great grandparents born in Japan
Gosei	Fifth	Born in U.S., great great grandparents born in Japan

The treatment of Japanese Americans during World War II marks an experience that sets apart the Japanese Americans from any other Asian American group. Following the Japanese bombing of Pearl Harbor, the U.S. government froze the bank accounts and other assets of Japanese Americans, financially immobilizing the Japanese American community (Kitano & Daniels, 1995). In 1942, the U.S. government then, under military auspices, rounded up Japanese Americans from their homes, regardless of their age, sex, and even citizenship, placing them in "assembly centers" and then to "relocation centers," places of **internment**. Confined to these internment camps without trial, and only because of ancestry, thousands of Japanese Americans lived and worked in the camps (Hoobler & Hoobler, 1995). You may know of Japanese Americans whose family members experienced the effects of World War II in this way. Only 10,000 Japanese Americans on the mainland who lived east of the prescribed area and 150,000 Japanese Americans who lived in Hawaii did not enter the internment camps. For the Japanese Americans in Hawaii, their labor for the United States was a "military necessity" (Kitano & Daniels, 1995). The federal government began clearing individuals to leave the internment camps in 1944, and all internees left by 1945.

A striking irony of the internment camp experience is that in 1943 the federal government began recruiting Japanese American men from these internment camps for service in the U.S. military.

Author of this chapter Gordon Nagayama Hall's uncle, David Ogawa, was part of the all-Japanese American 442nd Regimental Combat Team that valiantly fought in Europe. The 442nd was one of the most highly decorated military units in U.S. history. Meanwhile, Hall's mother Olive, who had been a college student, her parents, and younger siblings were somehow considered a threat to national security and were placed in an internment camp in Poston, Arizona.

Approximately half of those who were in the internment camps moved east beyond the Rocky Mountains for school, work, or military service following the war (Hing, 1993; Hoobler & Hoobler, 1995). Many continued to experience discrimination at work and school (Kitano & Daniels, 1995). Loo (1993) considers the repeated exposure to racism through internment and by daily encounters within U.S. society to be a form of **race-related trauma**. This type

Isamu Miyata grew up in Hawaii and was drafted into the army in 1945 at the age of 20. Meanwhile, mainland Japanese Americans were still being confined to internment camps. Isamu Miyata is pictured above at an army training camp in Alabama.

of trauma has been associated with silence and shame within the family, as it pertains to internment (Nagata & Cheng, 2003). Meg, a Japanese American woman, reveals how this silence affected her family:

> My parents were both interned, and I was born in the camp. However, I didn't really find out anything about my parents' experience until I was seventeen. They just did not talk about it. . . . My parents and others like them were experiencing a kind of amnesia about the facts of war, life in the camps. (Chow, 1998, p. 194)

Over time, the American public began to recognize the hardships of internment and to appreciate the Nisei U.S. military service in the war. Formal government acknowledgment of wrongs came only in the 1980s when the tireless efforts of a group of Sansei and other Asian American attorneys helped overturn the World War II convictions of Gordon Hirabayashi and Minoru Yasui, who refused to comply with curfew laws that applied to Japanese Americans but not to other U.S. citizens, and of Fred Korematsu, who refused to comply with the internment camp evacuation order. As a result of these legal victories, the federal government apologized and compensated each Japanese American individual who had been interned. By then, however, almost half of those placed in internment were dead (Kitano & Daniels, 1995).

Since the 1970s, generations of Japanese Americans have integrated into mainstream America. Even so, Japanese Americans continue to participate in ethnic organizations and adhere to values such as hard work and community solidarity passed down by previous generations (Hoobler & Hoobler, 1995). Despite their success at acculturation, discrimination remains. Japanese Americans continue to be stereotyped based on their Asian physical features, reflecting the hesitancy of mainstream America to accept that an American with an Asian background is also American.

South Asian Americans

The British colonial rule in India and unresolved racial classification by Americans during the 20th century characterize the experiences of South Asian immigrants. South Asian Americans are identified as those whose ancestry can be traced to the Indian subcontinent, which includes a number of countries: Bangladesh, Bhutan, India, Maldives, Nepal, Pakistan, and Sri Lanka (South Asian Association for Regional Cooperation, n.d.).

The first major wave of South Asian immigration to the United States took place after 1900 (Hing, 1993). These early South Asian immigrants originated from Punjab, an agrarian region of India. Because the overpopulated Punjab could not offer everyone a share of land, South Asian Americans sought to acquire their own land in the United States. Although some became tenants and proprietors, most of the immigrants became laborers on sawmills, farms, and railroads in the Pacific Northwest. Frustrated that the South Asian Americans were willing to work for lower wages, hate crimes were committed against these immigrants. In one incident, 500 European Americans attacked the "Hindus," forcing several hundred South Asian Americans to flee into Canada (Kitano & Daniels, 1995).

Most of the Punjabis were Sikhs, who characteristically wore turbans and unshaven beards (Takaki, 1998). This difference in dress may have been another contributor to the prejudice toward South Asian Americans, prompting some Americans to regard them as "the least desirable race of immigrants" (Kitano & Daniels, 1995, p. 97). By 1917, South Asian Americans, along with other Asian groups, were not allowed to immigrate to the United States if they could not pass a literacy test. Racially motivated hostilities and the strategic attempt to exclude South Asian Americans decreased South Asian immigration to the United States.

Racial classification for South Asian Americans over the first half of the 20th century proved inconsistent and generally discriminatory (Takaki, 1995). From 1910 to 1920, the government deemed South Asian Americans as Caucasian, which granted them naturalization. Although this did not allow them to sell or lease land, some South Asian Americans married Mexican American citizens to circumvent the restriction (Hing, 1993).

The 1917 Asiatic Barred Zone Act expanded exclusions of Asian immigration, paralleling the exclusion of immigrants from China. This act prevented South Asians and several other Asian nationals from coming to the United States (Campi, 2005). The 1923 Supreme Court case *U.S. v. Bhagat Singh Thind* was a major setback for South Asian Americans in their quest to obtain U.S. citizenship (Hing, 1993; Takaki, 1998). The Supreme Court ruling classified South Asian Americans as non-White, annulling the status of naturalized South Asian Americans. In a protest against this nullification of citizenship, Vaisho Das Bagai took his own life, leaving the message:

> I am no longer an American citizen. . . . What have I made of myself and my children? We cannot exercise our rights, we cannot leave this country. Humility and insults, who are responsible for all this? I do not choose to live a life of an interned person. . . . Is life worth living in a gilded cage? (Takaki, 1998, p. 300)

South Asian Americans began to lobby again for U.S. citizenship during World War II as America looked to India to establish alliances against the Germans and Japanese (Kitano & Daniels, 1995). The right for naturalization was obtained following Congressional approval in 1946. The act allowed wives and children to immigrate to the United States (Hing, 1993). Later, the Immigration Act of 1965 dramatically changed the immigration pattern for South Asian Americans, as an influx of South Asians entered the United States (Takaki, 1995).

Compared to other Asian immigrant groups, South Asian immigrants distributed themselves across the country somewhat more evenly. South Asian Americans currently primarily reside in the Midwest and Northeast, in addition to the West (Kitano & Daniels, 1995). Highly educated South Asian–American men and women occupy positions in medicine and engineering (Takaki, 1995), with many living and working within Silicon Valley. Dubbed part of the **brain drain**, many Indians initially came to the United States after receiving training in India because of the difficulty in obtaining profitable positions in their native country (Zia, 2000). Although Indian American workers in technological positions are paid significantly more than their Indian counterparts, Indian nationals are more able to obtain technological positions because many U.S. companies are now outsourcing technological positions to India (Pink, 2004). Attracted by the modernization and economic growth in India, many Indian Americans have returned to their native country (Waldman, 2004). Recent economic opportunities within South Asia have rapidly changed the motivations to immigrate to the United States.

Although many South Asians are able to obtain well-paying positions in the United States, South Asian–American men and women continue to face a **glass ceiling** when it comes to income and attainment of management positions (Fernandez, 1998). There is just a handful of South Asians in upper management, such as Amar Bose (founder of Bose Corporation), Kim Singh (CEO of PortaEnterprise and former executive of IBM, Ernst & Young, and Unisys), and Indra Nooyi (CEO of PepsiCo). As it currently stands, however, there are 4.4 percent of Asian Americans in the workforce, and only less than 1 percent in senior management. Only 1 percent holds board seats on a Fortune 500 company (Curry, 2006).

Not all South Asian Americans in the United States are educated and skilled technically. During the 1980s, an influx of South Asian Americans started businesses in the United States. South Asian Americans currently occupy the newsstand industry of New York, work as taxicab

Silicon Valley, an area within the San Francisco Bay area, is home to several high-tech industries. Many South Asian Americans, immigrants from the South Asian brain drain, work alongside Chinese American engineers.

drivers, and operate successful motel and hotel chains across the United States (Kitano & Daniels, 1995; Zia, 2000). Working-class South Asian Americans have borne the resentment of other ethnic groups due to their success in attaining these jobs. For instance, during the 1980s, members of the Puerto Rican community harassed South Asian–American business owners (Takaki, 1995). The Jersey City gang, "Dotbusters," in reference to the dot or bindi that Indian women often wear, have targeted and violently attacked South Asian Americans. After the September 11, 2001, terrorist attacks on the World Trade Center in New York City, South Asian Americans from all socioeconomic and educational backgrounds have been the target of hate crimes and racial profiling. South Asian Americans are commonly mistaken as illegal immigrants or terrorists (Novas, Cao, & Silva, 2004).

First- and second-generation South Asian Americans, like earlier generations, may continue to grapple with their identification as Americans. Due in part to the successful lobbying of the Association of Indians in America, the U.S. government counts South Asian Americans as Asian American (Novas, Cao, & Silva, 2004). Nowadays, South Asian Americans are the third largest Asian American group in the United States (U.S. Census Bureau, 2000). Even so, South Asian Americans often feel like outsiders to Asian Americans, especially since East Asian groups are not inclined to recognize South Asia as Asia. The debate as to whether South Asian Americans should consider themselves as Asian American remains, even among second-generation South Asian Americans. The decision to identify with being American is an issue even within the family. From one perspective, the task of second-generation South Asian Americans is to assimilate and succeed by attaining a good education and a well-paying job, but to also retain traditional values, such as marrying someone within their own group (Zia, 2000). As of now, a better understanding of the psychological adjustment among South Asian Americans, as it relates to issues of discrimination and identity in America, is still necessary.

Korean Americans

Korean Americans came to the United States in waves at the end of the 19th century. The Sino-Japanese War, which took place in Korea, propagated Korea's earliest wave of immigration to the United States (Kitano & Daniels, 1995). The poor living conditions in Korea, coupled with the need for laborers on the island of Hawaii, motivated approximately 7,000 Koreans to immigrate to Hawaii from 1903 to 1905 (Hing, 1993). Facilitated by Christian missionaries, sugar plantations recruited lower-class Koreans to work in the fields. Like the other ethnic minority laborers, these early Korean Americans faced poverty and hardship.

Japanese annexation in Korea prevented further migration of Koreans to the United States, consequently affecting the identity of Koreans in Hawaii (Zia, 2000). As a marginalized group in Hawaii without a homeland to return to, these Korean American "exiles" bonded together based on Korean nationalism, establishing Korean churches and schools that retained their home culture. During that period, one Korean writer from the *Sinhan Minbo* newspaper wrote: "If we want to start afresh our Korean community, we should give serious thought to our children's education and have schools that would give them Korean education" (Takaki, 1998, p. 279).

Korean women arrived as picture brides during this time, which helped to form Korean American families. Korean Americans also formed interethnic marriages in Hawaii, as they began to assimilate into mainstream culture (Novas, Cao, & Silva, 2004). In the early 20th century, Korean immigrants, like Chinese and Japanese laborers, left for the mainland and worked on farms and on the railroads.

After the Korean War in 1953, another wave of Korean immigrants arrived to the United States. These immigrants were predominantly the wives of servicemen and war orphans, with a small number of them students and professionals. Korean "war brides," accompanying their military husbands back to the United States, largely subsumed into American society (Kitano & Daniels, 1995). These women were not immune to the hardship of immigration according to the few studies conducted on this group (Yuh, 2002; Kim, 1972; Ratliff, Moon, & Bonacci, 1972; Jeong & Schumm, 1990). Attempted suicide and psychological maladjustments from abuse or "culture shock" characterized the experience of some wives (Yuh, 2002).

Approximately 150,000 of the immigrants from this wave were comprised of war orphans adopted by middle-class European Americans (Ministry of Health and Welfare, 1999). Korean adoptees faced a unique condition unlike other Asian American immigrants, appearing racially different from their European American families and from the communities they were raised in. As you might imagine, this often raised issues regarding their identity. Young Hee, a Korean adoptee describes: "Theoretically I was white, my family is white, the community I grew up in was white, and I could not point out Korea on a map, nor did I care about such a place. . . . I denied that I was Korean to everyone, most painfully, I denied it to myself" (Bishoff & Rankin, 1997).

Currently, Korean adoptees, their adoptive families, and others have raised issues specific to this experience, and have organized themselves, either in person or online, as a community, evidenced by the number of Web sites committed to support their unique experience.

The experiences of the most recent wave of Korean immigrants, arriving after the Immigration Act of 1965, are reminiscent of the second-generation Chinese and Japanese immigrants. With the exception of some Korean immigrants, such as doctors who successfully found work in New York (Takaki, 1995), language barriers and discrimination prevented many immigrants from obtaining professional positions even though many were professionally skilled in medicine or engineering. Instead, these Korean Americans chose to open small businesses, such as groceries, dry cleaners, and restaurants. The effect of the shift toward downward mobility included long working hours and the constant struggle to maintain an income. Due to the family-oriented nature of Korean Americans, all family members often contributed to the operation of the business (e.g., Min, 1984). Unlike traditional Korean gender roles, where women remain at home, many Korean American women found themselves working out of economic necessity (Kim & Kim, 1998; Lim, 1997). The lack of adherence to gender roles and occupational difficulties are sources of immigration stress for Korean American families. Immigration stress and psychological maladjustment may contribute to the high rate of domestic violence within Korean American families (Rhee, 1997).

Korean American-owned businesses are often located in large urban centers such as New York City or Los Angeles. Located within African American neighborhoods, Korean business owners faced a downside to their operations, as it became the center of racial tension between Korean Americans and other ethnic groups living in those areas. The impetus for the major conflict between the Korean Americans and African Americans involved the 1992 rioting following the verdict that found police officers not guilty of violating the civil rights of Rodney King, an African American beating victim (Novas, Cao, & Silva, 2004). The racial and economic conflict among minority groups manifested in massive looting and armed conflict, and took place at Korean American-operated stores, lasting three days (e.g., Min, 1996; Kim, 1999). **Sa-I-gu**, which literally means "April 29," denotes the riot that left financially and psychologically lasting effects on Korean Americans. One study found that the majority of riot victims experienced severe distress and symptoms of post-traumatic stress disorder (Kim-Goh, Suh, Blake, & Hiley-Young, 1995).

Currently, over 1 million Americans are of Korean descent (U.S. Census Bureau, 2000). Like other ethnic groups, Korean Americans predominantly reside in California and New York. A considerable number have also moved to areas such as Illinois, Washington, and Georgia. As middle-class entrepreneurs, many Korean immigrants have encouraged their American-born children toward upward mobility by attaining a better education and well-paying professions (Novas, Cao, & Silva, 2004). Given the relatively shorter immigration history of Korean Americans compared to other ethnic groups, greater research on immigration stress, discrimination, and psychological adjustment is needed for Korean American families.

Filipino Americans

The United States colonized the Philippines shortly after the conclusion of the Spanish-American War in 1898. As an official American colony, the Filipino people were considered "nationals" of the United States. As U.S. nationals, the Filipino people were not subjected to the same

A Korean American family from Maryland welcomes home their son and brother after his service in the Iraq War. AA/PIs continue to serve in the U.S. military, like previous generations. In 2005, 4.5% of all personnel on active duty and 3.4% of those in the National Guards and Reserves were AA/PIs. These numbers closely reflect the representation of military service age-eligible AAPIs (Williams, 2005).

exclusionary laws as other Asian ethnic groups. Until the Tydings–McDuffie Act in 1934, there was a high rate of immigration from the Philippines. Immediately after the establishment of the Philippine Independence Act in 1934, however, they were legally considered "aliens" (Sobredo, 1997). The Tydings–McDuffie Act restricted Philippine immigration to 50 people per year.

Having endured 377 years of Spanish colonization (1521 to 1898) and 50 years as a formal U.S. colony (1898 to 1946), Filipino culture is a mosaic of eastern and western influence, despite their geographical connection with Asia. Although colonization by the United States has facilitated their adaptation into mainstream culture, the unique relationship between the Philippines and the United States has been marred by ambivalence. The Philippines has tolerated over a century of extreme shifts from U.S. immigration and legal policy makers (Sobredo, 1997).

The migration history of the Filipino people reflects the heterogeneity of the culture. Filipinos entered the United States in three waves (San Juan, 1994). The first wave, which lasted from 1906 to 1946, was composed of a mix of agricultural workers, who settled throughout Hawaii and California, and college students sponsored by the United States. Following the success of hiring Japanese Americans to work on the plantations of Hawaii, sugarcane and pineapple plantation owners recruited Filipinos to work on their land. Not restricted to exclusionary laws that barred other Asian groups from entering the United States, over a hundred thousand Filipinos arrived in Hawaii between 1909 and 1934 in hopes of finding livelihood as field workers (Alcantara, 1981). The laborers, comprised mostly of men, served 3-year renewable contracts. These Filipino workers returned to the Philippines, stayed in Hawaii, or, like other Asian groups, moved toward the mainland for agricultural work (Espiritu, 1995).

Additionally, the U.S. government invited and funded **pensionados** to study in America. Over the course of 1903 to 1910, hundreds of Filipino students studied at universities across America, including prestigious Ivy League schools, such as Harvard and Yale. Several of those who succeeded in obtaining their degrees returned to the Philippines to work in government. However, not all pensionados were so fortunate. Many of those who did not complete their education ended up finding work in low-paid labor positions in the United States (Castillo-Tsuchida, 1979).

The second wave, from 1930 to 1964, was composed of the families of war veterans who fought alongside U.S. servicemen during World War II. Along with the Chinese Americans and Korean Americans, Filipino Americans shared the benefits of wartime prosperity and idealized Asian stereotypes created by the United States to separate Asian American groups from Japanese Americans. Despite their wartime allegiance to the United States, however, they entered the United States without American citizenship (Espiritu, 1995).

The third wave, from 1965 to 1984, included people from both the professional and working class. These Filipino Americans arrived to the United States under the Immigration Act of 1965, which gave Filipinos the opportunity to escape the hardships of their own country and seek out a better life. Motivated by political instability from the Philippines, Filipino immigrants sought better economic opportunities within the United States. Educated and professional, these Filipino immigrants shared similar characteristics with other Asian groups arriving at this time (Kitano & Daniels, 1995).

Filipino culture is often ignored when discussing Asian American issues, despite their status as the fastest-growing Asian American group (Flores, 1994). As the second largest Asian group (U.S. Census Bureau, 2000), their status as the "invisible Asian group" is ironic. The Filipino people's ease in adapting to American culture may contribute to their obscurity when discussing Asian American issues (Flores, 1994). Within the Asian groups, Filipino Americans demonstrate the greatest level of multiculturalism because of their history as a Spanish and U.S. colony. As such, they are often not thought of as Asian Americans. Today's Filipino Americans

A Filipino American grandmother and grandson visit San Francisco from their hometown of Los Angeles. When arriving to America, Filipino Americans resided largely in metropolitan cities on the West and East coasts. In the 1930s, many of them lived in "Little Manilas," small ethnic communities similar to Chinatown. Nowadays, Filipino Americans reside in both the cities and the suburbs across the United States.

include professionals, with many women specially trained in the medical field. However, these Filipino immigrants seem to lack cohesion compared to the East Asian groups that have organized themselves, and settle dispersedly the country.

Southeast Asians

There is incredible diversity among Southeast Asians, but they are often studied and discussed as one cultural group. Southeast Asians differ in their premigration histories, religious and philosophical ideology, worldviews, and language. Colonization created more cultural distance among the Southeast Asian groups than would be expected based on their geographic proximity. Laos itself is home to four different ethnic groups.

Broadly grouped, Southeast Asians can be understood in terms of their migration status. Ogbu (2002) distinguishes between refugees, or involuntary minorities, and immigrants, or voluntary minorities. Southeast Asian refugees include Cambodians, Vietnamese, and Laotians, which also include among them Mien, Hmong, and Meo ethnic groups. Other Southeast Asian groups have entered the United States under less coercive conditions. While some Southeast Asians, such as the Burmese, have entered the United States with refugee status, the majority have been voluntary immigrants. In the United States, their experiences reflect their cultural distinctness. Table 1.1 includes a breakdown of the different Southeast Asian groups currently living in the United States. This discussion will include a history of Southeast Asian refugees (Vietnamese, Cambodians, Hmongs) and other Southeast Asians (Thais, Indonesians, Malays, Singaporeans).

Southeast Asian Refugees The political turmoil that ensued shortly after the Vietnam War spread to the surrounding countries of Cambodia and Laos, forcing many of the inhabitants to flee their war-ravaged homelands. Although the Geneva Conference established Laos as a neutral country in 1954, North Vietnam relied on the **Ho Chi Minh Trail** in Laos to fight against South Vietnam (Conboy, 1995). To aid in the war without direct military involvement, the CIA covertly trained thousands of Hmong to fight against the North Vietnamese. Like the Vietnamese, the Hmong fled their war-torn country after the war. Fearing the Communist regime, over a hundred thousand Hmong people have entered the United States since 1975 (Office of Immigration Statistics, 2004). The United States also entered into Cambodia, bombing villages, and areas that housed the Vietnamese Communist camps and supply routes. Khmer Rouge, the Communist organization within Cambodia, overtook Cambodia during the 1970s, and shut down the country by confiscating property, closing institutions, and evacuating the cities (Chan, 2004). Khmer Rouge killed almost 2 million Cambodians through torture, execution, and starvation. Chanrithy Him, author of *When Broken Glass Floats* (2000), writes of her experiences during the Khmer Rouge:

> Throughout a childhood dominated by war, I learned to survive. In a country faced with drastic changes, the core of my soul was determined to never let the horrific situations take away the better part of me. I mentally resisted forces I could only recognize as evil by being a human recorder, quietly observing my surroundings, making mental notes of the things around me. There would come a day to share them, giving my voice to children who can't speak for themselves. Giving voice, as well, to my deceased parents, sisters, brothers, and extended family members, and to those whose remains are unmarked mass graves scattered throughout Cambodia, the once-gentle land. (p. 21)

Approximately 150,000 Cambodians have been admitted to the United States from 1974 to 1998, with the most recent wave of refugees escaping Cambodia after the mass defection of the Khmer Rouge in 1996 (Office of Immigration Statistics, 2004).

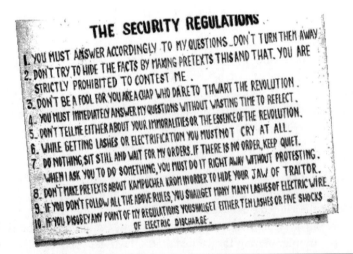

Pol Pot was responsible for the deaths of 2 million Cambodians. He frequently imprisoned those he considered enemies to Cambodia; this included educated Cambodians and anyone affiliated with the former monarchy. A sign hanging in Pol Pot's infamous prison, Tuol Sleng, reflects the years of intimidation and bloodshed that the Cambodian people experienced under his dictatorship. Many Cambodians fled to France, Canada, and the United States as a result of this experience.

Southeast Asian refugees entered the United States in three waves, each defined by a distinguishing set of circumstances and struggles. The first wave came immediately after the end of the Vietnam War from 1975 to 1978. During this time, President Gerald Ford authorized the entrance of 130,000 Southeast Asian refugees into the United States. This wave was composed mostly of Vietnamese and Cambodian individuals with social clout, such as political leaders, educated professionals, and the wealthy.

Approximately 700,000 Southeast Asians comprised the second wave of refugees arriving to the United States in 1978 (Office of Immigration Statistics, 2004). The fall of Saigon, which ended the Vietnam War, prompted hundreds of thousands of surviving Vietnamese, fearing reprisal from the Communists that had taken control of the country, to leave for countries such as China, France, and Canada. After the Vietnamese moved from their homes to asylum camps, U.S. military cargo ships transferred the Vietnamese to refugee-processing centers in the United States.

Additionally, the invasion of Cambodia by Vietnam marked the end of the "killing fields" and its associated trauma propagated by the Communist regime, the Khmer Rouge. Unlike their predecessors, this second wave included individuals from a variety of socioeconomic backgrounds, including less-educated farmers, and fisherman. The second wave brought with them a more traumatic history of war atrocities. Their adaptation to American culture was made difficult by their limited English proficiency and education (Takaki, 1995; Kitano & Daniels, 1995).

The third wave entered the United States after 1982, amidst changes in refugee policies. In collaboration with the Vietnamese government, individuals left Vietnam as part of the Orderly

Coauthor Sopagna Eap's family in a Thailand refugee camp. Eap's parents, Hwai and Heang Eap, and uncle, Harrison Pech, were part of the second wave of Cambodian refugees that entered the United States after the Cambodian civil war. Forbidden to leave the country, they narrowly dodged active minefields and Vietnamese soldiers as they rode bicycles to the Cambodian-Thai border.

Departure Program (ODP) and were granted immigrant status rather than refugee status. This group included released prisoners from reeducation camps and Amerasian children fathered by U.S. servicemen during the war (Kitano & Daniels, 1995).

Since the flight from war and political turmoil, Southeast Asians have had to reconcile their desire to go back to their homeland with living in and acculturating to American society. Cultural differences among the Southeast Asian groups have made this process particularly difficult. In particular, the Hmong have faced drastic cultural challenges, including a disruption in their agrarian lifestyle and ostracism toward their custom of marrying child brides (Kitano & Daniels, 1995). Among immigrant groups, the Hmong are among the poorest and most unemployed (Swartz, Lee, & Mortimer, 2003). Limited occupational skills and language competencies have prevented Southeast Asians from easily adapting to American culture (Ying & Akutsu, 1997).

Thais, Malays, Indonesians, Singaporeans, and Bruneian   Unlike their neighboring countries, the Thais were fortunate to not experience the political turmoil that characterized most of Southeast Asia. Instead, immigration to the United States by the Thai people was motivated more by military and trade connections than by political necessity (Novas, Cao, & Silva, 2004).

Other Southeast Asian groups from Indonesia, Malaysia, Burma, Brunei, and Singapore make up a small percentage of the Asian population in the United States (Novas, Cao, & Silva, 2004). The people of Indonesia, Malaysia, and Burma are no strangers to poverty and political instability in their own homelands, but poverty has prevented many of them from immigrating to the United States. The majority enter the United States through family preference provisions, and education. For this reason, only a little over 100,000 residents in the United States are from these three countries combined (U.S. Census Bureau, 2000).

In contrast, Singaporeans and Bruneian individuals enjoy some of the highest standards of living of any groups in the world. As a result, few come to the United States. These groups constitute a very small percentage of the U.S. population.

Pacific Islanders

Pacific Islanders have roots in Oceania, which includes islands in the Central and South Pacific Ocean. Oceania is composed of Polynesia (many islands), Micronesia (small islands), and Melanesia (black islands). Polynesia includes the Hawaiian Islands and American Samoa. Micronesia includes Guam, a U.S. territory, and the Marshall Islands, while Melanesia includes Fiji and Papua New Guinea. Among the Asian and Pacific Islander American population, Pacific Islanders have a particularly high risk for mental health problems and disabilities (Andrade et al., 2006; Cho & Hummer, 2001). However, Pacific Islanders are vastly understudied, and little is known about the protective and risk factors for mental illness and the most appropriate preventative measures and treatments for this heterogeneous group.

In the 2000 U.S. Census, 874,414 individuals identified themselves as Pacific Islanders, the majority of whom live in Hawaii and California. Pacific Islanders make up 0.3 percent of the U.S. population and are often of mixed heritage. Two-thirds of Pacific Islanders self-identify as biracial or multiracial. The four largest Pacific Islander subgroups in the United States (alone or in combination with one or more other races) are Native Hawaiians, Samoans, Guamanians, Chamarros, and Tongans (U.S. Census Bureau, 2000).

Native Hawaiians   Polynesians first settled on Hawaii approximately 1,500 years ago. It was not until January 18, 1878, that James Cook, an English explorer, first stumbled onto the shores of Hawaii. Initially, Captain Cook was showered with gifts from the Hawaiian people. However, in a later trip to the islands, he was stabbed to death over an incident involving a stolen boat

Brothers Justin, Jeris, and Jordan Orian are ¾ Japanese, ⅛ Filipino, and ⅛ Hawaiian. Like many children living in Hawaii, they are multiracial. This picture was taken in the mid-1980s. Justin is currently residing in Beaverton, Oregon, Jeris in Pearl City, Hawaii, and Jordan in Las Vegas, Nevada.

from one of his ships. Captain Cook was the first of several American and European explorers to exert a profound influence on the inhabitants of the previously isolated islands. At the time of his arrival, there were approximately 300,000 Hawaiians inhabiting the islands. By 1858, after numerous contacts with explorers and missionaries, the Hawaiian population had dramatically decreased in numbers to an estimated 60,000 due to the introduction of foreign, infectious diseases, such as syphilis (Novas, Cao, & Silva, 2004). Also by this time, the Hawaiians had largely abandoned their religion and their kapu (taboo) system, and adopted the Christian religion and many Western ideas. This was largely facilitated by King Kamehameha II, who had abolished the Hawaiian religion during his rule.

In 1848, King Kamehameha III signed an act called the **Great Mahele**, which divided the millions of acres of Hawaiian land between mostly the government and the Hawaiian chiefs. Before western influence, Hawaiians had no concept of land ownership and did not believe that the land belonged to anyone. Many Hawaiians sold their property for meager sums to foreigners, believing that this would not affect their use of the land. Foreigners soon seized the land for growing crops, hiring Hawaiians as cheap labor. Soon thereafter, wealthy plantation owners began recruiting workers from Asian countries to supplement Hawaii's dwindling native population, in effect creating one of the world's first "melting pots" (Novas, Cao, & Silva, 2004). On January 17, 1893, fearing the threat of taxation of their crops into the United States under the leadership of Queen Liliuokalani, plantation owners rallied for the dethroning of the queen by the U.S. government and staged a rebellion. The success of the rebellion led to the annexation of Hawaii to the United States, under President William McKinley in 1898. However, it was not until March 12, 1959, that Hawaii became the 50th state of the Union (Novas, Cao, & Silva, 2004).

Originally a healthy people, Native Hawaiians now face a multitude of physical and mental health problems (Cook, Withy, Tarallo-Jensen, & Berry, 2005). One study found that Native Hawaiian adolescents have significantly higher rates of psychiatric disorders than non-Hawaiians, particularly for anxiety disorders (Andrade et al., 2006). Interestingly, a strong ethnic identity in this population has been shown to be a protective factor for symptoms of depression and anxiety (Mccubbin, 2004), as well as a decreased risk of becoming a victim or perpetrator of violence (Austin, 2004).

Samoans, Guamanians, and Tongans　Similar to the Hawaiian Islands, the Samoan Islands were first inhabited by Polynesians and remained isolated until 1722 when Jacob Roggeveen, a Dutchman, first landed on its shores. Missionaries soon followed. In 1899, Germany and the United States essentially split the islands of Samoa between them. American (Eastern) Samoa went to the United States and was annexed on April 17, 1900 (Novas, Cao, & Silva, 2004). Around the same time, the Spanish-American War of 1898 concluded with the Treaty of Paris, in which Spain ceded Guam to the United States. The Spanish had ruled Guam since 1695 and much of the native population (the Chamarros) had been wiped out (Novas, Cao, & Silva, 2004). The Kingdom of Tonga, unlike Hawaii, Samoa, and Guam, is not owned by the United States. Rather, Tongans began immigrating to the United States in the 1960s with the backing and encouragement of the Church of Jesus Christ of Latter-day Saints, which had become a strong presence in Tonga (Novas, Cao, & Silva, 2004).

While very little research has been done on Pacific Islanders as a population, even less research has been conducted on Samoans, Guamanians, and Tongans. However, based on their histories, one would speculate that there exist differences in the psychological landscapes of these populations. Researchers should be careful not to overgeneralize their findings within one specific Pacific Islander group to the entire Pacific Islander population.

Socioeconomic Status

Asian Americans are often perceived as a group that has successfully utilized education for upward mobility. According to the 2000 U.S. Census Bureau, Asian Americans have the highest median household income of all ethnic groups. This figure, however, can be misleading. For instance, Asian American households are larger than European American households. The Asian American household includes more children and elderly people than the average European American household. When household income per capita is examined, Asian Americans are behind European Americans despite their higher rates of educational attainment. Even with a median income that is higher than the national average, Asian Americans still have a high rate of poverty. The Census shows that 13.5% of all Asian Americans live in poverty. This percentage is similar to the national average of 14% (U.S. Census Bureau, 2000). These dichotomous findings reflect the heterogeneity within ethnic minority populations. Table 1.4 shows data from the 2000 U.S. Census Bureau indicating median family income and percentage of those living in poverty in different Asian American groups. Southeast Asians and Pacific Islanders are over-represented in the lowest economic strata.

The "Model Minority"?

> In sixth grade Mrs. Walker
> Slapped the back of my head
> And made me stand in the corner
> For not knowing the difference
> Between persimmon and precision.
> How to choose
> Persimmons. This is precision…
>
> –Li Young Lee, "Persimmons" (1986, p. 17)

Table 1.4 Income Levels for Each Asian Ethnic Group

	Chinese	Japanese	Filipinos	Asian Indians	Cambodian/ Hmong/ Laotian	Koreans	Pacific Islanders	Vietnamese
Median family income	$58,300	$61,630	$65,400	$69,470	$43,850	$48,500	$50,000	$51,500
Median personal income	$20,000	$26,000	$23,000	$26,000	$16,000	$16,300	$19,100	$16,000
Percentage living in poverty	13.1	8.6	6.9	8.2	22.5	15.5	16.7	13.8

Source: U.S. Census Bureau. (2000). *Census 2000.* Washington, DC.

The popularity of the model minority myth largely stems from the educational success of Asian American students. Indeed, at first glance, evidence suggests that Asian Americans surpass all other ethnic groups in educational attainment. Eighty-five percent of all Asian American adults have attended college. Thirty-one percent of all Asian Americans 25 years of age or older hold a college degree, which is higher than the national average of 21% (Chang & Le, 2005). Asian Americans are also more likely to attain graduate degrees in higher education.

It is important to remember that figures suggesting the relative success of Asian Americans do not accurately reflect the academic experiences of all Asian Americans. Achievement discrepancies exist among various Asian American groups. Barriers experienced by refugee groups are obscured by evidence suggesting that Asian Americans are academically successful. Thus, social services and scholarships that are available to ethnic minorities often exclude Asian Americans from being eligible, despite the low achievement rates of Cambodians, Hmongs, Laotians, and Pacific Islanders.

Among Asian Americans, Southeast Asians and Asian Pacific Islanders do not experience the same level of academic success as their South Asian and East Asian counterparts, although Vietnamese American children are quickly bridging the academic gap (Zhou & Bankston, 1998). Southeast Asian Americans have lower college graduation rates than that of the national average. For example, only 6% of Cambodians, 7% of Laotian or Mien, and 17% of Vietnamese complete a college degree (Niedzwiecki & Duong, 2004). Twenty-six percent of Cambodians and 22.7% of Laotians have experienced no formal education. One reason for this discrepancy may be the conditions surrounding their immigration. Many Southeast Asian Americans have experienced various traumatic events and have had a more difficult time adapting to the host culture.

Explanations to account for the academic success of Asian Americans include both cultural and structural theories (Kim, 2002). Cultural theorists posit that the inculcation of the Confucian values of hard work, education, and social solidarity among Asian American children are responsible for their high rate of academic achievement. Structural explanations include the idea of relative functionalism (Sue & Okazaki, 1990). This explanation suggests that hardships experienced by immigrant groups result in an emphasis on education as a means of upward social mobility.

The idea that education may be the pathway for social leverage may perpetuate behaviors conducive to academic achievement among Asian American children. Indeed, Asian American youth are more likely to be involved in achievement-oriented peer groups (Steinberg, Dorn-busch, & Brown, 1992). Clearly Asian Americans place a high value on education. However, this high value comes at a cost to Asian Americans.

Even when Asian Americans do well, they must overcome obstacles not endured by Euro-pean Americans. Despite higher levels of educational attainment, evidence suggests that the economic payoff for the amount of education received by Asian Americans is lower than that of all other ethnic groups. For instance, found that Chinese Americans made less money than European Americans and African Americans when education, occupation prestige, and number of hours worked were equal, suggesting a glass ceiling effect that isn't revealed by descriptions of mean salary (Leong, 1998). Asian Americans are also less likely to be included in the ranks of management positions. Studies suggest that Asian values emphasizing social conformity and interpersonal harmony may work against Asian Americans when decisions regarding positions of authority are made (Leong, 1985). As Asian Americans acculturate and adapt more western values, stereotypes perpetuating Asian Americans as introverted and sub-missive may limit their ability to enter into more socially interactive fields such as law and psychology.

Summary

Who are Asian Americans? What does it mean to be Asian American? Answering these questions may have proven to be even more difficult than you first imagined. *Asian American* is an umbrella term for many ethnic groups and does not readily demonstrate the heterogeneous cultures, histories, and lifestyles for the members of these groups. Although many perceive Asian Americans to be well off economically, the socioeconomic status of Asian Americans must be couched in an understanding of the heterogeneous circumstances and cultural beliefs of each group. Generalized perceptions of the group as a whole have created the "model minority" myth, which has been found to affect psychological functioning. The question of how these perceptions might change remains, as the histories and experiences of Asian Americans continue to evolve.

Discussion Questions

1. Why is it important to study Asian Americans?
2. What is your cultural background? How has your background shaped who you are? How has your background influenced your personal habits?
3. How might the historical experiences of different ethnic groups impact their psycho-logical experiences?
4. When was the last time you observed or experienced discrimination? How did you come to determine it to be discrimination?
5. How might the "model minority" myth have a positive impact for Asian Americans? How might it have a negative impact? How might it positively or negatively impact other ethnic groups?
6. What will each of the different Asian American communities look like 50 years from now? How might individuals' ethnic identities change over time?
7. Imagine you are a refugee from another country coming to the United States. How similar or different would this experience be from that of a "voluntary immigrant"? What challenges or advantages might you face that "voluntary immigrants" may not experience?

8. The U.S. government dispersed many Southeast Asian refugees all over the country and settled them in small towns in the Midwest rather than big cities on the West Coast where there is a larger Asian American population. Can you think of the advantages and disadvantages of the U.S. government's approach to resettling Southeast Asian refugees? What emotional, psychological, and social issues might you face as a refugee living in California versus as a refugee living in Arkansas?

Key Terms

Brain drain: The loss of professionally trained labor from one environment to another environment considered more geographically or economically favorable. In the present day, many skilled South Asian Americans come to the United States to seek better opportunities.

Glass ceiling: Covert barriers experienced by minority groups in the workforce that precludes them from advancing in rank.

Great Mahele: An act signed by King Kamehameha III in 1848 dividing Hawaiian land between the royal family, chiefs, and the government. A small percentage of land went to commoners.

Ho Chi Minh Trail: A network of paths and roads used by the Viet Cong, a militant Communist group, to supply soldiers and supplies into South Vietnam during the Vietnamese War.

Internment: The imprisonment or confinement of individuals, in camps, without legal due process. For Japanese Americans, it refers to their experience of being forced to relocate by the U.S. government during World War II.

Paper sons: Young men, often in their teens, who came to the United States from China. These men posed as sons of an American-born or naturalized Chinese American in order to gain entry into the United States.

Pensionados: Filipino students sponsored by the U.S. government to receive a university education in the United States.

Picture brides: Women from primarily Japan and Korea chosen as brides by a matchmaker and paired with a groom living in the United States. Thousands of women during the 20th century married men whom they only "met" through photographs and family recommendations.

Race-related trauma: Experienced by stigmatized groups, such as Japanese Americans in internment, and it involves the repeated exposure to overt or covert racial discrimination, which can lead to interpersonal and psychological difficulties.

Sa-I-gu: A Korean term that refers to April 29, 1992, the day in which racially motivated riots targeted Korean American businesses in Los Angeles. Due to the acquittal of four members of the LAPD in the case of an African American man, Rodney King, riots involving fire and looting destroyed over 2,000 Korean American–operated stores. The riots prompted a city-wide curfew and over 30,000 law enforcement officers to maintain the area.

Sojourners: Immigrants who do not intend to stay in the new country permanently.

For Further Learning and Suggested Readings

1. Interview an Asian immigrant about his or her experiences entering the United States, preferably someone who is in your family or close to you in some way. You will be surprised at how much more you learn about them by focusing on such a vivid and often evocative experience. Here are some questions to consider asking: What were the most challenging aspects of immigrating to this country? Is there a story that sticks out in your memory that characterizes your experience as an immigrant? Who (if anyone) did you turn to for social support? What emotions did you personally

experience when you first entered this country? After a year living in this country? After 10 years?

2. Construct a family tree. Try to go back at least 4 generations. List where each family member was born and, if applicable, the year they immigrated to the United States.

3. Create a realistic dialogue between a man and a woman meeting for the first time on the shores of Hawaii. The Japanese man is an immigrant who emigrated to Hawaii to work in the sugar cane fields. The woman is a picture bride in search of a better life. This is their first meeting and they will be married later on that day.

4. What would it take to make you leave your country for good? Write down a list of possibilities and throw them into a hat. Draw one of the possibilities from the hat and identify the emotions associated with the situation you have created. Where would you go and why?

5. It is common to experience the symptoms of depression (i.e., sadness, fatigue, irritability, sleeplessness) when you move to a new place, especially if that place is very different from the place where you came from. Research treatments for depression in an Asian country and compare it to the treatments here (e.g., antidepressants and psychotherapy). Which treatments seem more appealing to you? If a recent Asian immigrant asks you to recommend help for his symptoms of depression, what would you tell him?

Chang, I. (2003). *The Chinese in America: A narrative history*. New York: Penguin Books.

Espiritu, Y. L. (2001). *Home bound: Filipino American lives across cultures, communities, and countries*. Berkeley: University of California Press.

Fadiman, A. (1998). *The spirit catches you and you fall down*. New York: Farrar, Straus and Giroux.

Hagedorn, J. T. (1993). *Charlie Chan is dead: An anthology of contemporary Asian American fiction*. New York: Penguin Books.

Hatta, K. (1994). *Picture Bride* [Motion picture]. Hawaii: Miramax Productions.

Houston, J. D., & Houston, J. W. (1973). *Farewell to Manzanar*. New York: Dell Laurel-Leaf.

Kim, I. J. (2004). *Korean-Americans: Past, present, and future*. New Jersey: Hollym International Corp.

Lahiri, J. (1999). *Interpreter of Maladies*. New York: Houghton Mifflin Company.

McCunn, R. L. (1989). *Thousand pieces of gold*. Boston: Beacon Press.

Novas, H., Cao, L., & Silva, R. (2004). *Everything you need to know about Asian American history*. New York: Penguin Group.

Pandya, P. D. (Director). (2001). *American Desi* [Motion picture]. United States: Blue Rock Entertainment.

Puttnam, D. (Director). (1994). *The killing fields* [Motion picture]. Thailand: Warner Bros.

Stone, O. (Director). (1993). *Heaven and earth* [Motion picture]. Thailand: Warner Bros.

Tajima-Pena, R. (Director). (1997). *Honk if you like Buddha* [Documentary]. United States: Independent Television Service.

Takaki, R. (1998). *Strangers from a different shore: A history of Asian Americans*. Boston: Little, Brown and Company.

References

Alcantara, R. (1981). *Sakada: Filipino adaptation in Hawaii*. Washington, DC: University Press.

Andrade, N. N., Hishinuma, E. S., McDermott, J. F., Johnson, R. C., Goebert, D. A., Makini, G. K., et al. (2006). The National Center on Indigenous Hawaiian Behavioral Health study of prevalence of psychiatric disorders in Native Hawaiian adolescents. *Journal of the American Academy of Child & Adolescent Psychiatry, 45*, 26–36.

Austin, A. A. (2004). Alcohol, tobacco, other drug use, and violent behavior among Native Hawaiians: Ethnic pride and resilience. *Substance Use & Misuse, 39*, 721–746.

Bishoff, T., & Rankin, J. (Eds.). (1997). *Seeds from a silent tree: An anthology by Korean adoptees*. San Diego: Pandall Press.

Campi, A. J. (2005). Closed borders and mass deportations: The lessons of the barred zone act. Retrieved September 24, 2006, from The American Immigration Law Foundation Web site: http://www.ailf.org/ipc/policy_reports_2005_barredzone.asp

Castillo-Tsuchida, A. (1979). *Filipino migrants in San Diego: 1900–1946.* San Diego, CA: San Diego Society.

Chan, S. (1991). *Asian Americans: An interpretive history.* CT: Twayne Publishers.

Chan, S. (2004). *Survivors: Cambodian refugees in the United States.* IL: University of Illinois Press.

Chang, I. (2003). *The Chinese in America: A narrative history.* New York: Penguin Books.

Chang, J., & Le, T. N. (2005). The influence of parents, peer delinquency, and school attitudes on academic achievement in Chinese, Cambodian, Laotian or Mien, and Vietnamese youth. *Crime and Delinquency, 51,* 238–264.

Cho, Y., & Hummer, R. A. (2001). Disability status differentials across fifteen Asian and Pacific Islander groups and the effect of nativity and duration of residence in the U.S. *Social Biology, 48,* 171–195.

Chow, C. S. (1998). *Leaving deep water: Asian American women at the crossroads of two cultures.* New York: Penguin Group.

Conboy, K. (1995). *Shadow war: The CIA's secret war in Laos.* CO: Paladin Press.

Cook, B. P., Withy, K., Tarallo-Jensen, L., & Berry, S. P. (2005). Changes in Kanak Maoli men's roles and health: Healing the warrior self. *International Journal of Men's Health, 4,* 115–130.

Curry, S. R. (2006, January/February). Fighting the glass ceiling: Why Asian Americans don't have more positions at the top. *Chief Executive.* Retrieved September 21, 2006, from http://www.committee100.org/initiatives/corporate_board/chief_executive_2006.htm

Espiritu, Y.-L. (1995). *Filipino American lives.* Philadelphia: Temple University Press.

Fernandez, M. (1998). Asian Indian Americans in the Bay Area and the glass ceiling. *Sociological Perspectives, 41,* 119–149.

Flores, P. V. (1994). Filipino students between two expectations. *Journal of the American Association for Philippine Psychology, 1,* 1.

Him, C. (2000). *When broken glass floats.* New York: W.W. Norton & Company.

Hing, B. O. (1993). *Making and remaking Asian America through immigration policy, 1850–1990.* Stanford, CA: Stanford University Press.

Hom, M. K. (1992). *Songs of Gold Mountain: Cantonese rhymes from San Francisco Chinatown.* Berkeley: University of California Press.

Hongo, G. (Ed.). (1993). *The open boat: Poems from Asian America.* New York: Doubleday.

Hoobler, D., & Hoobler, T. (1994). *The Chinese American family album.* New York: Oxford University Press.

Hoobler, D., & Hoobler, T. (1995). *The Japanese American family album.* New York: Oxford University Press.

Jeong, G. J., & Schumm, W. R. (1990). Family satisfaction in Korean/American marriages: An exploratory study of the perceptions of Korean wives. *Journal of Comparative Family Studies, 21,* 325–336.

Kim, B.-L.C. (1972). Casework with Japanese and Korean wives of Americans. *Social Casework, 53,* 273–279.

Kim, E. H. (2003). Preface. In J. Hagedorn (Ed.), *Charlie Chan is dead 2* (pp. vii–xix). New York, New York: Penguin Books.

Kim, K. C. (1999). *Koreans in the hood: Conflict with African Americans.* Baltimore: The Johns Hopkins University Press.

Kim, K. C., & Kim, S. (1998). Family and work roles of Korean immigrants in the U.S. In H. I. McCubbin, E. A. Thompson, A. I. Thompson, J. E. Fromer (Eds.), *Resiliency in Native American and immigrant families* (pp. 225–242). Thousand Oaks, CA: Sage Publications.

Kim, R. Y. (2002). Ethnic differences in academic achievement between Vietnamese and Cambodian children: Cultural and structural explanations. *The Sociological Quarterly, 43,* 213–235.

Kim-Goh, M., Suh, C., Blake, D. D., & Hiley-Young, B. (1995). Psychological impact of the Los Angeles riots on Korean-American victims: Implications for treatment. *American Journal of Orthopsychiatry, 65,* 138–146.

Kitano, H. H., & Daniels, R. (1995). *Asian Americans: Emerging minorities.* Englewood Cliffs, NJ: Prentice Hall.

Kwong, P., & Miscevic, D. (2005). *Chinese America: The untold story of America's oldest new community.* New York: The New Press.

Lee, L. (1986). *Rose.* Rochester, NY: BOA Editions.

Leong, F. T. (1985). Career development of Asian Americans. *Journal of College Student Personnel, 26,* 539–546.

Leong, F. T. L. (1998). Career development and vocational behaviors. In C. Lee and N. S. Zane (Eds.), *Handbook of Asian American Psychology.* Thousand Oaks: Sage Publications.

Lim, I.-S. (1997). Korean immigrant women's challenge to gender inequality at home: The interplay of economic resources, gender and family. *Gender & Society, 11,* 31–51.

Loo, C. (1993). An integrative-sequential treatment model for posttraumatic stress disorder: A case study of the Japanese American internment and redress. *Clinical Psychology Review, 13,* 89–117.

Loo, C. M. (1998). *Chinese America: Mental health and quality of life in the inner city.* Thousand Oaks, CA: Sage Publications.

McCubbin, L. D. (2004). Resilience among native Hawaiian adolescents: Ethnic identity, psychological distress and well-being. *Dissertation Abstracts International, 64*(01), 534B. (UMI No. 4050)

Min, P. G. (1984). From white-collar occupations to small business: Korean immigrants' occupational adjustment. *The Sociological Quarterly, 25,* 333–352.

Min, P. G. (1996). *Caught in the middle: Korean communities in New York and Los Angeles.* Berkeley: University of California Press.

Ministry of Health and Welfare. (1999). *Statistics from ministry of health and welfare.* Seoul: Ministry of Health and Welfare.

Nagata, D. K., & Cheng, W. J. Y. (2003). Intergenerational communication of race-related trauma by Japanese American former internees. *American Journal of Orthopsychiatry, 73,* 266–278.

Niedzwiecki, M., & Duong, T. C. (2004). *Southeast Asian American statistical profile.* Washington, DC: Southeast Asia Resource Action Center.

Novas, H., Cao, L., & Silva, R. (2004). *Everything you need to know about Asian American history.* New York: Penguin Group.

Office of Immigration Statistics. (2004). Refugees and asylees granted lawful permanent resident status by region and selected country of birth: Fiscal years 1946–2004. Retrieved May 1, 2006, from http://www.uscis.gov/graphics/shared/statistics/yearbook/YrBk04RA.htm

Ogbu, J. U. (2002). Cultural amplifiers of intelligence: IQ and minority status in cross-cultural perspective. In J. Fish (Ed.), *Race and intelligence: Separating science from myth* (pp. 241–278). Mawpah, NJ: Lawrence Erlbaum Associates.

Pink, D. H. (2004, February). The new face of the Silicon Age. *Wired Magazine.* Retrieved September 21, 2006, from http://www.wired.com/wired/archive/12.02/india.html?pg=1&topic=&topic_set=

Ratliff, B. W., Moon, H. F., & Bonacci, G. A. (1972). Intercultural marriage: The Korean American experience, *Social Casework, 59,* 221–226.

Reeves, T., & Bennett, C. (2003). The Asian and Pacific Islander population in the United States: March 2002, Current Population Reports (pp. 20–540). U.S. Census Bureau, Washington, DC.

Rhee, S. (1997). Domestic violence in the Korean immigrant family. *Journal of Sociology & Social Welfare, 24,* 63–77.

San Juan, E., Jr. (1994). The predicament of Filipinos in the United States: Where are you from? When are you going back? In R. Aguilar-San Juan (Ed.), *The state of Asian America: Activism and resistance in the 1990s.* Boston: South End Press.

Snyder, H. N., & Sickmund, M. (1999). *Jurenile offenders and victims: 1999 national report.* Washington, DC: Office of Juvenile Justice and Delinquency Prevention.

Sobredo, J. (1997). Filipino identity formation: Race, ethnicity and community in the United States. *Journal of Filipino American Studies, 1.*

South Asian Association for Regional Cooperation. (n.d.). Retrieved September 24, 2006, from U.S. Citizenship and Immigration Services Web site: http://www.saarc-sec.org/main.php?t=1

Steinberg, L., Dornbusch, S., & Brown, B. B. (1992). Ethnic differences in adolescent achievement: An ecological perspective. *American Psychologist, 47,* 723–729.

Sue, S., & Okazaki, S. (1990). Asian-American educational achievements: A phenomenon in search of an explanation. *American Psychologist, 45,* 913–920.

Swartz, T., Lee, J. C., & Mortimer, J. T. (2003). Achievements of first-generation Hmong youth: Findings from the Youth Development Survey. *CURA Reporter*, 15–21.

Takaki, R. (1995). *Strangers at the gates again.* New York: Chelsea House Publishers.

Takaki, R. (1998). *Strangers from a different shore: A history of Asian Americans.* Boston: Little, Brown and Company.

The house we live in. (2003). Retrieved September 24, 2006, from Race: The Power of an Illusion Web site: http://www.pbs.org/race/000_About/002_04-about-03.htm

This month in immigration history: December 1943. (2006). Retrieved September 24, 2006, from U.S. Citizenship and Immigration Services Web site: http://www.uscis.gov/graphics/aboutus/history/dec43.htm

U.S. Census Bureau. (2000). *Census 2000.* Washington, DC.

Waldman, A. (2004, July 24). Indians go home, but don't leave U.S. behind. *New York Times.* Retrieved September 21, 2006, from: http://www.nytimes.com/2004/07/24/international/asia/24indi.html?ex=1248321600&en=ca66fbfd9c35d682&ei=5090&partner=rssuserland

Williams, R. (2005, June 6). DoD's personal chief gives Asian-Pacific American history lesson. *American Forces Press Service.* Retrieved May 2, 2006, from http://www.emilitary.org/article.php?aid=3067

Ying, Y., & Akutsu, P. D. (1997). Psychological adjustment of Southeast Asian refugees: The contribution of sense of coherence. *Journal of Community Psychology, 25,* 125–139.

Yuh, J.-Y. (2002). *Beyond the shadow of camptown: Korean military brides in America.* New York: New York University Press.

Zhou, M., & Bankston, C. L. (1998). *Growing up American: How Vietnamese children adapt to life in the United States.* New York: Russell Sage Foundation.

Zia, H. (2000). *Asian American dreams: The emergence of an American people.* New York: Farrar, Straus, and Giroux.

2
History and Evolution of Asian American Psychology

FREDERICK T. L. LEONG and ARPANA GUPTA

OUTLINE OF CHAPTER

Introduction
Historical Context of Asian American Psychology
History of the Asian American Psychological Association
Developments in the Division on Women
Key Conferences
The Future of Asian American Psychology
Case Study
References

Introduction

In 1972, a group of Asian American psychologists attended the American Psychological Association (**APA**) convention in San Francisco and were discouraged by the fact that it was unreflective of Asian American psychological issues. This group of professors and clinicians flipped through the convention's program and found no presentations, papers, posters, or research findings on the issue of Asian Americans—and this in an association that claimed to represent 10,000 psychologists and mental health professionals. Thus, they began to wonder how the psychological needs of the Asian American population were being met or developed. As a result, ideas for an Asian American psychological association were born and then implemented through the efforts of these dedicated individuals.

This chapter summarizes the major events in the field of Asian American psychology from 1972 to 2005 by providing an overview of: (a) the historical context of Asian American psychology, (b) the history of the Asian American Psychological Association (**AAPA**), (c) the historical and recent developments in the Division on Women (**DoW**), (d) the significant regional conferences, and (e) a note about the evolution and future of Asian American psychology.

Historical Context of Asian American Psychology

In the 2000 U.S. Census, 4.2% of the U.S. population, approximately 11.9 million individuals, identified themselves as being fully or partly Asian. This population continues to rise as evidenced by the 2005 U.S. Census Bureau data, which show there are now 13.5 million individuals (5% of the population) of Asian ancestry in the United States. A large number of this Asian population comes from immigrant families—almost 64% (8.7 million) of these Asians were born in Asia.

An historical investigation indicates that U.S. immigration policy has greatly shaped and affected the patterns and size of the Asian American population, its ethnic composition, socio-economic welfare, and rights and privileges. These policies and dynamics have significant

31

Table 2.1 AAPA Presidents (1972–2005)

Terms	President
1972–1975	Derald Wing Sue
1975–1979	Robert Chin
1979–1982	Albert H. Yee
1982–1984	Harry Yamaguchi
1984–1988	Herbert Z. Wong
1988–1990	Katsuyuki Sakamoto
1990–1991	David S. Goh
1991–1993	Nolan W. S. Zane
1993–1995	S. Andrew Chen
1995–1997	Christine C. Iijima Hall
1997–1999	Reiko Homma True
1999–2001	Gayle Y. Iwamasa
2001–2003	J. C. Gisela Lin
2003–2005	Frederick Leong
2005–	Alvin Alvarez

Due to incomplete archival records, the start and end dates of Wong's presidential terms are uncertain. There are records that indicate Yamaguchi finished his term in the summer of 1984, that Wong was serving as the president in 1985 and 1986, and that Sakamoto's terms were 1988–1990.

implications in Asian American psychology due to the history of discrimination and abuse suffered by this group as a result of their race. A study of these experiences and the immigration legislation can offer psychologists a context within which to understand more contemporary experiences of Asian Americans.

As a result of the need for laborers on the sugar plantations in Hawaii and the expansion of railroads due to the gold rush in the early 19th century, an influx of Asian immigrants, especially the Chinese, occurred in America. By the 1880s, approximately 124,000 Chinese had moved to America, making up the largest ethnic minority group in the West. However, as early as 1854, the Chinese experienced legal discrimination and were not allowed to testify in courts. They were viewed as hostile and as unwelcome economic competitors. Further discrimination and denial of rights led to the Chinese Exclusion Act in 1882, which suspended immigration of Chinese laborers for 10 years and declared them ineligible for citizenship. Such treatment by American society was also eventually experienced by Japanese, Filipino, Korean, and Indian migrants (Leong & Whitfield, 1992; Endo, Sue, & Wagner, 1980).

These anti-Asian sentiments were clearly reflected in the legislative protocols and judicial rulings of the time. Other acts of discrimination and hardship included:

- The Geary Act in 1892, which was renewed in 1902 and made permanent in 1904, suspended Chinese laborers for another 10 years.
- The 1907 Gentleman's Agreement between Japan and the United States prevented Japanese workers from being issued passports.
- California's 1913 Alien Land Law prevented "aliens ineligible for citizenship" from purchasing agricultural land.

- The 1917 Immigration Act established an "Asiatic Barred Zone" that prevented further immigration from countries like India.
- The 1922 Supreme Court ruling on *Ozawa vs. United States* and the 1923 ruling on *United States vs. Thind* denied requests for naturalization by two Asians based upon their "non-white status."
- The 1924 Immigration Act excluded all immigration of aliens ineligible for citizenship, thus affecting nearly all Asian immigrants except Filipinos who were not considered aliens because the Philippines was a U.S. territory at the time.
- The 1934 Tydings–McDuffie Act, which created the commonwealth of the Philippines, ended the Filipinos' status as U.S. nationals.

Clearly the first part of the 20th century bore witness to many closed doors toward improved immigration status and opportunities (Leong & Whitfield, 1992; Endo, Sue, & Wagner, 1980). During World War II, individuals of Japanese ancestry were interned in camps, but it was also around this time that many of the naturalization, immigration, and legislative laws began to change. For instance, in 1943 the Chinese Exclusion Law was repealed. In 1946, Indian and Filipino immigrants gained the right to naturalize. In 1965, after the passage of the Hart–Celler Immigration and Naturalization Act, the restrictive per-country quotas for immigration were replaced by a priority for highly skilled workers (e.g., engineers, scientists, and medical workers). An emphasis was also placed on family reunifications and thus began the fast-paced growth of the Asian American population that we still bear witness to. In addition, due to the Vietnam War, the 1970s saw admittance of large numbers of refugees from Vietnam, Cambodia, and Laos (Leong & Whitfield, 1992; Endo, Sue, & Wagner, 1980; Leong, Okazaki, & David, 2007; Leong & Okazaki, under review).

Investigation of population trends suggests that from 1960 to 1980 there was a high concentration of Asian immigrants settled in the West and in Hawaii. Later, the federal government's refugee resettlement policies helped to increase the dispersion of the Asian American population by resettling refugees across the country. For instance, in 2000, 48% of Asians lived in the West compared to the earlier 71% in 1960, and the South experienced the greatest increase in the Asian American population. The ethnic composition of Asian Americans also saw dramatic shifts. Trends shifted from the 1960s to 2000 such that the Japanese were no longer the largest Asian group in the United States, but were replaced in numbers by Chinese, Filipino, and Asian Indians followed by Vietnamese and Korean Americans (Leong, Okazaki, & David, 2007; Leong & Okazaki, under review).

The dominant myth surrounding Asian Americans has been that of being a model minority, one that has attained both high economic and educational status and that has no or low rates of social problems (Sue, Sue, Sue, & Takeuchi, 1995). When aggregated across various ethnic groups, demographic profiles appear to support the notion of Asian Americans as a high-achieving group. However, the Asian American population also tends to show a wide range on many of these structural variables. In other words, the aggregate statistics that support the model minority image of Asian Americans betray the wide variability within this population.

The study of Asian American psychology can be traced back to the late 1960s and early 1970s. The field arose as part of the larger social and political movement at the time that challenged the marginalization of Asians in the United States and around the world. According to Omatsu (1994), the Asian American movement began as a parallel process to the black liberation movement led by Malcolm X. Asian American studies (**AAS**) arose out of activism on university campuses and as a reaction to racism displayed during the American wars in Southeast Asia.

Prashad (2005) writes that ethnic studies emerged out of an anti-racist and social justice tradition so that individuals of color could be integrated into the academic world. As such, it became recognized that the Asian community needed to participate in research as active participants versus simply as objects of study—the goal was that such action-oriented research would greatly influence the lives of Asians. Thus was born the field of Asian American psychology. In 1971, one of the earliest papers in Asian American psychology was written by Stanley Sue and Derald Wing Sue, entitled "Chinese American Personality and Mental Health," and was published in *Amerasia*, the first journal dedicated to AAS. This was the beginning of the era of Asian American studies and psychology (Leong, Okazaki, & David, 2007; Leong & Okazaki, under review).

One way to get a better overview of Asian American psychology is by focusing on the research of Asian American psychology and how this has evolved and changed over time. Leong (1995) used the PsychInfo database classification system to investigate key areas of research within Asian American psychology and found that the majority of journal articles were in the areas of social processes and social issues, followed by health, mental health treatment and prevention topics, then education psychology, and lastly psychological and physical disorders.

Another indirect method of viewing the field is a cursory look at Leong and Whitfield's bibliography on the psychology of Asians in America (1992), which highlights the major researchers and contributors to the Asian American psychological literature from 1967 to 1991. Just to name a few, these individuals include: Ronald C. Johnson (22 articles), Joseph Westermeyer (19 articles), Stanley Sue (18 articles), David Kinsey (18 articles), Craig T. Nagoshi (13 articles), Anthony Marsella (11 articles), Harry H. Kitano (11 articles), Donald Atkinson (10 articles), Jacquelyn H. Flaskerud (10 articles), Frederick T. L. Leong (10 articles), Kay Midlan (10 articles), and Joe Yamamoto (10 articles). Most of these researchers focused on mental health issues related to Asian Americans. Recently, the numbers of published work and topics in Asian American literature have grown. This is also reflected in the increasing number of courses that are being offered in AAS, since their inception into the higher education curriculum in 1968. According to the *Chronicle of Higher Education,* which used data collected by Cornell University in 1995, AAS have almost doubled over the last 8 years and courses are being offered at many more institutions as independent courses.

History of the Asian American Psychological Association

There is no doubt that the history of Asian American psychology is bigger than the AAPA, encompassing activities and persons that go beyond those advocated by the organization. However, the history of the organization is important to understanding the history of Asian American psychology in that it provides us with valuable insight, especially with regard to the intersection between the disciplines of advocacy, science, and practice of Asian American psychology.

The AAPA was founded on December 10, 1972, as a group effort spearheaded by a small but dedicated and influential handful of Asian American psychologists such as Derald Wing Sue, Stanley Sue, Roger Lum, Marion Tin Loy, Reiko True, and Tina Yong Yee. The association began as a way to meet informally, to stay connected, and to offer opportunities to exchange information and support among a select group of Asian American mental health professionals in the San Francisco Bay area. The AAPA is now a major ethnic minority psychological association that has enjoyed rapid growth—from 185 members in 1979 to over 500 members in 2005. The rise of the AAPA as an influential force within psychology has been dramatic, and it definitely reflects the growing needs and demands of the Asian American population, which is currently the fastest-growing ethnic minority group in the United States. In addition, the AAPA was able to define and establish the field of Asian American psychology, especially within the broader field of multicultural and ethnic minority psychology. This was because the AAPA has been influential in establishing and implementing culturally appropriate and culturally sensitive services for Asian Americans.

Derald Wing Sue became the first president of the association. A history monograph (Leong, 1995) of the association details interviews conducted with the two brothers and founders of AAPA, Derald Wing Sue and Stanley Sue. Derald Wing Sue, the older of the two brothers, humorously recalls how he became president of the then very small organization, which at the time did not have any formalized proceedings or rules. At the time the AAPA was formed, Derald Wing Sue was working as a psychologist at the University of California, Berkeley counseling center. Both Derald Wing and Stanley Sue recall that the impetus for forming the organization included their inadequate training in working with Asian American clients, their inability to effectively meet the needs of this population, and their isolation as professionals and scholars in the field. The organization started out very small and on a local level with the help of Stanley Sue's graduate students, Rod Kazama and Davis Ja. They decided to model the AAPA after the Association of Black Psychologists (**ABPsi**) because African American psychologists were the primary forces in advocating for the needs and concerns of all ethnic minorities within the APA at the time; they were bolstered by an awareness that Latinos were also planning to form their own professional organization.

For a more up-close look at the AAPA, a biography of its founders—brothers Derald Wing Sue and Stanley Sue—is provided here. In a recent interview (D. W. Sue, personal communication, January 21, 2006), we learned that the older of the two brothers, Derald Wing Sue, received his BS from Oregon State University. He went on to the University of Oregon to get his MS and then PhD in counseling psychology. He is currently a professor of Psychology and Education at Teachers College, Columbia University, in New York City. Dr. Sue has accomplished much in our field in his efforts to advance multicultural counseling and psychotherapy, some of which include the following: president of the Society for the Psychological Study of Ethnic Minority Issues; cofounder and first president of the AAPA; and president of the Society of Counseling Psychology (**APA's Division 17**). He was called upon by the White House during the Clinton administration to testify before the race advisory board in Washington, DC. Most important of all he was instrumental in creating with some other key individuals a new set of multicultural guidelines, which were eventually endorsed and used by the APA. They had a major impact on the accreditation and training in the field of multicultural and ethnic minority psychology (D. W. Sue, personal communication, January 21, 2006).

Dr. Stanley Sue is also a key figure in the history and the evolution of Asian American psychology. Sue (S. Sue, personal communication, January 21, 2006) indicated that currently he is a

Derald Wing and Stanley Sue (cofounders of AAPA).

distinguished professor of Psychology and Asian American Studies at the University of California, Davis. This charismatic and inspirational man received his PhD in cognitive dissonance from University of California, Los Angeles (UCLA). He notes that at the time he was a graduate student he was influenced by and very interested in the work of Harry Kitano, who later became a member of his dissertation committee. Stanley Sue then went on to serve in the psychology department at the University of Washington for 10 years. At the time he admits not knowing if a career could be built on ethnic research, but he was encouraged by Ned Wagner, full professor and director of the Clinical Psychology program, to conduct research in the area of Asian American issues. Sue says he felt good about taking on this path of scholarly work as it was clearly an understudied area, so it gave him a platform to make a difference and to break new ground. From the University of Washington, Stanley Sue moved on to join the faculty at UCLA for the next 15 years. While there, Sue received funding to establish the National Research Center on Asian American Mental Health, which has had a pivotal influence on the development of the field. The center was recently moved to the University of California, Davis when he took an appointment there. His pioneering work on the mental health of Asian Americans was also recognized at the national level when he was invited to contribute to a supplement to the Surgeon General's Report on Mental Health entitled, "Culture, Race, and Ethnicity" (U.S. Department of Health and Human Services, 1999, 2001). Sue has received numerous awards from professional associations, including two Distinguished Contributions Awards from the APA (S. Sue, personal communication, January 21, 2006).

The Sue brothers have worked on many projects together as well as independently. Clearly their dedication and contributions to the evolution of the Asian American psychology field are impressive. Their names are synonymous with AAPA.

Goals of the AAPA

Since its inception in the early 1970s, the AAPA has continued to grow and to struggle. The AAPA has managed to overcome many obstacles in order to become a highly visible organization with a clear identity. The organization has many goals and objectives, the main focus of which revolves around the mental and psychosocial health issues of Asian Americans. Other goals include advocacy, the promotion of research, policies, and current and culturally appropriate mental health practices. Another key objective of the organization includes the training and education of Asian American mental health professionals.

The AAPA has undertaken many important initiatives, especially as its leaders hoped to increase the organization's visibility from a local to a national level. During its formative years, the AAPA's leaders worked to increase awareness and advocacy of Asian American issues among the APA governance. In addition, they had to convince APA leaders that Asian Americans needed to be considered ethnic minorities. Through their efforts, the AAPA became known as the institution to which other psychology bodies, such as the APA and the American Psychological Society (APS), turned to for guidance and input regarding Asian American psychological issues. Examples of other important initiatives include the following: (a) advocating the U.S. Bureau of the Census to recognize and include Asian American subgroups in census data, (b) lobbying against the English-only language policy within California, (c) presenting state-of-the-art information on Asian Americans in various presidential commissions and surgeon general's reports, (d) pressing the APA to establish the Board of Ethnic Minority Affairs (now Committee on Ethnic Minority Affairs), and (e) promoting Asian American perspectives within the APA and other parts of organized psychology. It is obvious that the AAPA has consistently advocated on behalf of Asian American psychology and the welfare of Asian Americans.

Some of the AAPA's members have also achieved prominence in the APA's governance and leadership. To name a few: Dr. Richard Suinn was prominent and active in our profession. He served as chairperson of the APA Board of Ethnic Minority Affairs during its early years and as a member of the APA Board of Directors. In 1999, Suinn was also the first Asian American psychologist to serve as president of APA. Another person of prominence is Dr. Alice F. Chang who served on the board of directors for APA. Other AAPA members have also been able to serve as consultants in various governmental agencies. For instance, Dr. Stanley Sue directed the training for the National Asian American Psychology Training Center in San Francisco in 1980. Sue also established and served as the director of the National Research Center on Asian American Mental Health from 1988 to 2001 at UCLA and UC Davis.

AAPA Publications

From 1972 to 1979, as the AAPA formed an established identity, it published an official newsletter that disseminated association news and activities, editorials, and occasional publications of research or conceptual articles. Stanley Sue, at the suggestion of Robert Chin, requested a grant of $250 from the Society for the Psychological Study of Social Issues (**SPSSI**) to support the mailings of the newsletter in the early stages of the association. The newsletter was then renamed the *Journal of the Asian American Psychological Association* from 1979 to 1989 by the association's then appointed board of directors who felt that a journal would attract research articles of high caliber. In 1990, the journal then changed its format once again and reverted back to an association newsletter, now titled *Asian American Psychologist*. The newsletter is published on a regular basis, three times annually, and consists of topics revolving around AAPA news, events, advertisements, member announcements and accomplishments, and other pertinent issues pertaining to Asian American psychology. The goal of the newsletter is to communicate with the association's members. To receive the newsletter and join the AAPA, visit the Web site at http://www.aapaonline.org.

The association has been able to produce many journals, books, and newsletters that focus specifically on Asian American psychology and advocacy of service delivery to this population. Examples include Stanley Sue's (1982) pioneering *Mental Health of Asian Americans* and the landmark *Handbook of Asian American Psychology* (Lee & Zane, 1998). In addition, a history monograph has been edited by Frederick Leong in 1995 and it is the only monograph published by the AAPA to date. These publications have laid the groundwork for the development of the field of Asian

Stanley Sue, Alice F. Chang, and Richard Suinn (far right).

Richard Suinn.

American psychology. As a result various Asian American psychology courses, symposiums, and research are now being conducted at universities and conferences across the country.

Operating Structure of AAPA and Its Past Few Presidents

The AAPA currently holds a national convention on an annual basis a day before the APA convention. The convention features various programs related to Asian American psychology, training, research, policies, and education. The convention is designed to optimize interactions among the presenters and the participants so that levels of intimacy, learning, mentoring, and comradeship are established. The convention allows for the continued tremendous growth of its membership, and a strong and stable association in the long run. There has been a shift toward increasing and encouraging young membership in the association. For instance, the annual convention has established a book sale that provides the funds to support student scholarships and travel awards. A main feature of the annual convention is the mentor–mentee gathering, which fosters valuable and strong apprentice-type relationships, and the event also provides an opportunity for dissertation awards to be presented. A main award acknowledged at the AAPA annual convention is the fellowship funded by the Okura Mental Health Leadership Foundation, which was established by the late K. Patrick Okura and his wife, Lily Okura. This fellowship has allowed many young AAPA members to learn and become active in public policy issues in Washington, DC. Many other awards are presented at the convention. Some of these include the Distinguished Contributions Award, which was first presented to Dr. Robert Chin in 1985. In 1998, Dr. Frederick T. L. Leong, who was then appointed chair of the Awards Committee, decided with the support of the then president, Dr. Reiko True, to establish awards such as the Early Career Award and the Lifetime Achievement Award. The awards program has continued to grow and additional awards have been added, such as the Friend of AAPA

Photograph from the National Asian American Psychology Training Conference in 1976 in Long Beach, CA, sponsored by AAPA. Pictured in the 1st row (sitting, from right to left) are Roger Lum, ?, Henry Johnson, Ruby Takanishi, ?, Reiko True, Jim Cortez, Marion Tinloy, Bok Lim Kim, Pat Okura, Ai-Li Chin, William Liu, Yukio Okano, and Albert Yee; pictured in the 2nd row (standing, from left to right) are Gil Tanabe, ?, Sam Chan, ?, Max Callao, Ki-Taek Chun, Lloyd Inui, Stanley Sue, Harry Kitano, Ramsay Liem, Luke Kim, Lindberg Sata, Barbara Lui, Robert Chin, Helen Sing, Stanley Schneider, Norman Wong, Herbert Wong, Tim Dong, Tuan Nguyen, Richard Suinn, John Jung, Dalmas Taylor, Davis Ja, Harry Yamaguchi, and Bob Ryan. Five in the photograph would become AAPA Presidents, and many of the founders of AAPA can be seen.

Award, the Okura Award, and the Presidential Awards. The AAPA also maintains a Web page (http://www.aapaonline.org) and an active Listserv for discussion.

The AAPA operates through an executive committee and a board of directors. These are comprised of a president, vice president, past president, membership and financial affairs officer, secretary/historian, and four board members. Each executive committee is elected and appointed to serve a two-year term. In 1995 AAPA witnessed its first female president when Dr. Christine Iijima Hall was elected. This seemed to set a trend as Dr. Hall's presidency was followed by three other female presidents, namely, Dr. Reiko True (1997–1999), Dr. Gayle Iwamasa (1999–2001), and Dr. Jun-chih Gisela Lin (2001–2003). Each of the president's goals, missions, and accomplishments over the last 10 years of the organization are discussed in further detail in the following. See Table 2.1 for a list of all AAPA presidents from 1972 to 2005 (Leong, Okazaki, & David, 2007; Leong & Okazaki, under review).

Dr. Christine Iijima Hall was president of AAPA from 1995 to 1997. According to Hall (C. I. Hall, personal communication, December 27, 2005), her presidential goal was to improve the structure and functioning of the association in order to continue to stabilize its function and role in the field of Asian American psychology. For instance, she initiated the establishment of its headquarters in Phoenix, Arizona, with a permanent mailing address and voice mail. In addition, Hall established a permanent position of secretary/historian, which was at the time filled by Dr. Sumie Okazaki. Hall also attempted to regulate membership more closely. In 1996, with the help of Dr. Richard Kim, Hall was able to launch the AAPA Web site. This increased communication with its members, extending beyond the reach of the newsletter. In addition,

Table 2.2 Key Events in the History of Asian American Psychology

Year	Event
1965	Immigration law abolishes "national origins" as basis for allocating immigration quotas to various countries, and preferences are given to those with professional skills and to family reunification; this marks the start of an exponential growth in the Asian American population.
1968	Students on strike at San Francisco State University demand establishment of ethnic studies programs. First AAS course was offered.
1969	Students at the University of California, Berkeley, go on strike for establishment of ethnic studies programs.
1972	Asian American Psychology Association founded on December 10; Derald Wing Sue served as president until 1975.
	K. Patrick Okura organizes the first Asian American mental health conference in San Francisco.
1974	Richmond Maxi Center (later renamed Richmond Area Multi-Services, or RAMS), the first ethnic-specific outpatient mental health center for Asian Americans, opens in San Francisco.
1976	The National Asian American Psychology Training Conference, organized by Stanley Sue and funded by the NIMH meet in Long Beach, CA.
1978	At the National Conference for Increasing Roles of Culturally Diverse People in Psychology (the Dulles Conference), Asian American psychologists advocate for a better representation of Asian Americans in the APA; Robert Chin and Reiko True appointed to the ad-hoc Committee on Cultural and Ethnic Affairs (later to become the Board of Ethnic Minority Affairs).
1979	RAMS began operating the National Asian American Psychology Training Center (NAAPTC), the first training site for mental health professionals to provide culturally appropriate services to Asian Americans; AAPA began self-publishing the AAPA's journal (continued until 1989).
1980	The Asian focus unit, the first ethnic-specific inpatient psychiatric facility for Asian Americans, opened at the San Francisco General Hospital, headed by Francis Lu, M.D.
1982	Vincent Chin, a Chinese American draftsman, is clubbed to death with a baseball bat by two Euro American men; advocacy movement to bring legal justice renews Asian American community activism.
	S. Sue and J. Morishima publish *The Mental Health of Asian Americans.*
1987	The U.S. House of Representatives votes 243 to 141 to make an official apology to Japanese Americans and to pay each surviving internee $20,000 in reparations. (The U.S. Senate voted in 1988 to support redress for Japanese Americans in 1988, and President George H. W. Bush signs into law in 1989).
1988	Using their redress payments from the U.S. government paid out to former internees in Japanese American internment camps during WWII, K. Patrick Okura and Lilly Okura founded the Okura Mental Health Leadership Foundation to empower Asian American leaders with skills and knowledge in public policy and advocacy.
1995	Christine Iijima Hall elected as the first female president of the AAPA; DoW within the AAPA established by Alice F. Chang; AAPA publishes the *History of Asian American Psychology* monograph, edited by Frederick Leong.
1997	Richard M. Suinn elected as the first Asian American president-elect of the APA.
1998	The *Handbook of Asian American Psychology*, coedited by Lee C. Lee and Nolan W. S. Zane, published by Sage.
1999	Tiffany Ho convenes the Asian American Pacific Islander Mental Health Summit in Washington, DC.
2000	As a direct result of the 1999 Asian American Pacific Islander Mental Health Summit, the National Asian American Pacific Islander Mental Health Association (NAAPIMHA) was formed with D. J. Ida as its executive director.

(Continued)

Table 2.2 *(Continued)*

	Stanley Sue is invited to author the Asian American chapter in *Mental Health: Culture, Race, and Ethnicity, a Supplement to Mental Health: A Report of the Surgeon General.*
2002	Larke Huang is appointed as one of the commissioners within the president's New Freedom Commission on Mental Health.
	The AAPA celebrates the 30th anniversary of the founding of the association at its annual convention in Chicago, Illinois.
	G. C. N. Hall and S. Okazaki publish *Asian American Psychology: The Science of Lives in Context.*
2003	Karen Suyemoto taught a symposium on teaching Asian American psychology: Issues of content and pedagogy.
	Frederick Leong, as president of AAPA, and with the presidents of the other ethnic minority psychological associations is invited to the APA council of representatives to begin exploring the establishment of a seat on the council for these four associations.
2006	Contracts for important texts addressing Asian American psychology were signed: for example, *Handbook of Asian American Psychology*, edited by Leong, Inman, Ebreo, Yang, Kinoshita, and Fu, and *Asian American Psychology: Current Perspectives*, edited by Tewari and Alvarez.

the Listserv established by Richard Suinn at Colorado State University and then Alvin Alvarez at San Francisco State University helped improve member communication and involvement (C. I. Hall, personal communication, December 27, 2005).

From 1997 to 1999, Dr. Reiko True took on the presidency of the AAPA. Dr. True (R. True, personal communication, December 26, 2005) stated that she was able to establish financial stability within the association by expanding the monetary contributions made to the annual convention. During True's presidency, the DoW was formed and formally recognized. True also spearheaded the association's support for the appointment of Bill Lann Lee to the U.S. Civil Rights Commission. Other activities initiated by True include: (a) the support and formation of regional and networking groups, (b) the organization of the National Multicultural Summit and Conference, and (c) the publication of the Research Guidelines, which became a monograph series published by the Council of National Psychological Association for the Advancement of Ethnic Minority Interests (**CNPAAEMI**), of which AAPA is a member.

True was succeeded by Dr. Gayle Iwamasa as president of AAPA in 1999. It was the first time in the election history of AAPA whereby the president (Dr. Gayle Iwamasa) and the vice president (Dr. Yoshita Kawahara) joined forces and ran as joint-slate candidates. Dr. Iwamasa (C. I. Hall, personal communication, December 27, 2005) stated that during her presidency she attempted to further improve the structure and functioning of the association. Iwamasa consulted with an attorney and was able to incorporate the association by obtaining federal 501 (c)(3) tax-exempt status. She also increased the desirability of attending the annual convention by establishing firm procedures in order to offer attendees continuing education credits. However, at the same time she kept up with the tradition of organizing regional conferences such as the one in San Diego. Iwamasa also oversaw some significant changes in the association's bylaws. Additionally, Iwamasa established the AAPA Awards Committee and led the finalization of specific awards and award criteria.

Dr. Jun-chih Gisela Lin was president of AAPA from 2001 to 2003. Lin (J. G. Lin, personal communication, December 27, 2005) indicated that she oversaw the association's 30th anniversary celebration, a major event including a symposium and reception that took place at the 2002 annual convention in Chicago. During her presidency, Lin established various awards such as the Okura Community Leadership Award, Friend of the AAPA Award, the AAPA Student Grant for Dissertation Research, and she started the tradition of giving out the AAPA Presidential Award.

Lin also supported the trial run of the online mentor–mentee forum for student members, which was then moderated by Tai Chang and Cindy Fong. In addition, she supported the development of the AAPA regional networks. During her presidency, Lin's major initiative was commissioning the association's comprehensive needs assessment in 2001–2002 to aid in long-term and strategic planning for AAPA. The results of this needs assessment were reported in the Winter 2003 issue of the AAPA newsletter, the *Asian American Psychologist*. These results were also presented and discussed at a town-hall meeting at the 2002 AAPA convention in Chicago. Lin's second major initiative was to obtain and establish the current AAPA Web site http://www.aapaonline.org. Lin reports that the success of her initiatives was a result of the collaborative efforts of the Executive Committee, newsletter team, other AAPA committees, and the AAPA membership.

During his presidency from 2003 to 2005, Dr. Frederick T. L. Leong's primary goal was to continue to improve the structure and functioning of the association set forth by the previous AAPA presidents. This was accomplished by passing several important bylaws, such as the establishment of a new category for membership of fellows as a way to recognize outstanding member contributors to AAPA. As part of this process, he was able to get AAPA to grandfather in some of the most distinguished members, namely those who had been winners of the Lifetime Achievement Award, the Distinguished Contributions Award, and those who had been past presidents, as automatic fellows of the association. For instance, at the 2005 AAPA convention, Dr. D. J. Ida and Dr. Allen Ivey were inducted as new fellows of the association with Dr. Gordon Hall presiding as chair of the fellows committee. The second major bylaws change that was passed involved the formation of the Council of Past Presidents (**COPP**). This was established to recognize and benefit from the wisdom and advice of the "senior and important" members of AAPA. The third and final change in bylaws was to create a mechanism for the formation of new divisions. Soon after the passage of this bylaw, the student division under the leadership of Szu-Hui Lee was formed. This was followed by the formation of the South Asian American division under the leadership of Puni Kalra and Poonam Natha. There may be additional efforts to form other divisions along these lines in the near future. A fourth initiative undertaken by Leong has been to formalize the association's policies and procedures manual to ensure continuity between administrations.

Leong's other accomplishments during his presidency included the launching of the second edition of the *Handbook of Asian American Psychology* with several members of the AAPA's executive committee as coeditors (Drs. Arpana G. Inman, Angela Ebreo, Lawrence Hsin Yang, Lisa M. Kinoshita, and Michi Fu) and with many members as contributing authors. With the editorial team's support, Leong decided to donate the royalties from all future proceeds of the handbook to AAPA. Leong also initiated the production and distribution of the association's Digital History Project (**DHP**) with the help of the secretary/historian, Dr. Irene Kim. This was an attempt by Leong to prevent the loss of the association's important documents and historical archives, which were scanned and digitized onto a CD and made available to members for a nominal price.

Dr. Alvin Alvarez is the current president of the AAPA. His presidency objectives have focused on increasing the relevance, accountability, and visibility of AAPA within both the AAPA membership and the Asian community. This was done by developing member-driven task forces to meet the needs of professionals in the various domains and to increase dialogue between members, especially with regard to mentoring, advocacy, and public policy via the online forums. Another objective is to increase collaborative efforts with professional networks and the larger psychological community in order to raise the association's visibility and credibility. For instance, efforts were made to collaborate with practice-focused associations in the psychology community (Dr. D. J. Ida from the National Asian American and Pacific Islander Mental Health

Association, and Kavoos Bassiri from the Richmond Area Multi-Services in San Francisco). Other initiatives in this area have included coalition-building efforts with CNPAAEMI with the end goal of creating a permanent voting seat on the council. Lastly, a primary goal of the current president has been to strive for internal growth and maintenance within the association. This has been accomplished by initiating changes in the AAPA's structure in order to maximize its effectiveness. For example, three amendments were developed and approved to the association bylaws: creation of a president-elect position, creation of a communications officer position, and the availability of electronic distribution of AAPA materials. New divisions (e.g., Division of Students, **DoS**, and Division of South Asian Americans, **DoSAA**) and regional groups (e.g., Southern California, Northeast, Southeast, and Rocky Mountain) have also been recently developed to meet the specific needs of the diverse AAPA membership.

The future of AAPA seems clear: To continue with its efforts and goals to promote the well-being of all Asian Americans via training, research, and service; and to serve as the primary professional organization for Asian American psychologists and within the field of Asian American psychology.

Developments in the Division of Women

With the leadership of Dr. Alice F. Chang and others, the DoW was formed and inaugurated at the AAPA's August 1995 annual convention in New York. The formation of the division arose as membership within the AAPA increased, especially with regard to its women members. The division started with just a handful of women members but now includes over 100 women from divergent backgrounds and with diverse interests. In fact, according to Chang (A. F. Chang, personal communication, December 27, 2005), a few senior women, such as Drs. Reiko True, Barbara (Bobbie) Yee, and Maria Root, made the first major financial contributions along with a few women from the APA DoW to support the new division's efforts. In addition, the late Dr. K. Patrick Okura who at first thought the division was trying to get women removed from AAPA, actually matched the AAPA members' contributions to the division in 1996 in order to help build its financial base more quickly. The monetary effort was great, but even greater was the belief in the division's causes and what was needed by the division in order to become a substantial and equally identified part of the AAPA. Therefore, since its inception and formation, the DoW has been an important and integral part of AAPA.

The goal of DoW has focused mainly on the role of Asian American women in the field of psychology. The division allows an opportunity to celebrate the achievements of these women as well as to provide opportunities for mentorship and further collaboration on issues pertaining to Asian American women. The mission of the division includes: (a) celebrating the success of Asian, Asian American, and Pacific Island or Islander (**AAA & PI**) women, (b) developing social and political awareness about issues pertaining to this population, (c) increasing opportunities, visibility, and involvement of these women in the field and in professional organizations, (d) providing opportunities for regional networking and mentoring. The DoW's Internet efforts have also been helpful in this endeavor, by enhancing a sense of community within these women, and by researching and investigating psychological issues pertaining to this population.

The division seeks nominations for positions on a yearly or biannual basis, depending upon the term of the position. Positions include that of cochair, treasurer/membership coordinator, newsletter editor, mentor–mentee coordinators, secretary, and regional representatives. Past cochairs of DoW have included Dr. Karen Suyemoto, Dr. Kunya Des Jardins, Dr. Jeanette Hsu, Dr. Jeanne Lin, Dr. Soni Kim, Dr. Margaret Faye, Dr. Nita Tewari, Dr. Arpana Inman, Dr. Phi Loan Le, and Dr. Neesha Patel. The current DoW chairs are Dr. Susana Lowe and Dr. Juli Germer-Fraga.

Currently the division has regional representatives in the San Francisco Bay Area, Southern California, New England/Boston, New York/New Jersey, and the Midwest.

The benefits of joining the division include the valuable creation of lasting personal and professional relationships and support systems. In addition, the division puts out a newsletter on a regular basis to communicate with its members and keeping them abreast of upcoming DoW events. The atmosphere at the division is close, casual, and informal. The division also offers two awards annually that are presented at the AAPA convention: the Division on Women Award and the Alice F. Chang Student Scholar Award. The DoW Award is a $300 prize presented to an individual who highlights and celebrates work pertaining specifically to issues facing Asian American women. The second award is a $100 prize given to a student poster presented at the AAPA convention on women's issues.

Key Conferences

Networking is an important component for any member's professional development that can be accomplished by attending conferences. There were some key conferences that took place over the years within the field of Asian American psychology that were critical in enhancing the organization's networking efforts and increasing the organization's visibility. The 1972 meeting that took place in San Francisco was an effort by Asian American mental health professionals to provide a forum to discuss Asian American mental health issues. This meeting became recognized as a key conference that helped to unite the field for Asian American psychologists. This first meeting was made possible by some key individuals, such as Dr. K. Patrick Okura, who was the executive assistant director of the National Institute of Mental Health, James Ralph, who was chief of the Center for Minority Mental Health Programs, and the Asian American Social Workers Organization. They were able to secure funding from the National Institute of Mental Health (**NIMH**) that made this meeting possible. The conference was very successful and highlighted issues pertaining to Asian American mental health on a large scale, thus bringing these issues to the forefront of our field. Initially, the conference anticipated 81 delegates and 300–400 participants and observers. However, over 600 attendees were present. This meeting led to much tension and discussion as struggles, frustrations, and anger over inadequate mental health care to Asian and Pacific American communities were brought up. Details concerning some of the problems and tensions that arose during this conference have been documented by the Conference Report Committee and have also been briefly reviewed by Sue and Morishima (1982).

Another landmark conference was the National Asian American Psychology Training Conference (**NAAPTC**) that took place in 1976. With the encouragement and effort from some key figures such as Dr. Patrick Okura, Dr. Stanley Sue wrote a conference grant proposal to the NIMH for a national conference that would address the need for training mental health providers for the Asian American communities. This was an important move, as all of these efforts soon came to fruition and the conference was held in Long Beach, California, on July 31 to August 1, 1976. A report on the details of the conference was written by Sue & Chin (1976). Suggestions for training mental health providers that arose out of the conference included such things as increasing the number of bilingual, bicultural trainees, establishing a training center specific to meeting the needs of Asian American clients, exploring alternative models of psychological treatments for Asian American rather than relying solely on Western models of psychotherapy (Leong, Okazaki, & David, 2007; Leong & Okazaki, under review).

After the first Asian American mental health conference held in San Francisco in 1972, almost a quarter century later an Asian American Pacific Islander Mental Health Summit was finally held on July 10–12, 1999, in Washington, DC. This summit was put together by a Vietnamese American psychiatrist, Tiffany Ho, who worked at the Center for Mental

Health Services (**CMHS**) of the Substance Abuse and Mental Health Services Administration (**SAMHSA**). This conference was held in order to address the mental health needs of Asian Americans and Pacific Islanders across the country. As a result of discussions that took place at the conference it was decided that a strategic planning committee needed to be formed, which occurred in July 2000. This committee was known as the National Asian American Pacific Islander Mental Health Association (**NAAPIMHA**) and it was run by D. J. Ida who functioned as its executive director. More information about the goals and activities of NAAPIMHA are available on their Web site at http://www.naapimha.org.

Prior to 1985, AAPA held sporadic conferences based on where the annual APA convention was being held. The decision to hold an AAPA convention hinged on whether APA was being held in a city with significant numbers of Asian Americans, such as San Francisco, Los Angeles, or New York. However, since 1985, under the chairmanship of Dr. Nolan Zane and the presidency of Dr. Herbert Wong, AAPA has been holding an annual national conference that takes place a day before the annual APA conference. Each new convention brings together more members and more presentations that exemplify the growth and future direction of AAPA. In 2005, in Washington, DC, the association celebrated 20 years of consecutive annual conventions, which began in 1985. It is clear that the AAPA convention has achieved a level of continuity and stability that fosters considerable growth in the association, which in turn leads to a sufficient turnout at each convention—regardless of where the APA's convention is held (Leong, Okazaki, & David, 2007; Leong & Okazaki, under review).

The Future of Asian American Psychology

Forecasting the evolution and the future of Asian American psychology can be a hazardous undertaking for scientists since so many variables are involved in the development of a field. However, based upon the groundwork of past trends and facts in the field and the history of the Asian American Psychological Association (see Table 2.2 for a synopsis of key events) we can make some speculations about the future. What is clear from the historical review of Asian American psychology is that AAPA will continue to grow. Clearly, AAPA, with all of its associated organizations and sister agencies, is progressing along a trajectory of growth and development, especially as new and young Asian Americans continue to join the association and become involved in issues pertaining to this ethnic group. Therefore, we have taken the liberty to envision the future, especially of the AAPA.

Networking is an important and vital aspect of any organization. The AAPA is no different, especially as new professional relationships are fostered, professional opportunities are broadened, and both professional and personal support is provided and encouraged. Since its inception, regional networking has been an integral part of AAPA because it fosters an environment and opportunities for discussion of pertinent issues related to Asian Americans, collaboration on research, workshops, clinical outlets, and training and advocacy goals. Since 1985, the AAPA has been successful in continuing these opportunities as national annual conventions became the norm. This helped to further solidify and stabilize the association. What began initially as an effort to meet the diverse needs of all its members, has grown into something more powerful, more influential, and more effective for the growth of Asian American mental health issues. This will become even more of a reality as AAPA gets bigger and as we see more subgroups form within the association, especially with regard to increased recognition and involvement of other Asian subgroups.

Looking at the growth of APA and its now 55 divisions as a template for the growth of a successful organization, we can predict the same for AAPA. During Dr. Frederick T. L. Leong's presidency, we saw a change in the bylaws that allowed for the addition of new divisions. The

DoW was formed in 1995. A Division of Students is a recent addition, and the Division on South Asian Americans has formed through the South Asian Psychological Networking Association (**SAPNA**). If we use these cases as examples and as membership increases within AAPA with members who have diverse needs and interests, we foresee that other divisions will continue to form under the larger AAPA umbrella to combat the imbalance of representation of subgroups within the governance of the AAPA and at the same time to meet the needs of specific Asian American interest groups.

Last, but not least, we foresee that the AAPA and Asian American mental health professionals will grow in their representation, involvement, and presence in national and global governance regarding mental health issues. Already AAPA has become a member of CNPAAEMI, which operates out of the Office of Ethnic and Minority Affairs. Currently efforts are being spearheaded to secure a permanent seat for AAPA on the APA's Council of Representatives. If successful, this effort will help AAPA to communicate further and more effectively with other associations.

Summary

The current generation of Asian American mental health professionals is poised to make their mark on the field. Already great strides have been made. The future holds much promise to the growth, development, and evolution of the field of Asian American psychology. The bottom line: It is conceivable that most of the "possible futures" envisioned here will come true. Although the Asian American population as a whole is complex, diverse, and comprised of various subgroups, we can even hope that enough work will be done to give mental health professionals a better understanding of all the nuances pertaining to this population so that we can better serve and meet their needs. The groundwork has been set, and some great strides have been made, but there is still much more work to do in the future.

Discussion Questions

1. When was the AAPA formed and who were the instrumental players in making this happen?
2. Describe two of the laws that affected Asian Americans when they initially immigrated to the United States.
3. Name four of the presidents of the AAPA and their key initiatives.
4. What are some of the main goals mentioned for the DoW?
5. Name two key conferences pertaining to Asian Americans and explain why these conferences were important to the development of Asian American psychology.

Case Study

Prior to Asian American psychologists coming into fruition, most Asian Americans who entered therapy had to be seen by European American psychologists who at the time had limited understanding and experience in working with API populations. This is because not much was known about working with Asian Americans and culturally appropriate research or competencies had not been established. The probability was higher then for the European American therapist to use culturally incongruent techniques as it would be natural for them to rely on Eurocentric skills or approaches. Research now demonstrates that this incongruence is what led to the large numbers of early termination after the first session. In fact, such experiences for Asian American clients were common according the Seattle mental health research conducted in 1977 by Sue and Morishima, which was then followed up in 1989 in Los Angeles, and then in other studies.

Case Study Discussion Questions

1. What are some of your initial thoughts about meeting the therapeutic needs of Asian Americans in this case study?
2. What are your thoughts about the way Asian American psychology has progressed over the years and what do you anticipate the future will bring in relation to meeting the needs of Asian American clients?
3. What do you suggest mental health professionals do when working with Asian American clients to prevent premature termination?
4. How do you think ethnicity and gender influence working with Asian American clients?

Key Terms

AAA & PI: Asian, Asian American, and Pacific Island (or Islander).
AAPA: Asian American Psychological Association.
AAS: Asian American studies.
ABPsi: Association of Black Psychologists.
APA: American Psychological Association.
APA's Division 17: Society for Counseling Psychology.
APS: American Psychological Society.
CMHS: Center for Mental Health Service.
CNPAAEMI: Council of National Psychological Association for the Advancement of Ethnic Minority Interests.
COPP: Council of Past Presidents.
DHP: Digital History Project.
DoS: Division of Students.
DoSAA: Division of South Asian Americans.
DoW: Division on Women.
NAAPIMHA: National Asian American Pacific Islander Mental Health Association.
NAAPTC: National Asian American Psychology Training Center.
NIMH: National Institute of Mental Health.
SAMHSA: Substance Abuse and Mental Health Services Administration.
SAPNA: South Asian Psychological Networking Association.
SPSSI: Society for the Psychological Study of Social Issues.

For Further Learning and Suggested Readings

Asian American Psychological Association Web site: http://www.aapaonline.org.
Cao, L., & Novas, H. (1996). *Everything you need to know about Asian American history*. New York: Plume Books.
Gall, S., & Natividad, I. (1995). *The Asian American almanac: A reference work on Asians in the United States*. MI: Thomson Gale.
Leong, F. T. L. (1995). *A brief history of Asian American psychology*. A monograph series of the Asian American Psychological Association, vol. 1.
Takaki, R. (1998). *Strangers from a different shore: A history of Asian Americans*. Back Bay Books.

References

Endo, R., Sue, S., & Wagner, N. N. (1980). *Asian-Americans: Social and psychological perspectives* (Vol. 2). California: Science & Behavior Books.

Lee, L. C., & Zane, N. W. S. (1998). *Handbook of Asian American psychology.* Thousand Oaks: Sage Publications.

Leong, F. T. L. (1995). *A brief history of Asian American psychology.* A monograph series of the Asian American Psychological Association, vol. 1.

Leong, F. T. L., & Okazaki, S. (2006). History of Asian American psychology. Special issue of *Cultural Diversity and Ethnic Minority Psychology* on "History of racial and ethnic minority psychology." Manuscript submitted for publication.

Leong, F. T. L., & Whitfield, J. R. (1992). *Bibliographies in psychology, no. 11: Asians in the United States; Abstracts of the Psychological and Behavioral Literature, 1967–1991.*

Leong, F. T. L., Okazaki, S., & David, E. J. R. (2007). History and future of Asian American psychology. In Leong, Inman, Ebreo, Yang, Kinoshita, & Fu (Eds.), *Handbook of Asian American psychology, 2nd Edition.* (pp. 11–28). Thousand Oaks, CA: Sage Publications.

Omatsu, G. (1994). The "four prisons" and the movements of liberation: Asian American activism from the 1960s to the 1990s. In K. Aguillar-San Juan (Ed.), *State of Asian American activism and resistance in the 1990s* (pp. 19–70). Boston: South End Press.

Prashad, V. (2005). The man who confounded Congress. *Amerasia, 31,* 54–61.

Sue, S., & Chin, R. (1976, July/August). *Report to the National Asian American Psychology Training Conference.* Long Beach, CA.

Sue, S., & Morishima, J. (1982). *The mental health of Asian Americans: Contemporary issues in identifying and treating mental health problems.* San Francisco: Jossey-Bass.

Sue, S., Sue, D. W., Sue, L., & Takeuchi, D. T. (1995). Psychopathology among Asian Americans: A model minority? *Cultural Diversity and Mental Health, 1,* 39–54.

U.S. Census Bureau. (1993). *Statistical abstract of the United States* (113th ed.). Washington, DC.

U.S. Census Bureau. (2001). *Profiles of general demographic characteristics: 2000 Census of Population and Housing, United States.*

U.S. Census Bureau. (2005). *Profiles of general demographic characteristics: 2004 Census of Population and Housing, United States.*

U.S. Department of Health and Human Services. (1999). *Mental health: A report of the Surgeon General.* Rockville, MD: U.S. Department of Health and Human Services, Substance Abuse and Mental Health Services Administration, Center for Mental Health Services, National Institutes of Health, National Institute of Mental Health.

U.S. Department of Health and Human Services. (2001). *Mental health: Culture, race, and ethnicity, a supplement to mental health: A report of the Surgeon General.* Rockville, MD: U.S. Department of Health and Human Services, Substance Abuse and Mental Health Services Administration, Center for Mental Health Services, National Institutes of Health, National Institute of Mental Health.

3
Research Methods

ANNE SAW and SUMIE OKAZAKI

OUTLINE OF CHAPTER

Case Synopsis
Introduction
The Science of Psychology
Assumptions and Critiques of Modern Scientific Methods
Challenges and Conundrums
The Big Picture: What Differences Does Research Make?
References

Case Synopsis

Imagine that you are shopping at a local store. At the cash register, you write a check for your purchase and the sales clerk asks for your ID. Taking a look at your driver's license the sales clerk asks you, "Where are you from?" You answer, "New York," but the sales clerk is apparently not satisfied with this answer. The clerk asks, "No, where are you really from?"

For many Asian Americans, this is an all-too-familiar scene. And for some Asian Americans, being asked this very question evokes feelings of irritation or even anger at being perceived as a foreigner who can't possibly be from New York.

It may feel like their identity as an American and their sense of belonging in America are being threatened: But are Asian Americans truly perceived to be less American? How prevalent are these encounters in which Asian Americans are reminded that others see them as foreigners? And how do Asian Americans react in such situations? In a research paper recently published in the *Journal of Personality and Social Psychology*, social psychologists Sapna Cheryan and Benoît Monin (2005) reported on the results of a series of research studies to answer just these questions. In this chapter, we use the question "Where are you really from?" and some of Cheryan and Monin's studies as a starting point for our discussion about research methods in Asian American psychology.

Students often become interested in psychology because they are intrigued by people and human behavior. However, as students progress in their study of psychology at colleges and universities, many become disappointed to find themselves taking statistics classes and research methods courses. For students coming from Asian American studies or a humanities background, it may not be immediately apparent why there is so much discussion about research methods in psychology. Why must someone interested in Asian American psychology know research methods? What must we know about research methods in general for psychology, and unique to Asian American psychology? And what good does psychological research do for Asian Americans?

Introduction

This chapter is not intended to teach psychology research methods (see For Further Learning and Suggested Readings at the end of this chapter for such texts). Instead, the goal is to discuss

(From *Boston's Weekly Dig* with permission.)

the unique issues and dilemmas facing researchers in Asian American psychology as well as the underlying assumptions about psychological research. We will first explore the principles that make psychology a science and some assumptions and critiques of the scientific enterprise of psychology. Next, we will discuss some unique challenges that many researchers in Asian American psychology face, including how researchers select and obtain samples, what researchers are studying when they conduct research on Asian Americans (culture? race? ethnicity?), issues regarding studying psychological concepts between or within groups of Asian Americans, and language issues when collecting research data from Asian Americans. Finally, we will look at the big picture by discussing how research is useful and can make an impact on the daily lives of Asian Americans.

Although our lay knowledge about the psychological experiences of Asian Americans is often informed by our personal reflections or experiences, it is through the use of scientific research methods that psychology goes beyond description. Let us return briefly to our example about the question, "Where are you really from?" Suppose your friend Jay, who is a Chinese American born and raised in Texas and fresh out of college, is looking for a job. At every interview he attends, the interviewer starts with questions such as, "Where are you really from?" and "When are you going back to your country?" Jay finds himself emphasizing his American values and his turn as a varsity football player in high school. Is Jay's reaction typical or atypical? What if he hadn't been constantly asked those questions during the job interviews? Would he have behaved differently?

If we were interested only in Jay's behavior, applied psychologists (such as clinical and counseling psychologists) may be called in to conduct a psychological assessment of Jay and systematically gather data that might be relevant to answering questions just about Jay. Psychological research, on the other hand, typically does not answer questions about the behavior of any particular individual, but it helps to move us beyond anecdotal evidence or personal opinions. There are established scientific principles and corresponding research methods in psychology that help us describe, predict, control, synthesize, and explain what we observe about behavior. In doing so, research helps us make generalizations from the data gathered from a small number of research participants to a larger community (this is called **external validity**), so that we can be more confident that what holds for a small group of Asian Americans may hold for a larger community of Asian Americans.

The phenomenon of *identity denial* (Cheryan & Monin, 2005), which is discussed throughout this chapter as an example of contemporary Asian American research has been discussed from other disciplinary perspectives. Many Asian American writers have written about the experience of being asked "Where are you really from?" For example, Meena Kothari (1995) wrote eloquently about her evolving identity as a South Asian American woman in her essay aptly titled, "Where Are You From?" In law, Kenji Yoshino who teaches at Yale Law School and identifies as a gay Asian American legal scholar, discusses this from the legal perspective. Yoshino (2006) talks about the society's demand for *covering*— or the act of downplaying an aspect of self that is stigmatized in society, such as minority sexual orientation or minority racial status, so as to blend into the mainstream—as a threat to civil rights. Yoshino writes of his experience attending an elite boarding school where many students who were racial minorities (including himself) engaged in various types of covering behavior, such as avoiding ethnic organizations, "outprepp(ing) the preps, dressing out of catalogs that featured no racial minorities... Asian Americans got eyelid surgery, African Americans straightened their hair, Latinos planed the accents off their names" (p. 120).

Psychological phenomena of central interest to Asian Americans are found everywhere. What makes Asian American psychology distinct is our commitment to using scientific research methods to document and explain these common experiences.

The Science of Psychology

So what, then, are the scientific principles? According to Stanovich (2004), science is defined by three features: "(1) the use of systematic empiricism; (2) the production of public knowledge; and (3) the examination of solvable problems" (p. 9). What these features generally imply is that in building our knowledge, psychologists engage in systematic, structured, and theory-driven observations so that the results of the observations can say something meaningful about the underlying processes or mechanisms about the mind and the behavior.

Psychology research is typically conducted in a way that tests different explanations (or hypotheses) about some psychological phenomenon. Moreover, psychological knowledge produced by research must be publicly verifiable—that is, the findings are presented to the scientific community in a manner that can be replicated, critiqued, and extended by others. And finally, types of questions that psychologists ask in research must be potentially answerable using currently available methods. Questions such as "What is the meaning of life?" or "Is it wrong to react angrily in response to the question, Where are you really from?" are not solvable through scientific means. However, questions such as "Are Asian Americans perceived as foreigners?" or "Do Chinese Americans respond better to Traditional Chinese Medicine than to cognitive-behavioral therapy for depression?" are potentially testable questions.

Assumptions and Critiques of Modern Scientific Methods

The basic tenets of modern science just described arise from Western philosophy. Modernist empirical science as an epistemological system values objectivity, **operationalism**, parsimonious theories, logic of control and manipulation (as epitomized by true experiments), and so on. However, Asian American psychology, in its short history, has faced the limits of science-as-usual approach within psychology even while it has embraced its practice. (For one, we cannot randomly assign race, ethnicity, or culture to people!) We take the time now to discuss two examples of these tensions, because such critiques and internal dialogues within Asian American psychology as to its scientific foundation reveal issues central to the field.

Objectivity

Objectivity is a key assumption of scientific research. In conducting research, psychologists seek to leave out their own personal biases about the people they are studying and let the data speak for themselves. Researchers in psychology also assume that regardless of who is collecting the research data, participants will respond or behave in the same way. Replication of findings, or the process of repeating a study using different participants (and often, different researchers), is valuable in this regard.

However, some critics argue that it is impossible to be objective and bias-free in research. For example, postmodern theories, which have gained ground in Asian American studies and in many of the humanities disciplines, have challenged the notion that modernist science is neutral and value-free. Within Asian American psychology, Laura Uba (2002) has argued that in its allegiance to mainstream psychology's modernist scientific assumptions of objectivity and neutrality, Asian American psychology has failed to pay attention to the subjective voices of Asian Americans themselves. Uba argues that a postmodern approach to psychology may lead to new understanding of psychological constructs central to Asian American psychology such as racial, cultural, and ethnic identity, assimilation, and acculturation.

Research in Asian American psychology then faces a dilemma: At the risk of ignoring Asian Americans' experiences, should the field remain tied to the practice of psychology and its modernist scientific assumptions of objectivity and neutrality? If Asian American psychology focuses its research endeavors on being meaningfully applicable to Asian Americans, does it appear less scientifically rigorous? In an article titled, "Science, Ethnicity, and Bias: Where Have We Gone Wrong?" clinical psychologist Stanley Sue (1999) acknowledged that much of ethnic minority research (including Asian American psychology) is criticized by grant review panelists and journal reviewers for being descriptive (rather than theory-driven, hypothesis-testing), simple in research design, and lacking theoretical sophistication. In other words, Asian American psychological research is often perceived as not rigorous enough to be published in top psychology research journals or to be funded by granting agencies. There is some evidence that research articles on ethnic minority populations are not well represented in top psychology journals. For example, Hall and Maramba (2001) conducted an analysis of psychological research published in scholarly journals between 1993 and 1999 and found that only a very small percentage of publications in what are considered the first-tier academic psychology journals had any cross-cultural or ethnic minority content. Sue asked, "Does this mean that science is biased against ethnic research?" In responding to this question, Sue concluded that the "science and scientific methods are not the culprit" of ethnic minority psychology's state (p. 1070). Instead, Sue argued that psychology has erred in over-emphasizing **internal validity** (or the extent to which conclusions can be made about causal effects of the phenomenon) versus external validity (or the extent to which conclusions from one study can be applied to other populations). He argued that researchers should maintain high internal validity standards; however, we should pay more attention to external validity and make sure that the research we conduct can be applied to ethnic minority populations. We shall come back to this notion of external validity later in this chapter as a challenging methodological issue in Asian American psychology.

Operationalism

The doctrine of operationalism, as applied to psychology, means that concepts in psychological theories must be linked to observable events that can be measured. Translating concepts (such as anger) into observable and measurable events (such as questionnaire reports, observations of certain facial expressions and bodily postures or actions) allow the resulting knowledge to be publicly verified. In most instances, this is achieved through quantification. Quantification refers to the idea that researchers collect data that can be subjected to numeric qualification. In any field of science, researchers need to share a common language when talking about constructs or variables. Quantification of data gives us that common language and also allows us to easily summarize and make meaning out of similar data across individuals or groups of individuals.

For example, in their investigation of identity denial among Asian Americans, the first question Cheryan and Monin (2005) asked was, "Who is perceived as American?" To show whether individuals with Asian features were indeed perceived as less American than others, the researchers showed pictures of sample faces from four ethnic groups (White, Asian, Hispanic, and African American) to 111 participants, and asked the participants to give a numerical rating (from 1 indicating "not at all," to 7 indicating "extremely") on how American each face looked. The ratings were then averaged and compared, via statistical analyses. Not surprisingly, White American participants rated White faces as more American (with a mean rating of 5.76 out of 7) than the Asian American faces (with a mean rating of 4.20 out of 7). Interestingly, Asian American participants also rated the same set of White faces as more American (with a mean rating of 5.38 out of 7) than the same set of Asian American faces (with a mean rating of 3.92 out of 7)!

Using **quantitative methods** also helps us compare psychological phenomena across time points and individuals. For example, a common measure of ethnic identity is Jean Phinney's Multigroup Ethnic Identity Measure (MEIM; 1992). Examples of questions from the MEIM include: "I am happy that I am a member of the group I belong to" and "I have spent time trying to find out more about my ethnic group, such as its history, traditions, and customs." The responses across the 12 items on the MEIM are then summed into a single index of the strength of ethnic identity. Higher scores on the MEIM indicate higher levels of ethnic identity. However, you may wonder whether the MEIM, or any other quantitative measure of ethnic identity, really captures the full range of a person's ethnic identity or if scores are easily comparable across individuals.

Although quantitative research methods can tell us about relative levels of a psychological construct, these methods often cannot tell us detailed information about the phenomenology of a person's experience with the construct, or about the processes through which psychological constructs emerge. For example, what meaning does a person's ethnic identity have for him or her? What experiences lead a person to develop an ethnic identity? These questions may be

(Adapted from Cheryan & Monin (2005).)

better answered through **qualitative methods**, such as through interview narratives, because such methods are better suited for tackling complex and nuanced research questions.

Challenges and Conundrums

Every subfield within psychology has its own research demons that keep researchers up at night. For example, psychologists who study infant cognition must design studies suitable for babies who cannot read, speak, or understand complex instructions. Psychologists who study neurobiological bases of emotion must master the ever-evolving advances in brain imaging technologies, complex mathematical analyses of brain wave data or imaging data, as well as methods for eliciting desired emotions in a laboratory setting. Likewise, psychologists who study Asian Americans face a set of methodological issues that present particular challenges.

Sampling

Researchers typically cannot collect data from the entire population of interest. Instead, they carefully choose and collect data from a subset of the population—a sample—and use those data to make inferences about the entire population of interest. How one goes about **sampling** in Asian American psychological research is one of the research demons of the field.

Probability Sampling   In behavioral science research, there are two broad types of sampling. In **probability sampling**, every person in a given population has some probability of being included in the study, and that probability can be mathematically calculated and the results are weighted accordingly. Probability sampling has the major advantage in that **sampling errors** (i.e., the degree to which a sample differs from the population) can be calculated. An example of probability sampling that may be familiar to many readers may be various opinion polls that one might read in newspapers (e.g., Gallup polls). However, this type of sampling is quite complex, time-consuming, and typically expensive to carry out, and thus it is not commonly used in psychology research or in Asian American psychology. One exceptional example of the use of probability sampling in Asian American psychological research consists of a series of studies on the rates of psychiatric disorders among various Asian American communities conducted by sociologist David Takeuchi and his associates.

Nonprobability Sampling   In **nonprobability sampling**, research participants are not selected randomly from the population and the extent to which the research participants represent the population cannot be known. In nonprobability sampling, the degree to which the sample differs from the population remains unknown, and it becomes a judgment call on the part of the researchers (and consumers of the research) about how much the findings can speak to the more general population. One of the most common nonprobability sampling approaches is called a convenience sample where the researcher uses whatever individuals are available (e.g., college students, paid volunteers, prisoners, and so on). "Non-random" and "convenient" does not mean that participants are easy to recruit or that the researchers are being lazy. In fact, the bulk of psychological research uses convenience samples and researchers go about their sampling in a careful, purposive manner.

Selecting and Recruiting Participants   What makes Asian American psychology research particularly challenging is the need to balance the limits of convenience sampling with feasibility and access. First and foremost, the Asian American population is extremely diverse. Researchers must be clear about what segment of the Asian American population they wish to address in their study, and why. The researcher must also balance the theoretical questions with the

David Takeuchi, professor of Sociology and Social Welfare at University of Washington, has conducted a series of psychiatric epidemiology studies to determine the population estimates of rates of psychiatric disorders among Asian American populations using rigorous probabilistic sampling methods. The first study, the Chinese American Psychiatric Epidemiology Study (CAPES) gathered data from 1,747 individuals of Chinese descent in the greater Los Angeles area (Zheng et al., 1997; Takeuchi et al., 1998). The second study, the Filipino American Community Epidemiological Study (FACES) reported on data from 2,285 Filipino Americans in San Francisco and Honolulu (Gong, Gage, & Tacata, 2003; Abe-Kim, Gong, & Takeuchi, 2004). The most comprehensive study of this kind is titled the National Latino and Asian American Study of Mental Health (NLAAS), which Dr. Takeuchi conducted with Dr. Margarita Alegría at Harvard Medical School. NLAAS is the first nationally representative survey that estimates the prevalence of mental disorders and rates of service utilization for Latinos and Asian Americans. The NLAAS interviewed 2,554 Latinos (Puerto Ricans, Mexican Americans, Cubans, and Other Latinos) and 2,095 Asian American respondents (Chinese, Vietnamese, Filipinos, and Other Asians) across the United States in 2002. The data from each individual in the sample were collected in person via a structured interview, and the interviews were offered in Chinese, Vietnamese, Tagalog, or English for the Asian American respondents. In order to find eligible Asian American and Latino adults, the NLAAS project screened 27,026 households across the nation (Pennell et al., 2004)! Because the total population of Asian Americans in the United States is still relatively small (4% according to the 2000 U.S. Census), the NLAAS team sampled households from Census blocks of moderate to high (5+%) concentration of persons of targeted ethnicity. Still, imagine knocking on doors of houses after houses specifically selected to meet the probabilistic sampling scheme just to find if the persons living in those houses are Chinese American or Filipino American or Vietnamese American! Compare this to the 13,054 households across the nation screened to find 9,282 adults who completed a parallel survey of psychiatric epidemiology for mainstream American respondents (National Comorbidity Survey Replication) and you see what an extra effort it takes to collect data from Asian Americans and Latinos.

feasibility of recruiting the desired participants. In Asian American psychological research, *access* to research participants in the target population can be extremely challenging even when one is not studying families of Asian American individuals with schizophrenia (Okazaki, 2000), Asian American veterans of the Vietnam War (Loo, 1994), Japanese Americans whose parents were in the internment camps during World War II (Nagata, 1993), or other very specific segments of the Asian American population.

Say, for example, that you have a burning research question about the relationship between levels of acculturation and the openness with which Asian Indian American parents discuss sexuality with their adolescent children. Do you have access to a large number of Asian-Indian American parents of teenagers? Having or gaining access to many Asian American communities means that you have some type of an insider-status or are properly invited into the community through a relationship with the gatekeeper of the community. However, having access to potential participants does not necessarily guarantee that recruitment of participants would follow naturally. For example, even if you were given permission to make an announcement to a group of Asian Indian American parents at some occasion, how does one recruit them to volunteer in a psychology study that involves questions about discussion of sexuality with their children?

Another decision that a researcher must make is to determine who to include in the research and to set the **eligibility criteria** (or selection criteria) for the participants accordingly. Let us look at examples from two studies in Asian American psychology with different eligibility criteria.

EXAMPLE 1: Here is an excerpt from the description of research participants in a study conducted by Tsai, Simeonova, and Watanabe (2004) to examine cultural differences in the use of emotion words:

Thirty European Americans (EA) and 30 Chinese Americans (CA; 53.3% women) were recruited via flyers and announcements to participate in a study of family relationships. Participants were students from colleges and universities in Minnesota and received $20 for their participation in the study. To increase the cultural homogeneity of the EA sample, EA participants were required to (a) be born in the United States, (b) have EA parents and grandparents who were born and raised in the United States, and (c) be fluent in English. To increase the cultural homogeneity of the CA sample, CA were required to (a) be born in either the United States, China, Taiwan, or Hong Kong; (b) have Chinese parents and grandparents who were born and raised in China, Taiwan, or Hong Kong; (c) have been raised in households where a Chinese dialect (e.g., Mandarin, Taiwanese, or Cantonese) was spoken; (d) have at least 50% of their friends during childhood or adolescence be Chinese or CA; and (e) be fluent in English. (pp. 1228–1229)

Note the specificity of the eligibility criteria that Tsai and colleagues set for their study and the reason they give for their decision. In this case, it was to "increase the cultural homogeneity" within each group of participants, which means that the researchers wanted the European Americans in this research to be culturally similar to one another, and the Chinese Americans in this research to be culturally similar to one another with regard to language, national residency status, and family's nation of origin. This level of specificity gives the researchers more confidence that the group differences between EA and CA participants found in this study may be due to their cultural backgrounds (and more specifically, the differences between European American and Chinese cultural elements). It should be noted that there are also downsides to setting strict eligibility criteria for a research study. For one, it makes the data collection much more challenging to identify and recruit participants who meet all the criteria, especially if your research site is not located in an area densely populated by the target research sample. Another downside to strict criteria is that, with a research sample that has very specific sets of demographic characteristics, the research findings may be less *generalizable* to individuals or groups whose characteristics deviate from those of the participants in the study. For example, it is difficult to be certain how much the findings from Tsai et al.'s study about Chinese Americans may generalize to Korean Americans, Filipino Americans, or even other Chinese Americans who differ from Tsai et al.'s inclusion criteria.

EXAMPLE 2: Here is an excerpt from the description of research participants in a study conducted by Okazaki (2000) to examine cultural and family factors that may contribute to the delay of seeking treatment for Asian American patients with severe mental illness:

> Asian American patients receiving psychiatric treatment from one of five participating outpatient mental health clinics in the greater Los Angeles area were recruited for the study. All five referring clinics were receiving partial or total funding from the Los Angeles County Department of Mental Health, and four of the clinics were ethnic-specific or "parallel" services staffed by bilingual, bicultural Asian clinicians and serving primarily Asian American patients. Clinic staff was asked to approach all patients who met the following eligibility criteria: (a) of Asian or Asian American descent; (b) over age 18; (c) diagnosed (by psychiatric staff of the referring clinic) with DSM-III-R or DSV-IV schizophrenic disorder, schizoaffective disorder, mood disorder, or other psychotic disorder involving at least one past psychotic episode; (d) in regular contact with at least one family member; (e) psychosis not due to organic factors or substance abuse; (f) not currently diagnosed with an active case of post-traumatic stress disorder. (p. 59)

Now, the best estimate of the prevalence rate of schizophrenia is 1% of the general population (Regier et al., 1993). We also know from other research that Asian Americans with mental illness may not seek mental health services because of stigma and shame (Sue & Sue, 1999). These facts, along with the fact that Asian Americans still make up only 4% of the U.S. population (Reeves & Bennett, 2004), combine to make recruitment for the study described above quite challenging just in terms of locating participants who meet all the eligibility criteria AND are willing to volunteer in a psychology research study. The data collection for this study—which consisted of conducting individual interviews with 62 patients and 40 family members in 6 different languages (English, Cantonese, Mandarin, Vietnamese, Korean, and Japanese) took two years.

As the above example (Okazaki, 2000) shows, it is quite challenging to conduct research with Asian Americans in the community, especially if the research involves rare or stigmatized phenomena. Consequently, much research in Asian American psychology is conducted with college participants due to the convenience of recruiting these populations. For example, all five studies in Cheryan and Monin's (2005) research on identity denial were conducted with university students. Would you expect the results to be different if the same studies were conducted with people who were not college students?

On a different note, what does a researcher do if he or she is interested in Asian American participants who are not in college, or if he or she does not have ready access to any Asian American participants, perhaps because the research is conducted where there are few Asian Americans? A common method for many researchers who wish to recruit research participants from the community is called **snowball sampling**, whereby a researcher starts with a known group of participants who then recruits others to participate in the study. Often, researchers tap into intact ethnic organizations, such as kinship associations, professional associations, religious centers, and social clubs, for participants. While these organizations provide good sources of participants, they too represent a narrow subset of Asian Americans (Okazaki & Sue, 1995), and therefore the findings generalized from these samples should be interpreted with caution.

Surname-based telephone survey methodology has been used in several studies with Asian Americans. Telephone directories have been found to be reliable in identifying potential research participants because some Asian Americans have unique ethnic surnames that can be associated with specific groups (e.g., "Singh" or "Patel" for South Asians, "Kim" for Koreans, "Chan" or "Wang" for Chinese, "Tanaka" or "Suzuki" for Japanese, "Nguyen" for Vietnamese). Sasao (1994) also suggests that using this methodology can be cost effective (compared to face-to-face interviewing) and reliable as long as researchers use telephone lists with clearly identifiable surnames. He found that this methodology may not be quite as effective with the Filipino American community because many Filipino Americans have Hispanic surnames due to Spanish colonization of the Philippines from the 16th to 19th centuries.

What Do We Mean by "Asian American?"

In reflecting on appropriate research methods for studying the psychological experiences of Asian Americans, Tanaka, Ebreo, Linn, and Morera (1998) asked the following two questions: "What does the researcher assume when he or she sets out to study Asian American populations, and what do Asian American research participants believe about the extent to which their 'Asian Americanness' serves as a guide to their behavior?" (p. 22). These two questions also keep many Asian American psychology researchers up at night.

Pan-Asian American Concepts   In heeding Tanaka et al.'s (1998) suggested questions, we must ask ourselves what assumptions we are making by studying Asian Americans. What is it about being "Asian American" that we really care about, and to what extent does being "Asian American" affect how our research participants perform in our research study? When we construct a research study on Asian Americans, what is the "thing" that we are studying? Is "it" culture, race, or ethnicity? Is "it" minority status? One pitfall researchers in Asian American psychology often fall prey to is not being clear about what they mean when using the term *Asian American*. Sometimes researchers use the term as a demographic variable. Other times, researchers use the term as a proxy for something else that goes with "Asian American," such as culture, race, ethnicity, or minority status.

Shih, Pittinsky, and Ambady (1999) wanted to study how performance in a particular domain (in this case, math) is affected when an individual is conscious of a stereotype associated with that domain for the identity group to which they belong. They recruited Asian American women college students to be in their experiment. Before taking a difficult math test, some research participants were asked questions that elicited their ethnic identity in a subtle manner (e.g., "what language do you speak at home?") whereas other participants were asked questions that emphasized their gender (e.g., "do you live in a co-ed dorm?").

Which group of Asian American women do you think performed better on the math test in this experiment? Think about the stereotypes held about the math abilities of Asian Americans.

What about stereotypes about the math abilities of women? You can probably guess who performed better on a math test—those primed with their racial/ethnic identity or those primed with their gender identity. Yes, those who were primed with their racial/ethnic identity performed better than those primed with their gender identity. The authors argue that this is because women are negatively stereotyped as being worse in math than men and Asian Americans are positively stereotyped as being really good in math.

In the example given, what is it about being "Asian American" that the researchers care about? Clearly, the researchers are using "Asian American" as more than just a demographic variable. They know that something about being "Asian American" affects participants' performance. In the case of this study, being "Asian American" meant more than simply being Asian American but also being aware of the societal stereotypes about Asian Americans' math abilities and performing according to the stereotypes.

We must also think about the extent to which being "Asian American" affects the participants in our study. In the study presented above, being "Asian American" had a large impact on how participants performed on a math test. Let's discuss why it is important to consider how being "Asian American" or being, for example, Chinese American, affects research participants. Tsai, Ying, and Lee (2000) sought to understand the variations of meanings attached to "being Chinese" and "being American" among three different groups of Chinese Americans: those born in the United States, those who immigrated to the United States before or at age 12, and those who immigrated after age 12. They found that the three groups, despite all identifying as "Chinese American," derived different meanings from their Chinese and American identities. For example, whereas the American-born Chinese in the study felt that they could be both Chinese and American, immigrant Chinese Americans felt that being American meant being less Chinese and vice versa. This study shows us that it is important for researchers to understand not only what they mean by "Asian American," but also what their participants mean by "Asian American."

Ethnic Specificity   You will recall that at the start of the chapter, we mentioned that researchers in Asian American psychology often question whether many of the generalizations made in the field of psychology can be wholeheartedly applied to Asian Americans. As a racial group, Asian Americans represent diverse ethnic groups and cultures—that is to say, Asian Americans are a very heterogeneous population to study. Thus, one consideration researchers must think about is how specific a population they want to focus on in their research study. Do they want to examine Asian Americans as a group, or do they want to examine a specific ethnic group, such as Vietnamese Americans? Again, the answer to these questions depends on what it is that researchers want to study and why. If researchers believe that there is a common element that all Asian Americans share, they might be best served by studying a diverse sample of Asian Americans. If they believe that Asian Americans from one country of origin, such as Chinese Americans, might differ from Asian Americans from another country of origin, such as Japanese Americans, they might want to examine those two ethnic groups separately. Of course, researchers must have a good guess about what it is that makes their sample somewhat homogeneous, such as common cultural elements, religion, immigration status, or socioeconomic status.

It should be noted here that the body of knowledge of Asian American psychology has been built largely on studies that often only included East Asian Americans (especially Chinese Americans and Japanese Americans). A part of this is due to the fact that for the first two decades of Asian American psychology (the 1970s and the 1980s), Chinese Americans and Japanese Americans were most numerous on university campuses relative to other Asian ethnic groups, and thus most accessible to researchers. The demographic of the Asian American population in the United States, as well as at universities and colleges, in the past decade and a half have shifted to be increasingly diverse. Accordingly, we are starting to see more published research on other Asian American populations such as Vietnamese Americans, Asian Indian Americans, and Korean Americans.

Studying Psychological Concepts Within or Between Groups

Depending on the research question, researchers in Asian American psychology might want to study psychological phenomena within a particular group, or study phenomena across groups to look at similarities and differences. Culture is one of the most important influences on the psychological experiences of Asian Americans. Cross-cultural psychologists study the

E. J. R. David is an assistant professor at the University of Alaska. Born in the Phillippines, David immigrated to the United States at the age of 14 and lived in Alaska until graduate school. He is now back in Alaska as a professor, where his research focuses on colonial mentality, a set of psychological processes, and effects of colonization and oppression.

Q: Why are you interested in studying Filipino Americans?

A: Because most studies in Asian American psychology are based either on East Asian samples or on aggregate multiethnic samples that usually fail to capture the unique experiences of Filipino Americans. Filipinos compose the 2nd largest Asian group in the United States, but psychological research on this population is relatively fewer than other Asian groups. More importantly, there are many psychological concerns in the Filipino American community, including high rates of depression, suicide, alcohol and drug use, and school matriculation.

Q: Do you think that research with East Asian Americans can be applied to Filipino Americans?

A: Of course, in some ways, but not all East Asian concepts can be appropriately applied to Filipino Americans. Filipinos have unique historical and cultural characteristics that make their psychological experiences different from East Asians.

Q: What makes Filipino Americans' experiences different from that of other Asian Americans?

A: Well, I think the most important difference is colonial history. Filipinos were colonized by Spain for over 350 years and by the United States for about 50 years, and the fact that most Filipinos are Catholic and that many of them speak English are good examples of how Filipino culture has been strongly affected by such a colonial history. Colonial mentality, a more general psychological consequence of colonialism, is what I am studying. I believe that colonial mentality continues to exist among modern-day Filipinos because it has been passed along through generations by continued oppression and continued Americanization of the Philippines.

Q: How do you study the effects of colonialism on Filipino Americans? Is that even something that psychologists can study?

A: It is definitely something psychologists can and should study. Because of our rapidly diversifying society, psychology can no longer study people without taking into account people's historical, political, and cultural experiences. This is why I use a multidisciplinary approach in my efforts to understand colonial mentality by combining knowledge from multiple fields such as anthropology, history, sociology, political science, and psychology. In my studies, I use surveys, implicit association tasks, subliminal priming tasks, and interviews to better understand how colonial mentality operates within and affects Filipino Americans.

Q: What strategies do you use to find Filipino American participants?

A: I usually begin by enlisting the help of student and community organizations. From their contacts and influence, Filipino Americans across the country become aware of my projects. Through the Internet, I make sure that my projects are easily accessible so that Filipino Americans everywhere are given the opportunity to share their experiences.

Q: What do you do with your research data?

A: Aside from publishing it in scientific journals for other researchers and students to read, I make sure that I share my findings to the Filipino American community so that they can become more aware of how colonial mentality affects some of them. I do presentations and workshops for community and student groups. Also, I plan on conducting a series of workshops that will "decolonize" Filipino American mentalities.

influences of culture across different cultural groups by transporting and testing out current research knowledge in other, usually non-Western, cultures, examining how the new culture of study adds to existing knowledge about the phenomenon of interest, and attempting to integrate new and current knowledge in order to arrive at a more accurate universal truth about the phenomenon of interest (Segall, Lonner, & Berry, 1998). Thus, many cross-cultural psychologists believe that psychological phenomena are universal across different cultures.

In other cases, researchers may be interested in drawing a contrast between Asian Americans and White Americans with respect to their racial identity. For example, in their fourth study, Cheryan and Monin (2005) wanted to study how Asian Americans react to identity denial in a simulated situation. They recruited 20 Asian American and 26 White American Stanford University students to participate in the study. For half of the participants, a White American experimenter approached the participant and asked, "Do you speak English?" whereas the other half of the participants were not asked this question. Then all participants were asked to complete a questionnaire that asked them to "List as many American TV shows from the 80s as you can remember" (p. 723). The researchers timed how long the participants spent on this task. They found that Asian Americans spent a longer time generating American TV shows (an average of 3.11 minutes) after being asked "Do you speak English?" than Asian Americans who were not asked this question (an average of 1.34 minutes). However, White Americans who were asked the language question did not spend significantly more time naming the shows than White Americans who were not asked (on average, 2.11 and 2.88 minutes, respectively). In this case, the researchers were not interested in cultural variables associated with being Asian American (e.g., loss of face, collectivistic orientation) but in having their Americanness threatened. Cheryan and Monin suggested that when their identity (as American) was threatened, Asian Americans were motivated to spend more time and effort demonstrating their knowledge and familiarity with American popular culture.

Many times, researchers in Asian American psychology are less interested in how Asian Americans differ from other racial/ethnic/cultural groups. Instead, they are interested in describing or explaining phenomena within the racial group of Asian Americans, a particular ethnic group, such as Korean Americans, or a particular subset of an ethnic group, such as the elderly. For example, Pang (1998) sought to understand how depression is experienced among elderly Korean American immigrants, thus her sample was restricted to only elderly Korean American immigrants. Because Asian American psychology is an accumulation of research knowledge, we can use Pang's study to hypothesize how depression is experienced among other groups and conduct other within-group studies or a between-group study to look at how other groups might be similar or different from Pang's sample.

Etic and Emic Approaches   Researchers interested in the influence of culture on psychological phenomena will use **etic** or **emic** approaches. The etic perspective emphasizes the universal nature of psychological phenomena. Thus, psychologists who conduct research using an etic approach would need to study equivalent concepts and use equivalent standards to compare the phenomena they are studying. If two researchers wanted to study the prevalence of depression in two cultures, they would first define what they mean by depression, by, for example, using the definition and diagnostic criteria provided by the American Psychiatric Association's 1994 *Diagnostic and Statistical Manual* (DSM). They would then apply that conceptual definition to both cultures, using the same measurement tool, such as the Center for Epidemiologic Studies Depression Scale, or CES-D (Radloff, 1977). Notice that research from an etic approach focuses on the researcher's perspective.

In contrast, researchers oriented to an emic approach believe that psychological phenomena must be studied from the perspective of those within the culture. Emic approaches seek to understand psychological concepts and use measurement tools that are culturally appropriate and specific to their culture of study. Indigenous psychology is a subfield of psychology that emphasizes an emic research approach. Indigenous psychologists argue that each culture has its own indigenous psychology and if we would like to study those within the culture, we must use their concepts and methods rather than transplanting our own (Kim & Berry, 1993).

Researchers in Asian American psychology who conduct comparative studies of Asian Americans and other racial/ethnic groups may use both etic and emic approaches, depending on their research question. Deciding whether to use etic or emic approaches often helps researchers figure out which research methods are most appropriate for answering their research questions. Though this is not always the case, etic approaches tend to emphasize quantitative research methods, such as surveys, while emic approaches tend to emphasize more qualitative research methods, such as interviews. Oftentimes, emically oriented researchers will begin with qualitative methods to understand the phenomena and then translate their qualitative data into quantitative instruments.

Language Issues

Many of the established questionnaires used in psychological research are only available in English. However, the 2000 Census indicated that 79% of Asian Americans reported that they speak a language other than English at home (Reeves & Bennett, 2004). Thus researchers who are interested in conducting research with Asian Americans with no or limited English skills are taken to task to translate the material from English to the specific Asian language needed for that study. This is often easier said than done because many psychological terms and concepts do not translate easily across languages and cultures. Thus, when researchers do not have access to existing translated measures and must translate assessment measures themselves, they should use cultural or linguistic experts familiar with both languages to help with the translation in order to ensure translation equivalence. Brislin (1993) suggests that researchers use a multistep method that involves multiple translations and back-translations. Let's say that we want to translate a 20-item measure of ethnic identity from English to Tagalog. We should have one translator convert the measure from English to Tagalog, and another translator independently translate the measure back into English. Changes should be made to the new English version, and yet another round of translation and back-translation should occur. The end product should be an English version of the measure that is easily expressed in Tagalog.

The Big Picture: What Differences Does Research Make?

You may be wondering whether psychological research makes a real impact on Asian Americans' lives. One area of psychological research that has made an impact is in mental health

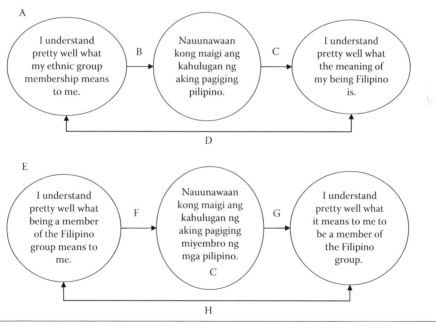

A. The researcher begins with an item in English.

B. The item, originally in English, is translated into Tagalog by Translator #1.

C. The item, in Tagalog, is translated back into English by Translator #2.

D. The researcher compares the two English versions. They certainly are not equivalent. First, the translators can not translate "my ethnic group" from English because there is no equivalent Tagalog term. More importantly, the translation derived from these steps does not quite capture the meaning of the English item, which asks the survey participant to describe what it means to be a part of his/her ethnic group.

service delivery. When Stanley Sue began his pioneering research in the 1970s, very little was known about Asian American psychology and about Asian Americans' utilization of mental health services. In examining the usage data for a countywide mental health system in King County (Seattle, Washington), Sue and McKinney (1975) noticed that Asian Americans were not using mental health services compared to the rate of usage by other ethnic groups. Sue began a program of research examining mental health service utilization and found many obstacles to Asian Americans' help-seeking for psychological problems. Some of these factors included shame and stigma surrounding mental illness, as well as the fact that existing services did not accommodate the linguistic and cultural needs of Asian American patients (Sue, 1993). Due in part to Sue's pioneering work, ethnic-specific mental health agencies that are staffed by bilingual, bicultural staff, have been created in many Asian American communities and have been found to be effective (Lau & Zane, 2000; Zane, Hatanaka, Park, & Akutsu, 1994). Although community activism played a part in the establishment of these culturally appropriate services, it would not have been possible without psychological research.

Summary

At the start of this chapter, we introduced identity denial as something that happens to many Asian Americans (Cheryan & Monin, 2005) and that has recently been studied in the field of Asian American psychology. Researching psychological phenomena that impact Asian Americans, such as identity denial or mental health service utilization, can be both challenging and rewarding. Asian Americans represent a heterogeneous group of communities that require researchers to employ innovative methods of study. This chapter discussed some of the most salient and vexing research challenges facing Asian American psychology research. We hope that as you learn more about research in Asian American psychology, you will be able to think critically about whether each study adequately answers the questions asked, how the researchers used the term *Asian American,* and how each study could be improved or extended to broaden our knowledge about Asian Americans. After all, you as consumers and users of psychological knowledge are essential members of the community.

Discussion Questions

1. Throughout this chapter, we talked about the identity denial research of Cheryan and Monin. How well do you think their studies can be applied to your own experiences?
2. How would you design a study to test the effects of identity denial? What are the advantages and disadvantages of your study's design?
3. Think of a psychological construct that interests you. How would you operationalize this construct so that it can be tested?
4. What are advantages and disadvantages of using quantitative methods? What are advantages and disadvantages of using qualitative methods?
5. If you wanted to conduct a research study at your school, how would you go about recruiting participants? How might the results you find be different if you conducted the same study in another part of the country?
6. If you were a researcher, how would you make your research accessible to the public?
7. If you were a clinician treating an Asian American adult client for depression, how would you apply research to your clinical work? If there was no research directly related to your client, how would you apply available research?

Key Terms

Eligibility criteria: Set of criteria that a researcher sets forth to determine the selection of research participants.

Emic: Focus on culture-specific concepts or processes.

Etic: Focus on culture-general or universal concepts or processes.

External validity: The extent to which conclusions from one study can be applied (or generalized) outside of specific research settings in which the research was carried out.

Internal validity: The extent to which conclusions can be made about causal effects of the phenomenon.

Nonprobability sampling: Method of sampling in which the chance of any given individual being selected for the study is not known.

Operationalism: A doctrine that states that concepts and variables are defined by the specific process or tests used to measure or manipulate them.

Probability sampling: Method of sampling in which random selection is used.

Qualitative methods: Research methods in which data are collected and analyzed without numerical or statistical analyses; often, the types of data that are involved in qualitative research involve interviews and other narrative data, participant observations, focus groups, and case studies.

Quantitative methods: Research methods in which collected data are quantified (converted into numbers) and statistically described or analyzed.

Sampling: Selection of individual observations in research that is intended to produce knowledge about a population of interest.

Sampling errors: Errors in estimation (or deviation from the truth about a population of interest) that occur by chance and that are attributable to the sample in the study.

Snowball sampling: Method of nonprobability sampling in which one participant or a small group of participants who meet the study's eligibility criteria are identified and then asked to refer others who also meet the eligibility criteria to the researcher.

For Further Learning and Suggested Readings

Benjafield, J. G. (1994). *Thinking critically about research methods.* Boston: Allyn & Bacon.

David, E. J. R., & Okazaki, S. (2006). Colonial mentality: A review and recommendation for Filipino American psychology. *Cultural Diversity and Ethnic Minority Psychology, 12,* 1–16.

Hall, G. C. N., & Barongan, C. (2001). *Multicultural psychology.* New York: Prentice Hall.

Stanovich, K. E. (2004). *How to think straight about psychology, 7th ed.* Boston: Allyn & Bacon.

Uba, L. (2002). *A postmodern psychology of Asian Americans: Creating knowledge of a racial minority.* Albany, NY: State University of New York.

Yoshino, K. (2006). *Covering: The hidden assault on our civil rights.* New York: Random House.

References

Abe-Kim, J., Gong, F., & Takeuchi, D. (2004). Religiosity, spirituality, and help-seeking among Filipino Americans: Religious clergy or mental health professionals? *Journal of Community Psychology, 32,* 675–689.

American Psychiatric Association. (1994). *Diagnostic and statistical manual of mental disorders* (4th ed.). Washington, DC.

Brislin, R. W. (1993). *Understanding culture's influence on behavior.* New York: Harcourt Brace Jovanich.

Cheryan, S., & Monin, B. (2005). "Where are you from?": Asian Americans and identity denial. *Journal of Personality and Social Psychology, 89,* 717–730.

Gong, F., Gage, S.-J. L., & Tacata, L. A., Jr. (2003). Help-seeking behavior among Filipino Americans: A cultural analysis of face and language. *Journal of Community Psychology, 31,* 469–488.

Hall, G. C. N., & Maramba, G. G. (2001). In search of cultural diversity: Recent literature in cross-cultural and ethnic minority psychology. *Cultural Diversity and Ethnic Minority Psychology, 7,* 12–26.

Kim, U., & Berry, J. W. (1993). *Indigenous psychologies: Research and experience in cultural context.* Newbury Park, CA: Sage.

Kothari, G. (1995). Where are you from? In G. Hongo (Ed.), *Under Western eyes: Personal essays from Asian America* (pp. 151–173). NY: Anchor Books/Doubleday.

Lau, A., & Zane, N. (2000). Examining the effects of ethnic-specific services: An analysis of cost-utilization and treatment outcome for Asian American clients. *Journal of Community Psychology, 28,* 63–77.

Loo, C. M. (1994). Race-related stress among Asian American veterans: A model to enhance diagnosis and treatment. *Cultural Diversity and Mental Health, 4,* 75–90.

Nagata, D. K. (1993). *Legacy of injustice: Exploring the cross-generational impact of the Japanese American internment.* New York: Plenum.

Okazaki, S. (2000). Treatment delay among Asian American patients with severe mental illness. *American Journal of Orthopsychiatry, 40,* 58–64.

Okazaki, S., & Sue, S. (1995). Methodological issues in assessment research with ethnic minorities. *Psychological Assessment, 7,* 367–375.

Pang, K. Y. C. (1998). Symptoms of depression in elderly Korean immigrants: Narration and the healing process. *Culture, Medicine & Psychiatry, 22,* 93–122.

Pennell, B., Bowers, A., Carr, D., Chardoul, S., Cheung, G., & Dinkelmann, K. (2004). The development and implementation of the National Comorbidity Survey Replication, the National Survey of American Life, and the National Latino and Asian American Survey. *International Journal of Methods in Psychiatric Research, 13,* 241–269.

Phinney, J. (1992). The Multigroup Ethnic Identity Measure: A new scale for use with adolescents and young adults from diverse groups. *Journal of Adolescent Research, 7,* 156–176.

Radloff, L. S. (1977). The CES-D scale: A self-report depression scale for research in the general population. *Applied Psychological Measurement, 1,* 385–401.

Reeves, T., & Bennett, C. (2004). *We the people: Asians in the United States, CENSR-17.* Washington, DC: U.S. Census Bureau.

Regier, D. A., Narrow, W. E., Rae, D. S., Manderscheid, R. W., Locke, B. Z., & Goodwin, F. K. (1993). The de facto mental and addictive disorders service system. Epidemiologic Catchment Area prospective 1-year prevalence rates of disorders and services. *Archives of General Psychiatry, 50,* 85–94.

Sasao, T. (1994). Using surname-based telephone survey methodology in Asian American communities: Practical issues and caveats. *Journal of Community Psychology, 22,* 283–295.

Segall, M. H., Lonner, W. J., & Berry, J. W. (1998). Cross-cultural psychology as a scholarly discipline: On the flowering of culture in behavioral research. *American Psychologist, 53,* 1101–1110.

Shih, M., Pittinsky, T. L., & Ambady, N. (1999). Stereotype susceptibility: Identity salience and shifts in quantitative performance. *Psychological Science, 10,* 80–83.

Stanovich, K. E. (2004). *How to think straight about psychology, 7th ed.* Boston: Allyn & Bacon.

Sue, S. (1993). Mental health issues for Asian ands Pacific Islander Americans. In N. Zane, D. Takeuchi, & K. Young (Eds.), *Confronting critical health issues of Asian and Pacific Islander Americans* (pp. 266–288). Newbury Park, CA: Sage Publications.

Sue, S. (1999). Science, ethnicity, and bias: Where have we gone wrong? *American Psychologist, 54,* 1070–1077.

Sue, S., & McKinney, H. (1975). Asian Americans in the community mental health system. *American Journal of Orthopsychiatry, 45,* 111–118.

Sue, D. W., & Sue, D. (1999). *Counseling the culturally different.* New York: Wiley.

Takeuchi, D. T., Chung, R. C.-Y., Lin, K.-M., Shen, H., Kurasaki, K., Chun, C.-A., et al. (1998). Lifetime and twelve-month prevalence rates of major depressive episodes and dysthymia among Chinese Americans in Los Angeles. *American Journal of Psychiatry, 155,* 1407–1414.

Tanaka, J. S., Ebreo, A., Linn, N., & Morera, O. F. (1998). Research methods: The construct validity of self-identity and its psychological implications. In N. Zane & L. C. Lee (Eds.), *Handbook of Asian American psychology* (pp. 21–79). Thousand Oaks, CA: Sage Publications.

Tsai, J. L., Simeonova, D. I., & Watanabe, J. T. (2004). Somatic and social: Chinese Americans talk about emotion. *Personality and Social Psychology Bulletin, 30,* 1226–1238.

Tsai, J. L., Ying, Y., & Lee, P. A. (2000). The meaning of "being Chinese" and "being American": Variation among Chinese American young adults. *Journal of Cross-Cultural Psychology, 31,* 302–332.

Uba, L. (2002). *A postmodern psychology of Asian Americans: Creating knowledge of a racial minority.* Albany, NY: State University of New York Press.

Zane, N., Hatanaka, H., Park, S., & Akutsu, P. (1994). Ethnic-specific mental health services: Evaluation of the parallel approach for Asian-American clients. *Journal of Community Psychology, 22,* 68–81.

Zheng, Y. P., Lin, K.-M., Takeuchi, D., Kurasaki, K. S., Wang, Y., & Cheung, F. (1997). An epidemiological study of neurasthenia in Chinese-Americans in Los Angeles. *Comprehensive Psychiatry, 38,* 249–259.

4

The Model Minority and the Perpetual Foreigner
Stereotypes of Asian Americans

**STACEY J. LEE, NGA-WING ANJELA WONG,
and ALVIN N. ALVAREZ**

OUTLINE OF CHAPTER

Case Synopsis
Introduction
Model Minority Origins
What's Wrong with the Model Minority Stereotype?
Perpetual Foreigner
Real World Experiences
Case Study
References

Case Synopsis

Mei Ling,[1] a student at a selective magnet high school, expressed a great deal of anxiety about living up to the **model minority** stereotype. Although she earned outstanding grades, participated in extracurricular activities, and got high SAT scores, Mei Ling lived in fear of failure. In talking with her counselor, she observed, "Everyone—teachers, other students, parents—expects Asians to be smart and get good grades. A lot of people think it just comes naturally and they look at you funny when you don't get 100% on a test. People don't know how hard it is (shakes head).... I study all the time, but I can't always get A's. I feel like a failure when I don't get all A's."

Introduction

Like other minority groups, Asian Americans encounter a multitude of stereotypes that constrain their identities, relationships with others, and their opportunities. The two most significant and persistent stereotypes of Asian Americans are the "model minority" stereotype and the stereotype that Asian Americans are **perpetual foreigners**. According to the model minority stereotype, Asian Americans have achieved enormous economic and academic success by working hard and following Asian cultural norms. Furthermore, the model minority stereotype suggests that Asian Americans have "made it" and no longer face any barriers to economic, social, or political success. The perpetual foreigner stereotype casts Asian Americans as inherently foreign and therefore not truly "American." In this chapter we will trace the origins of these two stereotypes and illustrate the way these stereotypic representations affect Asian American students and communities.

---

[1] The case of Mei Ling is a fictional composite of various students.

Model Minority Origins

Scholarly reports and the popular press typically represent Asian American students as valedictorians, music prodigies, and winners of math and science contests. According to these accounts, Asian American students achieve model success by working hard and staying out of trouble. The success of Asian American students has been attributed to Asian cultures and families. Recently, Asian American parents have been identified as being model parents. In *Top of the Class: How Asian Parents Raise High Achievers—and How You Can Too*, Kim Abboud and Kim (2006) suggest that Asian American parents hold "cultural high achievement" for their children—stressing involvement, encouragement, and discipline. The sisters use their own childhood experiences to explain the "Asian success" by revealing the 17 "secrets" Asian families hold. In doing so, the authors generalize "the Asian way" of raising children by saying their experiences represent all Asian Americans. In short, Asian Americans are understood to be good or model minorities. According to the stereotype, Asian Americans work hard, stay out of trouble, and earn success.

The term *model minority* was first used in the mid-1960s by sociologist William Petersen in an article entitled "Success Story: Japanese American Style" published in the *New York Times Magazine* on January 6, 1966. Shortly thereafter another article, this time focusing on Chinese Americans, appeared in *U.S. News and World Report* on December 26, 1966. Petersen concluded that Japanese and Chinese cultures/values/ethics of hard work and strong family ties enabled Japanese Americans and Chinese Americans to overcome racial barriers to achieve high academic and economic success in society. Various Asian American scholars have pointed out that these articles appeared during the civil rights era and that the model minority image of Asian Americans was being used to challenge the concerns of civil rights activists. According to the logic of the model minority stereotype, the "success" of Asian Americans proved that equal opportunities existed for all races. Furthermore, Asian Americans were held up as model minorities for other racial minorities to emulate.

During the 1980s, a handful of articles highlighted the success of Asian Americans in school. For example, articles such as *Newsweek's* "Asian Americans: 'A Model Minority'" (1982), "The Drive to Excel" (April 1984), *The New Republic's* "America's Greatest Success Story: The Triumph of Asian Americans," (July 1985), *Fortune's* "America's Super Minority" (November 1986), *Time's* "The New Whiz Kids" (August 1987), and *Parade's* "Why They Excel" (1990) all noted the Asian

Model minority myth compares Asian Americans to other racial groups.

American "success" story. These articles depicted Asians as the underprivileged Americans who have "made it" and achieved success by obtaining the American Dream. It was also during the 1980s that the focus included Southeast Asians. *Time's* "The New Whiz Kids" (August 1987) described the success of Southeast Asian students despite the enormous obstacles of fleeing wartime persecution in their or their parents' country. Thus, the media has "virtually equated the term, 'Asian American,' with 'success'" (Yun 1989, vii).

What's Wrong with the Model Minority Stereotype?

Some Asian Americans may ask, "What's wrong with being stereotyped as successful model minorities?" Others may even argue that the stereotype is better than stereotypes facing other racial groups. While the model minority stereotype may appear to be flattering and positive, it is extremely misleading and even harmful.

Masking Diversity

First of all, the stereotype hides diversity among Asian Americans. It masks the many concerns that Asian American individuals and communities face. Much of the scholarship that positions Asian Americans as high-achieving model minorities is based on **aggregate** data that lumps Asian Americans from various ethnic groups into one category. For instance, the top 10 largest ethnic groups that are categorized under the category of Asian American according to the U.S. Census (Reeves & Bennett, 2004), i.e., Chinese, Filipino, Asian Indian, Vietnamese, Korean, Japanese, Cambodian, Hmong, Laotian, and Pakistani, clearly have distinct immigration histories, as well as a diverse range of economic, social, and educational capital. By failing to recognize this diversity, the model minority stereotype allows policy makers as well as service providers to ignore many of their basic needs and often overlook the community as a whole. The model minority stereotype, for example, hides the social class diversity among Asian Americans. It hides the fact that some Asian American communities struggle with poverty. For instance, when one looks at the poverty rate for Asian Americans as an aggregate group, the rate for Asian Americans (i.e., 12.6%) is comparable to that of the general population (i.e., 12.4%) (Reeves & Bennett, 2004). However, when one looks at specific Asian ethnic groups, clear and powerful differences emerge. Whereas Filipino and Japanese Americans have poverty rates of less than 10%, the poverty rates for Hmong (38%) and Cambodian (29%) are among the highest of any community in the United States. In fact, Asians Americans are more likely to live in poverty than non-Hispanic Whites. In 2001, 1.3 million Asians and Pacific Islanders (10%) and 15.3 million non-Hispanic Whites (8%) lived below the poverty level (pp. 7–8). Some Asian Americans find themselves in desperate economic conditions. In the St. Paul and Minneapolis area, for example, there is growing concern regarding homelessness among the newer Hmong refugees (Demko, 2006).

Since the emergence of the model minority myth, the high median family income of Asian Americans has been interpreted as a key indicator of the community's economic success. Indeed, as shown in Table 4.1, the U.S. Census Bureau (2007) reported that the median income of Asian American families (i.e., $51,908) was considerably higher than that of non-Hispanic Whites at $45,367—a fact that seems to support the "accuracy" of the model minority myth and the presumption of uniform economic success. However, as with other demographic data on Asian Americans, the failure to critically analyze this aggregate data can lead to significant and incorrect assumptions. Therefore, closer scrutiny of Table 4.1 further reveals notable heterogeneity within the various Asian American communities.

As with other aggregate forms of data, ethnic group differences become masked. Whereas Asian Indian and Filipino families have median incomes higher than $60,000, Bangladeshi, Hmong, and Cambodian families have median incomes of less than $40,000—a sizable gap of

Table 4.1 U.S. Census (2000) Household Economic Figures

Groups	Median household, 1999	Per capita, 1999	Average household size
Racial groups			
American Indian/Alaskan Native	30,599	12,893	3
Asian	51,908	21,823	3
Black	29,423	14,437	3
Latino (any race)	33,676	12,111	4
White	45,367	24,819	2
Ethnic groups			
Asian Indian	63,669	27,514	3
Bangladeshi	39,321	13,971	4
Cambodian	36,155	10,366	5
Chinese	51,444	23,756	3
Filipino	60,570	21,267	3
Hmong	32,076	6,600	6
Japanese	52,060	30,075	2
Korean	40,037	18,805	3
Laotian	42,978	11,830	4
Pakistani	47,241	18,096	4
Thai	40,329	19,066	3
Vietnamese	45,085	15,655	4

Source: U.S. Census Bureau, 2007. *The American factfinder.* Retrieved May 19, 2007, from http://factfinder. census.gov.

$20,000 that is "hidden" in the aggregate data. Additionally, numerous scholars have pointed out that the focus on median **household income** fails to acknowledge that some Asian families are generally larger and therefore have more wage-earners within one family (Wu, 2002). For instance, compared with White families with an average household size of 2, Hmong and Cambodian families with 6 and 5 members respectively are quite large. Therefore, scholars have argued that it may be more useful to examine income per capita rather than household income. As a result, a more complex economic picture of Asian Americans begins to emerge. Specifically, whereas Japanese and Asian Indian clearly have higher **per capita incomes** than White individuals, it is also striking to note that Hmong, Cambodian, and Laotian individuals have the lowest per capita incomes of any racial or ethnic group. In fact, the Hmong per capita income is only 26% of Whites' total per capita income! Moreover, Asian American families are heavily concentrated in high-cost urban areas such as New York, San Francisco, and Honolulu, which may inflate their earnings. Lastly, scholars point to **income-to-education disparities** in which Asian Americans earn significantly less than White Americans despite equivalent educational levels. For instance, in California, Chinese American men earn 68% and Filipino American men earn 62% of the salaries that White Americans earn (Uy, 2004).

The model minority stereotype also hides differences in educational attainment and achievement among Asian ethnic groups (Um, 2003). For example, "while only 5.6 percent of Japanese Americans have only an elementary education or less, 61 percent of the Hmong Americans fall into such category" (Kim & Yeh, 2002). Parallel results can also be found in terms of higher education attainment. For instance, whereas 64% of Asian Indians and 48% of Chinese Americans have a college degree or higher, less than 10% of Cambodian, Hmong, and Laotian Americans have completed college. Moreover, as Lee and Kumashiro state in the 2005 NEA report, "[t]he differences in educational attainment and achievement across all AA/PI ethnic groups appear to be closely related to differences in social class" [because while] "Asian Americans and Pacific Islanders are more likely than whites to have incomes of $75,000 or more, they are also more likely than whites to have incomes below $25,000" (p. 2).

Contrary to the model minority implication that the equal opportunities provided in the United States are the source of Asian American's success, the educational and economic capital of Asian Americans may actually be reflective of resources and achievements that were obtained *prior* to their immigration into the United States. For instance, 65% of adult Indian immigrants, 62% of Taiwanese immigrants, and 43% of Filipinos come to the United States with a college degree in hand (Kao & Thompson, 2003). So, stop a moment to reflect on what advantages one would have if they arrived in this country with a college degree already in hand. In short, the credit for the educational success of some Asian Americans may have nothing to do with the American educational system and may be more reflective of selective immigration.

As with much of the data on Asian Americans, it is important to examine both interethnic and intraethnic differences when examining the educational capital of Asian immigrants. For instance, in contrast to the education levels of Asian Indian and Taiwanese immigrants noted above, only 5% of Cambodian and Laotian adult immigrants have a college degree (Kao & Thompson, 2003). Similarly, intraethnic educational and economic differences may also exist within a given ethnic group. For instance, Chinese American parents, who are highly educated, English-speaking, professionals from Hong Kong and Taiwan, will have different resources and expectations for their children in the United States than those with a low-level of educational attainment, who are non-English speaking, rural laborers from Guangdong Province and even more recently from Fujian (also known as Fukien) Province. Additionally, families with experiences of war, relocation, and family separation (e.g., Southeast Asians) will have different psychological and academic needs than East Asian (Chinese, Japanese, and Koreans) and South Asian (Indians, Pakistanis, Sri Lankans, etc.) families (Lee, 1994, 1996; Pang, Kiang, & Pak, 2003).

The unique needs of Asian American students are ignored when educational policy makers develop policies based on aggregate data that support the model minority stereotype (Pang, Kiang, & Pak, 2003). Under the No Child Left Behind Act (2001) also known as the reauthorization of the Elementary and Secondary Education Act (ESEA), for instance, American Indians, Blacks, and Latinos are mentioned as the targeted groups that need extra attention. There is, however, no mention of such commitment for Asian Pacific Islander American students. Asian Pacific Islanders, as the statement implies, are viewed as the ones who have "succeeded" into the dominant society. In other words, the assumption is that Asian American students do not need such support from the federal government.

Interracial Tension

The second major problem with the model minority stereotype is that it pits Asian Americans against other racial groups, for example, as what occurred during the L.A. Riots (the L.A. Riots was a result of the 1992 Rodney King case decision where Los Angelenos took to the streets in protest as a result of four White Los Angeles Police Department officers being acquitted of assault while arresting Rodney King, a Black motorist). Asian Americans are typically held up as *the* successful minority, and Asian American *successes* are implicitly and explicitly compared to the *failures* of other minority groups. When the dominant society holds Asian Americans up as model minorities it promotes antagonism between Asian Americans and other people of color. For instance, opponents of affirmative action have charged that affirmative action helps African Americans and Latinos and hurts Asian Americans. Here, Asian Americans are positioned as victims of "reverse discrimination." The assumption that Asian Americans no longer benefit from civil rights laws or government programs that promote equality is erroneous. In truth, many Asian Americans, particularly those who are low-income immigrants and refugees and not yet fluent in English, require policies, programs, and services to gain success in employment, education, and housing. The model minority stereotype therefore enforces the erroneous perception that Asian Americans no longer experience racism and discrimination and thus do not need social services like bilingual education, affirmative action, health care, welfare, and so on. The reality, however, is that Asian Americans have not achieved full equality with Whites and continue to experience racism. Asian Americans continue to earn less than Whites with equal educational backgrounds and experience. Furthermore, many Asian Americans struggle with poverty. The U.S. Census' 2003 Income, Poverty, and Health Insurance Coverage Report (DeNavas-Walt, Proctor, & Mills, 2004) show that "among people who indicated Asian as their only race, 11.8 percent were in poverty in 2003, higher than the 10.1 percent in 2002. The number in poverty also increased (from 1.2 million to 1.4 million)" (p. 11). By promoting interracial tension between Asian Americans and other people of color, the model minority stereotype prevents communities of color from joining in solidarity to fight racial inequalities.

Evidence for this interracial tension has already been found in the experiences of Asian American youth, who report being the targets of racially motivated verbal and physical harassment, presumably as a function of their perceived success as well as favored treatment from teachers and administrators. For instance, in their study of an urban high school in New York, Rosenbloom and Way (2004) observed that Asian American students were "being pushed, punched, teased, and mocked by their non-Asian American peers" (p. 433) as well as being robbed of money, jewelry, and clothes. In fact, Fisher, Wallace and Fenton (2000) found that East Asian high school students, relative to all other racial groups, reported the highest levels of **peer discrimination**, which includes incidents such as racial insults, social exclusion, and threats. To underscore the psychological implications of such incidents, Greene, Way and Pahl (2006) have found that the experience of discrimination from one's peers is associated with significant psychological effects such as decreased self-esteem and increased levels of depression.

Self-Silencing

Finally, the model minority stereotype may encourage Asian Americans to hide and silence issues or problems that may contradict the model minority image. Attempts to live up to the

The model minority myth serves as a racial wedge.

standards set by the model minority stereotype, for example, may lead Asian Americans to feel shame when they fall short of the model minority image. These feelings of shame may inhibit Asian Americans from seeking necessary assistance. For example, while relatively small numbers of Asian Americans utilize mental health services, research reveals that Asian Americans do suffer from mental health concerns (Lin & Cheung 1999). For instance, Asian American women have been identified as having among the highest suicide rates in the United States out of all racial groups (Centers for Disease Control and Prevention, National Center for Health Statistics, 2001). The model minority stereotype may encourage unhealthy efforts to achieve perfection. One study suggests that Asian American girls who attempt to be perfect may be at particular risk for eating disorders (Hall, 1995). Asian American students who attempt to live up to model minority standards may become depressed if they fall short of their goals.

Indeed, a notable study by Lorenzo, Frost, and Reinherz (2000) raises the issue of the relationship between academic success and psychological well-being for Asian Americans. In their study of Asian American high school students, Lorenzo et al. found that Asian American students had higher grade point averages, fewer expulsions and suspensions, and more academic awards than White students. Particularly since GPAs, expulsions, and awards are such observable behaviors and events, it is easy to see how one's reliance on these overt characteristics may lead to the conclusion that these students are successful and doing fine. However, Lorenzo and her colleagues found that these same Asian American students compared to White students were also reporting higher levels of depression, social isolation, as well as social and interpersonal problems such as being teased by peers. To exacerbate matters, these students also described having lower levels of social support in their lives, such as having a confidant. Moreover, Asian American students had significantly more negative perceptions of themselves relative to White students as indicated by lower levels of self-esteem, higher anxiety, and a stronger sense of being unpopular. Unfortunately, the psychological

Economic success does not equal psychological well-being.

characteristics such as low self-esteem, social isolation, or depression that were found in these students may be harder to detect and may be less overt than tangible characteristics such as grades and awards. Therefore, the likelihood that the psychological welfare of Asian Americans may be overlooked increases insofar as educators, parents, friends, and the general public focus exclusively on overt markers of academic and economic success. In short, it may be critical to realize that Asian Americans' academic and economic success is not equivalent to their psychological well-being and that there is a need to look beyond an individual's grades, degrees, and paychecks.

Perpetual Foreigner

In spite of the long history of Asian Americans in the United States, it continues to be assumed that the face of America cannot look Asian. Asian Americans are viewed as "the perpetual foreigners" or "the forever foreigners," who are unable to assimilate into dominant culture (Tuan, 1998; Wu, 2002). Tuan (1998) writes, Whiteness "is equated with being American; Asianness is not" (p. 139). In other words, the stereotype stresses that Asian Americans are different because they are viewed as "unassimilable." Moreover, Asian Americans are often overlooked in their right to civic participation, their right to have a voice in American democracy and laws that will affect their lives in their own country.

In *Yellow: Race in America Beyond Black and White*, Wu (2002) provides excellent examples of the perpetual foreigner as captured in the internment of innocent Japanese Americans [and Japanese Peruvians] during World War II. With the signing of Executive Order 9066, 120,000 Japanese Americans were forcibly evacuated and forced to sell or dispose of their homes, businesses, and farms without due process even though 62% of them were U.S. citizens (Chan, 1991). Imagine you, your parents, your grandparents, and your friends being given a week to get rid of all of your possessions and moving into a dusty and dirty assembly center simply because of your race and the presumption that you are guilty, rather than innocent. Consistent with the perpetual foreigner stereotype, Chan observed that Japanese Americans were regarded as an "enemy race" whose loyalties to Japan remained "undiluted" regardless of their years in the United States. Nevertheless, it is important to note that despite concerns about the national security risks posed by Japanese Americans, no incident of sabotage or espionage by Japanese Americans has ever been presented (Chan, 1991).

Even in times of peace, economic pressure in a community can dredge up ugly behavior as a consequence of this perpetual foreigner stereotype. For example, during the recession of 1982 autoworkers in Detroit, Michigan, symbolically sledged-hammered Toyotas and other Japanese brand imports. On June 19, 1982, using a baseball bat, two White autoworkers killed Vincent Chin, a Chinese American engineer celebrating his upcoming wedding because he "looked" Japanese and thus, Chin was the reason that they were out of work. Interestingly, "[i]n this tragedy, many of the symbols of America are present—Auto City USA, McDonald's, a murdered Chinese, and a white auto worker wielding a baseball bat" (Takaki, 1989, p. 23). As Wu (2002) clearly states, "Chin was singled out because of his race; his only connection to Japan was racial, and it was tenuous at that" (p. 71). This shows how Asian Pacific Islander Americans are identified as Other, and more specifically as the foreigner.

The perpetual foreigner image has been perpetuated by popular culture. For example, in the 1984 classic teen movie *Sixteen Candles*, the nerdish character Long Duk Dong (played by Gedde Watanabe), was portrayed as passive, smart, and nerdish. Not insignificantly, he spoke with a rather thick "Asian" accent. Throughout the movie he says things like, "Wassa happening hah-stuff?" in a fake Asian accent. Additionally, when any of the other characters in the movie mention his name the sound of a gong played simultaneously. The thick accent and the gong mark Watanabe's character as funny, foreign, and nerdish (i.e., the model minority). More recently Fox's "American Idol" season three contestant William Hung became known for his botched rendition of singer Ricky Martin's "She Bangs." Once again, the supposed foreignness of an Asian American became a joke. The 2005 Lions Gate Films' release of *Crash*, focused on race relations in Los Angeles. With the exception of the Asian American characters, all of the other characters were well developed and complex. Instead, the Korean American couple spoke frantically in a heavy Asian accent. They were depicted as only caring about making fast money by smuggling a van load of Asians into the country.

As we have shown thus far, despite the diversity among Asian Americans, they are still viewed as the model minorities and perpetual foreigners. These stereotypes "obscure the complexity of our experience, and make our contributions to the struggle against racism invisible" (Aguilar-San Juan, 1994, p. 4). Governmental services and programs for Asian Americans are often limited and/or overlooked because it is assumed that Asian Americans don't need help. Furthermore, both stereotypes contribute to anti-Asian sentiment. Thus, educators, policy makers, and others who work with children of immigrants should acknowledge such diversity and complexity as the number of children of immigrants continues to increase in our schools and communities.

Real World Experiences

> Anjela: Do you think people have this stereotypical image of Asians and Asian Americans?
> Alan: Some people, I think.
> Anjela: What kinds of stereotypes do you think they have?
> Alan: It's just like hatin'. Cuz, you know, all Asians have light skin and how the way we have our eyes thingy and the way we talk sometimes.
> Anjela: What do you mean the way you talk?
> Alan: I don't know, sometimes some Asian people can't pronounce some words, the right words, and they make fun of that.
> Anjela: Is there anything else?
> Alan: Yeah, they're like really racist like that. Like you're Asian, you're supposed to be smart. You're Asian, you're supposed to be like really good in math and drawing. All that crap.
> Anjela: How do you react then?
> Alan: I ignore them. Cuz it's annoyin'.
> Anjela: Who are the people who say these things?
> Alan: Like some White guys.
> Anjela: Are the majority of the students White?
> Alan: Yeah, like Whites everywhere. (Wong, 2005)

In this section we will provide in-depth snapshots of how Asian American students struggle with racism and stereotypes in their school settings. As Alan, an 8th grader who was born and raised in the United States, expressed above, the model minority and the perpetual foreigner stereotypes still affect Asian Americans students.

Model Minority

Research on Asian American youth reveals that the model minority stereotype influences the way non-Asians perceive Asian American students (Lee, 1996; Walker-Moffat, 1995; Wong, 2005). One of the common assumptions held by non-Asian students and teachers is that Asian

Americans are particularly good at math and science. Johnny, a Chinese American student in the Northeast, asserted that his problems in math were often overlooked because people assumed that "if you're Asian then you're smart in math" (Wong, 2005).

As we argued earlier, the model minority stereotype does not exist in isolation, but works in tandem with stereotypes of other racial groups. In schools, the academic success of Asian Americans is often compared to the academic struggles of other groups. One high school guidance counselor compared her Asian American and African American students like this, "Asians like U of P (University of Pennsylvania), M.I.T., Princeton. They tend to go to good schools.... I wish our blacks would take advantage of things instead of sticking to sports and entertainment" (Lee, 1996, p. 78). In this particular statement, the counselor erased the experiences of Asian American students who were struggling and blamed African American students for their struggles.

Asian American students often internalize racial stereotypes, including the model minority stereotype. Both high- and low-achieving Asian and Pacific Islander American students feel pressure to uphold the expectations of the model minority stereotype. And students who do not measure up to the stereotype often feel depressed and too embarrassed to ask for help. The tutoring coordinator of an East Coast community youth center that serves low-income Chinese American middle and high school students points out the harm of the model minority stereotype. She explained that the community center worked with many youth who were struggling in school:

> Even in math, I know there is this stereotype that has been ongoing that, "you're Chinese, you're good in math. How could you fail in math?" But there are students that we have who are struggling in math. Based on the youth that are here, I see there are youth who... I don't have to worry anything about them. But there are also youth who are struggling really really hard in order to get a passing grade. And I do see them. (Wong, 2005)

When another youth worker at the community center was asked if the model minority myth gets played out in schools, he responded with, "Oh yeah, of course. Yeah, some of the kids talk about it in terms of not doing well in math and sciences. And people are like 'what's wrong with you?' I mean, it's very prevalent." He went on to explain that some Asian American students feel too embarrassed to ask for help. In discussing his experience working with one Chinese American student, the youth worker reported, "He couldn't read. I mean he could barely read... he was embarrassed to ask for help so he just guessed on the exams... And I think in the long run [the model minority stereotype] usually really hurts these students."

Finally, the model minority stereotype can also damage Asian American students' self-image. As one Asian American high school student said about the model minority stereotype:

> They [whites] will have stereotypes, like we're smart.... They are so wrong, not everyone is smart. They expect you to be this and that and when you're not.... (shook her head) And sometimes you tend to be what they expect you to be and you just lose your identity... just lose being yourself. Become part of what... what someone else want[s] you to be. And it's really awkward too! When you get bad grades, people look at you really strangely because you are sort of distorting the way they see an Asian. It makes you feel really awkward if you don't fit the stereotype. (Lee, 1996, p. 59)

Although this particular student was a high-achieving student who went on to attend an elite university, she felt constrained by the stereotype. Like others who live under the veil of racial stereotypes, this student was not allowed to be an individual.

Perpetual Foreigner

Much of the racism that Asian Americans face in schools and in the workplace is expressed as anti-foreigner sentiment. The assumption is that Asian Americans are essentially foreign and therefore problematic. Asian American students, for example, face hostility for speaking their native languages or for speaking with Asian accents. Steven, an immigrant from Hong Kong, vividly remembers the racism he experienced while attending a middle school in the Northeast, "Like the first year I arrived in the U.S., I was at Madison and it was really serious there....Everyday they would yell at the Asian students...mostly the Black students because there are more Blacks there...Like especially when you speak English, you should speak better. Because at [my middle school], if they know you're in [the] bilingual [program] they would discriminate you. Like yelling at you or if you were talking with your friends in Chinese, they would laugh" (Wong, 2005).

Many Asian Americans internalize the belief that Asian Americans are not "real Americans." One Chinese American student, for example, explained, "Yeah, Chinese Americans are Chinese. Americans are Americans. We are Chinese American but they are American American. I don't know what I'm sayin' but...yeah, basically...yeah, Caucasians" (Wong, 2005). Another Chinese American student reported, "I hang out with African Americans and real Americans" (Wong, 2005). Not insignificantly, this student was equating Whites with "real Americans." Similarly, Tuan (1998) found; that "real" Americans are equated with white Americans while Asian Americans are viewed as un-Americans and thus are foreigners.

The perpetual foreigner stereotype also has a negative impact on intra-Asian relationships. A Chinese American immigrant enrolled in a bilingual class reported that her American-born peers often looked down on her:

> And sometimes some people think speaking to a [student in the] bilingual [program] is like...really embarrassing. Those, the ones who are born here think speaking to bilingual [students] is weird...I don't know how to explain. Like I have a friend who was born here and there's another person who asked her why she's hanging around with so many bilingual [program students] as friends. (Wong, 2005)

American-born Asians who are attempting to distance themselves from the foreigner image may reject their foreign-born peers (Lee, 2005). In their efforts to escape the perpetual foreigner label, some Asian Americans may even alter their bodies to appear more like European Americans. These efforts to look less Asian may include wearing colored contact lens, coloring hair, and even plastic surgery.

Summary

The stereotypes of Asian Americans as model minorities and perpetual foreigners continue to shape the way non-Asians view Asian Americans and the way Asian Americans see themselves. Stereotyped as model minorities and perpetual foreigners, Asian Americans are prohibited from being seen as individuals. They are prevented from being equal members of the larger American society. Moreover, these stereotypes obscure racial disparities and the heterogeneity within Asian American communities while also promoting racial divisions across racial groups. The insidious nature of both of these stereotypes make them difficult to challenge, but the experiences of Asian American students suggest that educators, social service providers, policymakers, and others must recognize and confront these stereotypes.

Discussion Questions

1. How does the perpetual foreigner stereotype harm Asian Americans?
2. How does the model minority stereotype harm Asian Americans?
3. What are some ways to debunk the model minority and perpetual foreigner stereotypes?
4. What are some reasons that people view the model minority stereotype as positive?
5. How would you define the model minority and perpetual foreigner stereotypes?
6. Why are the model minority and perpetual foreigner stereotypes so persistent and pervasive?

Case Study

The chapter has focused on the historical, conceptual, and empirical analysis of the model minority and perpetual foreigner stereotypes. To deepen our understanding of the psychological impact of these stereotypes, the following section continues with an examination of Mei Ling.

Client Information

Mei Ling is an 18-year-old, Chinese American high school senior in a local magnet school known for its focus on science and technology. She is the oldest of three children and her parents both work full-time. Her mother works at a restaurant and her father as a janitor during the week and a laborer during the weekend; however, her father was a physician back in China but is unable to practice in the United States. Her parents immigrated to this country 20 years ago. Her next oldest brother is a freshman in high school and works in the same restaurant as his mother, and her sister is in junior high.

Since last semester, Mei Ling has been complaining of headaches and difficulty in concentrating. A checkup with a physician found no physical cause for the symptoms and she was referred to a counselor. Additionally, Mei Ling's teachers have been concerned about her since she has exhibited a noticeable drop in her grades and appears to be increasingly withdrawn in her classes. Typically one of the brightest students in class, Mei Ling has not been turning in her homework and has been receiving C's and D's on the work she does turn in despite being an A–/B+ student. Although reluctant to see a counselor, she agreed to do so just to get everyone to stop bugging her. According to Mei Ling, she's "just tired and needs a break."

Case Study Discussion

Given Mei Ling's reluctance to see a counselor, a critical issue to address in the early phase of counseling is her motivation to seek help. To this end, the counselor begins with a psychoeducational focus to clarify and validate Mei Ling's concerns about counseling as well as to provide an explanation of how counseling works and the roles of both the client and the counselor. To engage Mei Ling in the counseling process, the counselor also focuses on the establishing trust and rapport with Mei Ling. In particular, addressing concerns around self-disclosure, confidentiality, and the perception that counseling is for "crazy people" may be topics that contribute toward both psychoeducational and rapport-building goals. Insofar as Mei Ling has a better understanding of how counseling works and its purpose, then there is greater likelihood that she will be intrinsically motivated to remain in counseling.

As Mei Ling commits to counseling, she begins to self-disclose more easily. She talks about the pressures that she has faced in her high-performing school, where teachers just assumed that Asian students all do well. Particularly, since her SAT scores have returned, her teachers have expected that Mei Ling will enroll in an Ivy League school and continue to pursue her strengths in science. Although her parents have encouraged Mei Ling to do what she wants, she feels some sense of guilt because she is painfully aware of all that her parents have sacrificed for their family. So, she feels torn. On one hand, she reports feeling resentful that people just assume that she will continue to succeed and that this success just comes easily for her. As she puts it, "they just want me to be their little prize on the shelf." But on the other hand, she is aware that her continued success also has an impact on her family. So, she talks about her frustration with being "stuck" and not being able to do what she wants.

Initial interventions focus on helping Mei Ling discuss and vent her most salient frustrations, which appear to center around the expectations that significant others have of her, particularly among her teachers. The counselor's ability to empathize with these frustrations combined with an awareness of model minority expectations of Asian Americans will be integral to forming rapport and trust with Mei Ling. Given the potential for underestimating the negative consequences of such a seemingly positive stereotype, the counselor's validation of the pressures that result from the model minority stereotype will be invaluable. This may take the form of an actual psycho-educationally focused discussion about the model minority stereotype and Mei Ling's understanding of this myth.

In addition, the counselor explores how Mei Ling has been coping with the pressures she has been facing as well as somatic symptoms she has been experiencing and their onset. Symptom relief and assessment of adaptive and maladaptive coping strategies are key goals at this point. The counselor may offer stress management techniques, thought-stopping interventions, and expansion of social support systems. In particular, it may be important to explore how Mei Ling utilizes her peers for social support, particularly other Asian Americans. Moreover, it will be critical to also assist Mei Ling in giving voice to her goals and wishes for her future. Given that she experiences her world as not attending to what she wants out of life and that there is a perceived lack of options, it is hoped that Mei Ling will feel empowered by an individual who is encouraging her to express what she wants. Hence, the focus shifts from Mei Ling's frustrations with her external world to an exploration and clarification of her personal goals.

It is the counselor's belief that in order to effectively negotiate and honor the multiple external factors that influence one's academic and career goals (i.e., family, friends, financial expectations, cultural expectations, etc.), the client also needs to have a grounded and clear understanding of their own personal goals. As Mei Ling begins to gain this clarity, the counselor initiates a discussion about the external expectations that Mei Ling is experiencing from various individuals in her life. In particular, the counselor assists Mei Ling in reflecting on these multiple expectations and how best to negotiate and integrate these expectations while also considering her personal goals. Hence, the counselor facilitates the client's decision-making process by honoring the multiple stakeholders in the decision and prioritizing their degree of influence. A key consideration of this decision-making process may involve an examination of Mei Ling's relationship with her parents and the extent to which she can communicate her concerns to them. Insofar as this is an issue, it may be helpful to assist Mei Ling in role-playing how she might approach her parents.

At a systems level, the counselor also explores additional opportunities to enhance the cultural and racial awareness of the school environment and its employees in regard to working with Asian American students. Consistent with a multicultural counseling perspective, the counselor recognizes that interventions within a larger system are as important as interventions with individual students. To this end, the counselor explores possible strategies, such as providing training to teachers and staff on working with Asian American students, developing programs during Asian Pacific Heritage month in May, writing an article in the school district newsletter, or even simply raising the issue during a faculty meeting.

Case Study Discussion Questions

For undergraduate students, please consider the following questions:

1. In what ways is Mei Ling's experience similar to and different from your own?
2. How would you deal with this situation if you were facing the same concerns?
3. If you were Mei Ling's friends, how might you be of help to her?
4. What options are available to someone in Mei Ling's position?
5. What would you need from a counselor who is trying to help you in such a situation?

For graduate students and/or beginning therapists, please consider the following questions:

1. How would you enhance Mei Ling's commitment to counseling?
2. How might you explain or address the model minority myth in this case? Or would you?
3. How might you involve the family in this case, if at all?
4. What additional resources might you recommend for Mei Ling?
5. How might you work with Mei Ling's teachers, if at all?

Key Terms

Aggregate: In regards to the model minority myth, this refers to the tendency to use data that portray Asian Americans as a single homogeneous community.

Household income: Income based on the entire household or family.

Income-to-education disparities: Individuals earning lower wages despite equivalent educational levels.

Model minority: Stereotype of Asian Americans that promotes the image of Asian Americans as uniformly successful in terms of economic, educational, and social capital.

Peer discrimination: Racial discrimination from one's peers as opposed to authority figures.

Per capita income: Income based on each wage-earning individual.

Perpetual foreigner: Stereotype of Asian Americans as being unassimilable into U.S. culture and as nonresidents regardless of their years in the United States.

For Further Learning and Suggested Readings

Books

Chan, S. (1991). *Asian Americans: An interpretive history*. Boston: Twayne.

Lee, S. (1996). *Unraveling the "Model Minority" stereotype: Listening to Asian American youth*. New York: Teachers College Press.

Reeves, T. J., & Bennett, C. E. (2004). *We the people: Asians in the United States, Census 2000 special reports CENSR-17*. Washington, DC: U.S. Department of Commerce.

Tuan, M. (1998). *Forever foreigners or honorary Whites? The Asian ethnic experience today*. New Brunswick, NJ: Rutgers University Press.

U. S. Commission on Civil Rights. (1992). *Civil rights issues facing Asian Americans in the 1990s.* Washington, DC.

Wu, F. H. (2002). *Yellow: Race in America beyond Black and White.* New York: Basic Books.

*Movies**

A.K.A. Don Bonus (1995)
Better Luck Tomorrow (2003)
Kelly Loves Tony (1998)
Wedding Banquet (1993)
* See also Center for Asian American Media at http://www.asianamericanmedia.org

Web Sites

Asian Nation—Asian American History, Demographics, and Issues: http://www.asian-nation.org
Media Action Network for Asian Americans: http://www.manaa.org
Model Minority—A Guide to Asian American Empowerment: http://www.modelminority.com

References

Aguilar-San Juan, K. (1994). *The state of Asian America: Activism and resistance in the 1990s.* Boston: South End Press.

Centers for Disease Control and Prevention, National Center for Health Statistics. (2001). *Health, United States.* Hyattsville, MD: U.S. Public Health Service.

Chan, S. (1991). *Asian Americans: An interpretive history.* Boston: Twayne.

Demko, P. (2006). The last place on earth. Retrieved May 19, 2007, from http://citypages.com/databank/27/1311/article14042.asp

DeNavas-Walt, C., Proctor, B. D., & Mills, R. J. (2004). *Income, poverty and health insurance coverage in the United States: 2003.* U.S. Census Bureau, Current Population Reports, P60–P226. Washington, DC: U.S. Government Printing Office.

Fisher, C. B., Wallace, S. A., & Fenton, R. E. (2000). Discrimination distress during adolescence. *Journal of Youth and Adolescence, 29*(6), 679–695.

Greene, M. L., Way, N., & Pahl, K. (2006). Trajectories of perceived adult and peer discrimination among Black, Latino, and Asian American adolescents: Patterns and psychological correlates. *Developmental Psychology, 42,* 218–238.

Hall, C. (1995). Asian eyes: Body image and eating disorders of Asian and Asian American women. *Eating Disorders: The Journal of Treatment and Prevention, 3*(1), 8–18.

Kao, G., & Thompson, J. S. (2003). Racial and ethnic stratification in educational achievement and attainment. *Annual Review of Sociology, 29,* 417–442.

Kim, A., & Yeh, C. J. (2002). *Stereotypes of Asian American students.* Eric Digests, ED462510.

Kim Abboud, S., & Kim, J. (2006). *Top of the class: How Asian parents raise high achievers–and how you can too.* East Rutherford, NJ: Berkeley Trade.

Lee, S. (1994). Behind the model minority stereotype: Voices of high and low achieving Asian American students. *Anthropology and Education Quarterly, 25*(4), 413–429.

Lee, S. (1996). *Unraveling the "Model Minority" stereotype: Listening to Asian American youth.* New York: Teachers College Press.

Lee, S. (2005). *Up against Whiteness: Race, school and immigrant youth.* New York: Teachers College Press.

Lee, S. J., & Kumashiro, K. (2005). *A report on the status of Asian Americans and Pacific Islanders in education: Beyond the "Model Minority" stereotype.* Washington, DC: National Education Association.

Lin, K., & Cheung, F. (1999). Mental health issues for Asian Americans. *Psychiatric Services, 50,* 774–780.

Lorenzo, M. K., Frost, A. K., & Reinherz, H. Z. (2000). Social and emotional functioning of older Asian American adolescents. *Child and Adolescent Social Work Journal, 17*(4), 289–304.

Pang, V. O., Kiang, P., & Pak, Y. (2003). Asian Pacific American students: Challenging a biased educational system. In J. Banks (Ed.), *Handbook of research on multicultural education* (2nd ed., pp. 542–563). San Francisco: Jossey-Bass.

Reeves, T. J., & Bennett, C. E. (2004). *We the people: Asians in the United States, Census 2000 special reports CENSR-17.* Washington, DC: U.S. Department of Commerce.

Rosenbloom, S. R., & Way, N. (2004). Experiences of discrimination among African American, Asian American, and Latino adolescents in an urban school. *Youth & Society, 35*(4), 420–451.

Takaki, R. (1989). *Strangers from a different shore: A history of Asian Americans.* New York: Little, Brown & Company.

Tuan, M. (1998). *Forever foreigners or honorary Whites? The Asian ethnic experience today.* New Brunswick, NJ: Rutgers University Press.

Um, K. (2003). *A dream denied: Educational experiences of Southeast Asian American youth.* Southeast Asia Resource Action Center (http://www.searac.org).

U.S. Census Bureau. (2007). *The American factfinder.* Retrieved May 19, 2007, from http://factfinder.census.gov

Uy, M. (2004). Tax and race: The impact on Asian Americans. *Asian Law Journal, 11,* 7–143, 129–138.

Walker-Moffat, W. (1995). *The other side of the Asian American success story.* San Francisco: Jossey-Bass.

Wong, A. (2005). *"Cuz they care about the people who goes there": A portrait of a community-based youth center.* Unpublished master's thesis, University of Wisconsin, Madison.

Wu, F. H. (2002). *Yellow: Race in America beyond Black and White.* New York: Basic Books.

Yun, G. (1989). *A look beyond the model minority image: Critical issues in Asian America.* New York: Minority Rights Group.

5
What Does That Behavior Mean?
Postmodern Perspectives

LAURA UBA

OUTLINE OF CHAPTER

What Does That Behavior *Mean?*: Postmodern Perspectives

1. I am more sensitive than most other people.
2. I am often hungry.
3. I am usually quiet.
4. I believe I am no more nervous than other people.
5. I like to attend ethnic festivals.
6. I mostly eat ethnic food.

Introduction

Statements like these often form the basis for modern psychological questionnaires. Questionnaires produce data at the heart of much of the research on Asian Americans because, like experiments, they are empirical, meaning that the research seeks knowledge by relying on the neutral collection of demonstrable data rather than on mystical beliefs or purely logical methods.

This chapter is going to look at some of the advantages and limitations of this traditional approach to understanding Asian Americans. In particular, it will challenge the plausibility of a major foundation of this approach, namely the **objective** (neutral and impartial) discernment of the meaning of human behaviors. Later, an alternative to the traditional research method will be presented. This alternative expands ways to analyze Asian Americans' behaviors and experiences. Finally, some of the implications of this alternative method for psychology, Asian Americans, and psychological and career interests will be discussed.

Traditional Psychological Research: Sources of Psychological Knowledge

Among the reasons that questionnaires or scales (i.e., clusters of questionnaire statements) are used is that the questionnaires are thought to be objective, reliable (i.e., producing the same results over time), and valid (i.e., measuring what they purport to assess). Questionnaires have been used to study a variety of issues, such as Asian Americans' anxiety levels and ethnic identity. (For examples, scan PsyLit.)

Consequently, this traditional research method—described in Chapter 3 and, along with observations of psychotherapists, dominant in Asian American psychology—is useful in ways that more informal investigative methods, such as casual observations of friends, would not be. Relying solely on years of casual observation would be an inefficient and unreliable approach to achieving unbiased knowledge. On the other hand, this **empirical research** method gives researchers a chance to study people in a more controlled and coherent way than would be naturally possible.

Even using a questionnaire to ask friends what they think about a topic or giving the questionnaire to every third person walking by on a campus, several biases could come into play, such as a tendency for the respondents to be similar in age, marital status, area of residence, and socioeconomic background. These types of biases would undermine efforts to generalize the findings to other Asian Americans. In contrast, respondents in empirical studies ideally are culled from randomly selected samples of Asian Americans to justify generalizing from the responses of that sample to other Asian Americans.

Empirical research is used to inform clinical (therapists) and research psychologists alike. When clinical psychologists form an understanding of, for instance, a client's ethnic identity, that understanding is based on their clinical experience, published clinical analyses, and existing empirical research. Likewise, research psychologists base their understanding on both clinical and empirical reports (albeit usually putting more emphasis on the latter) to inform their own research. Traditionally, both clinical and research psychologists give special attention to empirical research because it is thought to be objective, which has long been regarded to be a hallmark characteristic of science.

Psychology's Scientific Goals and Methods

At its inception as a discipline, psychology adopted scientific goals and methods. In so doing, it modeled itself after sciences like physics and, to a lesser extent, medicine.

A goal of research in physics, medicine, and other sciences is to discover timeless, universal relationships, such as a formulaic relationship between energy and mass or the effect of a chemical on a cell's functioning. Because of those relationships, a car in 1980 ran according to the same basic principles as a car today and chemotherapy administered in Washington works the same way when administered in Hong Kong. However, psychology has failed to find corresponding certitude or timeless relationships between variables because it studies humans with consciousness who individually interpret events and choose behaviors in varied ways that defy a parallel regularity.

Nevertheless, psychology clings to a self-ascribed identity as a "science," arguing that insofar as psychology uses the "same" scientific methods, albeit modified to study human behavior, its research findings are as objective and scientific as the findings in other sciences. That reasoning implies that as long as the data are gathered and interpreted without bias, the findings are objective. Is that objectivity really possible?

Objectivity is sought in the way a study is designed (e.g., in terms of how study participants are selected) and in the way the research is conducted. In particular, good researchers do not behave in ways that could bias the behaviors of study participants and, thus, the data produced. The data are not just impressions the researchers have of study participants, respondents ideally are selected without bias and the researchers do not try to sway the way respondents answer. Instead, it is assumed, researchers just try to uncover the objective meaning of questionnaire responses and other behaviors.

In their effort to be objective, researchers also let quantitative statistical analysis, the numerical analysis of the interplay of characteristics or behaviors, create data to interpret rather than twist responses to produce desired or expected results. This number-crunching is used to reveal patterns in the data that might otherwise be overlooked or misinterpreted, thereby suggesting bases for response patterns. For instance, statistical analysis is used to isolate the role of some variable, such as ethnicity, by holding in abeyance (i.e., controlling for) other variables, such as sex. Insofar as the results of the statistical analyses restrict the interpretations that can be drawn, statistical analyses add to the objectivity of the research.

When data are gathered in ways that are deemed objective and then statistically analyzed, psychologists assume the "same" response has the same meaning. One reason an identical meaning is assumed is that researchers are adhering to the useful but often misapplied **Ockham's razor**, later reincarnated as the Law of Parsimony, which dictates that the best scientific explanations are those that require the fewest assumptions. Another reason is that Ockham's razor and the desire to find lasting human behavior patterns have too often led to **reductionism**, the idea that when a complex phenomenon is properly understood, it will be exposed as an instance of a simpler phenomenon. For example, a synopsis of Freudian thought could say that Freud reduced the complex characteristic stubbornness to (really just being a result of) toilet training. Likewise, the model illustrated in Table 5.1 reduces adaptation to all-or-none attitudes toward one's own and other ethnic groups.

Questions About Objectivity

But is the meaning of a behavior, such as a response to a questionnaire, objective? Consider what happens in some middle school classes: A student repeatedly coughs and then other students, in the mistaken belief that they are witty, begin coughing to disrupt the class. Eventually, the teacher becomes angry and says "The next person to cough is going to the principal's office" and one student sitting there with a cold succumbs to an unstoppable need to cough. Those observing without bias would agree that the student coughed. However, the cough would not have the same meaning as the coughing of the witless classmates.

Unfortunately, psychological research rarely makes such a distinction. The "same" behavior—for example, a cough or the same response of "true" to a questionnaire statement—is regarded as having the same meaning.

For a questionnaire response to have an objective meaning and for the answers of one sample to generalize to other groups, the responses' meanings would need to be unambiguous and

Table 5.1 Traditional Model of Relationship Between Group Attitudes and Adaptation

		Maintaining ties with ethnic group	
		Valued	Not valued
Other groups	Valued	Integrated	Assimilated
	Not valued	Separated	Marginalized

Notice that this model's attempt to portray a universal relationship between acculturation attitudes and adaptation reduces the multidimensional complexity and individual variability of (a) attitudes toward one's ethnic group and other groups and (b) types of adaptation to the point of distortion and oversimplification. The model implies discrete, homogeneous, and static sets of attitudes toward one's ethnic group and all other groups.

stable. To see whether those criteria are met, imagine this chapter's listed opening statements were on a psychological test and answer each as true or false:

1. I am more sensitive than most other people.
2. I am often hungry.
3. I am usually quiet.
4. I believe I am no more nervous than other people.
5. I like to attend ethnic festivals.
6. I mostly eat ethnic food.

Were there any difficulties responding with complete accuracy?

When respondents think about their answer to the first statement, they might wonder about which meaning of sensitive—easily hurt or perceptive—should be applied. In responding to the second question, they might ask themselves "How often is often?" and "How hungry is hungry?" At one moment, they might choose "true" because they decide to use a fleeting definition they would not choose at another time and other respondents do not use. Although the responses would be the same, the meaning of those responses would not be. Traditional psychology would regard the data as objective but a respondent's self-report does not have the same kind of reliability or objective meaning as a liver cell's behavior when exposed to a particular chemical.

Analysis/Practice 5.1: For what reasons might responses to this chapter's opening third and fourth statements, often seen in personality and anxiety tests, not reflect personality or anxiety? Assuming that responses accurately reflect behaviors and values, for what reasons might responses to the last two statements, similar to those used on ethnic identity scales, not reflect ethnic identity?

As the foregoing has implied, objectivity is compromised by the fact that researchers must interpret the meaning of the data. Humans do not have a way of finding meaning independently of interpretations formed by their brains. People create meaning by relying on the brain's neural connections established through experience and learning: The human brain does not interpret information objectively. Like other humans, researchers cannot step outside of their consciousness to access objective meaning, existing outside of consciousness. Nor can the reliance on quantitative analysis simply produce objectivity because the numbers must be given meaning.

When trying to understand the lives and behaviors of Asian Americans, the answer to the lack of stable meanings and objectivity does not lie in using Asian research methods, as some have incorrectly argued. Modern research methods in Asia share many of the same **epistemological** (if not also **ontological**) assumptions (i.e., assumptions about what can be known and about the nature of reality, respectively) and using them would, at most, constitute a cross-cultural research method within a similar general framework. Another approach, though, avoids the fictional objective of **modernism** while still relying on careful, rigorous, reasoned analysis.

Postmodernism

Postmodernism, a subversive intellectual perspective influencing many fields (from architecture to history, literature, and sociology), has had a limited impact on psychology. It offers a perspective that places more emphasis on exposing complexity, contradictions, multiple meanings, and overlooked interpretations so often hidden by traditional **narratives** (e.g., descriptions and explanations, versions of reality). (Good references on postmodernism include Faulconer & Williams, 1990; Rosenau, 1992; Polkinghorne, 1988; Slife & Williams, 1995.) From a postmodern perspective, a narrative is a representation, and not simply a reflection, of characters and events, so a postmodern analysis would look beyond the surface.

Modernism

One way to illustrate postmodernism is to contrast it with modernism, a perspective that emphasizes neatly structured representations that hide underlying complexity. Modern buildings—like those big, rectangular downtown high-rises—look neatly straight-edged because they hide what was involved in their construction. In contrast, postmodern buildings take unexpected forms, jutting out at unexpected points; restaurants with a postmodern interior design have pipes and wiring clearly hanging over the customers' heads.

Perhaps closer to home, think about those term papers students often have to write: Come up with a theme, support it with evidence and reasoning that make the conclusion look irrefutable and inevitable. Along the way, even though the students are presumably seeking knowledge about the theme, they gloss over evidence and complexity that cast doubt on or complicate the thesis so that a neat conclusion can be written—even though they would not adopt that approach if they were seeking knowledge about how to resolve a personal problem. In contrast, a postmodern analysis, more in keeping with the way people try to understand personal problems, does not ignore inconvenient facts to serve a completely coherent conclusion because the orientation is more toward thoroughness than artificial coherence.

If a blind date asked a fellow to describe himself, to the extent that his self-portrayal is tightly coherent, he may feel slightly dishonest. Instead of saying "I am like this," he might be more accurate if he said "I'm like this; only sometimes, I'm not. Sometimes I'm like that. But if I'm in that situation, I usually do this. But not always...." A postmodern approach thrives on that complexity. It eschews a final, certain answer.

Traditional psychology ties its own hands by insisting on the form of empiricism it has adopted. Describing and explaining thoughts and behaviors solely in those terms is akin to asking people to describe their motivations or what they had for dinner last night but insisting that they limit their descriptions by only using the words purple, pink, blue, green, and gold: Study participants are given severely limited response options and researchers try to describe behavior patterns from that circumscribed data. Postmodernism expands the vocabulary.

Created Meanings

A postmodern psychology should appeal particularly to those who like to think about the meanings of behaviors. A lack of enthusiasm for statistics does not exclude them from psychology. Just as quantitatively comparing the alcohol content of a Manhattan and a highball would not reveal much about what makes the cocktails different from each other, how different people metabolize alcohol, which cocktail they prefer, why they drink it, and why they behave the way they do afterward, focusing on the quantitative narrows researchers' visual field. For instance, using a modernist, quantitative measure of acculturation occludes much of what makes acculturation relevant to the lives of Asian Americans. Rather than assume that ethnicity is best understood by self-reported ancestry or that Asian Americans associate their ethnicity with where their ancestors lived, researchers might listen to Asian Americans who think of their ethnicity in terms of links they form with others who have similar experiences, styles of communicating, and so on.

Analysis/Practice 5.2: Describe the girl depicted in the following story.

In response to unending conflicts with her neighbor and frustrated with her family's inability to understand her problems, a young teenage girl decides to run away. As she blows town, she finds herself in a completely new area. She gathers a posse of other unhappy, forgotten, ignored, and insecure souls who abuse the environment when not overdosing on a narcotic. Eventually, the group conspires with a mysterious guy who says he will help her get out of town (and help the posse members meet their needs) if the group kills a woman he does not like. The group kills her and all members of the group live happily ever after.

What impression of this girl makes sense? What is the moral of the story? Does the story have a clear, straightforward meaning?

Was the meaning created for this story similar to that of the Wizard of Oz, which was actually summarized? The reason for the probable difference in meaning is that the meaning was not inherent in the behaviors and events. As creatures with consciousness, humans create meanings. A postmodern perspective is conducive to examining the created meanings of events, situations, behaviors, and concepts. It informs in a way that is not accessible through traditional empirical research or clinical reports focusing on those seeking psychotherapy.

Illustrating the way that the meaning of events is created and that postmodernism offers new topics for study, Kylie, a 7-year-old girl who had taken *onigiri* (i.e., rice balls) to school, returned home upset because other children had made fun of her lunch (personal communication, Jennie Hasegawa). Kylie's mother told her that sometimes when children encounter unfamiliar food, they ridicule it because they do not know any other way to respond; so Kylie should tell them what *onigiri* is and offer some to them. Despite the teasing she encountered at school, Kylie, an *onigiri*-fan, that night chose it again for the next day's lunch. When Kylie returned home the next day, her mother began to unpack Kylie's lunch bag and noted, with concern, that the bag did not have the light feel it would have if it contained merely the remnants of a completely eaten lunch. As she unpacked, she was surprised to find several quarters at the bottom and asked Kylie about them. Kylie had charged her classmates 25 cents for each bite of her *onigiri*.

While for many Asian American children having their ethnic lunch ridiculed meant that their ethnic diet should be hidden, this mother created a meaning that the deficit was in the other children and that the situation was an opportunity to teach other children about what their family ate; to her entrepreneurial daughter, it was an opportunity to make money. A postmodern psychology might analyze those responses in terms of a number of issues, such as adaptation or what the responses tell us about the meaning of being Asian American. Anecdotes would not be drawn only from clinical settings. Mundane experiences and behaviors could be enlightening fodder for psychological analysis.

From a postmodern perspective, the meaning of human events, situations, and behaviors is not inherent in them and does not exist "out there" in the world; meaning is created, much as the meaning of cards is created and changes in the poker game Texas hold 'em as cards are revealed. The meaning constructed is intertextual: It is based on which **texts**, such as ways of responding to ridicule or new cards, are brought to bear. (Anything that can be analyzed—such as a phenomenon, concept, event, behavior—can be a text.) Instead of assuming that the "same" behavior or questionnaire response has the same meaning, a postmodern analysis digs deeply into multiple possible meanings.

Deconstructing

Inasmuch as meanings are constructed, they can be deconstructed, denuded so that what was hidden is exposed. Providing the opportunity to have in-depth understanding, **deconstruction** is a principal postmodern analytic approach described elsewhere (e.g., Uba, 2002).

Statements, concepts, events, or phenomena can be deconstructed by identifying underlying assumptions; **false choices** (e.g., your only choice is X or Y, valuing other ethnic groups or not valuing them); **privileged** (i.e., favored, valued, or dominant) and **unprivileged** (i.e., silenced, suppressed) meanings; possible unstable/multiple meanings; hidden complexity and contradictions; new frames of reference; how meanings are determined by what is absent; why particular dominant narratives are privileged; how and why alternative narratives are excluded; how well a narrative fits data; and the purposes, limitations, and consequences of particular narratives. By identifying the ideology behind narratives, the deconstruction of issues can lead to expanded understanding that ultimately can serve efforts to create a more fair society, an ultimate goal of much postmodern analysis.

Students have deconstructed statements, concepts, or phenomena they have heard or seen related to Asian Americans. (See a pedagogical method with student samples in Uba (2008).) The topics have included statements such as "I'm not racist, I have Asian friends" and "This is America, go back to your country"; the concepts of bananas and FOB; the idea that Asian American females are exotic; and phenomena such as the Abercrombie-Fitch T-shirts ridiculing Asian Americans, comedians making fun of Asian Americans, Asian American parents' physical punishment of their children, Latinos not viewing Filipino Americans as Asian Americans, and non-Asian Americans asking Asian Americans "What are you?" By doing so, the students learned more about the meanings of being Asian American as well as the meanings of their specific topic.

Deconstructing observed behaviors can help one to understand why particular individuals are behaving as they are, identify behavior patterns, contextualize events, and expose their roots. Take the following statement by a Filipina immigrant, for example.

> Because of racism, I decided to become as American as possible. I would learn their ways, associate with Euro Americans, engage in American recreation, and most importantly, I would learn to understand their sense of humor and wit. I remember staying up late every night to watch the "Tonight Show" because I thought if I could understand the humor, then I'll be just as smart and witty as any Euro American. I wanted so badly to be accepted. It came to a point where I disassociated myself from my own race. When I did come across any Filipinos, I would pretend not to know the language and culture.

One's understanding of her would be aided, for example, by identifying her assumptions that knowledge of American ways was indicative of intelligence and, implicitly, that her own acculturation "deficit" was a sign of stupidity and an underdeveloped sense of humor. One might note that she created a false choice of being who she was or being like white Americans whom she equated with "Americans." Learning about her thinking can be expanded by examining what she privileged—the ability to joke with European Americans; acceptance from those who, she

Identify several of the possible meanings of the posture depicted in this photograph.

believed, would only like her if she could joke with them; and the assumption that such people were worth trying to please.

Analysis/Practice 5.3: Try deconstructing the tendency of some police officers to hassle young Asian Americans (especially males). Perhaps begin by addressing just a few issues, such as the police officers' ideology and assumptions, ways in which alternative narratives are excluded, and possible multiple meanings of the behaviors of all involved. To begin deconstructing, do not fall into the trap of responding the way one might begin a typical term paper by providing reasons for behaviors and examples. Instead, focus on analyzing by identifying assumptions, false choices, and so on.

By addressing the aforementioned deconstruction issues, analyze the experiences of a fourth-generation Japanese American who, in his teenage years:

> …realized [for] the first time people looked at me as being Asian. I realized the stereotypes of being Asian and did not want to fit into it. Part of me trying to deny my culture was to join a gang of predominantly Mexicans. With them I felt protected from that stereotype […]. Hiding my culture was more important to me than staying out of all the trouble I knew I was going to get into…. [I] made more money than [I needed selling mail-ordered martial arts weapon to other students] but got even greedier. Later that year a group of us got arrested for breaking into someone's home.
>
> [In high school, my girlfriend] introduced me to a whole new set of [Asian] friends. With my new group of friends came the stereotype of being smart, quiet, and obedient….I was never good at being any of these. My family background was not the same as any of my friends that lived sheltered lives. It was very difficult to be around people who are smarter than me. Having a 2.7 GPA was considered failing to many of my friends' parents. Even though I have improved so much from Junior High, I was still looked at with disappointment. I always had a problem accepting my identity and wanted to avoid being Asian. I understood the restrictions of being Asian while traveling outside of L.A. every summer [on family vacations]. I feel like everyone is watching us. It seems so unfair…how unwelcome we are even in our own country.

While postmodernism encourages analyses from multiple perspectives, it need not lead to **relativism**, the belief that everyone's perspective is equally valid. If it did, it would be of little value. Although one of the many forms of postmodern is relativistic, a postmodern psychology should not be so. Instead, differing views would be challenged and deconstructed to produce a more comprehensive understanding than is currently created.

Implications for Psychology

A postmodern psychology need not ring a death knell for quantitative research. For example, comparing rates at which individuals of various racial and ethnic groups return to psychotherapy after their first encounter with a therapist remains useful because such data shed light on the appropriateness of the therapy offered to Asian Americans.

Despite viewing data differently, postmodernism is not antithetical to empiricism. Arguments do not necessarily trump data. However, a postmodern psychology would change the way much of the traditional research is interpreted and expand the repertoire of research methods. Instead of essentializing study participants by their ethnicity or age, for example, the complexity and multiple identities of study participants would be explored. The aforementioned 7-year-old *onigiri*-fan was not just a 7-year-old Japanese American. Understanding her behavior is enhanced by seeing other aspects of her identity: She is also smart, brave, and willing to be different to be true to herself. Likewise, a woman wouldn't say that she knows her close friends just because she knows their age and ethnicity; indeed, it is her understanding of them as individuals that distinguishes them from mere acquaintances and enables her to have a more complete understanding of her friends' behaviors. Accordingly, because individuals are not just representations of a demographic group, a postmodern psychology looks beyond those characteristics.

In addition, the voice of the researcher would not be so hyperprivileged. Hyperprivileging the researcher is similar to unnecessarily limiting one's understanding of friends' behaviors by relying only on one's own perspectives when one could get a different, if not more thorough, understanding by closely considering the friends' perspectives on their behavior. A postmodern psychology opens discussions by broadening the participation of study participants. (Traditionally, psychology treated and referred to study participants as "subjects" because the behavior of the latter were, like that of white mice in psychology laboratories, the subject of analysis by researchers. Several years ago, psychology shifted to referring to the people studied as "study participants" but still generally treats them as subjects.)

The insistence on traditional research methods has unduly limited psychology's research areas to those conducive to traditional empiricism or grounded in clinical concerns. A postmodern approach to psychology broadens the field. It is less tied to issues that can be addressed quantitatively. It is not restricted to a search for behavior tendencies found (or created) through statistical analysis (see Lee & Zane, 1998; Uba, 1994 for summaries of such research). A more in-depth analysis of behaviors and experiences is within the purview of serious study.

Although clinical psychologists' reports are typically qualitative, postmodern inquiry would not follow in the footprints of current qualitative clinical research, which still privileges many traditional assumptions and does not approach its subject with a postmodern orientation. Instead of just adopting methods used in clinical psychology, psychologists would reconsider their way of thinking about samples, methods, findings, and concepts.

For instance, rather than search for universal relationships between acculturation and ethnic identity, as might be the case in clinical research, or how an individual client's rejection of his or her ethnicity led to a poor self-concept, as might be done in a clinical case study, postmodern psychologists might examine everyday experiences—such as children pulling their eyes back to tease Asian Americans, biracial Asian Americans not being recognized as Asian American, non-Asian American females failing to seriously consider Asian American males in romantic ways, movies about Asians affecting the way Asian Americans are perceived and treated, teachers and others assuming academic prowess because of ethnicity—to expose the myriad, local (situation-specific) ways a variety of Asian Americans interpret events and how they construct their ethnic identity in the context of such events and other texts.

In addition, compared to most clinicians now, postmodern psychologists would think even more about the implications of their analysis for understanding where Asian Americans stand within society and ways to make society more equitable. For example, what does it say about the meaning non-Asian Americans assign to Asian Americans' ethnicity and the standing of Asian Americans that the movie *The Fast and the Furious* minimized the role of Asian Americans who created the car shows at the center of the film?

A postmodern psychology would knock down the boundaries of psychology and reshape it—and a postmodern psychologist could have a significant impact in changing psychology, postmodernism, and ethnic studies. Feminist psychology, research oriented toward understanding the identities of females, has had a large postmodern component for years (e.g., Gergen, 1988; Hare-Mustin & Marecek, 1990), but postmodernism has had little impact in psychological studies of minorities so a postmodern Asian American psychology could also lead research on the racially, culturally, and economically marginalized. (Insofar as postmodernism often focuses on what is usually unprivileged, it tends to analyze what has been marginalized, whether people or ideas.) White Americans would not be treated as universally normal humans, and Asian Americans would not be relegated to being cast as variations on the normal.

This redefinition of psychology would, in many cases, be easier for those new to the field than to their elders whose brains now might often overlook long-established assumptions and no longer consider the alternative methods they would have before they were disciplined. (Areas of study are called *disciplines* for a reason: Minds are taught to think in particular ways consistent with a field of study.)

A postmodern psychology could enter into interdisciplinary discussions in Asian American Studies where much of the research has a clear postmodern orientation and psychology is generally ignored. Anthropologists and sociologists have conducted postmodern studies on topics that could just as easily have been addressed with psychological concerns in mind, such as Asian Americans' role in import car shows (Kwon, 2004), ethnic identity (Kang & Lo, 2004; Ngô, 2005), and cultural portrayals of Asian Americans (Ongiri, 2002). For example, a psychological slant on the car shows could have led to an examination of the ways Asian Americans create avenues for expressing their ethnic identity; a psychological perspective could be taken on ways, both interpersonally and in terms of their ethnic identity, Asian Americans counter Orientalizing and marginalizing portrayals of Asian Americans. In such ways, a postmodern psychology could enter ethnic studies conversations.

Asian American psychology also offers a format in which ideas can be widely spread. The hundreds of Asian American Psychological Association members tend to be familiar with each other's work so instead of ideas and analyses being lost among the tens of thousands of studies regularly published in journals, they can spread to hundreds of psychologists relatively quickly, compounding their influence.

Summary

Asian American psychology has traditionally relied on quantitative empirical studies using questionnaires and qualitative clinical case studies. Both types of research are rooted in efforts to be objective.

This chapter challenges as a fiction the epistemological belief that behaviors have an objectively discernable meaning. It argues that meanings are not inherent characteristics of a behavior that observers objectively extract. The sensory feedback a human receives about the external world provides data; but inasmuch as humans cannot step outside of their brains to interpret, they must construct interpretations of that data using their minds. The interpretations of that data, their meanings, are constructed in the brain and the interpretation that is constructed depends upon the texts that have been brought to bear and the relevance those texts are thought to have.

Accordingly, postmodernism is described as an alternative to traditional psychological research paradigms. While not burdened by the fiction of objective meaning, postmodernism nevertheless is an intellectually rigorous perspective that seeks thorough understanding rather than artificial coherence.

The chapter points to some ways a postmodern psychology would expand understanding of Asian Americans' behaviors and experiences. It also suggests ways in which postmodern perspectives would be useful in understanding everyday experiences and events and expanding psychological discussions in Asian American Studies.

Discussion Questions

1. Psychology's traditionalists acknowledge that respondents sometimes behave or respond to questionnaires in ways that do not reflect their actual experiences, behaviors, and attitudes (e.g., by overemphasizing their recent experiences). For what other reasons might responses to a questionnaire not accurately reflect the respondent's behaviors, beliefs, experiences, and attitudes?

2. Deconstruct the following topics:
   a. The idea that Asian American males are not as masculine as other men
   b. Phenomena such as plastic surgery to look less Asian or Asian American parents telling their children they should not marry outside their ethnic group

3. What therapeutic effects can be produced when clients learn to deconstruct for themselves?

4. What kinds of psychological problems might be addressed using deconstruction?

Key Terms

Deconstruction: A subversive postmodern critical thinking method that exposes and disrupts whatever is assumed and accepted as true, natural, or undeniable.

Empirical research: Research seeking knowledge by relying on the neutral collection of demonstrable data.

Epistemological: Having to do with answering: What can be known?; how can it be known?; and how certain can one be of what is known?

False choices: Choices that do not reflect the true range of options available.

Modernism: A perspective that assumes ontological order and represents reality in orderly terms.

Narratives: Versions of reality; descriptions and explanations, recognized as being created rather than simply reflecting reality.

Objective: Impartial, neutral, transcending the mind.

Ockham's razor: The scientific rule that the best explanation has the fewest assumptions.

Ontological: Having to do with the nature of reality.

Postmodernism: An analytical perspective that regards knowledge about behaviors' meaning as intertextual, ultimately tentative constructions rather than objective understandings of universal principles underlying a fixed reality.

Privileged: Favored, emphasized, valued.

Reductionism: An analysis assuming that fully understanding complex phenomenon X will show that it is an instance of simpler phenomenon Y.

Relativism: The untenable view that everyone's view and position is equally valid.

Text: Anything that can be analyzed—such as a phenomenon, concept, event, or behavior.

Unprivileged: Silenced or suppressed meanings or narratives.

For Further Learning and Suggested Readings

Amerasia Journal

Journal of the Association of Asian American Studies

Robinson, D. N. (1976). *An intellectual history of psychology.* New York: MacMillan.

Uba, L. (2002). *A postmodern psychology of Asian Americans: Creating knowledge of a racial minority.* New York: SUNY Press.

Note: To see examples of deconstruction in other areas, one might start searching the Internet using the following search terms: "postmodern*" AND "deconstruct*" AND [any area of interest, such as] "architecture," or "litera*" or "histori*" or "film*" and so on.

References

Faulconer, J., & Williams, R. N. (1990). *Reconsidering psychology: Perspectives from continental philosophy.* Pittsburgh: Duquesne University Press.

Gergen, K. (1988). Feminist critique of science and the challenge of social epistemology. In M. M. Gergen (Ed.), *Feminist thought and the structure of knowledge* (pp. 27–48). New York: New York University Press.

Hare-Mustin, R. T., & Marecek, J. (1990). *Making a difference: Psychology and the construction of gender.* New Haven: Yale University Press.

Kang, M. A., & Lo, A. (2004). Two ways of articulating heterogeneity in Korean American narratives of ethnic identity. *Journal of the Asian American Studies Association, 7*(2), 93–116.

Kwon, S. A. (2004). Asian American youth and the import car scene. *Journal of the Asian American Studies Association, 7*(1), 1–26.

Lee, L. C., & Zane, N. (1998). *Handbook of Asian American psychology.* Thousand Oaks: Sage.

Ngô, F. (2005). A chameleon's fate: Transnational mixed-raced Vietnamese identities. *Amerasia Journal, 31*(2), 51–62.

Ongiri, A. (2002). "He wanted to be like Bruce Lee": African Americans, Kung Fu Theater and cultural exchange at the margins. *Journal of the Asian American Studies Association, 5*(1), 31–40.

Polkinghorne, D. (1988). *Narrative knowing and the human sciences.* Albany, NY: SUNY Press.

Rosenau, P. (1992). *Post-modernism and the social sciences: Insights, inroads, and intrusions.* Princeton, NJ: Princeton University Press.

Slife, B. D., & Williams, R. N. (1995). *What's behind the research? Discovering hidden assumptions in the behavioral sciences.* Thousand Oaks, CA: Sage.

Uba, L. (1994). *Asian Americans: Personality patterns, identity, and mental health.* New York: Guilford.

Uba, L. (2002). *A postmodern psychology of Asian Americans: Creating knowledge of a racial minority.* NY: SUNY Press.

Uba, L. (2008). A deconstructive pedagogy. *Journal of Excellence in College Teaching, 19*(1), 103–125.

6

Acculturation and Enculturation of Asian Americans

A Primer

BRYAN S. K. KIM

OUTLINE OF CHAPTER

Case Synopsis
Introduction
Diversity of Immigration History
Theories of Acculturation and Enculturation
Assessment of Acculturation and Enculturation
Research on Acculturation and Enculturation
Case Study
References

Case Synopsis

Consider the case of Linh, a 12-year-old Vietnamese girl who recently entered the United States with her parents. Linh's parents had long thought about migrating to the United States to escape their difficult lives in Vietnam and to take advantage of the economic opportunities. When an opportunity to enter the United States arose with the help of their distant relatives, Linh's parents decided to make the move. But unfortunately, Linh and her parents speak very little English and they do not have any definite plans for the kind of work they will do. As a short-term plan, Linh's father takes a job as a dishwasher at a Chinese restaurant and Linh's mother takes a job in house-keeping at a local hotel. As for Linh, she begins to attend a local high school where there are very few Vietnamese Americans. Because Linh and her parents are very unfamiliar with the cultural norms of the United States, they realize that they have a lot of cultural adjustments to make.

Introduction

As of this writing, millions of Asians have taken the awesome step of migrating to the United States. These Asians include individuals from relatively well-to-do backgrounds with existing sources of support in the United States in the form of many relatives and friends. But they also include others who are arriving in this country with no or little family ties, little money, and no proficiency in English, like Linh and her parents. Furthermore, the Asian American group includes descendants of Asians who arrived during the past 150 years who have lived in the United States all their lives as a member of the numerical minority. How have all of these persons adjusted to the dominant cultural norms of this country? And, what were the psychological ramifications of this adjustment process? These are the primary questions that will be addressed in this chapter.

The purpose of this chapter is to focus on the experiences of Asian Americans in their processes of adaptation to the U.S. culture and retention of the norms of their heritage cultures.

It will also describe the psychological consequences of these processes and research findings bearing on them. In so doing, the chapter will describe (a) the diversity of immigration history of Asian Americans, (b) the current theories on **acculturation** and **enculturation**, (c) the popular methods of assessing acculturation and enculturation, and (d) the research findings regarding acculturation and enculturation.

Diversity of Immigration History

Asian Americans are made up of individuals with diverse immigration histories. Many Asian Americans are five or six generations removed from immigration, whose ancestors entered the United States between the mid-1800s and early 1900s during the Gold Rush and transcontinental railroad eras in California and the time of sugar plantations in Hawaii. Also, there are other Asian Americans who are third- and fourth-generation Americans whose Asian ancestors entered the United States during World War II and the Korean War. This group is relatively small in number since the Immigration Act of 1924 effectively prevented association with the U.S. military (e.g., wives of soldiers). In fact, the total number of Asians who entered the United States during these two periods numbered just over 1 million (Chan, 1991). In comparison, the current number of Asian Americans is around 12 million!

In 1965, the U.S. Congress passed the Immigration Act of 1965 that swung wide open the doors. Based on the principles of family reunification and entry of skilled workers, this act increased the quota of migrants from Asian (and other Western hemisphere) countries to 120,000 from just a few thousand in the years previous to 1965. There are millions of Asian Americans, like Linh and her parents, who benefited from this act and were allowed to enter the United States. Also, a decade after the passing of the Immigration Act of 1965, the U.S. military forces pulled out of Southeast Asia that caused thousands of Asians from Vietnam, Laos, and Cambodia to flee these countries, due to fears of persecution from the victorious Communist forces, and enter the United States as refugees. This led to a large and visible presence of Southeast Asian Americans in the United States and further increased the number of Asian Americans as a group. The children to these immigration groups are now in their second (born in the United States) or third (parents were born in the United States) generations. In addition to these immigrants who had been in the United States for some time, there are also Asian Americans who entered the United States as recently as yesterday.

These varied migration histories of Asian Americans illustrate the diversity within the Asian American group in terms of how much time they have had to adjust and adapt to the lives in the United States. For individuals who migrated just yesterday, they have had very little opportunity to adapt to the U.S. culture. The cultural norms held by these persons might be very different from that of the dominant U.S. culture but very similar to that of their country of origin. For individuals who were born in the United States and who might be sixth-generation Americans whose ancestors migrated in the 1800s, their cultural norms may be very similar to the dominant U.S. cultural norms but whose norms may be very different than that of their Asian cultural heritage.

To try to understand these varied adaptation experiences of Asian Americans and the psychological implications of these processes, the construct of acculturation, one of the two major concepts in this chapter, has been a popular focus of study among psychologists and educators during the past 15 years. For example, at the time of this writing, a search of the PsycINFO database using "acculturation" and "Asian American" as keywords yielded 279 citations, with all but 13 references having the publication date of 1990 or later.

Theories of Acculturation and Enculturation

The previous section set the stage for describing the construct of acculturation and a related construct of enculturation. Because of the significant variations on migration histories among

Asian Americans, it is important to understand acculturation, or the extent to which these individuals have adopted the dominant cultural norms of the United States, as well as enculturation, or the degree to which they have retained the norms of their heritage cultures. In this section, more formal definitions of acculturation and enculturation will be provided, as well as the theories related to psychological functioning vis-à-vis these two constructs.

Construct Definitions

Redfield, Linton, and Herskovits (1936) first defined acculturation in the following manner: "Acculturation comprehends those phenomena which result when groups of individuals sharing different cultures come into continuous first-hand contact, with subsequent changes in the original culture patterns of either or both groups" (p. 149).

About 30 years later, Graves (1967) coined the term *psychological acculturation* to describe acculturation at the individual level and posited that acculturation includes the changes that an individual experiences in terms of their attitudes, values, and identity as a result of being in contact with other cultures. More recently, John Berry and his colleagues (e.g., Berry, 1980; Segall, Dasen, Berry, & Poortinga, 1999) developed a two-continua model of acculturation in which one continuum represents "*contact and participation* (to what extent should [people] become involved in other cultural groups, or remain primarily among themselves)" and the other continuum representing "*cultural maintenance* (to what extent are cultural identity and characteristics considered to be important, and their maintenance striven for)" (p. 305, Segall et al., 1999). Essentially, acculturation is defined as the extent to which people are participating in the cultural norms of the dominant group while maintaining the norms of their original culture.

However, there is a problem with this definition. In the context of cross-cultural psychology in which scholars, like John Berry and his colleagues, are examining the experiences of migrants from one country to another, this definition may be very accurate. However, for individuals who have not been originally socialized in their heritage culture, like many U.S.-born Asian Americans, the term *acculturation* may be insufficient. Rather, the term *enculturation* can be very helpful in more fully describing the experiences of these individuals. Herskovits (1948) described *enculturation* as the process of socialization to and maintenance of the norms of one's indigenous culture, including the salient values, ideas, and concepts. Based on this definition, it can be explained that the "cultural maintenance" process that is described above may be better represented with the broader terminology of enculturation. As mentioned above, although Segall et al.'s (1999) definition of acculturation in terms of cultural maintenance may be appropriate for immigrant Asian Americans who already have been socialized into their Asian cultural norms before arriving in the United States, it may not accurately describe the experiences of Asian Americans who were born in the United States. These Asian Americans may never have been fully enculturated into the Asian ethnic group's cultural norms by their parents and family. For these persons, the application of "cultural maintenance" process may be incorrect because they might have never been completely socialized in their Asian ethnic cultural norms in the first place. In addition, these persons may be socialized into their Asian heritage more fully later in life and hence engage in the process of enculturation during this time. Furthermore, another benefit of using the term *enculturation* is that it places an equal level of focus on the process of socializing into and retaining one's Asian cultural norms in comparison to acculturation, the process of adapting to the norms of the U.S. culture.

Based on this explanation, it has been proposed that the term *enculturation* be used to describe the process of (re)socializing into and maintaining the norms of the ancestral culture and the term *acculturation* be used to describe the process of adapting to the norms of the dominant culture (Kim & Abreu, 2001). For Asian Americans, therefore, acculturation refers to the process of adapting to the norms of the U.S. culture, and enculturation refers to the process of becoming socialized into and maintaining the norms of their heritage Asian cultures. Current theories of acculturation and enculturation suggest that Asian Americans who are further removed from migration will adhere to the mainstream U.S. cultural norms more strongly than Asian Americans who are recent migrants (Kim, Atkinson, & Umemoto, 2001). On the other hand, Asian Americans who are closer to migration will adhere to their heritage Asian norms more strongly than their counterparts who are several generations removed from migration.

Psychological Effects of Acculturation and Enculturation

So what does this mean for how Asian Americans function psychologically? This question will be the focus of attention in this next section. Specifically, a model will be presented that can be used to gain a helpful understanding of psychological processes and outcomes of acculturation and enculturation.

The model is known as the bilinear model of adaptation and it was proposed by John Berry and his colleagues (Berry, 1980; Segall et al., 1999). These authors theorized the following four acculturation "attitudes" based on combining either high or low levels of acculturation and enculturation: **integration, assimilation, separation,** and **marginalization** (see Figure 6.1). Integration is represented by individuals who become proficient in the culture of the dominant group while retaining proficiency in the heritage culture. People in this status are both highly acculturated and strongly enculturated. To illustrate, consider Michelle, a second-generation Hmong American college student in her final year as an international business major. Michelle's parents raised her to be fluent in the majority culture while maintaining a strong adherence to the cultural norms of the Hmong culture. Michelle was an active member of the Kiwanis Club while also attending a Hmong language school. Currently, she is the president of the Hmong Student Association on her college campus and actively participates in Hmong cultural festivals. Michelle plans to eventually earn an MBA and then become a CEO of a U.S. company conducting international business with Southeast Asian countries. Given the fluency across both cultures, Asian Americans in this status may be most psychologically healthy because it allows them to hold cultural norms that are functional in both European and Asian American cultures while being able to reconcile any conflicts that arise between the two cultural systems.

Separation occurs when an individual is not interested in learning the culture of the dominant group and maintains only one's heritage culture. Individuals in this status are strongly enculturated but not acculturated. To illustrate, consider Bharat, a first-generation Asian Indian American architect in his early fifties who migrated to the United States five years ago with his

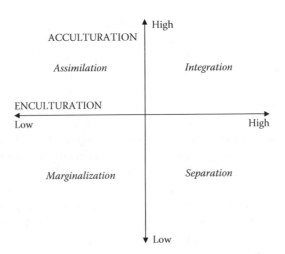

wife and lives in an Asian Indian enclave in Chicago. Upon arrival in the United States, Bharat had a very difficult time finding a position at an architectural firm due to cultural and language difficulties. As a result, Bharat, with the help of his relatives, opened a small grocery store specializing in goods from India and serving mainly other Asian Indian Americans. Although Bharat is disappointed about being unable to work as an architect, he is relieved that the store is making good profits. Bharat is a member of the local Hindu Mandir and maintains strong ties with the local Asian Indian community. Given his work and the area of residence, Bharat seldom has contact with members of the dominant group.

Assimilation, on the other hand, is represented by individuals who absorb the culture of the dominant group while rejecting the norms of the heritage culture. Individuals in this status are highly acculturated but not enculturated. Consider Cybil, a fifth-generation Chinese American lesbian woman in her thirties. Cybil came out to her family in her late teens but unfortunately her family rejected her. Her family simply could not believe that Cybil could be attracted to other women. As a result, Cybil moved out of her family's home and began to live on her own. Currently, Cybil socializes mainly with non-Asian Americans, typically with European Americans who are accepting of her sexual orientation. In considering this status, it is important to note that the degree to which Asian Americans are able to assimilate to the dominant U.S. cultural norm is a function of the level of acceptance by the U.S. society. Given the long history of having considered Asian Americans as "perpetual foreigners" by the dominant group, as well as other forms of stereotyping and discrimination, which are largely based on physical differences, it can be questioned whether full assimilation is possible.

Bilinear model of adaptation.

Marginalization represents the attitude of an individual with no interest in maintaining or acquiring proficiency in any culture, dominant or heritage. Individuals in this status are neither acculturated nor enculturated. Consider Jin-tae, a Korean American in his early teens who lives in a Midwestern state. Jin-tae arrived with his mother and father in the United States from Korea just four years ago. Since his arrival Jin-tae has had difficulty adjusting to the new life here. Although he had some English lessons in school in Korea, he has had a lot of trouble communicating with others at school. Jin-tae feels no connection to school or any aspects of the U.S. culture. Consequently, Jin-tae has tried to avoid interacting with members of the majority group. Unfortunately, Jin-tae also does not feel a strong connection to the Korean culture. Jin-tae did not have good socialization experiences with this culture, which he blames on his parents' strict upbringing. This perception is further exacerbated by the fact that both of his parents have had to hold two jobs to survive financially and hence had very little time to spend with Jin-tae. Recently, Jin-tae's parents have been very worried because he has begun to spend a lot of time with the "wrong crowd." In general, marginalization is perhaps the most problematic of the four statuses because marginalized Asian Americans will adhere to neither cultural systems and tend to reject both sets of norms.

As mentioned earlier, the integration (or biculturalism) status may be the psychologically healthiest status for Asian Americans. Related literature suggests that persons who can function effectively in both the heritage and dominant cultures may exhibit increased cognitive functioning and better mental health (LaFromboise, Coleman, & Gerton, 1993). LaFromboise et al. (1993) used the term **bicultural competence** to describe the process by which individuals are able to successfully meet the demands of two distinct cultures. These authors described bicultural competence as including (a) knowledge of cultural beliefs and values of both cultures, (b) positive attitudes toward both groups, (c) bicultural efficacy, or belief that one can live in a satisfying manner within both cultures without sacrificing one's cultural identity, (d) communication ability in both cultures, (e) role repertoire, or the range of culturally appropriate behaviors, and (f) a sense of being grounded in both cultures. LaFromboise et al. noted that individuals may experience difficulties adjusting to the different and sometimes opposing demands, but when they are able to obtain these skills they may be able to increase their performance in vocational and academic endeavors. Two recent research studies with Asian American college students showed that bicultural Asian Americans who adhere strongly to cultural values or behaviors of both the dominant U.S. and traditional Asian cultures tend to feel good about their membership to their Asian ethnic group (Kim & Omizo, 2005; Kim & Omizo, 2006). Hence, it can be seen that bicultural competence might be an attractive goal for Asian Americans in their processes of acculturation and enculturation.

In contrast to the positive effects of integration (biculturalism), another possible psychological outcome during the processes of adaptation is **acculturative stress**. Berry and Annis (1974) noted that members of immigrant minority groups, including Asian Americans, are vulnerable to stresses arising out of the acculturation process. For example, highly enculturated Asian Americans might experience severe acculturative stress when they attempt to balance the competing demands of two cultures; note that if the stress is successfully managed, the person typically would enter either the integration or assimilation status. Psychological symptoms of acculturative stress include mental health problems (e.g., confusion, anxiety, depression), feelings of marginality and alienation, heightened psychosomatic symptom level and identity confusion (Berry & Annis, 1974). In addition, Smart and Smart (1995) explained that people with acculturative stress tend to have difficulties making decisions with clarity and to carry them out effectively, largely due to heightened emotional stress, alienation, and a sense of hopelessness. The case of Jin-tae described above is a good example of someone who might be suffering

from acculturative stress. Without the support to acculturate to the dominant U.S. culture while maintaining strong connections to the Korean culture, Jin-tae might experience severe feelings of marginality and alienation, two hallmark symptoms of acculturative stress.

Assessment of Acculturation and Enculturation

Given the importance of acculturation and enculturation in understanding the varied experiences of Asian Americans, scholars have tried to devise various ways to psychologically assess these constructs. One of the more simple methods of assessing these is to ask individuals about their generation status. First-generation Asian Americans (i.e., migrants who were born in an Asian country) might be assumed to be at low acculturation and high enculturation. Conversely, fifth-generation Asian Americans might be assumed to be at high acculturation and low enculturation. However, this method is imprecise at best and offers only a crude measure of acculturation and enculturation. Fortunately, more sophisticated ways to assess these two constructs have been developed. Most of these methods involve quantitative measures involving self-report paper-and-pencil instruments. Another type of measurement is based on a qualitative method based on an interview format. This section will include descriptions of the various measurement models that have been used to assess these constructs and provide examples of quantitative and qualitative assessment methods.

Quantitative Assessment Method

Early adaptation theorists (Berry & Annis, 1974; Szapocznik, Scopetta, Kurtines, & Aranalde, 1978) conceptualized acculturation and enculturation as a process that takes place along a single, or unilinear, continuum. According to this model, adaptation occurs when a person moves from one end of a continuum, reflecting involvement in the culture of origin (i.e., enculturation), to the other end of the same continuum, reflecting involvement in the host culture (i.e., acculturation). A popular instrument that is based on this unilear measurement model is the Suinn-Lew Asian Self-Identity Acculturation Scale (SL-ASIA; Suinn, Rickard-Figueroa, Lew, & Vigil, 1987). The SL-ASIA items reflect language use, friendship choice, food preference, media preference, participation in cultural activity, generation and geographic history of life experiences, and ethnic/racial identity.

Despite the wide utility of the SL-ASIA, a number of scholars (e.g., Ramirez, 1984) have pointed out the limitations of basing instruments on the unilinear model. In the unilinear model, the midpoint might represent both biculturalism and marginalization, a situation that is theoretically impossible based on the adaptation model presented above. Consequently, most current methods of measuring acculturation and enculturation consider these two processes based on independent linearities, also known as a bilinear model. An instrument based on this model, for example, is the Asian American Multidimensional Acculturation Scale (AAMAS; Chung, Kim, & Abreu, 2004). The AAMAS assesses how Asian Americans might engage in the norms of one's Asian culture-of-origin, other Asian American cultures, and the European American culture. The first and the third factors represent enculturation and acculturation, respectively, and the second factor represents Asian Americans' adherence to the norms of a pan-ethnic Asian American culture. Largely adapted from the SL-ASIA, most of the items in the AAMAS are behavioral in nature and describe activities such as language usage, food consumption, practice of traditions, and association with people.

When assessing acculturation and enculturation, it is also important to consider how the constructs have been operationalized in observable terms. Szapocznik et al. (1978) first elaborated on ways of operationalizing acculturation (and enculturation) by proposing that it involved changes in two personal dimensions: behaviors and values. Kim and Abreu (2001) reviewed the item contents of 33 instruments designed to measure acculturation and enculturation and found that the items in these instruments tend to be mixtures of behaviors, values, knowledge, and identity. Having a mixture of dimensions is an important limitation because there is evidence to suggest that these dimensions tend to change at different rates. For instance, Kim, Atkinson, and Yang (1999) found that cultural behaviors tend to change more rapidly than cultural values.

Consequently, these authors recommended developing an instrument that separately assesses the following four dimensions: cultural behavior, cultural values, cultural knowledge, and cultural identity. Cultural behavior refers to friendship choice, preferences for television programs and reading materials, participation in cultural activities, contact with indigenous culture (e.g., time spent in the country of origin), language use, food choice, and music preference. The cultural value dimension refers to attitudes and beliefs about social relations, cultural customs, and cultural traditions, along with gender roles, attitudes, and ideas about health and illness. The cultural knowledge dimension refers to culturally specific information such as names of historical leaders in the culture of origin and the dominant culture, and significance of culturally specific activities. Finally, cultural identify refers to attitudes toward one's cultural identification (e.g., preferred name is in Mandarin), attitudes toward indigenous and dominant groups (e.g., feelings of pride toward the indigenous group), and level of comfort toward people of indigenous and dominant groups.

To date, there have been several instruments developed to assess a single dimension beyond cultural behavior. For example, an instrument that is designed to assess solely the cultural values dimension is the Asian American Values Scale—Multidimensional (Kim, Li, & Ng, 2005). The AVS is designed to assess the enculturation linearity of the bilinear model and contains items reflecting several dimensions of Asian values such as collectivism, conformity to norms, emotional self-control, family recognition through achievement, filial piety, and humility. Kim et al. reported evidence of reliability and validity of the AVS score. Complementing the assessment of Asian values enculturation are instruments to assess values acculturation. An example of this instrument is the European American Values Scale for Asian Americans—Revised (Hong, Kim, & Wolfe, 2005). This instrument contains items reflecting predominant U.S. attitudes regarding various situations including child-rearing practices, marital behavior, autonomy, and sexual freedom.

Qualitative Assessment Method

Another method of assessing a person's levels of acculturation and enculturation is to conduct an interview. Using the bilinear model and the four construct dimensions underlying acculturation and enculturation, an interviewer can ask questions about the person's behavioral and psychological functioning. For instance, along the behavioral dimension, a first-generation Chinese American who prefers to watch Mandarin-language television and eat Chinese food over watching U.S. television shows and eating American food could be said to be strongly enculturated but not very acculturated. A third-generation Japanese American who prefers to listen to U.S. music over Japanese music could be said to be strongly acculturated but low enculturated. On the other hand, a second-generation Korean American who equally prefers American and Korean food and music could be said to be bicultural (or integrationist).

Along the dimension of values, a first-generation Vietnamese American, similar to Linh's father, who strongly adheres to traditional Vietnamese cultural values but eschews U.S. values could be said to be strongly enculturated but not acculturated. But a fifth-generation Asian Indian American who strongly adheres to U.S. cultural values but does not endorse any traditional Asian Indian values could be said to be highly acculturated but not enculturated. Along the knowledge dimension, a first-generation Chinese American who understands the significance of fireworks and dragon dance during the Chinese New Year can be said to be highly enculturated. A fifth-generation Filipino American who understands the history behind the U.S. holiday of Fourth of July can be said to be highly acculturated. On the other hand, a second-generation Vietnamese American who understands the importance of both the Tet celebration and Christmas can be said to be both highly acculturated and enculturated, or bicultural. Lastly along the cultural identity dimension, a Pakistani American adult who prefers to be called by his indigenous name could be said to be strongly enculturated, whereas an Asian Indian American adult who prefers to be called only by his American name can be said to be highly acculturated.

Research on Acculturation and Enculturation

Mirroring the popular interest in the constructs of acculturation and enculturation as related to the lives of Asian Americans, there has been a growing body of research literature on these topics. Not only do acculturation and enculturation have important implications for psychological functioning as described above, research also has revealed important relations with vocational functioning, attitudes toward help-seeking and the counseling process.

Vocational Functioning

Regarding educational and occupational issues, six research studies were found that investigated the relations between acculturation and vocational experiences among Asian Americans. In an early acculturation study, Leong and Tata (1990) found that individuals with higher levels of acculturation tend to focus more on one's skills and talents in selecting their occupational pursuits. Park and Harrison (1995), based on data from Asian American college students, found that people who are highly acculturated may choose career goals that are different from individuals who are low acculturated, with the former group looking for more entrepreneurial opportunities. These findings were similar to those found in a study of Asian American college students by Tang, Fouad, and Smith (1999). Hardin, Leong, and Osipow (2002) surveyed Asian American and European American college students and found that, although as a group Asian Americans exhibited less mature career choice attitudes than European Americans, the high-acculturated Asian Americans did not differ from European Americans in maturity of career choice attitudes. In considering this finding, it is important to note that "mature" career choices include the extent to which individuals try to make autonomous and independent decisions. For Asian Americans who tend to focus also on the needs and wishes of their parents and family, the extent to which they can make "mature" choices may be culturally determined. Hence, a lack of "mature" choices does not indicate the presence of immaturity.

In another study, Chung (2001) found that Asian Americans who were more acculturated reported experiencing less conflict with their parents in the areas of education and career than both the low-acculturated and bicultural groups. This finding is consistent with the idea that Asian Americans' career decisions are not individual-based ones but also involve the wishes and opinions of parents and other family members.

Finally, in a study that sampled participants beyond the college population, Leong (2001) examined the relations between acculturation and career adjustment among Asian Americans working in several companies. The results showed that Asian Americans with high acculturation tended to be more satisfied and experience less stress and strain with their jobs than did their counterparts who were low acculturated. Also, the results showed that Asian Americans who were high acculturated tended to receive higher performance ratings from their supervisors than did their low-acculturated counterparts. In sum, all of these findings suggest that vocational behaviors of Asian Americans tend to be influenced by the degree to which they are acculturated and enculturated. Therefore, career counselors should be informed about these findings and tailor their services to meet the unique cultural needs of these Americans.

In further considering these findings, please consider what these findings suggest about the educational and career aspirations of Asian Americans. Also, how do the findings apply to your life? How consistent or inconsistent are the findings in comparison to your own experiences?

Attitudes Toward Seeking Psychological Services

Another growing body of research with Asian Americans involves their attitudes toward help seeking. A major impetus for this area of research is the findings from several epidemiological studies showing that Asian Americans tend to underutilize psychological services, even though their need for services is no less than other groups (e.g., Leong, 1994; Snowden & Cheung, 1990). In fact, given their experiences with stereotyping and discrimination, it can be reasoned that Asian Americans may be in greater need of psychological services.

Six research studies that contained significant findings regarding the reasons why Asian Americans tend to underutilize psychological services were identified. Atkinson and Gim (1989) found that the college students with high acculturation in comparison to those with low acculturation tended to be more likely to recognize a personal need for professional psychological help, be tolerant of the stigma, and open to discussing their problems with a service provider. This finding was replicated in Tata and Leong (1994) and more recently by Zhang and Dixon (2003). Hence, it is clear that more acculturated Asian Americans would be more likely to seek professional psychological help than their less acculturated counterparts.

However, in a study on the relations between acculturation and willingness to see a counselor, Gim, Atkinson, and Whiteley (1990) found that low–medium-acculturated individuals were more willing to see a counselor than high-acculturated Asian Americans, a result that seems to directly contradict the findings on help-seeking attitudes. To make sense of this finding, Gim et al. hypothesized that perhaps when less-acculturated students do acknowledge a problem, they are more willing to seek professional help. They speculated that this finding might reflect respect for authority on the part of less-acculturated Asian Americans.

In a similar study but focusing on values enculturation, Kim and Omizo (2003) examined the relations among Asian American adherence to Asian cultural values, attitudes toward seeking professional psychological help, and willingness to see a counselor. Based on the data for Asian

American college students, the results revealed that adherence to Asian cultural values was inversely related to both attitudes toward seeking professional psychological help and general willingness to see a counselor, above and beyond the effects of related demographic variables. In a partial replication of these results, Gloria, Castellanos, Park, and Kim (in press) observed a significant inverse relationship between adherence to Asian values and positive help-seeking attitudes.

In sum, these findings suggest that whether or not Asian Americans seek psychological services is influenced by their levels of acculturation and enculturation. An important implication of this finding is counselors may need to do a better job of "selling" their services to more traditional Asian Americans who are less likely to seek services than less traditional Asian Americans. Perhaps counselors can make efforts to normalize the counseling endeavor and decrease the level of stigma related to psychological difficulties through outreach services and materials (e.g., pamphlets and posters).

Counseling Process

While the research studies examining help-seeking attitudes and willingness to see a counselor are helpful in that they provide some explanations for Asian Americans' underutilization of services, they do not explain what occurs when they do enter treatment. Scholars on Asian Americans and mental health services have observed that Asian Americans tend to prematurely terminate counseling if they are not provided with culturally credible treatment (e.g., Leong, Wagner, & Tata, 1995). In light of these observations, researchers have investigated ways in which the counseling process can be modified to become more culturally relevant, sensitive, and effective in meeting the psychological needs of Asian Americans. In many of these studies, acculturation and enculturation were examined to investigate whether people of different adaptation levels may prefer different types of counseling intervention strategies.

In a study with Asian American college student clients, Kim and Atkinson (2002) investigated the effects of clients' adherence to Asian cultural values (values enculturation) on the counseling process. The results showed that clients with high adherence to Asian cultural values evaluated Asian American counselors as more empathic and credible than clients with low adherence to Asian values. On the other hand, clients who had low adherence to Asian values judged European American counselors to be more empathic than clients with high adherence to Asian values. In a similar study but with different results, Asian American college students who were experiencing career uncertainty engaged in career counseling with a European American female counselor (Kim, Li, & Liang, 2002). Clients with high adherence to Asian values perceived stronger counselor empathy and client-counselor working alliance than did clients with low adherence to Asian values, a finding that is inconsistent with that of Kim and Atkinson. To complicate the matter further, two similar studies with Asian American college student clients showed that client adherence to Asian values was not related to session outcome (Kim et al., 2003; Li & Kim, 2004).

These inconsistent findings are puzzling and have led researchers to speculate that there are perhaps other variables that may be moderating the relations between adherence to Asian values and counseling process. In a very recent study investigating this idea, Asian American volunteer clients with personal concerns engaged in single-session counseling with a European American female counselor (Kim, Ng, & Ahn, 2005). The results showed that adherences to both European American and Asian values were positively related to the client–counselor working alliance. These findings provided initial evidence that indeed Asian Americans' adherence to European American values needs to be taken into account when examining the relations between their adherence to Asian values and the counseling process. But of course, given the limited amount of research work in this area, additional studies are needed before firm conclusions can be made. Furthermore, all of these studies focused on assessing values acculturation and enculturation and other variables (e.g., severity of problem) need to be included in future research. Nonetheless, these findings offer initial information on ways in which counselors can be more effective with their Asian American clients.

Summary

The present chapter reviewed the current literature on acculturation and enculturation. The literature suggests that it is important to consider acculturation and enculturation as separate processes that influence how Asian Americans adjust to the norms of the dominant group and relearn or maintain their ancestral cultural norms. Acculturation and enculturation statuses for individuals can be assessed using both quantitative and qualitative methods. Extant research suggests that acculturation and enculturation play important roles in the areas of vocational functioning, attitudes toward help-seeking, and the counseling process.

Discussion Questions

1. In thinking about the situation with Linh and her parents at the beginning of the chapter, consider the following questions:
   a. What are some specific difficulties Linh and her parents might encounter in the United States?
   b. If you were in Linh's situation, how might you handle them? For example, how might you learn the new language and culture?

c. If you were in Linh's situation, how do you feel about what lies ahead for you?
d. If you were in Linh's situation, how long will you be able to survive in such a setting?
e. If you were in Linh's situation, what resources will you need to survive and eventually thrive in a foreign country?

2. Consider your current status in terms of your relations with the dominant and your heritage culture in terms of the discussion on acculturation and enculturation.
   a. What are your relations with both cultural norms?
   b. What level of bicultural competence do you have?
   c. How has it helped (or hindered) you in your social interactions?
3. Based on what was presented, how might you determine the levels of acculturation and enculturation for an Asian American person?
4. How might acculturation and enculturation levels influence an Asian American's vocational functioning, help-seeking attitudes, and involvement in counseling.

Case Study

So far this chapter has focused on the theory and research of how acculturation and enculturation impact Asian Americans in their personal lives and contribute to their psychological growth and development. The chapter will now shift its focus to a case study that illustrates how Asian Americans experience and cope with the issues discussed in this chapter. Moreover, the following case will also be presented to give readers a sense of what Asian Americans focus on in counseling.

It has been two months since Linh arrived in the United States with her parents. It has been a difficult time for her. Linh has had a very difficult time learning English, making friends, and making academic progress at school. Although the school offers bilingual education and has a Vietnamese-speaking instructor, Linh does not feel like she belongs in the school. The fact that there is very little racial diversity in her school, much less a presence of other Vietnamese American students, has made her situation worse. Linh feels sad, lonely, and hopeless at school. Yet, she feels as if there is nothing she can do. Her parents are at work all day and Linh feels like she has no one to turn to for help.

One day, the Vietnamese teacher approaches Linh and lets her know that she has been concerned about Linh's seemingly low mood. The teacher gently encourages Linh to talk to her about how she has been feeling. After much hesitation caused by not wanting to shame herself and her family, Linh begins to reveal her feelings about the difficulties she has had in adapting to her new life in the United States. After listening patiently to Linh, the teacher decides to refer Linh to a Vietnamese counselor in the community whom she hopes will be able to help Linh.

The counselor, who has had much experience working with clients dealing with acculturation and enculturation issues, begins her work with Linh by asking Linh questions regarding her experiences adapting to the norms of the U.S. culture. The counselor soon determines that Linh might be suffering from acculturative stress and begins to talk to Linh about the normality of her experiences and the ways in which Linh might cope with her difficulties by reshaping how she thinks about her situation through the use of cognitive therapy. After some time, the counselor is able to see that Linh can begin to see the brighter side of her situation in the school. In addition, the counselor encourages Linh to get connected with sources of support in the Vietnamese community, as well as social-oriented clubs in the school so that she can have better friendships and support systems.

It has been a year since Linh began meeting with the Vietnamese counselor and her mood has improved dramatically. Linh no longer feels sad, lonely, and hopeless. Linh also has been able to get involved with a Vietnamese youth group in the community. In addition, because her English proficiency has improved, Linh has joined a service club in school and befriended many other students. Linh now feels that she is beginning to move into a bicultural status where she can function well in the dominant culture as well as retaining her Vietnamese culture. And, Linh plans to continue her involvement in the Vietnamese youth group to maintain her ancestral culture, which suggests that she has achieved bicultural competence. As for the future, Linh wants to become a professional counselor who can help other immigrants who are experiencing similar types of problems.

Case Study Discussion Questions

For undergraduate students, please consider the following questions:

1. What are your initial reactions to this case regarding Linh?
2. Have you known anyone who was in a similar situation as Linh? How might you help the person with his or her difficulties?
3. What do you think about the counselor's approach in working with Linh?

For graduate students and/or beginning therapists, please consider the following questions:

1. What might be your clinical conceptualization of Linh's case?
2. How would you apply your theoretical orientation in Linh's case?
3. What might you do differently in comparison to the counselor to be more culturally sensitive with Linh?

Key Terms

Acculturation: The process of adapting to the norms of the dominant culture.

Acculturative stress: Psychological difficulties that arise out of the adaptation process.

Assimilation: An adaptation status in which individuals absorb the culture of the dominant group while they reject the norms of the heritage culture.

Bicultural competence: The skill with which individuals are able to successfully meet the demands of two distinct cultures.

Enculturation: The process of (re)socializing into and maintaining the norms of the ancestral culture.

Integration: An adaptation status in which individuals are proficient in the culture of the dominant group while they retain proficiency in the heritage culture.

Marginalization: An adaptation status in which individuals have no interest in maintaining or acquiring proficiency in any culture, dominant or heritage.

Separation: An adaptation status in which individuals are not interested in learning the culture of the dominant group and maintain only one's heritage culture.

For Further Learning and Suggested Readings

Atkinson, D. R. (2004). *Counseling American minorities* (6th ed.). Boston: McGraw-Hill.

Chun, K. M., Balls Organista, P., & Marin, G. (Eds). (2003). *Acculturation: Advanced in theory, measurement, and applied research*. Washington, DC: American Psychological Association.

Hall, G. C. N., & Okazaki, S. (2002). *Asian American psychology: The science of lives in context*. Washington, DC: American Psychological Association.

Segall, M. H., Dasen, P. R., Berry, J. W., & Poortinga, Y. H. (1999). *Human behavior in global perspective: An introduction to cross-cultural psychology* (2nd ed.). Boston: Allyn & Bacon.

Sue, D. W., & Sue, D. (2003). *Counseling the culturally diverse: Theory and practice* (4th ed.). New York: Houghton Mifflin.

References

Atkinson, D. R., & Gim, R. H. (1989). Asian-American cultural identity and attitudes toward mental health services. *Journal of Counseling Psychology, 36*, 209–212.

Berry, J. W. (1980). Acculturation as varieties of adaptation. In A. M. Padilla (Ed.), *Acculturation: Theory, models, and some new findings* (pp. 9–25). Boulder, CO: Westview Press.

Berry, J. W., & Annis, R. C. (1974). Acculturative stress: The role of ecology, culture and differentiation. *Journal of Cross-Cultural Psychology, 5*, 382–406.

Chan, S. (1991). *Asian Americans: An interpretative history*. Boston: Twayne Publishers.

Chung, R. H. G. (2001). Gender, ethnicity, and acculturation in intergenerational conflict of Asian American college students. *Cultural Diversity and Ethnic Minority Psychology, 7*, 376–386.

Chung, R. H. G., Kim, B. S. K., & Abreu, J. M. (2004). Asian American Multidimensional Acculturation Scale: Development, factor analysis, reliability, and validity. *Cultural Diversity and Ethnic Minority Psychology, 10*, 66–80.

Gim, R. H., Atkinson, D. R., & Whiteley, S. (1990). Asian-American acculturation, severity of concerns, and willingness to see a counselor. *Journal of Counseling Psychology, 37*, 281–285.

Gloria, A. M., Castellanos, J., Park, Y. S., & Kim, D. (in press). The role of adherence to Asian cultural values and cultural fit in Korean American undergraduates' help-seeking attitudes. *Journal of Counseling and Development*.

Graves, T. D. (1967). Psychological acculturation in a tri-ethnic community. *Southwestern Journal of Anthropology, 23*, 337–350.

Hardin, E. E., Leong, F. T. L., & Osipow, S. H. (2002). Cultural relativity in the conceptualization of career maturity. *Journal of Vocational Behavior, 58*, 36–52.

Herskovits, M. J. (1948). *Man and his works: The science of cultural anthropology*. New York: Knopf.

Hong, S., Kim, B. S. K., & Wolfe, M. M. (2005). A psychometric revision of the European American Values Scale for Asian Americans using the Rasch model. *Measurement and Evaluation in Counseling and Development, 37*, 194–207.

Kim, B. S. K., & Abreu, J. M. (2001). Acculturation measurement: Theory, current instruments, and future directions. In J. G. Ponterotto, J. M. Casas, L. A. Suzuki, & C. M. Alexander (Eds.), *Handbook of multicultural counseling* (2nd ed., pp. 394–424). Thousand Oaks, CA: Sage.

Kim, B. S. K., & Atkinson, D. R. (2002). Asian American client adherence to Asian cultural values, counselor expression of cultural values, counselor ethnicity, and career counseling process. *Journal of Counseling Psychology, 49*, 3–13.

Kim, B. S. K., Atkinson, D. R., & Umemoto, D. (2001). Asian cultural values and the counseling process: Current knowledge and directions for future research. *The Counseling Psychologist, 29*, 570–603.

Kim, B. S. K., Atkinson, D. R., & Yang, P. H. (1999). The Asian values scale: Development, factor analysis, validation, and reliability. *Journal of Counseling Psychology, 46*, 342–352.

Kim, B. S. K., Hill, C. E., Gelso, C. J., Goates, M. K., Asay, P. A., & Harbin, J. M. (2003). Counselor self-disclosure, east Asian American client adherence to Asian cultural values, and counseling process. *Journal of Counseling Psychology, 50*, 324–332.

Kim, B. S. K., Li, L. C., & Liang, C. T. H. (2002). Effects of Asian American client adherence to Asian cultural values, session goal, and counselor emphasis of client expression on career counseling process. *Journal of Counseling Psychology, 49*, 342–354.

Kim, B. S. K., Li, L. C., & Ng, G. F. (2005). The Asian American Values Scale—Multidimensional: Development, reliability, and validity. *Cultural Diversity and Ethnic Minority Psychology, 11*.

Kim, B. S. K., Ng, G. F., & Ahn, A. J. (2005). Effects of client expectation for counseling success, client-counselor worldview match, and client adherence to Asian and European American cultural values on counseling process with Asian Americans. *Journal of Counseling Psychology, 52*, 67–76.

Kim, B. S. K., & Omizo, M. M. (2003). Asian cultural values, attitudes toward seeking professional psychological help, and willingness to see a counselor. *The Counseling Psychologist, 31,* 343–361.

Kim, B. S. K., & Omizo, M. M. (2005). Asian and European American cultural values, collective self-esteem, acculturative stress, cognitive flexibility, and general self-efficacy among Asian American college students. *Journal of Counseling Psychology, 52,* 412–419.

Kim, B. S. K., & Omizo, M. M. (2006). Behavioral acculturation and enculturation and psychological functioning among Asian American college students. *Cultural Diversity and Ethnic Minority Psychology.*

LaFromboise, T., Coleman, H. L K., & Gerton, J. (1993). Psychological impact of biculturalism: Evidence and theory. *Psychological Bulletin, 114,* 395–412.

Leong, F. T. L. (1994). Asian Americans' differential patterns of utilization of inpatient and outpatient public mental health services in Hawaii. *Journal of Community Psychology, 22,* 82–96.

Leong, F. T. L. (2001). The role of acculturation in the career adjustment of Asian American workers: A test of Leong and Chou's (1994) formulations. *Cultural Diversity and Ethnic Minority Psychology, 7,* 262–273.

Leong, F. T. L., & Tata, S. P. (1990). Sex and acculturation differences in occupational values among Chinese-American children. *Journal of Counseling Psychology, 37,* 208–212.

Leong, F. T. L., Wagner, N. S., & Tata, S. P. (1995). Racial and ethnic variations in help-seeking attitudes. In J. G. Ponterotto, J. M. Casas, L. A. Suzuki, & C. M. Alexander (Eds.), *Handbook of multicultural counseling* (pp. 415–438). Thousand Oaks, CA: Sage.

Li, L. C., & Kim, B. S. K. (2004). Effects of counseling style and client adherence to Asian cultural values on counseling process with Asian American college students. *Journal of Counseling Psychology, 51,* 158–167.

Park, S. E., & Harrison, A. A. (1995). Career-related interests and values, perceived control, and acculturation of Asian-American and Caucasian-American college students. *Journal of Applied Social Psychology, 25,* 1184–1203.

Ramirez, M., III (1984). Assessing and understanding biculturalism-multiculturalism in Mexican-American adults. In J. L. Martinez Jr. & R. H. Mendoza (Eds.), *Chicano Psychology* (2nd ed., pp. 77–93). New York: Academic Press, Inc.

Redfield, R., Linton, R., & Herskovits, M. J. (1936). Memorandum on the study of acculturation. *American Anthropologist, 56,* 973–1002.

Segall, M. H., Dasen, P. R., Berry, J. W., & Poortinga, Y. H. (1999). *Human behavior in global perspective: An introduction to cross-cultural psychology* (2nd ed.). Boston: Allyn & Bacon.

Smart, J. F., & Smart, D. W. (1995). Acculturative stress: The experience of the Hispanic immigrant. *The Counseling Psychologist, 23,* 25–42.

Snowden, L. R., & Cheung, F. K. (1990). Use of inpatient mental health services by members of ethnic minority groups. *American Psychologist, 45,* 347–355.

Suinn, R. M., Rickard-Figueroa, K., Lew, S., & Vigil, P. (1987). The Suinn-Lew Asian self-identity acculturation scale: An initial report. *Educational and Psychological Measurement, 47,* 401–407.

Szapocznik, J., Scopetta, M. A., Kurtines, W., & Aranalde, M. A. (1978). Theory and measurement of acculturation. *Interamerican Journal of Psychology, 12,* 113–120.

Tang, M., Fouad, N. A., & Smith, P. L. (1999). Asian Americans' career choices: A path model to examine factors influencing their career choices. *Journal of Vocational Behavior, 54,* 142–157.

Tata, S. P., & Leong, F. T. L. (1994). Individualism-collectivism, social-network orientation, and acculturation as predictors of attitudes toward seeking professional psychological help among Chinese Americans. *Journal of Counseling Psychology, 41,* 280–287.

Zhang, N., & Dixon, D. N. (2003). Acculturation and attitudes of Asian international students toward seeking psychological help. *Journal of Multicultural Counseling and Development, 31,* 205–222.

7

Asian American Racial and Ethnic Identity

TAI CHANG and KWONG-LIEM KARL KWAN

OUTLINE OF CHAPTER

Case Synopsis

Jenny could remember the first time she felt ashamed of being Korean. It was in the first grade in the predominantly White school in the predominantly White suburb where she lived. It was show-and-tell day, and one of the other kids had forgotten to bring something to show, so he decided to tell a joke instead. He put his hands together, palms facing in, and said, "This is a refrigerator. Now open the door." He moved his fingers outward so that his hands made a "V" shape. "Now take the bottle of Coke from the refrigerator. Now open the bottle. Now drink from the bottle."

Then it happened... the boy made a mock Asian face by pushing his eyebrows up with his fingers, looked at Jenny, and said in a singsong voice, "Me Chinese, me play joke, me put pee-pee in your Coke." The class laughed. Jenny was not quite sure why they were laughing, but she understood that they were laughing at her and her "Chineseness." That was the first time she felt prejudice, the first time she felt different not because she spoke Korean or ate Korean food, but because she was perceived as "Chinese." That was the beginning of her identity as an Asian American. (This joke plays upon the stereotype of Asian Americans, particularly Asian American men, as cunning and devious. We telephoned the Consumer Affairs department at Coca-Cola's world headquarters to inquire about the origins of this racist joke, and a representative named Carol Ann assured us that the joke did not originate from The Coca-Cola Company.)

Introduction

Asian American. What is it—a **race**, an **ethnicity**, or both—and how does one become it? The process is complex: There is not a monolithic Asian American identity, nor is there a certain way of becoming and identifying oneself as Asian American, just as there is not a particular identity or developmental process for Chinese Americans, Filipino Americans, Indian Americans,

Vietnamese Americans, Korean Americans, Japanese Americans, or any of the dozens of other Asian ethnic groups represented by the term *Asian American*. In this chapter, we attempt to clarify what psychologists and other social scientists mean when they use labels like *Asian American* and *Chinese American* by defining the terms *race* and *ethnicity*. We then describe racial and **ethnic identity** development processes through which individuals identify themselves as Asian American, Chinese American, Indian American, or as members of any other Asian ethnic group. Common processes that drive both racial and ethnic identity development will be presented first, followed by a review of the main **racial identity** and ethnic identity models that apply to Asian Americans as well as an examination of how racial and ethnic identities are related. Finally, the case of Jenny will be presented and discussed to illustrate how racial and ethnic identity themes play out in clinical work.

Race and Ethnicity

Regardless of who we are, in the United States race and ethnicity are defined for us by institutions (e.g., the U.S. census, media), groups, and individuals (like the authors of this chapter), and these definitions have personal, social, and political consequences. This is not to say that how one defines these terms and the importance one gives to them are not important—they are; but for members of visible racial and ethnic groups, such as Asian Americans, the impact of external definitions and perspectives of race and ethnicity is impossible to avoid and has important consequences. Race, however, more so than ethnicity, confers societal power and status because of the political, social, and economic resources that are differentially distributed based on race.

Although there is some disagreement within psychology about what race and ethnicity are, as well as the differences between the two constructs, there is general agreement that race, as currently construed in the United States, is a sociopolitical construct, and not a genetic one. Historically, however, race has been conceived as a genetic construct. Even though racial groups have been identified by their surface physical characteristics (e.g., skin color, hair type, eye shape, body and facial form), racial groups have also been assumed to be genetically different in their nonsurface physical characteristics (e.g., intelligence, athletic ability, and sexual potency). However, the validity of the biological and genetic bases of racial categorization has been questioned since the practice began. According to Cavalli-Sforza (2000), scientists have never been able to agree on the number of races. First, different anthropologists have arrived at completely different numbers of races, anywhere from 3 to over 100. Second, racial classifications based on surface physical characteristics are primarily the result of climatic variation across geographic areas, and only a handful of genes are likely responsible for these surface physical characteristics. Because nonsurface characteristics are selected by factors other than climate, pure races do not exist, and this has been confirmed by more recent study of genetic variation. Third, most characteristics (e.g., height) vary as points on continuums, rather than as mutually exclusive categories, and thus any attempt to define races genetically requires creating arbitrary cutoff points and hence arbitrary racial categories.

If there are no meaningful genetic differences between races, what then is race, other than a convenient marker that designates people into groups based on surface physical characteristics? In the United States, race is a sociohistorical concept given meaning by social, economic, and political forces. Race is inherently unstable, and not fixed, as it is constantly being transformed by political and social change (Omi & Winant, 1994). For example, in 1910, the U.S. courts in *U.S. v. Balsara* determined that Asian Indians were Caucasians and, hence, White, and eligible for citizenship under the Naturalization Law of 1790. However, in 1923, in *U.S. v. Bhagat Singh Thind*, the Supreme Court ruled that, although Asian Indians were Caucasian, they were not White because that term was reserved for immigrants from Northern or Western Europe, in effect denying Asian Indians the right to citizenship (Takaki, 1998). According to Landrine and Klonoff (1996), "races are created from ethnic groups by applying and institutionalizing said criteria if and only if racial constructions are needed to justify the enslavement, exploitation or expulsion of one ethnic group by another. Races are created only when initial conditions of ethnic group differences in power exist" (p. 11). As such, racial groups in the United States are located at different places on the hierarchy of power and status, with Whites, who are at the top of the hierarchy, attaining, aggrandizing, consolidating, and preserving their power and status through the oppression of other racial groups.

Even though the dominant group has the power to define race for other groups, members of all racial groups can and do define what it means to be members of their groups. When Asian Americans define for themselves what it means to be members of their group, the term *Asian American* no longer denotes just an externally defined category—a race—but it engenders an internally defined identity as well. For Asian Americans, the civil rights movement of the 1960s united Americans of Asian descent to fight oppression and demand rights and resources. They chose the term *Asian American* to express solidarity among Americans of Asian descent based upon their common histories and experiences of discrimination and exclusion at the hands of Whites (Esperitu, 1992). *Asian American*, then, became a social and political identity—a racial identity—to fight racism, just as the term *Oriental* had been used in the propagation of racism.

Ethnicity is a social categorization based on the culture of an individual's ancestors' national or heritage group (Berry, Poortinga, Segall, & Dasen, 1992; Helms, 1994), who are seen by others and themselves as having a clearly defined sociocultural history and distinct cultural features that are transmitted across generations (Smedley, 1999). Members of an ethnic group share common ancestors or national origins, and can be identified by physical and visible indicators, such as name and genealogy (Atkinson, Morten, & Sue, 1989; Helms & Cook, 1999; Schaefer, 2000). Ethnicity defines the heterogeneity of Asian Americans, who are collectively distinguished from other racial groups (i.e., Blacks, Latinos, American Indians/Alaskan Natives, and Whites). Beyond the demographic label, ethnic group membership (e.g., Chinese, Filipino, Indian, Vietnamese, Korean, and Japanese Americans) helps delineate the vast cultural differences among Asian Americans. Although there are some cultural values shared by various Asian American ethnic groups, there are also values, worldviews, cultural customs and traditions, and histories that make each group distinct. An ethnic group can form the basis for an ethnic identity when individuals begin the process of deciding that they belong to that ethnic group and use their ethnic group membership to establish a sense of who they are.

Development of Racial and Ethnic Identities

As mentioned in the previous section, race and ethnicity are defined for us by external sources, but racial identity and ethnic identity are psychological constructs based on an individual's identification, attitudes, values, behaviors, and affiliation with her or his race and ethnicity. Psychological theories of racial and ethnic identity development describe the processes through which individuals explore their racial and ethnic identities as well as the concomitant changes in identity, attitudes, values, behaviors, and affiliation that occur during these processes. The predominant theories of racial and ethnic identities are, at their core, developmental in nature, borrowing the concept of stages, or statuses, from ego identity theory (Erikson, 1968; Marcia, 1980) and ultimately psychoanalytic theory. Developmental models propose that identity is not a static phenomenon. Instead, these models speculate that identity changes over time, and have traditionally proposed that there is a specific order by which it changes. This change is generally viewed as a progression through different stages of perceiving and relating to one's ethnic or racial group as well as the dominant group.

Most ethnic and racial identity theories acknowledge the importance of individuals' **regard** for their minority group in the identity development process. From the perspective of social identity theory (e.g., Tajfel & Turner, 1986), racial and ethnic groups are types of social groups, which are assumed to have status differences in our society. Evaluations of one's group, relative to other groups, influence the group's social prestige, which in turn influences the extent to which individuals identify with a group and the strategies they use to compare their racial or ethnic group to other groups, in other words, their racial and ethnic identity development. Ultimately, the goal for any individual is to enhance or preserve self-esteem and status. For example, an individual may "buy into" the dominant cultural stereotype that portrays Asian Americans as nerds and attempt to break that stereotype in an effort to enhance self-esteem. Another individual may question the premise that being a nerd is negative, reassign a positive value to being a nerd, and embrace his or her own nerdiness, thereby enhancing self-esteem. And yet a third individual may strive to enhance self-esteem for all Asian Americans, rather than just him- or herself, by participating in social activism to combat racist images in the media, thus elevating society's regard for all Asian Americans. These are but a few examples of the types of strategies that Asian Americans may employ to preserve or enhance self-esteem, and an individual's choice of which strategy to use is determined in part by his or her racial and ethnic identity development.

Identity development, however, is not just about enhancing or preserving esteem and status. Sellers and his colleagues (e.g., Sellers, Smith, Shelton, Rowley, & Chavous, 1998) proposed a very useful metatheory of racial identity, which has also been applied to ethnic identity (Yip, 2005). They argued that it is important to think about identity along four different dimensions: **salience, centrality, ideology**, and regard. Salience refers to how relevant an individual's race or ethnicity is to one's overall identity at a particular point in time. Kwan (2005) further defined racial salience as "the extent to which one's racial and ethnic features are perceived and experienced as conspicuous during cross-racial interactions" (p. 122). According to Kwan, racial salience is a psychosocial construct that can be triggered by external and internal catalysts. External catalysts refer to verbal and nonverbal behaviors that heighten the awareness of an Asian American's "Asianness" (e.g., a question about where one is "really from"; hate crimes directed at one's racial group). Internal catalysts, on the other hand, reflect the individual's conditioned sensitivity to the potential implications of racial salience during cross-racial interactions. When an Asian American is psychologically aware of the implications of his or her physical racial salience in a given environment (e.g., hostility toward Asians in a city where U.S. car manufacturing plants closed down due to foreign competition), such perception leads to certain behaviors (e.g., will not stop to dine or refill gas tank when driving through that city) that would otherwise not occur had Asianness not been salient. Centrality is determined by how large a role one's race or ethnicity plays in an individual's overall identity across time and over a wide range of situations. For one individual, her ethnic identity may be the most important aspect of her identity, whereas for another individual, his ethnic identity may be less important than his identity as a gay male, a pianist, and a boyfriend. Ideology consists of attitudes and beliefs that one holds about race, racism, and one's ethnicity; and regard refers to how one feels about being a member of a racial or ethnic group as well as perceptions about how others view that racial or ethnic group. Most racial and ethnic identity theories focus on the last two dimensions of Sellers' model—ideology and regard—and much of the remainder of this chapter will be devoted to describing the roles of ideology and regard in these theories.

Racial Identity

Racial identity refers to an individual's identification with a societally designated racial group and is influenced by racial socialization (Alvarez, Juang, & Liang, 2006; Helms, 1995; Helms

& Talleyrand, 1997). Racial identity describes how individuals deal with the effects of racism, give up dominant cultural views of their own racial group in exchange for self-definition, and develop positive attitudes toward their own racial group. Consider the excerpt below, in which the author, Eric Liu, a former speechwriter for President Clinton and later his deputy domestic policy adviser, began identifying himself as Asian American. (Liu was a speechwriter for President Clinton during his first presidential term, and thus, thankfully, no Asian Americans were responsible for the "I did not have sex with that woman" speech.)

> My own conversion, if I can call it that, is far from complete. Having spent so much of my life up through college soft-pedaling my Asianness, I began afterward to realize how unnecessary that had been. I began, tentatively, to peel back the topmost layers of my anti-race defenses. Did I have an epiphany? No: I think I simply started to grow up. I became old enough to shed the mask of perpetual racelessness: old enough, as well, to sense in myself a yearning for affinity, for affiliation. So I joined a couple of Asian American organizations, began going to their meetings and conventions. And I was welcome. Nobody questioned my authenticity, my standing. Mainly I encountered people quite like me: second generation, mainstream, in search of something else. Soon I was conversant in the patois of "the community." Soon I was calling myself, without hesitation, "Asian American." (Liu, 1998, pp. 66–67)

Helms's People of Color Racial Identity Model

One of the more well-known theories of racial identity for people of color is Helms's (1995) model of racial identity. Her model is a derivative of Cross's (1971) and Atkinson, Morten, and Sue's (1989) models, and is similar to Sue and Sue's (2003) racial/cultural minority identity development model. The main difference between Helms's model and Sue and Sue's model is that Helms focused primarily on the effects of race and racism on identity, whereas Sue and Sue theorized that racial and cultural aspects of identity develop in tandem. Sue and Sue posited that racial oppression experienced by minority group members in the United States not only influences their racial identities, but also the extent to which they endorse ethnic lifestyles, value systems, their cultural heritage, and a sense of cultural pride.

Helms's model describes five different statuses, formerly called *stages* (Cross, 1971; Helms, 1995), of racial identity. These statuses are thought to develop sequentially, from least mature or sophisticated to most mature or sophisticated; however, they are not mutually exclusive. Helms proposed that individuals can operate at multiple statuses at any given point in their lives, and the expression of any particular status depends on its centrality in the individual's overall identity, as well as the situational context. The **conformity**, or pre-encounter, status describes individuals who seek self-definition and self-esteem from Whites and feel no loyalty or obligation to people-of-color groups. Cross (1995) further proposed that the low salience of race in individuals' lives is more common in this status than the denigration of one's racial or ethnic group. Eric Liu's comment, from the excerpt above, about "soft-pedaling his Asianness" is an example of how individuals in the conformity status may minimize their race in order to feel more accepted by the White majority. Other theorists (Ibrahim, Ohnishi, & Sandhu, 1997) have argued that for many first-generation immigrants, particularly those from countries that were colonized, such as India or Pakistan, individuals often skip the conformity status entirely. These immigrants recognize that there are cultural differences between groups and are proud of their racial and ethnic identities. They move on to the **dissonance** status when they realize that hard work alone is not sufficient for attaining the "American dream." The dissonance, or encounter, status is where persons are confused about racial issues and their sense of belonging to either the majority group or their racial group. Individuals enter the dissonance status when their mode of seeking self-definition from Whites begins to conflict with their increasing awareness of racism. Black racial identity models (e.g., Cross, 1971) originally theorized that personal experiences with racism trigger movement into the dissonance status, but more recent models have deemphasized the role of these experiences.

The **immersion/emersion** status is where individuals idealize their racial group, denigrate Whites, and define themselves and others primarily according to race. Individuals in this status also look for positive characteristics of their racial groups and turn to those groups as a source of support. Joining Asian American social and community organizations, as in the case of Eric Liu, is one common way to attain this support. The **internalization** status is where individuals use internal criteria for their self-definition and practice acceptance and tolerance for their own racial group as well as for Whites. Self-definition requires both an understanding that Whites are the de facto standard of comparison, and a rejection of that standard. For example, instead of trying to break the stereotype that Asian Americans are nerds, an individual might question how that stereotype is used to preserve the status quo (e.g., Asian Americans study hard and work hard and do not make waves) and then decide for themselves what value to place on nerdiness. One might, for example, decide that nerdiness is a good thing and thus being a nerd is something to embrace, rather than reject. The **integrative awareness** status is where individuals integrate their identities as members of multiple groups, such as those defined by race, ethnicity, gender, sexual orientation, and religion. Individuals in this status feel a kinship with members of other racial groups as well as other oppressed groups, and attempt to eliminate racism and other forms of oppression. For example, many Asian Americans engage in social activism to fight for the civil rights (e.g., legalized gay marriage) of gay, lesbian, and bisexual persons.

Racial identity statuses have intuitive appeal because they describe the different phases of identity development that many people of color have experienced, but contemporary theorists acknowledge that racial identity development is not such a neat and orderly process. Parham (1989), for example, theorized that there is no end point in racial identity development; rather,

Mabel Teng: Individuals in the integrative awareness status of racial identity fight for the civil rights of other oppressed groups. San Francisco City Assessor Mabel Teng (second from left) officially married the first same-sex couple in the United States on February 12, 2004 (Courtesy Associated Press/Jakub Mosur, photographer.).

individuals can cycle through the various statuses many times throughout their lifespan. For example, an individual may have an identity in which integrative awareness attitudes are most central. For the most part, she may have come to terms with her personal experiences of racism to develop a strong sense of pride and self-confidence in being an Asian American, and she may use her experiences to fuel her work with like-minded Asian Americans and non-Asian Americans in combating racism and promoting racial and social equality. However, a new encounter with racism could trigger emotions of hurt and anger, causing her to retreat to having more self-protective attitudes (e.g., Whites are racists) and behaviors (e.g., seeking the support of other Asian Americans via friendships and community organizations) characteristic of the immersion/emersion status.

Other racial identity theorists have emphasized that the schemas, or cognitive frameworks for experiencing race and dealing with racism, that characterize each of the racial identity statuses can and do coexist within individuals (e.g., Helms, 1995; Carter, Helms, & Juby, 2004). They argue that people of color have in their repertoire multiple schemas, any one of which may be activated by a particular situation at a particular point in time. If a particular schema is especially effective for an individual, she or he may use it more frequently, and its repeated use makes it more accessible, which in turn increases the likelihood that it will be used again. This chronic accessibility, or dominance, of a particular schema is the defining characteristic of each racial identity status. In other words, individuals can have a repertoire of multiple racial identity schemas to access, but the dominant schema, the one that they use most frequently, defines their current racial identity status. For example, an Asian American in the internalization status might enter a new situation where everyone else is White. The situation might activate a conformity schema, which she had used in the past to minimize her Asianness and emphasize her similarity to other Whites, and which she can use again in the current situation to try to fit in. Thus, although she is currently in the internalization status, she has at her disposal schemas from other statuses (e.g., conformity) that she can use to deal with different racial situations, in this case, being the only Asian American in a predominantly White setting. Recent research (e.g., Carter, 1996; Carter et al., 2004; Chen, LePhuoc, Guzman, Rude, & Dodd, 2006; Worrell, Vandiver, Schaefer, Cross, & Fhagen-Smith, 2006) supports the idea that individuals endorse multiple racial identity schemas, and this research has even found consistent patterns in how much people endorse schemas of each status relative to one another.

Ethnic Identity

Ethnic identity consists of individuals' attachment to, sense of belonging to, and identification with members from their ethnic group as well as their ethnic culture (Phinney, 1989). Unlike racial identity, ethnic identity is not always conceptually grounded in oppression and racism. For many Asian Americans, ethnic group membership (e.g., Korean Americans or Vietnamese Americans) reflects the country of origin of their immigrant ancestors, historical settlement, or geographical regions in the United States (e.g., Hawaiians, Pacific Islanders). Ethnic group membership is often associated with the expectation and perception that the group member knows and practices various aspects of their ethnicity (e.g., language usage, food preference). Such expectations may come from family or extended family members of the immigrant generation who engage the later generations in activities (e.g., going to Chinese school during the weekends, celebrating Chinese New Year) that preserve the traditions and customs of their culture of origin. Expectations may also come from social peers, who presume that the ethnic label and visible physical features (e.g., skin and hair color) are associated with cultural knowledge and practice. In other words, members of Asian American ethnic groups are perceived to have some form of affiliation to their ethnic heritage. Their ethnic group membership and ethnic identity may have been heightened when their (grand) parents rebuked them for failing to say certain things in their Asian ethnic language, or when their White friends asked them how to say certain things in their Asian ethnic language.

In spite of the demographic label and familial and social expectations, individuals can have differential identification with or rejection of the traditions, customs, and cultural values of their ethnic group. They may or may not want to identify with the Asian heritage into which they were born and by which their family and peers expect them to live. Ethnic identity, therefore, involves a resolution between how a person is expected to see oneself as an ethnic being and how that person wants to see oneself as an ethnic being. When family demands, peer expectations, and personal preference of one's ethnic group affiliation are not congruent, the ethnic person may resort to various strategies, such as conformity, internalization, or rejection, to resolve the confusion and conflict. When Michael Woo was running for mayor of Los Angeles in 1993, Mr. and Mrs. Chou volunteered to participate in a telethon to recruit Asian American voters. The immigrant parents, in turn, demanded that their second-generation Chinese American children help with the telethon "because you are Chinese." Despite wanting to see Americans as raceless and "all the same," the oldest son conformed, whereas the youngest son refused to yield to the parents' command that "if you are Chinese, you ought to do it." Both decisions involved a negotiation between others' (the parents, in this case) expectations and one's personal choices about what it means to be Chinese American.

Two (Internal and External) Dimensions of Ethnic Identity

Isajiw (1990) delineated external and internal aspects of ethnic identity. **External ethnic identity** can be indicated by participation in ethnic activities and cultural practices including language

Kulintang: External aspects of ethnic identity include participation in cultural activities, such as traditional Filipino kulintang music. (Photo courtesy of Creative Work Fund; http://www.creativeworkfund.org/pages/bios/danongan_kalanduyan.html.)

usage, food preference, religious affiliation, observance of traditional customs and holidays, and dress.

Postmodern theorists (e.g., Uba, 2002), however, contend that these behaviors or activities are not merely indicators of ethnic identity; they *are* ethnic identity. From this perspective, ethnic identity is enacted not just through participation in ethnic practices like the ones denoted above, but also through new avenues not tied to ethnic tradition. For example, Michael, a fifth-generation Japanese American college student, participated regularly in a local Japanese American basketball league in Southern California. For him, these basketball leagues were distinctly Japanese American—most of the players in the leagues were Japanese American and there was a special connection for him between these modern-day leagues and the important role that sports have historically played in the Japanese American community, including during the Japanese American internment of World War II. For Michael, playing in these basketball leagues was a way for him to express his Japanese American identity—to feel Japanese American and to engender a sense of pride and solidarity in being Japanese American. Ethnic identity, therefore, is constructed inseparably from one's social and community contexts.

Internal ethnic identity encompasses a sense of attachment and a feeling of belonging that sustain group membership. Isajiw (1990) has further delineated three dimensions of internal ethnic identity. The cognitive dimension refers to the person's self-image of his or her ethnic group, knowledge of an ethnic group's heritage and historical past, and knowledge of an ethnic group's values. The affective dimension refers to feelings of attachment to one's ethnic group, and encompasses two types of feelings: sympathy and associative preference for same-ethnic-group

The Invaders: Asian American ethnic identities are constructed in cultures that are continually evolving. Organized Japanese American basketball leagues have existed for over 70 years. (Photo courtesy of Tai Chang.)

members over other-group members, and comfort with cultural patterns of one's ethnic group. The moral dimension refers to an ethnic group member's "feelings of group obligations...[that] account for the commitment a person has to his [or her] group solidarity that ensues" (Isajiw, 1990, p. 36). The moral dimension is considered the most important to a person's ethnic identity.

Psychologists (e.g., Isajiw, 1990; Sodowsky, Kwan, & Pannu, 1995) have contended that the internal and external aspects of ethnic identity can express themselves independently of one another. In other words, the attitudinal and behavioral expressions of one's ethnic identity do not always go hand-in-hand. A second-generation Chinese American can speak Mandarin and celebrate various Chinese festivities but not identify strongly as Chinese—he or she may engage in a *ritualistic form of ethnic identity* (Isajiw, 1990) to appease his/her immigrant (grand) parents. Another second-generation Chinese American can be deeply committed to his or her Chinese ethnicity without participating in cultural practices (e.g., language, ethnic festivities); he/she may practice an *ideological form of ethnic identity* to rediscover his/her ethnicity or to adapt to a racist and oppressive social environment (Isajiw, 1990). Using an internal-external ethnic identity model (Sodowsky et al., 1995), research has supported the independent functioning of two dimensions of ethnic identity (Chang, Tracey, & Moore, 2005; Kwan & Sodowsky, 1997). Kwan and Sodowsky proposed that future studies examine in what ways a significant discrepancy between internal and external ethnic identity may be related to various types of psychological adjustment and coping strategies.

Phinney's Three Stages of Ethnic Identity Development

Phinney's (1989, 1990) model of ethnic identity development is based on Marcia's (1980) adolescent identity model, which itself was derived from Erikson's (1968) theory of ego identity formation. Phinney proposed that ethnic group members progress through three stages (**unexamined ethnic identity, ethnic identity search**, and **achieved ethnic identity**) in their search for the meaning of ethnicity in their lives. Throughout each of the three stages, individuals must negotiate two primary tasks: **exploration** and **commitment** (Marcia, 1980). Exploration is when one actively questions and tries out various aspects of ethnic identity, whereas commitment refers to making firm, unwavering decisions about one's identity and engaging in activities to implement those decisions. Ethnic identity stages are formed based on various combinations of the exploration and commitment tasks.

The first stage, unexamined ethnic identity, is characterized by a lack of concern and/or a lack of thought about issues of ethnic identity (Phinney, 1989, 1990). This lack of exploration may be due to a disinterest in ethnicity, or to an absorption of ethnic attitudes passed down by parents or adults in the elder generation without questioning or evaluating the personal meaningfulness of ethnicity. Adapting Marcia's (1980) ego identity status model, the unexamined ethnic identity stage can be characterized by the ethnic person showing low exploration and low commitment to ethnicity (i.e., identity diffused), or low exploration and high commitment to one's ethnicity (i.e., foreclosed identity). A diffused ethnic identity can be characterized by an Asian American who does not care about ethnicity or who does not consider ethnicity to be a significant part of her or his identity. A foreclosed ethnic identity can be illustrated by an Asian American who has internalized an ethnic identity, be it total identification or rejection with the Chinese (or Japanese, Korean, Indian, Vietnamese, or any other Asian) ethnicity that is imposed by others (e.g., expectations of immigrant parents, opinions of social peers) rather than having gone through any personal evaluation to form the basis of such a commitment.

In the second stage, ethnic group members engage in an ethnic identity search. This search is usually triggered by a significant experience that forces the individual to confront one's ethnicity. The search process leads the ethnic person to immerse in activities (e.g., taking classes in

Asian American studies or an Asian language) and experiences (e.g., taking a trip to one's parents' or grandparents' country of origin) that facilitate understanding of the personal meaning of ethnicity. According to Phinney (1990), ethnic identity in this stage resembles Marcia's (1980) moratorium identity status, which is characterized by high exploration of the meaning of ethnicity but low commitment to an ethnic identity. While the realization that social groups as well as one's own identity can be defined along ethnic lines is personally enlightening, the individual is confronted with choosing an ethnic group as his or her identity reference group. An ethnic identity search and exploration leads to the realization that ethnicity is a basis by which social groups are categorized, and that one's ethnicity and perceived ethnic group membership has psychosocial and sociopolitical implications. When one's ethnic identity becomes more differentiated, it triggers a sense of confusion and ambivalence as the individual struggles to abandon a familiar identity and adopt a new one.

In the third stage, an ethnic group member progresses to develop an achieved ethnic identity, which corresponds to Marcia's (1980) identity achievement ego status. As a result of extensive exploration of the personal meaning of ethnicity, the person develops an appreciation of one's ethnicity and a commitment to that ethnic group. Rather than feeling confused and noncommittal, individuals come to terms with owning their ethnicity and resolving the confusion and ambivalence associated with their identities and ethnic group membership. Phinney (1990), however, noted that being clear and confident about one's ethnic identity does not necessarily imply a high degree of involvement and maintenance of one's ethnic customs.

The Impact of Majority/Minority Status on Ethnic Identity Development: Four Phases
of Ethnic Identity Conflicts

Smith (1991) contended that in a multicultural society with differential representation of visible racial and ethnic groups, members of both the majority (i.e., White Americans) and minority groups (e.g., Asian Americans, Chinese Americans, Filipino Americans, etc.) draw boundary lines to differentiate themselves from one another and to consolidate their own group membership. One of Smith's main tenets was that individuals' status as either minority or majority group members influences their ethnic identity development. Although we do not adhere to Smith's use of the term *ethnicity* to encompass race, we do agree with her notion that the minority status of one's culture (e.g., language, food, cultural customs, or values) can have an impact on one's ethnic identity. The acceptance or rejection of ethnic minority cultures by the majority group not only affects minority group members' racial identities, but also their ethnic identities, as individuals broaden, narrow, or crystallize their ethnic boundaries to determine who is in their ethnic group and the extent to which they want to identify with that group.

Smith postulated that the ethnic identification process involves four phases. Phase one is characterized by preoccupation with self or preservation of ethnic self-identity. Ethnic identity conflicts are triggered when ethnic contacts lead to the realization that group boundaries are defined in terms of majority and minority status. Ethnic contact may lead the minority group member to identify or avoid future contact with the majority group. Phase two is characterized by preoccupation with the ethnic group conflict. When an ethnic person feels rejected in his or her attempt to identify with the majority group, the ethnic person may feel anger, guilt, and remorse, and may retreat to his or her ethnic group as an identity reference group. The majority-minority boundary becomes clear and solidified in this phase. Phase three is characterized by attempts to resolve the ethnic identity conflicts. Minority group members who harbor resentment and mistrust may attempt to reconcile with or separate from the majority group, or may become marginalized when failing to identify with an ethnic reference group. In phase four, the person attempts to make sense of specific ethnic identity conflicts in light of other ethnic contact experiences. Rather than letting a particular ethnic identity conflict define the totality of ethnic contact experiences, the person attempts to take a more objective and optimistic approach to identifying his or her ethnic group as a positive reference group.

Relationship Between Ethnic and Racial Identities for Asian Americans

Researchers contend that individuals have both ethnic and racial identities and that the development of each is a continuous process. Theoretically, ethnic and racial identities develop side by side, but what is not clear is whether one tends to precede the other as well as the extent to which they influence one another. Identity theorists have acknowledged that the primacy of ethnic versus racial identity may vary depending on the group and the environment (Smith, 1991). For Asian Americans, ethnic or cultural aspects of identity may develop first, followed by the sense of oneself as a racial being. This may be especially true for first-generation immigrants, who make up over 60% of the Asian American population (Schmidley, 2001). Immigrants' acculturation needs, such as how much to retain or prevent the loss of their ethnic identity and cultural values and behavior, may take primacy over dealing with racism and discrimination. Moreover, Asian Americans as a group continue to face discrimination and racism on the one hand, but are simultaneously viewed as "model minorities" on the other; and these confusing racial messages may further contribute to racial identity taking a backseat to ethnic and cultural identity for many Asian Americans (Chen et al., 2006; Inman, 2006).

Even for American-born Asian Americans, a sense of ethnic awareness may precede any race-based identification. For example, Kim (1981) interviewed third-generation Japanese American women and noted that they all had some sense of being Japanese by the time they were 3 or 4 years old. Those whose families belonged to Japanese groups and participated in Japanese cultural activities had a positive sense of ethnic pride, whereas those who did not participate in these activities felt more neutral about being Japanese American. Kim found that after children entered elementary school, they began to experience prejudice and develop a sense that they were different. The realization that this prejudice and differentness was cued by their physical appearance marked the beginning of their awareness of race, particularly what it meant to be White and not White, as illustrated in the case study of Jenny. From this point on, ethnic identity and racial identity appear to develop simultaneously.

One common denominator that is thought to influence both ethnic and racial identity is one's minority/majority status (Smith, 1991; Sue & Sue, 2003). Coming to terms with one's identity as a minority member and in relation to the majority group is a central component of racial identity development (e.g., Helms, 1995) as well as ethnic identity development (e.g., Smith, 1991). Likewise, one's cultural heritage can serve to reinforce one's ethnic identity as well as his or her racial identity. For example, in the case of Michael, playing in the Japanese American basketball leagues was a cultural event for him and served as a way for him to express his Japanese American identity. At the same time, Michael may have taken pride in the fact that he was breaking racial stereotypes of Asian Americans as unathletic, thus asserting his racial identity as a not unathletic Asian American. The relationship between racial identity and ethnic identity is complex and not fully understood, and all of these complexities are embedded in the term *Asian American*.

To understand the relationship between racial and ethnic identities, one must consider the historical, contextual, and situational factors that influence the identity development process. The importance, or centrality, of one's ethnic and racial identities to one's overall sense of self may change over time, depending on one's stage of identity development. Nadal (2004) has suggested that there is a stage of identity development—*ethnocentric realization*—in which individuals reject their racial identities in favor of their ethnic identities. He proposed that this is especially true for members of doubly marginalized groups, such as Filipino Americans, who are oppressed by the dominant majority group, but are also marginalized within the racial minority group—Asian Americans—to which they are assigned. Nadal proposed that Filipino Americans feel marginalized and invisible because they do not have privileged status as "accepted" Asian Americans. This experience of being doubly marginalized is not limited to Filipino Americans, but is also pertinent to members of other groups, such as South Asian Americans (Chang & Yeh, 2003). These individuals may feel, for instance, that media portrayals of Asian Americans that focus primarily on East Asians do not include them and that the stereotype of the "model minority" does not apply to them. They may feel further excluded when their history and experiences are not included in the dialogue and literature (including the literature on Asian American racial and ethnic identities!) about Asian Americans or when social organizations that purport to represent all Asian Americans do not cater to them. Individuals in this stage reject being classified as Asian American and develop a strong sense of pride in their specific ethnic group (e.g., Filipino Americans) and advocate for the needs of that group.

In addition, the salience of an individual's ethnic and racial identities may also change, depending on the situational and relational context (e.g., Sellers et al., 1998; Yip, 2005). Individuals typically identify with more than one group, and whether or not a particular identity (e.g., Chinese, Chinese American, Asian American) is activated at a particular point in time depends on who else is around, where one is, and the meaning attached to that particular situation.

Nadal (2004) used the term *ethnocentric realization* to describe a stage of identity development in which members of marginalized Asian ethnic groups reject their Asian American racial identities in favor of their ethnic identities.

For example, an individual's ethnic identity as a Chinese American may be more salient when another Asian American asks the proverbial "what are you" question. However, that same individual's racial identity as an Asian American may be more salient if the same question were asked by a White person. It should be noted that salience is just one aspect of identity that can change, and researchers now theorize that identities themselves shift in response to changes in relational and cultural contexts (Yeh & Hwang, 2000).

Summary

Ethnic identity and racial identity are critical to understanding how Asian Americans develop a sense of who they are as they negotiate their ethnic heritage cultures, American culture, racial categorization, and racism. Racial identity refers to individuals' identification with and attitudes about their racial group, which is socially, politically, and historically constructed. Power and privilege in the United States are conferred on the basis of race, and *Asian American* is both a racial category and a sociopolitical identity that enables members of diverse Asian ethnic groups to achieve solidarity to combat oppression and racism. Ethnic identity is more concerned with a sense of belonging to and identification with one's ethnic group, which is typically defined by one's ancestors' national or cultural heritage group (e.g., Chinese, Filipino, Indian, Vietnamese, Korean, and Japanese Americans). Racial and ethnic identities consist of multiple components (e.g., internal, external) and vary along multiple dimensions (e.g., ideology, regard, centrality, salience) (Isajiw, 1990; Kwan & Sodowsky, 1997; Phinney, 1990; Sellers et al., 1998). Moreover, researchers generally believe that racial and ethnic identity development occurs as a progression through several distinct stages or statuses (e.g., Helms, 1995; Phinney, 1990). A summary of the main racial and ethnic identity models described in this chapter are provided in Table 7.1.

Racial identity and ethnic identity are important constructs not only because they are central to the identity development process, but also because they are intimately linked to adjustment and well-being for Asian Americans (e.g., Lee, 2003, 2005; Martinez & Dukes, 1997; Phinney & Alipuria, 1990; Yip & Fuligni, 2002). This relationship is complex, and research is only beginning to investigate what role racial and ethnic identities play in the pathway between stress and adjustment (e.g., Carter, Williams, Juby, & Buckley, 2005; Lee, 2005). One promising avenue of research examines how ethnic identity may serve to buffer individuals from the negative effects of racial discrimination (e.g., Lee, 2005; Yoo & Lee, 2005). Along similar lines, racial identity has been found to mediate the relationship between racial socialization and perceived racism (Alvarez et al., 2006). Future research should continue to investigate how ethnic and racial identities and their associated schemas are related to well-being and adjustment, as well as how the salience and centrality of these identities might influence those relations. In addition, because most of the extant research on racial and ethnic identity in the Asian American population has been conducted using East Asian samples, future research needs to address similarities as well as differences among diverse Asian ethnic groups in their racial and ethnic identity development processes.

Discussion Questions

1. What does being an Asian American mean to you?
2. Draw a timeline detailing key events in your own racial and ethnic identity development.

Table 7.1 Summary of Racial and Ethnic Identity Models

Phinney's (1990) Ethnic Identity Model	Helms's (1995) People of Color Racial Identity Model	Internal/external dimensions of identity (e.g., Isajiw, 1990)			
		Internal			External
		Dimensions of racial and ethnic identity (Sellers et al., 1998)			
		Ideology	Regard (for racial group)	Centrality	Salience	
Unexamined ethnic identity	Conformity	Idealize Whites	Positive or negative	Low	Variable	e.g., friendships with Whites
	Dissonance	Confusion about and search for the meaning of race/ethnicity in one's life	Ambivalence or confusion	Low	Variable	e.g., withdrawal from White friendships
Ethnic identity search	Immersion/emersion	Idealize own racial group; negative attitudes toward Whites	Positive	High	Variable, but generally high	e.g., friendships with Asian Americans
	Internalization	Self-definition; understand the meaning of race/ethnicity in one's life	Positive	High	Variable	e.g., friendships with Asian Americans and Whites
Achieved ethnic identity	Integrative awareness	Empathize with other oppressed groups; combat oppression	Positive	Moderate to high	Variable	e.g., social activism, friendships with members of other oppressed groups

Stages/statuses of ethnic and racial identity development

3. Which of the terms—*racial identity* or *ethnic identity*—is more meaningful for describing the identities of racial and ethnic group members in the United States? Which term is more meaningful for you?
4. At what point did you become aware of being similar to or different from other racial and ethnic groups?
5. What stages/statuses of identity development have you gone through, and what stage/status are you in now? What aspects of your thinking or behavior have exemplified each of those stages/statuses?

Case Study

Thus far, this chapter has focused on the key concepts of race, ethnicity, racial identity, and ethnic identity in understanding the experiences of Asian Americans. We now return to the case of Jenny to illustrate how identity is shaped by race and ethnicity and how racial and ethnic identities might influence the choices that an individual makes. The case study will also discuss how individuals' racial and ethnic identities can be used in therapy to more fully understand their problems.

Jenny, whose parents were both first-generation Korean immigrants, grew up in a predominantly White, working-class town and attended predominantly White schools during childhood. Throughout her school years, she became acutely aware, through incidents like the Coke episode in the first grade, that she was different, that being Korean or Asian was the source of this difference, and that this difference would often serve as the object of others' ridicule, taunts, and bullying. As a result, Jenny tried as best she could to fit in. She dressed, combed her hair, put on makeup, walked, and talked like all the popular White girls in school, and, although she felt proud to be Korean, she never openly talked about being Korean with her peers. In high school, she took pride in the fact that she did not fit the stereotypes of a "typical" Asian and actively tried to break those stereotypes. She was a cheerleader and vice-president of her senior class, dated the popular White "jocks," was not particularly good at math, and partied like a Hilton.

During Jenny's first year in college, she attended, for the first time in her life, a party sponsored by a Korean American club. She had fun there and met several other Korean Americans, who had also grown up in predominantly White towns, and with whom she felt a common bond. She participated in a few more of these parties and eventually joined the Korean Undergraduate Student Association (KUSA). By her sophomore year in college, she was an active member in the organization and attended all of its events as well as those of other Asian American organizations. Jenny's friendships with other Korean Americans and her participation in Korean American social and cultural activities gave her a sense of belonging and pride in being Korean American. She committed herself to learning more about Korean Americans, and took a couple of Korean language classes as well as an Asian American history class. Although she still felt good about not fitting into Asian American stereotypes, she no longer tried to break them. In fact, she was growing increasingly offended by stereotypes of Asian women as exotic and submissive.

During Jenny's junior year of college, she was walking home one night and crossed the street in front of an SUV that had stopped at a red light. The White female driver swore at Jenny as she walked in front of the SUV. When Jenny confronted her, the driver became increasingly belligerent and threatened to harm Jenny physically. Jenny and the driver had a loud and angry verbal confrontation in the middle of the street. Finally, as Jenny walked away, the driver called her a "Chink" and yelled, "You'll never be an American!" Following this incident, Jenny felt extremely "shook up," feared for her personal safety, and felt angry and agitated. A close friend of hers referred Jenny to the university counseling center.

In the discussion of Jenny's case that follows, a racially inclusive model of psychotherapy (Carter, 1995) will be used to examine the influences of race, culture, racial identity, and ethnic identity on the psychotherapeutic process. Therapists who conduct psychotherapy with racial minority group members like Jenny must understand their own racial and ethnic identities and how their identities might bias their perceptions of clients and their conceptualizations of clients' problems. In the case of Jenny, it would be beneficial for the therapist to have a working knowledge of racial and ethnic identity theories, and be able to consider Jenny's presenting problem within the context of her racial and ethnic identity development. Specifically, it appears that Jenny's dominant racial identity schemas might be immersion/emersion and, to a lesser extent, internalization and conformity. Jenny may still harbor feelings of anger and resentment toward Whites and blame them for the racism she suffered during her childhood. At the same time, Jenny may be struggling with having more objective views of White people that enable her to see both good and bad aspects of White individuals. Jenny's strides toward defining for herself what it means to be Korean American and Asian American, as evidenced by letting go of the need to break stereotypes, may also be threatened by the driver's racial epithets and taunting. The driver's slur that Jenny "will never be an American" may be especially hurtful because Jenny has spent so much of her life trying to be just that. Thus, her earlier conformity schema may be activated in her desire to prove that she is American, and this may conflict with her internalization schema to define for herself what it means to be American.

It is also important to understand how the interaction between the therapist's and client's racial identity statuses might influence the therapeutic process (Carter, 1995). If Jenny views this incident as a racist event, the therapist must be far enough along in his or her own racial identity development to be able to help Jenny process the event as a racist event. The therapist must also be aware of transference issues, that is, how Jenny perceives the therapist may influence how she presents herself and what she is willing to divulge. For example, if Jenny perceives the therapist as more Asian American and more advanced in terms of his or her own identity development, she may want to impress the therapist by intellectualizing about racism, and this may hinder the more therapeutic processing of her feelings evoked by the racist event. The therapist must also be aware of countertransference issues and what Jenny is "pulling" from the therapist. For example, a therapist responding to Jenny's transference reactions above may feel the need to mentor Jenny and help her progress in her racial and ethnic identity development. Trying to achieve this goal right away, however, may be counter to Jenny's most pressing and immediate needs—support and symptom relief following a traumatic experience. Thus, the therapist must be aware of his or her countertransference issues, and use them to help conceptualize Jenny's concerns and identify her needs.

Case Study Discussion Questions

For undergraduate students, please consider the following questions:

1. Do you see any parallels between your own racial and ethnic identity development and Jenny's?
2. How should Asian Americans respond to racist incidents like the one Jenny experienced during college? How would you have reacted?
3. How might Jenny's racial and ethnic identities have influenced her reactions to the driver? Her perceptions about the incident and the meaning she attaches to it?
4. To what extent is Jenny's problem a racial versus an ethnic identity "problem"?

For graduate students and/or beginning therapists, please consider the following questions:

1. How does your own racial and ethnic identity development influence your conceptualization of Jenny's case?
2. What might be important transference and countertransference issues for you to consider in working with Jenny?
3. What would you do to help Jenny emotionally process the incident with the White driver?

Key Terms

Achieved ethnic identity: The result of extensive exploration of the personal meaning of ethnicity, entailing an appreciation of one's ethnicity and a commitment to one's ethnic group.

Centrality: Determined by how large a role one's race or ethnicity plays in one's overall identity across time and over a wide range of situations.

Commitment: Another important task in ethnic identity development when one makes firm, unwavering decisions about one's identity and engages in activities to implement those decisions.

Conformity: Pre-encounter status of racial identity describing individuals who seek self-definition and self-esteem from Whites and feel no loyalty or obligation to person-of-color groups.

Dissonance: Encounter status of racial identity in which persons are confused about racial issues and their sense of belonging to either the majority group or the person-of-color group.

Ethnic identity: Consists of individuals' attachment to, sense of belonging to, and identification with members from their ethnic group as well as their ethnic culture.

Ethnic identity search: Immersion in activities and experiences that facilitate understanding of a personal meaning of ethnicity.

Ethnicity: Social categorization based on the culture of an individual's ancestors' national or heritage group.

Exploration: An important task in ethnic identity development in which one actively questions and "tries out" various aspects of ethnic identity.

External ethnic identity: Can be indicated by participation in ethnic activities and cultural practices including language usage, food preference, religious affiliation, observance of traditional customs and holidays, and dress.

Ideology: Attitudes and beliefs that one holds about race/racism or ethnicity.

Immersion/Emersion: Status of racial identity in which persons idealize their vision of persons-of-color, denigrate Whites, and define self and others primarily according to racial group.

Integrative awareness: Status of racial identity in which individuals feel a kinship with other members of other racial groups and other oppressed groups, and attempt to eliminate racism and other forms of oppression.

Internal ethnic identity: Encompasses a sense of attachment and a feeling of belonging that sustain group membership.

Internalization: Status of racial identity in which individuals use internal criteria for their self-definition and practice racial acceptance and tolerance for their own person-of-color groups as well as Whites.

Race: A sociohistorical concept given meaning by social, economic, and political forces.

Racial identity: An individual's identification with his or her societally designated racial group.

Regard: How one feels about being a member of a racial or ethnic group as well as perceptions about how others view that racial or ethnic group.

Salience: The extent to which an individual's race or ethnicity is perceived to be relevant or conspicuous at a particular time and place.

Unexamined ethnic identity: Characterized by a lack of concern and/or a lack of thought about one's ethnic identity.

For Further Learning and Suggested Readings

Books

Chan, J. (2001). *Chinese American masculinities: From Fu Manchu to Bruce Lee*. Routledge.

Lee, R. (1999). *Orientals: Asian Americans in popular culture*. Philadelphia: Temple University Press.

Liu, E. (1998). *The accidental Asian: Notes of a native speaker*. New York: Vintage Books.

Min, P.G., & Kim, R. (1999). *Struggle for ethnic identity: Narratives by Asian American professionals.* Walnut Creek, CA: Altamira Press.

Min, P.G. (2002). *The second generation: ethnic identity among Asian Americans* (pp. 129–152). Walnut Creek, CA: Altamira Press.

Root, M. P. P. (1996). *The multiracial experience: Racial borders as the new frontier.* Thousand Oaks, CA: Sage.

Takaki, R. (1998). *A history of Asian Americans: Strangers from a different shore.* Boston: Little, Brown and Company.

Uba, L. (2002). *A postmodern psychology of Asian Americans.* Albany, NY: State University of New York Press.

Zia, H. (2000). *Asian American dreams: The emergence of an American people.* New York: Farrar Straus Giroux.

Movies

American Sons (2008)
Bend It Like Beckham (2002)
Better Luck Tomorrow (2002)
Double Happiness (1994)
Pushing Hands (1992)
Who Killed Vincent Chin? (1987)

Web Sites

Asian Avenue: http://www.asianavenue.com
Digital History: http://www.digitalhistory.uh.edu/asian_voices/asian_voices.cfm
IMDiversity: http://www.imdiversity.com/villages/asian/village_asian_american.asp
Model Minority—A Guide to Asian American Empowerment: http://modelminority.com/index.html
Slip of the Tongue—a short film from the Media That Matters Film Festival: http://www.mediathatmattersfest.org./6/index.php?id=1
U.S. Asians: http://us_asians.tripod.com/new.html

References

Alvarez, A. N., Juang, L., & Liang, C. T. H. (2006). Asian Americans and racism: When bad things happen to "model minorities." *Cultural Diversity and Ethnic Minority Psychology, 12*, 477–492.

Atkinson, D. R., Morten, G., & Sue, D. W. (1989). A minority identity development model. In D. R. Atkinson, G. Morten, & D. W. Sue (Eds.), *Counseling American minorities* (pp. 35–52). Dubuque, IA: W.C. Brown.

Berry, J. W., Poortinga, Y. H., Segall, M. H., & Dasen, P. R. (1992). *Cross-racial psychology. Research and applications.* New York: Cambridge University Press.

Carter, R. T. (1995). *The influence of race and racial identity in psychotherapy: Toward a racially inclusive model.* New York: John Wiley & Sons.

Carter, R. T. (1996). Exploring the complexity of racial identity attitude measures. In G. R. Sodowsky & J. C. Impara (Eds.), *Multicultural assessment in counseling and clinical psychology* (pp. 193–223). Lincoln, NE: Buros Institute of Mental Measurements.

Carter, R. T., Helms, J. E., & Juby, H. L. (2004). The relationship between racism and racial identity for White Americans: A profile analysis. *Multicultural Counseling and Development, 32*, 2–17.

Carter, R. T., Williams, B., Juby, H. L., & Buckley, T. R. (2005). Racial identity as mediator of the relationship between gender role conflict and severity of psychological symptoms in Black, Latino, and Asian men. *Sex Roles, 53*, 473–486.

Cavalli-Sforza, L. L. (2000). *Genes, peoples, and languages.* New York: North Point.

Chang, T., Tracey, T., & Moore, T. (2005). The structure of Asian American acculturation: An examination of prototypes. *Self and Identity, 4*, 25–43.

Chang, T., & Yeh, C. J. (2003). Using On-line Groups to Provide Support to Asian American Men: Racial, Cultural, Gender, and Treatment Issues. *Professional Psychology: Research and Practice, 34*, 634–643.

Chen, G. A., LePhuoc, P., Guzman, M. R., Rude, S. S., & Dodd, B. G. (2006). Exploring Asian American racial identity. *Cultural Diversity and Ethnic Minority Psychology, 12,* 461–476.

Cross, W. E., Jr. (1971). Negro-to-Black conversion experience: Toward a psychology of Black liberation. *Black World, 20,* 13–27.

Cross, W. E., Jr. (1995). The psychology of Nigrescence: Revising the Cross model. In J. G. Ponterotto, J. M. Casas, L. A. Suzuki, & C. M. Alexander (Eds.), *Handbook of multicultural counseling* (pp. 181–198). Thousand Oaks, CA: Sage.

Erikson, E. (1968). *Identity: Youth and crisis.* New York: Norton.

Esperitu, Y. L. (1992). *Asian American panethnicity: Bridging institutions and identities.* Philadelphia: Temple University Press.

Helms, J. E. (1994). The conceptualization of racial identity and other "racial" constructs. In E. J. Trickett, R. J. Watts, & D. Birman (Eds.), *Human diversity: Perspectives on people in context* (pp. 285–311). San Francisco, CA: Jossey-Bass.

Helms, J. E. (1995). An update of Helms's white and people of color racial identity models. In J. G. Ponterotto, J. M. Casas, L. A. Suzuki, & C. M. Alexander (Eds.), *Handbook of multicultural counseling* (pp. 181–198). Thousand Oaks, CA: Sage.

Helms, J. E., & Cook, D. (1999). *Using race and culture in counseling and psychotherapy.* Boston: Allyn and Bacon.

Helms, J. E., & Talleyrand, R. M. (1997). Race is not ethnicity. *American Psychologist, 52,* 1246–1247.

Ibrahim, F., Ohnishi, H., & Sandhu, D. S. (1997). Asian American identity development: A culture specific model for South Asian Americans. *Journal of Multicultural Counseling and Development, 25,* 34–50.

Inman, A. G. (2006). South Asian women: Identities and conflicts. *Cultural Diversity and Ethnic Minority Psychology, 12,* 306–319.

Isajiw, W. W. (1990). Ethnic-identity retention. In R. Breton, W.W. Isajiw, W. E. Kalbach, & J. G. Reitz (Eds.), *Ethnic identity and equality* (pp. 34–91). Toronto: University of Toronto Press.

Kim, J. (1981). Processes of Asian American identity development: A study of Japanese American women's perceptions of their struggle to achieve positive identities as Americans of Asian ancestry. *Dissertation Abstracts International, 42*(4-A), 1551. (UMI No. 8118010)

Kwan, K.-L. K. (2005). Racial salience: Conceptual dimensions and implications for racial identity development. In R. Carter (Ed.), *Handbook of racial-cultural psychology* (pp. 115–131). New York: John Wiley.

Kwan, K.-L. K., & Sodowsky, G. R. (1997). Internal and external ethnic identity and their correlates: A study of Chinese American immigrants. *Journal of Multicultural Counseling and Development, 25,* 51–67.

Landrine, H., & Klonoff, E.A. (1996). *African American acculturation: Deconstructing race and reviving culture.* Thousand Oaks: Sage.

Lee, R. M. (2003). Do ethnic identity and other-group orientation protect against discrimination for Asian Americans? *Journal of Counseling Psychology, 50,* 133–141.

Lee, R. M. (2005). Resilience against discrimination: Ethnic identity and other-group orientation as protective factors for Korean Americans. *Journal of Counseling Psychology, 52,* 36–44.

Liu, E. (1998). *The accidental Asian: Notes of a native speaker.* New York: Vintage Books.

Marcia, J. (1980). Identity in adolescence. In J. Adelson (Ed.), *Handbook of adolescent psychology* (pp. 159–187). New York: Wiley.

Martinez, R. O., & Dukes, R. L. (1997). The effects of ethnic identity, ethnicity, and gender on adolescent well-being. *Journal of Youth and Adolescence, 26,* 503–516.

Nadal, K. L. (2004). Filipino American identity development model. *Multicultural Counseling and Development, 32,* 45–62.

Omi, M., & Winant, H. (1994). *Racial formation in the United States: From the 1960s to the 1990s* (2nd ed.). New York: Routledge.

Parham, T. A. (1989). Cycles of psychological nigrescence. *Counseling Psychologist, 17,* 187–226.

Phinney, J. S. (1989). Stages of ethnic identity development in minority group adolescents. *Journal of Early Adolescence, 9,* 34–49.

Phinney, J. S. (1990). Ethnic identity in adolescents and adults: Review of research. *Psychological Bulletin, 108,* 499–514.

Phinney, J. S., & Alipuria, L. (1990). Ethnic identity in college students from four ethnic groups. *Journal of Adolescence, 13,* 171–183.

Schaefer, R. T. (2000). *Racial and ethnic groups* (8th ed.). Upper Saddle River, NJ: Prentice Hall.

Schmidley, A. D. (2001). *Profile of the foreign-born population in the United States: 2000* [Electronic version] (U.S. Census Bureau, Current Population Reports, Series P23-206). Washington, DC: U.S. Government Printing Office.

Sellers, R. M., Smith, M., Shelton, J. N., Rowley, S. J., & Chavous, T. M. (1998). Multidimensional model of racial identity: A reconceptualization of African American racial identity. *Personality and Social Psychology Review, 2,* 18–39.

Smedley, A. (1999). *Race in North America: Origin and evolution of a worldview* (2nd ed.). Boulder, CO: Westview Press.

Smith, E. J. (1991). Ethnic identity development: Toward the development of a theory within the context of majority/minority status. *Journal of Counseling and Development, 70,* 181–188.

Sodowsky, G. R., Kwan, K.-L., & Pannu, R. (1995). Ethnic identity of Asians in the United States: Conceptualization and illustrations. In J. Ponterotto, M. Casas, L. Suzuki, & C. Alexander (Eds.), *Handbook of multicultural counseling* (pp. 123–154). Newbury Park, CA: Sage.

Sue, D. W., & Sue, D. (2003). *Counseling the culturally diverse: Theory and practice* (4th ed.). New York: John Wiley & Sons.

Tajfel, H., & Turner, J. (1986). The social identity theory of intergroup behavior. In S. Worchel & W. G. Austin (Eds.), *Psychology of intergroup relations.* Chicago: Nelson Hall.

Takaki, R. (1998). *A history of Asian Americans: Strangers from a different shore.* Boston: Little, Brown and Company.

Uba, L. (2002). *A postmodern psychology of Asian Americans: Creating knowledge of a racial minority.* Albany, NY: State University of New York Press.

Worrell, F. C., Vandiver, B. J., Schaefer, B. A., Cross, W. E., Jr., & Fhagen-Smith, P. E. (2006). Generalizing Nigrescence profiles: Cluster analysis of Cross Racial Identity Scale (CRIS) scores in three independent samples. *The Counseling Psychologist, 34,* 519–547.

Yeh, C. J., & Hwang, M. Y. (2000). Interdependence in ethnic identity and self: Implications for theory and practice. *Journal of Counseling and Development, 78,* 420–429.

Yip, T. (2005). Sources of situational variation in ethnic identity and psychological well-being: A palm pilot study of Chinese American students. *Personality and Social Psychology Bulletin, 31,* 1603–1616.

Yip, T., & Fuligni, A. J. (2002). Daily variation in ethnic identity, ethnic behaviors, and psychological well-being among American adolescents of Chinese descent. *Child Development, 73,* 1557–1572.

Yoo, H. C., & Lee, R. M. (2005). Ethnic identity and approach-type coping as moderators of the racial discrimination/well-being relation in Asian Americans. *Journal of Counseling Psychology, 52,* 497–506.

8
Religion and Spirituality

GENE G. ANO, ELIZABETH S. MATHEW, and MARY A. FUKUYAMA

OUTLINE OF CHAPTER

Case Synopsis

Jason, a 22-year-old Thai American student in his 4th year of college, was having considerable difficulty coping during the breakup with his ex-girlfriend. The couple dated for about 4 years and had planned on getting married. However, religious differences eventually tore the couple apart. Whereas Jason identified as Buddhist, his ex-girlfriend identified as a born-again Christian. Ironically, after the couple broke up, Jason had a conversion experience and thought this would help them get back together. But his ex-girlfriend had moved on. Jason felt sad, lonely, and depressed. Although he found tremendous comfort in his new spiritual identity and his relationship with God, he still had difficulty moving on with his life. Jason considered seeking professional help, but he was afraid that his therapist would either pathologize his newfound spiritual identity or minimize the importance of **religion** and **spirituality** in his life.

Introduction

Religion and spirituality are central to the Asian American experience. For example, about two-thirds of Asian Americans report that religion plays a very important role in their lives; the largest pan–Asian American movement is religious; Asian Americans more readily identify with a religion than a political party; the largest Asian American college and university student organizations are religious; and tens of thousands of Asian Americans have been persecuted and tortured as a result of their faith (Carnes & Yang, 2004). Despite the importance of religion and spirituality for Asian Americans, very little research has examined the nature, prevalence, and implications of their religious and spiritual beliefs and practices. As P. Scott Richards and Allen Bergin (2000) put it, "a lack of research on minority groups has plagued the mental health professions and in the area of religion the situation is no better" (p. 22). However, the picture is beginning to change. A small but growing body of literature has begun to examine Asian American religion and spirituality. The purpose of this chapter is to summarize some of this literature in order to provide a framework for understanding religion and spirituality within the context of Asian American psychology.

Definitions of Religion and Spirituality

In an attempt to clarify the constructs of religion and spirituality, Peter Hill and his colleagues (2000) provided some definitional criteria for the terms. While *religion* and *spirituality* both refer to thoughts, feelings, experiences, and behaviors that arise from a search for the sacred, religion involves "the means and methods (e.g., rituals or prescribed behaviors) of the search that receive validation and support from within an identifiable group of people" (p. 66). The **sacred** refers to those things that are holy, "set apart," transcendent, and of ultimate value to a person. According to these criteria, religion is defined as a broad construct that may involve organizational as well as individual beliefs, practices, and expressions that reflect a search for significance in ways related to the sacred.

In contrast, *spirituality* is defined as personal (rather than institutional) quests for the sacred that may or may not be religious. That is, one could be spiritual without considering themselves religious. However, religion assumes spirituality because spirituality is its most central function (Pargament, 1999). Thus, religion and spirituality as defined in this chapter are inclusive and overlapping, despite the apparent differences between the two terms. Both are multifaceted constructs, and both are centered around the sacred. Therefore, the terms *religion* and *spirituality* are used interchangeably throughout this chapter.

Asian American Religious Traditions

It is difficult to determine precise demographic information for Asian American religious affiliations due to the dearth of research and statistical data available. However, from 2000 to 2001, the Pilot National Asian American Political Survey (PNAAPS), one of the most comprehensive surveys of Asian American religious and political attitudes, attempted to clarify the religious and political affiliations of Asian Americans in the United States. According to the results of this survey, the vast majority (72%) of Asian Americans identify with a religious tradition. More specifically, 46% identified as Christian (including Catholicism); 15% identified as Buddhist; 6%

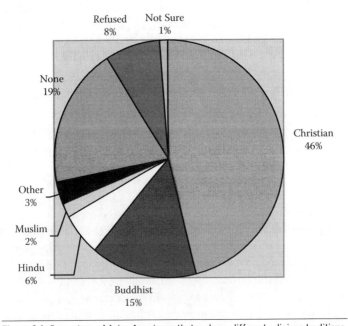

Figure 8.1 Percentage of Asian Americans that endorse different religious traditions.

identified as Hindu; 2% identified as Muslim; 3% endorsed "Other" religious affiliations; 19% endorsed "None"; 8% refused, and 1% endorsed "Not Sure" (Lien & Carnes, 2004). These statistics are summarized in Figure 8.1.

Although religious affiliation was not broken down among specific groups of Asian Americans, according to Siang-Yang Tan and Natalie Dong (2000), Korean Americans typically identify as Christian; Filipino Americans affiliate with Catholicism; Chinese Americans may endorse **Buddhism, Christianity,** or ancestor worship; Japanese Americans may follow Shintoism, Buddhism, or Christianity; Asian Indians and other Southeast Asians are likely to follow **Hinduism,** Buddhism, **Islam,** or Animism; and Vietnamese Americans are likely to affiliate with Buddhism or Christianity. A brief overview of some of these and other religious traditions relevant to Asian Americans is now presented, beginning with the oldest world religions (Hinduism and Buddhism), highlighting monotheistic traditions (Christianity and Islam), and including some relatively new religious movements (**Sikhism**).

Hinduism

Hinduism is one of the most ancient religions on earth and is often referred to as the *Santana Dharma*, meaning "ancient and eternal moral duty." Hinduism does not consist of an organized framework of doctrines. There is a great deal of diversity and flexibility within Hinduism. Nevertheless, certain principles and practices distinguish the Hindu tradition. Central to the Hindu belief system are the concepts of *atman*, the soul in all beings; *samsara*, the continuous flow of birth, death, and rebirth as the atman transmigrates; *dharma*, devotion or duty; and *karma*, the belief that all actions have consequences that result in either a "good" rebirth or a "bad" rebirth (Firth, 2005).

Photo of Krishna.

Hinduism states that the Universe and Knowledge were created simultaneously by Brahma, with no beginning or end (Hanna & Green, 2004). Hindus believe that there is one supreme God, Brahma, which manifests its self in different ways based on the needs of different people, resulting in thousands of divine images or deities. Some Hindu families may have traditions that worship only one of these deities, such as Krishna. However, ultimately, Brahma is the highest spiritual authority in Hinduism (Firth, 2005). Hindus believe that the goal of life is to reach Brahma (the ultimate reality) and escape the birth and death cycle (Hanna & Green, 2004). Relationships (to people and the universe) are essential to Hindu spirituality. As one East Indian participant in a qualitative focus group study of multicultural spiritual expressions put it, "Spirituality is a state of awareness where one feels connection to all and entails a mind/body practice/discipline that is shaped by culture and tradition and enables transcendence of ego (and the material plane) and connection to Ultimacy/Mystery" (Fukuyama et al., 2004, p. 6).

Implications for Working with Asian American Hindus   According to Anu Sharma (2000), certain Hindu principles have implications for psychological treatment. For example, belief in samsara, which involves the notion of reincarnation, can provide hope for a better life to come. Belief in karma implies a belief in personal responsibility. Because moral actions result in "good" consequences, Hindu clients may be empowered to make positive changes in their present lives and lives to come. In fact, research has shown that the karmic doctrine can provide individuals with a sense of control during stressful circumstances (Dalal & Pande, 1988). The concept of dharma (devotion or duty) may also be used therapeutically to further encourage adaptive change and has implications for psychological well-being. For example, Nalini Tarakeshwar and her colleagues (2003) found that Hindus who reported more use of the path of ethical action also experienced greater life satisfaction, greater marital satisfaction, and a less depressed mood.

Photo of Shri Swaminarayan Mandir, London, the largest Hindu temple outside India.

Buddhism

Buddhism was founded after the life and teachings of Siddhartha Gautama who lived in the 6th century BC near the border of Nepal and India. Buddhism is a philosophy of enlightenment. The emphasis is upon developing consciousness through realization of the Four Noble Truths, which are: (a) suffering is an inevitable part of life, (b) the cycle of rebirth is based on craving or desire or attachment, (c) when craving is overcome one attains peace, and (d) the way to achieve this peace is by following the Eightfold Path. The Eightfold Path is the prescription for becoming free of egocentrism and selfishness, through practices that develop intuitive wisdom, moral purity, and concentration. These eight steps can be summarized by the following: (a) right views or understanding, (b) right purpose or aspiration, (c) right speech, (d) right conduct, (e) right means of livelihood or vocation, (f) right effort, (g) right kind of awareness or mind control, and (h) right concentration or meditation (Boisselier, 1994). The result of realizing one's Buddha nature is compassion, selfless giving, wisdom, and transcendence, and ultimately, achieving *nirvana*, a state that transcends the cycle of death and rebirth.

The teachings of Buddhism were originally passed along orally for several centuries and then written in what are called the *Sutras*. Different interpretations of Buddhism have been brought to North America through Japanese, Chinese, Korean, Vietnamese, and Tibetan teachers. There are numerous variations in Buddhist practice, but they all share in the premise that the way to enlightenment is through the Three Jewels: the *Buddha*, the *Dharma* (teachings), and the *Sangha* (community).

Implications for Working with Asian American Buddhists   Because Buddhism emphasizes consciousness and attention to the workings of the mind, it is particularly compatible with Western psychology. According to Fred Hanna and Alan Green (2004), over 2,500 years ago, Buddhist monks were practicing skills that are today considered some of modern psychology's most advanced techniques, such as systematic desensitization, flooding, modifying beliefs, thought stopping, self-monitoring, and imagery techniques. One particular Buddhist spiritual discipline,

Photo of the Big Buddha structure in Hong Kong.

Photo of some Buddhist monks taking a break from the Dharma.

mindfulness meditation, has become quite popular in the treatment of stress-related physical symptoms and heart disease. Jon Kabat-Zinn (1990) and his colleague, Saki Santorelli (2000), have researched the positive effects of meditation practices for coping with stress. Furthermore, Acceptance and Commitment Therapy (ACT), a relatively novel treatment method that has been used to treat a variety of problems, is heavily influenced by Buddhist principles (Hayes, Strosahl, & Wilson, 2003).

Photo of an impressive Buddhist temple.

Christianity

Christianity began approximately 2,000 years ago and was founded on the life and teachings of Jesus, who originated from the Hebrew tradition in what is now called Israel or Palestine (Guthrie, 1993). Despite tremendous diversity within Christianity, which has resulted in various denominational differences, a few common themes emerge. Christians believe in one God, the Holy Trinity, eternally existent in three personas (Father or Creator, Son or Redeemer, and Holy Spirit or Sustainer). Christianity teaches that the universe was created by God and humanity is created in God's image. However, humanity is inherently sinful by nature and therefore separated from God. Christians believe that God has provided a means to establish a relationship with humanity through Jesus Christ. Jesus is viewed as fully human and fully divine. While on earth, Jesus spent time preaching acceptance and showing compassion to others. Christians believe that they must model God's behavior on earth by following Jesus's teachings and obeying the Ten Commandments. His death by crucifixion and resurrection from the dead represent for believers salvation from sin, death, and evil. Christianity also states that Jesus Christ will come back to earth and all those who believe will spend eternity in heaven. Christians view the *Bible* as Holy Scripture and a guide to everyday life (Guthrie, 1993).

Two sacred practices are typically found in most churches: *baptism* and *Eucharist or holy communion*. Baptism is a ritual of initiation when members join a Christian faith group, or in some traditions children are baptized as a sign of the family and community's commitment to raise the child in the church. It typically involves anointment or immersion in water. Communion is a ritual sharing of bread and wine (or grape juice) as a form of remembering Jesus's suffering and death.

Implications for Working with Asian American Christians   Asian American Christians, specifically those who immigrate, likely experience a shift from minority to majority religious status depending on where they settle in the United States. Yet, there are unique challenges with being an ethnic minority person who strongly identifies with a particular aspect of the majority culture. For example, identification with the majority religious perspective may complicate an Asian American Christian's cultural identity development. Consider the following testimony of

Photo from a cemetery showing a statue of Jesus.

Photo of some wine and bread that are used as symbols for the ritual of communion.

one Asian Indian Christian female: "My family can trace its Christian heritage to 2,000 years ago. I belong to the Mar Thoma Church—we're St. Thomas Christians from India. But, when I try to join the Christian organizations on campus, they're mostly White. They treat me like a 'new convert.' When I try to join in on the Indian Student Organization meetings—they're totally based on Hindu rituals. I can't relate. I just don't fit in" (personal reflection of an Asian Indian Christian female).

Such struggles are not uncommon for Asian American Christians. However, working collaboratively with God to solve one's problems, leaning upon the support of a congregation or church, or believing that there is a greater purpose for one's struggles are all spiritual resources that can be integrated into treatment in a culturally competent manner to promote healing and growth. In fact, Gene Ano and Erin Vasconcelles (2005) demonstrated that such practices are linked with a number of positive psychological outcomes.

Islam

Islam, which in Arabic means "peace" or "submission to the will of God" was founded by the Prophet Mohammad (Peace be upon him) around 600 CE in what is now known as Saudi Arabia.

Pages from the Qur'an, the Muslim Holy Scriptures.

Photo of some Muslims praying in a mosque.

The Prophet Mohammad, while meditating in the mountains, received the word of God from the Angel Gabriel. The Prophet Mohammad was illiterate, so he memorized the verses and they were later written down to form the Qur'an (Koran), the Islamic Holy Scriptures.

Central beliefs of Islam include the unity of God and all things, the recognition of Mohammad as prophet, the innate goodness of human beings, the importance of a community of faith, and the importance of living a devout and righteous life to achieve peace and harmony (Altareb, 1996). Islam is based on five pillars or fundamental obligations: faith, prayer, charity, fasting, and a pilgrimage to Mecca. Islam is found among immigrant groups from Pakistan, India, Indonesia, the Philippines, the Middle East, and Africa. The *Book of Hadith* consists of rules for living a righteous life based on guidance from the Prophet, called the *Sunna*.

Implications for Working with Asian American Muslims Islamic teachings are quite strict in contrast with U.S. American materialism and hedonism. For example, young women are not allowed to date, nor expose their bodies in public, such as by wearing sleeveless blouses. Tensions may exist between generations about what are appropriate behaviors, especially for families with adolescents growing up under the influence of American pop culture. For example, the pressures that college students face to date and party (i.e., drink alcohol and have sex) may go against Islamic teachings. Because of the differences between conservative Islamic teachings and liberal American values, Zari Hedayat-Diba (2000) stated that "most Muslims' view of the mental health field is negative, and consequently utilization of mental health services is unusual or rare" (p. 301). Still, depending upon education level and degree of acculturation, some Asian American Muslims may seek treatment. When working with Muslim clients, Fred Hanna and Alan Green (2004) assert that it is crucial for counselors to affirm Muslim clients' spiritual identities by promoting Islamic spiritual values that are consistent with Western psychology, such as benevolence, forgiveness, and personal development.

Sikhism

Sikhism was founded in northern India during the 15th century CE by Guru Nanak. Today, Sikhism is known as the fifth largest organized world religion, claiming approximately 20 million followers worldwide with about 85% to 90% of those living in the Indian state of Punjab in Asia (Richards & Bergin, 1997). There are approximately 490,000 Sikhs in North America, most of which are of South Asian descent.

Photo of the Golden Temple in Amritsar, India.

Sikhs believe in a genderless, formless, immortal, loving, and omnipotent God (Chilana, 2005). They believe that human beings were created by God and are free to choose between good and evil to show devotion to God by developing love, faith, and humility. Through dependence on God, people can achieve spiritual growth and overcome their ego and pride. Sikhs believe that five evil passions serve as the foundation for immoral behavior: lust, anger, covetousness, attachment to worldly things, and pride (Richards & Bergin, 1997). Instructions for moral living are found in the Sikh Holy Scriptures, known as the *Sri Guru Granth Sahib*. Sikhs refer to their places of worship as *gurdwaras*. The most sacred location for Sikhs is the Harimandar Sahib, or the Golden Temple, in Amritsar, India (Chilana, 2005).

Implications for Working with Asian American Sikhs   Due to their outward physical symbols of religious identity, Sikhs have been targeted for discriminatory practices and hate crimes throughout United States history. In California in 1994, three Sikh siblings were suspended for wearing a kirpan to school because it looked like a knife. Subsequently, the family sued the school district with the support of the ACLU on the basis that their right to exercise their religion had been violated. Although the case was won on appeal, the concern of religious minority groups to practice their religion remains a salient and potent issue (Lal, 1996). For example, the *New York Times,* on July 29, 2004, reported, "Amric Singh Rathour and Jasjit Singh Jaggi, two Sikhs in New York City who were told they could not wear turbans on the job as traffic enforcement agents, will be reinstated and allowed to wear their turbans in 2004" (Barron, 2004, p. B3). In light of such examples, much of the psychological distress experienced by Asian American Sikhs may be a result of racial prejudice and systematic discrimination. Therefore, when working with Asian American Sikhs, an advocacy approach that promotes social justice may be more warranted. However, within an individual treatment context, it may still be helpful to affirm one's spiritual identity and promote spiritual growth by encouraging the pursuit of virtue, a healthy reliance upon God, and the support of a religious community. As one Asian American Sikh client receiving treatment for drinking problems put it, "There was a void in my life which was filled up with drink, going to the temple fills that void" (Morjaria & Orford, 2002, p. 244).

Spirituality and Psychological Functioning

A significant body of research has investigated the relationship between spirituality and psychological functioning. Although this research has not exclusively focused on Asian Americans, the findings from this literature can be applied to Asian Americans because many of the studies have included samples (albeit small) of Asian Americans. Furthermore, one particular study demonstrated that Asian Americans rely more on spirituality to cope than Caucasian Americans do (Bjorck, Cuthbertson, Thurman, & Lee, 2001). In general, the findings from this literature suggest that spirituality typically has beneficial consequences for mental health. For example, in a recent meta-analytic review of the literature, more adaptive expressions of spirituality, such as the belief in a benevolent God, working collaboratively with God to solve one's problems, and seeking spiritual support from one's congregation, were associated with higher levels of positive affect, emotional well-being, life satisfaction, spiritual and stress-related growth, optimism, happiness, self-esteem, purpose in life, quality of life, resilience, and hope (Ano & Vasconcelles, 2005).

In reviewing this literature, Richards and Bergin (1997) offered some explanations for the positive influence of spirituality on health. First, spirituality may provide individuals with a secure sense of identity, which can make them more resilient to anxiety and stress. Second, spirituality provides a sense of meaning and purpose. As one Filipino American Christian stated, "My faith means everything to me. It defines who I am. Without it, life would be meaningless. But because of my faith, I know there is a greater purpose to the struggles I go through." Third, certain spiritual beliefs and practices may engender positive emotions of hope, faith, and optimism. Fourth, involvement in a religious community fosters a sense of belonging and provides access to social support and other valuable resources. Fifth, spiritual practices, such as prayer, meditation, and worship may produce inner experiences of peace and a sense of connectedness with a higher power, even if there is no higher power. Finally, many spiritual belief systems encourage lifestyles and behavioral habits that are healthy in and of themselves, such as an inner sense of responsibility and self-control. For example, one South Asian Hindu man stated, "It says in our holy book that we shouldn't drink, so we shouldn't be drinking anyway" (Morjaria & Orford, 2002, p. 242).

Despite the positive influences of spirituality on psychological functioning, certain forms of spiritual expression, such as spiritual struggles, may be a significant source of burden or distress. Examples of spiritual struggles include struggles with the Divine (e.g., anger at God, difficulty forgiving God, feelings of punishment, alienation, or abandonment by God), interpersonal spiritual struggles (e.g., conflicts and rifts with one's religious community), and intrapsychic spiritual struggles (e.g., spiritual doubts, fear, or guilt). Research has shown that such spiritual struggles are associated with various negative consequences, such as higher levels of anxiety, depression, hopelessness, distress, negative affect, callousness, hostility, social dysfunction, spiritual injury, and suicidality (Ano & Vasconcelles, 2005). For Asian Americans, another struggle may ensue when individuals experience conflict between their spiritual and ethnic identities. As one Chinese woman said, "sometime after I became a Christian, I wondered if Jesus was White and what he would think of Chinese. I felt uncomfortable being in a White church with these thoughts. Later, I started attending a Chinese Christian church, where I felt more at home."

Religion, Immigration, and Cultural Values

Religion and spirituality do not take place in a vacuum. Asian Americans carry out their religious beliefs and practices within the broader context of their lives. Thus, religion and spirituality are intricately interwoven with other aspects of Asian Americans' identities and life experiences. As Siang-Yang Tan and Natalie Dong (2000) put it, "traditional social values, acculturation, and religious beliefs and practices are closely interwoven, making it difficult to distinguish clearly among them" (p. 421). However, it is possible to examine how religion and spirituality influence and are reciprocally influenced by other aspects of the Asian American experience.

Immigration can be a very challenging and even traumatizing experience for many Asians, who either come to the United States in hopes of pursuing a better life for their family or seek refuge from political atrocities in their country of origin. Asian immigrants are faced with a variety of challenges, such as language barriers, value conflicts, identity confusion, intergenerational conflicts within the family, socioeconomic difficulties, and so on (see Chapter 1 of this text for further information). In such circumstances, spirituality can serve as a considerable resource, providing meaning, strength, inspiration, hope, a sense of community, social support, and even financial assistance. Furthermore, as strangers in a foreign land who are faced with the challenge of redefining their identities, religion provides a context for Asian Americans to renegotiate their boundaries and either practice incorporation or differentiation. "Asian Americans use religious conversations and religious spaces to face questions about their relation to their country of origin, personal and collective identities, and the organization of American society and culture" (Carnes & Yang, 2004, p. 3).

Although religion may be used to cope with the challenges of immigration, it may also be reciprocally impacted by assimilation. For example, traditional Eastern religious beliefs and practices may be challenged or even given up as Asian American immigrants are exposed to the religious beliefs, practices, symbols, and rhetoric of the mainstream culture. For Asian American immigrants who are faced with prejudice, racism, and discrimination, religious conversion may provide a sense of refuge and facilitate processes of assimilation and acculturation, which may explain why the majority of Asian Americans in the United States identify as Christian. However, it is important not to assume that Asian American immigrants adopt Christianity merely as a way to be accepted by the majority culture. Indeed, for some Asian American immigrants, Christianity is their religion of choice. For example, Tony Carnes and Fenggang Yang (2004) noted that some Asian Christians, particularly Koreans, actually immigrate to the United States as a means of seeking validation for their religious identity.

Religious beliefs and practices are also intricately interwoven with traditional Asian cultural values. Most East Asian countries are influenced by Buddhism, Confucianism, and Taoism that emphasize such traits as silence, nonconfrontation, moderation in behavior, self-control, patience, humility, and simplicity (Sodowsky, Kwan, & Pannu, 1995; Uba, 1994). These philosophies also value filial piety, restraint in emotional expression, respect for authority and elders, well-defined social roles and expectations, fatalism, inconspicuousness, conformity to norms, and the centrality of family relationships and responsibilities (Kim, Atkinson, & Yang, 1999). In addition, according to Siang-Yang Tan and Natalie Dong (2000), belief in spirits and the supernatural is consistent with a Christian worldview and Buddhist philosophies emphasize acceptance of suffering and the practice of self-restraint and control over one's emotions (see Chapter 4 of this text for more information on Asian American cultural values). In turn, traditional Asian cultural values also influence Asian American religious expressions as well, even when Asian Americans adopt Westernized Christian beliefs. As Tony Carnes and Fenggang Yang (2004) put it, "most Asian religious organizations bring a formalized, traditional, hierarchical, group-oriented culture with them. The emphasis is on religion as a doing—rather than a believing—of ritual, worship attendance, charity, and age hierarchy—and an especially strong patriarchy" (p. 5). Thus, religious principles influence and are mutually influenced by traditional Asian cultural values.

Summary

In exploring the themes of Asian American religion and spirituality, one word comes to mind—complexity! Religion and spirituality are multifaceted constructs. As such, they influence Asian American psychology, identity, and development in various ways, both positively and negatively. The forces of assimilation and stress of acculturation pose challenges for identity development and bicultural adaptation. Accordingly, religious affiliation may be a rich resource for inner strength and social support. For some Asian Americans, participation in a church, temple, or mosque may be one way to maintain ethnic roots and cultural values. On the other hand, religion may be a part of the pressure to assimilate to the new culture. By adopting mainstream religious values, beliefs, and practices, one may concurrently lose important parts of the culture of origin. When does participation in religion empower people and when does it co-opt them? What accountability does organized religion have in ministering to ethnic minority congregations? These are some of the questions that still prevail. In this chapter, the major religions that have influenced Asian Americans have been summarized and cross-cultural issues have been discussed, but religion and spirituality are not limited only to the faiths discussed in this chapter. Indigenous (folk) beliefs and other forms of worship and prayer exist in Asian American communities. It is evident that religion and spirituality, however they are expressed, are connected to culture and cultural adjustments for Asian Americans.

Discussion Questions

1. What has your faith/spiritual journey been like? Have you had particular high points and low points or is spirituality nonexistent for you?
2. How are your religious and spiritual beliefs related to your ethnic identity?
3. How do you envision a religiously diverse and pluralistic society allowing for complex life choices?
4. As a counselor, do you think it would be important to collaborate with religious professionals for some clients? How would you do so?
5. What are some of the ethical implications of integrating spirituality into counseling?

Case Study

So far this chapter has focused on the theory and research of how religion and spirituality impact Asian Americans and how religion and spirituality contribute to their psychological growth and development. The chapter will now shift its focus to a case study that illustrates how Asian Americans use religion and spirituality in their daily lives to cope with some of the issues discussed in this chapter. Moreover, the following case will also be presented to give readers a sense of how religion and spirituality might be integrated into therapy with Asian Americans.

Jason is a 22-year-old, Thai American senior in college majoring in psychology. He reluctantly referred himself for therapy because he was having considerable difficulty dealing with the breakup with his ex-girlfriend, Jennifer, a 21-year-old, Filipina American junior majoring in nursing. The couple broke up because of religious differences. Whereas Jason identified as Buddhist, his ex-girlfriend identified as a born-again Christian. Throughout the course of their relationship, Jason ridiculed Jennifer for her faith, accusing her of being weak-minded and calling her a Jesus freak. Jason vowed that he would never become a born-again Christian because for him "to be Thai meant to be Buddhist." After their breakup, Jason felt sad, lonely, and depressed and experienced a "profound emptiness" that he had never felt before. As a Buddhist, Jason had always been taught that suffering is a part of life, but now his suffering felt unbearable. He remembered previous conversations (or arguments) that he had with his ex-girlfriend about how Jesus suffered on the cross for the salvation of humanity. Thus, he felt like God could relate with his suffering. At this point, Jason ironically had his own religious conversion, despite previous vows never to do so.

After converting to Christianity, Jason thought he and his ex-girlfriend would be able to work out their differences and get back together, but his ex-girlfriend had moved on with her life. Nevertheless, Jason continued to cultivate his new spiritual identity with fervor and excitement. He prayed often, read the Bible daily, and sought comfort in his relationship with God. However, deep down inside, Jason still felt depressed and had difficulty moving on with his life. He considered seeking professional help, but as a psychology major, he remembered how many of his professors taught that "religion is a crutch for the weak." As a result, Jason was afraid that a professional counselor might minimize the importance of his spirituality or even ridicule his religious beliefs. He finally decided to seek professional counseling when he found out that his ex-girlfriend was now engaged to her new boyfriend.

Case Study Discussion

The counselor that worked with Jason used a spiritually sensitive, integrative approach to treatment that incorporated techniques from humanistic-existential, cognitive-behavioral, and developmental orientations. Jason's counselor recognized that he might have some reservations about participating in therapy due to the stigma against mental health services in the Asian American culture. Therefore, the counselor made painstaking attempts to build the therapeutic alliance before even addressing Jason's symptoms by exploring his reservations about treatment and how they might be related to his cultural background, normalizing his concerns, and providing an atmosphere of genuineness, acceptance, and empathy. As Jason became more comfortable with the process, he also articulated his fears about having his spiritual beliefs and practices either ridiculed or ignored in counseling. The counselor disclosed how she often relied upon spirituality in her own life and attempted to reassure Jason that religion and spirituality were "safe" topics to address in their work together.

In light of Jason's presenting concerns and spiritual disposition, the counselor conceptualized his case from a bio-psycho-social-spiritual model. According to this model, problems may arise from biological, personality, social, cultural, historical, or spiritual contexts. However, this case discussion will emphasize some of the spiritually integrated interventions that the counselor used because the spiritual dimension is often overlooked in secular psychotherapy.

First, the counselor conducted a spiritual assessment and encouraged Jason to tell his testimony (i.e., the story of his religious conversion). As Jason discussed the ironic circumstances that led to his conversion, it became apparent that he harbored a lot of guilt about ridiculing his ex-girlfriend for her faith. Thus, Jason's counselor drew upon resources from his own spiritual frame of reference, such as the belief in a loving and merciful God in order to promote forgiveness (from God and himself). Furthermore, while Jason reported that he experienced tremendous comfort in his relationship with God by praying and reading the Bible, he was essentially isolated because he was not involved in any religious community. Therefore, his counselor helped him find a congregation that would provide him with the spiritual and social support he needed to heal from his pain, yet was also sensitive to some of the unique issues of being an Asian American Christian.

It was crucial for Jason's counselor to be sensitive to the various ways spirituality was intertwined with his case. For example, initially, spirituality was a source of struggle for Jason because spiritual differences were the reason he and his ex-girlfriend broke up. However, afterward, spirituality became a significant resource for Jason, helping him cope and serving as a major component of his identity. While it was helpful for Jason's counselor to have some knowledge about various spiritual traditions and their relation to Asian American cultural values, it was also crucial for her to be aware of her own spiritual worldview and how it might impact treatment. She had to be particularly careful not to impose her own spiritual values upon Jason.

Case Study Discussion Questions

For undergraduate students, please consider the following questions:

1. What are your initial reactions to this vignette?
2. Do you think it was appropriate for Jason's counselor to mention that she often uses spirituality in her own life? Explain.
3. Would you feel comfortable talking about your spiritual beliefs with a counselor? Why or why not?

For graduate students and/or beginning therapists, please consider the following questions:

1. Do you think it is appropriate to integrate spirituality into counseling? Explain.
2. What is your reaction to Jason's religious conversion? How do your own spiritual beliefs (or lack thereof) influence your reaction?
3. If you were Jason's therapist, how would you respond if Jason insisted that the solution to his problems was "to just trust more in God"?

Key Terms

Buddhism: Religious tradition founded by Siddhartha Gautama that teaches principles such as the Four Noble Truths and the Eightfold Path.

Christianity: Religious tradition founded on the life and teachings of Jesus that promotes the belief in God as the Holy Trinity and the salvation of humanity from sin through the crucifixion, death, and resurrection of Jesus Christ.

Hinduism: One of the oldest religious traditions that espouses concepts such as the *atman, samsara, dharma,* and *karma.*

Islam: Religious tradition founded by the Prophet Mohammad that is based upon "five pillars": faith, prayer, charity, fasting, and pilgrimage to Mecca.

Religion: Institutionalized, objective thoughts, feelings, experiences, beliefs, and behaviors that arise from a search for the sacred.

Sacred: Objects, principles, or ideas that are holy, "set apart," transcendent, and of ultimate value to a person.

Sikhism: Religious tradition founded by Guru Nanak that contains a mixture of Hindu and Islamic teachings, such as the belief in one God, reincarnation, and the ability/duty of human beings to choose good over evil.

Spirituality: Personal, subjective thoughts, feelings, experiences, beliefs, and behaviors that arise from a search for the sacred.

For Further Learning and Suggested Readings

Chodron, P. (2001). *The places that scare you: A guide to fearlessness in difficult times*. Boston, MA: Shambhala.

Fontana, D. (2001). *Discover Zen: A practical guide to personal serenity*. San Francisco: Chronicle Books.

Kabat-Zinn, J. (1994). *Wherever you go, there you are: Mindfulness meditation in everyday life*. New York: Hyperion.

Kushner, H. S. (1989). *When bad things happen to good people*. New York: Avon Books.

Lesser, E. (1999). *The seeker's guide: Making your life a spiritual adventure*. New York: Villard Books.

Walsh, R. (1999). *Essential spirituality: Exercises from the world's religions to cultivate kindness, love, joy, peace, vision, wisdom, and generosity*. New York: John Wiley & Sons.

References

Altareb, B. Y. (1996). Islamic spirituality in America: A middle path to unity. *Counseling and Values, 41*, 29–38.

Ano, G. G., & Vasconcelles, E. B. (2005). Religious coping and psychological adjustment to stress: A meta analysis. *Journal of Clinical Psychology, 61*(4), 461–480.

Barron, J. (2004, July 29). Two Sikhs win back jobs lost by wearing turbans. *New York Times, 153*, B3.

Bjorck, J. P., Cuthbertson, W., Thurman, J. W., & Lee, Y. S. (2001). Ethnicity, coping, and distress among Korean Americans, Filipino Americans, and Caucasian Americans. *Journal of Social Psychology, 141*(4), 421–442.

Boisselier, J. (1994). *The wisdom of the Buddha*. New York: Harry N. Abrams.

Carnes, T., & Yang, F. (2004). *Asian American religions: The making and remaking of borders and boundaries*. New York: New York University Press.

Chilana, R. S. (2005). Sikhism: Building a basic collection of Sikh religion and culture. *Reference and User Services Quarterly, 45*, 11–21.

Dalal, A. K., & Pande, N. (1988). Psychological recovery of accident victims with temporary and permanent disability. *International Journal of Psychology, 23*, 25–40.

Firth, S. (2005, August 20). End-of-life: A Hindu view. *The Lancet, 366*, 682–686.

Fukuyama, M., Ahmad, M., Freytes, M., Hickey, J., Kane, A., Leever, B., et al. (2004, August). A qualitative investigation of multicultural expressions of spirituality. Poster presentation at the American Psychological Association Convention, Honolulu.

Guthrie, S. (1993, February 8). Hinduism gains a foothold in America. *Christianity Today, 37*, 48–52.

Hanna, F. J., & Green, A. (2004). Asian shades of spirituality: Implications for multicultural school counseling. *Professional School Counseling, 7*(5), 326–333.

Hayes, S. C., Strosahl, K. D., & Wilson, K. G. (2003). *Acceptance and commitment therapy: An experiential approach to behavior change*. New York: The Guilford Press.

Hedayat-Diba, Z. (2000). Psychotherapy with Muslims. In P. S. Richards & A. E. Bergin (Eds.), *Handbook of psychotherapy and religious diversity* (pp. 289–314). Washington, DC: American Psychological Association.

Hill, P. C., Pargament, K. I., Hood, R. W., McCullough, M. E., Swyers, J. P., Larson, D. B., & Zinnbauer, B. J. (2000). Conceptualizing religion and spirituality: Points of commonality, points of departure. *Journal for the Theory of Social Behavior, 30*(1), 50–77.

Kabat-Zinn, J. (1990). *Full catastrophe living: Using the wisdom of your body and mind to face stress, pain and illness*. New York: Delta.

Kim, B. S. K., Atkinson, D. R., & Yang. P. H. (1999). The Asian values scale: Development, factor analysis, validation, and reliability. *Journal of Counseling Psychology, 46*, 342–352.

Lal, V. (1996). Sikh kirpans in California schools: The social construction of symbols, legal pluralism, and the politics of diversity. *Amerasia Journal 22*(1), 57–89.

Lien, P., & Carnes, T. (2004). The religious demography of Asian American boundary crossing. In T. Carnes & F. Yang (Eds.), *Asian American religions: The making and remaking of borders and boundaries* (pp. 38–51). New York: New York University Press.

Morjaria, A., & Orford, J. (2002). The role of religion and spirituality in recovery from drink problems: A qualitative study of Alcoholics Anonymous members and South Asian men. *Addiction Research and Theory, 10*(3), 225–256.

Pargament, K. I. (1999). The psychology of religion and spirituality? Yes and no. *International Journal for the Psychology of Religion, 9*(1), 3–16.

Richards, P. S., & Bergin, A. E. (1997). *A spiritual strategy for counseling and psychotherapy.* Washington, DC: American Psychological Association.

Richards, P. S., & Bergin, A. E. (2000). *Handbook of psychotherapy and religious diversity.* Washington, DC: American Psychological Association.

Santorelli, S. (2000). *Heal thy self: Lessons on mindfulness in medicine.* New York: Bell Tower.

Sharma, A.R. (2000). Psychotherapy with Hindus. In P. S. Richards & A. E. Bergin (Eds.), *Handbook of psychotherapy and religious diversity* (pp. 341–365). Washington, DC: American Psychological Association.

Sodowsky, G. R., Kwan, K. K., & Pannu, R. (1995). Ethnic identity of Asians in the United States. In J. G. Ponterotto, J. M. Casas, L. A. Suzuki, & C. M. Alexander (Eds.), *Handbook of multicultural counseling* (pp. 123–154). Thousand Oaks, CA: Sage.

Tan, S-Y., & Dong, N. J. (2000). Psychotherapy with members of Asian American churches and spiritual traditions. In P. S. Richards & A. E. Bergin (Eds.), *Handbook of psychotherapy and religious diversity* (pp. 421–444). Washington, DC: American Psychological Association.

Tarakeshwar, N., Pargament, K. I., & Mahoney, A. (2003). Measures of Hindu pathways: Development and preliminary evidence of reliability and validity. *Cultural Diversity and Ethnic Minority Psychology, 9*(4), 316–332.

Uba, L. (1994). *Asian Americans: Personality patterns, identity, and mental health.* New York: The Guilford Press.

9

Colonialism
Societal and Psychological Impacts on Asian Americans and Pacific Islanders

KEVIN L. NADAL

OUTLINE OF CHAPTER

Case Synopsis

Kristine is a 26-year-old Filipina American who has been dating her Filipino American boyfriend Joel for quite some time. While Joel is a handsome, polite, and successful engineer, he is darker skinned than Kristine and her family members. This causes conflict in the family when Kristine becomes pregnant, as her family reprimands her for bringing a darker-skinned Filipino in their lineage.

Yeun Mi is an 18-year-old Korean international student, who was raised to be a devout Christian. Upon moving to the United States, she encounters new friends of different religions that she does not understand or agree with. She is conflicted because she does not want to believe that her new friends are sinners and are therefore going to hell, but wants to stay true to the tenets of her religion.

Introduction

In the late 1400s, several European countries began to explore different parts of the world in search of wealth and natural resources (Osborne, 2000; Sardesai, 1997; Ty, n.d.). Upon the discovery of a sea route around Africa's southern coast in 1488 and of the Americas in 1492, Europeans discovered that there were vast lands where different civilizations owned resources that were unavailable in Europe. Trade began with different countries, and eventually Europeans sought foreign lands in order to expand and contribute to their empires. Thus, the era of **colonialism** began in Africa, the Americas, and in Asia and the Pacific Islands.

Colonialism can be defined as the control by one power over a dependent area or people ("Colonialism," 2006). Usually this is manifested through exploitation by a stronger country of a weaker one, with the use of the weaker country's resources to strengthen and enrich the stronger country. European **colonization** affected Asian countries in different ways. For some Asian countries that have been colonized by a European nation (like India, the Philippines, or Vietnam), colonialism has shaped the culture, history, economics, and politics of these countries.

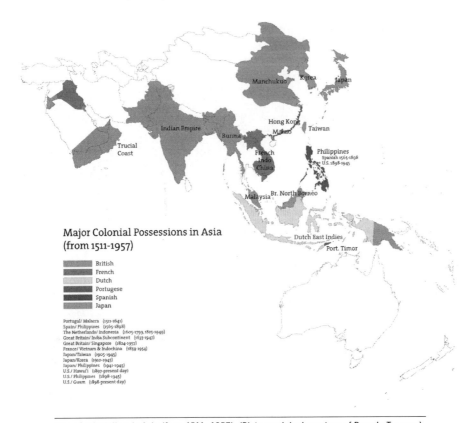

Map of colonialism in Asia (from 1511–1957). (Picture original courtesy of Pamela Tamayo.)

For other countries that were not directly colonized by a European nation (like China or Japan), colonialism has been less prevalent and only indirectly impacted the nations' cultures or history. Moreover, the colonization of one Asian empire onto other Asian countries, as well as American colonization, have societal and psychological implications for Asian and Asian American individuals. This chapter will explore several aspects of colonialism, including the historical and contemporary effects of colonialism on the mental health of Asians and Asian Americans. Let's examine why colonialism is important to Asian American psychology.

History of European, Japanese, and American Colonization in Asia

History of European Colonialism in Asia

Europeans began to colonize Asian countries as early as the 1500s (Osborne, 2000; Sardesai, 1997; Ty, n.d.). Some of these colonizing countries include Portugal, Spain, the Netherlands, Great Britain, and France; some of the countries that were colonized by Europeans include the Philippines, Vietnam, India, Indonesia, China, and Singapore. Colonizing usually began for economic reasons, particularly with the trade of raw materials that were unavailable in the colonizers' home countries. As the demand for raw materials increased, European countries sought to colonize areas all over the world, in order to bring economic wealth to their respective empires. As European countries began to expand their territories, competition began between European leaders to gain more land for power and prestige. Often, this competition led to violence and hostility between colonizing countries. Table 9.1 describes the major types of European colonization that took place in Asia during 400 years.

Table 9.1 History of European Colonization of Asia

Colonizing/colonized country	Historical context
Portugal/Malacca (1511–1641)	Portugal captured Malacca in 1511, holding it until the Dutch seized it in 1641. Subsequently, they maintained only a small piece of territory on the island of Timor, southeast of Bali.
Spain/Philippines (1565–1898)	Spain ruled the Philippines from 1565–1898. After the Spanish-American War, the Philippines was granted independence from Spain before it became a territory of the United States from 1899–1946.
The Netherlands/Indonesia (1605–1799, 1825–1949)	The Dutch arrived in Indonesia in 1596. Dutch colonialism was carried out initially by the Dutch East India Company (V.O.C.) from 1605–1799. When the V.O.C. collapsed, the Dutch government took control of its assets in 1825. After World War II, the Indonesians fought for national liberation from 1945–1949 and were granted independence by the United Nations.
Great Britain/India subcontinent (1633–1947)	Britain established bases in India as early as 1633, acquired Bombay (now known as Mumbai) from Portugal in 1661, and established Calcutta in 1690. After the Sepoy Mutiny in 1858, the British transferred the administration of India from the East India Company to the British government. In 1876, Queen Victoria was proclaimed empress of India. India was finally to achieve complete independence in 1947.
Great Britain/Singapore (1824–1957)	Britain governed Penang, Singapore, and Malacca as the Straits Settlements (later termed Malay Peninsula) from 1874–1914. The Malay States negotiated and gained independence in 1957.
France/Vietnam and Indochina (1859–1954)	The French seized Saigon, Vietnam in 1859. By 1867, the French annexed Cochin China (the South) and Cambodia. By 1907, they completed their conquest of French Indochina (Annam, Laos, Tonkin). In 1954, Vietnam gained its independence.

There are many reasons why colonialism ensued during this period of time; these motives have been identified as political, economic, and cultural (Ty, n.d.). Some of the political motivations for colonialism involve the need for European countries to expand territory, increase national pride and military, or to gain status as a world power. As various empires started to acquire new colonies in and near Europe, it became more important for countries such as Great Britain, France, and Spain to expand their territory in further lands in order to gain more power and world status. As a result, Great Britain and France attained colonies in Africa, North America, and Southeast Asia, while Spain conquered most of South America and the Philippines.

There were also several economic motives for colonization. Some of these motives include the desire for commercial enterprise, international trade, and rare raw materials. For example, many European explorers sought to find spices or precious metals that they could bring back to their respective countries. By taking resources from these colonized countries for cheap prices, colonizers could gain more wealth for their home countries. As a result, the colonizing country would increase the economy of their home country, without much regard for the societal implications their activities would have on the colonized countries.

Finally, there were several cultural reasons that influenced the drive for Europeans to colonize other countries in these far-off lands in Africa, Asia, or the Americas. Rudyard Kipling (1899) coined the term *White Man's Burden,* the notion held by many colonizers, believing that their way of life was better than that of the colonized. Because Europeans viewed these indigenous cultures as "savages," they felt it was their duty to civilize and educate them to become better human beings. Moreover, because these many European countries also viewed indigenous cultures as having immoral and inferior religious beliefs, they also forced religion (particularly Christianity) onto these cultures as well. Because of their White Man's Burden, they believed it was not only their obligation to colonize these indigenous countries, but their responsibility as moral, privileged Christians.

Activity 9.1: *Self-Reflection*
Read Rudyard Kipling's (1899) "White Man's Burden":

>Take up the White Man's burden—
>Send forth the best ye breed—
>Go bind your sons to exile
>To serve your captives' need;
>To wait in heavy harness,
>On fluttered folk and wild—
>Your new-caught, sullen peoples,
>Half-devil and half-child.
>
>Take up the White Man's burden—
>In patience to abide,
>To veil the threat of terror
>And check the show of pride;
>By open speech and simple,
>An hundred times made plain
>To seek another's profit,
>And work another's gain.
>
>Take up the White Man's burden—
>The savage wars of peace—
>Fill full the mouth of Famine
>And bid the sickness cease;
>And when your goal is nearest
>The end for others sought,
>Watch sloth and heathen Folly
>Bring all your hopes to nought.
>
>Take up the White Man's burden—
>No tawdry rule of kings,
>But toil of serf and sweeper—
>The tale of common things.
>The ports ye shall not enter,
>The roads ye shall not tread,
>Go mark them with your living,
>And mark them with your dead.
>
>Take up the White Man's burden—
>And reap his old reward:
>The blame of those ye better,
>The hate of those ye guard—

The cry of hosts ye humour
(Ah, slowly!) toward the light:—
"Why brought he us from bondage,
Our loved Egyptian night?"

Take up the White Man's burden—
Ye dare not stoop to less—
Nor call too loud on Freedom
To cloke your weariness;
By all ye cry or whisper,
By all ye leave or do,
The silent, sullen peoples
Shall weigh your gods and you.

Take up the White Man's burden—
Have done with childish days—
The lightly proferred laurel,
The easy, ungrudged praise.
Comes now, to search your manhood
Through all the thankless years
Cold, edged with dear-bought wisdom,
The judgment of your peers!

Questions for Discussion:

1. What are some of your reactions to the poem?
2. How would a person with an ancestry from a colonized country/land (i.e., India, Philippines, Hawaii) react to the poem?
3. How would a person with an ancestry from a colonizing country (i.e., Great Britain, Spain, France) react to the poem?

As noted in Table 9.1, the amount of time that these different European countries spent in these Asian countries varied. Moreover, because there is such a diversity of the colonizing European countries as well as the colonized Asian countries, the impact of colonization was different for each place and time. For example, because the Philippines were conquered by Spain for almost 350 years, the Spanish were able to have a significant impact on the Philippines' language and culture (Nadal, 2004). Many Filipino words, customs, food, music, and clothing have been impacted by Spanish culture; in fact, a majority of Filipinos today have Spanish surnames. This is different from the French impact on Vietnamese language and culture, which might be viewed as comparatively less pervasive, as colonization lasted for less than 100 years.

To help us better understand the influence of colonization on different countries, let's examine three major eras of European colonization of Asian countries: the Philippines, which were colonized by Spain from 1550 to 1898; India, which was colonized by Great Britain from 1633 to 1947; and Indochina (i.e., Vietnam, Cambodia, Laos), which was colonized by the French from 1859 to 1954. Exploring these three types of colonization is valuable because they were the largest and longest European settlements in Asia and because each created a distinct historical and cultural impact.

Economics   Let's examine how colonialism in these Asian countries affected them economically. While all of these Asian countries were being exploited of their raw goods and natural resources, colonial supporters viewed the colonization as **modernism** (and therefore beneficial) because it led to modern economic and technological growth within these countries (Said, 1993). For example, as a result of French colonial rule and the construction of irrigation systems, the Vietnamese were able to quadruple the amount of land used for rice cultivation ("Vietnam," 2006). However, although the nation may have been able to produce more rice, the people who benefited directly from this modernism were the colonizers. Not only did French colonizers gain more profit by increasing productivity, but the Vietnamese people were treated with disdain and left impoverished (Le, 2006). A similar phenomenon occurred in India. British colonization brought several things to India, including the development of railways and irrigation, as well as the cultivation of significant products, such as tea, coffee, and silk (Said, 1993). However, not only did the citizens of India not receive the financial benefits of these products, but they continued to live in poverty and experience significantly increased margins between social classes. So while modernism may have been a direct benefit of colonialism, the economic rewards would not be seen by the colonized country. This is similar to what happened in the Philippines, where Spanish and American colonialism increased production of natural goods, and spurred on technological expansion, but where almost half of the entire population still remains in poverty (Balisacan, 1994).

Education   There are several impacts that colonialism had on the education within these Asian countries. The push for these countries to be more educated by Western standards has had both positive and negative implications. First, some might view the educational agenda of the colonizer as imposing and uninvited, especially as the new educational institutions glorified the colonizers' values, while denigrating the values or cultures of the colonized. The notion that the ideals and intellect of European society was more important than that of indigenous Asian cultures is presumptuous.

Another negative effect of Western education is that it created a tension between those who were educated and those who were not. Hierarchies and competition for power were created in these formerly collectivist cultures. Educational privileges were granted to the wealthy, including the opportunity to study in the colonized land (i.e., Gandhi was able to study law in Great Britain). By encouraging this competition among the colonized, colonizers were able to maintain a sense of power and control of the colonized.

However, there are a few positive effects of colonialism. It is through colonialism that different Asian countries were able to generate some of the greatest writings, which combined Western thought with indigenous Asian ways of thinking. For example, the writings of Jose Rizal of the Philippines and Mahatma Gandhi of India would not be possible without colonialism. Now noted as great world leaders, these two were able to use their Western educations to reach the rest of the world and educate others about their home countries. One of Gandhi's famous quotes is: "Among the many misdeeds of the British rule in India, history will look upon the Act of depriving a whole nation of arms, as the blackest." While Gandhi is remembered for his protest against colonialism, it is ironic that he would not be as influential without the tools he used from the colonizer.

Culture, Language, Values, and Standards of Beauty   European colonialism influenced the culture of these colonized countries in many ways. These cultural effects take different forms— language, food, standards of beauty, and shift in values. Language affected all of these colonized countries in different ways. In both India and the Philippines, it was encouraged for the natives to learn the language of the colonizers (i.e., English for Indians and Spanish for Filipinos); however, it is more likely that those of higher social classes spoke the language of the colonizer. Food affected all of these colonized countries as well; for example, it is very likely for Southeast Asians to incorporate the French influence of bread into their meals (i.e., Vietnamese sandwiches).

A shift in cultural values may also occur as a direct effect of colonialism. For example, while all of these indigenous Asian countries may have valued collectivism over individualism, European colonialism encouraged citizens of these colonized countries to be more competitive and individualistic. Moreover, hierarchies in previously collectivist cultures were now created, and those groups who were most similar to the colonizer were valued, while those who were least similar were devalued. For example, Vietnamese persons with a lighter skin tone and who were educated would be the most valued, while Vietnamese persons with a darker skin tone and no formal education would be least valued. These hierarchies often led to tensions within the society where Asians of colonized countries would turn against others of their same ethnic group, simply because some benefited from colonial teachings and values. This type of value within colonized Asian cultures would be similar to the "slave mentality" phenomenon that is often exhibited with Black American culture, in which darker-skinned slaves would work as field slaves on the plantations, while lighter-skinned slaves would be allowed to work as house slaves, serving their masters inside the house (Haley, 1976).

Colonialism also affected cultural standards of beauty, in which a lighter skin tone was valued in all of these countries, although it had not previously been a concern. For example, in all three of these colonized regions, light-skinned celebrities (musicians, actors, etc.) are historically and contemporarily favored in entertainment and media. In fact, in Southeast Asia and the Philippines, actors who are biracial (mixed with White/European) are the most favored and are often the highest paying actors in their respective countries.

Religion   The degree of religious influence may directly reflect the duration of time that the colonizer occupied the colonized country, as well as the motivation for colonization. For example, the Philippines were colonized by Spain for over 350 years, with religion as one of the main motivations for colonization. Filipino national hero Jose Rizal describes how the Spanish Catholic friars would brutally force Filipinos to accept Christianity as their religion. He writes (in a first-person point of view) about a religious friar who was taught to physically abuse Filipino children in order for them to learn:

> It soon became known throughout the town that I did not whip the children. . . .[The curate] said that I was exposing the children to destruction, that I was wasting time, that I was not fulfilling my duties, that the father who spared the rod was spoiling the child—according to the Holy Ghost—that learning enters with blood, and so on. (Rizal, 1997, p. 105)

This passage exemplifies the cruelty that was delivered to the native Filipino people. As a result, over 90% of the Filipino population is currently either Catholic or Christian (Agbayani-Siewert & Revilla, 1995). While Filipinos in pre-colonial times may have held more indigenous spiritual views or may have been Muslim, the proselytizing of Spanish missionaries significantly impacted the religion of the Philippines, even into the present day.

Religion may have had a different influence in both India and Indochina. Because the French may have conquered Vietnam and other Southeast Asian countries primarily for economic reasons (and not religious reasons), the presence of Christianity in Vietnam is growing at 10% of the population ("Vietnam," 2006), but this number is nowhere near as significant as the Philippines. This trend is similar in India, where the majority of the population still remains its pre-colonial Hindu (Seegobin, 1999).

Finally, it is important to recognize that with European colonization, Catholic and Protestant missionaries have made extensive movements in other noncolonized countries, in an effort to expand Christianity. For example, there is a growing and rapid increase in Korean Christianity (both Catholic and Protestant), in which there was a rise from 5% in 1965 to 25% to 30% of the South Korean population today (Buswell & Lee, 2005). Although Korea was not formally colonized by European countries, the influence of Christianity has significantly impacted the culture and values of both North and South Koreans. In fact, Christianity has such an influence in Korean culture, that Korea holds 11 out of the 12 largest Christian congregations in all of the world, and produces the second largest amount of Christian missionaries, following the United States (Buswell & Lee, 2005).

History of Japanese Colonialism in Asia

Alongside European colonization in Asia, Japan began to colonize different Asian countries as well, forming what was called Imperial Japan or the Empire of Great Japan (Cumings, 2005). From 1871 to the end of World War II in 1945, Japan sought to create an empire in order to increase economic and global power. As a result, Japanese colonized both Taiwan and Korea from 1910 to 1945, while invading parts of China and occupying other countries such as the Philippines and Indochina from 1942 to 1945. Through this time, many describe the treatment of Japanese soldiers toward Koreans, Philippines, and other people in Southeast Asian countries as atrocious, brutal, and murderous (Cumings, 2005). The Japanese empire ended with Japan's surrender to the Allied forces in 1945.

There are many effects of Japanese **imperialism** on different Asian countries. It can be argued that Japanese colonialism should be viewed as modernism, due to the notion that the presence of Japanese colonizers in many Asian countries has led to an increase in modern thought and economic expansion. For example, although Japanese colonialism in Korea may be viewed as harsh and brutal, modern aspects of Korean society, such as rapid urban and industrial growth, the expansion of commerce, and growth of media culture (i.e., radio and cinema) emerged during the 35-year period of colonial rule (Cumings, 2005). So while Koreans may have negative feelings about the treatment they received from Japan in the past, they may also feel positively about Korea becoming the second most-industrialized nation in Asia.

In fact, the experiences of brutality during the Japanese occupation have led to an anti-Japanese sentiment by many Asian countries. This may result in tension within the Asian and Asian American community that is twofold. First, non-Japanese Asian Americans (i.e., Chinese, Koreans, Filipinos, Taiwanese, and Southeast Asians) may harbor negative and resentful thoughts toward Japanese people today. Second, Japanese people may be taught that they are superior to other Asians because of the history of their empire, economic capital, and world power.

Although Japanese imperialism may have occurred several generations ago, the impact on the current generations is still considerable. The history of Japan as an imperialist country has influenced the country's modern-day capitalism and economic power. As a result, while Japan may not be directly colonizing any Asian countries today, its economic and political force still dominate other Asian countries.

History of American Colonialism in Asia and the Pacific Islands

As a result of the Spanish American War, the Philippines gained its independence with the help of the U.S. military in 1898 (Schirmer & Shalom, 1987). However, immediately following this war, the United States acquired the newly independent Philippines (as well as Guam and Puerto Rico), and liberated Cuba from Spain. That same year, the U.S. Congress passed the Newlands Resolution, which annexed Hawaii as an American territory. Immediately thereafter, the U.S.

Table 9.2 History of Japanese and American Colonization in Asia

Colonizing/colonized country	Historical context
Japan/Taiwan (1905–1945)	Following its defeat in the First Sino-Japanese War (1894–1895), Taiwan and Penghu (the Pescadores) was ceded to Japan. In 1935, the Japanese began an island-wide assimilation project to bind the island more firmly to the Japanese Empire. Ended with defeat in WWII.
Japan/Korea (1910–1945)	After the Sino-Japanese and Russo-Japanese Wars, Korea was dominated by Japan. In 1910, Japan forced Korea to sign the Japan-Korea Annexation Treaty. Military Rule continued from 1910–1919, Cultural Rule from 1920–1935, and Imperial Subjectification from 1936–1945. Ended with defeat in WWII.
Japan/Philippines (1941–1945)	After the bombing of Pearl Harbor in 1941, Japan occupied the Philippines during WWII, taking over most of the country by force. Many reported brutal killings and rape by Japanese military. Ended with defeat in WWII.
U.S./Hawaii (1897–present day)	In June 1897, U.S. President McKinley signed a treaty of annexation with the Republic of Hawaii. The Newlands Resolution was passed by the House June 15, 1898, and by the Senate on July 6, 1898, formally annexing Hawaii as a U.S. territory. On August 21, 1959, Hawaii became the 50th state of the U.S.
U.S./Philippines (1898–1945)	On June 12, 1898, the Philippines were granted independence from Spain, following the Spanish-American War. Instead of allowing freedom of the Philippines, Spain was forced in the negotiations to hand over the Philippines to the U.S. in exchange for $20 million, which the U.S. later claimed to be a "gift" to Spain. After the end of WWII, the U.S. granted the Philippines freedom on July 4, 1946.
U.S./Guam (1898–present day)	The U.S. took control of Guam in 1898 after the Battle of Guam of 1898 in the Spanish-American War. The Guam Organic Act of 1950 established Guam as an unincorporated organized territory of the United States, provided for the structure of the island's government, and granted the people United States citizenship.

military took control of the sugar industry in Hawaii and built several naval bases in order to build a fortress in the Pacific Ocean (Laenui, 1993).

When the Philippines and Hawaii were taken over by the United States in 1898, American colonialism began in Asia and the Pacific Islands. In this era, Filipinos and Hawaiians (as well as Puerto Ricans and Guamanians) were encouraged to replace their native identities with American identities, by changing their indigenous names, speaking English, and pledging to the American flag (Laenui, 1993; Strobel, 2001). Members of these countries were viewed as less sophisticated than Europeans/Americans again, and were encouraged to become more civilized and less savage. In fact, Filipinos were often referred to as America's "little brown brothers," in that the U.S. government felt a paternalistic need to educate Filipinos to develop more Western values and become more American (Miller, 1982). Reflecting a similar sentiment as mentioned in Rudyard Kipling's "White Man's Burden" (1899), the U.S. government continued to colonize the Philippines until the end of World War II in 1946. Hawaii remained a U.S. territory until it became the 50th state in the union in 1959 (Laenui, 1993).

There are many consequences of U.S. colonization of the Philippines and Hawaii. First, because American education had been promoted in both regions, English was now a dominant language in both the Philippines and Hawaii. In fact, English is currently the second national language of the Philippines and most Filipinos will speak English at greater levels than any other Asian country (Nadal, 2004). Some may view this as a negative consequence because Filipinos and Hawaiians were being educated in a language that was not their native language. Moreover, because of American colonialism, both Filipinos and Hawaiians were being encouraged to speak English and to stop speaking in their native dialects. As a result, many Filipino immigrants will not teach their children Tagalog or native Filipino languages, because of the belief that English is a superior language and that the English language that is necessary for success (Posadas, 1999).

However, for Hawaii, there are many more negative consequences of American colonization, which include the loss of native Hawaiian culture, as well as the increase of poverty as a result of tourism (Trask, 1993). While many assume that the tourism and corporate presence in Hawaii have led to economic growth, the U.S. presence in Hawaii has done quite the opposite. Not only does Hawaii have the worst average family income to average housing costs ratio, but nearly one-fifth of Hawaii's resident population was classified as "near-homeless" (Trask, 1993). Moreover, during the 1970s and 1980s, the Census Bureau reported that personal income growth in Hawaii was the lowest by far compared to any of the other 50 states (Trask, 1993). Finally, the population of Hawaii has changed considerably as a result of colonialism. In the 1960s, Hawaii residents outnumbered tourists by more than 2 to 1. In the 1990s, tourists outnumbered residents by 6 to 1, while outnumbering native Hawaiians by 30 to 1 (Trask, 1993). Not only has colonization led to a change in culture, language, and politics as it has in other countries, but it is also leading to the significant decrease in native Hawaiians in their own land.

A final consequence of American colonialism is the degree to which the American presence in Asia continues to influence different Asian cultures. For example, although the Philippines were granted independence in 1946, the United States has continued to have an American military and media presence. Moreover, after the Korean War and the Vietnam War, the United States has also maintained a military and media presence in both Korea and Vietnam. Through its military presence, the United States continues to influence the culture, values, and belief systems of these Asian countries without directly governing them. This can be manifested through these Asian countries in many ways. For example, because of a military presence, Americans may be viewed as strong or bullying (i.e., American soldiers are taught to be feared and respected in Korea and the Philippines). Moreover, the media presence in Asian countries may influence the standards of wealth and beauty. For example, although Korea had not been directly colonized by the United States, Koreans are taught from American media that blond hair and round blue eyes are ideal; this may lead to many Koreans seeking eyelid surgery to make their eyes look more like those of White Americans (Kaw, 1993). Likewise, it is likely that Asians of many different countries may listen to popular American musical artists like Michael Jackson or Britney Spears, while Americans are most likely unfamiliar with musical artists in the Philippines, Vietnam, Korea, or India.

Effects of Colonialism on Mental Health

There are many ways in which colonialism may impact an Asian American individual's mental health. Let us recall that one of the motivations of colonization was cultural, in that colonizers believed it was their responsibility to teach "inferior" citizens of colonized countries to become more "superior" like the colonizers. As a result, many individuals of the colonized countries may develop what is called a **colonial mentality**. With a colonial mentality, the colonizer's values and beliefs are accepted by the colonized as truths, and the mores of the colonizer are accepted as being superior to those of the colonized (Strobel, 2001). It is important to recognize that colonial mentality can affect both Asian nationals (those born in Asia) and Asian Americans (those born in the United States). An Asian or Asian American with a colonial mentality may believe that the indigenous practices and rituals of the native country may be savage and uncivilized. For example, an Indian with colonial mentality may believe that indigenous Indian religions (i.e., Hinduism or Islam) are primitive or inferior. Because the colonized society has taught its members to be more like the colonizers, the individual has learned that indigenous practices (in this case, religious practices) are unworthy and inferior.

Colonial mentality may affect an Asian American individual on many levels, which include denigration of one's self, denigration of one's culture, discrimination against those that are less acculturated, and tolerance and acceptance of contemporary oppression of one's ethnic group (David & Okazaki, 2006). A person's self-esteem and the ways of perceiving oneself may be affected by colonial mentality. For example, an individual may have low self-esteem because he is not more like the colonizer in terms of physical appearance, cultural values, family prestige, or educational background. This may lead to self-hatred, directed toward any personal characteristic deemed inferior, such as skin tone, eye shape, facial structure, or hair texture.

Oftentimes, Asian and Asian American individuals try to change their physical attributes to be more like the colonizer. For example, many Filipinos and Indians will buy skin-bleaching cream in order to appear more light-skinned like their Spanish and British colonizers. Other Asian ethnic groups like Koreans or Japanese may have eyelid surgery, in order to look more European, while South Asians and Filipinos may straighten their hair in order to have more of a European appearance. Asians and Asian Americans who suffer from low self-esteem due to these types of appearance issues often experience further difficulties functioning in everyday life.

Asian American individuals with colonial mentality may also discriminate against others who are less acculturated or less similar to the colonizer. For example, Asian Americans often view recent immigrants as less Americanized or FOB (fresh-off-the boat), leading to in-group stereotypes of being stupid or backward (Revilla, 1997). Finally, colonial mentality may take the form of individuals who tolerate and accept oppression, admiring the colonizer and adopting the belief that the colonizer is superior. This manifests as Asian Americans who view the colonizers as civilizing, freedom-giving, or unsanctified heroes. One problem with this viewpoint is that these Asian Americans become colorblind and deny racial discrimination because they want to believe the United States is truly the land of opportunity and that they are living the American dream. The following is an example of one Asian American's experience:

> I know many Filipinos (in America who) would deny that they have been discriminated against. Too many are so thankful to be (in America) that they shut their eyes to avoid seeing the injustices, political and economic injustices. Then there are those who simply do not care. This type of attitude stifles our community. (Villa, 1995, p. 179)

Often, colonial mentality may also influence Asian Americans of certain colonized countries to deny their actual ethnic makeup. For example, some Filipino Americans may deny their Filipino heritage and tell others that they are Spanish, Hispanic, Latino, or Hawaiian. In fact, many famous Filipino celebrities (i.e., actress Tia Carrere, *American Idol* finalist Jasmine Trias, and baseball player Benny Agbayani) have claimed either a Spanish, Hawaiian, or Chinese identity over a Filipino identity (Jorge, 2004). Filipino Americans often refer to this as the IMSCF syndrome, otherwise known as the "I-am-Spanish-Chinese-Filipino" syndrome (Jorge, 2004).

Perhaps in their perspective, being Spanish, Hawaiian, or Chinese is more marketable than being Filipino. Perhaps their colonial mentality prevents them from being proud of their Filipino heritage, particularly if these Filipinos are originally from Hawaii, a land where Filipinos are at the bottom of the racial hierarchy, often seen as uncivilized savages.

Other times, members of other colonized Asian American groups may tell others that they are "mixed" or only a certain percentage of their ethnic group. For example, a lighter skinned Southeast Asian American may be seen as more beautiful or respectable if others would perceive them to have European blood. By telling others that they are mixed, they feel a false sense of pride or supremacy. However, in doing so, they are really masking their true feelings about being a member of their actual colonized group, which might include shame, embarrassment, and inferiority.

Colonial mentality also affects the way that an individual perceives others. These individuals may treat others as either more superior or more inferior based on colonial beliefs. For example, a South Asian American with a lighter skin tone may treat a darker-skinned South Asian American as inferior to herself, and vice versa. Although these two individuals may be of the same ethnicity, they buy into colonial mentality and subject themselves to a hierarchy based on skin tone alone. Because of this, colonial mentality also leads to intraethnic prejudice and discrimination. Group members who are more similar to the colonizer may hold prejudiced beliefs about group members

MANILA'S FINEST.
The new native policemen.

© 2001 HARPWEEK®

Intraethnic tension among Filipinos. (From HarpWeek, 2006. Retrieved on January 5, 2006 from http://www.harpweek.com/09Cartoon/BrowseByDateCartoon.asp?Month=December&Date=30.)

who are less similar to the colonizer. For example, a Filipino American with more Spanish qualities (i.e., skin tone, language, last name) may discriminate against a Filipino American with less Spanish qualities. This often takes form in discriminating against a whole region of people who may have similar characteristics (i.e., Filipinos who speak Tagalog are from Luzon, may discriminate against Ilocanos who tend to be darker-skinned or Mindanaoans who are predominantly Muslim). As a result, colonial mentality may turn people of the same ethnic group against each other, leading to competition, lack of unity, and tension between subgroups.

Internalized Racism

Colonial mentality may have similar definitions to **internalized racism**, but it is different in many ways. Internalized racism is defined as the acceptance by a member of an oppressed racial group, of negative messages about their abilities and intrinsic worth. Both terms involve the idea of self-hatred about oneself and one's racial/ethnic group, based on the beliefs and standards of a dominant group. However, the self-hatred that is discussed in colonial mentality goes above and beyond race. Colonial mentality includes beliefs about race, ethnicity, religion, language, cultural practices, traditions, and standards of beauty. Colonial mentality also differs from internalized racism in that it can lead to a hierarchy within an ethnic group. For example, while an African American with internalized racism may have hatred toward all African Americans,

A British man with Indian servants is an example of the hierarchy of colonial India. (From Edwardes, M, *Bound to Exile*, Praeger Publishers, Westport, CT, 1970.)

an Asian Indian American individual with colonial mentality may only have hatred toward dark-skinned Asian Indian and South Asian individuals. At the same time, this Asian Indian American, for example, may also possess internalized racist views, believing that Whites/ Europeans are superior, while maintaining self-hatred toward his own Asian Indian group. Individuals can maintain varying levels of internalized racism and colonial mentality at the same time.

Colonial mentality may also lead to further internalized racism, as it may create a hierarchy and tension within the Asian American community as a whole. Oftentimes, East Asian Americans are viewed by Asians and by non-Asians as the most superior Asian group for reasons such as their perceived "model minority" intellect and education, and economic and political power from their home countries. On the contrary, Filipinos, Southeast Asians, and Pacific Islanders are often viewed as the inferior Asian group, for their lack of educational attainment and less economic and political power of their home countries (Okamura, 1998). In fact, South Asians are often not recognized as Asian Americans at all, as they have only been documented as Asian American since the 1980 U.S. Census (Espiritu, 1992).

Colonialism may be a major influence for this perceived hierarchy. Both China and Japan have qualities that are treasured in colonial thinking, including vast geographic size and/or territory, military expansionism, modern technology, and economic advancement. Additionally, because light skin is highly valued by the colonizer, it is important to notice that these two East Asian groups generally have a lighter skin color than Filipinos, South Asians, Southeast Asians, and Pacific Islanders.

Colonialism has affected how Asian Americans perceive themselves and each other, oftentimes leading individuals to rank themselves as either superior or inferior to other Asian American groups of different ethnicities. This may take the form of East Asians being more represented (specifically in leadership positions) in Asian American community and student organizations, as well as having a higher presence in the American media despite the growing population of Filipinos, South Asians, and Southeast Asians.

Summary

This chapter focused on ways that colonial mentality impacts Asian Americans' and Pacific Islanders' psychological functioning. European countries began to colonize Asian countries since the early 1500s. As a result, colonialism has affected Asian countries economically, culturally, politically, religiously, and sociologically. Psychologically, colonialism still affects Asian and Asian American individuals in a myriad of ways. First, colonialism may lead to a hierarchy among members of specific colonized Asian American ethnic groups—those who are most similar to the colonizers are most valued, while those who are least similar to the colonizer are least valued. Second, an individual may develop a colonial mentality, in which the individual learns to dislike aspects about the self that are unlike those of the colonizer. Finally, colonialism may lead to tension within the Asian American community, in which different ethnic groups may feel either superior or inferior to one another.

The chapter will now present two case studies that demonstrate how colonial mentality may affect an Asian American's ability to function in everyday situations. These examples are also offered to help the reader understand how colonial mentality might manifest in therapy. Upon reading these examples, reflect on the major themes involving colonialism. Explore what you think is going on for the individuals involved, and try to imagine what it would be like if you were to go through their experience.

Discussion Questions

1. In your opinion, have any Asian countries benefited from colonialism? Why or why not?
2. How would you feel or act if your country of origin was colonized?
3. Think about other countries and lands that have been colonized (i.e., Puerto Rico, Cuba, Guam). In what ways has colonialism affected their people politically, economically, and culturally?
4. How do you feel about present-day colonialism (i.e., Iraq, Kuwait, etc.)? In what ways has the United States continued to colonize other countries?
5. If you are a member of a colonized country, think about how colonialism has affected your behavior in your everyday life. The values of your family and friends. Messages that you have been taught by your community.

Case Study

Case Example #1: The Case of Kristine and Her Darker-Skinned Boyfriend

Kristine is a 26-year-old second-generation Filipina American woman who enters therapy at a community center. Her parents are from Manila, the capital city of the Philippines, where both Spanish and American colonization affected the Philippines most. Her parents have always taught her to value her light brown skin tone and large eyes, and often told her to stay out of the sun to avoid "getting dark." Kristine was also taught that it would be best for her to marry someone White or light-skinned so that her children would be "mestizo" (the Filipino word for fair-skinned and/or biracial Filipino/White). A year ago, Kristine entered a relationship with Joel, a second-generation Filipino American whom she went to college with. When she first brought Joel home to meet her family, the first thing that her parents commented on was his dark-brown skin. Although Joel was respectful, handsome, and intelligent, as well as a successful engineer, Kristine's parents were not happy that she was dating someone who had darker skin than her. Although he was Filipino American, the fact that he was dark was enough for her parents to disapprove of the relationship.

Kristine entered counseling because she had told her parents that she is pregnant. Her parents were very disappointed in her, not only because they think she is ruining her life, but because they are not happy that their grandchild is potentially going to have a dark skin tone. During her pregnancy, Kristine's parents have referred to their unborn grandchild as "the ugly duckling" or "darkie." She is distraught because she does not want her child to be subjected to teasing by her parents or family members. She also does not understand how her parents could be so "racist" and hurtful toward her, her boyfriend Joel, and even her unborn baby. She seeks counseling because she wants her parents to be more supportive, but also because she does not feel that she can ever express her true feelings of anger and resentment toward her parents.

Case Example #2: The Case of Yeun Mi and Her Non-Christian Friends

Yeun Mi is an 18-year-old Korean international student who came to the United States to pursue her undergraduate degree in premed biology. She grew up in a very traditional Korean family in Seoul, and wanted to study in the United States in order to have the best education possible. She is the youngest of three children, and is the only female child of her parents. Yeun Mi was raised to be a devout Christian, and upon arriving in the United States she has continued to make Christianity a salient part of her life.

Because Yeun Mi lived in a homogeneous area all of her life, she had been exposed only to Koreans who were also Christian. As a result, when she first entered college, she experienced a complete culture shock. She expected to encounter a lot of White American students, but was unaware that her college would have so many Asian Americans. Many of these Asian American students lived in her dorm, and she was always pleased with the small, positive interactions that she had with them. Shortly after attending classes, Yeun Mi discovered that one of her dorm mates, Sophia, was in a few of her classes. Sophia was a Chinese American who grew up in a suburb just outside of their college. The two talked about homework assignments and eventually became friends. Sophia introduced Yeun Mi to her good friend Kathleen, a Cambodian American, who had been friends with Sophia since high school. Yeun Mi was hesitant to become friends with Kathleen, as she had heard negative things about Cambodians, such as that they were uncultured, unintelligent, and dishonest. However, she thought that Kathleen was a nice person and continued to be friendly with her.

As Yeun Mi became better friends with Sophia and Kathleen, she invited Sophia to come to her church. It was at this point that Sophia told Yeun Mi that she was Buddhist, while Kathleen revealed that she was Muslim. Yeun Mi felt very conflicted because she had strong feelings about people who were not Christian. She learned from an early age that anyone who was not Christian would go to hell. Moreover, she was taught that Christianity was the only religion, and that other Asian religions were unsophisticated and primitive.

Yeun Mi is confused. She does not want to believe that her new friends are going to hell, but she does not want to question or doubt her Christian faith either. When she first moved to the United States, her mother warned her not to become "too American" or "less Christian." Now, she fears that she would be compromising a part of her identity that is very important to her. She also feels frustrated because cognitively she does not want to stop being friends with people because of their religion, but emotionally believes that her friends belong to the sinful religions and will not be "saved."

As a result, Yeun Mi begins to avoid her emotions, by shunning herself from all other students, including Sophia and Kathleen. She does not want to take the risk of becoming friends with someone and then discovering that they are not Christian like her. She rationalizes that she came to the United States for an education, not to make friends. However, she also feels very lonely and depressed because she does not have any social support in the United States and she doesn't feel that anyone back in Korea would be able to understand her. Her resident advisor noticed this depression in Yeun Mi and recommended that she go to the counseling center for help.

Case Study Discussion

Through these two cases, we notice that colonialism affects the mental health of these two clients in many ways. In both cases, we notice how colonialism has built hierarchies between members of similar racial/ethnic groups. With the case of Kristine, we see how skin tone plays a role in determining a person's value and importance. Although Kristine's boyfriend is Filipino American like her family members, the fact that he has a darker skin tone is enough for him to be deemed unattractive and unworthy of Kristine's love. Moreover, the value of light skin is so engrained in Kristine's family values that they even minimize the worth of her unborn baby, already assuming that he will be "ugly" and not as worthy regardless that the child is an innocent infant entering the world.

In the case of Yeun Mi, we notice how colonialism affects the perceptions between two different Asian groups on the basis of religion. Because Yeun Mi grew up with deep-rooted Christian values, she has learned that non-Christian religions are not only flawed and less worthy, but that they are evil. The colonial values that Christianity is more superior than indigenous Asian religions have affected Yeun Mi so much that she is unable to maintain friendships with those who are different from her. These conflicting emotions have led Yeun Mi to feel distressed and unable to function.

In both cases, we notice how colonialism has been passed down from generation to generation. Kristine's parents taught her from an early age that in order to be beautiful, it would be important for her to keep her skin lighter and to avoid going in the sun. These standards of beauty may have affected Kristine in so many ways that she may not even be completely aware of them. Perhaps she has internalized that light skin is better and is genuinely concerned that her baby will be treated differently because of his dark skin. Perhaps she may purposely be trying to rebel against her parents by getting together with a man that she knows they would not approve of. Nonetheless, it would be important for Kristine's counselor to help her explore not only how she feels about her parents' and family's colonial mentalities, but also how her own colonial values may affect her cognitions and emotions.

In terms of Yeun Mi's situation, we also notice how different generations are affected by colonial mentality. Because Yeun Mi is the only one in her family who is in the United States, she does not feel that her parents or family in Korea would be able to provide her with any support or empathy, because they are comfortable maintaining their Korean Christian values. At the same time, she is unable to share her experience with her new Asian American friends, for she fears feeling judged and misunderstood. As a result, Yeun Mi feels very isolated and does not know who to talk to about her situation. In therapy, it would be important for her counselor to provide support for her and validate her conflicted experience. Moreover, it would be important for Yeun Mi to explore how her colonial views have both strengths and limitations. In doing so, it is hoped that she would be able to have a stronger understanding of herself and her values.

There are many ways that a counselor or therapist might approach these two cases. First, in using a multicultural counseling competence model, it is imperative for counselors to (a) be aware of their own cultural values and biases, (b) have knowledge of clients' diverse worldviews, and (c) to provide culturally appropriate intervention strategies to better serve their clients (Sue, Arredondo, & McDavis, 1992). When either of these clients enters therapy, it is necessary for the therapist to be aware of his or her own biases about Asian Americans and colonial mentality, in order to prevent projection of one's values onto the client. The therapist must be aware of his own racial/cultural being, and how this might affect the therapy. For example, an Asian American individual who interacts with a White therapist might be hesitant in becoming vulnerable, due to the assumption that the therapist would not understand; furthermore, an Asian American individual with colonial mentality may idealize a White therapist because of her "colonial" physical features. In addition to awareness, a therapist must have the knowledge or willingness to learn about the culture of the client, in order to provide culturally appropriate skills and interventions.

The counselor may use an integrative approach with the client, utilizing strategies from different theoretical orientations. Borrowing from person-centered therapy, the therapist may utilize unconditional positive regard with the client, as well as empathy as a way to assist the client to feel comfortable, which will help the client to connect with her emotions. In utilizing psychoanalytic therapy, the therapist may also explore transference and countertransference with the client, in order to support the client in understanding how colonial mentality may manifest in daily life and impact all of her relationships, including the therapeutic relationship. Finally, in using a family systems approach, the therapist may encourage the client to explore the different roles within the family, to facilitate understanding how one's colonial mentality has been passed from one generation to the next, as well as to explore the feelings that the client may have about these messages.

Through these interventions, it is hoped that both clients will be able to understand how colonial mentality has impacted their lives, while alleviating the clients' internalized feelings of blame, guilt, or shame. It is also expected that therapy will provide an opportunity for the clients to process their thoughts and emotions, which they may or may not be able to share directly with their family or friends.

Case Study Discussion Questions

For undergraduate students, please consider the following questions:

1. What are your initial reactions to these two case examples?
2. What are your thoughts or reactions to the messages that Kristine received about skin color? How may this relate to your own experiences?
3. What are your thoughts or reactions to the messages that Yeun Mi received about religion? How may this relate to your own experiences?

For graduate students and/or beginning therapists, please consider the following questions:

1. What would be difficult for you in working with Kristine or Yeun Mi as her counselor? What might be some of your transference or countertransference issues?
2. Would the counselor's ethnicity and gender make a difference in the counseling relationship and work with Kristine or Yeun Mi? What might be some of those differences?
3. What is your theoretical orientation? Would you use the same orientation in working with Kristine and Yeun Mi?

Key Terms

Colonialism: The exploitation by a stronger country of a weaker one, with the use of the weaker country's resources to strengthen and enrich the stronger country.

Colonial mentality: The concept that the colonizer's values and beliefs are accepted by the colonized as a belief and truth of their own; that the mores of the colonizer are superior to those of the colonized.

Colonization: The act or process of establishing a colony or colonies.

Imperialism: The policy of extending a nation's authority by territorial acquisition or by the establishment of economic and political hegemony over other nations.

Internalized racism: The acceptance, by members of an oppressed racial group, of negative messages about their abilities and intrinsic worth; self-hatred about one's racial group.

Modernism: The conformity to modern ideas, practices, or standards, while employing a deliberate departure from tradition.

For Further Learning and Suggested Readings

The following readings are by authors from colonized Asian countries. Through these firsthand accounts, one may learn about the psychological impact of both Asian American/Pacific Islanders on both an individual and societal level.

Gandhi, M. K. (1983). *Autobiography: The story of my experiments with truth.* New York: Dover Publications.

Lam, T. B. (2000). *Colonialism experienced: Vietnamese writings on colonialism, 1900–1931.* Ann Arbor: University of Michigan Press.

Rizal, J. P. (1997). *Noli me Tangere: A novel.* Honolulu: University of Hawaii Press.

Trask, H-K. (1993). *From a native daughter: colonialism and sovereignty in Hawai'i.* Monroe, ME: Common Courage Press.

References

Agbayani-Siewert, P., & Revilla, L. (1995). Filipino Americans. *Asian Americans: Contemporary trends and issues.* Thousand Oaks, CA: Sage.

Balisacan, A. M. (1994). *Poverty, urbanization and development policy.* Quezon City, Philippines: University of the Philippines Press.

Buswell, R. E., & Lee, T. S. (Eds.), (2005). *Christianity in Korea.* Honolulu: University of Hawaii Press.

Colonialism. (2006). *Encyclopedia Britannica.* Retrieved January 21, 2006, from Encyclopedia Britannica. http://www.britannica.com/eb/article?tocId=9361159.

Cumings, B. (2005). *Korea's place in the sun: A modern history.* New York: W. W. Norton.

David, E. J. R., & Okazaki, S. (2006). Colonial mentality: A review and recommendation for Filipino American psychology. *Cultural Diversity and Ethnic Minority Psychology, 12*(1), 1–16.

Espiritu, Y. L. (1992). *Asian American panethnicity: Bridging institutions and identities.* Philadelphia: Temple University Press.

Haley, A. (1976). *Roots.* New York: Doubleday and Company.

Jorge, R. (2004, October 10). Everyone's idol. *The Manila Times.* Retrieved January 22, 2006, from http://www.manilatimes.net/national/2004/oct/10.

Kaw, E. (1993). Medicalization of racial features: Asian American women and cosmetic surgery. *Medical Anthropology Quarterly, 7*(1), 74–89.

Kipling, R. (1899). White man's burden. In P. Brians, M. Gallwey, D. Hughes, et al. (Eds.), *Reading about the world* (3rd ed., Vol. 2). New York: Harcourt Brace Custom Publishing.

Laenui, P. (1993). One hundred years of colonization in Hawaii. *Fourth World Bulletin, 2*(3).

Le, C. N. (2006). The lessons of colonialism. *Asian-nation: The landscape of Asian America.* Retrieved January 29, 2006, from http://www.asian-nation.org/colonialism.shtml.

Miller, S. C. (1982). *Benevolent assimilation: The American conquest of the Philippines, 1899– 1903.* New Haven, CT: Yale University Press.

Nadal, K. L. (2004). Pilipino American identity development model. *Journal of Multicultural Counseling and Development, 46*(2).

Okamura, J. Y. (1998). *Imagining the Filipino American diaspora: Transnational relations, identities, and communities.* New York: Garland Publishing.

Osborne, M. (2000). *Southeast Asia: An introductory history* (8th ed.). Sydney: George Allen & Unwin.

Posadas, B. M. (1999). *The Filipino Americans.* Westport, CT: Greenwood Press.

Revilla, L. A. (1997). Filipino American identity: Transcending the crisis. In M. P. P. Root (Ed.), *Filipino Americans: Transformation and identity* (pp. 316–323). Thousand Oaks, CA: Sage.

Rizal, J. P. (1997). *Noli me Tangere: A novel.* Honolulu: University of Hawaii Press.

Root, M. P. P. (1997). Contemporary mixed-heritage Filipino Americans: Fighting colonized identities. In M. P. P. Root (Ed.), *Filipino Americans: Transformation and identity.* Thousand Oaks, CA: Sage.

Said, E. W. (1993). *Culture and imperialism.* New York: Vintage Books.

Sardesai, D. R. (1997). *Southeast Asia: Past & present* (4th ed.). Boulder, CO: Westview.

Schirmer, D. B., & Shalom, S. R. (1987). *The Philippines reader: A history of colonialism, neocolonialism, dictatorship, and resistance.* Boston: South End Press.

Seegobin, W. (1999). Important considerations in counseling Asian Indians. In Kit S. Ng (Ed.), *Counseling Asian Families from a systems perspective* (pp. 83–94). Alexandria, VA: American Counseling Association.

Strobel, L. M. (2001). *Coming full circle: The process of decolonization among post-1965 Filipino-Americans.* Manila: Giraffe Books.

Sue, D. W., Arredondo, P., & McDavis, R. J. (1992). Multicultural counseling competencies: A call to the profession. *Journal of Counseling and Development, 70,* 477–486.

Trask, H-K. (1993). *From a native daughter: colonialism and sovereignty in Hawai'i.* Monroe, ME: Common Courage Press.

Ty, R. (n.d.). *Colonialism and nationalism in Southeast Asia.* Retrieved December 20, 2005, from http://www.seasite.niu.edu/crossroads/ty.

Vietnam. (2006). *Encyclopedia Britannica.* Retrieved January 12, 2006, from http://www.britannica.com/eb/article-52739.

Villa, D. (1995). I offended many Filipinos because I was an FOB. In Y. L. Espiritu (Ed.), *Filipino American lives* (pp. 169–180). Philadelphia: Temple University Press.

10
Managing Multiple Social Identities

GRACE A. CHEN

OUTLINE OF CHAPTER

Case Synopsis
Introduction
Background
Factors in Identity Development
Multiple Oppressions
Case Study
References

Case Synopsis

Chi is a 21-year-old Vietnamese American junior sociology major. She has done well in her courses so far and gets along with her classmates fairly well. However, she has been feeling lonely and disconnected from people lately. Chi recently came out to her family as a lesbian, and their reaction was mixed. Her older brother and sister have been supportive and understanding, but her parents have been silent and distant. Chi has been "out" to her faculty advisor since she declared her major a year ago, and she receives support from both queer and straight faculty and students. She doesn't completely feel comfortable around them, though, as she is one of a few Asian American students in her major, and there are only a handful of other students of color. She broke up with a girlfriend about two months ago, which was difficult for her as she has struggled to form a close group of friends since starting college. Chi decided to go to the university counseling center as she was feeling depressed and was having difficulty falling asleep at night, which was affecting her schoolwork.

Introduction

Psychological research currently focuses on single aspects of identity that reflect social group membership, such as ethnicity and gender. Since there are multiple social groups with which individuals can identify in addition to ethnicity and gender—such as religious affiliation, racial background, and sexual orientation—an understanding of **identity development** in Asian Americans needs to incorporate the perspective of the intersection of **multiple social identities**. Having multiple social identities means that an individual subjectively experiences being part of more than one social group. For instance, one person may identify with being a man, a Cambodian, an Asian American, and a Buddhist while another person may only identify with being a Christian. This chapter provides background information about identity development as well as factors that affect identity development. Additionally, the chapter discusses theories and research on different ways that individuals manage their multiple social identities.

Background

When studying any racial or ethnic group in psychology, it is important to acknowledge that there is great variation within a group. This is seen in personal characteristics (e.g., personality, self-esteem, intelligence) as well as in how individuals identify with various aspects of themselves related to social categories, such as ethnicity, gender, race, sexual orientation, religion, and socioeconomic class status. Recognition of **within-group differences** in the Asian American population regarding psychological processes will aid researchers and clinicians in conceptualizing Asian American identity in a more complex manner.

Identity development research focuses on individuals' subjective experiences of who they are, based on personal characteristics or social group memberships. Both social context and personal meaning influence identity development. **Personal identity** refers to qualities that make one feel unique. Marilynn Brewer (2001) defined personal identity as "the individuated self—those characteristics that differentiate one individual from others within a given social context" (p. 246). William Cross Jr. (1987) considered personal identity factors, such as self-esteem and self-worth, as "so-called universal components" that are found in all humans regardless of race, sex, social class, or culture. Personal identity, then, relates to personal characteristics, such as personality and self-esteem, and individual relationships.

Social identities, in contrast, are related to meaning associated with various social group memberships, such as ethnicity, gender, race, sexual orientation, religion, and socioeconomic status. Social identities expand the meaning of identity beyond the individual in that they represent "categorizations of the self into more inclusive social units that depersonalize the self concept" (Brewer, 2001, p. 246). The aim of **social identity** development models is to theorize individuals' psychological processes related to social group memberships. This includes the individuals' internal understanding of how various demographic variables are integrated into their self-concept. For example, a person's demographic variables may include being "female" and "Taiwanese"—her social identity development would involve how she views herself as a woman and as Taiwanese. For the purposes of this chapter, social identities will be defined as the incorporation of meanings associated with social group memberships into the personal self-concept.

Increasingly, psychologists have noted that individuals often do not experience themselves in discrete categories of identity (Constantine, 2002; Greene, 2000; Parks, Carter, & Gushue, 1996; Reynolds & Pope, 1991; Robinson, 1999). Beverly Greene (2000) commented on the limitations of American psychology in which "identity is rarely viewed as an integrated whole in which one component can only be understood in relation to and in the context of others" (p. 2). Because psychological research follows this tendency of isolating social identities in empirical studies, psychotherapists are often influenced to operate similarly with their clients. For instance, Tracy Robinson (1999) noted that counselors may have difficulty viewing a client as "an integrated whole" because "when an identity status deviates from a normative standard, it tends to dominate and thus render invisible other equally viable components of a person's identity" (p. 75). Robinson's point speaks to the problem of concentrating only on the marginalized aspects of identity at the cost of considering other valid aspects of identity for the individual. For example, a client or student is not likely to state, "I am learning disabled" or "I am a Hmong refugee"; instead the client might state, "I am a college student trying to graduate." The client may happen to have a learning disability and be a Hmong refugee, but those characteristics alone do not define the individual's experience. Clinically, considering that **salience** of identity may vary for different individuals, it is essential that therapists explore individuals' subjective (i.e., internal) experience of which aspect(s) of identity will be most relevant to the therapeutic process.

Factors in Identity Development

Not only has identity development traditionally been conceptualized in singular categories (e.g., racial identity, ethnic identity, and sexual identity), it has been examined mainly as an internal psychological process. Increasingly, identity development scholars are recognizing factors in identity development, namely (a) identity salience, (b) internal definition versus external definition of identity, and (c) the role of context. This next section discusses these factors in identity development, which are an essential foundation to understanding how individuals manage multiple social identities.

Salience of Various Social Identities

Salience refers to the most prominent—and often most relevant—characteristic, which in this case refers to social identity. Research on Asian Americans has assumed ethnicity or race as the most salient social identity. This assumption is based on the recognition that people of color and ethnic minorities have been psychologically impacted by the oppression of racial and ethnic groups in the United States. Also, people tend to focus on the most visible characteristics, usually regarding race and sex, which tap into racial and gender identities. This limits our understanding of identity development in Asian Americans because it does not consider the diversity within the group in terms of ethnicity, class, sex, religion, age, and sexual orientation. Furthermore, individual differences in the salience of different aspects of identity may exist (Fouad & Brown, 2000; Rotheram & Phinney, 1987). Recognizing salience as a factor of social identity development allows for the possibility that individuals deal with multiple social identities and that some are more prominent in their self-identity than others.

Although race is "a salient collective identity" for many people of color (Helms, 1994), this may not always be the case for Asian Americans because of the "model minority myth." This conspicuous distinction pits Asian Americans against other visible ethnic and racial minority groups and encourages them to strive toward becoming as close to the White ideal as possible. Hence, it may be easier for Asian Americans to disregard racial discrimination when given the opportunity to live the privileged life of being the "exception" of racial and ethnic minority groups. In other words, Asian Americans are often rewarded by the dominant society for not identifying as being part of an oppressed group (Ancheta, 1998). Another reason that race may not be as salient for Asian Americans is that many White Americans buy into the "model minority myth" and may be more tolerant of and less (overtly) discriminatory toward Asian Americans such that Asian Americans do not perceive racial discrimination as being a major issue in their lives. Thus, their racial identity may not be the most salient aspect of their identity.

Kathleen Ethier and Kay Deaux (2001) outlined three bases of influence of salience on social identity: (a) having "chronic levels of group identification" makes it more likely that the individual will experience that identity as salient, independent of the situational context (e.g., growing up with a strong Korean identity); (b) the more contrast between the individual's self-definition and the current context, such as having minority status, makes that identity more salient (e.g., being female in a predominantly male profession); and (c) the more contrast between the individual's past background and the current context (e.g., moving from a predominantly White neighborhood to a racially diverse university) makes that identity more salient (pp. 255–256).

An exploratory qualitative study (Chen & Guzmán, 2003) investigating identity salience and multiple identities with an Asian American sample has provided preliminary results addressing the validity of the Multidimensional Identity Model (Reynolds & Pope, 1991) with this population. The outcomes suggest that although ethnicity and race are the most salient social identities for many Asian Americans, other social identities—such as gender, religious affiliation, and class—are also salient for many others. Additionally, some participants listed personal identity characteristics, such as "personality," "human being," and "career," as being most salient.

Because the open-ended question was originally part of a larger study on racial and ethnic identity, the participants may have been primed to think more about those social identities, so the outcomes may be biased. However, the results of this preliminary study indicate the need for further research on the salience of multiple aspects of identity. Many respondents described difficulty in choosing just one salient identity and listed multiple social identities as salient in their lives, which reflects the complexity of how individuals experience self-identity with regards to social group memberships.

The Role of Context

Social identity salience can depend on the context (i.e., social, cultural, and political environment). Depending on the context, some social identities may be more salient than others. Rotheram and Phinney (1987) noted that changes in the "sociocultural milieu" also influence identity salience. For example, in the 1960s, the "Black is beautiful" movement encouraged Blacks to be proud of their identity as Blacks; this in turn influenced the salience of this social identity in a positive manner. Similarly, popular culture in the past decade has embraced Chinese characters and Indian patterns on clothing and accessories, which may allow Chinese Americans and Indian Americans to feel more comfortable with and proud of their ethnic heritage.

In a study with Asian American females, Shih, Pittinsky, and Ambady (1999) examined how stereotypes about females and Asian Americans influenced math performance. They suggested that salience of social identity for Asian Americans depended on the social context, which would prime different social identities given the nature of the situation. Two conditions were presented—the stereotype of females having lower math aptitude, and the stereotype of Asian Americans as excelling in mathematical tasks (Shih, Pittinsky, & Ambady, 1999). The Asian American female participants performed better when their Asian American identity was made more salient than their gender identity. In a related study, Pittinsky, Shih, and Ambady (1999) investigated identity adaptiveness (i.e., shifting social identity salience) in different situations. The results of the study suggest that social contexts priming social identities to be salient can have effects on emotions related to social identification, especially if stereotypes exist for those social identities.

Several participants in Grace Chen's (2005) study indicated that they viewed their social identities differently based on different social contexts. Entering a particular occupational field made certain social identities more salient for the following respondent:

> I am very aware of being an Asian American woman. I never used to think twice about it, but there's something about law school that's changed that. In my interactions with my profs, the admin, opposing counsel, judges, other classmates, I am aware of stereotypes they may have of Asian American women and for the most part I try not to conform to them. For example: In law school, many of the Asian American women are seen as quiet, shy, meek, sweet, petite, giggly, etc. The stereotypes sicken me and the women who perpetuate them irritate me. (26-year-old heterosexual Korean American female)

In this example, not only did the participant become more aware of stereotypes about Asian American women; she also was bothered by people who seemed to emulate or perpetuate those stereotypical images. Similarly, Asian American students may behave differently and have a different level of self-efficacy based on the makeup of their classes. For example, they may feel more comfortable speaking in an Asian American Studies course than in a course mainly comprised of White students.

A shift in geographical location—primarily a change in the demographics' racial and ethnic diversity—also prompted many participants to think about race and ethnicity in more salient ways (Chen, 2005):

> These [race, ethnicity, gender] are the top three ways I am viewed. The actions of others impact how I see myself. When living in Los Angeles, I didn't particularly identify racially/ethnically first. There were always Asians and Chinese around me, but moving to a place that is primarily White affected me. All of a sudden, I began thinking of myself as a racial being because I was being treated as such—as an Other. So many times being asked where I was from or to explain my nationality and culture. I began to feel like an Other and have now embraced it as a sense of resistance and pride. (40-year-old heterosexual Chinese American female)

Similar to the previous respondent's experience, the following respondent indicated that social identity salience was affected by many contextual considerations—geography, racial diversity, and others' attitudes and knowledge about Asian Americans:

> Society's standards and values definitely affect the way I identify with social groups. Some factors that influence my identity is largely determined by my environment, geography of

where I live, the percentage of other Asian Americans or Filipinos in my immediate surroundings, and the views, knowledge, and exposure that individuals may or may not have
about Asian Americans or Filipinos. (32-year-old heterosexual Filipina American female)

These examples illustrate how many Asian Americans shift their behaviors and attitudes
related to their social identities based on social situations, geographical location, and others'
identity development. Thus, their social identities had different levels of salience depending on
the context (e.g., family function, work, geographical location).

Internally Defined Versus Externally Defined Identity

One dimension of the Multidimensional Identity Model (Reynolds & Pope, 1991) regarding
identification with multiple identities involves either passive acceptance of societal views or personal conscious choice (see Figure 10.1). Passive acceptance of societal views reflects an **externally defined identity**, while personal conscious choice indicates a more **internally defined
identity**. While Amy Reynolds and Rachele Pope originally included passive acceptance versus
conscious identification as a dimension of identifying with a single aspect of identity, the concept of internally defined versus externally defined identity seems to be applicable to individuals
identifying with multiple social identities as well.

In Grace Chen and Michele Guzmán's (2003) exploratory qualitative study on identity
salience, participant responses indicated that the salience of identity was often influenced by
societal context. One individual commented on the salience of race as being affected by external
views:

I would suppose my race to be the most salient aspect of my identity. Others notice that
I'm not 100% Asian and therefore that triggers conversation. When others take note of a
particular aspect of you, I think you tend to identify with that more often. (21-year-old
Korean American female)

In this example, the respondent indicated that the external factor of how others have treated
her impacted how she personally identified with that particular social identity. However, even if
identification with a social identity was influenced by societal views, it did not necessarily negate
personal meaning or conscious choice. Another response revealed the complex nature of defining one's identity within a sociocultural context:

My ethnicity is the most salient. I believe since the world is still very superficial, my face will
be a first-time determinant of how others decide to treat me. I believe I am who I am because
of my background (Chinese) especially since my mother instilled a great deal of Chinese values and customs in me ever since I was a child. . . . (23-year-old Chinese American female)

Here, the respondent acknowledged that society's reaction to her has influenced her ethnicity to be more salient but that there is also a lot of personal meaning and value associated with
being Chinese. In order to deal with the reality that society still treats people differently based
on social group memberships (e.g., race, gender, socioeconomic status), external definitions of
identity may be incorporated into internal definitions of identity.

In sum, the concept of internally defined versus externally defined identity has been included
in theories of identity but has not been empirically investigated. Scholars have advocated that
identity development be conceptualized within the sociocultural context (Ellemers, Spears, &
Doosje, 2002; Neville & Mobley, 2001). This points to the need for identity researchers to consider the impact of external definitions of social group membership on internal definitions of

identity. Clinically, therapists need to consider how clients define themselves and are affected by societal views.

Multiple Social Identities and Development

Identity development models regarding single aspects of social identity, such as ethnicity, race, or sexuality, often do not take into consideration the intersection or salience of that aspect of identity relative to other aspects of identity (Cass, 1979; Helms, 1994; Phinney, 1989). However, several models include comments on the importance of considering context and relationship with other aspects of identity (Helms, 1994; Worthington, Savoy, Dillon, & Vernaglia, 2002). Unfortunately, few theoretical models address the issue of multiple social identities directly. The integration of various aspects of identity into a self-concept is important to consider, especially among individuals who are members of multiple oppressed groups (Greene, 2000; Lowe & Mascher, 2001; Reynolds & Pope, 1991).

In contrast to identity models tracing a developmental process, the Multidimensional Identity Model (Reynolds & Pope, 1991) considers how individuals manage multiple identities. Drawing on biracial identity development models that address the intersection of multiple identities, Reynolds and Pope (1991) developed the Multidimensional Identity Model as a categorical identity model. This model is based on the reality that individuals often experience multiple oppressions because of their various social group statuses, such as being a woman and a person of color. Although their model focuses on marginalized social identity statuses, the concepts of the Multidimensional Identity Model seem applicable to dominant identity statuses as well. Thus, the concepts of the Multidimensional Identity Model are utilized in this chapter's discussion of marginalized as well as dominant social identity statuses.

There are several theoretical models and research studies that have delineated similar concepts regarding multiple social identities. This section presents a summary of theories and research regarding multiple identities. The theories and research discuss how individuals manage their multiple social identities in the following ways:

- Focusing on a single social identity, such as gender, ethnicity, or religion
- **Compartmentalizing** multiple social identities into separate categories
- **Integrating** identities into a holistic identity

Additionally, some individuals do not identify with any social identity (at least not consciously) and focus on their personal identity instead. The following sections discuss the various ways in which individuals manage their social identities.

Focusing on a Single Social Identity

When individuals focus on a single social identity, they are identifying with the most salient social group membership. In her review of research on identity development in adolescents, Phinney (1993) described how some adolescents engage in dualized thinking (i.e., all-or-nothing), where they feel they must choose one identity over another. In this sense, individuals believe they must identify with only one social identity, such as identifying either as a woman or as a Vietnamese American, but not both. However, other individuals may choose to identify with only one social identity because that social identity's salience is so fundamental to their overall sense of self and not necessarily because they feel they must choose one social identity over others.

The choice of one salient social identity may be based on the identity development factor of internally defined versus externally defined identity. Passively accepting a societal definition (externally defined) means that individuals agree with what they perceive to be the most salient social identity that society seems to notice about them. For example, in Chen and Guzmán's (2003) research on Asian Americans and identity saliency, one respondent indicated that race has been made most salient in his identity by others' reactions to him: "It's right there and obvious that you look different; most of the other [identities] aren't easily known from a glance" (19-year-old Chinese American male).

In contrast, individuals who consciously identify with a social identity (internally defined) often have developed an internal sense of meaning related to that social group. Another respondent in Chen and Guzmán's (2003) study specified that his Taiwanese ethnicity is salient because it is personally meaningful to him: "I can speak my native language and am well aware of events happening here and there and I advise at a Taiwanese camp. I'm pretty adamant about not being called Chinese and at the same time try to explain to everyone who questions me the difference" (18-year-old Taiwanese American male).

In this example, the respondent discussed his ethnicity with a sense of pride and seems intentional in integrating it in his life through various behaviors.

If you had to choose only one salient social identity, which would it be? Why?

Compartmentalizing Multiple Social Identities

Individuals also can identify with more than one social identity, such as identifying with being a man as well as a Christian. One way in which individuals manage their multiple identities is to separate them into different compartments. Reynolds and Pope's (1991) Multidimensional Identity Model described this as "identifying with multiple aspects of self in a segmented fashion" (p. 179). In this sense, the multiple aspects of self are not necessarily interacting with each other. Some individuals may separate and experience their multiple social identities in parallel processes, where there are no overlaps among the social identities (Uba, 1994). Individuals may do this to simplify how they understand their social identities as others may not recognize the complexities of their identity. Individuals may not feel validated by others in identifying with more than one social identity, so identifying in a segmented fashion is a way for them to manage

their multiple social identities. Phinney (1993) observed that some individuals separate their multiple identities because the salience of various social identities depended on the context.

In one example from Chen and Guzmán's (2003) research on Asian Americans and identity saliency, a respondent described how she experiences a couple of her social identities in different ways:

Race is salient only in that that's what others will see first and any assumptions they have about Asians will then be attributed to me, and I have become more aware of this phenomenon and how that affects me and my life. Personally, the most salient aspect of my life is my sexual orientation, and that was something I had to struggle with for such a long time that it has become almost instrumental in my development of self-identity, self-esteem, and other aspects of my life. (21-year-old Taiwanese American female)

This respondent indicates how her internal definition of her identity is related to her sexual orientation while she feels others externally define her identity to be related to her race. The way she discusses race and sexual orientation reflects a segmented manner in which she views her social identities.

When individuals identify with more than one social identity, there may be conflict among the social identities. Thus, individuals may try to cope by compartmentalizing their social identities in an effort to decrease conflict. In Chen's (2005) research on Asian Americans and multiple social identities, individuals were asked if they experienced conflict as a result of identifying with multiple social identities. The following examples reflect how some respondents in the study experienced conflict and how they managed that conflict:

Not identifying as Catholic but remaining respectful of my Filipino parents by not deliberately telling them of my negative views of the Catholic church. [Follow-up question: How do you manage this conflict?] Culture switching. You turn off one part of your identity when you are in a situation that doesn't support it. (26-year-old Filipino American male)

As the daughter of Taiwanese parents, I'm expected to be obedient and respectful—which is often in conflict with me being a woman who expresses herself and is vocal about her opinions. I'm also expected to do little else than study really, really hard, which is often in conflict with my conception of what a 23-year-old should do. [Follow-up question: How do you manage this conflict?] I often feel like I lead a double life—one that my parents are aware of, and another that I lead when I am away at school. The geographical separation is substantial, so I am able to do so. (23-year-old Taiwanese American female)

Another way individuals compartmentalize their social identities is in a hierarchical fashion, where some social identities are more salient than others, but they all are relevant in how individuals identify themselves with social groups. Phinney (1993) described how some individuals have a master identity that organizes a hierarchy of identities. In another example from Chen and Guzmán's (2003) research on Asian Americans and identity saliency, a respondent described the varying salience of multiple social identities:

I am a female first and foremost. Then follows my Indian American identity. I feel that gender is really the most defining characteristic because patriarchy is everywhere, regardless of culture and ethnicity. It is how others identify me (usually in a negative sense such as guys on the street catcalling). My Indian American identity has made me more aware of race, race relations, etc., but it hasn't necessarily made people treat me any differently than they'd treat a white person (I think). It is important to me in that much of my life's work has been devoted to it. (23-year-old Indian American female)

The master identity for this respondent seems to be gender, which she feels to be an overarching feature of her identity, including her ethnicity.

In thinking about your own identity, do you use a particular hierarchy? How does this help you manage various situations?

Integrating Multiple Social Identities

Individuals who identify with multiple social identities and try to make sense of how those social identities are incorporated into their self-concept are trying to integrate their multiple social identities. Individuals' sense of self is often quite complex, and they may want to have a more holistic self-concept in which they can incorporate social identities with their personal identity characteristics. Reynolds and Pope's (1991) Multidimensional Identity Model attempts to understand how people merge multiple social identities. Although some individuals may try to integrate multiple social identities, they may not necessarily try to integrate all of their social identities. They may be integrating the social identities that are most salient to them.

In Chen and Guzmán's (2003) research on Asian Americans and identity saliency, some respondents indicated that the intersection of multiple social identities was most salient to their identities:

To me race and gender go hand in hand. Being an Asian male, it is a constant struggle to deal with how the media and our society has [sic] mentally castrated the Asian male. Our masculinity is stripped from us and sometimes it is such a [sic] uphill battle. (23-year-old Chinese American male)

For me, being Cambodian is [in]extricably linked with being Buddhist. Growing up in a religious household, I have been immersed in the Cambodian culture and have noticed that it has shaped most of my values and thoughts, although I know that living in America and interacting with Americans has made my experience different than my parents. (20-year-old Cambodian American female)

Both respondents described how their social identities were intertwined with how they viewed themselves as they do not experience those social identities as discrete categories of their self-concept.

It is important to note, though, that in Phinney's (1993) research with adolescents of color, she found that the integration of identities may increase internal conflict if social group values are in opposition to one another. On the other hand, at this sophisticated level of cognition, Phinney observed, adolescents may also have increased tolerance for ambiguity and may be able to handle contradictory messages. As Phinney viewed managing identities as a developmental process, she suggested that, through maturation, individuals can reach the level of abstract, integrated thinking in which the complexity of identity across contexts is understood. Thus, individuals are able to achieve differentiation among multiple social identities, which then helps them integrate their multiple social identities.

An example of the conflict one can experience while trying to integrate identities is in Chen's (2005) study, where one respondent discussed the conflict she often had regarding her social identities:

An example would be race and gender. I am very active on campus, but I often feel like I have to choose between representing my people or representing my gender. To represent my gender would be viewed as creating division within my race. But to place my race before my gender is just imposing the same kind of oppression. [Follow-up question: How do you manage this conflict?] I try to not suppress one over the other. I don't really know. I feel like I'm just doing the best I can in creating a holistic identity that doesn't require me to choose one or another. I don't know how successful I am though. (21-year-old Chinese/ Vietnamese American female)

This respondent felt torn between her gender and race, as many women of color have experienced. Esther Chow (1989) discussed how Asian American women may not participate in the feminist movement as much because it seems like a "double bind for them because it pits ethnic identity against gender identity" (p. 367). Trying to integrate multiple social identities into one's self-concept can be challenging when one's social environments do not support or recognize the intersection of these conflicting social identities.

In Susan Jones and Marylu McEwen's (2000) conceptual model of Multiple Dimensions of Identity, the core identity (i.e., personal identity) interacts with fluid and dynamic aspects of social identity within changing contexts, which include family background, sociocultural conditions, and career decisions (see Figure 10.1). Their model recognized the interplay among personal identity and multiple social identities, such as culture, gender, race, class, religion, and sexual orientation, as well as the importance of understanding the interactions within varying contexts. The dots represent the relative salience of each social identity at a particular moment in time; the closer the dots are to the core, the more salient that social identity is at that moment for the individual. For instance, in a family where the daughter attended Chinese language school on the weekends and the parents insisted on speaking Chinese at home, the daughter's ethnic identity (being Chinese) may be more salient and closer to her core identity. Jones and McEwen (2000) indicated that although the model does not illustrate a developmental process, the model

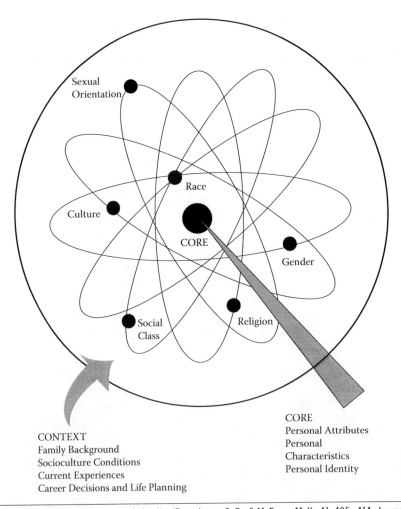

Figure 10.1 Model of Multiple Dimensions of Identity. (From Jones, S. R., & McEwen, M. K., 41, 405–414, *Journal of College Student Development*, 2000. Reprinted with permission from the American College Personnel Association.)

could be used as a "developmental snapshot" to understand the salience and intersections of social identities. Integrating multiple social identities seems to require cognitive and emotional complexity as well as supportive environments that allow for individuals to develop a more multifaceted sense of self.

More recently, the model of Multiple Dimensions of Identity was updated to consider how individuals filter contextual influences through a meaning-making process in terms of how they conceptualize their self-identity (Abes, Jones, & McEwen, 2007). While the original model conceptualized the relationship among individuals' multiple identities and core identity (within various contexts), the updated model takes into account the meaning-making process that individuals use to filter and incorporate contextual influences (in varying degrees) into their self-identity. See Figure 10.2 for the updated model of Multiple Dimensions of Identity.

Focusing on Personal Identity

An approach to managing social identities that is not often discussed is focusing on personal identity and not identifying with any social identity. For many individuals, they do not incorporate meanings of their social group memberships into their overall self-concept. This may be because personal identity characteristics, such as values and personality, are most salient in their identity. However, it could also be based on individuals' denial of or avoidance of dealing with social issues, especially if their social group memberships highlight their "otherness."

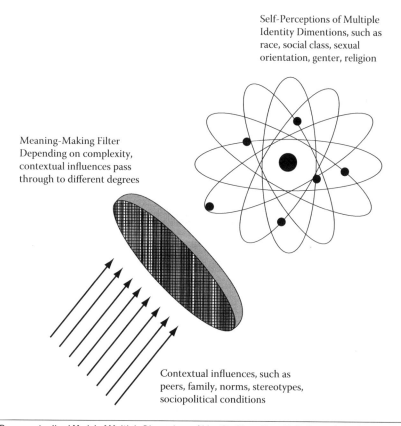

Self-Perceptions of Multiple Identity Dimentions, such as race, social class, sexual orientation, genter, religion

Meaning-Making Filter Depending on complexity, contextual influences pass through to different degrees

Contextual influences, such as peers, family, norms, stereotypes, sociopolitical conditions

Figure 10.2 Reconceptualized Model of Multiple Dimensions of Identity (From Abes, E. S., Jones, S. R., & McEwen, M. K., 48, 1–22, *Journal of College Student Development*, 2007. Reprinted with permission from the American College Personnel.)

In this sense, it may be a coping mechanism for some individuals to focus on personal identity attributes over social identities.

A respondent in Chen's (2005) study on multiple social identities discussed how he did not really identify with social groups:

> To be honest, I don't identify myself that strongly with any of the above groups. I think it is more coincidence that my friends/peers are of the same socioeconomic status, sexual orientation and age. I identify most strongly with similar family situation (married, kids of same age, etc.) and coworkers (people who are in my business or work with me). (31-year-old heterosexual Chinese American male)

This respondent seems to identify based on personal characteristics, such as his familial and occupational roles, rather than any social identities. Similarly, the next example is of a respondent who identifies with an immediate context: "I think I most identify myself as part of my immediate family" (21-year-old Hmong American female).

The respondent focuses on her role in her family, which is undoubtedly embedded in some kind of cultural context, but she does not seem to identify with broader social groups. Another respondent in Chen's (2005) study emphasized her personal values as what defines her identity: "My values of being honest and open-minded" (23-year-old Chinese American female). These examples reflect how some individuals base their self-concept more on their personal identity and not on any social identities.

Think for a moment about your personal identity characteristics and your social identities— what stands out to you most? How much is your self-concept based on personal identity characteristics, and how much is based on your social identities?

Multiple Oppressions

Having **multiple oppressed identity statuses** can be difficult to manage, can amplify issues of oppression and discrimination, and can cause feelings of conflict within an individual in terms of identity development. Many scholars have discussed the burden of "double jeopardy" (e.g., being a woman of color) and "triple oppressions" (e.g., being a gay man of color with a disability) and how multiple oppressions affect individuals (Alarcon, 1997; Chow, 1989; Crawford, Allison, Zamboni, & Soto, 2002; Greene, 2000; Reynolds & Pope, 1991). For instance, Greene (2000) described how gay, lesbian, and bisexual people of color can feel marginalized by their gay, lesbian, and bisexual community and/or their racial and cultural community. In addition, multiple oppressions are often overlooked in psychology as research tends to focus on one aspect of identity (e.g., being gay, lesbian, or bisexual) to the neglect of other aspects of identity (e.g., being a woman and a person of color). In Greene's (2000) review of lesbian and gay psychology, she detailed its "omissions of diversity" regarding age, sexuality (e.g., bisexuality), class, ethnicity and race. She described many individuals dealing with "multiple stigma," who felt they had to compartmentalize their identities or hide aspects of identity in order to be accepted into one community or another. Thus, managing multiple aspects of identity, especially oppressed social identity statuses, can create conflict within individuals.

Two key points to consider when discussing multiple oppressions are that (a) oppressed identity statuses are not necessarily more salient; and (b) multiple oppressions are not necessarily "additive." First, oppressed social identity statuses are not necessarily more salient to an individual than more privileged social identity statuses. Regarding a counseling context, Robinson (1999) strongly cautioned against therapists making assumptions about their clients' problems based on their seemingly "oppressed" group statuses. Instead, the client should be considered as having "multiple and textured identities" without assuming that "oppressed" group statuses have caused distress or are at the root of their problems (Robinson, 1999). For example, even though being male is considered a privileged identity, an Asian American man may feel that his gender is quite salient to his identity in light of the fact that he constantly has to deal with stereotypes about "weak and nerdy Asian men."

Second, having multiple oppressed identity statuses is not by default equivalent to adding up oppressions. Ayesha Vernon (1999) argued that having multiple oppressed social identity statuses should not automatically be considered "additive" oppressions. The interactions of multiple social identities—oppressed and privileged—are complex, and individuals experience them in diverse ways, so it is not sufficient to assume that multiple oppressions are simultaneous and additive (Chow, 1989; Vernon, 1999). For instance, an Asian American woman who identifies as a bisexual may feel that her race is more salient to her in her school environment because her math teachers always assume she is good at math; in this case, her identity as a bisexual woman is less salient. Certainly, managing multiple oppressed identity statuses can be difficult for individuals, but the salience of the various social identities needs to be considered when understanding how individuals create and manage their self-identity.

Summary

The diversity of how Asian Americans manage multiple social identities reflects the diversity within the Asian American population. The manner in which individuals manage their multiple social identities is complex as their social identities interact with their personal identity within constantly changing contexts. This chapter described multiple factors that affect identity development—the salience of various social identities, the role of context, and internally defined versus externally defined identity. Additionally, the chapter outlined how individuals may create their self-identity in a variety of ways—by focusing on a single social identity, compartmentalizing their multiple social identities, integrating their multiple social identities, or focusing on personal identity. Furthermore, many Asian Americans are dealing with multiple oppressed social identity statuses, which may or may not affect their self-identity significantly, depending on the context and the salience of various social identities. Overall, the chapter discussed how individuals' subjective experiences are crucial in understanding how Asian Americans manage multiple social identities.

Discussion Questions

1. Create your own model of multiple dimensions of identity (see Figure 10.1 for an example). What personal attributes, characteristics, and identities define your core? Which aspects of social identity are close to your core identity? Which are further away? Describe the context which influences you most.

2. Now that you have created your own model of multiple dimensions of identity, think about how others might perceive you—your family, your friends, your classmates, your professors, and people in public. Which personal identity characteristics and social identities do you think others associate most with you? How do you think that affects your relationships with people?

3. Sometimes individuals experience conflict as a result of identifying with multiple social identities. What might be some of the consequences of such conflicts (psychological or interpersonal)? What are some ways you would cope with these conflicts?

4. Based on the concepts of this chapter, discuss the following case studies in terms of how the individuals are managing their multiple identities. What are the social identities with which they identify? How do they manage their social identities?

Charlene, 20-year-old, heterosexual, Christian, Korean American female: I hold my faith in God above everything else. The color of people's skin doesn't really matter—it's how you relate to each other and the values you hold. I see the Christian faith as something that transcends cultural differences and past hurts. There's no point to focus on race so much. I believe that my religion has taught me to treat people with respect, and ultimately that's what's most important in life.

Raj, 23-year-old, heterosexual, Hindu, Indian American male: I am so tired of people calling me "Apu"—I hate the stupid stereotypes that all Asian Indians are either convenience store owners or cab drivers. But then sometimes I feel guilty—why am I trying so hard to distance myself from the working class? My family is upper middle class, and I know I grew up privileged. After 9/11, I'm angry and scared that ignorant Americans view South Asians as Arab terrorists. I get so frustrated with my family because they don't seem to understand that racism is alive and well in the United States. My parents just tell me not to make waves, that we are guests in this country. They want me to focus on marrying a nice Hindu girl so we can pass on our cultural traditions. I don't really know how I feel about that; I can't even think that far ahead.

Case Study

So far this chapter has focused on psychological theories and research on how Asian Americans manage multiple social identities. The chapter will now focus on a case study to help illustrate how Asian Americans might experience and cope with these issues. Additionally, the case will present factors that may be of concern for Asian Americans in counseling.

Chi is a 21-year-old, Vietnamese American, female undergraduate student who decided to go to the university counseling center since she wasn't doing very well in school lately. She stated that her main concerns were feeling depressed and having difficulty concentrating and sleeping. Chi has not been studying very much, and her grades started dropping. Chi lives off campus in an apartment with an acquaintance. Her parents, who are refugees, initially wanted her to live at home and commute to her classes, which is an hour and a half away. With support from her older brother and sister, Chi convinced her parents to let her live on campus.

When Chi was a sophomore in high school, she realized that she identified as a lesbian. She came out to her female best friend, who was very supportive. In college, Chi had her first serious relationship with another student, Maya, who is White. They broke up after a year of dating because they were constantly arguing about politics and social issues. Chi is active with the Asian American Student Association, and Maya could not understand what "the big deal was" about race relations on campus. Chi was very frustrated with Maya's "color-blind" attitude, especially since she had come out to her family under pressure from Maya, who accused Chi of being embarrassed about their relationship. Chi felt she was respectful of Maya's view about being openly gay with family even though she knew her family would have difficulty accepting her being gay; yet Maya did not respect that it was important to Chi to fight racism. Because she spent so much time with Maya before, Chi doesn't have very many close friends and feels lonely.

Chi always felt close to her parents and enjoyed spending time together as a family growing up. When she came out to her family a few months ago, her brother and sister were supportive. Chi's parents were unhappy with her disclosure and expressed discomfort and concern about her "choosing such a difficult lifestyle." They are devout Catholics, and they disapprove of her being gay. They told her that they love her but wish she could be "normal" and get married and have kids. Their relationship is now strained, and Chi wishes her family was the way it used to be. Out of respect for her parents, Chi hides her "lesbian self" when she's around family and the Vietnamese community. Chi doesn't feel completely comfortable as an Asian American in the gay and lesbian community as it seems like people don't see that stereotypes and racism still exist. Although she is out to members of the Asian American Students Association, Chi doesn't feel comfortable around anyone enough to talk to about her feelings. Her faculty advisor isn't as familiar with Asian American studies as he is with queer studies, so he encourages Chi to focus more on queer issues in her honors thesis.

Case Study Discussion

The counselor who met with Chi used a person-centered approach to counseling as well as feminist and multicultural perspectives to provide support and understanding. The person-centered approach to counseling helps the counselor to establish a genuine, unconditional, and empathic therapeutic relationship with Chi. The feminist and multicultural perspectives encourage the counselor to understand Chi's experience within cultural, social, political, and historical contexts. Furthermore, based on her feminist and multicultural perspectives, the counselor maintains awareness of her own experiences and biases that may impact her work with Chi. For example, the counselor is aware of her privilege as a heterosexual woman, so she wants to be careful not to minimize Chi's experience of alienation from her family and the Asian American community since she identifies as lesbian.

The challenges that Chi faced were related to the intersections of her multiple identities as a woman, a lesbian, an Asian American, and a Vietnamese American. Because all these social identities were salient to Chi, she experienced conflict with her family and various communities. Chi did not like feeling as if she had to compartmentalize her social identities; she could not and did not want to separate her lesbian self from her Vietnamese/Asian American self. However, she did not have strong social support and was not close to anyone who could understand how she felt.

Because Chi was feeling isolated and did not have anyone to talk to about her concerns, the counselor provided support through the use of empathy, which helped Chi feel more connected to the counselor. The counselor also validated Chi's feeling of not being completely accepted by her family, by the Asian American community, or by the lesbian, gay, and bisexual community. Often in subcommunities, such as the Asian American community, and lesbian, gay, and bisexual community, the most salient concerns reflect the defining nature of the community (i.e., ethnicity, race, and sexual orientation) even though there is much diversity within these communities. The counselor explicitly acknowledged the difficulty of having multiple social identities and feeling pressured by various groups to identify only in certain ways. This acknowledgment helped Chi realize that she indeed was struggling with difficult issues; previously she thought maybe there was something wrong with her since she did not have very many close relationships.

Based on feminist and multicultural perspectives, the counselor aimed to empower Chi to define her own identity and to make decisions that benefited her as well as her relationships with others. The counselor pointed out that even though Chi's advisor was urging her to focus mainly on queer issues, Chi should consider what she is really interested in studying for her honors thesis and not make decisions based on her advisor's discomfort with Asian American Studies. Chi decided that she would suggest to her advisor to arrange for a co-advisor who could advise her on Asian American issues for her honors thesis. The counselor was aware of the need to be culturally sensitive in that Chi's culture values included being close to family and respecting her elders. Because Chi's relationship with her family is extremely important to her, the counselor discussed with Chi that perhaps Chi may have to compartmentalize her social identities a little so that she can maintain her relationship with them. Through counseling, Chi determined that compartmentalizing her social identities was reasonable because she values her family so much—she decided that she would not be very expressive about being lesbian when she is around her family, but she also would not deny nor hide her lesbian identity just to make her family happy. The counseling experience helped Chi feel more comfortable with managing her multiple social identities. For the most part, she viewed and expressed her social identities in an integrated fashion. However, around her family, Chi was willing to compartmentalize her social identities—without denying any of them—in order to maintain her relationship with her family.

Case Study Discussion Questions

For undergraduate students, please consider the following questions:

1. What aspects of Chi's identity do you identify with? What aspects of Chi's identity do you feel you have difficulty identifying with? How would that impact how well you understood her feelings and experience?
2. What are you reactions to how Chi decided to compartmentalize her identity around her family? What would you have done in her situation?
3. What do you think of the counselor's approach to working with Chi?

For graduate students and/or beginning therapists, please consider the following questions:

1. Imagine that Chi is your client—which of your social identities are similar to Chi and which differ? How would that impact your work as a counselor?
2. What is your theoretical orientation? How would you approach working with Chi?
3. How familiar are you with Vietnamese culture? Lesbian, gay, and bisexual issues? Asian American issues? Gender issues for Vietnamese and Asian Americans? What areas would you like to learn more about? How would you learn more about these topics and communities?

Key Terms

Compartmentalizing: Separating multiple social identities into different parts and identifying with each social group in a segmented fashion.

Externally defined identity: Passive acceptance of societal views about one's identity characteristics.

Identity development: The process in which individuals develop a sense of who they are, based on personal characteristics or social group memberships.

Integrating: Incorporating multiple social identities into a holistic sense of self.

Internally defined identity: Personal conscious choice of how one views himself/herself.

Multiple oppressed identity statuses: When an individual has more than one oppressed or marginalized social identity (e.g., being female, gay, person of color, etc.). Also referred to as "double oppressions" or "triple oppressions."

Multiple social identities: Individuals' subjective experience of being part of more than one social group (i.e., in terms of ethnicity, gender, race, religious affiliation, sexual orientation, and socioeconomic status).

Personal identity: Characteristics that make an individual feel unique, such as personality and self-esteem.

Salience: How prominent a feature is.

Social identity: Incorporation of meanings associated with social group memberships, such as gender and race, into the personal self-concept.

Within-group differences: Differences that exist within one social group (as opposed to differences found between two social groups).

For Further Learning and Suggested Readings

Abes, E. S., Jones, S. R., & McEwen, M. K. (2007). Reconceptualizing the Model of Multiple Dimensions of Identity: The role of meaning-making capacity in the construction of multiple identities. *Journal of College Student Development, 48,* 1–22.

Cho, M. (2001). *I'm the one that I want.* New York: Ballantine Books. (also a motion picture)

Espiritu, Y. L. (1996). *Asian American women and men: Labor, laws, and love.* Thousand Oaks, CA: Sage.

Greene, B., & Croom, G. L. (2000). *Education, research, and practice in lesbian, gay, bisexual, and transgendered psychology: A resource manual.* Thousand Oaks: Sage.

Okazaki, S. (Producer). (1995). *American sons* [Motion picture].

References

Abes, E. S., Jones, S. R., & McEwen, M. K. (2007). Reconceptualizing the Model of Multiple Dimensions of Identity: The role of meaning-making capacity in the construction of multiple identities. *Journal of College Student Development, 48,* 1–22.

Alarcon, M. C. (1997). *The relationship between womanist identity attitudes, cultural identity, and acculturation to Asian American women's self-esteem.* Unpublished doctoral dissertation, Ball State University, Muncie, IN.

Ancheta, A. N. (1998). *Race, rights, and the Asian American experience.* New Brunswick: Rutgers University Press.

Brewer, M. B. (2001). The social self: On being the same and different at the same time. In M. A. Hogg & D. Abrams (Eds.), *Intergroup Relations: Essential Readings* (pp. 245–253). Philadelphia: Psychology Press.

Cass, V. C. (1979). Homosexual identity formation: A theoretical model. *Journal of Homosexuality, 4,* 219–235.

Chen, G. A. (2005). *The complexity of "Asian American identity": The intersection of multiple social identities.* Unpublished doctoral dissertation, University of Texas, Austin, TX.

Chen, G. A., & Guzmán, M. R. (2003). *Identity saliency in Asian Americans.* Unpublished manuscript, University of Texas, Austin, TX.

Chow, E. N.-L. (1989). The feminist movement: Where are all the Asian American women? In *Making waves: An anthology of writings by and about Asian American women* (pp. 362–377). Boston, MA: Beacon Press.

Constantine, M. G. (2002). The intersection of race, ethnicity, gender, and social class in counseling: Examining selves in cultural contexts. *Journal of Multicultural Counseling and Development, 30,* 210–215.

Crawford, I., Allison, K. W., Zamboni, B. D., & Soto, T. (2002). The influence of dual-identity development on the psychosocial functioning of African-American gay and bisexual men. *Journal of Sex Research, 39,* 179–189.

Cross, W. E., Jr., (1987). A two-factor theory of Black identity: Implications for the study of identity development in minority children. In J. S. Phinney & M. J. Rotherham (Eds.), *Children's Ethnic Socialization: Pluralism and Development* (pp. 117–133). Newbury Park, CA: Sage.

Ellemers, N., Spears, R., & Doosje, B. (2002). Self and social identity. *Annual Review of Psychology, 53,* 161–186.

Ethier, K. A., & Deaux, K. (2001). Negotiating social identity when contexts change: Maintaining identification and responding to threat. In M. A. Hogg & D. Abrams (Eds.), *Intergroup relations: Essential readings* (pp. 254–265). Philadelphia: Psychology Press.

Fouad, N. A., & Brown, M. T. (2000). Role of race and social class in development: Implications for counseling psychology. In S. D. Brown & R. W. Lent (Eds.), *Handbook of counseling psychology* (3rd ed., pp. 379–408). New York, NY: John Wiley & Sons.

Greene, B. (2000). Beyond heterosexualism and across the cultural divide: Developing an inclusive lesbian, gay, and bisexual psychology: A look to the future. In B. Greene & G. L. Croom (Eds.), *Education, research, and practice in lesbian, gay, bisexual, and transgendered psychology: A resource manual* (Vol. 5, pp. 1–45). Thousand Oaks, CA: Sage.

Helms, J. E. (1994). The conceptualization of racial identity and other "racial" constructs. In E. J. Trickett, R. J. Watts & et al. (Eds.), *Human diversity: Perspectives on people in context* (pp. 285–311). San Francisco: Jossey-Bass.

Jones, S. R., & McEwen, M. K. (2000). A conceptual model of multiple dimensions of identity. *Journal of College Student Development, 41,* 405–414.

Lowe, S. M., & Mascher, J. (2001). The role of sexual orientation in multicultural counseling: Integrating bodies of knowledge. In J. G. Ponterotto, J. M. Casas, L. A. Suzuki, & C. Alexander (Eds.), *Handbook of multicultural counseling* (2nd ed., pp. 755–778). Thousand Oaks, CA: Sage.

Neville, H. A., & Mobley, M. (2001). Social identities in contexts: An ecological model of multicultural counseling psychology process. *The Counseling Psychologist, 29,* 471–486.

Parks, E. E., Carter, R. T., & Gushue, G. V. (1996). At the crossroads: Racial and womanist identity development in Black and White women. *Journal of Counseling & Development, 74,* 624–631.

Phinney, J. S. (1989). Stages of ethnic identity in minority group adolescents. *Journal of Early Adolescence, 9,* 34–49.

Phinney, J. S. (1993). Multiple group identities: Differentiation, conflict, and integration. In J. Kroger (Ed.), *Discussions on Ego Identity* (pp. 47–73). Hillsdale, NJ: Lawrence Erlbaum Associates.

Reynolds, A. L., & Pope, R. L. (1991). The complexities of diversity: Exploring multiple oppressions. *Journal of Counseling & Development, 70,* 174–180.

Robinson, T. L. (1999). The intersections of dominant discourses across race, gender, and other identities. *Journal of Counseling & Development, 77,* 73–79.

Rotheram, M. J., & Phinney, J. S. (1987). Introduction: Definitions and perspectives in the study of children's ethnic socialization. In J. S. Phinney & M. J. Rotherham (Eds.), *Children's ethnic socialization: Pluralism and development* (pp. 10–28). Newbury Park, CA: Sage.

Shih, M., Pittinsky, T. L., & Ambady, N. (1999). Stereotype susceptibility: Identity salience and shifts in quantitative performance. *Psychological Science, 10,* 81–84.

Uba, L. (1994). *Asian Americans: Personality patterns, identity, and mental health.* New York, NY: Guilford Press.

Vernon, A. (1999). The dialectics of multiple identities and the disabled people's movement. *Disability & Society, 14,* 385–398.

Worthington, R. L., Savoy, H. B., Dillon, F. R., & Vernaglia, E. R. (2002). Heterosexual identity development: A multidimensional model of individual and social identity. *Counseling Psychologist, 30,* 496–531.

11

Asian American Women
The Nail That Sticks Out Is Hammered Down

CHRISTINE C. IIJIMA HALL

OUTLINE OF CHAPTER

Case Synopsis

Emily is a 22-year-old second-generation Japanese American college student who is dating a 28-year-old White American male. She reports that she is very serious about this man. Sam is of a lower social class, did not attend college, and works at the university copy center. Her parents are unhappy because they wish her to marry a Japanese man. Her parents have tried to introduce her to the Japanese men they know and have attempted to set her up with a matchmaker from the Japanese community. Sam has asked Emily to move in with him, but she is not sure how to tell her parents. Emily is experiencing symptoms of anxiety, depression, and negative self-esteem.

Introduction

Writing a chapter on Asian American women is like writing a chapter on the number of ways to cook and prepare rice. That is, there are so many aspects of Asian American women that cannot be completely conveyed in a single chapter. Thus, this chapter will focus on a few main issues, specifically historical background, **gender** roles and stereotypes, and racism and **sexism**. These tie together because they represent the many aspects of the psychology—social, developmental, cultural, family, gender, counseling—of Asian American women. (Please note that issues of sexual orientation are touched upon briefly in this chapter because lesbian, bisexual, gay and transgendered issues are addressed in more detail in another chapter in this book.)

Brief History of Asian Women in America

Asian and Asian American women were systematically excluded from entering the United States through immigration laws (Espiritu, 1996). In fact, legislation is an excellent barometer of the sentiment expressed about the group since "legislation both influences and is influenced by the values and attitudes of the American people" (Tien, 2000, p. 29).

Late 1800s and Early 1900s

Originally, Asian men and women were excluded from entering the United States and from becoming U.S. citizens through anti-immigration laws such as the Chinese Exclusion Act of 1882, the Immigration Act of 1917, and the National Origins Act of 1924. These laws were modified along the way to satisfy capitalist needs. That is, in the late 1800s, the Chinese Exclusion Act of 1882 was changed to allow large numbers of Chinese, Japanese, Korean, and Filipino men to immigrate as cheap labor (Espiritu, 1996; Tien, 2000). They primarily worked in laundries, restaurants, and for railroads. Many of the Asian men were married and left their wives behind. However, a large number were single with no possibilities of finding spouses in the United States because the exclusion acts (such as the Alien Wife Bill) directly prohibited Asian women from entering the United States (Espiritu, 1996; Tien, 2000).

The United States purposely excluded Asian women from immigrating into the United States because families could be threats to the "efficiency and exploitability of the workforce" (Espiritu, 1996, p. 16). That is, employers housed and fed Asian male workers as cheap labor, and the costs to maintain families (housing, food, clothing, education) were greater than for single workers.

In the late 1800s and early 1900s, the U.S. began to allow Asian women to immigrate to the United States through such laws as the Gentleman's Agreement (True & Guillermo, 1996). Many of these women were spouses joining their husbands, single women searching for work and marriage, or picture brides (women who were matched with men via exchange of photos). Many of the women worked side by side with their men. Asian women labored in agriculture and service sectors as farm workers, prostitutes, cooks, domestic servants, laundresses, and seamstresses (Espiritu, 1996).

Most of the immigrated women were prostitutes brought in by the United States to fulfill the sexual needs of the Asian men while simultaneously hindering marriages. Due to this large

Asian pioneer woman in the United States. (From the Idaho State Historical Society.)

number of prostitutes, the stereotype of Asian women being sexually permissive, hypersexual, and sexually **subservient** began to flourish (Espiritu, 1996). This image was in stark contrast to that of European women who were viewed as "pure." Thus, negative perceptions of Asian women added fodder to keep "undesirable" Asian women out of the United States.

Back in Asia, the lives of the married women whose husbands had migrated to the United States changed tremendously. Many became quite assertive and self-sufficient and took control of the family governance (Espiritu, 1996). To limit the independence of these "married widows," many husbands sent money home, not to their wives, but to other family members to dole out appropriately so the women would not become too independent (Espiritu, 1996). Many women, however, did maintain their independence and when they were able to join their husbands in America, these independent behaviors continued and caused marital problems.

Post World War II

After World War II, many U.S. servicemen were stationed in Europe and in the Pacific. Between 1944 and 1950, 50,000 to 100,000 marriages involving these servicemen in Asia, and 150,000 to 200,000 in Europe, took place (Tien, 2000). However, a large discrepancy existed in how the U.S. treated these war brides. Servicemen were allowed to return with their White European wives (War Bride Act of 1945 and Fiancée Act) but not with their "colored" Asian wives (primarily from Japan, China, and the Pacific Islands). It was not until 1947 when the Alien Wife Bill was reintroduced and passed as the "Soldier's Bride Act." While this law allowed for wives' entry into the United States, the U.S. government continued to make it difficult (with additional paperwork, approvals, counseling, etc.) to marry an Asian woman and bring her into the United States (Hall, 1987; Tien, 2000).

Upon arriving in the United States, these Asian women, their American husbands, and their children faced much discrimination. One particular form of discrimination was anger from

Chapter author Christine C. Iijima Hall's parents in the 1940s. Married for more than 50 years.

White and Black American women because these Asian women had married *their* men. That is, many young men died during WWII, thus reducing the number of eligible men. The Asian women became the "foreigners" who "stole" the few marriageable American men who returned from the war (Hall, 1987).

Discriminatory treatment was also enacted on the Japanese living inside the United States during WWII. Following the bombing of Pearl Harbor in 1941 by the Japanese, 110,000 Japanese Americans were interned by the United States for four years (Nagata, 2000). Due to this inappropriate confinement, many Japanese Americans tried to separate themselves from Japan as much as possible by choosing not to teach their children the Japanese language or other customs in order to prove their affinity to the United States (personal conversation with the author's Japanese mother). Others developed a distrust of the U.S. government that has been passed down to each new generation.

Similar to post WWII, the post Vietnam War era resulted in many Southeast Asian war brides entering the United States with their military husbands. While the process for marrying Vietnamese women was not as difficult as the process following WWII, the discrimination upon entering the United States was just as great. Again, these women were perceived as the "enemy" who married the few eligible American men who did not die in the war. Additional Asian groups also began to arrive into the United States such as Cambodians, Laotians, and other Southeast Asians. Many of these individuals were refugees escaping their oppressive governments. Some individuals were from well-to-do families, while others were poor and found ways to escape. The difficulties of these newly immigrated women were financial, emotional (culture shock), and physical (health and domestic violence).

The history of immigration to the United States sets the stage for the stereotypes and images of Asian American women today, as well as their relationships.

Question: Do you know the history of how your ancestors arrived in the United States? Was there racism or sexism upon their arrival?

Racism and Sexism in America

Women represent 51.3% (6.41 million) of the Asian Pacific Islander population living in the United States (Reeves & Bennett, 2003). They experience a complicated interaction of racism, sexism, and **classism** that must be taken into account when understanding the lives of Asian American women (Espiritu, 1996).

Gender Roles of Asian American Women

The traditional Asian culture is commonly a patriarchal one. The role of women is primarily to honor and serve men. The "three obediences"—obedience to the father, submission to the husband, and indulgence of the son—are the measures of a woman's value (Fu, 2006). While this role may be seen as "old world," these traditional beliefs still set the standards for many of the behaviors of Asian American women such as being a good wife, mother, elder caretaker, conveyer of traditions and customs, and homemaker while also performing nontraditional functions such as working outside the home. Thus, balancing the traditional with the nontraditional has become a major stress factor for Asian American women.

Many individuals in the United States may be surprised to hear that while education is promoted in most Asian cultures, there is usually a dual standard for men and women. That is, women are expected to obtain an education because education is important for displaying wisdom and good genes, and for ensuring adequate provisions for the women and their families. However, it is important for a woman not to become *too* educated because it may reduce her "female attributes" of wife, mother, etc. because a man may not want to marry a woman more educated than himself, and a career may cause her to focus on work rather than family duties.

For example, the young Japanese women in Japan were extremely disappointed with Masako Owada when this Harvard-educated and career-minded woman chose to forgo a promising career with the Japanese Ministry of Foreign Affairs to become Princess of Japan in 1993. Her worth became solely based on her ability to produce a male heir to the throne. The reader will agree with the irony of this since it is the man who contributes the chromosomes to produce a male, not the female! The couple, now in their late 40s, has one child—a girl.

The three obediences and priorities of wife and mother are obvious examples of oppression and control of Asian women by a patriarchal society. Another example of oppression and control can be seen in the ancient Chinese tradition of feet binding. It was marketed as a way of making women more attractive (the smaller feet, the more beautiful) while in reality it transformed women into powerless and weak beings under the control of their husbands (Levy, 1991). Women with bound and deformed feet could not walk and therefore were totally reliant on their husbands or servants for mobility.

Clothing can also be a cultural tradition that serves to oppress and control. For example, the Japanese obi binds and flattens the breasts and the Korean hanbok is tent-like and camouflages all secondary sex characteristics. Similar to the Islamic burka, these concealing costumes may have been designed to reduce men's thoughts of sex and to control women.

Stereotypes

Oppression of Asian women worsened when they arrived in the United States as now they faced racism and stereotypes. Stereotypes maintain oppression. They deny individuality, and they

Wedding photo of Erica Sugiyama-Hill, "Case Study" author for this chapter and third-generation Japanese American.

prejudice people to the valuable characteristics of individuals and groups. Common stereotypes that have plagued Asian and Asian American women have been those of exoticism and objectification commonly conveyed through media images.

These images of Asian women range from the "dragon lady" who is evil, inscrutable, sinister, and dark with long fingernails, to the ingénue who is innocent, sweet, subservient, fragile, and needs to be rescued. These images developed through different mechanisms. The negative and even evil stereotypes began in the 1800s and early 1900s when their immigration was prohibited or severely limited into the United States. Images of prostitution and oversexuality were prominent. As the United States interacted with Asia militarily (WWII, Korea, Vietnam), the dehumanization and sinisterization of Asians were emphasized, encouraging the United States to fight and kill the enemy. Evil images of dragon ladies were further developed through movies such as the Charlie Chan and James Bond series.

At the conclusion of these military confrontations with Asia, American males began viewing Asian women differently. American men saw Asian women as being (unlike American women) subservient, "dutiful, obedient, and sexually accessible" to their men (Danico & Ng, 2004, p. 122). American men especially enjoyed the image of the "geisha," professional prostitutes who served upper-class men with baths, massages, tea, dancing, and sex. The geisha is an example of a perfect woman constructed by a patriarchal culture. Traditionally in Japanese culture, a geisha is "raised" from a young age to become the cultured, elegant, beautiful, and sexually pleasing "perfect" woman. She is a fantasy. American men bought into the fantasy and mistakenly believed that all Japanese and Asian women were like geisha.

The "perfect woman" image is further promulgated by the small stature, facial features, and extremities (hands and feet) of Asian women (Hall, 1995; Root, 1990). Smaller women are seen as less powerful and "childlike" (Root, 1995, 1998). Childlike images convey weakness and innocence. A powerless individual does not argue or question authority; she obeys the authority figure—men.

Winners of the annual Vietnamese beauty contest in Phoenix, AZ.

This oppressive physical image of Asian women may influence the body image of Asian American women (Hall, 1995). For example, if an Asian American woman is overweight, she may develop an eating disorder such as anorexia or bulimia. Body image difficulties may also develop if she feels she is not beautiful enough by White American standards. This may be exhibited in a desire for cosmetic surgery on her eyes and nose, breast enhancement, or skin lightening. (Body image is discussed in more detail in another chapter of this book.) The reader should keep in mind that these oppressive criteria for beauty are predominantly placed on women and are based on sexist, racist, and classist guidelines. What do you think an Asian American woman experiences if she does not fit the stereotype of the quiet, subservient geisha? Is she seen as being too aggressive, a dragon lady, or as "acting White"? What television shows and movies have you seen that involved Asian or Asian American women (such as *Mulan*, Margaret Cho, Lucy Liu, Tia Carrere, and Sandra Oh)? What types of roles do they play—stereotypical or could someone of any race play the same role?

Education and Professional Life

A gender difference exists in educational attainment of Asian Americans (Reeves & Bennett, 2003). Females are more likely to have less than a high school education, while males have a greater percentage of bachelor's degrees or higher (see Table 11.1).

With the differences in education attainment and gender roles/stereotypes, it is not surprising that career choices may differ between Asian American men and women. There is a higher proportion of Asian American men in the labor force than women (75% vs. 59%). There is also a bimodal distribution of career choices/employment of Asian American women similar to the bimodal distribution of educational attainment. Women are employed in lower-paying positions more often than men. For example, a large disparity exists between Asian American women and men in technical, sales, and administrative support jobs with women representing 34% and men 23% (Reeves & Bennett, 2003). The other large disparity is in the higher-paying jobs of precision, production, crafts and repair category. Almost 9.4% of Asian American men compared to 3.4% of Asian American women were employed in this category. There is no gender difference in the unemployment rate.

At the other end of the curve, 37% of Asian American women are employed in managerial and professional fields (Reeves & Bennett, 2003). This includes such occupations as doctors, lawyers, nurses, engineers, managers, and so on (41% of Asian American men are in this professional category). The statistic of 37% may surprise the reader in one respect but fit some of the stereotypes in another. That is, many Asian American women have high education attainment and high work standards so therefore enter into professional work. However, the image of the Asian woman as docile and nonassertive may cause problems for Asian American women wanting to move into executive positions in these professional fields (Danico & Ng, 2004). In fact, there are very few Asian American women in leadership positions in business and higher

Table 11.1 Educational Attainment of Asian American Females and Males

	Less than high school (%)	High school graduate (%)	Some college or Associate of Arts degree (%)	Bachelor's degree or more (%)
Females	14.5	23.2	18.5	43.8
Males	10.5	20.5	18.1	50.9

Source: From Reeves, T., & Bennett, C. in *The Asian and Pacific Islander population in the United States: March 2002*, Current Populations Reports, U.S. Census Bureau, Washington, DC, 2003, P20–P45.

Poster used for campaign against sweatshop abuses (circa 1993). Poster says "Justice" in Chinese.

education. Very little social science research could be found on the issue of Asian American women and work in the United States. Most publications simply quote work statistics.

Economics

Economically, the "APA community has the largest gap between rich and poor" (Lai & Arguelles, 2003, p. 220). Overall, 12.7% of Asian American women live in poverty compared to 9.1% Whites, 24.2% Latinos, and 26.7% Blacks (Lai & Arguelles, 2003). Many Asian women are employed in sweatshops. In the Northern California Bay Area (which has a large Asian population), the 20,000 sweatshops have large numbers of Chinese and Hong Kong women working in them. In New York, Asian women represent the majority of sweatshop workers. In Los Angeles, 15% of the sweatshop workers are Asians. This large number of sweatshop workers is due to discrimination, poverty, and immigration.

Households maintained by Asian American males without spouses had higher incomes than those headed by Asian American women without spouses present (Reeves & Bennett, 2003). Of these males, 51.5% had incomes over $50,000 compared to the 31% of the women with incomes over $50,000 (see Table 11.2). On the other end of the income spectrum, families with Asian American female heads of households had lower incomes, with 14.6% living at the poverty level compared to 9.1% of the male-headed households (Reeves & Bennett, 2003). Thus, women continue to bear a large brunt of the socioeconomic hardship of the Asian American population.

In terms of the gender gap in income, Asian American women earn approximately 80% of what an Asian American man earns (Lai & Arguelles, 2003). Thus, financial inequities exist

Table 11.2 Asian Female and Male Income Comparison

	Less than $25,000 (%)	$25,000–$34,999 (%)	$35,000–$49,999 (%)	$50,000–$74,999 (%)	$75,000 and above (%)
Females	32.0	20.4	16.5	14.0	17.1
Males	24.8	13.2	10.5	20.5	31.0

Source: From Reeves, T., & Bennett, C. In *The Asian and Pacific Islander population in the United States: March 2002*, Current Populations Reports, U.S. Census Bureau, Washington, DC, 2003, P20–P45.

between men and women among Asian American populations similar to the gender inequities in the overall U.S. workplace.

Family

Relationships and Family

Asian American men are less likely to marry than Asian American women (Reeves & Bennett, 2003). This statistic is contrary to the White population, in which more men are or have been married than women. These never-married statistics include individuals of different sexual orientations. While there may be no valid estimate of the Asian American gay, lesbian, bisexual, and transgendered demographics, there are Census data on unmarried Asian couples living together. Of the 4.7% Asian American households with two unmarried individuals living together as significant others, 0.7% is of the same sex and 4.0% are of the opposite sex (U.S. Census, 2000a).

One reason more Asian American women are married than men may be that Asian American women are more likely than Asian men to marry outside the Asian population (U.S. Census, 2000). In 1990, Asian American women were three times more likely to have White husbands (18%) than Asian American men were to have White wives (7%). (These individuals are more likely to marry Whites and also African Americans, Hispanics, and other Asians/Asian Americans.) Adding to this number, in 2000, among cohabiting couples, there were twice as many White male–Asian female couples as Asian male–White female couples.

Interracial marriage between the males from the dominant culture and females from the minority population is a tricky one especially when the dominant culture has traditionally been the oppressor. Many believe this type of marriage epitomizes the assimilation and domestication of the oppressed group through "the assimilation of the 'ethnic' woman into the benevolent paternalism of American society" (Lee, 1999, p. 171). Thus, the Asian/Asian American women who enter these interracial marriages may be seen by the Asian/Asian American community as sellouts or bananas (yellow on the outside, white on the inside) who are prostituting themselves to the enemy and White men may be viewed as the ultimate oppressor who now owns, enslaves, and rapes the oppressed woman. This negative stereotype of interracial relationships is an overreaction because research shows that the majority of the Asian American women who date White men are not the subservient, stereotypical Asian woman. In fact, most of these women view themselves as having strong personalities and independence (Fujino, 1997). This overreaction may also be a sexist response because Asian American men who marry and date White women are not seen as being enslaved or owned by these White women.

The White, dominant culture may also be unhappy with these mixed marriages. As seen after WWII, White women were hostile toward these relationships since these "foreigners" were marrying White men who potentially could have been their spouses. Similarly, when Asian men marry White women, the White men may view it as the oppressed culture infiltrating their "territory."

The relationship between a White American man and an Asian woman has been the fodder of many a book, movie, and opera. Most of these stories end in trauma and drama because this union is not seen as acceptable. *Sayonara*, a post-WWII movie in which an American soldier falls in love with a Japanese woman, is an example of this. In the movie, the United States does not allow the couple to marry and return to the United States so they both commit suicide. This double suicide is unusual because in most stories, only the Asian woman commits suicide, such as in *Madame Butterfly* and *Miss Saigon*. What do you think about when you see a White man with an Asian female? Is it different from seeing an Asian man with a White female?

Family Size

Family size for Asian Pacific Islanders is a difficult statistic to report on since Asians traditionally have multiple generations living in one household. That is, children, parents, grandparents, uncles/aunts, and other extended family members may be living under a single roof. The 2002 statistics show 72% of married couples had more than two individuals living in the household and 20% had more than five members (Reeves & Bennett, 2003). Interestingly, single (unmarried, widowed, or divorced) Asian women have more individuals living in the household than single Asian men. Some of these individuals may be contributing to the household income while many may not. The Asian woman may also be caring for elders and children. Thus, as the traditional family caretaker, Asian women may have physical, emotional, and financial stress placed on them added to their nontraditional role of breadwinner. Because society expects the Asian American woman to perform these duties, she may have few support networks to understand and help her navigate the stress of a multigenerational and multiperson household.

In terms of children, the majority of Asian American children live with both parents in the home (U.S. Census, 2000b). Very few children are born to single Asian American mothers (Lai & Arguelles, 2003). Only 15% of Asian American children are born out of wedlock compared to 26% White, 62% Black, and 30% Hispanic. This is perhaps due to the strong family ties, family obligations, and the need not to "shame" the family with a child out of wedlock.

Domestic Violence

Another major health threat among Asian American women is domestic violence. Because traditionally Asian women are required to be obedient, it is not a far stretch to understand the belief that a disobedient woman needs to be controlled through physical means. Thus, in some Asian cultures, violence against wives and daughters is not uncommon.

Disproportional high rates of domestic violence among Asian American immigrants have been reported (Hall, 2002). Domestic violence may be exacerbated due to multiple stressors experienced by immigrant men. These stressors may include lack of work, work that emasculates or asexualizes men (such as laundry and restaurant work), and the trauma of war (such as for Southeast Asian refugees). Immigration may also lower the socioeconomic status of Asian men

Wedding photo of a Muslim American East Indian bride and her sisters.

to a point where they are equal to women (Espiritu, 1996, p. 8). This lowering of status "erodes men's patriarchal authority and empowers women to challenge the patriarch" (p. 8). Immigrant men may take the anger of this new status out on their families through domestic violence.

These episodes of domestic violence may go unreported by the Asian American woman due to her fear of not being believed, fear of jeopardizing her financial dependence on men, and self-blame for precipitating the attacks. It may be further difficult for an Asian/Asian American woman to report violence against herself or her children because "airing" personal information in public is not acceptable in the Asian community (Hall, 2002). She would be further victimized by her community for not following the cultural mores. Thus, the Asian woman may not report the violence to the police, seek alternative living arrangements, or pursue mental health counseling. She is, therefore, at risk for continued violence and stress.

Health

Asian American women have the highest average life expectancy (85.8 years) of any other ethnic group in the United States (Office of Minority Health Research Council, 2006). These numbers vary somewhat by Asian groups such as Filipino (81.5 years), Japanese (84.5), and Chinese (86.1). These are remarkable statistics considering the stresses experienced by Asian women. Poverty, language, lack of health insurance, and cultural barriers to health services are just a few factors that can affect the health and life expectancy of API women (Intercultural Cancer Council, 2006).

The top two illnesses that affect Asian American women are cancer and diabetes. Cancer has been the leading cause of death for Asian American females since 1980 (ICC, 2006). Cervical and breast cancer are especially high. Asian American women are 1.5 times as likely as White women to have cervical cancer (OMHRC, 2006), with Korean American and Vietnamese American women having rates five times higher than White women (ICC, 2006). A large contributor to this statistic is young Asian women not routinely performing self-breast exams and receiving Pap smears (ICC, 2006).

Filipino family celebrates their matriarch's 80th birthday.

Type 2 diabetes is increasing in the Asian community (National Institute of Health, 2006). Major contributors to this are the loss of the traditional Asian diet of vegetables and fruits, an increased intake of animal protein and processed carbohydrates, and a lack of exercise that leads to increased weight.

The field of psychology can contribute to the physical health of Asian American women by researching ways that encourage Asian American women to follow good health practices such as self-breast exams, yearly well-woman exams, prenatal care, and a healthy diet and regular exercise. With what you have read about the Asian/Asian American family structure and values, what ideas do you have for encouraging Asian American women to follow good health practices?

Mental Health

Very little research has been conducted on the mental health prevalence and help-seeking behaviors of Asian American women. Of these few male and female immigrants (20%) who utilize mental health services, women tend to seek help more frequently than do Asian men (Chui, Ganesen, & Clark, 2005; Kimerling & Baumrind, 2005). The multiple stressors on Asian American women may cause them to seek help in larger numbers.

In searching psychology publication databases, common themes that bring Asian/Asian American women into therapy include immigration adjustment, domestic violence, shame, living and raising children in a bicultural world, discrimination effects, shame, and eating disorders. In terms of cultural adjustment, at a recent Asian American Psychological Association Division on Women conference, psychologist Dr. Phi Loan Le (2006) stated that many of the Asian immigrant women in therapy had lived in predominantly Asian areas where one does not notice being different from the mainstream. "It's like the air you breathe." Then upon immigration, the immigrant woman enters another culture and feels like she is smothering and unable to breathe.

Little is known about the interaction of race, gender, and socioeconomic status in relation to treatment methods (Chui, Ganesen, & Clark, 2005). It does appear that Asian American women prefer a wider range of treatment and support options. They tend to seek non-Western methods for dealing with mental health issues such as faith healing and other spiritual avenues. Some may use a combination of both Western and traditional healing methods. With Asian American women, these options may include complementary and alternative therapies that include a spiritual component. If mental health providers are able to offer a variety—a multicultural approach—of therapeutic options, perhaps more Asian American women would consider seeking help in the form of psychological counseling.

Asian American Women's Movement

Asian American women have experienced racism and sexism for many decades, and they have fought back in various ways. The movement began as early as the time of the first "married widows," who remained behind in Asia to care for the family and cultivated their independent thoughts and actions.

The more established Asian American women's movement in the United States began as a unification of Asian American women and as a reaction to the racism of the Women's Movement (Ng, 1998: Shah, 1997; Wei, 1993). The reaction of Asian American women to the women's liberation movement of the 1960s and 1970s was similar to that of other ethnic women's movements. That is, the predominantly White women's movement began as a struggle for equal rights to work outside the home. However, most ethnic women already worked outside the home as a necessity, usually in low-paying occupations in a racist and sexist America.

Thus, Asian American women had different issues such as equal pay, equal rights (based on sex *and* race), and respect as women and Asians. Many White women activists did not understand these different needs because they believed sexism transcended racism. But as Bettie Luke Kan stated: "No matter how hard you fight to reduce the sexism, when it's all done and over with, you still have the racism. Because white women will be racist as easily as their male counterparts. And white women continue to get preferential treatment over women of color" (cited from Espiritu, 1996, p. 6). Thus, the Asian American women's movement was about the intersection of racism and sexism in their lives—about improving the role and status of Asian American women.

Several early organizations emanated from the Asian American women's movement. These included the Organization of Asian Women (OAW), Asian Women United–San Francisco, and the National Network of Asian and Pacific Women (Wei, 1993). As with many other political movements, universities and colleges played a major role in the movement. In the 1970s and 1980s, many higher education institutions began offering courses on Asian American women through the Asian American or women's studies departments. These courses produced such publications as the *Asian Women Journal, Making Waves: An Anthology of Writings by and about Asian American Women,* and the video series *With Silk Wings* (Wei, 1993). From other organizations emerged media such as the Organization of Women's audiovisual history of Asian American women called *Tapestry.*

Cultural and literary groups began, such as the Pacific Asian American Women Writers–West (PAAWWW) and Unbound Feet (primarily Chinese). During this time, Asian American writers began publishing top-selling books such as Maxine Hong Kingston with *Woman Warrior* and Amy Tan with *Joy Luck Club.* These authors portrayed Asian and Asian American women as strong, feminist, intelligent, and independent women, counter to their powerless stereotypes. A movie released in 2005, written and directed by Alice Wu, *Saving Face,* is also an excellent example of breaking the stereotype of Asian American women. The movie focuses on a second- generation Chinese American young woman discovering her lesbian sexuality while living in a close Chinese American community. The interactions with her first-generation mother, the expectations of the community for her to marry, and the relationship with her Chinese American lover provide a wonderful understanding of a modern Asian American young woman. An additional subplot of the movie is her mother's interaction with her own parents and their expectations of her. It is truly a multigenerational/multicultural story.

Summary

The field of psychology focusing on Asian American women encompasses history, politics, stereotypes, culture, and relationships. Asian American women have exhibited flexibility in order to navigate through these different worlds and issues. "People carry multiple identities whose salience may be triggered by different contexts and goals" (Okazaki, 2002, p. 24). These women have done this well.

The title of this chapter comes from an Asian adage that is taught to young Asian children early in their lives. "The nail that sticks out is hammered down" means that one should not act as an individual or act differently from others. If you do so, you will be controlled or punished. Asian American women who protest sexism, racism, and classism may stick out. However, as Dr. Michi Fu stated at the 2006 Asian American Psychological Association Division on Women Conference, "Sometimes the nail gets hammered down regardless" just because you stick out as a woman. Thus, you might as well be yourself and do what needs to be done.

Discussion Questions

1. What gender inequities have you observed? If you are a male, what can you do to facilitate gender equality?
2. If you are a female, have you experienced double standards or sexism? How can you prevent sexism individually and in society? How do you personally manage the standards of women placed upon you?
3. As a man, what have you been taught about what women can and can't do?
4. What have your mothers, aunts, and grandmothers taught you about being an Asian American woman?
5. What has American society taught you about being a woman?

Case Study (Contributed by Erica Sugiyama Hill, M.C.)

Emily is a 22-year-old Japanese American woman with anxiety and dysthymia (chronic mood disorder). She is from an upper middle class family, is second-generation Asian American and is in her last year of her bachelor's degree program. Emily is able to speak Japanese fluently but feels she is forgetting the language because she speaks English most of the time.

Emily is dating a 28-year-old White American male, Sam, whom she met at a party two months ago. She reports that she is very serious about this man. Sam is of a lower social class, did not attend college, and works at the university copy center. There are times when Emily and Sam have conflicts in their relationship due to cultural differences but they are able to discuss and resolve them. Emily told her parents that Sam is the man she would like to marry someday. However, her parents would like her to marry someone who is Japanese. Her parents have tried to introduce her to the Japanese men they know and have attempted to set her up with a matchmaker from the Japanese community. Emily's mother has begun to "talk up" how proud she is of Emily's brother who married a Japanese American woman, and her mother stated that he is worthy of many of the family heirlooms.

Emily feels rejected by her family. She reports feelings of worthlessness, guilt, anger, and loss of interest in usual activities. She has significant weight gain, insomnia, anxiety, fatigue, and difficulty concentrating at work. Emily reports she just wants her parents to understand it is her life and she should be able to make decisions on her own without their interference. Sam has asked Emily to move in with him but she is not sure how to tell her parents. Emily reports that she has always felt alone in her own family and feels her family has never approved of the men she has dated because they are not Japanese. She has increased anxiety when she has to be with her family and is not sure what she should do.

Emily has been referred to the university's counseling center by a friend. Although she is resistant in seeking therapy because she feels embarrassed, she has agreed to see a counselor who is trained in cognitive behavioral therapy (CBT). CBT's theoretical foundation is that the client's thoughts can be powerful and affect behaviors and beliefs. By understanding how one's thoughts and beliefs can dominate and even control behaviors, a person can better understand how flawed assumptions can bias thoughts, distort situations, and lead to distress and pathology. By confronting flawed assumptions and problematic thoughts, the client and therapist can work to change the client's thought processes, which will in turn affect the client's behavior (Beck & Weishaar, 2000).

CBT appears to be an appropriate counseling technique for Japanese and Japanese Americans because it is very structured, present centered, and short term. By identifying a client's maladaptive thought processes, the therapist and the client can then work on "decatastrophizing" the situation, explore other possibilities of the cause and effect of her situation, and help her understand that she cannot control all situations that occur in her life (Beck & Weishaar, 2000).

This restructuring of her cognitive processes can allow Emily to apply her new skills to her behavior and alleviate her anxiety. One excellent tool used in CBT is role-playing. Using this technique with her therapist, Emily would play out different situations and reexamine ways to handle the problems within her own cultural context.

The counselor also needs to be aware of his or her own understanding and beliefs about Asians and Asian Americans. That is, if the counselor assumed Emily was from Japan and did not understand English well, this misinterpretation could disrupt the therapeutic process and greatly damage Emily's view of therapy. The counselor needs to have some knowledge of the Asian/Japanese culture but also understand there are great variations between families and generational differences.

Case Study Discussion Questions

For undergraduate students, please consider the following:

1. Does the generational issue play a role in Emily's life?
2. What makes Emily's situation different from a White American college student?
3. How would you help Emily to deal with her situation if she were your friend? How would you help her if you were a mental health counselor?

For graduate students and/or beginning therapists, please consider the following:

1. How would you evaluate the possibility of suicide, especially since the stories of Asian women in dramatic mixed relations are always contemplating suicide?
2. How much does Emily consider the Japanese/Japanese American community as her referent group?
3. Because her parents have difficulty with Emily dating outside of her race and ethnicity, how would that affect you if you were a non-Asian therapist?
4. Emily is very anxious about her family finding out she is coming to counseling because she fears she will be rejected by them, especially her mother. How would you approach this situation to alleviate her anxiety?
5. What therapeutic approaches would be applicable to Emily's situation?

Key Terms

Classism: Discrimination based on socioeconomic status.
Gender: The behavioral, cultural, and political perspective of a person's or group's sex or sexual identity.
Interracial: Couple or family that consists of persons of different racial backgrounds.
Sexism: Discrimination based on sex or gender.
Subservient: Inferior, subordinate, submissive.

For Further Learning and Suggested Readings

Chin, J. L. (2000). *Relationships among Asian American women.* Washington, DC: American Psychological Association.

Espiritu, Y. L. (1996). *Asian American women and men*. Thousand Oaks, CA: Sage Publications.

Gupta, S. (Ed.). (1999). *Emerging voices: South Asian American women redefine self, family and community*. Thousand Oaks, CA: Sage.

Hune, S., & Nomura, G. M. (Eds.). (2003). *Asian/Pacific Islander American women*. New York: New York University Press.

Lai, E., & Arguelles, D. (2003). *The new face of Asian Pacific America: Numbers, diversity and change in the 21st century*. San Francisco: Asianweek.

Root, M. P., & Kelley, M. (2003). *Multiracial child resource book: Living complex identities*. Seattle: Mavin Productions.

Women of the South Asian Diaspora Collective (Eds.). (1993). *Our feet walk the sky*. San Francisco: Aunt Lute Books.

References

Beck, A., & Weishaar, M. (2000). Cognitive therapy. In R. Corsini & D. Wedding (Eds.), *Current psychotherapies*. Itasca, IL: F. E. Peacock Publishers.

Chui, L., Ganesen, S., & Clark, N. (2005). Spirituality and treatment choices by South and East Asian women with serious mental illness. *Transcultural Psychiatry, 42*(4), 630–656.

Danico, M. Y., & Ng, F. (2004). *Asian American issues*. Westport, CT: Greenwood Press.

Espiritu, Y. L. (1996). *Asian American women and men*. Thousand Oaks, CA: Sage Publications.

Fu, M. (2006). *Hear our voices: Empowering Asian American women*. Asian American Psychological Association's Southern California Division on Women Conference, Long Beach, CA.

Fujino, D. (1997). The rates, pattern and reasons for forming heterosexual interracial dating relationships among Asian Americans. *Journal of Social and Personal Relationships, 14*(6): 809–828.

Hall, C. I. (1987). Japanese war brides. *Asian American Psychological Association Journal, 12*(1), 3–10.

Hall, C. I. (1995). Asian eyes: Body image and eating disorders of Asian and Asian American women. *Eating Disorders: The Journal of Treatment and Prevention, 3*(1), 8–19.

Hall, G. C. N. (2002). Culture-specific ecological models of Asian American violence. In G. Hall & S. Okazaki (Eds.), *Asian American psychology: The science of lives in context*. Washington, DC: American Psychological Association.

Intercultural Cancer Council. (2006). http://iccnetwork.org/cancerfacts/cfs3.htm.

Kimerling, R., & Baumrind, N. (2005). Access to specialty mental health services among women in California. *Psychiatric Services, 56*(6), 729–734.

Lai, E., & Arguelles, D. (2003). *The new face of Asian Pacific America: Numbers, diversity and change in the 21st century*. San Francisco: Asianweek.

Lee, R. G. (1999). *Orientals: Asian Americans in popular culture*. Philadelphia: Temple University Press.

Levy, H. (1991). *The lovers: The complete history of the curious erotic tradition of feet binding in China*. New York: Prometheus Books.

Le, P. (2006). *Hear our voices: Empowering Asian American women*. Asian American Psychological Association's Southern California Division on Women Conference, Long Beach, CA.

Nagata, D. (2000). World War II internment and the relationships of Nisei women. In J. Chin (Ed.), *Relationships among Asian American Women*. Washington, DC: American Psychological Association.

National Institute of Health (2006). *Diabetes and Asian Americans and Pacific Islanders*. Retrieved April 28, 2006. http://www.ndep.nih.gov/diabetes/pubs/FS_AsAm_Eng.pdf from http://diabetes.niddk.nih.gov/dm/pubs/asianamerican.

Ng, F. (Ed.). (1998). *Asians in America: Asian American women and gender*. New York: Garland Publishing.

Office of Minority Health Resource Council. (2006). http://www.omhrc.gov.

Okazaki, S. (2002). Beyond questionaires: Conceptual and methodological innovations in Asian American psychology. In G. Hall & S. Okazaki (Eds.), *Asian American psychology: The science of lives in context* (pp. 13–39). Washington, DC: American Psychological Association.

Reeves, T., & Bennett, C. (2003). *The Asian and Pacific Islander population in the United States: March 2002*, Current Populations Reports, P20-540. Washington, DC: U.S. Census Bureau.

Root, M. M. P. (1990). Disordered eating in women of color. *Sex Roles, 22*, 525–536.

Root, M. M. P. (1995). The psychology of Asian American women. In H. Landrine (Ed.), *Bringing cultural diversity to feminist psychology: Theory, research, and practice* (pp. 265–301). Washington, DC: American Psychological Association.

Root, M. M. P. (1998). Women. In L. C. Lee & N. W. S. Zane (Eds.), *Handbook of Asian American psychology* (pp. 211–231). Thousand Oaks, CA: Sage.

Shah, S. (Ed.). (1997). *Dragon ladies: Asian American feminists breathe fire.* Boston, MA: South End Press.

Tien, L. (2000). U.S. attitudes toward women of Asian ancestry: Legislative and media perspectives. In J. Chin (Ed.), *Relationships among Asian American women.* Washington, DC: American Psychological Association.

True, R. H., & Guillermo, T. (1996). *Asian/Pacific Islander American women.* In M. Bayne-Smith (Ed.), *Race, Gender and Health* (pp. 94–120). Thousand Oaks, CA: Sage Publications.

U.S. Census (2000a). *Married-Couple and Unmarried-Partner Households: 2000.* Retrieved April 28, 2006. http://www.census.gov/prod/2003pubs/censr-5.pdf

U.S. Census (2000b). *Children and the Households They Live In: 2000.* Retrieved April 28, 2006. http://www.census.gov/prod/2004pubs/censr-14.pdf

Wei, W. (1993). *The Asian American movement.* Philadelphia: Temple University Press.

12

Asian American Men and Asianized Attribution
Intersections of Masculinity, Race, and Sexuality

DEREK KENJI IWAMOTO and WILLIAM MING LIU[1]

OUTLINE OF CHAPTER

Case Synopsis
Introduction
History
Major Issues
Women's Perceptions of Asian American Men
Asian American Masculinities
The New Asian American Male
Case Study
References

Case Synopsis

Terrell is a 19-year-old Chinese American college freshman attending a large West Coast university. He joined a Greek fraternity that is known for members who are athletic, who drink and party excessively, and who are predominately European American. Terrell's fraternity brothers comment about how they did not expect him to be athletic, outgoing, assertive, carefree, and a womanizer. They have also stated that he is "unlike other Asians." In the past he felt very proud about these comments, because of his athletic ability, physique, and since he did not want to be like the "Asian kids." But recently, these descriptions have left him feeling conflicted. Meanwhile his grades have also suffered, he has lost interest in activities he usually enjoys, and he has been increasingly annoyed and critical of his fraternity friends. His friend suggested that he make an appointment at the counseling center, so reluctantly he did.

Introduction

For over 200 years, the masculinity of Asian American men has been subjected to ridicule and feminization in American popular culture and society (Pierson, 2004). Asian Americans have been demonized, caricatured as foreign-born buffoons (Chan, 2000), the Yellow Peril invaders, an enemy's Fifth Column (Chua & Fujino, 1999), and asexualized or impotent (Chan, 2000). These forms of marginalization and invisibility further the stereotypic and distorted notions of Asian American masculinity (Chan, 2000). The glaring lack of famous Asian American men in the public eye, for instance, is both symptomatic and reinforcing of these biased gender notions. There are relatively few nationally known political figures (e.g., Gary Locke, the former governor of Washington; Daniel Inouye, a senator from Hawaii), sports figures, and Asian American movie stars. Of the few nationally recognized sports (e.g., Yao Ming in basketball, Ichiro Suzuki

---

[1] Both authors contributed equally to this chapter.

in baseball) and movie stars (e.g., Jet Li, Jackie Chan), many are Asian international figures or were born abroad. Given the lack of prominent political and positive media figures and the public derision of Asian male masculinity through the propagation of stereotypes and discriminatory media images, the question emerges, how do these images or lack thereof impact Asian American males? Although there has been little empirical attention on the prevalent issues that Asian American men face and how this group formulates a self-identity, this chapter highlights some salient issues and the identity developmental processes of Asian American men. The term *Asian American* will be used in this chapter since American society tends to "racialize" Asian Americans (i.e., despite one's own ethnic identification and the fact that people with certain phenotypic features are perceived and categorized in specific racial groups) (Kim, 2001; Liu, 2002).

The focus of this chapter is to understand the study of masculinity, especially among Asian American men, as a multicultural competency (Liu, 2005). In addition, this chapter will explore the prevalent issues faced by this population such as: the historical and current status, work discrimination and model minority stereotypes that are perpetuated in the media, and relationships with Asian American women. The authors also discuss heterosexual issues related to Asian American men and masculinity. There are limitations of this approach, but to discuss all aspects of sexuality and masculinity in one chapter would be far too broad. The following section describes how these sociocultural factors psychologically impact how Asian American men formulate their masculinity and how this process potentially affects an individual's mental health. The authors discuss **Asianized attribution** as the intersection of masculinity, race and racism, and sexuality—an important multiple identity for Asian American men. The following section will describe the new masculine identity Asian Americans are developing. At the conclusion of the chapter, a clinical case study is provided for illustration of certain concepts being presented.

History

To understand the dynamic issues that Asian American males currently experience, it is vital to understand the role of immigration history, racist governmental laws, and media images in shaping the Asian American male identity (Chua & Fujino, 1999). Throughout the mid to late 1800s and early 1900s and even today, Asian American men have been emasculated and exploited by American industry. During these periods, the Asian laborers who were recruited to work were exploited by American industry since they provided cheap labor (Chan, 1991; Liu, 2002). Asian male laborers were perceived as nonmasculine labor hands and were relegated to "women's work" such as cooking, laundering, and domestic duties (Chua & Fujino, 1999). As Asian immigrant numbers grew, hostility and anti-Asian sentiment erupted. There were race riots, lynching, anti-miscegenation laws (some specifically forbidding Asians to marry European Americans), job exclusion, denial of citizenry and landownership, and exclusionary immigration policies that were passed throughout the late 1800s into the early half of the 1900s (Chan, 1991; Chua & Fujino, 1999; Lee, 1998; Liu, 2002; Takaki, 1990). Further, as a consequence of the political turmoil in Southeast Asian countries (e.g., Vietnam, Cambodia, Laos) in the 1970s and early 1980s, the men who immigrated to the United States during this period, "lost their families, jobs and earning ability, lost their status and authority" (Liu, 2002, p. 108), had minimal support systems, and were relegated to lower-paid menial positions.

During this period, new evolving forms of racism and stereotypical images emerged that affected Asian Americans. The **model minority myth** was introduced as a divisive tool against African, Latino, and Native American communities during civil rights, labor rights, identity, and immigration reform protests. The intent was to suggest to non-Asians that the best way to succeed in America was to emulate Asian Americans—be quiet and work hard. The model minority image of Asian Americans is assumed to be organic, genetic, or cultural. Unfortunately, the model minority myth instilled the erroneous impression that all Asian Americans are financially well-off and do not experience as much racism and discrimination as other ethnic and racial groups (Lee, 2003). The Asian American male was then seen as the "family man" who does need governmental assistance (Chua & Fujino, 1999). Paradoxically, the model minority myth further painted the Asian American male as the frugal business-type, nerdy, prudent, accented, and foreign as well as asexual (Chan, 2000; Chua & Fujino, 1999; Okazaki, 1998).

Major Issues

Workplace Discrimination

Workplace discrimination is muted by the notion that Asian American men do not experience as much workplace discrimination as African Americans or Latinos. In a Gallup poll of 1,252 adults conducted in May 2005, Asian Americans reported the highest workplace discrimination (31%), followed by African Americans (26%) (Joyce, 2005). Asians on the other hand were least likely of any group to report discrimination. Paek and Shah (2003) suggest that the stereotype of the Asian American as a model minority may lead to workplace exploitation whereby Asian Americans may be "viewed as disposable workers who may be hired and fired at will because they are complacent about how they are treated and too passive to complain" (p. 238).

The mainstream perception that Asian Americans are perpetual foreigners, and permanent aliens (e.g., Asian Americans are often asked "What are you?" "Where are you from?" or receive comments such as "You speak good English"), and not "real" Americans could explain why Asian Americans are perceived as upwardly mobile in the corporate sector (Liang, Li, & Kim, 2004; Liu & Chang, 2006). However, Asian Americans face the same macro-level patterns of discrimination as other minority groups in America. Friedman and Krackhard (1997) suggested that Asian Americans are "excluded from social networks" in predominately White organizations because they are "different" or considered foreign (Paek & Shah, 2003, p. 238). Although Asian Americans are often stereotyped as being diligent workers, they are often perceived as being poor leaders and passive (Sue, 2005; Young & Takeuchi, 1998).

Furthermore, like other ethnic minority groups and women, Asian Americans experience the **glass ceiling**, an invisible barrier that allows disempowered groups to "see and strive for high-level management positions" (Paek & Shah, 2003, p. 238) but systemically prevents these groups from obtaining these higher-level managerial jobs. Consequently, Asian Americans are less likely to hold managerial positions than Whites with comparable education and work experience, and they also earn less than Whites when controlled for age and education (Leong, 1998; Young & Takeuchi, 1998). Sue (2005) noted that some "Asian American managers used tactics such as working harder, working more hours . . . and modesty (not drawing attention to their self for accomplishments), all of which did not impress their supervisors" (p. 361). Therefore, although there is a perception of Asian American men as being well-represented in managerial positions, there are significant barriers that hinder advancement up the corporate ladder for Asian American professionals. This lack of advancement could explain why some young Asian American men experience distress balancing work and family pressures (Liu & Iwamoto, 2006).

Negative Portrayal in the Media

Asian Americans not only experience discrimination and racism in the work environment, but they are also subjected to stereotypes and negative images, and are marginalized in the popular media. There is a lack of positive Asian American role models and images in the media for

Asian Americans (Iwamoto & Caldwell, 2006; Lee & Yeh, 2002). In the major TV markets Asian American men remain invisible. In the top 25 TV markets (e.g., Los Angeles, New York, Chicago) in the United States in 2002, there was only 1 male Asian American news anchor, while there were 13 Asian American women (Riley & Kennard, 2002). Although Asian American women have earned some prominent roles as news anchors and reporters at major TV news stations (though still many Asian American women are subjected to fit the "Connie Chung" mold), Asian American men on the other hand are only designated to news reporting duties (18 Asian American men compared to 57 Asian American women total in the top 25 TV markets) (Riley & Kennard, 2002).

Asian American men are also negatively and stereotypically portrayed on television and film (Lee & Yeh, 2002). In movies and television shows, Asian Americans view a limited range of media figures who resemble their physical features, and when these figures/characters do exist they are usually villains, martial artists, submissive, gardeners, restaurant workers, and convenience store owners with a thick accent (Lee & Yeh, 2002). The quintessential Asian stereotype was the *American Idol* (2003) contestant, William Hung. A former UC Berkeley student, Hung gained mass popularity after he sang in an off-note and attempted to dance to Ricky Martin's "She Bangs" in an *American Idol* audition. Many Asian Americans had mixed sentiments about William Hung's mass popularity since by music industry standards he is not a talented singer, and he soon began to embody, represent, and reinforce Asian male stereotypes: short, geeky, and unfashionable (Le, 2006a). His heavy accent continued to conflate the image of Asian American men as perpetual foreigners or unassimilable aliens. Hung's popularity in the mainstream media is indicative of the media's appetite for simplified and stereotypic images of Asian men and could be a reason why people find him amusing and an easy target for ridicule. Some have defended William Hung's popularity by stating that Asian Americans represent many images (Le, 2006a). While many may agree with this notion, in fact William Hung had become the contemporary Asian American equivalent of an African American minstrel singer. That is, William Hung represented how the masculinity of Asian American males has long been the subject of

Roger Fan, star of *Finishing the Game* and *Better Luck Tomorrow*.

ridicule (comedic entertainment) and humiliation (see Long Duk Dong character in 1984 movie *Sixteen Candles*).

Conversely, Asian American men are also generally invisible in comparison to Asian American women in popular media. While Asian American women are fetishized and exoticized as objects of "consumption" and "desire" within a White dominant and patriarchal society, no such cultural space is allotted for Asian American men. Left relatively invisible and voiceless, Asian American men are ineffective and impotent—the less-than-ideal male figure in comparison to the White male exemplar.

Thus, in the popular media Asian American men are often subjected to secondary roles and are rarely cast as the leading man. Asian American male entertainers, actors, and models are unable to find a nonstereotypical role in America so they end up having to go overseas to Asian countries to find lead roles or to be featured models (Hua, 2005). The few Asian men who have starred in lead roles are Asian international movie stars who often portray stereotypical roles such as martial arts experts (e.g., Jackie Chan, Jet Li, Chow Yun-Fat). Even in those leading roles played by Jackie Chan, Jet Li, and Chow Yun-Fat, their characters are one-dimensional and they do not play the romantic leads (Feng, 1996; Sue, 2005). For example, Jet Li "did not kiss his Juliet in *Romeo Must Die* (2000)" (Im, 2000). Even in the movie *The Joy Luck Club*—a movie about the plight and intergenerational conflicts of Chinese American women—Chinese culture and men are depicted as dominant, controlling, unromantic, and patriarchal (Feng, 1996). Another implicit message in *The Joy Luck Club* was that the "White man provides the romantic freedom that Asian unions would squash" (p. 32). That is, the message is that the White man is a more romantically desirable and better alternative spouse than the controlling and oppressive Asian American man.

These negative messages are also explicitly depicted in pop-culture magazines. A featured spread in an April 2004 *Details* magazine, titled "Gay or Asian," which was "meant to be satirical," managed to perpetuate stereotypes of Asians and equate being gay with being an Asian American male.

One cruises for chicken; the other takes it General Tso-style. Whether you're into shrimp balls or shaved balls, entering the dragon requires imperial tastes. So choke up on your chopsticks, and make sure your labels are showing. Study hard grasshopper: A sharp eye will always take home the plumpest eel.

Dolce and Gabbana suede jacket: keep the last samurai warm and buttoned tight on the battlefield.

Ladyboy fingers: soft and long. Perfect for both waxing on and waxing off, plucking the koto, or gripping the Kendo stick.

Metallic sneakers: when the Pink Lady takes the stage, nothing should be lost in translation.

This overtly racist, stereotypical, and offensive spread by *Details* magazine depicted an Asian American man with his name-brand attire—arrows pointing at various body parts and products the model is wearing, and instructs the reader how to delineate a gay male from an Asian male (e.g., "Delicate features: refreshed from a hot tea or a hot night of teabagging"). The magazine picture's overt racial remarks and stereotypical sexual innuendoes—"whether you're into shrimp balls or shaved balls"—compares Asian male genitals to the size of shrimps (Sakai, 2004). The spread feminizes the model's features, "ladyboy fingers: soft and long," and "Pink Lady takes the stage," which is symbolic and reflective of how America and the media depicts Asian American men—emasculated, gay, and feminized. The implied connection between homosexuality and Asian American masculinity tapped into a history of **emasculinization**, marginalization, and alienation that has shaped contemporary constructions of Asian American men.

These one-dimensional portrayals reflect the stereotypical attitudes, beliefs, and values of larger society (Iwamoto, 2003). These limited and negative roles and images can be a source of embarrassment, frustration, and anger for Asian American men. They can take an emotional toll on Asian American men. Some Asian American men, especially those living in predominantly White communities, might begin to despise their appearance and begin to idealize the Euro-centric or Western forms of beauty and attractiveness such as being blonde and having large blue eyes. According to Liu (Pierson, 2004), "some [Asian American men] might court non-Asian women exclusively as a sign of status because they are able to overcome stereotypes and cultural prohibitions." In contrast, other Asian American male bachelors may experience some frustration since they feel that their dating pool is limited since many women of different races as well as some Asian Americans consider Asian American men unattractive and undesirable dating/marriage partners.

Women's Perceptions of Asian American Men

The controversial topic discussed both in empirical research and popular culture is how general stereotypes have affected romantic partner selection especially for heterosexual Asian American men. Recent scholarly articles (Okazaki, 1998), popular literature, and Internet blogs have discussed the phenomenon and resentment that a minority of Asian American men feel about Asian American women dating White men. This is a very complex phenomenon in which *some* Asian American men feel "their masculinity is challenged and undermined" (Chua & Fujino, 1999, p. 393) in regards to Asian American women who *exclusively* date White men. The minority of Asian American men critiquing this phenomenon believe that some Asian American women overlook them as potential marriage partners and have the same stereotypical gendered notions about Asian men as the majority group. For example, some Asian women might think or feel an Asian American boyfriend or spouse would not be romantic, spontaneous, or willing to share in the household chores, for example. For other Asian American women, dating non-Asians is related to the perception that other racial groups are less interpersonally controlling and less adherent to traditional **gender role** norms and expectations. Finally, some Asian

American women do not want to date Asian American men because they are "like my brother or father." Meaning that, for some Asian American women who had negative experiences with significant Asian American men in their lives such as a father or brother, they generalize this experience and perceive (stereotype) all Asian American men as being similar to a particular man they know.

With these sentiments in mind, it is not surprising that some discussion has focused on outmarriage and interracial relationships among Asian Americans. Asian American women outmarry at a much higher rate than Asian American men, and both groups outmarry at a higher rate than other racial groups (e.g., African Americans, Latino/a Americans) (Le, 2006b). According to Le's (2006) analysis of the U.S. Census data in 2004, both 1.5 generation (immigrated to the United States at the age of 13 years or younger) and second-generation (born in the United States), Asian American *men and women* are both more likely to outmarry to European Americans and/or other Asian ethnic groups (pan-Asian) than Asian immigrants. Some ethnic groups among Asian American women in general have the highest outmarriage rates to Whites. In the past Japanese American women had the highest rates of outmarriages, though this trend has changed. Currently, Korean American 1.5 and second-generation women have the highest rate of outmarriage to White men (47%), followed by Filipinos (40.5%), Chinese (30%), and Japanese Americans (28%). Out of the Asian American men, Filipinos have the highest outmarriages (28.1%), followed by Korean Americans (23.9%), Japanese Americans (19.7%), and Asian Indian Americans (20.5%) (Le, 2006b).

There are a number of possible explanations why Asian Americans and, more specifically, Asian American women outmarry. For Fujino (1997), the selection of marriage partners is a matter of propinquity or the availability of potential partners given a certain context. So, for some Asian American men and women in an environment where there is a lack of other Asian Americans from which to select, the obvious choice may be to marry a non-Asian. For Okazaki (1998), the gender stereotypes have "potentially damaging effects to Asian Americans' self-concept as well as for dating and marriage patterns" (p. 46). In Lee and Vaught's (2003) study with Hmong American female high school students, the stereotypes of Asian American men were pervasive: more traditional, unappealing, and emasculate. One participant stated that "I'm attracted to White men. Not attracted to Asian men at all" (Lee & Vaught, 2003, p. 457). Similarly the women in this study also thought that Asian men were too short and unattractive, financially poor, emotionally distant, and boring (Lee & Vaught, 2003). The researchers concluded that the women in this study who rejected Asian men tended to endorse the stereotypes ascribed by popular culture. These participants therefore favored and idealized White men and the hegemonic form of masculinity—"the right manhood, both racially and economically," and one who is strong, rational, and emotionally and economically stable (Lee & Vaught, 2003, p. 457).

Similarly, Fong and Yung's (1995/1996) study unraveled some aspects of the complex dynamics and phenomenon of interracial marriage by Asian Americans. One significant finding was the "aversion to marrying within the same race." Many Asian American men and women in this study had negative feelings and stereotypical perceptions of Asian Americans of the opposite sex. The participants were influenced by Western notions of attractiveness and privilege, and many felt that traditional Asian culture was too patriarchal (Fong & Yung, 1995/1996; Okazaki, 1998). The **feminist**-identified participants tended to perceive non-Asian men as more **egalitarian**, whereas some participants felt that marrying a White spouse would increase their social status and felt that European American culture was better than Asian culture (Okazaki, 1998).

Another study by Chua and Fujino (1999) examined how Asian American men form their masculinity and looked at how various groups of women (Asian-international students, Asian American, and White women) perceived Asian American men. Chua and Fujino's study revealed that among all the women, the three groups had ambivalent views of Asian American masculinity—more than what was hypothesized. The researchers indicated that these women did not have strong stereotypical notions of Asian American masculinity, but at the same time they viewed Asian American masculinity cautiously. All the women made a clear distinction between White and Asian American men: Asian American men were perceived as adhering to traditional gender roles and were more nurturing, while White men were seen as more independent, physically attractive, masculine, and outgoing. On one hand many of the women participants wanted a partner who was caring, egalitarian, and did not adhere to traditional patriarchal roles, yet the hegemonic masculinity was idealized.

In the three studies mentioned, the dominating or **hegemonic male** characteristics were traits of an ideal mate. The hegemonic male refers to a man who is independent, self-reliant, assertive, masculine (i.e., tall, lean, muscled, with chiseled jaw), confident, ambitious, tough, and financially and emotionally stable. Generally Asian American men across these studies were perceived as adhering to traditional patriarchal values, less emotionally receptive, and physically unattractive. Consequently the "gender stereotypes of the Asian American male makes this population less desirable marriage partners" (Espiritu, 1997, p. 97).

Some scholars believe that the historical racism, discrimination, emasculation, and perceptions by some women of Asian men have deeply impacted how Asian Americans formulate their masculinity (Chan, 2000; Truong, 2006). This next section will describe how the salient issues of discrimination, racism, stereotypes, and cultural factors have and continue to shape the masculinity formation of Asian American men.

Asian American Masculinities

Asian American men's struggles and negotiations of masculinity may be understood by masculinity theories, cultural factors, and racial identity development theory. As mentioned previously, the historical and contemporary marginalization and constant bombardment and reinforcement of pervasive stereotypes of Asian men have significant gendered consequences (Liu & Chang, 2006). Since Asian American men are often stereotyped as passive, feminine, nerdy, asexual (e.g., myth of small penises), or even as deviant sexual aggressors (i.e., wife beater, frequent patron of the strip club), they are then perceived as embodying "extreme and deviant forms of masculinity" (Liu & Chang, 2006). Yet the Eurocentric notions of masculinity and the hegemonic masculine characteristics of "being in control, decisive, aggressive and assertive, ambitious, analytical, competitive, athletic, independent and self-reliant, and individualistic with strong personality" remain ideal and normalized (Truong, 2006, p. 324). Asian American men are then left in ambivalence: either conform to the White male norm, or be typecast as having deviant forms masculinity and not being what society considers a "real man" (Chan, 1998; Truong, 2006). This poses a major dilemma for Asian American men, who are left to create a new form of masculinity, even though there are few models of masculinity for them.

Masculinity Myth and Gender Role Conflict

While some Asian American men might create a new form of masculinity or conform to White norms, Asian American men remain similar to other men because they live in a society that expects them to endorse and adhere to the **masculinity myth** and gender roles (Levant, 1996; Pleck, 1995). The masculinity myth posits a dominant form of masculinity, which carries with it contradictory and inconsistent expectations as well as negative consequences for men who live up to or attempt to live up to the expectations (Levant, 1996). The typical and idealized portrayal of a "real man" in U.S. society suggests that the male has to be anti-feminine (opposite of "traditional" female characteristics such as openness, vulnerability, emotionally expressive), tough, aggressive, daring, and physically strong (Brannon, 1976). Men are also encouraged to have an "emphasis on sexual prowess, sexual conquest, and sexual aggression" (Lindsey, 1997, p. 225). These expectations place a demand on men that have been characterized as "strain and conflict."

Gender roles are "behaviors, expectations, and values defined by society as masculine and feminine" (O'Neil, 1990, p. 24). The gender role strain theory, which has been heavily studied through **gender role conflict**, posits four empirical factors in which men experience conflict (O'Neil, Helms, Gable, & Wrightsman, 1986). In the first factor—**success, power, and competition** (SPC)—success refers to a man's focus on wealth and accomplishments as a means of gaining self-worth; power implies the need for the man to have authority over another person; and competition refers to the man's need to "win" over another individual. The second factor, **restrictive emotionality** (RE), is defined as a man's inability to express his emotions, while simultaneously denying others their right to express emotions. The third factor, **restrictive affectionate behavior between men** (RABBM), refers to a man's difficulty (i.e., limited ways) of expressing intimacy, sexuality, and affection toward men and women. Finally, the fourth factor, **conflict between work and family** (CWF), refers to a man's inability to balance the demands of work and home (i.e., family) (O'Neil et al., 1986). According to some scholars, gender role conflicts potentially hinder "human potential and cause psychological distress" (Blazina, Pisecco, & O'Neil, 2005, p. 39). Given that gender role conflict and strain are related to a culture's expectations of men, it is unclear how Asian American men, who may have to navigate two cultures, contend with these bicultural expectations.

Cultural Values and Acculturation

Since cultural expectations are intertwined with gendered expectations, adherence to cultural values and level of acculturation can play a significant role in how Asian American men form their identities. Examples of cultural values include a focus on group harmony and **filial piety** (Liu & Iwamoto, 2007) and prominence in the family (Tang, 1997), risk taking, and courageous behavior (Nghe & Mahalik, 1998). Related values are keeping the adoration and admiration of the family, which entails fulfilling their filial duties such as carrying on their family name, taking care of aging parents, conforming to the expectations of the parents, and advancing the culture (Tang, 1997). Since a majority of Asian Americans have been living in America for two or fewer generations, cultural factors such as values, beliefs, and worldview (Kim, Ng, & Ahn, 2005) greatly influence how Asian American men deal with and navigate their multiple identities. Other recent immigrants may experience **acculturative stress** as they learn to cope and thrive (Roysircar & Maestas, 2002). These stressors may cause psychological distress for Asian American men. For instance, depending on the level of acculturation and generation since immigration, some Asian American men may subscribe to strict gender role expectations and the violation of these expectations could be met with social ostracization.

There are also economic pressures related to filial piety. Asian Americans have one of the highest rates of family-owned business compared to other races; this is especially true for first-generation Asian Americans and immigrant Korean Americans (28% own their own businesses) (Le, 2006). Consequently, for many children of first- and second-generation Asian American parents who own their own businesses, there could be additional pressure to assist their parents with the family business. Often, the need to please parents and the parental pressure to succeed lead to academic stress, poor self-image, poor academic and job performance, and psychological distress (Wong & Halgin, 2006). These social pressures to inculcate and maintain specific gender role behaviors may lead some Asian men, especially those in their native countries, to endorse "traditional" gender roles more than Asians in America (Levant, Wu, & Fischer, 1996; Nghe & Mahalik, 1998).

Generally, there is limited research examining how Asian American men conceptualize and define their masculinity. Research results from one study suggested that Asian American men tended to see their masculinity differently from White men; White men tended to consider the hegemonic masculinity notion very important to their identity as men (Chua & Fujino, 1999). Conversely, Asian American men did not necessarily see their masculinity in opposition to femininity: masculinity was tied to being polite, obedient, and a willingness to do domestic tasks (Chua & Fujino, 1999). Chua and Fujino contend that Asian American men are forming a more flexible notion of masculinity. Moreover, Asian American men also believed that their ability to achieve high occupational status was intrinsically tied to masculinity. Furthermore, the results suggested that some Asian American men continue to construct and emulate the hegemonic definition of masculinity to counteract the effeminate images of Asian American men. Thus, culture and gender expectations are intimately connected.

Additionally, there is limited research examining how cultural values and acculturation relate to gender role conflict for Asian American men. Kim, O'Neil, and Owen (1996) examined the relationship between gender role conflict and levels of acculturation among Asian American men (Kim et al., 1996). The researchers found no differences between Chinese, Japanese, and Korean American men's acculturation levels along the four patterns of gender role conflict (Kim et al., 1996). However within-group effects were uncovered. Specifically, individuals who were more acculturated tended to feel more pressure to be successful, have power, and be competitive. Furthermore, compared to less acculturated individuals, higher acculturated individuals were less likely to restrict their emotions, or were able to express their emotions easier (Kim et al., 1996).

In a similar study, Liu and Iwamoto (2006) examined the relationships among Asian cultural values, psychological distress, self-esteem and gender role conflict among Asian American men. Liu and Iwamoto found adherence to traditional Asian values (i.e., enculturation), as measured by the Asian Values Scale (Kim, Atkinson, & Yang, 1999), was related to higher scores on gender role conflict subscales (GRCS). For instance, individuals who endorsed more traditional Asian values tended to endorse certain gender role schemas, and conversely, individuals who did not endorse Asian values did not adhere to the gender role schemas. The researchers also found that individuals with higher self-esteem did not experience as much psychological distress (i.e., anxiety, depression); and those who were more distressed endorsed the GRCS subscales. These findings are supported by previous investigations on this link with other men (i.e., European American) (Liu, Rochlen, & Mohr, 2005).

In conclusion, contrary to stereotypes of Asian American men, the findings suggest that this population is a very heterogeneous group. The findings reveal that many Asian American men do not adhere to gender role schemas and are well-adjusted. Furthermore, individuals are affected by gender role conflict and psychological distress depending on their level of acculturation and adherence to Asian values. It also appears that Asian American men are similar to other men of different ethnicities and races insofar as higher adherence to gender roles relates to more psychological distress.

Racial Identity

The studies reviewed suggest a connection between acculturation and Asian values to gender role conflict and masculinity formation. Some believe these "masculine identities are inseparable from racial identities, and the motivational and developmental forces that influence Asian American masculine identities need to also capture the sociopolitical dynamics from which race and racial identity are formed" (Liu & Chang, 2006). Chen (1999) describes three masculine identity strategies used by Chinese American men to combat stereotypes and racism. Some Chinese American men idealize and conform to the hegemonic masculinity, while others attempt to deflect attention away from the perceived stereotypes by overcompensating (e.g., for men who were not fluent in English, they would work extra hours) (Chen, 1999). Others deny the existence of racism and stereotypes, and feel they are the exception to the stereotype of Asians or consider themselves unlike other Asians (Chen, 1999). Strategies that describe individuals who are coping with internalized racism, can be further explained by racial identity development theory—how individuals react to social dynamics and racial oppression. Racial identity theory describes how racism and discrimination impact the individual intrapsychically. Therefore to elucidate how racial identity and masculinity are intertwined, a case is presented to illustrate the dynamic process of how an Asian American male might simultaneously develop, experience, and form his racial identity and masculine identity.

A Case of Asian American Men's Racial Identity and Masculinity Development

According to the Minority Identity Development Model (Atkinson, Morten, & Sue, 1998), the first status is **conformity**. During the conformity status, the Asian American male usually has a color-blind attitude and his group frame of reference is the White/European Americans. This individual is not comfortable about, and is ashamed of, being Asian. He might involve himself in everything that is perceived as "non-Asian" like eating only American food, not studying as hard (to counter the model minority myth), socializing with only European American peers, exclusively dating White girls (completely dismissing Asian girls), and dressing and attempting to look as White as possible (bleach hair, get colored contacts). Although this individual might have color-blind ideology, he may try to shed the model minority image consciously and unconsciously by being highly active in sports in order not to be perceived as the "wimpy" guy. He might adhere to hegemonic attitudes (e.g., highly independent, dominant, anti-feminine), and do anything to not look like the "Asian nerd." Consequently, since this individual does not recognize the overt and covert racism he is experiencing and how it is affecting himself interpersonally, he is likely to be negatively impacted intrapsychically (e.g., low self-esteem).

In the **dissonance** status, the individual begins to realize that he (and Asian Americans) is not fully accepted by society. He may become conscious of the racism and oppression that Asian Americans and other ethnic/racial groups experience. He begins to realize his own prejudice and stereotypical attitudes he has toward other Asians, and become more aware how he might be overcompensating (i.e., highly adhering to certain masculine notions such as acting tough, restricting his emotions, or trying to be a ladies' man or playboy). Furthermore, he might establish his first close relationship with a fellow Asian American(s), and may begin to discuss, become more educated about, and appreciate his cultural roots with his newly acquired peer groups. At the same time, he feels that he is in an ambiguous state; his idealized notions of White America might begin to shatter, which he feels very confused about.

Resistance immersion is a status in which the individual's reference group shifts solely to Asian Americans, and he becomes completely immersed in the Asian culture, though this immersion is somewhat superficial. For the first time he begins to think about what it is to be Asian and begins to feel slightly more comfortable about who he is. The pent-up frustration and anger toward Whites are quite evident and the individual expresses to others these bitter feelings toward Whites. He might exert his dominant masculinity characteristics by overtly and subtly challenging White men at work, in sports, and intellectual activities. The individual attempts to act and be as "Asian" as possible (e.g., associate with only Asians, involve himself in Asian/Asian American politics), and idealize the Asian culture which could entail adhering to traditional gender roles (Liu, 2002). He also might begin to be interested in exclusively Asian partners, yet is bitter about Asian women and men who date White men and feels these individuals are selling out.

Introspection marks a status in which he begins to truly reflect and understand what it means to be Asian. He re-assesses his feelings toward Whites, though retaining some bitterness. In regards to his masculinity, he is still attempting to balance, negotiate, and become more flexible (e.g., by not attributing certain characteristics such as being strong, assertive, thoughtful, sensitive as being either feminine or masculine characteristics) about what it means to be an Asian American man.

The last status, **integrative awareness**, represents a time when the individual has a positive notion of what it means to be Asian and feels comfortable with his new identity. The negative feelings toward Whites subside, and positive aspects of Whites are for the most part accepted (Sue & Sue, 1999). This individual is still involved in exploring Asian American issues such as racism and discussing the emasculation and marginalization of Asian American men. Concurrently, he becomes aware of how his old notions of masculinity shaped how he used to perceive things. Furthermore, he redefines and develops a new progressive form of nonhegemonic masculinity by having egalitarian relationships, being an attentive and emotionally involved partner/parent (Chua & Fujino, 1999).

In conclusion, this section on racial identity illuminates how an Asian American male's racial identity may also parallel one's gender and masculine development. That is, when someone operates in specific racial identity status such as conformity status, they idealize, adhere to, and identify with the White culture and Western notions of masculinity such as the hegemonic notions. But as one transitions through racial identity development, they might begin to challenge (resistance immersion) notions of White culture. For example, they may unconsciously/consciously advocate against the White power structure by becoming more resentful and competitive (i.e., at work) toward White males as a way to "fight" against this power structure. However, as one gains more awareness of how racism impacts them, they realize that hegemonic notions are a racialized concept (applies to primarily White males) that do not include Asian American men. Therefore, Asian American males begin to accept and become more comfortable in their own skin and reflect upon their strengths and characteristics. Consequently, they form and shape their own progressive notions of masculinity identity.

Asianized Attribution

Although many of the constructs such as racial identity development capture elements related to Asian American men's experiences, the intersections of masculinity, racism and race, and attributed masculinity and sexuality are not discussed. To understand this intersection, the authors offer the term *Asianized attribution* for consideration. To illustrate, research has emerged in explaining why there is a paucity of Asian Americans holding managerial positions (Xin, 2004). Xin suggests that there are different impression management strategies used by Asian Americans that are not congruent with what managers and evaluators expect (Sue, 2005). We believe that regardless of the criteria managers and evaluators have, if the evaluators have conscious or unconscious stereotypic notions of Asian Americans, they will have an Asianized attribution of Asian American individuals.

Asianized attribution is the evaluation process in which attributes or characteristics of an Asian American man are racialized and negatively evaluated. An individual (e.g., supervisor, managers, colleagues of an Asian American male worker) or outsider (an individual interacting with an Asian American) with stereotypical notions of Asian Americans will automatically attribute certain characteristics as "Asian" and the subsequent evaluation will be inherently negative.

Table 12.1 Asianized Attribution

Asian American male characteristics/ attributes	Stereotypical notions held by evaluator, and transformation/ interpretation process	Outsiders' evaluation
1. Asian American worker is polite, modest, agreeable, and grateful →	1. Fits schema and stereotype of Asians (e.g., passive) →	1. While these characteristics are positive, for leadership roles or managerial positions, they are not ideal, and the evaluation of the Asian American individual is that he is too *differential, nonassertive,* and *not an ideal leader*
2. Asian American male has some gender role notions and expectations →	2. Fits schema of how Asian males are stereotypically →	2. Regardless of ethnic or racial identity, these characteristics are perceived as "too traditional," patriarchal, and inherent of the "Asian culture"; for example, the Asian American male could be completely assimilated to European American culture and has "conformity" ideology, but these characteristics are racialized and are attributed to the Asian culture

For example, if an Asian American male has characteristics of being polite, modest, agreeable, and grateful, the individual's manager/supervisor with stereotypical notions of Asians might perceive the Asian American employee as a diligent and good worker, but lacking the ideal characteristics of a manager because he is too deferential, and nonassertive. Moreover, in the process of evaluating the characteristics of the Asian American worker, these characteristics (e.g., polite, agreeable, grateful, and modest) adhere to the evaluator's schema or stereotypic notions of "how Asian workers are"; though concurrently, the detrimental stereotypes of Asians as too passive and not good leaders are then simultaneously activated in the evaluation process and associated with the "Asianized" characteristics. Consequently, the evaluator will ultimately have a negative evaluation of the Asian American worker.

Similarly, another example is when an Asian American male believes that the man should be the breadwinner and the woman should focus on household and domestic responsibilities. A non-Asian may have an Asianized attribution of this Asian American male. The non-Asian's Asianized attribution will be that these characteristics and values fit the non-Asian's stereotypical notions of Asian males. That is, regardless of the individual's ethnic or racial identity, these characteristics are perceived by the non-Asian as "too traditional," patriarchal, and inherent of the "Asian culture." Even if the Asian American man is highly acculturated to the dominant cultural norms (e.g., European American culture), the Asian American man's attributes (e.g., gender role expectations) are racialized and perceived as natural to the individual's Asian cultural heritage even if the individual completely rejects his cultural heritage. Alternatively, if a White/European American male has the exact same attributes (i.e., gender role expectations), the non-White evaluator might perceive these characteristics as patriarchal but the evaluator may not racialize the individual's characteristics (i.e., the non-White will not make the generalization that all European Americans are "traditional and patriarchal"). Accordingly, it is unlikely the outside evaluator will attribute these characteristics as endemic of the European culture, thus the White male will not be evaluated as harshly.

Transgressive Attribution

Another phenomenon that some Asian Americans have experienced is when specific attributes are expressed (i.e., assertive) by Asian Americans but the expressions are interpreted negatively or seen as threatening. The authors term this phenomenon **transgressive attribution** or a process in which attributes of an Asian American individual are incongruent with the evaluators' stereotypical notions of Asians and are consequently negatively interpreted.

For example, if an evaluator has stereotypical beliefs of Asians as being passive or nonassertive, and if an Asian American man is assertive, the evaluator's conception is challenged but at the same time, the assertive behavior is perceived as deviant (the assertive attribution deviates from the stereotypical belief of "how Asians are") or violates the evaluator's stereotypical

Table 12.2 Transgressive Attribution

Asian American male characteristics/ attributes	Stereotypical notions held by evaluator, and transformation/ interpretation process	Outsiders' distorted evaluation
1. Asian American male asserts himself during a meeting	1. The assertive attribute is unexpected and does not fit evaluator's stereotype; hence, this attribute deviates from the evaluator's schema of Asians and is thus viewed as threatening	1. Asian American male is perceived as aggressive, defensive, and anxious
2. Asian American male has some gender role notions and expectations	2. Does not fit stereotype of Asian males not being good leaders	2. Since it is not expected, the advancement of the Asian American male is perceived as threatening; the Asian American male's accomplishments are minimized, and every characteristic is scrutinized by evaluators
3. Asian American male is confident and mentions his accomplishment to his colleagues in a humble manner	3. The Asian American male's colleagues expect Asians to be quiet and to not verbally highlight their accomplishments	3. The Asian American male is perceived as being cocky and arrogant

notions. Subsequently, these attributes of the Asian American man are then interpreted and characterized negatively. The Asian American man's attributes are distorted by the evaluator, and consequently the assertive Asian American male is perceived as aggressive, defensive, and anxious. Transgressive attribution is similar to how women's attributes are often misinterpreted in a sexist workforce. Sometimes when women assert themselves in the work environment, they are seen as "too aggressive" or "bitchy." For Asian American men, this phenomenon, or the transgressive attribution that evaluators have, often limit these men from climbing the corporate latter.

The New Asian American Male

In the face of all the obstacles experienced by Asian American men, this group has fought adversity and has started to form an identity for themselves. Asian American men are a unique group since they have to balance and deal with multidimensional identities, juggling acculturative factors, bicultural expectations, and internalized racism, on top of forming a new and evolved formed of masculinity. Despite their marginalized status of not fitting into the Eurocentric hegemonic mold, the current trend is that many second- and higher generation Asian American men are changing and challenging the hegemonic masculine notions (Chan, 2000; Chua & Fujino, 1999). Asian American men are thriving and their voices are growing stronger as evidenced by watchdog organizations and individuals (http://www.angryasianman.com, http://www.asiannation.org) who are speaking up for Asian Americans and Asian men in particular and who are being nationally recognized (i.e., the creator of Angryasianman.com has been on National Public Radio and in national newspapers). Likewise, as the research reviewed in this chapter indicates, Asian American men are developing psychologically healthy and flexible identities in which they are not adhering to gender role and masculine norms. In particular, these men are developing nonhegemonic masculinities, which includes being emotionally involved in their relationships, being sensitive, demonstrating assertiveness without being demanding and controlling, willing to contribute to household responsibilities, striving for egalitarian relationships and non-gendered identities (Sue, 2005). Similarly, Chan (2000) suggests that in order to counter the hegemonic model, constructing an ambiguous model of masculinity is necessary. That is, if both men and women have more flexible notions of what masculinity means (i.e., men can be sensitive and emotionally expressive and that does not make him "gay" or "feminine") or even eliminate gendered identities (e.g., that men are supposed to be strong and women are supposed to be sensitive), then conflict surrounding masculine and gender issues would not arise as frequently.

Summary

This chapter highlighted the discrimination and marginalization that Asian American men have endured in America. The historically derogatory views of Asian American men as the foreigner, invader, asexual, and feminine, still exist today. Many scholars believe this lack of positive images and stereotypes has made Asian American men less desirable marriage and dating partners (Fong & Yung, 1995/1996; Lee & Vaught, 2003; Okazaki, 1998). Several studies have supported this assertion by illuminating that European American, Asian American, and Asian immigrant women have a clear delineation between Asian American men and European American men, and have stereotypically gendered notions of Asian American men as traditional, passive, emotionally restricted, and less desirable than White men (Lee & Vaught, 2003; Okazaki, 1998). For Asian American men, some of the sources of psychological distress could be explained by cultural-specific factors such as cultural values, level of acculturation, and level of racial identity awareness. Asianized attribution and trans-gressive attribution elucidate how the intersection of masculinity, racism, race, and sexuality are captured in negative attributions or evaluations of Asian American men.

In spite of the bombardment of negative images, discrimination and marginalization, Asian Americans have been resilient in many ways. There are a steadily growing number of nationally recognized figures and outspoken advocates who are bringing attention to the plight of this population. Additionally, contrary to popular stereotypes, Asian American men report that their masculine identity is less important than European American men. Finally, the new generation of Asian American men has begun to form positive and progressive identities that are less gendered, more egalitarian, and flexible.

Discussion Questions

1. Are you aware of an instance when you or others had an Asianized attribution or trans-gressive attribution of an Asian American male?
2. How many famous Asian American males do you know? What are the implications, and how might this affect the psyche of Asian American males?
3. Have you ever noticed the lack of Asian American men news anchors and reporters (and how there are greater numbers of Asian American women)? What are the reasons for this?
4. If you are a male, what are some of the pressures you face? If you are a female, are there areas in which you have found that males experience double standards?
5. What are your stereotypes of Asian American males? Make a list. Does this fit with some of the stereotypes that were presented in this chapter?
6. List some of the strengths of being an Asian American male. What do you bring to the table, and add to this society as an Asian American male?

Case Study

This chapter focused on the historical and current background of the emasculation, marginalization, and multiple masculine and racial identities Asian American men experience. This next section focuses on illustrating how some of these issues and con-cepts might apply in a clinical case.

Terrell is a 19-year-old college freshman attending a large Southern California uni-versity. He is from Petaluma, California, a small, predominately White, middle-class city in Northern California. In high school, he was the star baseball player and was in the popular partying crowd. He wanted to continue his partying lifestyle and attend a prestigious school, which was how he chose this particular university. When he ini-tially joined the fraternity, he partied hard by playing drinking games (who can drink the most), stayed up all night, dated multiple women, and occasionally skipped a class or two since he was so tired in the mornings. A month into the quarter, Terrell real-ized the partying was catching up with him since he began to receive C's and D's on tests he felt were not too difficult. He was confused, guilty, and worried that he might be placed on academic probation, which would not settle well with his parents. Terrell also started to get annoyed and irritated at his fraternity brothers. He noticed they often mad racial comments, and when he would attempt to lead activities, they were not as responsive to him and would sometimes ignore his suggestions. The more he asserted himself, the more negative evaluations he received, thus causing Terrell to feel overwhelmed, alienated, and withdrawn. Because he felt he could not talk with his frat brothers about his concerns and because he did not want to be perceived as weak, he opted to talk with his female friends. When that did not help him get out of his "funk," he "dreadfully" decided to try counseling.

Case Study Discussion

In the intake session, Terrell listed his concerns such as how he feels overwhelmed, irritated, and uninterested in things he normally enjoys. After assessing for possible depression, the therapist proceeded to normalize his feelings that he is not alone and that college life is challenging for many students because one has to balance all the daily responsibilities such as school, social, work, and family life. The therapist mentioned that when the demands increase and become off-balanced, one begins to feel pressured, anxious, and overwhelmed. She instilled hope for Terrell by pointing out his strengths such as his active coping style and his ability to be vulnerable by sharing all the information with her. She presented him with therapeutic techniques (i.e., teaching him stress reduction techniques) and provided him with information about sleep hygiene and other health tips. After the first session, Terrell felt good about the session and decided to continue to attend since he felt heard, he gained valuable information about how to manage his stress, and because he felt confident that the therapist could continue to help him out.

In later sessions, the therapist worked on having Terrell make emotional connections with his daily experiences and interactions with people. He began to realize that throughout his life he did not want to be perceived as the "whiz kid," which he was called in grade school. Ever since then he focused his energy on excelling athletically, to be the popular kid and keep his high grades on the "DL" (down-low). However, despite his efforts he never fit in and he was constantly reminded that he was Asian. Since the few Asians that attended his high school were international students and were not viewed as "cool" by his peers, he attempted to further disassociate himself from all Asians. The therapist asked him what he did to distance himself and he replied that he would work out daily, wear sports jerseys and designer jeans, would not study as hard since he did not want to be perceived as a nerd, and attempted to prove that he was "smooth with the ladies," unlike the "other" Asian guys. When his parents would take him to "ethnic events" he animatedly resisted going because he thought all the Asian kids were "different" from him and the adults were "gossipy." He would actively prove how different he was from other Asian kids by taking everything to the extreme (i.e., showing off athletically at the functions, being obnoxiously loud, and making sure he was well dressed).

Successive sessions focused on issues surrounding masculine and racial identity development. Terrell did experience some dissonance and resistance immersion ideology toward his White peers since he became aware of why he was feeling annoyed and snapping at his White fraternity brothers. He realized that (a) they constantly reminded him that he was different (because he is Asian); (b) they stereotype Asians and other people of color; and (c) he was angry that despite all his efforts to fit in with the White crowd he was never fully accepted. Future sessions focused on these issues and the therapist facilitated Terrell's navigation through his dissonance feelings (i.e., anger, frustration). She continued to help him deconstruct his masculine ideology by pointing out the consequences of masculine ideology (i.e., his risk-taking behaviors, playboy ways) and assisted in facilitating his racial identity development by providing Terrell with activities and papers that helped him learn and discuss with her and others what it means to be Chinese American—the pros and cons.

Case Study Discussion Questions

For undergraduate students, please consider the following questions:

1. What are your reactions to the vignette? Can you relate or know of any men like Terrell?
2. Do you think the therapist handled the case well? What might have been an alternative way of approaching Terrell's situation?
3. What are some other issues you noticed that men of color face?

For graduate students and/or beginning therapists, please consider the following questions:

1. What is your approach in working with Asian American men? Is it different from (or the same as) working with men of different ethnic/racial backgrounds?
2. How might your stereotypes impact your work with Asian American men?
3. If you are a male therapist, what are some challenges you experience in working with other men? If you are a female therapist, what are some challenges in your experiences of working with men?

Key Terms

Acculturative stress: Stress due to the immigration process. Some factors that contribute to acculturative stress are the process of adjusting and adapting to a new culture, and overcoming language, cultural, and financial barriers (Roysircar & Maestas, 2002).

Asianized attribution: The process of when certain attributes or characteristics (e.g., modest, humble, agreeable) of the Asian American individual adheres to the evaluator's schema or stereotypic notions of "how Asian workers are"; the detrimental stereotypes of Asians (e.g., such as being too passive or not good leaders) are then simultaneously activated in the evaluation process, is associated with the "Asianized" characteristics. Consequently, the evaluator will ultimately have a negative evaluation of the Asian American individual.

Conflict between work and family: Refers to a man's inability to balance the demands of work and home (i.e., family) (O'Neil et al., 1986).

Conformity: Characterized by racial identity attitudes which trivialize race-related issues and racism (Alvarez & Helm, 2001). Individuals in this status tend to have a color-blind attitude and idealize White culture norms, beliefs, and values.

Dissonance: Status that marks a period when an individual starts to question White cultural norms and the individual becomes distressed and confused about prior notions regarding race and racial dynamics in America.

Egalitarian: Having a balanced and equal relationship (i.e., equal decision-making power in major decisions such as buying a car or house, splitting household duties) with a partner/significant other.

Emasculinization: To degrade, disempower, strip away any credibility to a man, and to attribute feminine characteristics to a male.

Feminist: "Believes that patriarchal aspect of U.S. society is responsible for many of the problems faced by women. They believe women show a variety of reactions to their subordinate status in society" (Sue & Sue, 1999, p. 318).

Filial piety: Includes taking care of aging parents, conforming to the expectations of the parents and cultural beliefs and traditions (Lee, 1996).

Gender role: "Behaviors, expectations, and values defined by society as masculine and feminine" (O'Neil, 1990, p. 24).

Gender role conflict: Posits four empirical factors in which men experience conflict (O'Neil et al., 1986). In the first factor, SPC, success refers to a man's focus on wealth and accomplishments as a means of gaining self-worth; power implies the need for the man to have authority over another person; and competition refers to the man's need to "win" over another individual. The second factor, RE, is defined as a man's inability to express his emotions, while simultaneously denying others their right to express emotions. The third factor, RABBM, refers to a man's difficulty (i.e., limited ways) of expressing intimacy, sexuality, and affection toward men and women. Finally, the fourth factor, CWF, refers to a man's inability to balance the demands of work and home (i.e., family) (O'Neil et al., 1986).

Glass ceiling: An invisible barrier that allows disempowered groups to "see and strive for high-level management positions" (Paek & Shah, 2003, p. 238) but systemically denies these groups access to these higher-level managerial jobs.

Hegemonic male: Refers to a male who is independent, self-reliant, assertive, masculine (i.e., tall, lean, muscle tone, chiseled jaw), confident, ambitious, tough, financially and emotionally stable.

Integrative awareness: The individual has a positive notion of what it truly is to be a member of one's racial group and feels secure and proud about it. Furthermore, the individual has more "cognitive complexity and flexibility around race and racial issues" (Alvarez & Helms, 2001, p. 221).

Introspection: Characterized by the individual reflecting upon and starting to truly understand what it means to be a member of a racial or ethnic group. The person reevaluates personal feelings toward Whites, though is still cautious and somewhat distrustful of Whites.

Masculinity myth: Posits a dominant form of masculinity, which carries with it contradictory and inconsistent expectations as well as negative consequences for men who live up to or attempt to live up to the expectations (Levant, 1996).

Model minority myth: Was introduced as a divisive tool against African, Latino, and Native American communities during civil rights, labor rights, identity, and immigration reform protests. The intent was to suggest to non-Asians that the best way to succeed in America was to emulate Asian Americans—to be quiet, and to work hard. The model minority image of Asian Americans is assumed to be organic, genetic, or cultural. The model minority myth also instilled the erroneous impression that Asian Americans are all financially well-off and that Asians do not experience as much racism and discrimination as other ethnic and racial groups (R. M. Lee, 2003).

Resistance immersion: Proceeds dissonance status and is characterized by the individual learning about his or her culture and race, and represents a time of hypersensitivity toward issues about race (Alvarez & Helm, 2001). In addition, the individual is angry, resentful, and distrusts White culture.

Restrictive affectionate behavior between men: Refers to a man's difficulty (i.e., limited ways) of expressing intimacy, sexuality, and affection toward men and women.

Restrictive emotionality: Defined as a man's inability to express his emotions, while simultaneously denying others their right to express emotions.

Success, power, and competition: Success refers to a man's focus on wealth and accomplishments as a means of gaining self-worth; power implies the need for the man to have authority over another person; and competition refers to the man's need to "win" over another individual.

Transgressive attribution: The transformative evaluation process in which attributes of an Asian American individual is incongruent with the evaluators' stereotypical notions of Asians and is consequently negatively interpreted. That is, if an Asian American is displaying certain attributes that challenge the evaluator's stereotypical notions of Asians, the attribution is perceived as deviant (the assertive attribution deviates from the stereotypical belief of "how

Asians are") or violates the evaluator's stereotypical notions. Subsequently, these attributes of the Asian American male are then interpreted and characterized negatively.

For Further Learning and Suggested Readings

http://www.angryasianman.com

http://www.asian-nation.org

Cajayon, G. (2003). *The Debut* [Motion picture].

Chua, P., & Fujino, D. C. (1999). Negotiating new Asian-American masculinities: Attitudes and gender expectations. *Journal of Men's Studies 7*(4), 391–413.

Espiritu, Y. L. (1997). *Asian American women and men*. Thousand Oaks, CA: Sage Publications.

Lin, J. (Director). (2003). *Better Luck Tomorrow* [Motion picture].

Okazaki, S. (1995). *American Sons* [Motion picture].

References

Alvarez, A., & Helms, J. E. (2001). Racial identity and reflected appraisals as influences on Asian Americans' racial adjustment. *Cultural Diversity and Ethnic Minority Psychology, 7*, 217–231.

Alvarez, A., & Piper, R. E. (2005). Integrating theory and practice: A racial-cultural counseling model. In R. T. Carter (Ed.), *Handbook of racial-cultural psychology and counseling* (Vol. 2). Hoboken, NJ: John Wiley.

Atkinson, D. R., Morten, G., & Sue, D. W. (1998). *Counseling American minorities* (5th ed.). Boston, MA: McGraw-Hill.

Blazina, C., Pisecco, S., & O'Neil, J. M. (2005). An adaptation of the Gender Role Conflict Scale for Adolescents: Psychometric issues and correlates with psychological distress. *Psychology of Men and Masculinity, 6*, 39–45.

Brannon, R. (1976). The male sex role: Our culture's blueprint of manhood and what it's done for us lately. In D. David & R. Brannon (Eds.), *In the 49% majority*. Reading, MA: Addison-Wesley.

Chan, J. W. (1998). Contemporary Asian American men's issues. In L. R. Hirabayashi (Ed.), *Teaching Asian America: Diversity and the problem of community issues* (pp. 93–102). Lanham, MD: Rowman and Littlefield Publishers.

Chan, J. W. (2000). Bruce Lee's fictional models of masculinity. *Men and Masculinities, 2*(4), 371–387.

Chan, S. (1991). *Asian Americans: An interpretive history*. Boston: Littlefield Publishers.

Chen, A. S. (1999). Lives at the center of the periphery, lives at the periphery of the center: Chinese American masculinities and bargaining with hegemony. *Gender and Society, 13*, 584–607.

Chua, P., & Fujino, D. C. (1999). Negotiating new Asian-American masculinities: Attitudes and gender expectations. *Journal of Men's Studies 7*(4), 391–413.

Espiritu, Y. L. (1997). *Asian American women and men: Labor, laws, and love*. Thousand Oaks, CA: Sage.

Feng, P. (1996). In search of Asian American cinema (race in contemporary American cinema, part 3). *Cineaste 21*, 32–35.

Fischer, A. R., & Moradi, B. (2001). Racial and ethnic identity. In J. G. Ponterotto, J. M. Casas, L. A. Suzuki, & C. M. Alexander (Eds.), *Handbook of multicultural counseling*. (2nd ed., pp. 341–370). Thousand Oaks, CA: Sage Publications.

Fong, C., & Yung, J. (1995/1996). In search of the right spouse: Interracial marriage among Chinese and Japanese Americans. *Amerasia Journal, 21*, 77–98.

Friedman, R. A., & Krackhard, D. (1997). Social capital and career mobility. *The Journal of Applied Behavioral Science, 33*, 316–334.

Fujino, D. C. (1997). The rates, patterns and reasons for forming heterosexual interracial dating relationships among Asian Americans. *Journal of Social & Personal Relationships 14* (6), 809–28.

Helms, J. E., & Cook, D. A. (1999). *Using race and culture in counseling and psychotherapy: theory and practice*. Needham Heights, MA: Allyn and Bacon.

Hua, V. (2005, November 27). Asian American entertainers find demand for their talent overseas very rewarding. *San Francisco Chronicle*, pp. 21, 24.

Im, S. (2000). The great divide: Interracial romance divides Asian Americans. Retrieved from http://www.poppolitics.com/articles/2000-12-19-divide.shtm

Iwamoto, D. K. (2003). Tupac Shakur: How do you see it? Understanding the identity formation of hyper-masculinity of a popular hip-hop artist. *Black Scholar, 33*(2), 44–49.

Iwamoto, D. K., & Caldwell, L. D. (2006). Asian American identity in the classroom. In W. R. V. O. Pan (Ed.), *Race, ethnicity, and education: The influences of racial and ethnic identity in education.* Westport, CT: Greenwood/Praeger.

Joyce, A. (2005, December 9). The bias breakdown. *Washington Post,* p. 1.

Kim, B. S., Atkinson, D. R., & Yang, P. H. (1999). The Asian Values Scale: Development, factor analysis, validation, and reliability. *Journal of Counseling Psychology, 46,* 342–352.

Kim, B. S. K., Ng, G. F., & Ahn, A. J. (2005). Effects of client expectation for counseling success, client-counselor worldview match, and client adherence to Asian and European American cultural values on counseling process with Asian Americans. *Journal of Counseling Psychology, 52,* 67–76.

Kim, E. J., O'Neil, J. M., & Owen, S. V. (1996). Asian-American men's acculturation and gender-role conflict. *Psychological Reports, 79,* 95–104.

Kim, J. (2001). Asian American identity development theory. In C. L. Wijeyesinghe & B. Jackson III (Eds.), *New perspectives on racial identity development: A theoretical and practical anthology* (pp. 67–90). New York: New York University Press.

Le, C. N. (2006). Asian small businesses. *Asian-Nation.* Retrieved February 12, 2006, from http://www.asian-nation.org/small-business.shtml

Le, C. N. (2006a). Behind the headlines: APA news blog. *Asian-Nation.* Retrieved February 7, 2006, from http://www.asian-nation.org/headlines/index.php

Le, C. N. (2006b). Interracial dating and marriage: U.S. raised Asian Americans [Electronic Version]. *Asian-Nation.* Retrieved February 5, 2006, from http://www.asian-nation.org/interracial2.shtml.

Lee, A., & Yeh, C. (2002). Stereotypes of Asian Americans. *Educational Resources Information Center,* 1-6.

Lee, L. C. (1998). An overview. In L. C. Lee & N. W. S. Zane (Eds.), *Handbook of Asian American psychology.* Thousand Oaks, CA: Sage Publications.

Lee, R. M. (2003). Do ethnic identity and other-group orientation protect against discrimination for Asian Americans? *Journal of Counseling Psychology, 50*(2), 133–141.

Lee, S. J., & Vaught, S. (2003). "You can never be too rich or too thin": Popular and consumer culture and the Americanization of Asian American girls. *The Journal of Negro Education, 72*(4).

Leong, F. (1998). Career development and vocational behavior. In L. C. Lee & N. W. C. Zane (Eds.), *Handbook of Asian American psychology.* Thousand Oaks, CA: Sage Publications.

Levant, R. F. (1996). The new psychology of men. *Professional Psychology: Research and Practice, 27,* 259–265.

Levant, R. F., Wu, R., & Fischer, J. (1996). Masculinity ideology: A comparison between U.S. and Chinese young men and women. *Journal of Gender, Culture, and Health, 1,* 207–220.

Liang, C., Li L. C., & Kim B. S. K. (2004). The Asian American Racism-Related Stress Inventory: Development, factor analysis, reliability, and validity. *Journal of Counseling Psychology, 51,* 103–114.

Lindsey, L. (1997). *Gender roles: A sociological perspective.* Englewood Cliffs, NJ: Prentice Hall.

Liu, W. M. (2002). Exploring the lives of Asian American men: Racial identity, male role norms, gender role conflict, and prejudicial attitudes. *Psychology of Men and Masculinity, 3,* 107–118.

Liu, W. M. (2005). The study of men and masculinity as an important multicultural competency consideration. *Journal of Clinical Psychology, 61,* 685–697.

Liu, W. M., & Chang, T. (2006). Asian American men and masculinity. In F. Leong, A. Inman, A. Ebreo, L. Yang, L. Kinoshita, & M. Fu (Eds.), *Handbook of Asian American psychology* (2nd ed., pp. 197–212). Thousand Oaks, CA: Sage Publications.

Liu, W. M., & Iwamoto, D. K. (2006). Asian American men's gender role conflict, distress, self-esteem, and Asian values. *Psychology of Men and Masculinity, 7,* 153–164.

Liu, W. M., & Iwamoto, D. K. (2007). Conformity to masculine norms, Asian values, coping strategies, peer group influences and substance use among Asian American men. *Psychology of Men and Masculinity, 8,* 25–39.

Liu, W. M., Rochlen, A., & Mohr, J. (2005). Real and ideal gender role conflict: Exploring psychological distress among men. *Psychology of Men and Masculinity, 6*(2), 137–148.

Nghe, L. T., & Mahalik, J. R. (1998, August). *Influences on Vietnamese men: Examining gender role social-ization, acculturation, and racism.* Paper presented at the meeting of the American Psychological Association, San Francisco, CA.

O'Neil, J. M. (1990). Assessing men's gender role conflict. In D. Moore & F. Leafgren (Eds.), *Men in conflict: Problem solving strategies and interventions.* Alexandria, VA: American Association for Counseling and Development.

O'Neil, J. M., Helms, B. J., Gable, R. K. D., & Wrightsman, L. S. (1986). Gender-role conflict scale: College men's fear of femininity. *Sex Roles, 14,* 335–350.

Okazaki, S. (1998). Teaching gender issues in Asian American psychology. *Psychology of Women Quarterly, 22,* 33–52.

Paek, H. J., & Shah, H. (2003). Racial ideology, model minorities, and the "not-so-silent partner": Stereo-typing of Asian Americans in U.S. magazine advertising. *The Howard Journal of Communications 14,* 225–243.

Parham, T., White, J. L., & Ajamu, A. (1999). *The psychology of Blacks: An African centered perspective* (3rd ed.). Upper Saddle River, NJ: Prentice Hall.

Pierson, D. (2004, May 12, 2004). Sex and the Asian man. *Los Angeles Times.*

Pleck, J. H. (1995). The gender role strain paradigm: An update. In R. F. Levant & W. S. Pollack (Eds.), *A new psychology of men* (pp. 11–32). New York: Basic Books.

Riley, P., & Kennard, C. (2002). *Asian male broadcasters on TV: Where are they?* Los Angeles, CA: University of Southern California School for Communications.

Roysircar, G., & Maestas, M. L. (2002). Assessing acculturation and cultural variables. In K. Kurasaki, S. Okazaki, & S. Sue (Eds.), *Asian American mental health: Assessment theories and methods* (pp. 77–94). Norwell, MA: Kluwer Academic.

Sakai, K. (2004). Gay or Asian? Spread causes minority uproar [Electronic Version]. *Gay Asian Pacific support network.* Retrieved February 5, 2006, from http://www.gapsn.org/project2/discussion/sakai.asp.

Sing, B. (1989, February 13). Toward equality exploring a world of difference backlash against the "model minority": Asian-Americans find themselves resisting a "demure" stereotype. *The Los Angeles Times,* pp. 12–14.

Sue, D. (2005). Asian American masculinity and therapy: The concept of masculinity in Asian American males. In G. R. Brooks & G. E. Good (Eds.), *New handbook of psychotherapy and counseling with men: A comprehensive guide to settings, problems, and treatment approaches.* San Francisco, CA: Jossey-Bass.

Sue, D. W., & Sue, S. (1999). *Counseling the culturally different: Theory and practice* (3rd ed.). New York: John Wiley and Sons.

Suinn, R., Rickard-Figueroa, K., Lew, S., & Vigil, P. (1987). The Suinn-Lew Asian Self-Identity Accultura-tion Scale: An initial report. *Educational and Psychological Measurement, 47,* 401–407.

Takaki, R. (1990). *Iron cage: Race and culture in 19th century America.* New York: Oxford University Press.

Tang, J. (1997). The model minority thesis revisited: (Counter) evidence from the science and engineering fields. *Journal of Applied and Behavioral Science, 33,* 291–315.

Truong, N. (2006). Constructing masculinities and experiencing loss. *Men and Masculinities, 8*(3), 321–330.

Xin, K. R. (2004). Asian American managers: An impression gap? An investigation of impression man-agement and supervisor-subordinate relationships. *The Journal of Applied Behavioral Science, 40*(2), 160–181.

Wong, F., & Halgin, R. (2006). The "model minority": Bane or blessing for Asian Americans? *Journal of Multicultural Counseling and Development, 34*(1), 38–49.

Young, K., & Takeuchi, D. (1998). Racism. In L. C. Lee & N. W. S. Zane (Eds.), *Handbook of Asian American psychology.* Thousand Oaks, CA: Sage Publications.

13
Lesbian, Gay, Bisexual, and Transgender Asian Americans

Y. BARRY CHUNG and ANNELIESE A. SINGH

OUTLINE OF CHAPTER

Case Synopsis

Sonali is a 23-year-old Asian American university student currently living in the South. She is struggling with her sexual identity. She remembers being attracted to females from the age of 5 years old, and currently has a crush on her best female friend at the university. Sonali has only shared her attractions to women with her male friend. Her parents are from Gujarat, India, and they are expecting her to get married after she completes her graduate studies. Sonali is the middle child and the only girl in her family. Her older brother was married last year, and her parents are in the process of arranging the marriage of her younger brother.

Introduction

Within Asian American psychology, the study of **lesbian, gay, bisexual**, and **transgender** (LGBT) issues is a relatively new area of inquiry. Proclaimed as the fourth force in psychology (Pedersen, 1988), the multicultural movement has just begun to examine the complexity of intersecting cultural identities such as those of LGBT racial and ethnic minorities. The limited amount of literature available on LGBT people of color leaves psychologists ill-equipped to work effectively with these populations (Greene, 1997a). Both racial/ethnic minorities and sexual minorities (i.e., LGBT persons) have to deal with social oppression and identity development issues (Israel & Selvidge, 2003). With a dual minority status, LGBT people of color may experience multiple layers of oppression. Some may struggle between their racial/ethnic and sexual/gender identities (Diaz, Ayala, & Bein, 2004; Harper, Jernewall, & Zea, 2004).

This chapter provides an introduction to Asian American LGBT psychology, beginning with definitions of key concepts, followed by an overview of LGBT issues in Asia and America. The chapter further focuses on LGBT Asian Americans with regard to (a) oppression and discrimination, (b) religion and worldview, and (c) duel identity development. The discussion is based on current theoretical and empirical literature, as well as the professional and personal experience of the authors with the LGBT Asian communities. After a summary of the chapter, discussion questions are posed and a case study is provided in order to facilitate thinking and understanding. The chapter concludes with exercises and learning activities as well as resources for further learning and readings.

Definitions of Key Concepts

The term **sexual orientation** refers to a person's affective/emotional and physical/sexual attraction to members of both sexes (Chung & Katayama, 1996). Lesbian and gay persons are females and males, respectively, whose sexual orientation is primarily toward people of the same sex. Although the word *gay* is sometimes used to include both gay men and lesbian women, this chapter limits its use to refer to gay males only so that lesbians are not rendered invisible due to the term's historical usage and strong association with men. Bisexual persons are those who are strongly attracted to both males and females, regardless of whether this attraction is equally to both sexes. Although an estimate of 10% of all Americans have a primary same-sex orientation and a majority of Americans are bisexual (Kinsey, Pomeroy, & Martin, 1948, 1953), it is impossible to determine the exact percentage of LGB persons in the larger population.

The definition of transgender is more complicated with fewer consensuses. Contrary to common misconception, transgenderism (the noun form of transgender) is not about one's sexual orientation, but **gender identity** and behavior. Gender identity is a person's identification of being male or female, regardless of one's biological sex. Transgender persons are broadly defined in this chapter as (a) persons whose gender identity or behavior differs significantly from what traditional culture deems congruent with their biological sex at birth or (b) those who have ambiguous or multi-sex genitalia. This definition includes transvestites and transgenderists (part-time and full-time cross-dressers, respectively), transsexuals (pre and post sex-reassignment operations), and androgynous and intersex persons (those with ambiguous or multi-sex genitalia; Carroll & Gilroy, 2002; Feinberg, 1996, 1998; Gainor, 2000). Other less academic but popular terms among the LGBT communities include drag kings (male impersonators), drag queens (female impersonators), MTF (male-to-female transsexuals), and FTM (female-to-male transsexuals). The word *queer*, although once a derogatory term, is now an accepted or affirmative term used among the LGBT communities for self-reference.

It is important to make a distinction between sexual orientation and gender identity because LGB people are not necessarily transgender, whereas transgender people do not necessarily identify as LGB. The confusion between the two concepts may stem from (a) the fact that the cultures associated with LGB and transgender people are often intertwined due to their shared experience of departing from traditional ideation of gender norms and behaviors and (b) stereotypes about LGBT persons (e.g., gay men are effeminate, lesbians are masculine, female impersonators prefer to have sex with men).

LGBT Issues in Asia

Given the fact that Asian Americans are influenced by Asian cultures and a large percentage of Asian Americans were born in Asia, it is important to examine the cultural context of LGBT issues in Asia in order to better understand the experience of LGBT Asian Americans. This section provides an overview of homosexuality, bisexuality, and transgenderism in Asia.

Homosexuality and Bisexuality

Although LGB persons seem largely invisible in Asian countries, the existence of homosexuality and bisexuality can be traced back to almost the beginning of all Asian histories (Leupp, 1995; Pope & Chung, 1999). Same-sex love and intimacy have been noted in historical accounts, literature, and artwork in Asian countries (e.g., homosexual and bisexual behaviors of emperors as well as concubines and servants living within the confine of royal palaces, military warriors and their younger mentees; Ruan, 1991). For example, there is a well-known story about a Chinese man who woke up and cut off his sleeve on which his male partner was resting so as not to awake him. Japan's kabuki and takarazuka (i.e., live theaters featuring all-male or all-female casts, respectively) feature same-sex love in their performances (Robertson, 1998). In many Asian cultures it is acceptable for same-sex persons to show affection for each other (e.g., holding hands, sleeping in the same bed) because such behaviors are not considered sexual in nature. On the other hand, Asian cultures tend to be intolerant when a person self-identifies as LGB because an LGB identity is largely a Western concept and unaccepted in Asian cultures (Chung & Katayama, 1998).

In recent history, Asian countries ruled by Communist parties have used more severe measures to treat LGB persons such as public humiliation, physical assault, imprisonment, or even execution. Countries with a primary religion of Islam (e.g., Indonesia and Malaysia) may also forbid homosexual practice. Homosexual acts are still illegal in India, Malaysia, and Singapore. Significant changes toward acceptance of homosexuality and bisexuality occurred in the 1990s and 2000s. In 2001, homosexuality was excluded as a psychological disorder in the *Chinese Classification and Diagnostic Criteria of Mental Disorders*. In the contemporary LGB movement, affirmative terms are developed in Asian countries for self-identification as LGB (e.g., *tongzhi* or *lala* in China, *doseiaisha* in Japan, *Bakla* in the Philippines).

Transgenderism

Transgenderism also has a long history in some Asian cultures. From Thailand to India, transgender people have been exalted as having unique spiritual powers because they possess both

Figure 13.1 Female impersonation. (Photograph by Jeff Boggs.)

Figure 13.2 Male impersonation.

masculine and feminine qualities. In China, early Beijing operas only employed male actors. Therefore, all female roles were played by males. On the other hand, Cantonese operas (in southern China) are known to have actors and actresses play the roles of the opposite sex. *Bianxing* is a Chinese term that translates to "one who changes sex," and is inclusive of transgender people regardless of the decision to seek sex-reassignment surgery. With an increasingly active transgender community in China, both traditional routes (e.g., academia, conferences) and technological approaches (e.g., Internet support groups, Web sites) are utilized to further understand these communities. These resources also target transgender community members to provide information on sex-reassignment surgery, hormone therapy, and other daily living issues (e.g., clothing, safety).

Hijras are known as the "third sex" in India, as they claim to be neither male nor female. Born biologically male, their manner and dress are distinctively female. Although their history includes being both exalted and feared by society, hijras also face real danger from hate crimes and other forms of violence in contemporary India. Since 2000, hijras have made true political gains despite this danger. Hijras such as Asha Devi and Kamla Jaan have been elected to mayoral positions, while Shabnam Mausi was elected as a legislative representative of her state (Nanda, 1990).

Finally, Thailand is a land of contradictions for transgender people. Drag queen performance is a major entertainment industry in Thailand, featuring female impersonators (see Figures 13.1 and 13.2). The term *katoey* (lady boy) is used to describe transvestites and transsexuals in this country. However, this term is considered extremely offensive in other countries such as China, because its translation is also understood as "human monster." Although many accounts of mistreatment of transgender people in Thailand exist, the country is also home to one of the most thriving sex-reassignment surgery centers in the world. Transgender people from all over the world come to Thailand for such surgeries, including those from the United States.

LGBT Issues in America

The experience of LGBT Asian Americans is influenced by their statuses as racial minorities and sexual minorities, as well as the interaction between the two identities. The experience of Asian

Americans as racial minorities is discussed in other chapters; thus, this next section focuses on LGBT persons' experience as sexual minorities in America.

U.S. Laws and Partnerships

U.S. laws regarding homosexual acts and same-sex relationships have changed significantly in the past few decades. In 1971, homosexual sex was illegal in most states, punishable to life imprisonment in five states (Weinberg & Williams, 1974). Currently, there are 1,128 federal protections and benefits that are available only to couples who are legally married (National Gay and Lesbian Task Force, 2006). Massachusetts is the only state where same-sex marriage is legal, while five other states (California, Connecticut, District of Columbia, New Jersey, and Vermont) recognize same-sex civil unions or domestic partnerships with benefits equivalent to heterosexual couples. Hawaii and Maine's domestic partnership laws afford same-sex couples fewer benefits than heterosexual couples. However, unlike heterosexual marriages, other states do not recognize or honor same-sex marriages or civil unions from the aforementioned states. Therefore, if a same-sex couple moves to another state, the benefits from the marriage or civil union become invalid. Because marital status is required in federal law to petition for a partner to immigrate to the United States, LGBT people cannot petition to bring their life partner to the United States.

LGBT individuals face other obstacles in America because there are no federal recognition and benefits for same-sex couples. They do not have automatic access to hospital visitation, which can be especially damaging psychologically in cases of sudden medical illness of partners. There are also significant financial barriers in terms of estate and taxation benefits, because same-sex couples are not allowed automatic financial decision-making power on their partner's behalf. Other rights and responsibilities not afforded to LGBT individuals in America are in the areas of social security and veteran's benefits, which are not accessible to LGBT couples. National organizations, such as the National Gay and Lesbian Task Force and the Human Rights Campaign, are advocacy groups that lobby on behalf of the rights of LGBT people. However, these groups face an uphill battle, as there was a backlash against LGBT people after their fight for marriage rights in recent years. In many states, legislatures are introducing legislation that specifically forbids LGBT people the rights to adopt or foster children. Therefore, many LGBT families live with the fear that their rights to build a family will be taken away from them.

Discrimination and Prejudice

Beyond legal, marriage, and family issues, LGBT Americans contend with societal discrimination in the form of hate crimes, such as violence and bullying. Hate crimes have tripled from the year 1993 to 2001 (Human Rights Campaign, 2004), and violence toward transgender people continues to rise. These rates are alarming, especially because FBI reporting on hate crimes based on sexual orientation is underreported. The tragic deaths of Matthew Shepherd in 1998, who was viciously beaten and left to die because he was gay, and Teena Brandon, a transgender man murdered because of his gender identity, have brought national attention to hate crimes against LGBT people. Fortunately, state and federal legislation is beginning to be passed, with sexual orientation and gender identity being included in hate crime legislation.

Discrimination against LGBT people also exists within the counseling and psychology professions. Homosexuality was categorized as a mental disorder in the *Diagnostic and Statistical Manual of Mental Disorders* until its removal in 1973 (Chernin & Johnson, 2003). Additionally, gender identity disorder remains labeled as a mental illness in this same text despite the significant body of research asserting the distinct biological and medical basis of gender identity issues. Categorizing gender identity as a mental disorder creates significant barriers for transgender people, as access to medical procedures that allow their sex and gender identities to be congruent (e.g., chest surgery for a female-to-male) are more difficult because it is viewed primarily as a psychological illness.

LGBT Asian Americans

This section focuses on the interaction between the two minority statuses of LGBT Asian Americans (i.e., being racial and sexual minorities). It discusses this experience by examining external factors (oppression and discrimination), internal factors (religion and worldview), and the management of their cultural identities (dual identity development). Because of the absence of psychological literature on transgender Asian Americans (Singh, Chung, & Dean, 2006), some discussions below apply to LGB Asian Americans only.

Oppression and Discrimination

In addition to being discriminated against by the dominant cultural groups of White Americans and heterosexual persons, LGB Asian Americans report being oppressed by the heterosexual Asian community and the White LGB community (Chan, 1989; Newman & Muzzonigro, 1993; Wooden, Kawasaki, & Mayeda, 1983). Being rejected by one's own cultural group members (i.e., Asians and LGB persons) can be particularly damaging to LGB Asian Americans because people tend to rely on support from their own cultural group members when facing oppression from other cultural groups. The lack of such support may contribute to feeling marginalized from all cultures.

Countering this marginalization and lack of support, Asian American LGBT persons form their own social groups in major U.S. cities to support each other (see Figures 13.3 and 13.4). Drag shows have become an integral part of social functions within Asian American gay male groups. As discussed previously, transgender behavior has a long history in some Asian countries such as China, Japan, and Thailand. Asian men also have some advantages for female impersonation, compared with other racial groups in America, because of their biological features such as shorter height, facial hair and bone structure, and hairless body. Associated with

Figure 13.3 LGBT Asian American social gathering (a). (Photograph by Y. Barry Chung.)

Figure 13.4 LGBT Asian American social gathering (b). (Photograph by Y. Barry Chung.).

this drag culture are stereotypes about Asian gay men being effeminate and submissive, sexually or otherwise. Less is known about other forms of transgenderism among the Asian American community, and their experience with discrimination awaits future studies.

Another form of oppression or discrimination is the overshadowing factor of race in how LGBT Asian Americans are sexualized (Chung & Katayama, 1998). Asians (especially males) are often perceived to be asexual or sexually unattractive in America. On the other hand, a small portion of White Americans are particularly, if not exclusively, attracted to Asians. The term *rice queen* is used to refer to White gay men who are predominantly attracted to Asian men. It can be frustrating and upsetting to feel that one's attractiveness (or lack of) is largely because of one's race. Preliminary research (Chung & Szymanski, 2006) suggested that a significant portion of LGBT Asian Americans tend to seek romantic relationships with White Americans, which may be a result of internalized racial oppression. These Asian Americans may have subscribed to Western standards of aesthetics and see other Asians as unattractive; or they may find White Americans to be superior or more desirable as mates than Asians. Chung and Szymanski's study found that some Asian gay men consider other Asians to be competitors for White men as potential mates. Some Asian men also jokingly characterize the act of having an Asian lover as "incestuous."

Religion and Worldview

When considering the issues that face LGBT Asian Americans, it is critical to understand the influence of Eastern religions and worldviews on their lives. Some Asian countries are dominated by certain organized religions such as Buddhism (Thailand), Hinduism (India), Christianity (Korea), and Islam (Indonesia). In other countries, people's belief system and worldview are often influenced by traditional philosophies (e.g., China). Buddhism does not specifically address homosexuality and transgenderism. Hinduism has similar views as Taoism, such as recognizing the importance of balance between female (shakti) and male (shiva) qualities in the world. However, Hinduism does not have the same stringent belief system against homosexuality. Although Hindu texts do not specifically endorse homosexuality, there are portrayals of same-sex relationships and behaviors in Hindu temples. Christianity and Islam faiths, as interpreted by fundamentalists, consider homosexuality a sin. However, certain denominations or individual churches do not hold the same negative belief about homosexuality, and some may be affirmative of people of all sexual orientations and gender identities.

Traditional Asian philosophical teachings (e.g., Confucianism and Taoism) emphasize straight adherence to prescribed gender roles and male-female relationships in hierarchical social structures. These teachings also include complementarity between "Yin" (female, darkness, softness, etc.) and "Yang" (male, light, strength, etc.), as well as continuation and expansion of the family through reproduction. Therefore, transgender behavior and same-sex relationships are considered inappropriate and counterproductive (Chan, 1989; Chung & Katayama, 1998).

Depending on their cultural roots and acculturation to LGBT mainstream culture, LGBT Asian Americans may have different attitudes regarding their sexual orientation or gender identity. Those who are influenced by religions or worldviews that oppose homosexuality and transgenderism may hold more negative attitudes about their sexual or gender identities, whereas those who are more acculturated to mainstream American and LGBT cultures may be less negative. Another important cultural value among Asian Americans is collectivism. Asian cultures are known for their focus on collectivistic values (i.e., valuing family and community benefits over individual gain), in contrast to individualistic values (i.e., valuing individuals and independence) among White Americans (Sue & Sue, 1990). These collectivistic values can affect LGBT Asian Americans' decisions regarding coming out or how they manage their identities. LGBT Asian Americans who hold individualistic values may be more likely to be totally out to family, friends, and coworkers because they value the pursuit of individual happiness, dignity, and autonomy. Those who are collectivistic may manage their identity differently across different social contexts (e.g., being out to LGBT friends but not to family, heterosexual friends, and coworkers) because they value the well-being of their community and significant others over their self-fulfillment. For example, a bisexual Asian female who is second generation in the United States and individualistic in her values may participate in a public LGBT pride parade and march with her Asian LGBT peers. On the other hand, a bisexual Asian female who is first generation in the United States and collectivistic in her values may feel more comfortable attending a small gathering during a LGBT pride festival at a friend's private home. It is important to understand this cultural value so as not to judge these LGBT Asian Americans as developmentally immature or unhealthy. A multiculturally sensitive approach is to understand that people from different cultures have their own coping strategies that may not resemble a linear development model (e.g., Cass, 1979, as described below).

Dual Identity Development

One important and complex issue facing LGBT Asian Americans is their development and management of their racial and sexual/gender identities. As racial minorities, Asian Americans have to deal with how they acculturate to the mainstream American culture as well as their Asian cultural heritage. Sue and Sue (1990) proposed four stages to describe this racial identity development process. In the first stage, Conformity, the Asian person identifies with the majority cultural group and devalues his or her own cultural group. The person enters the Dissonance stage when encountering conflicts between one's attitudes toward the majority group and one's own group. The third stage, Resistance/Immersion, involves identifying with one's own cultural group and devalues the majority cultural group. Finally, in the Integrative Awareness stage, the person realizes that all cultures have their strengths and weaknesses and opposes all forms of racism. Regarding the development of a homosexual identity, Cass (1979) described six stages: Confusion, Comparison, Tolerance, Acceptance, Pride, and Synthesis. In the beginning, children or adolescents assume a heterosexual identity because of socialization. When sexual feelings begin to emerge, homosexual adolescents become confused because their attraction toward people of the same sex is in conflict with their assumed heterosexual identity. During the Comparison stage, homosexual persons feel different and alienated from others. These persons enter the Tolerance stage when they become more able to tolerate their increasing emotional and behavioral affiliation with a homosexual identity. Increased sexual exploration and formation of sexual relationships with people of the same sex facilitate the persons' movement toward the Acceptance stage when they are able to accept homosexual orientation as an identity. Some people advance to the Pride stage when they devalue heterosexuality and take pride in being homosexual. In the final stage of Synthesis, homosexual persons integrate their homosexual identity with other identities and appreciate diversity in sexual orientation. Although several other homosexual identity development models have been proposed since Cass's (1979) publication, they depict a similar process that can be summarized in Figure 13.5. In this model, a person first assumes a heterosexual identity because of socialization, then goes through stages of confusion and identity pride during the coming-out process, and finally achieves identity synthesis.

Models of racial or sexual identities have generally been developed with a focus on one dimension of identity only (e.g., race or sexual orientation), with less attention to an integration of multiple identities. Chan's (1997) review of literature indicates that Asian American LGB persons are often seen more as sexual minorities than racial minorities, even though they desire both identities to be acknowledged. Chung and his colleagues (Chung & Katayama, 1998; Chung & Szymanski, 2006) suggested that LGB Asian Americans' development of racial and sexual identities involves a parallel and interactive process. Their research provides preliminary support for this theoretical model. The parallel process follows this sequence: (a) identification with the mainstream cultural group (i.e., White Americans or heterosexuals), (b) awakening and conflicting feelings due to increasing awareness of self (i.e., being racial minority or sexual minority), (c) immersion to one's own cultural group (Asians or LGB people), and (d) identity integration. Furthermore, Chung and Szymanski proposed that the development of one identity interacts with the development of the other identity. Because of Asian cultures' relative intolerance of homosexuality and because an LGB identity is largely a Western concept, the coming-out process for Asian Americans naturally begins with Westernization. Through association with White LGB persons and alienation from one's Asian cultural group members, the LGB Asian American is able to obtain role models and resources for establishing one's LGB identity without having to face Asian culture's oppression against homosexuals. However, exposure to racism within the mainstream LGB community also inflicts conflicts associated with racial and

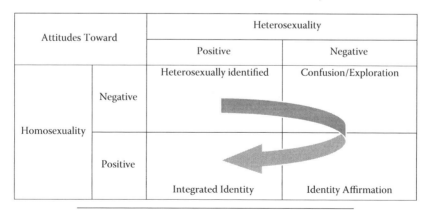

Figure 13.5 Integrative model of homosexual identity development.

sexual identities. Such experience may contribute to feeling marginalized from all worlds, without any community to anchor one's identity. Upon further strengthening one's LGB identity, the Asian American is able to find comfort and community with other LGB Asian Americans. Continued development of one's racial and sexual identity results in an integrated LGBT Asian American identity where both identities are complementary to each other, contributing to a unique holistic identity.

Summary

This chapter provides an overview of the psychology of LGBT Asian Americans. It began with definitions of key concepts and an introduction of LGBT issues in Asia and America to give the reader a context for understanding LGBT Asian Americans. The chapter further discussed the experience of LGBT Asian Americans, focusing on external factors (oppression and discrimination), internal factors (religion and worldview), and the management of cultural identities (dual identity development). Discussion questions are posed below to facilitate learning, followed by a case study that is an application of materials covered in this chapter. The chapter concludes with exercises and learning activities as well as resources for further learning and readings. Readers are encouraged to engage in self-reflection and cultural exploration with LGBT Asian American issues, keeping in mind that multicultural competence involves looking inward, taking risks, thinking outside of the box, and being empathic.

Discussion Questions

1. How do you think and feel about LGBT people in general and LGBT Asian Americans in particular?
2. What are the advantages and disadvantages of being LGBT Asian American?
3. How do you imagine your relationship with your parents, other members of your family, and your friends may change if you were an LGBT Asian American?
4. What help or resources would you suggest or provide in your community to LGBT Asian Americans who are having difficulty in adjustment?
5. If you had to develop a brochure for LGBT Asian Americans, what would you include?

Case Study

So far, this chapter has focused on the history and research of how being LGBT impacts Asian Americans in their personal lives and contributes to their psychological growth and development. The chapter will now shift its focus to a case study that illustrates how LGBT Asian Americans experience and cope with these issues. Moreover, the following case study will give readers a sense of what LGBT Asian Americans may focus on in therapy.

Sonali was referred to the university counseling center by her gay male friend who was currently seeing a counselor there. She is a 23-year-old Asian American student who is struggling with her sexual identity. She is currently in graduate school in a large public university in the South. She told her counselor that she remembered being attracted to females since she was 5 years old. Sonali currently has a crush on her female best friend at the university, and she has only disclosed her attraction to her male friend. Sonali's parents were born in Gujarat, India, where gender roles tend to be quite strict. Her family is Muslim and devout, attending mosque weekly and participating in prayer (salas) five times daily. Sonali is the middle child and the only girl in her family. Her older brother was married last year, and her parents are in the process of arranging the marriage of her younger brother.

Sonali has always known that her parents would arrange for her marriage. However, now that her younger brother is in the marriage process, she is beginning to feel tremendous pressure from her parents to begin a search for a groom. Sonali feels scared to talk about being attracted to women and does not want to marry a man. It is her last year in her graduate program, but she no longer feels as motivated to succeed in her studies as she did when she first came to the university. She has been sleeping more than usual and crying daily about the prospect of beginning the arranged marriage process. Sonali has also been staying in her dorm room alone, rather than spending time with her friends, which she used to enjoy.

Case Study Discussion

The counselor who works with Sonali used an affirmative approach in order to create a safe and therapeutic environment in which to explore her sexual identity. The counselor had previously thought about maintaining his office as a safe space for LGBT students in general, and has a "Safe Zone" sticker posted in his office along with LGBT books and magazines. Aware of the dual identity issues that Sonali may experience as a South Asian female questioning her sexual identity, the counselor shared with Sonali the diverse experiences of LGBT Asian Americans. He also validated Sonali's concerns about pleasing her parents, in addition to her fear of an arranged marriage with a man.

The counselor also explored the social support systems that Sonali currently had in her life. She shared the importance of her friendship with a gay Asian male, and the counselor helped Sonali identify the qualities of their friendship that allowed her to tell him about her struggles. The counselor then asked Sonali to list other people in her life that had similar qualities. Sonali shared that her sociology professor had reached out to her after Sonali wrote a paper on gay marriage, but she was scared the professor might "judge" her if she knew Sonali was "gay and messed up." The counselor validated Sonali's fears and brought up the systemic inequalities that LGBT individuals face in the United States and the world. In each session, the counselor paid close attention to her mood and affect, in order to monitor potential symptoms of depression due to her internalized homophobia. He also reassured Sonali that LGBT Asian Americans have a unique coming-out process, due to the tension that can come from wanting to maintain a "proper" family image, but also wanting to individually express one's self.

Sonali was unaware that other LGBT Asian Americans existed, as she had always heard her parents say, "America has gay people, not India, and there are no gay Muslims." The counselor had access to the Internet in his office, and showed Sonali the Web site of a support group for South Asian LGBT people in addition to various books and resources on LGBT people and the coming-out process. Throughout therapy, the counselor paid careful attention to Sonali's values, assessing the tension or balance between an individualistic and/or collectivistic orientation. During one session, Sonali asked the counselor if he was "gay." The counselor answered that he was not, and validated the reason she would ask this question. He then explored the thoughts and feelings behind her question, which allowed Sonali to share further about how "good" it would feel to "talk to other gay people." The counselor and Sonali used this exploration to guide future sessions exploring her coming-out as it related to her dual identity, religious values, and sexual identity.

Case Study Discussion Questions

For undergraduate students, please consider the following questions:

1. What are the stressors that Sonali faces currently in her life? Are you concerned for her?
2. What are the strengths that Sonali has that could help her?
3. What advice would you give to Sonali if you were her friend?

For graduate students and/or beginning therapists, please consider the following questions:

1. What type of information and community resources (within and outside of the LGBT Asian American community) would be helpful to Sonali?
2. What are the systems (e.g., race/ethnicity, family) operating on Sonali's life on the micro and macro levels?
3. How would you talk to Sonali about her coming-out process? Would you advise her to come out? Why or why not?

Key Terms

Bisexual: Those who are strongly attracted to both males and females, regardless of whether the attraction is equal to both sexes.

Gay: Males whose sexual orientation is primarily toward other males.

Gender identity: A person's identification of being male or female, regardless of one's biological sex.

Lesbian: Females whose sexual orientation is primarily toward other females.

Sexual orientation: A person's affective/emotional and physical/sexual attraction to members of both sexes.

Transgender: Persons whose gender identity or behavior differs significantly from what traditional culture deems congruent with their biological sex at birth or those who have ambiguous or multisex genitalia.

For Further Learning and Suggested Readings

To learn more about Asian American LGBT issues, you may engage in the following learning activities in order to gain more knowledge and awareness about this population.

Search the Internet for Asian American LGBT issues. Notice the degree of difficulty or ease as you attempt to search for helpful information about this community. List the categories of information that you find about Asian American LGBT people, and list categories of information that you think are missing as a result of your Internet search.

Initiate a discussion with a friend or family member about Asian American LGBT people. Notice what common stereotypes about Asian Americans and LGBT people arise in your discussion. Explore where these stereotypes come from, and how they impact how you both view the Asian American LGBT community.

Visit an Asian American or LGBT community organization. Assess whether their organization's literature (e.g., brochures, newsletters) are inclusive of Asian American LGBT people. Interview a staff member about how they conduct outreach to the Asian American LGBT community. Notice and list the presence of stereotypes, challenging questions, and level of comfort in this discussion. Consider writing a brief article about your experience and submit it for publication in their newsletter.

Visit the Web sites of national LGBT organizations in the U.S. (e.g., the National Gay and Lesbian Task Force, Human Rights Campaign), and search for Asian American LGBT information. Notice what information you find on culture, coming out, and other LGBT issues (e.g., adoption, marriage). Compare the differences in Asian American LGBT concerns and the concerns of the mainstream LGBT movement in the U.S.

Asian movies that feature LGBT themes are often showcased at the San Francisco International Lesbian and Gay Film Festival. Some famous movies include *Lan Yu, Fish & Elephant, Bungee Jumping of Their Own, Formula 17, The Wedding Banquet,* and *Farewell, My Concubine.* These films portray the stories of lesbian or gay relationships in the context of traditional and contemporary Asian cultures, some with spices of tragic or comedy themes.

Readers may consult three notable publications related to LGBT Asian Americans: (a) Greene's (1997b) special issue on *Ethnic and Cultural Diversity among Lesbians and Gay Men*; (b) Fassinger's (2003) special issue on *Multicultural Counseling with Gay, Lesbian, and Bisexual Clients*; and (c) Zea and Harper's (2004) special issue on *Lesbian, Gay, and Bisexual Racial and Ethnic Minority Individuals: Empirical Explorations.*

For books, readers may be interested in Leong's (1995) *Asian American Sexualities: Dimensions of Gay and Lesbian Experience,* Sullivan and Jackson's (2001) *Gay and Lesbian Asia: Culture, Identity, Community,* and Eng and Yom's (1998) *Q & A: Queer and Asian in America.*

For magazines, *Bamboo Girl* (Queer Asian American urban girls' perspective), *Flavor* (explores racism and homophobia from Asian queer perspective), and *Trikone* (South Asian LGBT perspective) have engaging articles on the LGBT Asian American experience.

For Web sites, helpful resources are http://www.exoticizemyfist.com (Queer Asian American women), http://www.trikone.org (South Asian LGBT organization), http://www.xiasl.net (transgender support in China), as well as the Web sites of "Asians and Friends" in major cities (Asian American gay men social groups).

References

Carroll, L., & Gilroy, P. J. (2002). Transgender issues in counselor preparation. *Counselor Education and Supervision, 41,* 233–242.

Cass, V. C. (1979). Homosexuality identity formation: A theoretical model. *Journal of Homosexuality, 4,* 219–235.

Chan, C. S. (1989). Issues of identity development among Asian-American lesbians and gay men. *Journal of Counseling and Development, 68,* 16–20.

Chan, C. S. (1997). Don't ask, don't tell, don't know: The formation of a homosexual identity and sexual expression among Asian American lesbians. In B. Greene (Ed.), *Ethnic and cultural diversity among lesbians and gay men* (pp. 240–248). Thousand Oaks, CA: Sage Publications.

Chernin, J. N., & Johnson, M. R. (2003). *Affirmative psychotherapy and counseling for lesbians and gay men.* Thousand Oaks, CA: Sage Publications.

Chung, Y. B., & Katayama, M. (1996). Assessment of sexual orientation in lesbian/gay/bisexual studies. *Journal of Homosexuality, 30*(4), 49–62.

Chung, Y. B., & Katayama, M. (1998). Ethnic and sexual identity development of Asian-American lesbian and gay adolescents. *Professional School Counseling, 1*(3), 21–25.

Chung, Y. B., & Szymanski, D. M. (2006). Racial and sexual identities of Asian American gay men. *Journal of GLBT Issues in Counseling, 1*(2), 67–93.

Diaz, R. M., Ayala, G., & Bein, E. (2004). Sexual risk as an outcome of social oppression: Data for a probability sample of Latino gay men in three U.S. cities. *Cultural Diversity and Ethnic Minority Psychology, 10,* 255–267.

Eng, D. L., & Yom, A. Y. (1998) *Q & A: Queer and Asian in America.* Philadelphia, PA: Temple University Press.

Fassinger, R. E. (Ed.). (2003). Multicultural counseling with gay, lesbian, and bisexual clients [Special issue]. *Journal of Multicultural Counseling and Development, 31*(2).

Feinberg, L. (1996). *Transgender warriors: Making history from Joan of Arc to Dennis Rodman.* Boston, MA: Beacon Press.

Feinberg, L. (1998). *TransLiberation: Beyond pink or blue.* Boston, MA: Beacon Press.

Gainor, K. A. (2000). Including transgender issues in lesbian, gay and bisexual psychology: Implications for clinical practice and training. In B. Greene & G. L. Croom (Eds.), *Education, research, and practice in lesbian, gay, bisexual, and transgendered psychology: A resource manual* (pp. 131–160). Thousand Oaks, CA: Sage Publications.

Greene, B. (1997a). Ethnic minority lesbians and gay men: Mental health and treatment issues. In B. Greene (Ed.), *Ethnic and cultural diversity among lesbians and gay men* (pp. 216–239). Thousand Oaks, CA: Sage Publications.

Greene, B. (Ed.). (1997b). *Ethnic and cultural diversity among lesbians and gay men.* Thousand Oaks, CA: Sage Publications.

Harper, G. W., Jernewall, N., & Zea, M. C. (2004). Giving voice to emerging science and theory for lesbian, gay, and bisexual people of color. *Cultural Diversity and Ethnic Minority Psychology, 10,* 187–199.

Human Rights Campaign. (2004). *Equality state by state: Gay, lesbian, bisexual, and transgender legislation.* Retrieved January 30, 2006, from http://www.hrc.org/Content/ContentGroups/Publications1/Equality_State_by_State.pdf

Israel, T., & Selvidge, M. M. D. (2003). Contributions of multicultural counseling to counselor competence with lesbian, gay, and bisexual clients. *Journal of Multicultural Counseling and Development, 31,* 84–98.

Kinsey, A. C., Pomeroy, W. B., & Martin, C. E. (1948). *Sexual behavior in the human male.* Philadelphia, PA: W. B. Saunders.

Kinsey, A. C., Pomeroy, W. B., & Martin, C. E. (1953). *Sexual behavior in the human female.* Philadelphia, PA: W. B. Saunders.

Leong, L. (1995). *Asian American sexualities: Dimensions of gay and lesbian experience.* New York: Routledge.

Leupp, G. P. (1995). *Male colors: The construction of homosexuality in Tokugawa Japan.* Berkeley, CA: University of California Press.

Nanda, S. (1990). *Neither man nor woman: The hijras of India.* New York: Wadsworth Publishing.

National Gay and Lesbian Task Force. (2006). *Why civil unions are not enough.* Retrieved January 30, 2006, from http://www.thetaskforce.org/reslibrary/list.cfm?pubTypeID=2#pub269.

Newman, B. S., & Muzzonigro, P. G. (1993). The effects of traditional family values on the coming out process of gay male adolescents. *Adolescence, 28,* 213–226.

Pedersen, P. B. (1988). *A handbook for developing multicultural awareness.* Alexandria, VA: American Association for Counseling and Development.

Pope, M., & Chung, Y. B. (1999). From bakla to tongzhi: Counseling and psychotherapy with gay and lesbian Asian and Pacific Islander Americans. In D. S. Sandhu (Ed.), *Asian and Pacific Islander Americans: Issues and concerns for counseling and psychotherapy* (pp. 283–300). Commack, NY: Nova Science Publishers.

Robertson, J. (1998). *Takarazuka: Sexual politics and popular culture in modern Japan.* Berkeley, CA: University of California Press.

Ruan, F. F. (1991). *Sex in China: Studies in sexology in Chinese culture.* New York: Plenum.

Singh, A., Chung, Y. B., & Dean, J. K. (2006). Acculturation level and internalized homophobia of Asian American lesbian and bisexual women: An exploratory analysis. *Journal of GLBT Issues in Counseling, 1*(2), 3–19.

Sue, D. W., & Sue, D. (1990). *Counseling the culturally different: Theory and practice.* New York: John Wiley & Sons.

Sullivan, G., & Jackson, P. A. (2001). *Gay and lesbian Asia: Culture, identity, community.* New York: Harrington Park Press.

Weinberg, M. S., & Williams, C. J. (1974). *Male homosexuals: Their problems and adaptations.* New York: Oxford University Press.

Wooden, W. S., Kawasaki, H., & Mayeda, R. (1983). Lifestyles and identity maintenance among gay Japanese-American males. *Alternative Lifestyles, 5,* 236–243.

Zea, M. C., & Harper, G. W. (Eds.). (2004). Lesbian, gay, and bisexual racial and ethnic minority individuals: Empirical explorations [Special issue]. *Cultural Diversity and Ethnic Minority Psychology, 10*(3).

14
Sexuality

GRACE A. CHEN and SARA CHO KIM

OUTLINE OF CHAPTER

Case Synopsis

Lisa is a 21-year-old, Asian American, heterosexual female who seeks counseling because she is feeling extremely anxious. She recently went to the student health center due to vaginal discomfort, and she is worried that she may have a **sexually transmitted infection** (STI). Lisa confides to her counselor that she has been sexually active with a number of men and was embarrassed in discussing the matter. She is afraid if her parents find out, she will be forced to transfer schools or possibly be disowned. Lisa finds out a week later that she has a viral STI, which can be treated but not cured. She is unsure of what steps to take next.

Introduction

This chapter was almost the shortest chapter in the book—when one of the authors mentioned to her cousin that the chapter topic was on Asian Americans and **sexuality**, the humorous response was, "We don't have sex! We don't talk about sex! There's your chapter!" A common stereotype and perception is that Asian Americans are not sexual and do not discuss sexuality openly with others. To a certain extent, this has been true among Asian Americans in traditional communities. Generally speaking, there is a silence about sex and sexuality in the Asian American community. Given the lack of discussion regarding this area, this chapter will bring forward issues that are present in the community and not often discussed. The chapter will discuss a range of issues regarding Asian Americans and sexuality, such as identity development, socialization, behaviors, sexual health, and **sexual violence**. The chapter will also cover how social and cultural issues impact sexuality for Asian Americans.

"Now let's talk about sex, baby...." Although there has been increased discussion about sexuality in Asian Americans in the humanities, there are few empirical studies in psychology on sexuality and the **sexual identity** of Asian Americans (Okazaki, 2002). The extant studies on Asian Americans mainly examined sexual attitudes and behavior and not sexual identity development (Chng & Geliga-Vargas, 2000; Cochran, Mays, & Leung, 1991; Huang & Uba, 1992; Meston, Trapnell, & Gorzalka, 1996). The silence in the Asian American community surrounding sexuality presumably preserves this reality as sacred and pure, with one author commenting that the "invisibility and silence ironically create certain attitudes among Asian Americans toward sexuality, such as separation, shame, homophobia, and fixed gender roles" (Lee, 2006). Therefore, researching, discussing, and examining Asian American sexuality and sexual identity in depth is important to break the silence around this commonly taboo subject.

Sexuality is more than one's **sexual orientation**—it is a continuum of identities, desires, fantasies, behaviors, and attractions, which can range from homoerotic to heterosexual (Takagi, 1994). Sexuality is the "total expression of the attempt to discharge energy from sexual drives" (Gilbert & Scher, 1999). So, why is sexuality such an important topic in psychology? Sexuality is a fundamental aspect of an individual's identity and how one relates to others. Asian American sexuality is an important topic to discuss given the stereotypes and assumptions that Asian Americans are less sexually active or, on the other extreme, sexually deviant. Oftentimes Asian Americans are understudied in sexuality research, which is problematic especially with regards to sexual health concerns, including sexual behavior, HIV, and other associated risks.

Sexual Identity

Sexual identity involves one's subjective experience and development as a sexual being, whether one is bisexual, gay, lesbian, or heterosexual. For the most part, the literature on sexual identity development focuses on the development of one's sexual orientation identity. Sexual orientation refers to one's sexual object choice based on sexual and affective desires, attractions, and behaviors—these include attractions to the same sex (gay, lesbian), both sexes (bisexual), and a different sex (heterosexual).

The majority of theory and research on sexual orientation identity development focuses on minority sexual identity development, such as that of lesbian and gay individuals (Worthington, Savoy, Dillon, & Vernaglia, 2002). However, more recently, scholars have identified the need to examine heterosexual identity (Mohr, 2002; Worthington et al., 2002). The chapter "Lesbian, Gay, Bisexual, and Transgendered" in this textbook discusses LGBT issues in depth, so this chapter will not focus on LGBT issues for Asian Americans in detail. However, a general overview of lesbian/gay identity development as well as heterosexual identity development is provided in this section.

Susan McCarn and Ruth Fassinger (1996) and Ruth Fassinger and Brett Miller (1996) proposed a model delineating both individual and social aspects of sexual minority identity development. The model for Sexual Minority Identity Formation (Fassinger & Miller, 1996; McCarn & Fassinger, 1996) addressed group identity in addition to individual sexual identity development in four phases: (a) awareness, (b) exploration, (c) deepening/commitment, and (d) internalization/synthesis. According to this model, individual sexual identity development and group membership identity are separate (yet related) processes, and the model takes into consideration attitudes toward other lesbians/gays and attitudes towards heterosexuals. For example, a woman who is questioning her sexual orientation meets gay and lesbian individuals for the first time in college and is interested in understanding their experiences as a group, which places her in the "exploration" phase of her group identity; however, she feels attracted to one woman and is unsure of what that means for herself, so her individual sexual identity is in the awareness phase. The **Sexual Minority Identity Formation Model** removed the emphasis in other models on political awareness and disclosure of being lesbian/gay as part of lesbian/gay identity development.

Until recently, most sexuality research on heterosexual individuals focused on sexual attitudes and behavior without exploring the development of heterosexual *identity*. However,

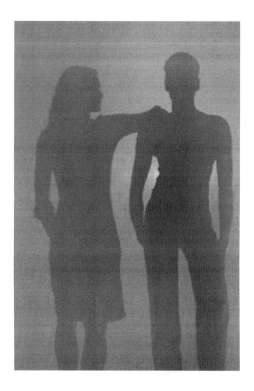

several researchers have begun theorizing and researching heterosexual identity development (Eliason, 1995; Mohr, 2002; Sullivan, 1998; Worthington et al., 2002). Heterosexual identity development is defined as "the individual and social processes by which heterosexually identified persons acknowledge and define their sexual needs, values, sexual orientation and preferences for sexual activities, modes of sexual expression, and characteristics of sexual partners" (Worthington et al., 2002, p. 510). The **Multidimensional Model of Heterosexual Identity Development** (Worthington et al., 2002) is based on several other identity development models (Downing & Roush, 1985; Helms, 1995; Sullivan, 1998) and consists of five identity statuses: (a) unexplored commitment, (b) active exploration (goal-directed, excludes "naïve behavioral experimentation"), (c) diffusion (no commitment or exploration), (d) deepening and commitment, and (e) synthesis (congruence of individual identity and integration with other social identities). For example, a young man who seeks out women to date because he feels that is what is expected of men his age may be in the "unexplored commitment" status as he has not actively considered what his sexual orientation is. This model should be considered within a biopsychosocial context, including the cultures of gender, ethnicity, and religion. In particular for Asian Americans, it is important to consider cultural influences (e.g., ethnic traditions, religious values, media messages, etc.) on sexual identity development; these cultural influences are often evident in Asian Americans' socialization by parents, schools, and peers within the context of the dominant U.S. culture.

Socialization

Sexual identity of Asian Americans is influenced by several factors—parents, culture, religion, and media. In many Asian American homes, the topic of sexuality is rarely discussed. Traditional Asian values emphasize the importance of chastity and disapprove of nonmarital sexual behavior (Kim & Ward, 2007). The fact that the *Kama Sutra* (an ancient text on love and sex) originated in India does not preclude that, in actuality, "sex is shrouded in a veil of secrecy" in

South Asian culture and is not discussed openly in families (Devji, 1999). Due to strong Asian cultural influences, Asian American adolescents and young adults rarely have an opportunity to seek information regarding sexual matters for fear of shaming their family by exposing a private topic in a public manner (Hahm, Lahiff, & Barreto, 2006). As such, Asian Americans learn about sexuality mainly through their peers and the media (Lee & Vaught, 2003; Okazaki, 2002).

Few studies have been conducted on the socialization of Asian Americans regarding sexuality, especially regarding parental communication about sexuality (one exception is Kim & Ward, 2007). Messages about sexuality are mixed based on gender and levels of acculturation (Kim & Ward, 2007). For Asian American females, maintaining self-control through abstinence and modesty is highly valued in Asian cultures as well as in U.S. American culture. For Asian American males, underlying messages of independence and sexual prowess are received from Asian culture, while conflicting images of Asian American men being either hypersexual or asexual are received from U.S. American culture.

Parents

Parents provide implicit messages about sexuality through discussions around dating and marriage. Parents are more likely to discuss with their children dating expectations than actual sexual behavior (Kim & Ward, 2007). In South Asian cultures, dating is often deemed unacceptable as it is seen as "inevitably involving sex" (Leonard, 1999). Arranged marriages have been the cultural norm of many South Asian (e.g., Asian Indian and Pakistani) and Southeast Asian ethnic groups (e.g., Hmong), and discussions about dating and sexuality are unlikely to occur in those traditions. However, attitudes and beliefs may be shifting from traditional Asian views as Asian immigrants and Asian Americans become acculturated to U.S. dominant culture (Devji, 1999).

In examining parental sexual communication among Asian Americans, Janna Kim and Monique Ward (2007) found that the types of messages and the amount of communication were based on gender (of both children and parents), parents' acculturation levels, religion, and language differences within the home. Daughters received significantly more communication about sexual topics than sons did, and both sons and daughters received more communication from their mothers and very little from their fathers. Daughters received more prohibitive messages regarding abstinence until marriage, sex as a taboo topic, and gendered sex roles. Sons tended to receive messages about STIs and contraception, which assumed they were sexually active. Parents who were more acculturated conveyed a greater number of messages that premarital sex was acceptable. In families where parents spoke in an Asian language but children spoke in English to their parents, the daughters and sons received significantly less communication from their mothers. Although Asian immigrant parents tended to focus discussions on dating and qualities of good marriage partners, some parents did discuss safer sex practices regarding pregnancy and STIs with their children (primarily discussed with male children) (Kim & Ward, 2007).

The participants in Kim and Ward's (2007) study indicated that the messages they received from their parents tended not to be a result of direct, explicit discussions about sexual topics. Thus, although Asian American parents may not discuss sexual topics explicitly with their children, they nevertheless communicate their values and thoughts about sexual topics through indirect means. Ironically, a result of parental restrictions on dating (which, in essence, is used as a means to restrain sexuality) is that many young Asian Americans do not tell their parents about their relationships (Espiritu, 2001; Leonard, 1999). Thus, their parents end up possibly having less influence and control over their children's sexuality than they believe and wish they have.

In what ways did your parents or other family members indirectly inform you of appropriate and acceptable sexual practices and behaviors?

Studies reveal that when Asian American parents do discuss sexuality with their children, Asian Americans are more likely to have greater awareness of STIs, abortions, pregnancy-related information, and HIV/AIDS (Hahm et al., 2006). Discussions within Asian American families regarding coming-out experiences for LGBT youth and adolescents are much less frequent. Heterosexual dating and marriage are presumed to be the normal course of development for Asian American children. With the seldom-discussed issues around dating, sexual behaviors, and sexual education, lesbian/gay/bisexual/queer identity discussions are not even on the radar for most parents raising Asian American children (Hom, 1994). So, if you were Asian American, and you were thinking of coming out, who would you turn to, and where would you go?

Culture

Socialization of Asian Americans regarding sexuality also occurs through cultural expectations espoused by or implied in their families and ethnic communities. An overarching message in various Asian American communities (whether East Asian, South Asian, or Pacific Islander) is that women in particular are expected to remain virgins until marriage (Devji, 1999; Lee, 2006; Leonard, 1999). Boyung Lee (2006) discussed a 2003 ABC News *20/20* report in which young women (a large proportion of them Chinese American and Korean American) were undergoing surgery for "hymen restoration" in order to appear as virgins for their weddings as they feared ramifications (shame and ostracism) if they were not perceived as pure. In East Asian cultures (i.e., Chinese, Japanese, and Korean), traditional Confucian values dictate that a woman's chastity and honor are intimately linked to her family's honor and reputation; thus, women are expected to stay virtuous (i.e., remain virgins until marriage). Similarly, in South Asian cultures, a common theme in cultural messages regarding gender and sexuality is that women must remain chaste and pure for their husbands and for the honor of their families (Abraham, 1999). Traditional South Asian culture links dating closely to serious commitment (i.e., marriage), and thus casual dating has not been seen as an option. Often, the behaviors of girls and young women are perceived to affect the family's reputation and honor; thus, girls and young women are more controlled by their parents than boys and young men are (Leonard, 1999). More recently, second- and third-generation Indian Americans generally feel they have more options regarding their sexuality and are developing new values about dating and sexuality that are more reflective of dominant U.S. cultural values (Devji, 1999).

The messages for Filipina Americans were similar to those for East Asian American and South Asian American women—remain a virgin until marriage (and continue to be "sexually modest"), have children, and honor and serve the family (Espiritu, 2001). Yen Le Espiritu (2001) discussed how messages regarding gender and culture converged for young Filipina Americans. The idea of being a virtuous woman was closely tied to upholding the values of the Filipino culture. For instance, if a Filipina were to make sexual choices contrary to her parents' wishes, she would not only be perceived as an immoral young woman, she would be a "bad Filipina." Thus, it was implied that she was less "authentic" of a Filipina than a chaste Filipina woman. Additionally, there were double standards in their families—boys were allowed to do whatever they wanted while girls were far more restricted by their parents. The Filipina American women in the study expressed frustration and great pain in feeling pressured to conform to a cultural ideal of what a "good Filipina" should be.

Although various Asian ethnic groups differ in culture in many ways, the common theme was that girls and young women were greatly restricted by their parents and expected to be chaste and maintain sexual purity, while boys and young men were expected to be "boys." What are some of the cultural messages you have received from your families and ethnic communities? How are they similar to or different from the traditional values described above?

Religion

Another way that Asian Americans are socialized about sexuality is through religion. Religion can be a significant influence on individuals' perspective on sexuality as well as their sexual behavior. In Kim and Ward's (2007) study, participants from religious families received more messages regarding abstinence until marriage and sex as a taboo topic. For many Asian American young females, chastity is held in the highest esteem by their cultures and religions (Espiritu, 2001; Lee, 2006). In fact, the intersection of religion and culture often restricts what is deemed as acceptable sexual practice for Asian Americans (Lee, 2006). In the Korean American community, for example, males and females who are active members of Korean American Protestant church groups are encouraged to refrain from sexual immorality based on both biblical principles and cultural messages that extol the virtues of abstinence and sexual modesty. In Hindu, Sikh, and Muslim religions (which are the main religions that a large proportion of South Asians identify with), women are to remain virtuous and refrain from dating, while men are not expected to. Some young adults date regardless of this norm and "hide" their relationships and keep them secret from their parents (Leonard, 1999).

In addition to the explicit religious messages young Asian Americans receive about sexuality, the void of information and discussion on certain sexuality topics in religion also conveys messages and values about sexuality. Lee (2006) discussed how these avoided topics are part of a "null curriculum" that excludes certain options, and thereby "narrows students' perspectives and the range of their thoughts and action" (p. 404). Although the silence around sexuality is presumably to avoid embarrassment, by establishing sexuality as a taboo topic, it thereby suggests that sexuality is to be associated with "separation, shame, homophobia, and fixed gender roles" (Lee, 2006, p. 405). Thus, the consideration of sexuality as a natural part of human life is disregarded. By not dealing with sexuality directly, Asian Americans create and receive messages that often do not allow for individuals to think critically about their sexual identity, especially in relation to their spiritual identity.

Media

The media also send messages about sexuality, which can affect sexual behavior (Ward, 2003). Messages about Asian American sexuality are often gendered, with images of Asian American men as paradoxically asexual and hypersexual and images of Asian American women as hypersexual beings (Espiritu, 1996; Mok, 1999). These messages may impact the sexual behavior of Asian American adolescents, such as permitting or pressuring girls to be more sexually active with sexy and coy images, and restricting boys' opportunities for sexual activity with nerd stereotypes (Hahm et al., 2006; Huang & Uba, 1992). In the April 2004 issue of *Details* magazine, an article depicted a stylish Asian American man and posed the question, "Gay or Asian?" Although supposedly meant to be satirical, the article reinforced the stereotypical image of an effeminate Asian man. The unspoken message in society is that gay is effeminate (i.e., like a woman), and therefore, undesirable (Pharr, 1988). Thus, in associating Asian (and Asian American) men with being gay, they are relegated to being seen as effeminate and incompatible sexual partners for women, which is the asexual image often portrayed of Asian men. Although L.T. Goto's (1995) discussion of the myth of Asian men having small penises was humorous, it also reflected how pervasive the myth was and how it negatively impacted Asian American men. A Korean American man interviewed for the essay commented that "after a while, it plays on your psyche" (Goto, 1995).

The hypersexual image of Asian and Asian American women is often linked to the perception of them being demure and submissive as well (Espiritu, 1996; Marchetti, 1993). Not only does the hypersexualization of Asian American women objectify them such that they are seen

as less than human, these images may place them at greater risk to be victims of sexual violence. When individuals are depicted as objects—especially as sexual objects—others can distance themselves in the situation by disregarding their feelings and rights as people.

Before jumping to conclusions that Asian Americans are sexually frustrated and sexually inept, it is important to consider the broad spectrum of sexual behaviors and images found in

the Asian American community. On one end of the continuum, sexual practices may be prohibited based on religious and cultural values. On the other end, images of Asian American females as hypersexual inanimate objects dominate popular media images (Kawahara & Fu, 2007; Lee & Vaught, 2003). Both extremes are problematic in that stereotypes and misrepresentations may be used to further objectify and dehumanize Asian Americans as an Other. The various messages that Asian Americans receive about sexuality—from their parents, culture, religion, and media—inform their sexual identity, which is invariably related to the decision-making process involved in choosing to engage in sexual behaviors.

Take a moment to think about your own sexual development. When did you first think about your sexuality? In what context? Where did you learn about sexuality? What or who influences how you think about your sexuality?

Sexual Behavior

This section discusses research on Asian Americans, sexual behavior, and factors that may influence Asian Americans' decisions regarding sexual behavior. Research on sexual behavior tends to focus on adolescents and risk behavior, such as alcohol use and contraception. Furthermore, the studies are concerned about health issues and tend to examine sexual behavior from a risk perspective rather than a developmental perspective. However, some literature discussed possible factors that affect Asian Americans' decisions to engage in various sexual behaviors (Cochran et al., 1991; Huang & Uba, 1992; Regan, Durvasula, Howell, Ureno, & Rea, 2004). The following section will discuss the factors influencing sexual behaviors.

Many studies have found that Asian American adolescents are less likely to have sexual intercourse and tend to engage in sexual activities later in age than their White, Black and Latino peers (Feldman, Turner, & Araujo, 1999; Hahm et al., 2006; Hou & Basen-Engquist, 1997; Okazaki, 2002). In a Canadian study, Asian Canadian college students, compared to non-Asians, engaged significantly less in light petting, heavy petting, oral sex, and sexual intercourse (Meston et al., 1996). Similar results were found in another recent study in that Asian Americans were less experienced in kissing and sexual intercourse than non-Asian Americans (Regan et al., 2004). Various surveys on Asian American adolescent sexual behavior indicate a range of

20% to 28% prevalence rate of sexually active Asian American adolescents (Hahm et al., 2006), and for Asian American college students 35% (Meston et al., 1996) to 40% (Huang & Uba, 1992). In two additional studies on Asian Americans' sexual behavior (Feldman et al., 1999; Regan et al., 2004), findings indicated that the average age of Asian American adolescents first engaging in sexual intercourse was 18 years old and almost 19 years old, respectively. Studies on gender differences found the mean age of first engaging in sexual intercourse to be 17.9 for Asian Canadian males and 18.2 for Asian Canadian females (Meston et al., 1996) and 18.5 for Asian American males and 18.8 for Asian American females (Huang & Uba, 1992). Being sexually active differed by generation though. First-generation Asian immigrant youth engaged in sexual intercourse at a lower rate compared to U.S.-born Asian Americans and were, on average, older when they did first engage in sexual intercourse (Cochran et al., 1991; Hussey et al., 2007).

Once Asian Americans become sexually active, their sexual behavior patterns are similar to those found in other racial and ethnic groups, such as number of lifetime partners and condom use (Cochran et al., 1991; Hou & Basen-Engquist, 1997). For instance, sexually active Asian American adolescents were comparable to other adolescents in the use of birth control—ranging from a third to half of the time using birth control (Cochran et al., 1991; Hou & Basen-Engquist, 1997). However, one national survey of high school students revealed that Asian American adolescents were less likely than other racial groups to have used a condom during their first sexual intercourse experience (Dye & Upchurch, 2006). Another study identified links between multiple risk behaviors and found that smoking, alcohol use, and drug use are possibly related to engaging in sexual behaviors—including sexual risk behaviors, such as having sex without a condom (Hahm et al., 2006; Hussey et al., 2007). The following section on sexual health discusses implications of sexual risk behavior further.

The experience of dating and engaging in sexual behaviors for Asian Americans is often shadowed by implicit messages that carry the tone that sex is inappropriate outside of marriage—a

marriage that is: (a) approved or arranged by your parents and/or (b) acceptable based on religious standards (e.g., maintaining virginity, marrying a born-again believer) (Espiritu, 2001; Leonard, 1999). Cultural values and religious beliefs play a significant role in Asian American women's decision not to engage in sexual behaviors (Cochran et al., 1991). Moreover, Asian American adolescent girls with higher parental attachment and school attachment are less likely to have sexual intercourse (Hahm et al., 2006). However, more highly acculturated Asian American females feel less inhibited, and have patterns of sexual behavior that are similar to females in other ethnic groups (Hahm et al., 2006; Okazaki, 2002). In contrast, sexual behavior of Asian American males has not been found to be related to acculturation level, parental attachment, or school attachment (Hahm et al., 2006). Nonetheless, both Asian American women and men are more permissive and approving of premarital sex the more acculturated they are (Huang & Uba, 1992). Asian Americans tend to find sexual intercourse more acceptable in committed relationships than in casual contexts (i.e., no affection between partners) (Huang & Uba, 1992), and they are older (as compared to Caucasians, African Americans, and Latinos/as) when they are first involved in a romantic relationship (Regan et al., 2004). Sexual behavior patterns—and what influences them—are important to study and understand as sexual risk behaviors are linked to various consequences, such as pregnancy and STIs.

What are your values about sexual behavior? What influences your decisions regarding sexual behavior? How is your sexual behavior related to your sexual identity and your overall self-concept?

Sexual Health

Asian Americans have generally been understudied in sexual health research compared to other racial groups (National Asian Women's Health Organization, 1997). Because of this, it is important to examine the sexual health implications of misinformation (or lack of information) on potential health risks for women and men. Sexual health encompasses concerns such as STIs, HIV/AIDS, and reproductive health. This section discusses sexuality as it relates to prevalence and risk of contracting STIs and HIV/AIDS as well as reproductive health.

STIs

The use of the term *sexually transmitted infection* or STI is preferred by many health educators over the term *sexually transmitted disease* (STD) since oftentimes individuals can be infected without showing any symptoms of a "disease"; additionally, the term *infection* is less stigmatizing than *disease* (American Social Health Association, 2007b). Sexual health literature currently uses both terms, which refer to the same thing—STIs include bacterial (e.g., chlamydia, gonorrhea), viral (e.g., herpes, hepatitis A and B, human papillomavirus, HIV), and parasitic (e.g., trichomoniasis) infections that are transmitted through sexual activity. In this section as in other health literature, HIV/AIDS is discussed separately from other STIs.

The Centers for Disease Control and Prevention (CDC) estimates that 19 million new cases of STIs occur each year (2005). Although the incidence of STI cases among Asian Americans is relatively low compared to other racial groups, the incidence of certain STIs, such as gonorrhea and syphilis, is increasing at a faster rate for Asian Americans (Centers for Disease Control and Prevention, 2005; National Asian Women's Health Organization, 2000). Additionally, the data on the incidence of STIs in Asian Americans are most likely an underestimation of the actual incidence of STIs as there is underreporting for the Asian American population and not all STIs are reportable (for surveillance purposes) (National Asian Women's Health Organization, 2000). Asian American women have higher STI rates than Asian American men, which may be a result of STIs being transmitted more easily from men to women (National Asian Women's

Health Organization, 2000). Because many STI cases are asymptomatic (i.e., no apparent symptoms), the STIs may go untreated, which can have serious consequences, especially for women. These include pelvic inflammatory disease, infertility, tubal pregnancy, chronic pain, and cervical cancer (American Social Health Association, 2007a).

Education, prevention, and treatment of STIs are important for the Asian American population because of the likely underestimation of prevalence of STI cases, and thus perceived low risk. In terms of STI prevention, the National Asian Women's Health Organization's survey on reproductive and sexual health for Asian American women found that 45.0% of the sample used condoms for protection against STIs while 29.2% did not engage in protective behaviors (National Asian Women's Health Organization, 1997). Additionally, when it comes to utilizing health services, Asian Americans may be less likely to seek medical care "due to lack of access to medical care, language barriers, and cultural taboo" (Asian American and Pacific Islander Women's Health, 2005).

Is your knowledge about STIs complete and accurate? Where can you learn more about the prevention and treatment of STIs? How likely are you to get tested for STIs? What would prevent you from getting tested for STIs?

HIV and AIDS

Acquired Immune Deficiency Syndrome (AIDS) is caused by the Human Immunodeficiency Virus (HIV). An individual may be HIV-positive (and exhibit no symptoms) but not have an AIDS diagnosis. An AIDS diagnosis occurs during advanced stages of HIV infection when an individual's immune system is severely compromised (National Institute of Allergy and Infectious Diseases, 2005). HIV cases among Asian Americans and Pacific Islanders may be underestimated because of underreporting or racial group misclassification (Centers for Disease Control and Prevention, 2006) and because five states (California, Hawaii, Illinois, Massachusetts, and Washington) with high percentages of the Asian American/Pacific Islander population in the United States are not included in current estimations by the CDC. There are many ways to contract the HIV virus, with sexual contact being one of the main ways HIV is transmitted. See Table 14.1 for information regarding HIV transmission.

At the end of 2004, Asian Americans and Pacific Islanders constituted less than 1% of all AIDS cases in the United States (while Asian Americans and Pacific Islanders made up 4.9% of the U.S. population overall) (Centers for Disease Control and Prevention, 2006; U.S. Census Bureau, 2005). Although Asian Americans and Pacific Islanders are diagnosed with HIV/AIDS at a lower rate than other racial groups, the number of AIDS cases has increased in recent years (Centers for Disease Control and Prevention, 2006). See Table 14.2 for HIV/AIDS statistics for Asian Americans and Pacific Islanders.

Research on college students and HIV risk has revealed that many college students have limited HIV knowledge (So, Wong, & DeLeon, 2005). Cochran et al. (1991) reported that a high proportion of their Asian American college student sample (93%) had engaged in vaginal intercourse without a condom at some point in their lifetime. Additionally, although So et al. (2005) found that Asian American college students have a relatively low HIV risk, they reported a 37.1% lifetime prevalence of unprotected sex in their sample. Thus, Asian American college students are still engaging in sexual behaviors that may place them at risk for HIV and other STIs.

Studies on sexual risk behaviors among Asian American and Pacific Islander (API) men who have sex with men (MSM) have found that API MSMs are more likely to engage in unprotected sex when they have not been in the United States for very long or do not identify as being gay (Chng & Geliga-Vargas, 2000; Do, Hudes, & Proctor, 2006). Additionally, API MSMs may be less likely to get tested or treated for HIV/AIDS because they perceive their risk as low, fear

Table 14.1 What Do You Know About HIV Transmission?

Mode	HIV transmission
Risky sexual behavior	The most common way HIV is transmitted is through sexual contact—vaginal, anal, or oral sex without using a condom with an infected partner or a partner whose HIV status is unknown
Contaminated needles	HIV can be transmitted through injection drug use—sharing needles or syringes with contaminated blood can spread HIV; rarely do patients or health care workers contract HIV through accidental needle sticks from contaminated needles
Mother to child	HIV-infected women can transmit HIV to their babies during pregnancy and birth; however, with drug treatment during pregnancy and delivering by caesarean section, the risk of HIV transmission can be as low as 1%
Infected blood	HIV infections can be spread through blood transfusions of contaminated blood; currently, there is blood screening and heat treatment of donated blood, so the risk of HIV transmission through blood transfusions is now extremely low
Sexually transmitted infections	Having a sexually transmitted infection increases the risk of contracting HIV during sex from an infected partner
Saliva	No evidence exists for HIV transmission through saliva contact (e.g., kissing) even though HIV has been found in the saliva of infected people; however, HIV can be in the lining of the mouth, and it can be transmitted through oral sex
Casual contact	HIV is *not* spread through touching, hugging, sharing food/utensils, swimming pools, bedding, telephones, toilets, or insect bites

Source: National Institute of Allergy and Infectious Diseases, 2005.

deportation if they are undocumented immigrants, or lack health insurance (Chng, Wong, Park, Edberg, & Lai, 2003; Do et al., 2006). Thus, API MSMs' understanding of sexual health issues is not only about lack of knowledge; other barriers include perceptions of low risk, fear of deportation as an undocumented immigrant, and lack of health insurance.

How likely are you to get tested for HIV? What would prevent you from getting tested for HIV? Do you know where you can get anonymous HIV testing? What questions would you ask

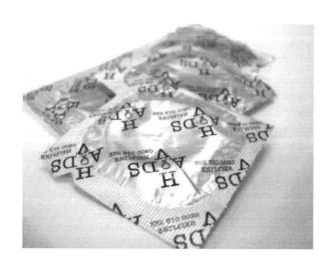

Table 14.2 HIV and AIDS Cases Among APIs in the United States

	Total	Men	Women	Children[b]
APIs given AIDS diagnoses in 2004[a]	486	392 (80.7%)	92 (18.9%)	1 (0.2%)
Total APIs living with HIV (not AIDS) at end of 2004 (based on 42 states)[a]	1,306	Men 975 (74.7%)	Women 331 (25.3%)	
Estimated number of APIs living with HIV/ AIDS[c] at end of 2004[a]	2,765[d]	Men 2141 (80.7%)	Women 596 (18.9%)	Children 27 (0.2%)
Total APIs living with AIDS in U.S. at end of 2004[a]	4,045	Men 3384 (83.7%)	Women 644 (15.9%)	Children 17 (0.4%)
Total APIs given AIDS diagnoses 1981–2004[e]	7,317	*		

[a] Centers for Disease Control and Prevention (2004).
[b] Children <13 years old.
[c] Includes diagnosis of HIV infection only, diagnosis of HIV infection and a later AIDS diagnosis, and concurrent HIV infection and AIDS diagnoses.
[d] Includes one person of unknown sex.
[e] Centers for Disease Control and Prevention (2006).
* No information available on sex.

to learn about a potential partner's sexual history? How would you talk about engaging in safer sex practices? Consider including questions about birth control, condom use, and history of STIs or current HIV status.

Reproductive Health

When discussing sexuality and how it relates to one's health, reproductive health must be included as an important consideration. Although the topic of reproductive health is broad, this section focuses on the reproductive health issues of accessing reproductive and sexual health services and sexual health education (see the chapter "Physical Health" regarding other topics of reproductive health, such as cancer screening for women). Resources about other topics of reproductive health are included at the end of the chapter.

In a reproductive and sexual health survey of Asian American women, the National Asian Women's Health Organization (1997) found that half of the women surveyed had not seen a medical provider in the last year for reproductive or sexual health services, and a quarter had never received any reproductive or sexual health services. Not only is it important for Asian American women to access reproductive and sexual health services as a matter of routine health care, but if they are experiencing sexual dysfunction, they may need some treatment. This is particularly concerning since sexual dysfunction and depression often coexist in Asian American women, either as a symptom of depression or as a side effect of anti-depressant medication (Dobkin, Leiblum, Rosen, Menza, & Marin, 2006). Additionally, 89% of Asian American men surveyed by National Asian Women's Health Organization (1999) had never received reproductive health services regarding family planning or STIs.

Sexual health education and treatment is important for Asian Americans as they tend to be underserved in health services. Asian American girls and women may be more likely to engage

in risky sexual behaviors due to a lack of sexual health education and the cultural taboo of discussing sexual issues in their families (Kao, 2006). Similarly, Asian American men may engage in risky sexual behaviors due to a lack of perceived personal risk of having or contracting STIs or HIV (National Asian Women's Health Organization, 1999). As mentioned previously, barriers to sexual health care and safer sexual practices may be related to language barriers, cultural taboo surrounding sexual issues, lack of economic resources, and perception of low risk. For instance, Asian American adolescents may not seek or receive appropriate sexual health education and treatment because of "health care providers' misconceptions, stereotyping, racism, sexism, and bicultural gaps between the adolescents' home culture and environmental culture" (Kao, 2006).

Sexual Violence

As noted, discussions regarding sexuality are rarely held in Asian American households. To a greater degree, acts of sexual violence are not discussed as they are considered shameful to the family and community. An unfortunate consequence is that fewer Asian Americans may be aware of the prevalence of sexual violence within the community and may not know where to turn should they need assistance (Leonard, 1999). This section discusses the experience of sexual violence and how it relates to sexuality for Asian Americans.

Sexual violence is defined as "any sexual act that is forced against someone's will . . . [including] physical, verbal or psychological" acts (Centers for Disease Control and Prevention, 2007). Victims do not consent and are unable to consent or refuse (i.e., too young, mentally disabled, under the influence of alcohol or drugs, etc.). The use of the term *sexual violence* reflects a broader range of sexually abusive and violent behaviors, including **sexual abuse**, unwanted touching, acquaintance **rape**, and stranger rape (Centers for Disease Control and Prevention, 2007; Koss & Dinero, 1988). Sexual abuse includes causing another person to engage in a sexual activity by threatening or placing that person in fear and engaging in a sexual act when that person is incapable of declining participation in, or communicating unwillingness to engage in that sexual activity. Sexual abuse includes child sexual abuse and sexual abuse in an intimate relationship (e.g., marriage), where usually the perpetrator has more authority and power (i.e., psychologically, physically, and/or economically). **Sexual assault** encompasses a broader range of inappropriate sexual behavior and refers to any unwanted sexual contact, ranging from touching to rape, whether through force or coercion. Rape is defined as nonconsensual vaginal, oral, and anal penetration. Sexual violence is perpetrated by males and females just as victims of sexual violence are both males and females. However, the vast majority of victims of sexual violence are female (Centers for Disease Control and Prevention, 2007).

Data regarding the prevalence of child sexual abuse in the Asian American community are limited, and estimates are that the incidence is relatively low as compared to other ethnic and racial groups (Kenny & McEachern, 2000; Okazaki, 2002). Nonetheless, it is likely that sexual abuse is underreported in Asian American communities. Possible reasons may be because there is a lack of awareness of social services, tendency to keep sexual issues private, filial piety preventing children from reporting, shame about losing one's virginity, and caretakers not believing children's reports of sexual abuse (Futa, Hsu, & Hansen, 2001; Kenny & McEachern, 2000). Additional barriers to obtaining mental health and social services include language barriers, limited financial resources, and lack of trust in American public services (Futa et al., 2001). Lack of research on sexual abuse in Asian American communities is concerning as the consequences of sexual abuse include depression, anxiety, anger, lower self-esteem, and suicidality (Futa et al., 2001; Kenny & McEachern, 2000).

Sexual abuse often is a component of the larger issue of domestic violence, which includes physical, psychological, and sexual abuse (Malley-Morrison & Hines, 2004). Like physical and psychological abuse, sexual abuse in an intimate relationship is related to the abuser trying to maintain power and control over the partner. A study of women of Japanese descent in Los Angeles (about a quarter of whom were immigrants) estimated that 20% of the participants had experienced sexual abuse (e.g., coercion, unwanted touching, forced sex, etc.) in their marriage in their lifetime; 43% of their partners at the time of the worst abusive incident were of non-Japanese descent (Yoshihama, 1999). In a qualitative study of South Asian immigrant women who experienced domestic violence in their marriage, 60% of the 25 women interviewed had experienced sexual abuse by their husbands in addition to physical or psychological abuse (Abraham, 1999). A study on Korean immigrant women reported almost 37% of the participants had experienced their partner forcing them to have sex (Song, 1996). All of these studies indicate a substantial number of Asian immigrant and Asian American women have experienced sexual abuse in an intimate relationship. The implications for mental health and social services include understanding women's subjective experiences of abuse within their cultural context and addressing barriers to seeking help, such as fear of dealing with immigration, language barriers, and cultural norms of not seeking outside help (Abraham, 1999; Yoshihama, 1999). In terms of sexual identity, Asian and Asian American women's sexuality can be negatively impacted by sexually abusive experiences in intimate relationships in that sexual behaviors become associated with pain (physical and emotional), fear, and powerlessness.

Rape can be committed by a stranger or, as often is the case, by someone known to the victim. Reports of rape are made from individuals of all racial groups, but most studies have studied rape in adult women. In a study by Linda Kalof (2000), findings revealed no significant difference in reports of rape among college students representing different ethnic groups: 18% of Black women, 19% of Asian women, 21% of Hispanic women, and 24% of White women indicated they had experienced behavior that is considered rape. However, when asked directly if they had ever been raped, only 11% of Asian American college women said yes. Additionally, 9% of the Asian

American women had experienced attempted rape (Kalof, 2000). Furthermore, 10% indicated that they had been coerced or manipulated into having sex when they did not really want to. However, in a study based on the National Violence Against Women Survey, Asian and Pacific Islander females were the least likely to report incidents of rape compared to females of other U.S. racial/ethnic groups (Tjaden & Thoennes, 1998). Similar findings were reported in an earlier study where Asian women reported the lowest incidents of rape (Koss, Gidycz, & Wisniewski, 1987). The inconsistencies in the number of rapes reported by Asian American females over time may be due to a number of factors. On one hand, older studies may indicate less awareness and language barriers as possible reasons for lower reporting of rape. Additionally, shame, privacy, and concern for loss of face are barriers to women reporting sexual assault (Lee & Law, 2001; Sable, Danis, Mauzy, & Gallagher, 2006). On the other hand, more recent studies (i.e., Kalof, 2000) indicate the possibilities that there is greater awareness around issues of rape and sexual assault and there is a greater number of rapes occurring in the Asian American community.

Attitudes toward rape differ by racial groups and immigration status. In a study of Asian American and Caucasian college students' attitudes toward rape, results revealed that Asian Americans were more likely than Caucasians to believe it is the women's responsibility to prevent rape, that the main motivation for rape is sex, and that rape is committed by strangers (Lee, Pomeroy, & Yoo, 2005). These findings indicated that some Asian American college students have negative attitudes toward rape victims (i.e., such as blaming victims for the rape), overlook other motivating factors beyond viewing rape as only about sex, and fail to consider the broader definition of rape to include acquaintance rape. In another study on attitudes toward rape, Neetha Devdas and Linda Rubin (2007) found that while first-generation South Asian American women were more accepting of rape myths (i.e., prejudiced or stereotyped beliefs about rape), second-generation South Asian American women were similar to European American women in being less accepting of rape myths (Devdas & Rubin, 2007). Implications of the study included

the possibility that more acculturated South Asian American women were less accepting of rape myths and that first-generation South Asian American women may be more likely to blame the victim, which would decrease the likelihood of South Asian American women seeking help. It seems that education about rape and rape myths would be useful for Asian Americans, especially those who are less acculturated, to help them understand the nature of rape better.

In addition to rape, Asian Americans experience other acts of sexual assault against them. In a recent study on U.S. college students, 23.4% of Asian American women reported unwanted sexual contact as compared to 28.1% of Black women, 34.6% of White women, and 36.8% of Hispanic women (Kalof, 2000). Although Asian American women reported the fewest instances of unwanted sexual contact as compared to non-Asian American women, the finding that close to one quarter of the Asian American female sample experienced unwanted sexual contact is noteworthy and concerning.

Very little data are available regarding Asian American men's experience of sexual violence (Tjaden & Thoennes, 2000). Because men are less likely to be victims of sexual violence, there is less focus on research on male victims of sexual violence, and there is little available data on the relatively smaller population of Asian Americans. In a review of literature on male sexual assault victims, findings estimated the prevalence of male victims of sexual assault in the United States to range from 3% to 22.2% (Tewksbury, 2007). The available research shows that barriers to men reporting being a victim of sexual violence include guilt, shame, stigma, fear of not being believed, and having their sexuality questioned (Sable et al., 2006; Tewksbury, 2007). Unfortunately, the studies did not specifically examine race or ethnicity, so it is difficult to discuss Asian American men's experiences of being sexual assault victims. Even though there is a dearth of research on male victimization, it is important to keep in mind that men are victims of sexual assault, and they experience many consequences just as female victims do although the nature of the consequences may vary (Tewksbury, 2007).

Due to the prevailing notions that an Asian woman's value is strongly connected to the preservation of her virginity, it is not surprising that reports of sexual abuse and sexual assault in the Asian American community may go unreported. Additionally, media images tend to hypersexualize Asian American women, and some inappropriate sexual behavior (i.e., those that could be defined as sexual assault) toward Asian American women may be perceived as normal and acceptable because they are portrayed as such. Thus, some victims of sexual abuse and sexual assault may not be aware that the behaviors they experienced are considered sexual abuse or sexual assault and do not report inappropriate sexual behavior. Unfortunately, a corollary is that some perpetrators of sexual abuse and sexual assault may not be aware that their behavior is inappropriate and considered sexual abuse or sexual assault. Research on sexual abuse, sexual assault, and rape suggests a greater need for awareness, intervention, and prevention regarding sexual abuse, sexual assault, and rape in the Asian American community.

Consider the case of Amy who was coerced by an acquaintance to have sex even though she did not want to. She does not think of herself as having been raped, but she has become withdrawn, has difficulty sleeping, and gets easily startled when people are near her. At the urging of one of her friends, she comes to counseling to seek help because she cannot concentrate at work. Amy is surprised to learn that what happened to her is considered rape; she decides not to report it though. During most sessions, she often blames herself for the rape and is afraid no Asian American man will want to marry her if he finds out that she put herself in that situation. Cases such as this one are all too familiar for victims of acquaintance rape. The added cultural layers include guilt, fear of bringing shame to one's family, and worrying about future prospects for marriage.

Take a moment and consider ways the Asian American community can openly discuss issues related to sexuality, especially sexual assault. From what you know, do you have a clear sense of what constitutes sexual assault and rape (including date rape)? What steps would you take if you or someone you know is raped by an acquaintance or a date?

Summary

Sexuality is an integral part of an individual's identity. To examine and understand Asian Americans and sexuality, it is important to take into consideration issues such as ethnic culture, parental influences, gender, religion, and media images of Asian American women and men. This chapter discussed how those issues are related to Asian Americans and the broad topic of sexuality, which includes sexual identity development, socialization, behavior, health, and violence. The discussions in this chapter represent only some of the major aspects of sexuality, and readers are encouraged to continue learning about Asian Americans and sexuality by exploring the suggested resources provided at the end of the chapter.

Discussion Questions

1. What were/are the messages you receive about sexuality: (a) from your parents? (b) from your friends? (c) from your religion? (d) from the media (TV, movies, magazines, news)?
2. How has your understanding about sexuality changed over time?
3. If you have questions regarding sex, who do you go to? How confident are you that the information is correct?
4. What are your thoughts about how race and sexuality intersect for Asian Americans? For yourself?
5. How would you talk to a sexual partner about his/her sexual history? What questions would you include? When would you ask those questions?
6. What are your inhibitions and fears about sexuality that might impact your mental or physical/sexual health?

Case Study

This chapter has presented theory and research of how sexuality impacts Asian Americans in their personal lives and contributes to their psychological growth and development. The chapter will now shift its focus to a case study that illustrates how an Asian

American might experience and cope with sexuality concerns. Moreover, the following case will also be presented to give readers a sense of what Asian Americans might focus on in counseling.

Lisa is a 21-year-old, Asian American college student who seeks counseling because she just found out she has an STI. During a gynecological checkup, Lisa learned that she has a viral STI, which can be treated but not cured completely. She feels extremely anxious about having an STI and is more worried about the stigma of having an STI than about having an infection. Lisa's parents are immigrants from South Korea, and they raised her as a Christian. Her parents never discussed sexuality directly with Lisa and her younger brother, but she knew the unspoken expectation was that she remains a virgin until she is married. Lisa first had sex when she was 18 years old with her boyfriend of 7 months during her freshman year of college. She felt comfortable with her decision and was happy in the relationship, but she didn't talk to her Christian Asian American friends about it because she was afraid they would disapprove. Since then, Lisa has had more casual sexual encounters. She had a couple of one-night stands after meeting guys at parties, and sometimes she couldn't remember clearly what happened because she'd had a few drinks during the night. Although Lisa learned about contraception and STIs, she did not always use condoms in her sexual encounters because they weren't available or she and her partner were too drunk to remember to use them. She took the morning-after pill after each one-night stand to prevent pregnancy.

Lisa fears that her parents will disown her if they find out she has an STI. She believes she is being punished by God for engaging in premarital sex. Although Lisa once felt connected to other Asian American Christians through her participation in church, she has now distanced herself and feels lonely, ashamed, and unsure of what to do next.

Case Study Discussion

The counselor who meets with Lisa utilizes a cognitive-behavioral approach to address Lisa's anxiety, as well as a person-centered approach to establish rapport and provide support. The cognitive-behavioral approach to counseling involves the counselor helping the client understand that how she thinks about a situation affects how she feels and behaves; thus, if the client shifts her thinking, she can change how she feels and acts about a situation. The cognitive-behavioral approach is useful with Asian Pacific Americans because it provides concrete strategies to deal with a problem, which is often preferred by Asian Pacific Americans who may not be familiar with counseling. The person-centered approach to counseling entails the counselor establishing a genuine, unconditional, and empathic therapeutic relationship with the client. Additionally, the counselor provides psychoeducation (i.e., information about psychological issues) regarding sexual health and alcohol use. The counselor also aims to be culturally competent by being aware of and knowledgeable about sociocultural issues related to Lisa being a young Korean, Christian, heterosexual female with immigrant parents. The counselor pays attention to any bias she may have about Korean culture and Christianity so that she can try to avoid judging Lisa as a person.

Lisa's guilt is connected to both her Christian and Korean upbringing that premarital sex is not acceptable. She feels guilty for letting down her parents and disobeying them by being sexually active (even though her parents' values about sex were implied and not spoken). Lisa personally feels comfortable with being sexually active although she is starting to become concerned about having too many casual sexual encounters, especially since she acquired an STI as a result. She also feels very anxious about whether to talk to her parents about her STI. Lisa fears being disowned by them, but she's afraid of dealing with her treatment alone since it is a viral STI, which will never be cured completely (but the symptoms can be treated). The counselor normalizes Lisa's guilt and internal conflict about her decision to be sexually active. The counselor supports and encourages Lisa to weigh the costs and benefits of discussing her situation with her parents. They also explore other ways Lisa can get support in managing her STI.

Lisa also is questioning her Christian identity because she has not followed the value of abstinence. She wonders what her behavior and values mean about her religious faith. Lisa's counselor provides support for Lisa to explore her spiritual beliefs because her behavior is incongruent with her religious beliefs about sex, although it is congruent with her personal beliefs about sex. Her counselor encourages her to talk with a spiritual leader whom she trusts if she feels she needs more spiritual guidance.

The counselor uses cognitive-behavioral techniques, such as thought-stopping techniques and reframing cognitive distortions, to help Lisa manage her constant worrying and anxiety. She also provides educational information to Lisa about sexual health and communicating with potential sexual partners. In addition, the counselor discusses how alcohol can affect judgment, specifically with regard to risky sexual behavior (e.g., no condom use). Throughout their sessions, the counselor tries to value Lisa's concern about her relationship with her parents and religious faith while validating Lisa's wish to be sexually active in a healthy manner.

Case Study Discussion Questions

For undergraduate students, please consider the following questions:

1. How would you feel if you were in Lisa's situation?
2. If you were Lisa's friend, what resources might you suggest for her?
3. What suggestions would you make to Lisa about how to discuss sexual history with a potential sexual partner?

For graduate students and/or beginning therapists, please consider the following questions:

1. What do you think is the impact of Lisa's religious upbringing on how she feels and how she is handling this situation? The influence of her Korean cultural background?
2. What are the cultural implications for Lisa if she chooses not to tell her parents about her STI? And if she chooses not to tell anyone?
3. What are your reactions to Lisa? What are your reactions to Lisa's therapy? How would you work with Lisa?

Key Terms

Multidimensional Model of Heterosexual Identity Development: Model that describes heterosexual identity development within a biopsychosocial context in five statuses: (a) unexplored commitment, (b) active exploration, (c) diffusion, (d) deepening and commitment, and (e) synthesis.

Rape: Nonconsensual vaginal, oral, and anal penetration either by a stranger or someone known.

Sexual abuse: Causing another person to engage in a sexual activity by threatening or placing that person in fear; engaging in a sexual act when that person is incapable of declining participation in, or communicating unwillingness to engage in, that sexual act.

Sexual assault: Any unwanted sexual contact, ranging from touching to rape, whether through force or coercion.

Sexual identity: One's subjective experience of oneself as a sexual being.

Sexuality: Continuum of desires, fantasies, behaviors, attraction—ranging from homoerotic to heterosexual.

Sexually transmitted infection: Bacterial, viral, and parasitic infections transmitted through sexual activity.

Sexual Minority Identity Formation Model: Model that describes individual sexual identity and group sexual identity (i.e., being part of the gay/lesbian category) development for gay and lesbian individuals in four phases: (a) awareness, (b) exploration, (c) deepening/commitment, and (d) internalization/synthesis.

Sexual orientation: Sexual object choice (sexual and affective desires, attractions, and behavior)—same sex (gay, lesbian), both sexes (bisexual), or different sex (heterosexual).

Sexual violence: Any nonconsensual sexual act, including physical, verbal, or psychological acts, committed against someone.

For Further Learning and Suggested Reading

Books

Espiritu, Y. L. (1996). *Asian American women and men: Labor, laws, and love.* Thousand Oaks, CA: Sage.

Kudaka, G. (Ed.). (1995). *On a bed of rice: An Asian American erotic feast.* New York: Anchor Books.

Leong, R. (Ed.). (1995). *Asian American sexualities: Dimensions of the gay and lesbian experience.* New York: Routledge.

Movies

Kama Sutra (1996)
Pillow Book (1996)

Web Sites

American Social Health Association: http://www.ashastd.org/learn/learn_overview.cfm

The Centers for Disease Control and Prevention: http://www.cdc.gov/std/default.htm, http://www.cdc.gov/hiv/, and http://www.cdc.gov/ncipc/factsheets/svfacts.htm

National Asian Pacific American Women's Forum: http://www.napawf.org

National Asian Women's Health Organization: http://www.nawho.org

Rape, Abuse, and Incest Network: http://www.rainn.org

References

Abraham, M. (1999). Sexual abuse in South Asian immigrant marriages. *Violence Against Women, 5,* 591–618.

American Social Health Association (2007a). *Overview fact sheet on sexually transmitted diseases.* Retrieved March 26, 2007, from http://www.ashastd.org/pdfs/STDOverview_factsheet.pdf

American Social Health Association (2007b). *STD vs. STI.* Retrieved March 26, 2007, from http://www.ashastd.org/learn/learn_statistics_vs.cfm

Asian American and Pacific Islander Women's Health. (2005). *Asian women's health topics: Sexually transmitted infections.* Retrieved March 26, 2007, from http://www.sph.umich.edu/apihealth/2005/sti2.html

Centers for Disease Control and Prevention. (2004). *HIV/AIDS Surveillance Report.* Retrieved July 13, 2007, from http://www.cdc.gov/hiv/topics/surveillance/resources/reports/2004report/table11.htm

Centers for Disease Control and Prevention. (2005). *STD surveillance 2005: Special focus profile.* Retrieved March 26, 2007, from http://www.cdc.gov/std/stats/05pdf/2005-special-focus.pdf

Centers for Disease Control and Prevention. (2006). *HIV/AIDS among Asians and Pacific Islanders.* Retrieved March 10, 2007, from http://www.cdc.gov/hiv/resources/factsheets/PDF/API.pdf

Centers for Disease Control and Prevention. (2007). *Sexual violence: Fact sheet.* Retrieved June 19, 2007, from http://www.cdc.gov/ncipc/factsheets/svfacts.htm

Chng, C. L., & Geliga-Vargas, J. (2000). Ethnic identity, gay identity, sexual sensation seeking and HIV risk taking among multiethnic men who have sex with men. *AIDS Education & Prevention, 12,* 326–339.

Chng, C. L., Wong, F. Y., Park, R. J., Edberg, M. C., & Lai, D. S. (2003). A model for understanding sexual health among Asian American/Pacific Islander men who have sex with men (MSM) in the United States. *AIDS Education & Prevention, 15,* 21–38.

Cochran, S. D., Mays, V. M., & Leung, L. (1991). Sexual practices of heterosexual Asian-American young adults: Implications for risk of HIV infection. *Archives of Sexual Behavior, 20,* 381–391.

Devdas, N. R., & Rubin, L. J. (2007). Rape myth acceptance among first- and second-generation South Asian American women. *Sex Roles, 56,* 701–705.

Devji, M.S. (1999). The paradoxes of the Kama Sutra and the veil: Asian-Indian women and marital sexuality. In S. R. Gupta (Ed.), *Emerging voices: South Asian American women redefine self, family, and community* (pp. 169–192). Walnut Creek, CA: Alta Mira Press.

Do, T. D., Hudes, E. S., & Proctor, K. (2006). HIV testing trends and correlates among young Asian and Pacific Islander men who have sex with men in two U.S. cities. *AIDS Education & Prevention, 18,* 44–55.

Dobkin, R. D., Leiblum, S. R., Rosen, R. C., Menza, M., & Marin, H. (2006). Depression and sexual functioning in minority women: Current status and future directions. *Journal of Sex and Marital Therapy, 32,* 23–36.

Downing, N. E., & Roush, K. L. (1985). From passive acceptance to active commitment: A model of feminist identity development of women. *The Counseling Psychologist, 13,* 695–705.

Dye, C., & Upchurch, D. M. (2006). Moderating effects of gender on alcohol use: Implications for condom use at first intercourse. *Journal of School Health, 76,* 111–116.

Eliason, M. J. (1995). Accounts of sexual identity formation in heterosexual students. *Sex Roles, 32,* 821–834.

Espiritu, Y. L. (1996). *Asian American women and men: Labor, laws, and love.* Thousand Oaks, CA: Sage Publications.

Espiritu, Y. L. (2001). "We don't sleep around like White girls do": Family, culture, and gender in Filipina American Lives. *Signs: Journal of Women in Culture and Society, 26,* 415–440.

Fassinger, R. E., & Miller, B. A. (1996). Validation of an inclusive model of sexual minority identity formation on a sample of gay men. *Journal of Homosexuality, 32,* 53–78.

Feldman, S. S., Turner, R. A., & Araujo, K. (1999). Interpersonal context as an influence on sexual timetables of youths: Gender and ethnic effects. *Journal of Research on Adolescence, 9,* 25–52.

Futa, K. T., Hsu, E., & Hansen, D. J. (2001). Child sexual abuse in Asian American families: An examination of cultural factors that influence prevalence, identification, and treatment. *Clinical Psychology: Science and Practice, 8,* 189–209.

Gilbert, L. A., & Scher, M. (1999). *Gender and sex in counseling and psychotherapy.* Boston, MA: Allyn and Bacon.

Goto, L. T. (1995). Asian penis: The long and short of it. In G. Kudaka (Ed.), *On a bed of rice: An Asian American erotic feast* (pp. 177–184). New York: Anchor Books.

Hahm, C. H., Lahiff, M., & Barreto, R. M. (2006). Asian American adolescents' first sexual intercourse: Gender and acculturation differences. *Perspectives on Sexual and Reproductive Health, 38,* 28–36.

Helms, J. E. (1995). An update of Helms's White and people of color racial identity models. In J. Ponterotto, L. A. Suzuki, & C. Alexander (Eds.), *Handbook of multicultural counseling* (pp. 181–198). Thousand Oaks, CA: Sage Publications.

Hom, A. Y. (1994). Stories from the homefront: Perspectives of Asian American parents with lesbian daughters and gay sons. *Amerasia Journal, 20,* 19–32.

Hou, S.-I., & Basen-Engquist, K. (1997). Human Immunodeficiency Virus risk behavior among White and Asian/Pacific Islander high school students in the United States: Does culture make a difference? *Journal of Adolescent Health, 20,* 68–74.

Huang, K., & Uba, L. (1992). Premarital sexual behavior among Chinese college students in the United States. *Archives of Sexual Behavior, 21,* 227–240.

Hussey, J. M., Hallfors, D. D., Waller, M. W., Iritani, B. J., Halpern, C. T., & Bauer, D. J. (2007). Sexual behavior and drug use among Asian and Latino adolescents: Association with immigrant status. *Journal of Immigrant and Minority Health, 9,* 85–94.

Kalof, L. (2000). Ethnic differences in female sexual victimization. *Sexuality & Culture, 4,* 75–97.

Kao, T.-S. A. (2006). Ask the expert: Sexual health education disparities in Asian American adolescents. *Journal for Specialists in Pediatric Nursing, 11,* 57–60.

Kawahara, D. M., & Fu, M. (2007). The psychology and mental health of Asian American women. In F. T. L. Leong, A. Ebreo, L. Kinoshita, A. G. Inman, & L. H. Yang (Eds.), *Handbook of Asian American psychology* (2nd ed., pp. 181–196). Thousand Oaks, CA: Sage Publications.

Kenny, M. C., & McEachern, A. G. (2000). Racial, ethnic, and cultural factors of childhood sexual abuse: A selected review of the literature. *Clinical Psychology Review, 20,* 905–922.

Kim, J. L., & Ward, L. M. (2007). Silence speaks volumes: Parental sexual communication among Asian American emerging adults. *Journal of Adolescent Research, 22,* 3–31.

Koss, M. P., & Dinero, T. E. (1988). Stranger and acquaintance rape. *Psychology of Women Quarterly, 12,* 1–24.

Koss, M. P., Gidycz, C. A., & Wisniewski, N. (1987). The scope of rape: Incidence and prevalence of sexual aggression and victimization in a national sample of higher education students. *Journal of Consulting and Clinical Psychology, 55,* 162–170.

Lee, B. (2006). Teaching justice and living peace: Body, sexuality, and religious education in Asian-American communities. *Religious Education, 101,* 402–419.

Lee, J., Pomeroy, E. C., & Yoo, S.-K. (2005). Attitudes toward rape: A comparison between Asian and Caucasian college students. *Violence Against Women, 11,* 177–196.

Lee, M. Y., & Law, P. F. M. (2001). Perception of sexual violence against women in Asian American communities. *Journal of Ethnic and Cultural Diversity in Social Work, 10,* 3–25.

Lee, S. J., & Vaught, S. (2003). "You can never be too rich or too thin": Popular and consumer culture and the Americanization of Asian American girls and young women. *Journal of Negro Education, 72,* 457–466.

Leonard, K. (1999). The management of desire: Sexuality and marriage for young South Asian women in America. In S. R. Gupta (Ed.), *Emerging voices: South Asian American women redefine self, family, and community* (pp. 107–119). Walnut Creek, CA: Alta Mira Press.

Malley-Morrison, K., & Hines, D. A. (2004). *Family violence in a cultural perspective: Defining, understanding, and combating abuse.* Thousand Oaks, CA: Sage Publications.

Marchetti, G. (1993). Romance and the "Yellow Peril". Berkeley, CA: University of California Press.

McCarn, S. R., & Fassinger, R. E. (1996). Revisioning sexual minority identity formation: A new model of lesbian identity and its implications for counseling and research. *The Counseling Psychologist, 24,* 508–534.

Meston, C. M., Trapnell, P. D., & Gorzalka, B. B. (1996). Ethnic and gender differences in sexuality: Variations in sexual behavior between Asian and non-Asian university students. *Archives of Sexual Behavior, 25,* 33–72.

Mohr, J. J. (2002). Heterosexual identity and the heterosexual therapist: An identity perspective on sexual orientation dynamics in psychotherapy. *Counseling Psychologist, 30,* 532–566.

Mok, T. A. (1999). Getting the message: Media images and stereotypes and their effect on Asian Americans. *Cultural Diversity and Mental Health, 4,* 185–202.

National Asian Women's Health Organization. (1997). *Expanding options: A reproductive and sexual health survey of Asian American women.* Retrieved March 25, 2007, from http://www.nawho.org/pubs/NAWHOOptions.pdf

National Asian Women's Health Organization. (2000). *Community solutions: Meeting the challenge of STDs in Asian Americans and Pacific Islanders.* Retrieved March 25, 2007, from http://www.nawho.org/pubs/NAWHOSolutions.pdf

National Institute of Allergy and Infectious Diseases. (2005). *HIV infection and AIDS: An overview.* Retrieved March 27, 2007, from http://www.niaid.nih.gov/factsheets/hivinf.htm

Okazaki, S. (2002). Influences of culture on Asian Americans' sexuality. *The Journal of Sex Research, 39,* 34–41.

Pharr, S. (1988). *Homophobia: A weapon of sexism.* Inverness, CA: Chardon Press.

Regan, P. C., Durvasula, R., Howell, L., Ureno, O., & Rea, M. (2004). Gender, ethnicity, and the developmental timing of first sexual and romantic experiences. *Social Behavior and Personality: An International Journal, 32,* 667–676.

Sable, M. R., Danis, F., Mauzy, D. L., & Gallagher, S. K. (2006). Barriers to reporting sexual assault for women and men: Perspectives of college students. *Journal of American College Health, 55,* 157–162.

So, D. W., Wong, F. Y., & DeLeon, J. M. (2005). Sex, HIV risks, and substance use among Asian American college students. *AIDS Education & Prevention, 17,* 457–468.

Song, Y. I. (1996). *Battered women in Korean immigrant families: The silent scream.* New York: Garland Publishing.

Sullivan, P. (1998). Sexual identity development: The importance of target or dominant group membership. In R. L. Sanlo (Ed.), *Working with lesbian, gay, bisexual, and transgender college students: A handbook for faculty and administrators* (pp. 3–12). Westport, CT: Greenwood.

Takagi, D. Y. (1994). Maiden voyage: Excursion into sexuality and identity politics in Asian America. *Amerasia Journal, 20,* 1–17.

Tewksbury, R. (2007). Effects of sexual assaults on men: Physical, mental and sexual consequences. *International Journal of Men's Health, 6,* 22–35.

Tjaden, P., & Thoennes, N. (1998). *Prevalence, incidence, and consequences of violence against women: Findings from the National Violence Against Women Survey* (No. NCJ No. 172837). Washington, DC: U.S. Department of Justice.

Tjaden, P., & Thoennes, N. (2000). *Full report of the prevalence, incidence, and consequences of violence against women.* Washington, DC: National Institute of Justice.

U.S. Census Bureau. (2005). *Annual estimates of the population by sex, race and Hispanic or Latino origin for the United States: April 1, 2000 to July 1, 2005.* Retrieved March 29, 2007, from http://www.census.gov/popest/national/asrh/NC-EST2005/NC-EST2005-03.xls

Ward, L. M. (2003). Understanding the role of entertainment media in the socialization of American youth: A review of empirical research. *Developmental Review, 23,* 347–388.

Worthington, R. L., Savoy, H. B., Dillon, F. R., & Vernaglia, E. R. (2002). Heterosexual identity development: A multidimensional model of individual and social identity. *Counseling Psychologist, 30,* 496–531.

Yoshihama, M. (1999). Domestic violence against women of Japanese descent in Los Angeles: Two methods of estimating prevalence. *Violence Against Women, 5,* 869–897.

15
Dating, Partnerships, and Arranged Marriages

MUNINDER K. AHLUWALIA, LISA A. SUZUKI, and MADEEHA MIR

OUTLINE OF CHAPTER

Case Synopsis
Introduction
Historical Context for Relationships
Rates of Asian American Interracial and Interethnic Marriage and Divorce
Relationships and Dating
Marriage
Stressors and Complications
Case Study
References

Case Synopsis

Annie, a single, 18-year-old Korean American female is a freshman at a large, urban university. Annie lives in university housing with two roommates and is involved in university activities. Her boyfriend, Sam, is Korean and they have been dating for one and a half years. She said Sam was very good-looking, charming, and her parents loved him, "in fact, everyone loved him." While visiting Sam for a week during winter break, Annie and Sam got in an argument. Annie felt that he was upset because she told him that she wasn't really interested in getting married in the near future because she wanted to go to graduate school, pursue a career, and see the world first. Sam told her that she was being selfish because his parents and hers were hoping they would marry after college and they were anxiously awaiting their first grandchildren. This was one of the few times that Annie and Sam could not reconcile their differences and reach a compromise. Annie was very upset because Sam had always told her in the past that she should follow her dreams and that he would always support her. As a result of this argument they have not spoken in over a month. Annie came to the university's counseling service because she was feeling "angry, hurt and panicky."

Introduction

A common assumption is that relationships between individuals from the same ethnic group will not experience conflicts due to cultural differences. This case above illustrates potentially complex issues that can exist between partners from the same ethnic group because of the complex interaction of both of their historical, economic, and social contexts. These factors impact all dating, partnership, and marital relationships.

The dating and marital practices among various Asian groups in the United States have been the subject of historical and contemporary interest. Articles have appeared in the popular press exploring the complexity of dating and marriage for Asian Americans. The purpose of this chapter is to provide an informed examination of relationships within diverse Asian communities in the United States. This chapter will focus on Asian American communities with respect to dating, partnering, and marriage. The chapter begins with a discussion of the historical context of Asians in America that serves as the backdrop to understand how various practices evolved. Then, it proceeds to address dating and marriage, and stressors impacting relationships among Asian Americans. Statistics regarding the rates of **intraethnic, interethnic**, and **interracial** relationships, clinical case examples, and practice exercises are also provided. It is beyond the scope of this chapter to comprehensively address the unique histories and practices that may exist for each of the 25 different Asian subgroups (Uba, 1994). Therefore, this chapter highlights dating, partnering, and marriage practices for various Asian subgroups in the hope that the reader will gain an understanding of the complex array of factors that impact the formation of intimate relationships within Asian communities.

Historical Context for Relationships

The unique history of each Asian subgroup has contributed to the formation of **intraracial** and interracial partnership traditions. This section highlights major historical events that have directly impacted relationship patterns of Asians in the United States including immigration policies, antimiscegenation laws, and the U.S. military occupation and wartime maneuvers in Asian countries (i.e., World War II, the Korean War, and the Vietnam War).

Immigration Policies

Most reviews of the literature on Asian relationships begin with a discussion of the early immigration of Asians to America. A seminal work by Xie and Goyette (2004) entitled, "A Demographic Portrait of Asian Americans," begins by highlighting the history of various Asian groups in the United States (i.e., Chinese, Japanese, Filipino, Korean, Indian, Vietnamese, and "Other" Asian ethnic groups). The history of these groups generally includes attention to the immigration policies of the U.S. government, antimiscegenation laws, and the impact of U.S. occupation and wartime maneuvers in Asian countries. For example, Exclusion Acts were put into effect at particular times barring particular Asian ethnic groups from immigrating to the United States (e.g., Chinese Exclusion Act 1882–1943; Kitano, Yeung, Chai, & Hatanaka, 1984; Japanese immigration restricted from 1907–1908, all Asian immigration prohibited with exception of Filipinos by National Origins Act 1924; Xie & Goyette, 2004). For decades, Asian immigrants were not allowed to become naturalized citizens (Lee, 1998). As noted by Lee (1998), "it is quite evident that the ebb and flow of Asian immigration to the United States closely followed historic legislative events" (p. 4).

Immigration policies had a direct impact on the formation of marital relationships in Asian communities. Fujino (2000) notes that between 1850 and 1930, Asian immigrants were mainly single or unaccompanied married men as the United States required an inexpensive source of labor to meet growing demands in the agrarian (e.g., plantation) and industrial (e.g., mining and construction; Lee, 1998) sectors. Immigrants came from China, Japan, Korea, the Philippines, and India as young men sought economic opportunities in the United States. Immigration of Asian women was strictly limited given that the U.S. government did not want to expend resources to support children and families, and did not want to grant permanent residency to Asian immigrants. Chinese, Japanese, and Asian Indian immigrants were barred from citizenship in 1878, 1922, and 1923, respectively (Lee, 1998).

A number of exclusion laws were put into effect prohibiting in some cases, and severely limiting in other cases, the number of Asian women allowed to gain entry into the United States (Fujino, 2000). Thus, thousands of Asian men were unable to find female partners within their

own racial and ethnic group. During the 1850s to 1870s, the majority of Asian women who immigrated came from poor families and were sold into prostitution (Lee, 1998).

Asian communities created unique practices to address the imbalance in the male–female ratios (i.e., in the Chinese community the ratio was 1:26; Yung, 2005). For example, Japanese and Korean women immigrated as picture brides following the passage of the Gentlemen's Agreement Act (1907–1908), which limited the immigration of Japanese laborers but allowed wives and families to join Japanese men already in the United States (Yung, 2005). Women in Japan and Korea exchanged photographs with potential husbands in the United States. If a match was determined, the bride's name was entered into the family registry and they were issued passports to travel to meet their husbands. Twenty thousand Japanese women and 1,000 Korean women arrived in the United States based upon this marital practice (Yung, 2005). Many of the picture brides were met in the United States by men who were much older than their pictures and less wealthy than initially implied in correspondence.

Prior to 1965, only highly skilled individuals immigrated. It was not until 1965 and the passage of the Immigration and Naturalization Act that large-scale immigration from Asia resumed. It should be noted that this legislative act allowed entry for highly skilled Asians and for family reunification.

Antimiscegenation Laws

For Asian Americans, establishing relationships with White partners was not possible due to U.S. antimiscegenation laws that made interracial marriage illegal (Fujino, 2000). California, where a large Asian immigrant community was established, passed an antimiscegenation law preventing marriage between Whites and "Mongolians" in 1880. This law was not overturned until 1948. Interestingly, Filipinos who were considered Malay rather than Mongolian were allowed to intermarry until 1933 (i.e., when Malays were also included). Fujino notes, "antimiscegenation laws generally were successful in thwarting the formation of Asian-White unions" (p. 183). Thus a large percentage of men within particular Asian communities (i.e., Asian Indian) married Latina, African, or women from other Asian ethnic groups. It should be noted that during this time more Asian men intermarried than women given the limited number of Asian women who were allowed to immigrate. In states where antimiscegenation laws were not present or not enforced, some Asian American men intermarried with White women (Shinagawa & Pang, 1996). In 1967, antimiscegenation laws were eliminated by the U.S. Supreme Court.

U.S. Military Occupation and Wartime Maneuvers

Prior to and during World War II, there were more men than women for all Asian subgroups residing in the United States (Shinagawa & Pang, 1996). Between the late 1940s to 1965 a large percentage of Asian immigrants were women. During overseas military conflicts (i.e., World War II, the Korean War, the Vietnam War), American servicemen married Asian women and then brought them over to the United States following the War Brides Act of 1946, 1948, and 1958, which allowed these marriages without concern regarding the race/ethnicity of the bride (Shinagawa & Pang, 1996).

By 1967, when antimiscegenation laws were abolished, Asian Americans could legally intermarry members of the White community. During the civil rights era, a larger proportion of Asian women intermarried to members of the White community in comparison to Asian men (Shinagawa & Pang, 1996).

While it is beyond the scope of this chapter to address the impact of military actions that occurred between Asian countries, it is important to note that these historical conflicts may continue to exert a major influence between members of various Asian communities. For example, the Rape of Nanking (December 1937–March 1938), during which 369,366 Chinese civilians and prisoners of war were killed and 80,000 women and girls were raped and killed by invading Japanese troops, is still recalled in many families (Yin & Young, 1997).Thus, a marital alliance between a member of these families and a partner of Japanese descent may not be supported. In addition, it is important to note that one cannot assume similarity between all Asian subgroups. For example, Filipino and White cultures are much more similar than Filipino and Chinese (Agbayani-Siewert, 2004) or Indian cultures in terms of histories (e.g., colonization), political ideology (e.g., democracy), and cultural ideals (e.g., attitudes toward women).

Rates of Asian American Interracial and Interethnic Marriage and Divorce

Rates of marriage and divorce among Asian American ethnic groups are presented in Table 15.1 (Reeves & Bennett, 2004; Xie & Goyette, 2004). Xie and Goyette (2004) provide information regarding marriage rates from the 2000 U.S. Census, noting a greater percentage of Asian Americans are married in comparison to White and Black Americans between the ages of 35 to 44. Seventy eight percent of Asian men and 80% of Asian women were married in comparison to 69% of White men, 52% of Black men, 71% of White women and 42% of Black women. Members of the Japanese community had relatively lower marriage rates (men 64%, women 74%) in comparison to Koreans (85% men, 84% women) and Asian Indians (88% men, 90% women) who had the highest marriage rates.

In addition, Xie and Goyette (2004) presented information regarding percentages of Asians interracially and interethnically married based upon the 2000 U.S. Census. In terms of interracial marriage, 12% of all married Asian men and 23% of all married Asian women were married to non-Asians (Xie & Goyette, 2004). Asian women clearly marry outside of their racial group more often than men with the exception of Asian Indians.

Examination of interracial marriages between Asian ethnic groups yields major differences. In particular, Filipino women marry non-Asians three times as often as men from this community (33% and 13% respectively). Similarly, Korean women marry outside of their racial and ethnic group over eight times as often as Korean men (27% and 4% respectively). Xie and Goyette (2004) note that these disparities by gender are in part due to the fact that military men met and married their wives overseas and then returned with them to the United States. They note that

Table 15.1 Intermarriage and Divorce Rates Among Asian Americans by Ethnic Group and Gender

| Race/ethnicity | Spouses race/ethnicity (marriage)[a] | | | Divorce[c] |
	Non-Asian (%)	Same Asian ethnicity (%)	Other Asian[b] (%)	
All Asians	—[d]	—	—	4.2
Men	12	—	—	—
Women	23	—	—	—
Chinese	—	—	—	3.8
Men	6	90	5	—
Women	13	83	4	—
Japanese	—	—	—	6.7
Men	20	69	11	—
Women	41	51	8	—
Filipino	—	—	—	5.2
Men	13	83	4	—
Women	33	63	4	—
Korean	—	—	—	4.6
Men	4	93	3	—
Women	27	69	4	—
Asian Indian	—	—	—	2.4
Men	8	90	3	—
Women	5	92	3	—
Vietnamese	—	—	—	4.1
Men	3	92	4	—
Women	10	86	4	—
Other Asian	—	—	—	4.4
Men	9	—	—	—
Women	18	—	—	—
Multiethnic Asian	—	—	—	—
Men	13	—	—	—
Women	26	—	—	—
Multiracial Asian	—	—	—	—
Men	44	—	—	—
Women	54	—	—	—

Source: From Xie, Y., & Goyette, K. A. (2004), http://paa2004.princeton.edu/download. asp?submissionId= 40245

[a] Marriage data provided by ethnic group and gender. Based upon 2000 U.S. Census 5% Public Use Microdata Sample (PUMS).

[b] "Other Asian" for spouse's race/ethnicity includes multiethnic and multiracial Asians.

[c] From http://www.census.gov/prod/2004pubs/censr-17.pdf (Divorce). Data not provided by gender. Based upon 2000 U.S. Census special tabulation.

[d] —, data not applicable or not available.

"While it is difficult to pin down precisely the social processes that underlie this gender difference, the social barrier for intermarriage is lower for Asian American women than for Asian American men" (Xie & Goyette, 2004, p. 24). The relative social barriers for men and women's interethnic and interracial marriages may relate to perceptions and stereotypes of Asian American men and women (e.g., see section on "Attractiveness and media influences").

Other findings from this census data indicate that intermarriage rates among U.S.-born Asian Americans are higher than immigrant Asian Americans. Also, assimilation seems to also play a role given that Japanese Americans (viewed as the most assimilated Asian ethnic group) have high **outmarriage** rates to non-Asians (20% men, 41% women). Japanese as a whole appear to "exhibit marriage and family behaviors that closely resemble those of whites" (Xie & Goyette, 2004, p. 25).

There is some evidence for Asian panethnicity (Xie & Goyette, 2004). "If Asian Americans had no preference for other Asians over non-Asians except for those in their own ethnicity, we would expect the ratio of "other Asians" to "non-Asian" to be comparable to that of the general population" (Xie & Goyette, 2004, p. 61). This, however, is not the case. The ratio of other Asians to non-Asians among spouses of Asian Americans is much higher than that of the general population (0.04). For example, the ratio among Vietnamese men is 1.24. This suggests that if Asians do not marry intraethnically, they are much more likely to marry interethnically than interracially.

According to the 2000 U.S. Census special tabulation, among the population 15 years and older (Reeves & Bennett, 2004), "Asians were less likely than the total population to be separated, widowed, or divorced: less than 10 percent compared with 19 percent of the total population" (p. 7). Xie and Goyette (2004) note that "With respect to divorce…Asian Americans have a nontrivial divorce rate, albeit low relative to the rates of whites and blacks" (p. 25). The percentages provided in Table 15.1 represent only that of divorce not including those who indicated "separated" or "widowed." The highest rate of divorce is noted among Japanese Americans at 6.7 percent. The reader is referred to Xie and Goyette's publication for more detailed information on divorce rates for other Asian ethnic groups. Examination of overall rates of separated, widowed, and divorced status indicate that "Between 10 percent and 15 percent of all Cambodians, Filipinos, Koreans, Laotians, and Thai were separated, widowed, or divorced, with about 15 percent of Japanese in these categories" (p. 7).

Relationships and Dating

Many factors have been identified as impacting Asian Americans' dating, partnership, and marital choices, including acculturation, ethnic identity, attractiveness, media images, interracial dating and friendship experiences, parental and community influences, density, and propinquity.

Acculturation

Acculturation is the process of cultural change and adaptation that occurs when an individual from one culture comes into contact with other cultures. Acculturation appears to impact openness to discussion of intimate facets of relationships. For example, in most traditional Asian cultures, sexuality is not often discussed. However, as Asian American individuals within these communities become more acculturated in the United States, discussions regarding sexuality and dating have become more open. For example, Fujino (2000) noted that dating patterns are related to acculturation. Asian Americans' level of acculturation is a positive predictor of interracial dating with White Americans and is negatively related to dating other Asian Americans (Mok, 1999).

Generational status has been positively related to level of acculturation. Within particular second-generation Asian American communities (e.g., South Asians), there may be a preference for traditional attributes in mate selection (Lalonde, Hynie, Pannu, & Tatla, 2004). Lalonde and colleagues suggest further that women may abide by family expectations because they tend to be more relational, whereas men, who may be more collective, might do this because of a sense of identity and interdependence with their family and their ethnic group.

Ethnic Identity

Ethnic identity refers to an individual's level of involvement and identification with one's own ethnic group and culture. Ethnic identity has been hypothesized to be linked to dating patterns in that the stronger the ethnic identity, the less likely one is to date or marry interracially. This is based upon the assumption that the more closely one is tied to their own ethnic group the more likely they will choose a partner who shares their same ethnicity. However, while some studies found that Asian American ethnic identity was positively related to dating Asian Americans (e.g., Mok, 1999), others found that Asian Americans married to White Americans had strong pride in their ethnicity (e.g., Sung, 1990). There is no definitive explanation for these inconsistent findings, but one can hypothesize that other factors moderate ethnic identity.

Attractiveness and Media Influences

Perception of attractiveness is an important variable in the selection of a mate and images of race and attractiveness are shaped by the media (Fujino, 2000). Stereotypic perceptions of Asian Americans among non-Asian Americans may affect dating and marital relationships. Both Asian American and Asian biracial men and women are often labeled as exotic (Chua & Fujino, 1999; Root, 1998). Stereotypes about Asian American women are often perpetuated in the media (e.g., movies, magazines, books) with descriptions of being passive (e.g., a subservient "lotus blossom"), a sex object, a prostitute, or the opposite of passive, the evil "dragon lady" (Fujino, 2000; Homma-True, 1990). Asian American men, on the other hand, are seen as both hyper-sexualized, and desexualized or emasculated (Chua & Fujino, 1999). Media representations are of "the feminized Asian American male" (Chua & Fujino, 1999, p. 391), small in stature and subservient. These depictions clearly may also impact Asian American self-image and influence one's engagement in interracial and intraracial relationships.

Chua and Fujino (1999) suggest that Asian Americans may not think they are as physically attractive as White Americans and attribute more positive qualities to White Americans. Asian American college students' self-perceptions of heterosexual attractiveness were negatively related to dating Asian Americans and positively related to interracial dating (Mok, 1999).

Experiences with Interdating and Friendships

Individuals tend to date interethnically and interracially more often than they intermarry (Fujino, 1997). This may relate to the idea that marriage is seen as a more serious, permanent commitment than dating. However, dating members of a particular ethnic group makes future dating with individuals from that ethnic group more likely (Weiss, 1970; Kikumura & Kitano, 1973). In a study of Asian American college students, Mok (1999) found that individuals with past experience dating interracially and who have friendships with non-Asian Americans are more likely to date interracially, while having predominantly Asian American friends was positively related to dating Asian Americans. So, the more diverse their friends, the more likely Asian Americans will date outside their own racial and ethnic group.

Family Influence

Families have a great amount of influence in the lives of Asian Americans. Asian American adolescents may be not be encouraged to date by their parents as much as Whites (Mok, 1999). Attitudes toward dating and marriage are often brought over from the native homeland and parental objections may be the biggest obstacle in interracial dating (Kitano et al., 1984; Sung, 1990). These attitudes are traditionally collectivist in their countries of origin, wherein the welfare and happiness of the group is regarded as more important than that of the individual (Khandelwal, 2002). In the case of Asian families, the wishes and expectations of parents and extended family are to be respected and adhered to as much as possible, even within the Diaspora. Asian parents who discourage their children from dating and are more involved in partner choice will have children who are less likely to date interracially (Mok, 1999). Immigrant parents may pressure their children to partner within their ethnic community and some will ostracize or even "cut off" members of the family that interdate or intermarry (Kitano et al., 1984). Extended family members may also have a great deal of influence in identifying potential suitors in particular communities. For example, in the South Asian community in the United States, it is most common for family members (e.g., uncles and aunts) abroad to post matrimonial advertisements rather than the individuals themselves.

Community Influence

As mentioned previously, Asians and Asian Americans are often identified as interdependent and collectivistic. These worldviews are noted to be influential in the formation of dating and marriage patterns. For example, in Indian culture, other members of the community are all seen in terms of familial relationships; children are raised to think of other girls as sisters, other boys as brothers, and elders as aunts and uncles. Educational and other nonfamily socialization, however, impact collectivism. In Barber's (2004) study of a collectivist culture (i.e., Nepal), she found that increased exposure to nonfamily institutions (e.g., schools) transform marriage from an experience controlled by family to an experience controlled by the individual. This information can also be applied to Asian communities in the United States, that is, as exposure to nonfamily institutions increase, the influence of family and community may decrease. The educational system in the United States is one example of a highly individualistic institution, reinforcing independence, personal decision making and autonomy. Asian Americans' identities and life choices are influenced by living in the context of such individualistic values. For example, if a young Korean woman attends college away from home, plays on the soccer team, and works as a waitress at the local coffee shop, she may see romantic relationships as more of an individualized choice than if she lived at home and commuted to school. Being socioeconomically independent while being exposed to a depth and breadth of philosophies, worldviews, cultures, and sociopolitical ideas through college courses and lectures may expand one's relationship choices.

Density or Propinquity

Research has suggested that dating behavior is related to density (i.e., the relative proportion of an individual's ethnic group in comparison with other ethnic groups in the neighborhood; Mok, 1999) and propinquity (i.e., the physical distance between groups; Fujino, 2000; Kitano, Fujino, & Sato, 1998). The lower the density of Asian Americans and the greater the propinquity, the opportunity for intraracial dating is lowered and the chance of interracial dating becomes higher. Fujino (1997) found propinquity to be the strongest predictor of interracial dating. This relationship is not absolute given that geographic region has a great impact on relationships and dating choices as well. Interracial and interethnic relationships on the coasts (e.g., Hawaii and California) are more common than the Midwest because of the amount of interethnic and interracial contact. For example, all Asian American groups had outmarriage rates of more than 60% in Hawaii (Kitano et al., 1998).

Gay, Lesbian, and Bisexual Relationships

In addition to the above listed factors, other variables impact dating in Asian American gay, lesbian, and bisexual communities. Asian countries, such as China, Korea and Japan, have long histories of tolerance for same-sex attraction (as long as familial obligations, such as marriage and procreation, are fulfilled), but Western influence has replaced that tolerance with ideals that same-sex relationships are abnormal (Kimmel & Yi, 2004). Interestingly, homophobia has been found to be greater in Asian cultures than in United States and same-sex relationships are considered to be problematic, sinful, and unnatural (Chung & Katayama, 1998). Because sexuality is linked to procreation in many Asian cultures (Okazaki, 2002), for gay and lesbian Asian Americans, dating and partnership can be more challenging than for heterosexuals. Many gay and lesbian Asian Americans hide their sexual identity and are not "out" in their families and communities. One study found that Asian American gays and lesbians fear disapproval more than White Americans (Lippa & Tan, 2001).

Because marriage and family are so central to many of the ethnic groups, not getting married and subsequently not having children is seen as a deficit. In fact, most gay and lesbian Asians do get married and have children (Chung & Katayama, 1998). Bisexuals may leave same-sex attraction unexplored because of cultural pressure to be in a relationship with someone from the opposite sex.

Asian American gay men tend to be more involved in the gay culture than the Asian culture (Matteson, 1997). Although the gay and lesbian community is more tolerant of diversity than mainstream U.S. culture (e.g., interracial couples), it is still predominantly White and middle class (Matteson, 1997). Gay and lesbian Asian Americans may experience ethnic discrimination or exoticization within the larger gay and lesbian community.

Marriage

There are differences between Asian and Western views on both love and **arranged marriages** (Naidoo & Davis, 1988). There are gender differences as well as cultural differences involved in the selection of a marital partner (Buss et al., 1990). In many cultures, marriage is seen as an alliance between two families (Dion & Dion, 1993), with love coming after marriage (Goodwin & Cramer, 2000). Details on the motivations, nature, and process of arranged marriage, a particularly unique and often misunderstood social construct, will be presented in the following sections.

Arranged Marriages

Historically, many Asian American ethnic groups practiced arranged marriage, but South Asians are often most associated with arranged marriage practices today. This section covers reasons for arranged marriage, corresponding practices, and the concept of introduced or semi-arranged marriages. Traditionally, South Asian countries such as Pakistan, Bangladesh, India, Nepal, Sri Lanka, and Malaysia experience the highest proportion of arranged marriage (Zaidi & Shuraydi, 2002). South Asians tend to be reared in traditional, patriarchal communities that emphasize spirituality, family, and permanence of the marriage bond (Vaidyanathan & Naidoo, 1991). These values play a pivotal role in maintaining the traditional social framework of procreation (Ayyub, 2000; Khandelwal, 2002).

Marriages that are arranged are typically **inmarriages** or intraethnic unions, which are valued by South Asians because of similarity in ethnicity, religion, language, region, and customs.

In addition, there is often a belief by family members that individuals will be more compatible if they are from similar ethnic backgrounds. Marriages can be arranged based on factors such as region (e.g., Indians from Gujrat), caste (e.g., Indian Brahmins), or socioeconomic status. Sometimes, however, ethnicity or nationality is less important than religious affiliation (e.g., Muslim Pakistani with Muslim Indian).

In Western societies, a person wishing to marry generally searches for a partner through means of dating, courtship, and often cohabitation, which is the fundamental difference between arranged marriages and **love marriages** (Batabyal, 2001). In societies where there is minimal socialization between genders due to religious and cultural parameters, parents, relatives, friends, and matchmaking intermediaries take upon themselves the task of looking for suitable mates for individuals (Batabyal, 2001). This custom has existed for centuries and has had only slight variations in its implementation in recent years. Thus, the essence of the practice is still maintained both in South Asia and the Diaspora (Mullatti, 1995).

Reasons for Arranged Marriage

In general, expressions of sexuality outside of marriage are considered highly inappropriate in most Asian cultures (Okazaki, 2002). Further, Islamic religion prohibits premarital dating, sex, and cohabitation, reinforcing the practice of arranged marriage among Muslims. In some cases, both religion and culture combine to create a strong pressure to follow this tradition, such as among Indian Hindus and Sikhs. In contrast to second- and third-generation East Asians (e.g., Chinese and Japanese Americans) who are more assimilated (Penn, Hernandez, & Bermudez, 1997), South Asians retain many ideals such as strict adherence to regional language, food, caste (e.g., Hindus), religion (and subsects of religion), and other cultural aspects are maintained, including the practice of arranged marriage.

Arranged marriages are based on the collective good rather than the individuals' choice (Goodwin & Cramer, 2000), and love or chemistry between the partners is not considered a critical factor. It is often said in South Asian communities, for example, that love comes after marriage or through marriage. The difference can be posed as "you fall in love with the person you marry vs. you marry the person you fall in love with." Marriage is considered to be a contractual agreement between two families implemented to maintain strong social and cultural ties within a community (Khandelwal, 2002). Although the individual does play a role, the degree to which one is involved in the process of spousal selection may vary (e.g., among different families, communities, religious groups).

In line with collectivist cultural norms, partners in arranged marriages are often joined in the celebration of two families, tribes, or castes, and others may become involved in marital matters and decisions (Khandelwal, 2002), such as child-rearing, financial planning, and domestic responsibilities. Living with extended family is common in Asian families; examples include elderly parents living with one family or two brothers with their respective families living together. Individuals engaged in these types of marriages may subsequently face unique stressors such as conflicts with extended family and in-laws, societal expectations, and strong gender roles.

Methods/Practices of Arranged Marriage

Arranged marriages take place only with parental approval. Prospective mates are often sought and found through the use of newspaper and magazine matrimonial advertisements placed by parents as well as word-of-mouth in the local and national South Asian community (Mullatti, 1995). Many **matchmakers** may align partners' astrological signs and horoscopes in creating compatible couples (e.g., Hindus often engage in this practice). Some South Asian families will also return to their "homeland" of India, Pakistan, and Bangladesh to seek potential mates for their children (Khandelwal, 2002). Pre-arranged "meetings" are set up, often following e-mail or telephone communication. A variety of reasons may motivate such international matchmaking, including the hope that such a union will cement the affiliation to South Asian culture and familial ties. There is also a belief that "native" men and women are more chaste, adaptable, respectable, and desirable marriage candidates than their Westernized South Asian counterparts.

Further, the use of Internet matrimonial advertisements, predominantly written by individuals other than the marriage candidate, speaks to Asians' adaptability to a rapidly evolving technological society. Modern-day matchmaking, particularly in the past decade, has manifested in the numerous Web sites catering to the religious, cultural, regional, educational, and financial criteria outlined by South Asian parents. The Web contains a number of sites for potential partners (e.g., http://www.shaadi.com). An example of a matrimonial ad is below.

Matrimonial Ad: Girl Seeks Boy
Parents of 23 year old fair, beautiful, B.A. educated, slim Hindu Bengali Brahmin girl seeks Hindu Brahmin boy who is tall, educated, green card holder or U.S. citizen. Girl residing in U.S. Parents of girl own home in the U.S. and have extensive land in India. Girl's family currently visiting India. Early marriage. Contact uncle in Delhi.

Placing high value on parental and community approval is considered acceptable in most South Asian immigrant groups. However, this practice may not be as desired by South Asians raised in or having spent a significant amount of time in the United States, who have been influenced by Western ideals of love and marriage. As one young Pakistani American woman voiced in an interview, "Marriage shouldn't begin with marriage and end in love, it should begin with love and end in marriage" (Zaidi & Shuraydi, 2002, p. 509).

Introduced/Semiarranged Marriage

South Asian Americans have begun to redefine the meaning and paths to marriage. In some communities and families, the practice of arranged marriage has been modified to include any combination of chaperoned interactions, open courting, or dating under the watchful eyes of parents and relatives (Zaidi & Shuraydi, 2002). The result of this transformation is the **introduced/semiarranged marriage**, in which parents introduce potential candidates to their children in formal or informal meetings, with the premise that the individual holds the right to "accept" or "reject" the suitor. Parents grant a degree of freedom to their children with respect to marriage without leaving the matter entirely up to them. This "modern arranged marriage" (Khandelwal, 2002) appears to be a compromise between an arranged and love marriage, and appears to be a relatively recent phenomenon for immigrants and their children attempting to cope with cultural differences.

Love Marriages

Though the concept of a "love marriage" may seem redundant to those in the West, in the context of South Asian culture, it is still seen as a conscious choice to be made over others, such as an arranged or introduced/semiarranged marriage. Zaidi and Shuraydi (2002) define the

Western mate selection process as a self-choice system based on the factor of love. The "self" in American society is an individualized unit that creates a new, private relationship (Khandelwal, 2002) through marriage (as compared with traditional Asian cultures where marriage is seen as a joining of families). Marriage is a function of greater self-expression and personal gratification within which the individuals in question are in control (Zaidi & Shuraydi, 2002).

Intraethnic Marriage

Intraethnic love marriages (both partners are of the same ethnicity), similar to intraethnic arranged marriages, may occur due to a number of factors. For example, the individuals in question may be attracted to, seek or value similar cultural backgrounds; likewise, residing in or socializing with one's own ethnic group may increase proximity and accessibility to other Asians.

Often, non-Asians may assume that an intraethnic couple (i.e., both being Filipino) will have a smooth transition in terms of dating, parental approval, and marriage. However, regional differences such as varying language dialects, cuisine, and social customs as well as religious differences can become a point of contention for the families involved, despite the affection, mutual respect, and personality compatibility that may be expressed in a marriage based on love. Moreover, pressure to marry within the parameters of one's race, ethnicity, religion, community, and socioeconomic class regardless of personal choice may lead to frequent conflict and interpersonal distress within the family and the individual. Individuals of a marriageable age may struggle to find a compromise when their significant others do not fulfill parental standards or requirements. It is not uncommon for romantic relationships to be dissolved in light of ultimatums given on the part of the parents, because the family's shame of a love marriage is more than the parents can bear, and thus children opt to alleviate their parents' distress. Because a love marriage presumes one to be engaged in a relationship prior to marriage, it may by definition be perceived as a threat to family honor, associated with chastity, and hence be less valued by family members, the community, and society (Zaidi & Shuraydi, 2002). Many Asian Americans may have to decide whether they want to marry someone their parents disapprove of or sacrifice their own romantic interests for the family. For many Asian Americans, the family's welfare and happiness is held in higher esteem than that of the individual (Khandelwal, 2002).

Interethnic and Interracial Marriage

According to Fujino (2000), five patterns exist related to Asian American intermarriage (i.e., both interracial and interethnic): (a) the majority of Asian Americans marry intraethnically, (b) acculturation (as measured by generational or immigrant status) is directly related to outmarriage rates (e.g., third generation outmarries more than the second generation, which outmarries more than first-generation immigrants), (c) Asian Americans are outmarrying at increasingly higher rates, with greater numbers of interethnic or **Pan Asian** marriages (i.e., Asians marrying other Asians from different ethnic groups), (d) Asian American women outmarry at higher rates than Asian American men, and (e) when outmarrying, Asian American men tend to marry other Asians, but Asian American women tend to marry White men.

Stressors and Complications

Some of the issues that arise between two individuals dating/marrying interethnically or interracially include issues of prejudice, acceptance within families and communities, "cutting off" individuals from families and communities, and gaining or losing status in the community. In many Asian communities, family honor is closely tied to the performance and activities of the children. If a person marries outside the ethnic group or outside the religion, that may be seen by the family or community as a failure of the parents to instill Asian values, which brings shame to the family. As a result, these may be ostracized or even cut off by their families.

Hiding Relationships

To prevent or postpone some of the conflict that can emerge with their families when dating interethnically or interracially (and for some, when dating at all), some Asian Americans may avoid discussing or actively hide their relationships. Wear (2000) studied Asian and Pacific Islander women and found that one of the major areas of stress was hiding relationships that involved dating someone outside their culture. This included not only interethnic and interracial dating, but also differences relating to caste, religion, national origin, and regional origins within the home country. Hiding a relationship is difficult because of close networks within specific communities (e.g., Indian Punjabis). One medical student explained, "We can't go out because somebody you know might see you and they're going to tell their parents and their parents will tell mine" (Wear, 2000, p. 162). Another student described her mother's reaction to finding out that one of her daughter's friends was seriously dating someone:

> She started to cry. She took my hand and said, "Promise me you'll never kiss a boy until you decide to marry him." It was like, OK, Mom. She doesn't get that dating is a part of the culture here. I don't want to hide it from my parents, but I feel like I don't have any choice. (Wear, 2000, p. 162)

Abuse in Relationships

Asian Americans share some similar cultural values that influence their experiences with abuse in relationships. Tolerance of abuse and violence in dating and marital relationships, however, varies greatly between and within Asian ethnic subgroups. Women are sometimes seen as second-class citizens, inferior to men, or even the property of men. When a woman behaves in a manner that is perceived by the man (and society) to be humiliating (e.g., drinking, infidelity), violence in dating and marital relationships may be seen as justified because of the man's need to save face (Agbayani-Siewert, 2004). This perception of justification varies among Asian ethnic groups. For example, Filipino college students were found to be more egalitarian in their attitudes toward women, tended to justify acts of violence against women less, and defined physical aggression as violence more often than Chinese students (Agbayani-Siewert, 2004).

It is important to recognize, however, that a number of variables [e.g., different cultural beliefs, generational status (i.e., immigrant, second generation), socioeconomic status] can impact the occurrence of, attitudes toward, interpretations of, and responses to relationship violence (Bhuyan, Mell, Senturia, Sullivan, & Shiu-Thornton, 2005). As Bhuyen and colleagues explain, in certain cultures (e.g., Khmer), enduring an abusive relationship is seen as part of a woman's karma or fate. The following quote illustrates the complex factors contributing to violence. It is a Cambodian woman's story about her experiences with her husband (Bhuyan et al., 2005, p. 910):

> Since I have been living in the U.S., my husband's feeling is not the same when he was in Cambodia. [His] work and money took care of that. I stayed home taking care of the kids. But we both have to work here. My husband emotionally and physically mistreats me. First emotionally, he doesn't want me to go to school. I go to work and can't speak English. . . . He doesn't allow me to have friends. . . . He doesn't let me know what the income and expenses are. When he wants to send money to his relatives, he never tells me. He never talks with me about anything. When he comes back from work, he would start a fight.

This case highlights the stress impacting this couple's relationship after their immigration to the United States. In particular, issues of socioeconomic status, social support, and language are notable.

Divorce

Most Asian cultures are traditional and patriarchal, with religion, culture, and family playing significant and positive roles in individuals' lives. Dissolution of marriage complicates the family situation as lines become blurred and discontinuous (Yee, Huang, & Lew, 1998), and among Asian Americans, divorce is still uncommon except for the younger and more acculturated individuals.

Divorce is generally viewed negatively by Asians across subgroups, likely influenced by a number of sociocultural and religious factors. In a study by Tien (1986) assessing attitudes about divorce among Korean Americans, Chinese Americans, and European Americans, European Americans had the most positive attitudes toward divorce, with Chinese Americans next and Korean Americans last.

However, because of the rapid social, economic, cultural, and gender role changes, the various Asian interpretations of the institution of marriage are undergoing a major transformation (Huang, 2005). Along with this are the swiftly rising divorce rates among various Asian cultural communities living in the United States (Wong, 1995; Huang, 2005), despite the fact that divorce is still a stigmatized construct. Among Asian Americans, divorce has gone from less than 4% in 1994 to about 5% in 2002 (*USA Today*, May 28, 2003).

Though some have attributed the historically smaller number of actual reported divorces among couples in Asian arranged marriages to a stronger emphasis on familial harmony (Yee, Huang, & Lew, 1998), these rates may not necessarily be indicative of healthy, happy relationships but possibly a hesitation to break cultural norms by leaving problematic marriages. There appears to be a shift in personal values and social norms for Asian Americans: Despite seemingly low proportions, South Asian divorce rates are on the rise as children of immigrants are getting divorced at a higher rate than that of their conservative parents (Valiante & Rome, 2005). Muslims in North America (including Asians of Indian, Pakistani, and Bangladeshi descent) have the third-highest divorce rate at 33 percent (Valiante & Rome, 2005), conflicting with previous low reports of divorce. The shame and stigma associated with divorce, particularly surrounding divorced women, may not translate as strongly for more acculturated Asians living in the United States. This gradual transformation of cultural practices will likely have powerful implications for the framework and dynamics of Asian American relationships and families across ethnic subgroups.

Summary

This chapter began with an overview of Asian American dating, partnerships, and marital relationships. It then proceeded to identify important historical events impacting the emergence of relationship patterns in the United States, including immigration and antimiscegenation laws, along with U.S. military actions. The rates of interracial and interethnic marriages and divorce in Asian communities are discussed. Factors that relate to Asian American relationships and dating include acculturation, ethnic identity, attractiveness and media influences, interracial dating and friendships, family and community influence, and density and propinquity. In particular, gay, lesbian, and bisexual Asian Americans face unique challenges in relationships. Marriages among Asian Americans range from being completely arranged to being based on love with no family involvement. Finally, it is important to remember that stressors and complications in Asian Americans' relationships can include abuse and divorce.

Discussion Questions

1. Reflect on these questions yourself and then interview others (e.g., a peer and an elder) regarding their beliefs and values surrounding the formation of intimate relationships, dating, and marriage. Compare the results. What are areas of similarity? Areas of difference?
2. Growing up, did you discuss sexuality, dating, and relationships with your family?
3. Who did you grow up around (ethnically and racially)?
4. When you think of "Asian," what comes to mind?
5. At what age do you think someone should start dating? What do you consider to be a marriageable age? What developmental milestones must be met before a person should consider getting married?
6. Have you been told who you can or can not marry? How do you understand where these ideas come from?
7. What is your ideal relationship? What are the qualities you are looking for in a partner?
8. Ethnically and racially, who do you think is attractive?
9. Culturally, who would be most compatible with you, your interests and lifestyle?
10. Would you enter an interracial relationship? Why or why not? Are there particular racial/ethnic groups that you would find more acceptable than others? Where does this acceptance or nonacceptance come from?
11. What are some of the challenges that would emerge for gay and lesbian Asian Americans? What ethnic groups do you think would be most accepting? The least?

Case Study

Thus far, this chapter has focused on history, theory, and research of Asian Americans' dating, partnership, and marital relationships and their impact on psychological growth and development. The case of Annie will now be continued to give readers a sense of what an Asian Americans may focus on in therapy.

Background Information

Annie is an 18-year-old Korean American female college freshman. She was referred to the university counseling service by her academic advisor after she told him that she was upset about the "fight" she had with her boyfriend, Sam, and that she couldn't concentrate on her midterm exams. Annie told her counselor that there were times she felt "sad," "anxious," and "empty," especially now that she was not talking to Sam. Annie stated that she "adored" Sam, but was terrified of them getting in a fight. She said that when they would begin to disagree about something, she would not know what to say to him and would disengage.

Annie's father is an engineer and her mother works as a nurse at night. She said her father was normally a quiet man and was "well-liked" in the community, but he had a temper that went on like a "switch" when he was drinking; one moment he would be keeping to himself and the next minute he would be yelling and hitting her, her brother, or her mother. Annie's mother insisted that there was nothing wrong with her father's "discipline," that she should be a "good, quiet girl," and that it is a woman's job to "endure." Annie initially said her relationship with her mother was very close, but then stated that when she disagreed with her, her mother would give her "the silent treatment" and not speak to her for days.

Theoretical Orientation

The counselor's theoretical stance is influenced by Sullivan's interpersonal theory, and she actively inquires into current and past interactions because they allow her to understand her client's life in context. The counselor introduced their difference in culture as a variable because it has an impact on relationships and how one sees oneself. When asked in the first session about the relevance of the Korean culture in her life, Annie said that it did not have an impact on her. Throughout the therapy, however, Annie began to understand ways in which culture influenced her life and relationships (i.e., gender roles).

Through counseling, Annie is able to improve the functioning of her self-system, the way she gains self awareness, interacts with others, controls anxiety, and shapes impressions of herself and others. The therapeutic relationship acts as an important tool in the therapeutic process. The key interactional patterns that constitute Annie's personality are reenacted in all areas of her life, including the therapeutic relationship. As patterns in other relationships are identified, the counselor looks for ways in which they emerge in their relationship and tries to resist transformation.

Case Conceptualization

The counselor considered the possibility that Annie was having difficulties adjusting to changes in her relationship with Sam. Her symptoms of anxiety were interfering with her daily activities because of difficulty concentrating. Annie spoke about how problems with her boyfriend paralleled her relationship with her parents. As a child, she received conditional approval and acceptance from her parents, who did not give her the sense of security she needed to grow, instead encouraging dependence. While this was partially a cultural influence, it also counteracted her tendency toward growth and autonomy as a bicultural woman. Eventually, Annie's sense of self was shaped by her parents' needs and designed to keep anxiety at a minimum. Her relationship with Sam reenacts and reinforces the conflict between her need for security and her desire for growth. When she asserted herself in the relationship by sharing her "dreams" for the future with Sam, he responded negatively given his desire to get married and begin a family after they graduated. Sam reminded Annie that their parents had met and jokingly said they were ready to plan the wedding. When Annie told her mother that she wanted to go to graduate school and have a career first, her mother asked her, "Why do you want to do that? Men aren't attracted to women that are more educated than they are. Sam will make enough to support you so you don't have to work."

Prior to this argument, when Annie and Sam would have a disagreement, Annie would "back off" and Sam would get frustrated. As a result, she stopped being open with him.

Intervention Strategies

The counselor began therapy with an exploration of her thoughts and feelings about the therapeutic process. Because Annie was skeptical, the counselor explained the nature and benefits of therapy. Annie expressed hesitation because her traditional Korean parents did not believe in counseling and discouraged discussing personal issues both outside and within the home; she therefore pursued counseling as a last resort.

Gradually, Annie was able to use the counseling relationship as a safe, secure environment where she could explore her needs for security, self-acceptance, and self-esteem along with her concerns about identity, interdependence, and autonomy. The counselor worked toward enabling her to tell her story and understand her life events in a new way. She explored her relationship with Sam in greater depth. She shared that her "dreams" were viewed by him as "too ambitious" and that she thought he felt threatened when she asserted herself. Annie stated that she loved Sam but she didn't want to be "trapped" in what she felt would be a "traditional Korean marriage" like her parents. She realized the role of her parents and culture in shaping ideas about relationships. Annie shared her feelings and thoughts with Sam and while he "understood" where she was coming from he expressed that he felt torn between wanting to support her and the pressure coming from their parents that they should marry upon graduation.

Additional Clinical Considerations

The counselor should be aware of her own intersecting identities and cultural background and how that impacts her work with Annie. She must take care not to impose her culture onto Annie through the clinical work. For example, the counselor must try to understand Korean culture and the experience of being a bicultural daughter of immigrant parents in the United States.

Case Study Discussion Questions

For undergraduate students, please consider the following questions:

1. What are your initial reactions to this vignette?
2. What are your thoughts or reactions to Annie's hesitations about counseling? How does this relate to your understanding?
3. What do you think about the counselor's approach to working with Annie?

For graduate students and/or beginning therapists, please consider the following questions:

1. What would be challenging for you when working with Annie as her counselor? What may be some of the transference and countertransference issues?
2. As the counselor, how would your identities (e.g., race, ethnicity, gender, socioeconomic status) impact your relationship and work with Annie?

3. What is your theoretical orientation? Would you apply this theory when working with Annie?

Additional Case Study Examples

1. Intraethnic   Alima, a 23-year-old, second-generation Pakistani American, Muslim female, has become engaged to Iqbal, a Pakistani, Muslim male. Alima's parents arranged the marriage during their last visit to their village near Multan and Iqbal agreed to move to the United States after they got married. Alima had agreed to engagement and marriage, but when she returned to her home in Philadelphia, she began to have second thoughts. She worried that she did not know enough about Iqbal.

2. Interethnic   Raj is a 25-year-old South Indian man who has been dating Carol, a Korean American female for 4 years. They met while working at an accounting firm in San Francisco. Raj is concerned about their cultural and religious differences (Carol is Protestant and he is Hindu) and wonders how this will impact their future together. Conflicts have already arisen as Raj has asked Carol to become a vegetarian given his religious background.

3. Interethnic   Mei is a 21-year-old international student from Hong Kong who is studying at a state university. She has been dating Robert, a 22-year-old, third-generation Japanese American man for the past 2 years. Her parents are planning to visit her for 3 weeks and she is anxious about their arrival and unsure of how her parents will respond to Robert. She knows that her parents have expressed a great deal of hatred toward the Japanese due to the occupation of China by the Japanese and the atrocities that were committed during this time.

4. Interracial   Anna is a 28-year-old, biracial Filipina and Dominican female, who has been dating Sandra, a 30-year-old African American female for 6 months. Anna has not told her family she is a lesbian and refuses to introduce Sandra to her family. Sandra is out to her own family and is becoming impatient with Anna's resistance. Anna thinks that Sandra is not being understanding of her cultural and religious background.

Key Terms

Arranged marriage: Marriage in which matchmakers or parents look for and arrange suitable mates for the individuals involved, with little to no premarital contact between the man and woman (Batabyal, 2001; Khandelwal, 2002; Vaidyanathan & Naidoo, 1991).

Inmarriage: Marriage within an individual's specific nationality group (e.g., Korean and Korean; Kitano, Yeung et al., 1984).

Interethnic: Relationship with a partner from a different ethnicity but same racial group (e.g., Japanese and Indian; Fujino, 2000).

Interracial: Relationship between racially different partners (e.g., Chinese and Latino; Fujino, 2000).

Intraethnic: Coethnic union or relationship between individuals of the same ethnic group (e.g., Vietnamese and Vietnamese; Fujino, 2000).

Intraracial: Relationship between partners of the same race but possibly ethnically different (e.g., Pakistani and Indian; Fujino, 2000).

Introduced/semiarranged marriage: Marriage in which parents and the prospective spouse are active together in the process of finding a mate, with "open courting" or arranged "dates" between individuals (Zaidi & Shuraydi, 2002).

Love marriage: Marriage in which a partner typically courts, dates, and sometimes cohabits before marrying a person with little or no parental involvement (Batabyal, 2001).

Matchmaker: A go-between who is either paid or volunteers to match prospective spouses in accordance with religious, regional, cultural, and socioeconomic and sometimes astrological criteria outlined by both families (Batabyal, 2001). Called *Vichola* in Indian culture.

Outmarriage: Marriage outside an individual's specific racial or ethnic group (e.g., Filipino and White; Fujino, 2000).

Pan Asian: Relationship between two individuals from different Asian ethnicities (e.g., Chinese and Korean; Shinagawa & Pang, 1996).

For Further Learning and Suggested Readings

The following films and books depict intraethnic, interethnic, and interracial relationships within Asian American communities.

Intraethnic Relationships

Books: *Yellow: Stories, The Namesake, The Village Bride of Beverly Hills, For Matrimonial Purposes, Arranged Marriage*
Movies: *The Joy Luck Club, Mulan, Monsoon Wedding*
Web sites: http://www.shaadi.com

Interethnic and Interracial Relationships

Books: *The Foreign Student: A Novel, Sharmila's Book*
Movies: *Mississippi Masala, Bride and Prejudice, Bend It Like Beckham, Touch of Pink, The Wedding Banquet, Shogun, The Last Samurai, The Karate Kid II, Between Heaven and Earth*

References

Agbayani-Siewert, P. (2004). Assumptions of Asian American similarity: The case of Filipino and Chinese American students. *Social Work, 49*(1), 39–51.

Ayyub, R. (2000). Domestic violence in the South Asian immigrant Muslim population in the United States. *Journal of Social Distress & the Homeless, 9*(3), 237–248.

Barber, J. S. (2004). Community social context and individualistic attitudes towards marriage. *Social Psychology Quarterly, 67*(3), 236–256.

Batabyal, A. A. (2001). On the likelihood of finding the right partner in an arranged marriage. *Journal of Socio-Economics, 33*, 273–280.

Bhuyan, R., Mell, M., Senturia, K., Sullivan, M., & Shiu-Thornton, S. (2005). "Women must endure according to their karma": Cambodian Immigrant Women Talk About Domestic Violence. *Journal of Interpersonal Violence, 20*(8), 902–921.

Buss, D. M., Abbott, M., Angleitner, A., Asherian, A., Biaggo, A., Blanco-Villasenor, A., et al., (1990). International preferences in selecting mates: A study of 37 cultures. *Journal of Cross-Cultural Psychology, 21*, 4–47.

Chua, P., & Fujino, D. C. (1999). Negotiating new Asian American masculinities: Attitudes and gender expectations. *The Journal of Men's Studies, 7*(3), 391–413.

Chung, Y. B., & Katayama, M. (1998). Ethnic and sexual identity development of Asian American lesbian and gay adolescents. *Professional School Counseling, 1*(3), 21–25.

Dion, K.K., & Dion, K.L. (1993). Individualistic and collectivistic perspectives on gender and the cultural context of love and intimacy. *Journal of Social Issues, 49*(3), 53–69.

Fujino, D. C. (1997). The rates, patterns, and reasons for forming heterosexual interracial dating relationships among Asian Americans. *Journal of Social and Personal Relationships, 14*(6), 809–828.

Fujino, D. C. (2000). Structural and individual influences affecting racialized dating relationships. In J. L. Chin (Ed.), *Relationships among Asian American women* (pp. 181–209). Washington DC: American Psychological Association.

Goodwin, R., & Cramer, D. (2000). Marriage and social support in a British-Asian community. *Journal of Community and Applied Social Psychology, 10*, 49–62.

Homma-True, R. (1990). Psychotherapy issues with Asian American women. *Sex Roles, 22*, 477–486.

Huang, W. (2005). An Asian perspective on relationship and marriage education. *Family Process, 44*(2), 161–173.

Khandelwal, M. S. (2002). *Becoming American, being Indian: An immigrant community in New York City.* New York: Cornell University Press.

Kimmel, D. C., & Yi, H. (2004). Characteristics of gay, lesbian and bisexual Asians, Asian Americans, and immigrants from Asia to the USA. *Journal of Homosexuality, 47*(2), 143–172.

Kitano, H. H. L., Fujino, D. C., & Sato, J. T. (1998). Interracial marriages: Where are the Asian Americans and where are they going? In L. C. Lee & N. W. Zane (Eds.), *Handbook of Asian American psychology* (pp. 233–260). Thousand Oaks, CA: Sage Publications.

Kikumura, A., & Kitano, H. H. L. (1973). Interracial marriage: A picture of the Japanese Americans. *Journal of Social Issues, 29*, 67–81.

Kitano, H. H. L., Yeung, W., Chai, L., & Hatanaka, H. (1984). Asian American interracial marriage. *Journal of Marriage and the Family, 46*(1), 179–190.

Lalonde, R. N., Hynie, M., Pannu, M., & Tatla, S. (2004). The role of culture in interpersonal relationships: Do second generation South Asian Canadians want a traditional partner? *Journal of Cross-Cultural Psychology, 35*(5), 503–524.

Lee, L. C. (1998). An overview. In L. C. Lee & N. Zane (Eds.), *Handbook of Asian American psychology* (pp. 1–19). Thousand Oaks, CA: Sage Publications.

Lippa, R. A., & Tan, F. D. (2001). Does culture moderate the relationship between sexual orientation and gender-related personality traits? *Cross-Cultural Research, 35*, 65–87.

Matteson, D. R. (1997). Bisexual and homosexual behavior and HIV risk among Chinese-, Filipino-, and Korean American men. *Journal of Sex Research, 34*(1), 93–104.

Mok, T. A. (1999). Asian American dating: Important factors in partner choice. *Cultural Diversity and Ethnic Minority Psychology, 5*(2), 103–117.

Mullatti, L. (1995). Families in India: Beliefs and realities. *Journal of Comparative Family Studies, 26*, 11–25.

Naidoo, J., & Davis, J. C. (1988). Canadian South Asian women in transition: A dualistic view of life. *Journal of Comparative Family Studies, 19*, 311–327.

Okazaki, S. (2002). Influences of culture on Asian Americans' sexuality. *Journal of Sex Research, 39*(1), 34–41.

Penn, C. D., Hernandez, S. L., & Bermudez, J. M. (1997). Using a cross-cultural perspective to understand infidelity in couples therapy. *The American Journal of Family Therapy, 25*(2), 169–185.

Reeves, T. J., & Bennett, C. E. (2004). *We the People: Asians in the United States: Census 2000 Special Reports.* Retrieved February 3, 2006, from http://www.census.gov/prod/2004pubs/censr-17.pdf.

Root, M. P. P. (1998). Multiracial Americans: Changing the face of America. In L. C. Lee & N. W. Zane (Eds.), *Handbook of Asian American Psychology* (pp. 261–287). Thousand Oaks, CA: Sage Publications.

Shinagawa, L. H., & Pang, G. Y. (1996). Asian American panethnicity and intermarriage. *Amerasia Journal, 22*(2), 127–152.

Sung, B. L. (1990). Chinese American intermarriage. *Journal of Comparative Family Studies, 21*(3), 337–352.

Tien, J. (1986). Attitudes towards divorce across three cultures: Implications for community mental health. *Asian American Psychological Association Journal*, 55–58.

Uba, L. (1994). *Asian Americans: Personality patterns, identity, and mental health.* New York: Guilford Press.

USA Today. (2003, May 28). *Census: Divorce rate up among Asians.* Retrieved July 24, 2006, from http://www.usatoday.com/news/nation/census/2003-05-28-asians-census_x.htm.

Vaidyanathan, P., & Naidoo, J. (1991) Asian Indians in Western countries: Cultural identity and the arranged marriage. *Contemporary Issues in Cross-Cultural Psychology*, 37–49.

Valiante, W. C., & Rome, N. (2005). *Family therapy and Muslim families: A solution focused approach.* Retrieved May 19, 2005, from http://www.crescentlife.com/articles/islamic%20psych/family_therapy_and_muslim families.htm

Wear, D. (2000). Asian/Pacific Islander women in medical education: Personal and professional challenges. *Teaching and Learning in Medicine, 12*(3), 156–163.

Weiss, M. S. (1970). Selective acculturation and the dating process: The patterning of Asian-Caucasian interracial dating. *Journal of Marriage and the Family, 32,* 273–278.

Wong, R. R. (1995). Divorce mediation among Asian Americans: Bargaining in the shadow of diversity. *Family & Conciliation Courts Review. Special Issue: Domestic Violence, 33*(1), 110–128.

Xie, Y., & Goyette, K. A. (2004). *The American People Census 2000: A demographic portrait of Asian Americans.* New York: Russell Sage Foundation. Retrieved February 5, 2006, from paa2004.princeton.edu/download.asp?submissionId=40245.

Yee, B. W. K., Huang, L. N., & Lew, A. (1998). Families: Life-span socialization in a cultural context. In L. C. Lee & N. W. Zane (Eds.), *Handbook of Asian American psychology* (pp. 83–135). Thousand Oaks, CA: Sage Publications.

Yin, J., & Young, S. (1997). *The rape of Nanking: An undeniable history in photographs.* Chicago, IL: Innovating Publishing Group.

Yung, J. (2005). *Picture brides.* Retrieved February 7, 2006, from http://college.hmco.com/history/readerscomp/women/html/wh_02600_picturebride.htm.

Zaidi, A. U., & Shuraydi, M. (2002). Perceptions of arranged marriages by young Pakistani Muslim women living in a Western society. *Journal of Family and Comparative Studies, 33*(4), 495–514.

16

Asian American and Pacific Islander Families

BARBARA W. K. YEE, JENNY SU, SU YEONG KIM,
and LORIENA YANCURA

OUTLINE OF CHAPTER

Case Synopsis

John, a 17-year-old Chinese American high school student, was placed on probation after punching another student in the face during an argument at lunch. During a home visit and interview, the school psychologist learned that John has never acted aggressively, was seen as cooperative and somewhat shy, was a straight-A student throughout high school, and an active member of the student council and the school debate team. Given John's congenial personality and excellent academic achievements, his parents were extremely surprised and upset about his aggressive outburst in school. They did not notice any obvious signs of distress in their son prior to this incident and simply could not understand why he could have acted in such an inappropriate way.

Introduction

Asian American and Pacific Islanders (AAPIs) have been described as a "model minority," who are well educated and financially stable, value family relationships and hard work, and exhibit positive behaviors or other attributes. Positive AAPI family characteristics have been identified as important protective factors underlying the development of resiliency among many AAPIs in the United States. An important caveat is that there are wide variations in academic and career advancement, social, health, and family outcomes across AAPI ethnic groups such as Hmong, Cambodian, or Native Hawaiians (Yee, Huang, & Lew, 1998). Positive stereotyping of the AAPI population may lead to ignoring problems that some families face. This chapter reviews how AAPI family strengths are mobilized to protect and diminish risk for family members as they adapt to life's challenges. AAPI families may hide dysfunction behind cultural familial norms that consider family life as private and extremely confidential, which creates increased risk among AAPI families. This chapter highlights cross-cutting family themes and examples of diversity in health and mental health outcomes across AAPI families.

The family literature seeks to understand how families socialize and develop the human capital of younger family members, while nurturing family relationships (i.e., social capital) over the lifespan. Families and schools have been given the responsibility to nurture the development of human capital among children (i.e., enhancement of life skills, knowledge, and abilities). Societies and cultural practices, through families and schools, seek to insure that future actions of its citizens are effective and adaptive. Family relationships may be a primary source of social capital that contributes to resiliency and provides a lifelong source of social support, or they may serve to increase burdens.

This chapter examines how the current status of Asian American and Pacific Islander families can be explained by risk and protective factors seen in the AAPI demographic profile. This chapter will then describe common AAPI family types and that relationship to **acculturation**. Family developmental issues arise during socialization of children and adolescents, in family interactions with adult children, or when caring for frail, elderly family members. This chapter ends by summarizing what we know about Asian and Pacific Islander families and provides supplementary materials to enhance the reader's knowledge of Asian American and Pacific Islander families living in the United States.

Demographic Profile of AAPI Families in the United States

According to the 2000 U.S. Census, there are approximately 2.6 million Asian American and Pacific Islander (AAPI) families living in the United States. The vast majority of families (80.3%) are maintained by married couples and 60% of these families include children younger than 18 years of age. A high percentage of intact and stable AAPI families are a protective social environment for children and adolescents. As Table 16.1 shows, the percentage of larger family households (i.e., those with three or more people) tends to be higher among the AAPI population (3.6 people) than the general U.S. population (3.14) (U.S. Bureau of the Census, 2000).

On average, AAPI families appear highly successful on important protective factors related to a family's socioeconomic status. For example, 42.7% of AAPIs 25 years and over had four or more years of college compared to only 24.4% in the general U.S. population. AAPI families earned a median of $57,874 as compared to family median income of $50,046 for U.S. families in 1999, with a greater number of workers contributing to the AAPI family income. A comparison of median per capita income (see Table 16.1) shows that AAPIs as a group actually earn less than the general U.S. population. AAPI wages have not been commensurate with their higher educational attainment and AAPIs may experience a glass ceiling or racial barriers to positions in the upper echelons of management and leadership (Woo, 2000).

Although AAPIs as a group exceed the U.S. population at the upper educational spectrum, a few AAPI ethnic groups cluster at the bottom. Approximately 60% of Hmong adults 25 years and older, for instance, have less than a high school education, much higher in comparison to the rate of 19.6% for the total U.S. population. As indicated previously, higher education levels do not automatically translate into incomes that are commensurate with level of educational attainment or work history of AAPIs.

Immigration, limited English speaking abilities, and foreign-born status are underlying challenges for many Asian American (AA) and Pacific Islander (PI) families. In the 2000 U.S. Census (Reeves & Bennett, 2004), 69% of all AAs were foreign born, and 79% spoke a language other than English at home with 40% speaking English less than "very well." Many Pacific Islander Americans are native to the United States (Native Hawaiians) or island areas (American Samoa, Guam, Commonwealth of Northern Mariana Islands) and have U.S. citizenship at birth. However, another 42% of PIs are foreign born with significant numbers immigrating between 1990 and 2000 (Harris & Jones, 2005). Forty-four percent of the Pacific Islander population spoke a language other than English at home, with Fijians and Tongans, and Marshallese having the highest limited English proficiency and Natives Hawaiians having the highest English speaking

Table 16.1 Selected Characteristics of Asian Pacific Islander Families Compared to the Total U.S. Average

Characteristics	Asian and Pacific Islander		Total U.S.	
	Number	%	Number	%
Family households	2,616,085	100.0	72,261,780	100.0
Married-couple families	2,124,995	81.2	55,458,451	76.7
Female householder, no spouse present	325,146	12.4	12,500,761	17.3
Male householder, no spouse present	165,944	6.3	4,302,568	6.0
Nonfamily households	899,111	100.0	33,277,342	100.0
Education (persons 25 years and over)	7,351,229	100.0	182,211,639	100.0
Less than high school	1,426,961	19.4	35,715,625	19.6
High school graduates	1,212,080	16.5	52,168,981	28.6
Some college	1,572,645	21.4	49,864,428	27.4
Four or more years of college	3,139,543	42.7	44,462,605	24.4
Number of people in family households	2,616,085	100.0	72,261,780	100.0
Two	694,773	26.6	29,295,526	40.5
Three	632,619	24.2	16,658,604	23.1
Four	655,603	25.1	14,776,948	20.4
Five	333,126	12.7	6,993,101	9.7
Six	169,717	6.5	2,785,740	3.9
Seven or more	130,247	5.0	1,751,861	2.4
Subfamilies[a] in household	3,515,196	100.0	105,539,122	100.0
None	3,319,400	94.4	102,796,354	97.4
One	182,522	5.2	2,652,953	2.5
Two	12,344	0.4	85,071	0.1
Three	859	0.0	4,467	0.0
Four or more	71	0.0	277	0.0
Workers in family in 1999	2,616,085	100.0	72,261,780	100.0
None	188,424	7.2	9,148,427	12.7
One	786,087	30.0	21,981,637	30.4
Two	1,186,995	45.4	32,520,874	45.0
Three or more	454,579	17.4	8,610,842	11.9
Median family income in 1999 (dollars)	57,874		50,046	
Per capita in 1999	20,719		21,587	
Families in poverty in 1999	260,467	10.0	6,620,945	9.2

Source: U.S. Bureau of the Census (2000). *U.S. Census 2000 Summary File 4,* http://www.census.gov/Press-Release/www/2003/SF4.html

[a] Subfamilies: Married couples or a single parent with minor children living in a home maintained by somebody else.

abilities of the Pacific Islander ethnic groups. The demographic characteristics of AAPI ethnic groups portray a wide range of protective and risk family profiles. The following section describes how family values and acculturation may be considered to be risk or protective factors that shape health and mental health outcomes for AAPI families.

Family Values and Acculturation

Some common cultural values are shared by AAPI family members, but the emotional reactions and specific behavioral expressions may be heavily influenced by acculturation. Yee, DeBaryshe, Yuen, Kim, and McCubbin (2006) discuss four cultural themes that appear to be shared by Asian American and Pacific Islander families: **collectivism, relational orientation, familism, and family obligation**. The value of collectivism may be defined as putting the needs of the family as a whole above the needs of its individual members. The value of relational orientation refers to the tendency to define the self in terms of relationships with others instead of focusing on the individual. The value of familism defines the family system as the most important social group that is hierarchical (e.g., men have greater power than women, older over younger family members) and central for culture and society. The value of family obligation refers to strong emotional, physical, and behavioral ties between children and their parents throughout the lifespan. The extent to which AAPI families subscribe to the traditional values of collectivism, relational orientation, familism, and family obligation, and corresponding family behavioral practices will shape the nature and quality of their family relationships.

Immigration and acculturation are challenges for AAPI families, and they differ in their attempts to negotiate acculturation experiences. **Traditional AAPI families** generally speak their native language in the home while practicing traditions and holding values of their heritage culture; they are highly collectivistic; and they adhere to clearly defined positions in the patriarchal family hierarchy based on age, gender, and birth order (Wong, 2002). Placing the needs of the family ahead of one's own desires and ambitions, and showing respect for elders are behaviors that are valued. Any behaviors or emotional expressions that might disrupt familial harmony are discouraged. Traditional families prefer to associate with people from their heritage culture, have limited contact with mainstream U.S. society, are recently arrived, or live in ethnic Asian communities.

Besides traditional AAPI families, there are *assimilated families* and *bicultural families*. **Assimilated AAPI families** generally speak English in the home and live according to the values of mainstream U.S. culture such as adopting an individualistic and egalitarian orientation; they relinquish their ethnic identities, cultural values, and traditions; they seek relationships primarily with Anglo Americans; and they usually disengaged from their ethnic communities. Many assimilated families consist of members who are born and raised in the United States.

Bicultural AAPI families generally speak English and the native Asian language, and affiliate with their ethnic and mainstream American communities. Bicultural families embrace

Table 16.2 Traditional, Assimilated, and Bicultural Family Typology and Examples of Possible Associated Features

	Primary language spoken in the home	Value orientation	Social network
Traditional	Native Asian language	Primarily traditional/ collectivistic	Prefer to associate with other members in their ethnic community; little contact with mainstream U.S. society
Assimilated	English	Primarily mainstream/ individualistic	Prefer to associate with Anglo Americans; little contact with their ethnic community
Bicultural	English and Native Asian language	Uphold both traditional and mainstream values; able to shift values according to social context	Affiliates with both ethnic community and mainstream American society

aspects of their heritage culture and the mainstream U.S. culture, and adopt behaviors and values that are integral features of American life, while striving to maintain the values and traditions of their ethnic heritage. With the ability to shift their values and behaviors according to the situational and cultural context, members of bicultural families can function effectively at home and in the outside world. Family relationships are typically more egalitarian than those of traditional families, but the extent to which it is revealed in public depends on whether they are in or outside of their ethnic community. Bicultural families tend to have larger households than assimilated families but smaller ones than traditional families. Most bicultural families consist of immigrant parents who are well-acculturated or American-born Asians who were raised in traditional families. The following section discusses important developmental tasks and challenges faced by AAPI families over the lifespan.

AAPI Family Development Over the Lifespan

Young Families

As the United States becomes increasingly diverse, there is more interest in how children from diverse backgrounds grow, develop, and adjust to life's challenges. Asian children are an important segment of this group, as the high migration rate of Asian families to America is likely to continue into the future (White, Fong, & Cai, 2003).

Developmental Issues in the Study of Asian American Children   An important developmental issue for children and their families is school achievement and academic performance. Asian parents emphasize the importance of children's high academic performance, and socialize children about the honor and respect that high academic performance brings to the family (Chen, Liu, & Li, 2000). For immigrant parents, a chief reason for migrating to the United States is to provide educational opportunities for their children (Min, 1995) and so these children are pressured to succeed. Under these circumstances, if students perform poorly in school, it meant that parents' investment and sacrifices for their children was not fruitful (Fuligni & Yoshikawa, 2004). Asian parents highly value and regard educational attainment as a way to achieve social mobility and economic security (Song & Glick, 2004; Sue & Okazaki, 1990).

Another significant developmental issue for Asian American families is how they deal with the socio-emotional problems experienced by their children. Asian children in the United States report higher levels of depressive symptoms than both White and other minority adolescents (Bankston & Zhou, 2002). At the same time, Asian students may be less likely to receive services for emotional problems because they are perceived as model minorities without problems (Chang & Sue, 2003). This gap between higher incidence of depression and underutilization of mental health services suggests that Asian American families are trying to handle these issues within the family. This may create high family stress and poor mental health outcomes for Asian American children. The following section will discuss a primary family relationship—the relationship between parents and their children.

Parenting   Parents are the primary socializers of their children (Collins, Maccoby, Steinberg, Hetherington, & Bornstein, 2000). **Authoritarian** and **authoritative** parenting styles are the most widely studied parenting constructs (Baumrind & Black, 1967). Authoritative parents are affectionate with their children, but firm in their disciplinary practices (Baumrind & Black, 1967). Authoritarian parents discipline their children with a set of standards, they emphasize respect for authority and order, and discourage democratic exchanges between the parent and child (Baumrind & Black, 1967). Authoritative parenting is associated with fewer depressive symptoms, while authoritarian parenting is associated with more depressive symptoms in Asian

American (Kim & Ge, 2000) and European American adolescents (Steinberg, Mounts, Lamborn, & Dornbusch, 1991). The relationship between parenting style and depression is consistent for Asian and European adolescents. While authoritative parenting is associated with higher academic achievement for European American adolescents (Dornbusch, Ritter, Leiderman, Roberts, & Fraleigh, 1987), this is not the case for Asian Americans (Chao, 1994). According to Ruth Chao (2001), this may be because parental warmth and closeness plays a negligible role in the academic performance of Asian American children, in contrast to its importance for European Americans adolescents. Acculturation may lessen this difference.

Culture and Parenting   Ruth Chao (1994) sought to explain why authoritative parenting was not related to the level of academic achievement by Asian American children. Parenting may vary across cultures. Chinese parents may endorse *"guan" or* a **training** parental style in which

children are expected to follow a standard of conduct. It resembles, but may be distinct from, the authoritarian parental style. "Training" is accomplished through the Chinese parental role as teachers of acceptable behavior with expressions of parental devotion and sacrifices to support the child. Academic success is viewed as a positive reflection of successful "training" by parents and helps to explain the academic successes of children who have Asian immigrant parents.

Ruth Chao (1995) also notes that cultural values shape parenting goals. Specifically, Asian American parents emphasize the collective value of school success as a positive reflection of the family, while European American parents emphasize individual well-being and development of a high level of self-esteem in their children. According to Lieber, Nihira, and Mink (2004), a major challenge confronting immigrant parents of Asian American adolescents is the need to modify some traditional values, such as **filial piety** in the new host country, yet they believe in the importance of teaching their children other traditional values.

Parenting by Mothers and Fathers   Asian children are more likely to have immigrant parents (88%), than White (18%) or Hispanic (65%) children in the United States (U. S. Census, 2001), and this has a profound influence on Asian American family life. Upon migration, Asian women typically gain more economic independence, while the opposite is true for men in Asian immigrant households (Espiritu, 1999). The traditional patriarchal role of fathers as breadwinners is more difficult to achieve after migration (Pessar, 2003).

Parke et al. (2004) suggested that fathers' disciplinary strategies, although more infrequent, are more intense and shown to be more influential than mothers' parenting. Asian immigrant fathers appear to exert a stronger influence than mothers in the development of children's depressive symptoms (Kim, Gonzales, Stroh, & Wang, 2006). Culture influences the parenting role in which fathers and mothers have distinct family roles and contribute in different ways to the development of Asian American children.

Sibling Relationships in AAPI Families   Parents play a central role in the socialization of life skills and family support network in AAPI families. Siblings may have another vital role in the socialization of younger siblings because older siblings are the first peers that children encounter. Although siblings provide a source of conflict and sibling rivalry, they can be a great source of support and comfort over a lifetime. For instance, sibling relationships allow younger siblings to

practice and sharpen social skills, while nurturing the emotional relationships between family members. These skills and role modeling enhance younger siblings' ability to adapt and function in important social spheres over the life course.

Birth order appears to influence the acculturation level of siblings in Vietnamese and Korean American families (Pyke, 2005). First-born siblings are afforded higher status, are disciplinarians to younger siblings, and have more traditional viewpoints and behaviors that are closer to those of their parents than younger siblings. Pyke (2005) described first-born and older siblings as "generational deserters and black sheep" because they differed from more acculturated younger siblings. Pyke (2005) argued that diversity in acculturation across siblings may enhance a family's ability to adapt in new cultural environments. Younger acculturated siblings expressed relief when older siblings accepted the traditional family obligations, felt that older siblings provided help when needed, viewed their older siblings as mediators between their traditional parents and themselves, and appreciated when family traditions were maintained by older siblings. Younger, more acculturated siblings served as an effective bridge to the mainstream American culture. Although the different acculturation levels within and across generations may be a source of family tension, it may also serve an adaptive function for immigrant families. Given that sibling relationships may be one of the longest family relationships that humans have, more research must examine this important family relationship.

Families in the Middle

Asian and Pacific Islander cultures endorse the value of family interdependence and this value systematically impacts the AAPI family environment across the lifespan. Unlike their European American counterparts, AAs are socialized to consider intergenerational support and dependence—whether emotional, instrumental, or financial—as lifelong obligations (Fuligni, Tseng, & Lam, 1999). In traditional Asian cultures, parents believe that they have the responsibility to offer their children protection and guidance throughout their lifetime. The children, in turn, are expected to repay their parents by assisting their family and fulfilling their filial duties as obedient sons or daughters (Ho, 1992). Although these mutual obligations reinforce collective values and help foster family solidarity and interdependence, family obligations may be a source of persistent intergenerational conflict within AA families.

Equipped with greater facility of the English language and better understanding of U.S. cultural norms, children living in AA immigrant families often become the primary caretaker of the family. As children become older, they bear heavier burdens in handling interpersonal interactions on behalf of their parents in the English speaking world. As the family's cultural broker, they spend a lot of time on family affairs, and therefore have fewer opportunities to engage in autonomous activities such as socializing with peers or participating in extracurricular events compared to their peers (Tseng, 2004).

AA parents often rely on their children to be responsible for household duties, such as taking care of younger siblings and paying bills. This situation may create **role reversals** within the family (Kibria, 1993). Role reversals may challenge traditional family roles or the balance of power within immigrant families (Zhou, 1997). Parents and older family members rely on the younger generation to help the family cope with the logistics of daily living and everyday survival in the American society. AA parents who are lacking in acculturative resources, such as English skills or knowledge about American ways, and exclusively depend on younger family members find that their parental authority is diminished and there is an erosion of elderly centered Confucian family values. In some cases, the power and status acquired by children may even lead to being disrespectful toward their parents and members of older generations who remain traditional, less fluent in English, and less familiar with the mainstream American way of life (Ho, Rasheed, & Rasheed, 2004).

Aside from shifts in family roles, tension arises between older and younger generations when AA adolescents begin to seek autonomy and freedom from parental control. Traditionally, AA parents tend to exercise a great deal of control over their children. Close supervision not only allows parents to guard the safety of their children, it is also considered by AA parents as a way to communicate their care and affection to their children (Uba, 1994). Unfortunately, many AA children who grew up among mainstream American values do not understand this and instead see their parents as overly protective and controlling.

Asian American young adults are still expected, by older more traditional family members, to obey parental authority and to prioritize family obligations over personal choice (Fuligni & Pedersen, 2002). During the college years, as AA young adult children are exposed to more Western values and ideals, the cultural schism between the generations may grow. While living away at college, it is more difficult for parents to monitor their children's daily activities. However, many AA parents continue to provide strong parental guidance over their children's academic and social affairs, such as decisions over course selection or college major, dating, and potential marriage partners.

AA college students not only face increased pressure to excel academically, but they may be compelled to major in culturally sanctioned fields—namely medicine, science, or business— because these careers are perceived to be most economically viable and socially rewarding by the family. In some cases, decisions to pursue careers that have been rejected by their AA parents would subject young adult children to loss of financial and emotional support (Wong & Mock, 1997). Sadly, many AA young adult children may relinquish their personal career desires and life ambitions in order to comply with their parents' wishes and authority.

Asian American and Pacific Islander Dating and Marriage

Academic and career pursuits may create intergenerational tension, but they are by no means the only sources of conflict for AA families with adult children. Another source of stress comes from dating and marital preferences of the younger generation.

Cultural scripts and acculturation shape who may be considered an eligible marriage partner, marital role expectations, or whether marriage results from romance or other factors such as family or financial status of the potential marital partner. An examination of marriage and divorce in AAPI families reveals extensive cultural variations in contemporary society.

Romantic attachment is the primary reason behind the selection of a marital partner in contemporary Western society. This creates a dilemma for recent immigrants whose culture may consider financial situation, family status, or continuity of family lineage to be a major reason underlying selection of a marriage partner. For example, second-generation Muslim Pakistani American women may want to select a husband based upon romantic attraction, but feel ambivalent or conflicted because family traditions exert enormous pressure to marry a mate who had been selected by the family elders (Zaidi & Shuraydi, 2002). Interracial mate selection has been used as an indicator of racial discrimination and acculturation, but mate selection is the result of ethnic composition and availability of potential mates in the surrounding community (Fujino, 2000). Interethnic marriages were encouraged and fostered in the Native Hawaiian community to address the alarming decline in the Hawaiian population by Western-introduced diseases in the late 1800s and for political reasons (McCubbin & McCubbin, 2005). In contemporary society, acculturated AAPIs may be more willing to choose partners outside their own race (non-Asian) and among other AAPI ethnic groups than are their less-acculturated peers (Aguirre, Saenz, & Hwang, 1995).

Marital satisfaction is largely a function of spousal agreement on gender roles and marital expectations, both of which are highly influenced by culture (Lebra, 1976). Marital conflicts and tensions may arise as a result of differences in culture, gender, and marital role expectations; disapproval of the marriage from the family of origin; or intrusiveness of in-laws in the family unit (Inman, Altman, & Kaduvettoor, 2004).

Information on marital violence in AAPI families is both scant and contradictory (Malley-Morrison & Hines, 2004). National and statewide studies of victimization and domestic violence rarely report statistics for AAPI. National self-reported rates in domestic violence were lowest for both AAPI women (15%) and AAPI men (3%). By contrast, the Asian and Pacific Islander Institute on Domestic Violence (Kim, 2005) finds that studies with smaller AAPI subgroup community samples show rates as high as 80% and suggest that Japanese, Vietnamese, and South Asian women are most at risk for domestic violence. Many AAPI groups define abuse in a way that excludes emotional maltreatment. Cultural values such as patriarchy, or encouraging forbearance and saving face, as well as demographic characteristics such as linguistic isolation and refugee status, may be responsible for the widely disparate reported rates or poor detection of domestic violence in AAPI families. To date, no studies have examined whether family interdependence tends to reduce the risk of violence in AAPI families (e.g., closely connected family members may intervene when abuse is threatened) or increase the risk (e.g., family members avoid seeking help from outsiders). AAPI families can be an important source of protection or a source of risk, such as hidden domestic violence.

Older Families

As discussed throughout this chapter, there is much diversity across Asian American and Pacific Islander families. Yee, DeBaryshe, Yuen, Kim, and McCubbin (2006) discuss four cultural themes that are reflected in the adaptation and coping mechanisms of AAPI families: collectivism, relational orientation, familism, and family obligation. This section will discuss how these cultural themes are woven into several AAPI family caregiving scenarios.

Collectivism is practiced by older women in AAPI families by doing unpaid household work to enhance their family well-being. Many Chinese American and Korean American elderly women move to the United States to take care of their grandchildren so their daughters or daughters-in-law can work in family businesses (Yoon, 2005). Older AAPI individuals are family resources because they contribute valued household or babysitting services, but they also can drain the resources of the family during illness or disability.

Relational orientation concerns the perception and treatment of vulnerable family members. In Native Hawaiian families, the health of the family depends upon the health of each of its members. Caring for a frail, elderly family member is an expression of family interdependence and a natural part of the life cycle (McCubbin, McCubbin, Thompson, & Thompson, 1998). Therefore decisions to place a family member in a long-term care facility or use government assistance do not make sense and are rarely made except as a last resort. Familism is expressed by the relatively high rates of intergenerational households among AAPI, as compared to White families (Simmons & O'Neill, 2001). From 20% to 40% of Asian Americans aged 55 or older lived in the same household as their children, compared to 4.5% of non-Hispanic Whites (Kamo, 1998). Immigrants who do not speak English fluently and are at least 60 years old when they move to the United States are more likely to live with family members (Wilmoth, 2001). Japanese immigrants are less likely than immigrants from China, Taiwan, or India to live with family members.

A family obligation value puts family concerns before one's own needs. This value is often expressed as filial piety and has similar terms across Asian languages: *xiao* in Mandarin Chinese, *haau* in Cantonese, *oya koko* in Japanese, and *hieu thao* in Vietnamese. In traditional Asian societies, adult children were expected to provide care for their aging parents when they became too frail to take care of themselves.

In this country, behavioral expressions of family obligation and filial piety are influenced by acculturation and may be a source of intergenerational conflict (Asai & Kameoka, 2005; Wang & Gallagher-Thompson, 2005). The responsibility to provide care for aging parents is not held as strongly by mainstream American culture; nearly three-fourths (73%) of AAPI adults believe that it is their children's responsibility to care for aging parents, while less than half of all Americans (49%) endorse the same belief (AARP, 2003).

Grandparenting The relationship between grandparents and their grandchildren is an important, but understudied family relationship. Slightly over one-third of all Asian American respondents over age 65 reported that they looked after their grandchildren (Asian American Federation of New York, as cited in Yoon, 2005). Asian American grandparents have a high degree of involvement in the lives of their grandchildren. Anecdotal evidence from AAPI students at the University of Hawaii suggests that Asian American grandparents stay very involved in the upbringing of their grandchildren by doing such things as cooking their meals or taking them to and from school.

There are different patterns of co-residence within AAPI families. Upward co-residence occurs where the grandparents move into the household of the middle generation. Upward co-residence is typical for the majority of Asian cultures, especially among recent immigrants such as Vietnamese American families. Downward co-residence occurs where the grandchildren and their parents move into the grandparents' already established household. Downward co-residence is more typical of Japanese Americans, who immigrated to the United States earlier than other Asian cultures (Kamo, 1998).

There are also differences between the grandparents and their grandchildren on immigration status. Some AAPI grandchildren living in the United States do not have regular contact with their grandparents because their grandparents are still living in another country. Differences in acculturation status may also influence the relationship between grandparents and their grandchildren. Grandparents who identify with traditional value systems might be perceived as cold

and distant by their more acculturated grandchildren. A recent survey of Chinese American and Korean American immigrant grandparents found that 48.5% felt that they had cultural differences with their grandchildren and 41.6% felt that language barriers adversely influenced their communication with their grandchildren (Yoon, 2005). However this generation gap due to immigrant status might not apply to Japanese American grandparents because they are the least likely of any API group to be immigrants (Kamo, 1998).

Caring for Older Family Members   The values of relational obligation and familism figure in the care that many Asian American families give for frail and elderly members. Asian American families are twice as likely as White families to provide care for relatives aged 50 and over, instead of relying on formal services. For many families from cultures where it is traditional for young couples to live with the male's family, this duty falls on the daughters-in-law, who are expected to take care of older members of their husband's family (Lee & Sung, 1998). Differences in expectations of filial piety by older versus younger generations can be a source of stress in AAPI families.

Intergenerational conflict is not uncommon in Japanese American (Braun & Browne, 1998) and Chinese American (Kane & Houston-Vega, 2004) families. It may result from differences between the generations in acculturation to mainstream American values. An example of intergenerational conflict is provided by a case study of an acculturated and college-educated Chinese American woman who works full time and comes home to clean and cook for her frail mother and her elderly retired father. Her parents will not to eat leftovers or take-out food, because they feel it is not healthy. Her father is able to cook, but will not do so because he feels it is the daughter's duty to cook (Wang & Gallagher-Thompson, 2005). This situation is a source of stress for both generations who have different views of the value of family obligation.

High levels of intergenerational conflict, as well as feelings of guilt when they cannot provide the high level of care that their older family members expect, may be possible reasons why many Asian American caregivers show symptoms of depression. Asian American caregivers have been shown to be more depressed and less healthy than their non-Hispanic White counterparts (Pinquart & Sörensen, 2005). Poor physical health may be due to the tendency for many individuals of Asian descent to somaticize emotional distress (McDermott, Tseng, & Maretzki, 1980). It might be easier for caregivers to admit to experiencing physical ailments than to admit having shameful emotional difficulties in caring for an older family member.

Feelings that it is their responsibility to provide care might also help to explain why Asian American families who are caring for older relatives are less likely to reach out to formal community services. As a whole, caregivers from Asian cultures rely on help from inside their network of family and friends, and not on community resources (Pinquart & Sörensen, 2005). This self-reliance may be due to several factors: cultural beliefs that care should be provided by the family, difficulties in accessing services, or language barriers (Dilworth-Anderson, Williams, & Gibson, 2002). Another barrier to formal service use might be cost, which may be especially prohibitive for Southeast Asians, such as Cambodians and Hmong, because they have the lowest median incomes of all Asian groups (Reeves & Bennett, 2004).

Summary

The experiences, issues, and challenges of AAPI families are vastly different based on the family's ethnic background. In this review of Asian American and Pacific Islander families, evidence suggests that a subset of AAPI families comes close to a model minority, however there is great diversity across AA and PI families, across generation, historical time, and through acculturation. Cultural values of collectivism, relational orientation, familism, and family obligation influence how families and individual family members relate to each other. Acculturation influences how these cultural values shape feelings, family behavior, and expectations.

Family members are challenged by developmental tasks and stressors that may result in an increase of family tensions. The focus of much family research examines how families cope with these normative (e.g., school transitions and adolescent transitions) and non-normative life events (e.g., divorce, migration); however, more family research must examine these processes for AAPI families. A primary function of parents is to socialize their children in the acquisition of important knowledge, life skills, and development of social capital. This is a more complex task for AAPI parents in a new cultural environment. Young AA families train children for achievement, but it is unknown whether these relationships will generalize to PI families. Siblings help to socialize younger family members, and varying acculturation levels across sibling birth order may be an adaptive strategy developed by immigrant families to cope with a foreign culture. Family expectations and demands are greater among AA college students than European American students, and may delay the adolescents' individuation from the family. Culture also shapes who may be considered an eligible dating and marital partner, marital role expectations, and basis for marriage. Through high rates of intergenerational living, AAPI grandparents contribute important household and babysitting services to their families. Through strong AAPI family obligation and familism, AAPI families provide much care for family members needing medical or home-care assistance. Through acculturation, the specific behavioral expression of filial care may shift from daily hands and around-the-clock care to use of professional services when needed.

As the outcome trajectories of Asian American families show divergent paths that vary by ethnicity, findings that are observed in one group may not necessary generalize to another (Glick & White, 2004). This means that family research conducted primarily on East Asian American groups in the United States may not generalize to Pacific Islander groups such as Native Hawaiians or Micronesians in the United States. Moreover, not all people and families internalize cultural values in the same manner or to the same extent. This in turn can be a source of family variability across Asian American and Pacific Islander American communities.

Discussion Questions

1. In your family, who was most influential in your socialization? Was this person also the family disciplinarian? How much did this person affect your social, cognitive, and emotional development?
2. How much did you interact with extended family members? What was your relationship with each member?
3. During your childhood and adolescence, what kinds of family traditions or activities taught you important cultural values?
4. Think back to your childhood and adolescence. What types of conflict with your family did you experience? How old were you when these conflicts first emerged? Did any of them persist into college? Do you still experience some of these family conflicts today?
5. What do you think are the main causes for these family conflicts?
6. How did you cope with these conflicts? What were the most and least helpful strategies you used to deal with them?

Case Study

Many AA young adults are connected with their family, but struggle to balance parental expectations with the need for autonomy. High familial expectations may create undue stress on young adult children, and create feelings of guilt and shame if they fail to meet their parents' expectations. The lack of verbal encouragement for achievement from parents may result in children feeling that their efforts are not acknowledged. To illustrate the intergenerational struggles commonly experienced by Asian American young adults, we will now shift to the case study described at the beginning of the chapter. We will also provide an example of how a therapist works with the complex issues presented by this Asian American client.

John, a 17-year-old Chinese American high school student, was referred to therapy for punching a student at school. John came from a lower-middle-class Chinese immigrant family. As the oldest child in the family, he was frequently asked to take care of his younger siblings and do household chores after school. John usually did not mind these family responsibilities. He believed that having these family responsibilities helped him in his schoolwork. Doing well in school was regarded by his parents as an important vehicle for success in life.

After a few individual therapy sessions, the therapist believed that John's aggressive behavior at school was a way to relieve frustration that he had toward his parents. John told the therapist that his parents wanted him to be the best at everything, but never acknowledged his effort. The therapy sessions were conducted in English because John felt more comfortable describing his thoughts and feelings in English. As John began identifying sources of stress and describing his relationship with his parents, he realized that he was struggling to be a good Chinese son. Although he wanted to have greater control over his life, he was fearful of disappointing his parents.

The therapist recommended bringing his parents into the therapeutic process. Feeling highly responsible for their child's aggression at school, John's parents agreed. They were surprised to learn that their son did not feel their pride in his accomplishments in school and admitted that, unlike "American" parents, they rarely praise or compliment their children. They explained that most Chinese do not express their approval and affection to their children directly. By opening the dialogue between John and his parents, the therapist helped John to understand the cultural context of his struggle.

Case Study Discussion Questions

For undergraduate students, please consider the following questions:

1. What are your initial reactions to this case study?
2. What are your thoughts or reactions when John said that his parents did not acknowledge his achievements? How may this relate to your own experiences?
3. What do you think about the therapist's approach in working with John? Do you think it is a good idea to invite his parents to therapy?

For graduate students and/or beginning therapists, please consider the following questions:

1. What do you see are the most challenging issues presented in this case?
2. What are your views pertaining to the roles of parents and children that are relevant to this case? How might your values affect your work with John?
3. When working with Asian American immigrant parents and their children, how could therapists respect the cultural values of each generation and at the same time help to decrease the amount of intergenerational conflict?

Key Terms

Acculturation: The process of adapting to a new culture that is different from the culture of origin.

Assimilated AAPI families: AAPI families in which its members disengage from their ethnic culture and adopt the values, norms, and beliefs of the mainstream U.S. culture.

Authoritarian parenting: Disciplining children with a set of standards that emphasize respect for authority and order and discourage democratic exchanges between the parent and child.

Authoritative parenting: Authoritative parents are affectionate with their children but firm in their disciplinary practices.

Bicultural AAPI families: AAPI families in which its members identify with values, norms, and beliefs of both their ethnic group and the mainstream U.S. culture; the bicultural family interacts with both cultures and integrates the two into its daily practices.

Collectivism: In terms of AAPI families, when individual members place the needs of their families above their individual needs.

Familism: The family value placing the family at the center of the social system and specifying its hierarchical structure.

Family obligation: A family value underlying strong emotional ties between children and their parents throughout the lifespan.

Filial piety: The notion of respect and responsibility for care of older family members, often reflected in responsibility for their care.

Relational orientation: A tendency to define the self in terms of one's relationships with others instead of attributes of the individual.

Role reversal: A process in which many critical roles traditionally assigned to parents are given to the children. In the case of immigrant families, role reversal occurs because children acculturate faster than their parents, which often undermines traditional authority that parents have over their children.

Traditional AAPI families: AAPI families in which its members identify strongly with their ethnic group's values, norms, and beliefs; there is little desire to adopt the values and practices of the mainstream U.S. culture.

Training: An indigenous style of Asian American parenting described by Ruth K. Chao (1994) that emphasizes parental teachings, devotion, and sacrifice to promote child success.

For Further Learning and Suggested Readings

Classroom Exercises in Small Groups

Case Study for Small Group Discussion (Adapted from Neufeld et al., 2002)   Mary and her husband came from Hong Kong at 30 years of age. For 5 years, she has been looking after her husband, who has Alzheimer's disease, high blood pressure, and diabetes. Although Mary has three adult children, she and her husband live by themselves. She would like her children to spend more time taking care of her husband because her health is not good. Besides, she believes that taking care of elderly parents is the job of adult children. However, her children say that they are very busy in their work. Her children have suggested sending their father to a nursing home. Mary is very angry at this suggestion. Mary, like many other immigrant women, said that she would like to get more services for her husband. However, she can speak only Cantonese and doesn't know much about health care in the United States.

Case study for small group discussion questions

1. What API family values are represented by this scenario?
2. What is the source of the intergenerational conflict in this case?
3. What types of assistance do you think Mary would be willing to accept in caring for her husband?
4. What are some possible barriers to Mary's acceptance of outside services?
5. What would you do if you were one of Mary's children or grandchildren?

Please organize students in groups of three to four and have them discuss the following questions:

1. What was your mother's or father's predominant style of parenting? What were the differences between your mother and father?
2. Are there any findings presented that surprises you?
3. If you are an Asian American, how similar or different are the descriptions of Asian American families and relationship from your own families?
4. How would you design a study to elucidate the inconsistent findings about the role of parenting on adolescent outcomes among children of Asian Americans?
5. What would be the advantage or disadvantage of designing a study that samples various Asian American ethnic groups?
6. What would be the advantage or disadvantage of designing a study that includes a sample of European Americans?
7. What would be the advantage or disadvantage of designing a study that samples Asian groups outside of the U.S.?

Create Your Family Genogram The family genogram is a pictorial representation of all the members of a family over several generations. It is a tool used by counselors and therapists for understanding intergenerational relationships and structures. Follow the three steps below to complete your own family genogram.

Step 1: Draw a family tree to map the structure of your family (see Figure 16.1 for a sample of a family genogram). Include all members in your family over at least three generations. Use squares to represent males and circles to represent females. If a person is deceased, put an "X" through the square or circle. For example:

☐ Male Family member   ☒ Deceased male family member

◯ Female family member   ⊗ Deceased female family member

☐ ◯ You

Step 2: Add information about each person by including their age, year of death (if applicable), family immigration history (e.g., voluntary immigrants vs. refugees), and generation status (e.g., first generation).

Step 3: Use the following lines to illustrate patterns of relationships among family members.

═══════════ Strong relationship

- - - - - - - - - - - - - Weak relationship

∨∨∨∨∨∨∨ Conflicted relationship

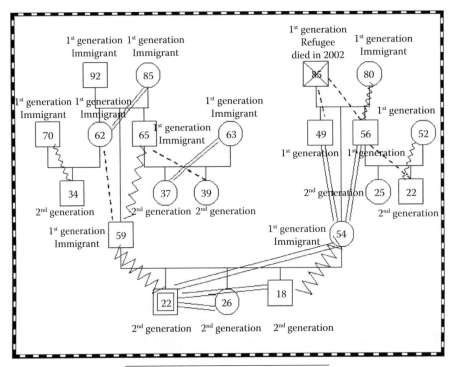

Figure 16.1 A three-generation family genogram.

Suggested Books, Movies, and Television Programs

Books

Fiction
In Full Bloom by Caroline Hwang
Mona in the Promised Land by Gish Jen
The Joy Luck Club by Amy Tan

Nonfiction
Leong, F. T. L., Inman, A. G., Ebreo, A., Yang, L. H., Kinoshita, L., & Fu, M. (Eds.). (2007). *Handbook of Asian American psychology* (2nd ed.). Thousand Oaks, CA: Sage Publications.

Movies

Better Luck Tomorrow (2002): Asian American youth delinquency
Bride & Prejudice (2004): marriage in Indian family
Grace Lee Project (2005): Asian American stereotypes
The Joy Luck Club (1994): Chinese American family
The Wedding Banquet (1994): marriage in Asian American culture

Television Programs
Gilmore Girls (depicts a Korean American family)

References

AARP (2003). Lean on me: *Support and minority outreach for grandparents raising grandchildren*. [Electronic Version]. Washington, DC: AARP.
Aguirre, B. E., Saenz, R., & Hwang, S. (1995). Remarriage and intermarriage of Asians in the United States of America. *Journal of Comparative Family Studies, 26*, 207–215.

Asai, M. O., & Kameoka, V. A. (2005).The influence of sekentei on family caregiving and underutilization of social services among Japanese caregivers. *Social Work, 50*(2), 110–118.

Bankston, C. L., & Zhou, M. (2002). Being well vs. doing well: Self-esteem and school performance among immigrant and nonimmigrant racial and ethnic groups. *International Migration Review, 36*, 389–415.

Baumrind, D., & Black, A. E. (1967). Socialization practices associated with dimensions of competence in preschool boys and girls. *Child Development, 38*, 291–327.

Braun, K. L., & Browne, C. V. (1998). Perceptions of dementia, caregiving, and help seeking among Asian and Pacific Islander Americans. *Health & Social Work, 23*(4), 262–274.

Chang, D. F., & Sue, S. (2003). The effects of race and problem type on teachers' assessments of student behavior. *Journal of Consulting and Clinical Psychology, 71*, 235–242.

Chao, R. K. (1994). Beyond parental control and authoritarian parenting style: Understanding Chinese parenting through the cultural notion of training. *Child Development, 65*, 1111–1119.

Chao, R. K. (1995). Chinese and European American cultural models of the self reflected in mothers' childrearing beliefs. *Ethos, 23*, 328–354.

Chao, R. K. (2001). Extending research on the consequences of parenting style for Chinese Americans and European Americans. *Child Development, 72*, 1832–1843.

Chen, X., Liu, M., & Li, D. (2000). Parental warmth, control, and indulgence and their relations to adjustment in Chinese children: A longitudinal study. *Journal of Family Psychology, 14*, 401–419.

Collins, W. A., Maccoby, E. E., Steinberg, L., Hetherington, E. M., & Bornstein, M. H. (2000). Contemporary research on parenting: The case for nature and nurture. *American Psychologist, 55*, 218–232.

Dilworth-Anderson, P., Williams, I. C., & Gibson, B. E. (2002). Issues of race, ethnicity, and culture in caregiving research: A 20-year review (1980-2000). *Gerontologist, 42*(2), 237–272.

Dornbusch, S. M., Ritter, P. L., Leiderman, P. H., Roberts, D. F., & Fraleigh, M. J. (1987). The relation of parenting style to adolescent school performance. *Child Development, 58*, 1244–1257.

Espiritu, Y. L. (1999). Gender and labor in Asian immigrant families. *American Behavioral Scientist, 42*, 628–647.

Fujino, D. (2000). Structural and individual influences affecting racialized dating relationships. In J. L. Chin (Ed.), *Relationship among Asian American women* (pp. 181–209). Washington, DC: American Psychological Association.

Fuligni, A. J., & Pedersen, S. (2002). Family obligation and the transition to young adulthood. *Developmental Psychology, 38*, 856–868.

Fuligni, A. J., Tseng, V., & Lam, M. (1999). Attitudes toward family obligations among American adolescents with Asian, Latin American, and European backgrounds. *Child Development, 70*, 1030–1044.

Fuligni, A. J., & Yoshikawa, H. (2004). Investments in children among immigrant families. In A. Kalil & T. C. DeLeire (Eds.), *Family investments in children's potential: Resources and parenting behaviors that promote success* (pp. 139–162). Mahwah, NJ: Lawrence Erlbaum Associates.

Glick, J. E., & White, M. J. (2004). Post-secondary school participation of immigrant and native youth: The role of familial resources and educational expectations. *Social Science Research, 33*, 272–299.

Harris, P. M., & Jones, N. A. (2005, August). *We the people: Pacific Islanders in the United States.* Census 2000 Special Report (CENSR-26). Washington DC: U.S. Census. Retrieved May 20, 2006, from the U.S. Census home page: http://www.census.gov.prod/2005pubs/censr-26.pdf.

Ho, M. K. (1992). *Minority children and adolescents in therapy.* Newbury Park, CA: Sage Publications.

Ho, M. K., Rasheed, J. M., & Rasheed, M. N. (2004). *Family therapy with ethnic minorities* (2nd ed.). Thousand Oaks, CA: Sage Publications.

Inman, A. G., Altman, A., & Kaduvettoor, A. (2004, April). *South Asian interracial marriages and marital satisfaction.* Poster session presented at the annual meeting of the American Counseling Association, Kansas City, MO.

Kamo, Y. (1998). Asian grandparents. In M. E. Szinovacz (Ed.), *Handbook on grandparenthood* (pp. 97–112). Westport, CT: Greenwood.

Kane, M. N., & Houston-Vega, M. K. (2004). Maximizing content on elders with dementia while teaching multicultural diversity. *Journal of Social Work Education, 40*(2), 285–303.

Kibria, N. (1993). *Family tightrope: The changing lives of Vietnamese Americans.* Princeton, NJ: Princeton University Press.

Kim, M. (2005, March). *The community engagement continuum: Outreach, mobilization, organizing and accountability to address violence against women in Asian and Pacific Islander Communities.* Asian and Pacific Islander Institute on Domestic Violence. Retrieved May 20, 2006, from http://www.apiahf.org/apidvinstitute/ResearchAndPolicy/publications.htm

Kim, S. Y., & Ge, X. (2000). Parenting practices and adolescent depressive symptoms in Chinese American families. *Journal of Family Psychology, 14,* 420–435.

Kim, S. Y., Gonzales, N. A., Stroh, K., & Wang, J. J.-L. (2006). Parent-child cultural marginalization and depressive symptoms among Asian American family members. *Journal of Community Psychology, 34,* 167–182.

Lebra, T. S. (1976). *Japanese patterns of behavior.* Honolulu: University of Hawaii Press.

Lee, Y., & Sung, K. (1998). Cultural influences on caregiving burden: Cases of Koreans and Americans. *International Journal of Aging & Human Development, 46*(2), 125–141.

Lieber, E., Nihira, K., & Mink, I. T. (2004). Filial piety, modernization, and the challenges of raising children for Chinese immigrants: Quantitative and qualitative evidence. *Ethos, 32,* 324–347.

Malley-Morrison, K., & Hines, D.A. (2004) *Family violence in cultural perspective: Defining understanding and combating abuse.* Thousand Oaks, CA: Sage Publications.

McCubbin, E. A., Thompson, A. I., & Fromer, J. E. (Eds.), *Resiliency in Native American and immigrant families* (pp. 3–48). Thousand Oaks, CA: Sage Publications.

McCubbin, H. I., McCubbin, M. A., Thompson, A. I., & Thompson, E. A. (1998). Resilience in ethnic families: A conceptual model for predicting family adjustment and adaptation. In H. I. McCubbin, E. A. Thompson, A. I. Thompson, & J. E. Fromer (Eds.), *Resiliency in Native American and immigrant families* (pp. 3–48). Thousand Oaks, CA: Sage.

McCubbin, & H. McCubbin (2005). Culture and ethnic identity in family resilience: Dynamic processes in trauma and transformation of indigenous people. In M. Unger (Ed.), *Pathways to resilience* (pp. 27–44). Thousand Oaks, CA, Sage Publications.

McDermott, J. F., Tseng, W., & Maretzki, T. W. (1980). *People and cultures of Hawaii: A psychocultural profile.* Honolulu: University Press of Hawaii.

Min, P. G. (1995). *Asian Americans: Contemporary trends and issues.* Thousand Oaks, CA: Sage Publications.

Neufeld, A. (2002). Immigrant women: Making connections to community resources for support in family caregiving. *Qualitative Health Research, 12*(6), 751–768.

Parke, R. D., Coltrane, S., Duffy, S., Buriel, R., Dennis, J., Powers, J., et al. (2004). Economic stress, parenting, and child adjustment in Mexican American and European American families. *Child Development, 75,* 1632–1656.

Pessar, P. R. (2003). Engendering migration studies: The case of new immigrants in the United States. In P. Hondagneu-Sotelo (Ed.), *Gender and U.S. immigration: Contemporary trends* (pp. 20–42). Berkeley, CA: University of California Press.

Pinquart, M., & Sörensen, S. (2005). Ethnic differences in stressors, resources, and psychological outcomes of family caregiving: A meta-analysis. *Gerontologist, 45*(1), 90–106.

Pyke, K. (2005). "Generational deserters" and "black sheep": Acculturative differences among siblings in Asian immigrant families. *Journal of Family Issues, 26,* 491–517.

Reeves, T. J., & Bennett, C. E. (2004, December). *We the people: Asians in the United States.* Census 2000 Special Report (CENSR-17). Washington, DC: U.S. Census. Retrieved May 20, 2006, from the U.S. Census home page: http://www.census.gov/prod/2004pubs/censr-17.pdf

Simmons, T., & O'Neill, G. (2001). *Census 2000 brief: Households and families 2000.* Retrieved June 8, 2006, from http://www.census.gov/prod2001pubs/c2kbr01-8.pdf

Song, C., & Glick, J. E. (2004). College attendance and choice of college majors among Asian American students. *Social Science Quarterly, 85,* 1401–1421.

Steinberg, L., Mounts, N. S., Lamborn, S. D., & Dornbusch, S. M. (1991). Authoritative parenting and adolescent adjustment across varied ecological niches. *Journal of Research on Adolescence, 1,* 19–36.

Sue, S., & Okazaki, S. (1990). Asian-American educational achievements: A phenomenon in search of an explanation. *American Psychologist, 45,* 913–920.

Tseng, V. (2004). Family interdependence and academic adjustment in college: Youth from immigrant and U.S.-born families. *Child Development, 75,* 966–983.

Uba, L. (1994). *Asian Americans: Personality patterns, identity, and mental health.* New York: Guilford Press.

U.S. Bureau of the Census (2000). *U.S. Census 2000 Summary File 4.* Retrieved May 12, 2006, from http://www.census.gov/Press-Release/www/2003/SF4.html

U. S. Census. (2001). *Current population reports, school enrollment in the United States—Social and economic characteristics of students, P20-533.* Washington, DC.

Wang, P.-C., & Gallagher-Thompson, D. (2005). Resolution of intergenerational conflict in a Chinese female dementia caregiver: A case study using cognitive/behavioral methods. *Clinical Gerontologist, 28*(3), 91–94.

White, M. J., Fong, E., & Cai, Q. (2003). The segregation of Asian-origin groups in the United States and Canada. *Social Science Research, 32,* 148–167.

Wilmoth, J. M. (2001). Living arrangements among older immigrants in the United States. *Gerontologist, 41*(2), 228–238.

Wong, B. (2002). Family and traditional values: The bedrock of Chinese American business. In N. V. Benokraitis (Ed.), *Contemporary ethnic families in the United States: Characteristics, variations, and dynamics* (pp. 212–220). Englewood Cliffs, NJ: Prentice Hall.

Wong, L., & Mock, M. R. (1997). Asian American young adults. In E. Lee (Ed.), *Working with Asian Americans: A guide for clinicians* (pp. 196–207). New York: Guilford Press.

Woo, D. (2000). *Glass ceilings and Asian Americans.* Lanham, MD: Alta Mira Press.

Yee, B. W. K., DeBaryshe, B., Yuen, S., Kim, S. Y., & McCubbin, H. (2006). Asian American and Pacific Islander families: Resiliency and life-span Socialization in a cultural context. *Handbook of Asian American psychology* (2nd ed., pp. 69–86). Thousand Oaks, CA: Sage Publications.

Yee, B. W. K., Huang, L. N., & Lew, A. (1998). Families: Life-span socialization in a cultural context. In L. C. Lee & N. W. S. Zane (Eds.), *Handbook of Asian American psychology* (pp. 83–135). Thousand Oaks, CA: Sage Publications.

Yoon, S. M. (2005). The characteristics and needs of Asian-American grandparent caregivers: A study of Chinese-American and Korean-American grandparents in New York City. *Journal of Gerontological Social Work, 44*(3–4), 75–94.

Zaidi, A. U., & Shuraydi, M. (2002). Perceptions of arranged marriages by young Pakistani Muslim women living in a Western society. *Journal of Comparative Family Studies, 33,* 495–514.

Zhou, M. (1997). Growing up American: The challenge confronting immigrant children and children of immigrants. *Annual Review of Sociology, 23,* 63–95.

17
Parenting and Raising Families

DIANE S. HAYASHINO and SAPNA BATRA CHOPRA

OUTLINE OF CHAPTER

Case Synopsis

June and Gary are Asian American immigrant parents who are bringing their 15-year-old daughter Cindy in for individual counseling. They are worried that their daughter is becoming increasingly defiant and disrespectful and is losing her cultural roots. They want the best for their daughter, and are confused by her recent acts of disobedience. Counseling is a last resort for them, and they are hoping the counselor can get Cindy "back on track." Cindy feels bad to hurt her parents, but also feels that her parents are "too traditional" and unaware of social customs appropriate for teenagers in the United States. After meeting with the counselor for a few sessions, she hopes the counselor will talk to her parents for her.

Introduction

The overall goal of this chapter is to increase our understanding of Asian American **parenting** from a strengths-based multicultural perspective. More specifically, we will address existing parenting research and raising children in Asian American families. This chapter provides a review of some of the unique factors that influence Asian American families, including cultural values, the role of extended family, gender roles, **acculturation** and **enculturation**, role reversal, social support, parental expectations for academic performance, religious and spiritual values, ethnic identity development, and racism. This chapter also utilizes Bronfenbrenner's ecological perspective to understand the contextual influence of culture that shapes parenting and the parent-child relationship. The chapter will conclude with a case study, suggestions for practice, discussion questions, and resources for further learning.

An ecological framework focuses on the bidirectional influences among children, parents, school, community, and culture, and places the individual as an active agent in his or her environment (Bronfenbrenner, 1979). Bronfenbrenner stated "the greatest limitation in the study of human development is the failure to go beyond the individual, and not take into account the social ecology of the individual" (1989, p. 216). According to Bronfenbrenner (1989), the ecological environment is comprised of a series of nested systems: the micro-, meso-, exo-, and macrosystem. The microsystem includes the individual and his or her interactions with those in the immediate environment, such as the parent(s), siblings, family members, and peers. The family is considered among the more important settings for the child, in terms of social, cognitive, and emotional development. The mesosystem involves the linkages between these immediate settings, such as the interactions between the child and parent and/or the interaction between the child and peers. The exosystem encompasses those factors that do not directly include the child but are indirect influences, such as the parent's ethnic identity. The macrosystem is the broader societal, cultural and political environment, and includes political ideologies, religious and spiritual beliefs, cultural norms and values. These systems are embedded within a chrono-system, in that these influences are continually changing over time. An ecological approach to understanding parenting provides a comprehensive understanding of the individual and envi-ronment that in turn allows for a richer and more strengths-based approach to understanding and working with Asian American parents and families.

An example of how the exo- and macrosystems may impact parenting and families across generations is the internment of 110,000 Japanese Americans from the West Coast during World War II. In the internment camps, families were placed with several other families in barracks, thereby decreasing family cohesion and parental control. Children spent more time with peers, and therefore parents lost their influence as primary socializing agents. The strong ties and attachment to the immediate family unit were reduced, as parents were silenced by their own shame for being treated as prisoners, considered disloyal, and discriminated by society, and as

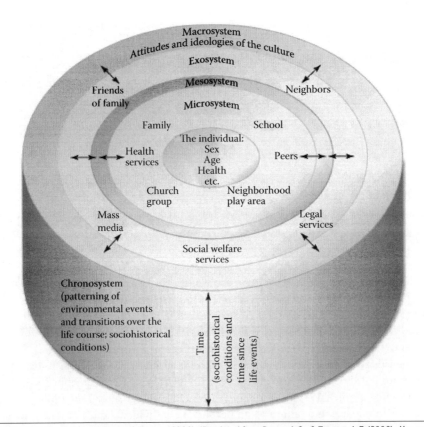

Bronfenbrenner's Ecological Model (Dacey & Travers, 2006). (Reprinted from Dacey, J. S., & Travers, J. F. (2006). *Human develop-ment: Across the lifespan* (6th ed.). Copyright 2006. Reproduced with permission of The McGraw-Hill Companies.)

they experienced heavy financial and emotional losses (Spickard, 1996). Among third-generation Japanese Americans whose parents had been interned, the effects were transmitted from generation to generation through increased cautiousness, and a high degree of silence and communication within the family about the internment experience (Nagata & Takeshita, 1998). Therefore, an understanding of parenting and families must occur by taking into account the contextual influences on the child, parent, and family system.

Definitions and Demographics

Parenting involves caring and providing for children, keeping children healthy and safe, passing down social and cultural customs and values, and guiding children's social, emotional, and cognitive development. An individual's parenting style is influenced by her or his own experiences growing up, the child's temperament and personality, the parent's personality, the parent's emotional and psychological resources, the parent's social and community support, and the parent's own cultural socialization and background (Parke, 2004).

Although parenting and raising children is universal across cultures, the process may look different from one culture to the next. The goals that parents hold for their children and the methods they use in raising their children are impacted by cultural values, beliefs, and behaviors. Indeed, variations in parenting styles and behaviors across cultural groups have been well-documented (Reid, Webster-Stratton, & Beauchaine, 2001). Thus, in order to provide an accurate overview of parenting, this chapter must also review some of the relevant demographics of Asian American families.

Asian Americans are a diverse population originating from countries such as China, Japan, Korea, the Philippines, Vietnam, Cambodia, and India. Asian Americans vary in terms of language, religion, reasons for immigrating, generational status, educational level, socioeconomic status, acculturation and enculturation levels, and unique customs and practices. In terms of family size, Asian American households have more people per household. For example, 33.1% of Asian American and Pacific Islander families have 4 or more people per household compared to 24.3% of all American families (U.S. Bureau of the Census, 2002). Asian Indians, Chinese Americans, Korean Americans, and Japanese Americans tend to have a relatively low percentage of female-headed households (7% to 13%) (U.S. Public Health Service, 2001). Vietnamese, Filipinos, and other Southeast Asian ethnic groups each have a rate of approximately 18% of female-headed households. In general, Asian American women tend to have fewer children and start their families at a later age than women of other ethnic groups (U.S. Public Health Service, 2001). The number of reported cases of child physical abuse is increasing (Lum, 1998), however, the incidence continues to be lower as compared to European Americans. The rates of child abuse are misleading due to cultural factors that may impact reporting, such as avoiding shame, preserving the hierarchical structure of family, language barriers in reporting the abuse. Therefore, the rates may be higher than what is reported.

Table 17.1 Family Demographics (Asian American and National Average)

	Asian American	U.S. national average
Family size per household	3.61	3.14
Married-couple families[a]	82.2%	76.7%
Female-headed households	11.4%	17.3%
Child poverty rate	14.3%	16.6%

Source: Lai, E., & Arguelles, D., *The new face of Asian Pacific America: Numbers, diversity, and change in the 21st century*, AsianWeek, San Francisco, 2003.
[a]Data for same-sex households not available.

In this chapter, we recognize that parenting can take many forms, including single-parent families, grandparents and extended family, gay and lesbian parents, intercultural couples, blended or stepfamilies, families in which one parent resides in another country, and adoptive or foster parents. There is very little research on the rich diversity within Asian American families. Existing studies have focused primarily on immigrant, heterosexual, two-parent Chinese American and Japanese American samples. Research on families in other Asian ethnic groups as well as second- or third-generation Asian American parenting is lacking.

Parenting Research and Assessment

Literature on parenting has historically focused on middle-class, European American, heterosexual families. Most parenting research has used European American middle-class samples as the norm by which other groups are compared (Jambunathan, Burts, & Pierce, 2000; Julian, McKenry, & McKelvey, 1994; Kim & Wong, 2002). For example, in Jambunathan, Burts, and Pierce's (2000) study of European American, African American, immigrant Asian American, immigrant Asian Indian, and Latina mothers of preschoolers, the European American mothers responded to the instruments with more "appropriate" responses (e.g., they had a clearer understanding of what to expect of their child, had more empathy for their child). The authors acknowledged that given that the research instruments were designed and normed with European American samples, it is no wonder that the European American parents embodied more positive parenting traits in the research findings.

Research on parenting frequently refers to Baumrind's (1971) classification of three parenting styles: **authoritative, authoritarian,** and **permissive.** Authoritative parents are warm and responsive, encourage open communication, set firm boundaries, and respect their child's individuality. Authoritarian parents expect obedience and compliance from their children, and are described as being strict and rigid. Permissive parents are warm and sensitive to the child, but do not establish and enforce rules and boundaries. Baumrind posited that the authoritative parenting style is the optimal approach for positive child outcomes. Research on the parenting styles of Asian immigrant parents has consistently documented that these parents tend to adopt an authoritarian style of parenting (e.g., Chao, 1994; Jambunathan et al., 2000; Kawamura, Frost, & Harmatz, 2001; Kelley & Tseng, 1992; McLoyd, Cauce, Takeuchi, & Wilson, 2000).

Chao (1994) challenged this classification of parenting as being ethnocentric and questioned its applicability to Asian American families. For Asians, parental control may not have the negative connotations of hostility and dominance that it does for European Americans. Instead, parental control may serve to maintain unity and functioning within the family. Chao (2001) suggested that perhaps parental warmth and responsiveness in Asian American families is expressed through investment, devotion, and sacrifice for children in contrast to a European American conceptualization of warmth as praise and outward affection.

Asian American parents tend to rely more on internal rather than external controls when disciplining their children. Children may be motivated to behave because of a fear of punishment (external control), but they may also be motivated to behave because of fear of isolation, shame, rejection, and guilt placed upon them by their family. As one Asian American student stated in a class with one of the authors, "sometimes I wished my mom would have just yelled at me rather than giving me the look, because it made me feel so bad." Due to the strong internalization of the cultural values of filial piety, collectivism, and saving face by the child, this form of discipline by the parents may be viewed as effective in controlling their child's behaviors. It is important that mental health service providers remain attentive to the possible long-term emotional consequences of utilizing this type of discipline.

Raising Children in Asian American Families

Cultural Values

There is not one homogeneous parenting style that characterizes all Asian American parents. However, there are certain common traits and cultural values among traditional Asian families that have been documented in the literature (e.g., Baptiste, 2005; Jambunathan et al., 2000; Parke, 2004; Serafica, 1990; Wu, 2001). Family needs generally take precedence over individual needs. There is an emphasis on maintaining harmony in the family, saving face (avoiding bringing shame to the family), filial piety (the child's duty to respect and honor parents' wishes and to care for them in old age), as well as interdependence and collectivism rather than independence and individualism. The shared cultural values, beliefs, and behaviors provide stability and cohesiveness for the family system (Bush, Bohon, & Kim, 2005). For the Asian American family, an emphasis on family goals over individual goals, filial piety, and family cohesion contributes to a broad network of support.

Parents may induce shame, guilt, and concern for family obligation (saving face) in reinforcing cultural values and disciplining their children (Baptiste, 2005; Jambunathan et al., 2000; Serafica, 1990). For example, a 24-year-old second-generation Chinese American stated: "My grandparents were always close by. When we lived in an apartment they were always a few floors up. Now my parents have a two-family house, and my grandparents live next door. So this was always pointed out to me. Maybe they are fearful that one day we would become too Americanized and not take care of them" (Hom, 1992, p. 153). In this example, the parents are reinforcing the value of filial piety.

Role of Extended Family

Grandchild-grandparent relationships have traditionally held an important presence in Asian families where three-generation households are not uncommon (Smith & Drew, 2004). Asian American households are more likely to include extended family members as compared to European American and African American families (McLoyd, Cauce, Takeuchi, & Wilson, 2000). However, empirical research on parenting in Asian American families fails to address the role that grandparents and extended family members might play in the childrearing process.

Chinese American and Korean American families are more likely to have greater involvement of grandparents in child-rearing than Japanese American families (Shibusawa, 2001). One possibility for this finding is that most Japanese American older adults were born in the United States and tend to be acculturated in terms of valuing and respecting their adult children's independence (Shibusawa, 2001). Immigrant Asian Indian parents who work outside the home and have young children often arrange for their parents or in-laws to come from India to live with them and assist in raising children. Generally, most grandparents enjoy being involved with the family and caring for their grandchildren. However, on the other hand, conflict can ensue between the parents and in-laws regarding child-rearing practices. Most commonly, the conflict occurs between the primary caretakers who are usually the mother and the grandmother in the family. Clearly, with the involvement of additional caretakers involved in raising children, family dynamics shift, often creating a household environment where both support and tension exist within the family.

Gender Roles

As more Asian American women are contributing to the family's income and demanding a higher status in their families, gender roles are changing. In traditional Asian families, the family structure tends to be patriarchal with the father being the head of the household, while

Grandfather and grandson.

mothers exercise more authority in regards to child-rearing. Researchers suggest that as Asian American families become more acculturated, their child-rearing practices begin to look more like those of European Americans (McLoyd et al., 2000). For example, Chinese American families are beginning to change as they become more acculturated. These changes include a shift from extended to nuclear family, more shared decision making between mothers and fathers, and less favoring of sons over daughters (Lee & Mock, 2005). In a study of Asian Indian immigrant families, Jain and Belsky (1997) found that the fathers who were more highly acculturated were the most involved with their children in caregiving, playing, teaching, and disciplining. Additionally, the husband-wife dyad is becoming more important with increased acculturation, whereas traditionally the parent-child dyad is primary (Kim & Ryu, 2005). More recent studies are finding that fathers who are more involved with their children tend to hold nontraditional gender roles and more egalitarian beliefs (McLoyd et al., 2000). Therefore, the stereotype of Asian American fathers as distant and uninvolved with their children is being challenged as more fathers are actively participating in the daily care of their children.

Acculturation and Enculturation

Acculturation refers to changes in one's culture-specific behaviors, values, knowledge, and identity along the norms of the dominant culture (Kim & Omizo, 2005). Enculturation refers to changes in one's culture-specific behaviors, values, knowledge, and identity along the norms of the indigenous culture (Kim & Omizo, 2005). A person can be highly acculturated to mainstream U.S. values, and hold on to some traditional values as well. It is not an "all or nothing"

Father and son.

process. For example, a person could be acculturated in some domains or settings (e.g., in the workplace) and hold traditional values in other areas (e.g., family relationships).

Asian American parents may be selective in which values they choose to adopt and which traditional values they choose to retain (Wu, 2001). Even through the process of acculturation, Asian American families tend to retain a value for collectivism and family, and pride in one's

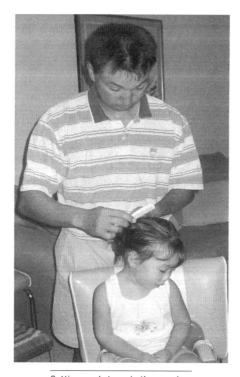

Getting ready to go in the morning.

native culture (Julian, McKenry, & McKelvey, 1994). Serafica (1990) argued that immigration is not likely to significantly alter traditional child-rearing beliefs. However, parents who carry guilt or anxiety about leaving the homeland tend to cling more strongly to tradition when raising their children. For example, Asian Indian immigrant parents often idealize traditional values to the extent that they actually become even more rigid in adhering to tradition in their expectations for their children (Baptiste, 2005). This idealization of traditional values in turn can lead to intergenerational conflict and stress for both the parents and the children.

Furthermore, the acculturation level within families contributes to conflicts between family members (Sluzki, 1979). Conflicts between parents and their children may include disagreements over the use of praise and reinforcement, dating, career choice, religion and spiritual values, and gender roles. For example, if an Asian American parent holds a more traditional Asian value in terms of expressing support to their child through involvement and investment, this may contrast with the more European American parenting practices of physical or emotional affection (praising) that their children may be exposed to in schools and through interactions with their peers' families. The difference between these values may create tension, misunderstanding, and confusion for the parents and children.

Asian American children exposed to the majority culture learn that the path to popularity, success, and happiness lies in being more like their European American peers. Parents then view this as the children being disrespectful and turning their backs on their family and culture, while the children start to feel like their parents do not know anything about how to make it in this country. From the authors' experiences in working with college students, children often keep secrets from their parents because of the perception that their parents would disapprove of their Western behaviors. The struggle between the parents' desire to maintain traditional values and the pressure children feel to acculturate to the majority culture can be painful for both children and parents.

Cheung and Nguyen (2001) discussed the struggles of Vietnamese parents and children in particular. Children are often unaware of their parents' struggles to survive as refugees, and parents are unaware of children's struggles to negotiate between parents, peers, and school. To further complicate this, parents and children do not talk openly about their experiences with each other. For Koreans, the Korean language consists of special words used to designate respect to people of varying levels of status. Tension may develop as second-generation children lose fluency and understanding of the nuances of the language and are not able to communicate to their parents in a way they deem respectful and appropriate (Kim & Ryu, 2005). Some children may feel disconnected from their parents as a result of language barriers. For example, a Chinese American college student expressed: "Even with the Chinese I speak, I am limited to the normal yet shallow 'everyday' conversations I have with my parents and do not have enough of a vocabulary to have meaningful talks with them. Such was the case just the other night when they asked me what my major at Berkeley was but I did not know the phrase for "biology," much less, 'Molecular and Cellular Biology.' The best I could manage was 'science' in Chinese and explained the rest in English; I could not communicate to them why I selected this major, what I was going to do with it, and so forth. We ended the discussion by changing the subject" (http://www.cal.org/resources/digest/involuntary.html). Some common parental fears are that their children will become too Americanized, that they will lose control over their children, and that their children will make them lose face in front of the rest of their community. Thus, acculturation and enculturation play significant roles in parenting and raising children.

Role Reversal

Asian American parents must often rely on their children to assume adult roles such as translators, managers of the family's budget, and caregivers for their siblings. For example, a 1.5-generation Vietnamese American child may have to negotiate multiple roles in the family, leading to uncertainty, guilt, and confusion. Thus, the parent-child relationship and parenting practices are affected by migration experiences and the ongoing stresses of acculturation and changing family dynamics. Status inconsistency and lowered employment status of the parents also contribute to their loss of power within the family, and their own feelings of insecurity and confusion (Lee, 1996). For adolescents, this role reversal may lead them to view their parents as poor role models and they may feel ashamed of their parents' limited English skills, low socioeconomic status, and ignorance of U.S. culture (Lee, 1996). Immigrant refugee parents rely heavily on their children for daily activities such as paying bills, answering phone calls, and communicating with teachers, which contributes to the parents' loss of direct control of their children.

Social Support

A lack of community social support systems may pose additional challenges for Asian American parents and contribute to increased feelings of isolation. For example, due to the involuntary disbursement of many Southeast Asian immigrant and refugee families, they experienced difficulty adjusting to their new environment (Zhou & Bankston, 1998). The Vietnamese, Cambodian, Laotian, and Hmong groups (among others) who were dispersed in isolated neighborhoods experienced more trauma and adjusted to their new country much slower than those who were resettled as groups (Boehnlein & Kinzie, 1995). Social isolation and a disruption of support systems for parents are sources of significant stress for these families who often rely on the support and presence of extended family and close friends in parenting (Lin, 1986). Research has shown that those families who have strong community and family ties experience fewer problems in the parent-child relationship (McLoyd, 1998; Mehta, 1998). As a first-generation Vietnamese American parent shared, "we come here [U.S.] and are busy making a living, and we don't have time to tell them [children] why we came, so they don't understand their parents. So, we depend

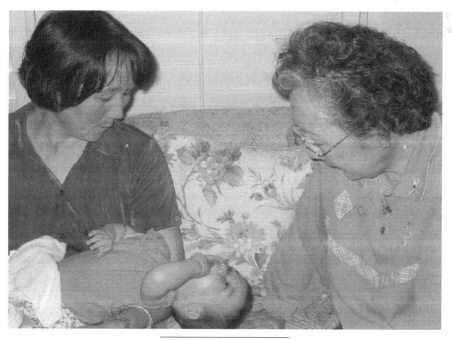

Mother, child, and grandmother.

on the older children and others to teach the younger children about our history and values" (Hayashino, 2003). The reliance on family support and extended kinship ties serves a protective function by reducing the sense of powerlessness and isolation. Thus, families who are connected to their ethnic communities and socialize with them, tend to be more effective with the coping and parenting behaviors.

A group that faces a considerable amount of stress is gay and lesbian parents. Asian American gay and lesbian parents face additional sources of stress from the lack of social support in their communities, and often hold multiple minority statuses. Clearly, gay and lesbian parents of color share feelings of oppression and marginalization from some of the parenting community who hold cultural beliefs that gays and lesbians may "recruit" children into their "deviant life-style" (Armesto, 2002). Specifically for Asian American gay and lesbian parents who hold multiple or **triple minority** statuses, the lack of support within their own families and communities is evident. For example, as the co-founder and coordinator of the Asian Pacific Islander-Parents, Families and Friends of Lesbians and Gays (API-PFLAG) stated, "we are most concerned about our family and the huge fear of rejection that we may face" (Lai & Arguelles, 2003, p. 247). Additionally, gaining immigration status for same-sex partners is a challenge since immigration policies continue to be heterosexist.

Parental Expectations for Academic Performance

Several researchers have found that Asian American parents have high expectations for their children's academic success and time spent studying (e.g., Chao, 2001; Julian, McKenry, & McKelvey, 1994; Kim & Ryu, 2005; Okagaki & Frensch, 1998; Phinney & Chavira, 1995; Shibusawa, 2001; Sijuwade, 2003). Indeed, good grades are expected rather than rewarded by many Asian American parents (Cheung & Nguyen, 2001). In their study of Asian American, European American, and Latino parents of 4th and 5th graders, Okagaki and Frensch (1998) found that the Asian American parents, mostly immigrants, had higher academic expectations for their children and were less satisfied with grades of B's or C's. Children are often expected to honor their duty to their family through their academic accomplishments, and school success is viewed as a positive reflection on the parents (Chao, 2001; Cheung & Nguyen, 2001; Serafica, 1990). Chao (2000) found that Chinese immigrant parents tend to explain their children's academic success as being connected to their respect and honor to the family. Baptiste (2005) found that Asian Indian children who do not meet their parents' high academic expectations may feel that they have failed. In a study of Asian American and European American parents of children with high achievement test scores, Sijuwade (2003) found that the Asian American parents had fewer demands on their children to participate in household chores. Parents would rather have children focus on their studies than spend time on chores or activities not contributing to their academic success. Japanese American parents compared to European American parents hold higher expectations for their children's academic achievements due to both the cultural value on education and the belief that school success will lead to better career prospects and offset racial discrimination in the workplace (Shibusawa, 2001). Moreover, Japanese American parents tend to attribute school performance to the child's effort, whereas European American parents attribute it to ability. This may result in Asian American parents not recognizing learning disabilities that their child may be struggling with because they presume that with enough hard work, anyone can get good grades. Based on the authors' experience in university counseling centers, it is worth noting that some Asian American students struggle with their internalized belief that they should succeed academically to the high levels expected of themselves as well as their families and communities. In some cases, these students can experience intense pressure to succeed, and extreme guilt and shame when they are unable to fulfill such high academic expectations. Therefore, second- and third-generation Americans need to be aware of their cultural expectations and the impact their values may have on their children.

Religious and Spiritual Values

For many Asian American families, religion and spirituality serve as primary sources of social support, provide a sense of belonging, and preserve cultural traditions (Min, 1991). Asian Americans are represented among faiths such as Christianity, Buddhism, Shintoism, Taoism, Catholicism, Islam, and Hinduism. With respect to resolving family problems, often parents and extended family members seek the advice of their religious or spiritual leaders. Church involvement provides many Asian American families with a coherent sense of identity and belonging. For example, some Asian American parents who are concerned with their child's perceived loss of cultural values through acculturation rely on the church as a resource for preserving culture and ethnic identity (Kim & Ryu, 2005). Among Korean Americans, church membership is significantly higher as compared with membership in Korea (Kim & Ryu, 2005). Korean and Korean American parents of children with disabilities who closely identified with their ethnic church and received strong emotional and social support were less likely to engage in self-blame regarding their child's disability (Cho, Singer, & Brenner, 2000). Therefore, for many Asian American families, faith and religion provide support, a sense of community, and hope in times of isolation and parenting difficulties.

Instilling Positive Ethnic Identities in Children

Ethnic minority parents strive to raise their children with a positive sense of ethnic identity (Jambunathan et al., 2000; Julian, McKenry, & McKelvey, 1994). Asian immigrant parents make a concerted effort to teach their children the practices and beliefs of their native culture (McLoyd et al., 2000). However, when children are in school and exposed to influences outside the family, children may begin to perceive that their group is not as valued as the dominant culture. Serafica (1990) reviewed various studies that have documented that Chinese American, Japanese

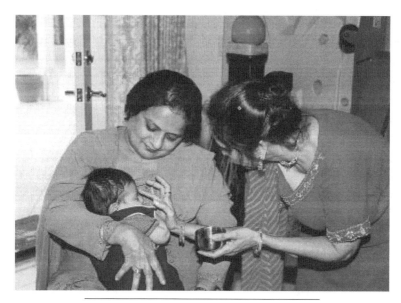

Traditional Hindu ceremony offering blessings to the baby.

328 • Asian American Psychology

American, and Korean American children's ratings of their physical features were lower than those of others. Asian American youth also tend to have a lower body image and self-concept than their European American peers (Shibusawa, 2001) as discussed in Chapter 12.

Children are impacted by both overt and subtle messages in fairy tales, children's television programming, and other forms of media. The authors recall their own experience growing up in the United States when non-White dolls, puppets, and popular children's characters were not widely available and accessible. It is important for Asian American parents to provide a range of toys and storybooks for their children that depict Asian Americans (and other racial/ethnic minority group members) in a positive way.

For some Asian Americans, parents' ability to pass down cultural values and practices to their children is interrupted by outside oppression. For example, after World War II and the internment of Japanese American families, many Japanese American parents made a conscious effort to Americanize their children in an attempt to protect them from the very real threat of racism in their lives. A Japanese American man wrote, "There is no way we could teach our children Japanese at home. We speak English. It wasn't a conscious effort that we did this. It was more a question of circumstances, because of the closing of the schools during the war. Certainly some parents discouraged it because of the war, but we didn't make it a point to learn Japanese. It was more important to be accepted. I can speak a little Japanese, but I can't read or write it. My son can speak. He studied the language in college. I feel proud about that. Before the war, 90% of the Japanese children went to Japanese school. But that was stopped with internment" (Moritsugu, 1992, p. 99).

Racism

Racism, prejudice, and discrimination are realities that ethnic minorities and Asian Americans often face. In child-rearing, Asian American parents are often challenged with how to respond when their child experiences any form of prejudice, racism, and discrimination. For example, a 2nd grade Asian Indian girl, in a predominantly upper-middle-class, European American school, is playing with her classmates when they decide to play "Home Owner and Maid" (a rather classist version of the children's make-believe game of "House"). The Asian Indian girl's classmates agreed that she should be the maid because she is "brown." Upon the Asian Indian girl's request that they take turns being the maid, the Asian Indian girl was told, "you're brown, you're the maid," and was later harassed by other classmates with "you're brown, you're poor, you're the maid. . . . " When the Asian Indian girl reported this incident to her mother, a second-generation Asian Indian American, she was at a loss for how to support her daughter. Thus, preparing children for the reality of prejudice, racism, and discrimination is an integral part of raising families who are members of a minority culture.

Racial/ethnic minority parents face additional challenges in parenting their children. They need to teach their children about their own native culture, about the dominant culture, and about racism and prejudice (Phinney & Chavira, 1995). Most of the empirical research that examines how minority parents focus on these three areas in socializing their children focuses on African American parents. Several researchers have documented that African American parents, more so than other racial minority parents, discuss race with their children and help prepare them to survive and cope with racism and prejudice (Julian et al., 1994; McKown, 2004; McLoyd et al., 2000; Phinney & Chavira, 1995). Immigrant parents may not provide as much support for their children in dealing with racism for a number of reasons. They may be unaware of potential racism their children might encounter because they themselves grew up in a very different society or were raised in an ethnic-specific community. They may not know how to talk about and handle discrimination, or they may be struggling with their own adjustment issues.

The authors speculate that second-, third-, or fourth-generation Asian Americans may be more likely to openly dialogue with their children about racism and prejudice.

Asian Americans are a unique racial minority group in that they are the recipients of both negative and positive stereotypes. However, even these "positive" stereotypes can be damaging for Asian American children. For example, Asian American students are viewed by teachers as more passive and unassertive, and are called on less than Caucasian students in class (Chang & Sue, 2003). Asian American children are often resented or bullied at school by other students because of their perceived or actual academic success (Shibusawa, 2001). In a study of Korean American parents and children, B. Kim (cited in Serafica, 1990) found that 30% of the sample reported that the children had faced racial bullying or name calling at school. Kim reported a range of parents' responses to children's experiences of racism, including telling the child to have pride in their culture, taking karate classes, improving academically, or fighting back.

In a sample of African American, Japanese American, and Mexican American adolescents and their parents, Phinney and Chavira (1995) found that 38.9% of the Japanese American students reported receiving verbal slurs, as compared to 29.2% of the Mexican American and 6.3% of the African American students. The parents' responses indicated that two thirds of the Japanese American parents indicated that they try to teach their children about their native culture. The Japanese American parents were significantly less likely than the other two groups of parents to guide their children in how to get along in White America and in a diverse society and how to cope with discrimination and racism. Only 22.2% reported that they talked to their children about discrimination, as compared to 75% of African American and 58.3% of Mexican American parents.

While parents cannot isolate their children from these messages and influences, parents can provide a safe and open environment for children to talk about their encounters with discrimination and how to deal with them (Reynolds, 2005). When parents are able to openly discuss experiences of racism and how to deal with them, children are better equipped to respond to their own encounters with racism (Phinney & Chavira, 1995). Tatum (1999) encourages parents of minority youth to listen to their children and affirm their identities so that their children can resist internalizing racist messages and develop positive racial and ethnic identities. Carter (1999) offered suggestions for parents of color to protect their children from the harmful influences of racism, such as attending to the child's self-esteem and positive ethnic identity, and connecting with others of the same cultural group to give the child a sense of belonging and support. More research is needed on how parents can help their children maintain a positive ethnic identity and self-concept in an environment in which their culture may be demeaned.

Summary

This chapter has sought to provide an overview of parenting among Asian Americans by highlighting some of the unique factors that impact these families. We discussed how these factors contribute not only to the similarities among Asian American ethnic groups and parenting, but also provide some understanding of the within-group differences due to generational differences, level of acculturation, and ethnic identity. Thus, an Asian American parent may be negotiating and balancing not only the dominant White culture's values, beliefs, and attitudes about parenting but their native culture as well. As we mentioned in this chapter, this process may lead to strengthening the family unit as well as creating stress and conflict.

In working with Asian American parents who may be experiencing stress and conflict, it is crucial that some of these specific issues such as intergenerational conflict, role

Mother and son.

reversal, and language barriers be addressed in services provided. It may not be effective to simply provide parenting education and support focused on parenting skills. Instead, facilitating improved communication between parents and children may lead to more positive outcomes in the family.

Discussion Questions

1. What do you think are the basic characteristics of an ideal parent? Where does this definition come from?
2. What do you think might be some of your parenting challenges?
3. Which cultural values do you want to keep and pass on to your children? Which cultural values do you wish to not pass on to your children?
4. Reflect on your own experiences growing up being or feeling "culturally different"? Did you talk to your parents about this, and if so, how did they react?
5. How might you prepare your children for racism and prejudice?

Case Study

Thus far, this chapter has focused on research related to the experiences of Asian Americans in parenting and raising children. The chapter will now shift its focus to a case study that illustrates how Asian Americans experience and cope with the issues discussed in this chapter, as well as how therapists might work with such a family.

June and Gary married in their native country, and immigrated to the United States soon thereafter because of promising work opportunities. Both worked long hours to establish themselves as successful physicians. Two years later, their first child Cindy was born. June and Gary felt great joy and excitement to be parents but were also fearful about their lack of family support. June left her practice at that time to stay home and care for Cindy. Two years later, their son Dave was born. June and Gary were pleased to now have both a daughter and a son. Shortly after Dave was born, June's mother

Eileen joined the family household to help with childcare. June resumed employment as a physician at a local hospital, and Gary continued to work at his private practice. As the children started school, June and Gary began to worry that their cultural traditions would be lost in their children. The family currently lives in a predominantly White suburban neighborhood in Orange County. Cindy and Dave are now 15 and 13 years old, respectively.

Over the past year, Cindy and her parents have had numerous clashes over Cindy's choice of clothing, time spent with friends, and her desire to begin dating. June and Gary have tried lecturing and scolding her, taking away privileges like the telephone and Internet, and forbidding her to go out with friends. They recently caught Cindy after she lied and snuck out with her boyfriend to attend a large concert 40 miles away from home. Both parents feel disrespected by her and scared of the path they see Cindy taking. They wonder aloud to her, "How could you do this to us?" and "What did we do as parents to deserve this?" They feel lost and confused. They are also worried about what others in their community may be thinking about their family. They want the best for their children, and are now worried about their daughter's future.

Cindy feels hurt, angry, and misunderstood. She loves her family, and feels guilty for making her parents feel so upset. However, she also feels like she has no choice but to lie to her parents because they do not support most of her choices. She also feels embarrassed and defensive of her family in front of her mostly White friends who do not understand why her parents are so strict. More recently, she has been having difficulty sleeping and concentrating on her homework. After a record of straight A's, her grades are now falling.

Cindy's younger brother, Dave, has always been obedient to his parents. He does well in school, plays on a soccer team, and has friends in the neighborhood. Although Cindy and Dave fought a lot growing up, over the past year, Cindy began confiding in Dave about the battles she was having with their parents, and the two have grown close. However, now Dave feels caught between his sister and their parents. June and Gary discovered that Dave knew about Cindy's plan to sneak out with her boyfriend to the concert. They feel betrayed that he lied to them and did not look out for his sister's safety and well-being. As a result, Dave and Cindy have stopped talking about the situation.

Although their grandmother Eileen is disappointed that Cindy and Dave lied to their parents, she also perceives June and Gary to be overly restrictive and punitive. She trusts Cindy and Dave, and wants them to enjoy social activities with their peers. She is saddened to see Cindy feeling so bad. Cindy has confided in her that she is having difficulty concentrating and that her grades are dropping. Eileen is worried, and tries to lift Cindy's mood by cooking her favorite foods and allowing her to sneak in phone calls to her friends.

No one in the family has ever sought counseling services before, but June and Gary feel like they do not know what else to do. They are bringing Cindy in for individual counseling due to their concerns that she is "out of control" and jeopardizing her future. They are hoping that the counselor, who is of the same ethnicity, can help get Cindy "back on track." In the first session, Cindy tells the counselor that she thinks her parents need counseling because they are "so stuck in their ways." She reveals that she feels badly about hurting her parents but does not know what to do. Over the next two sessions, Cindy begins to feel a strong connection with the counselor, and asks the counselor to talk to her parents for her and convince them to be less restrictive.

Case Study Discussion

In working with Cindy, the counselor utilized an integrated systems approach within a multicultural framework. The counselor's awareness of her own cultural worldview as well as the cultural worldview of Cindy (and her parents) was important in understanding and developing culturally appropriate counseling interventions with Cindy. The importance of being aware of cultural differences as well as similarities between the counselor and Cindy was a starting place in the therapeutic process and goal setting. The counselor started by first meeting with Cindy to explore the presenting issue, her expectations about counseling, and goals for counseling. It was especially important that the counselor remained nonjudgmental and refrained from taking sides with either Cindy or her parents, given some of the identified intergenerational conflicts. It was important for the counselor who was trained in the United States to avoid supporting Cindy in her desire to acculturate rather than with the parents who appeared more resistant to change. Doing so would have failed to recognize the conflict that both sides experience, and may have led to premature termination if the parents felt misunderstood and blamed.

The counselor focused on establishing trust and credibility in the therapeutic relationship. For example, in the initial sessions, Cindy was somewhat reluctant to share details about her family and the conflicts they were experiencing. When the counselor acknowledged that for many Asian Americans, it is difficult to share family secrets with an outsider, Cindy gradually opened up, shared her story, and developed greater trust in the therapeutic relationship. A cultural genogram was used by the counselor to identify resources within the family and community, as well as problems across generations. Cindy acknowledged her maternal grandmother as someone that she felt very close to and that they had talked in the past about the conflicts that she was experiencing with her parents. She shared that her grandmother would sometimes mediate conflicts with her parents, and was effective in "getting them to be less traditional." As the counselor and Cindy worked toward having a session with her parents, they also agreed it would be important to include her grandmother in the session.

The counselor was also knowledgeable about the cultural values of filial piety and collectivism, and how these values were impacting the parent-child relationship as Cindy's parents perceived a loss of parental authority over Cindy and her brother. The counselor explored Cindy's level of adherence to her cultural values (enculturation) as well as her level of adherence to U.S. dominant cultural values (acculturation). Cindy shared how she had negotiated and balanced these two aspects of herself at home with her parents, and this was effective in providing her with a greater understanding of not only herself but her parents as well. In a session with Cindy, her parents, and her grandmother, the counselor provided some psychoeducation by explaining the acculturation and conflicts that can commonly arise between parents and their children to normalize and validate their experiences. Cindy's parents developed a clearer understanding that they had not failed as parents but rather were facing the normal processes of adjustment and acculturation. In addressing the parents' fear that Cindy might "lose her cultural traditions," it was important for the counselor to explain that although Cindy may be resisting her native culture in favor of mainstream culture at the present time, many racial minority children go through a developmental process of initially rejecting their own culture to eventually integrating aspects of both their native and mainstream culture into their identity. This allowed some relief to Cindy's parents and validated the unique and stressful challenges of raising children in a culture different from their own.

Finally, in working with Cindy within the context of her family, the counselor needed to attend to sociopolitical factors (e.g., immigration, acculturation level, intergenerational conflict, socioeconomic level). By addressing the broader issues that were impacting Cindy's relationship with her parents, she was able to externalize some of the conflicts rather than blame herself for "making her parents upset." Over time, she was also able to embrace the cultural differences between her and her White friends, and felt less ashamed for having "overprotective parents."

Case Study Discussion Questions

For undergraduate students, please consider the following questions:

1. What are your thoughts or reactions to the conflict between Cindy and her parents? How may this relate to your own experiences?
2. What would you do if you were in Cindy's shoes? What would you do if you were in Cindy's parents' shoes?
3. What do you think about the counselor's approach in working with this family? How would you have reacted to the counselor?

For graduate students and/or beginning therapists, please consider the following questions:

1. What might be challenging for you in working with Cindy? What may be some of the transference or countertransference issues?
2. What is your theoretical orientation? Would you use the same orientation in working with this family?
3. How would your work with these parents be different if they were an interracial couple? If they were a gay or lesbian couple? Were of lower income? Single parent?

Key Terms

Acculturation: Changes in the individual's attitudes, beliefs, and behaviors along the norms of the dominant culture.

Authoritarian: Strict and rigid interactions between parent and child, with the parent expecting obedience and compliance from the child.

Authoritative: Firm and consistent boundaries between the parent and child, with open communication that is warm and responsive to the child's needs.

Enculturation: Changes in the individual's attitudes, beliefs, and behaviors along the norms of one's indigenous culture.

Parenting: Caring and providing for children, keeping children healthy and safe, passing down social and cultural customs and values, and guiding children's social, emotional, and cognitive development.

Permissive: Inconsistent and flexible boundaries between the parent and child.

Triple minority: Holding multiple minority statuses in terms of gender (e.g., female), race (e.g., Asian American), and sexual orientation (e.g., lesbian).

For Further Learning and Suggested Readings

Books

Asian American Coalition (1995). *Children of Asian America*. Chicago, IL: Polychrome Publishing.
Lee, J. F. J. (1992). *Asian Americans*. New York: The New Press.
McGoldrick, M., Giordano, J., & Garcia-Preto, N. (2005). *Ethnicity and family therapy* (3rd ed.). New York: Guilford Press.
Tatum, B. D. (1999). *"Why are all the Black kids sitting together in the cafeteria?" and other conversations about race*. New York: Basic Books.

Movies

American Desi: Asian Indian acculturation and academic pressures
Bend It Like Beckham: Asian Indian family issues and interracial relationships
Double Happiness: Chinese Canadian woman attempts to balance her parents' wishes with her own
Kelly Loves Tony: two teenaged Southeast Asian American parents raising a child
My Brown Eyes: Korean American boy's adjustment to school in America
The Namesake: acculturation gap between parents and children
Rabbit in the Moon: Japanese American internment and impact on family
Wedding Banquet: cultural values and coming out in an Asian family

Web Sites

Asia for Kids: http://www.asiaforkids.com

References

Armesto, J. (2002). Developmental and contextual factors that influence gay fathers' parental competence: A review of the literature. *Psychology of Men and Masculinity, 3*(2), 67–78.

Baptiste, D. A. (2005). Family therapy with East Indian immigrant parents rearing children in the United States: Parental concerns, therapeutic issues, and recommendations. *Contemporary Family Therapy, 27*, 345–366.

Baumrind, D. (1971). Current patterns of parental authority. *Developmental Psychology Monographs, 4*(1, Part 2), 1–103.

Boehnlein, J. K., & Kinzie, J. D. (1995). Refugee trauma. *Transcultural Psychiatric Research Review, 32*, 223–252.

Bronfenbrenner, U. (1979). *The ecology of human development.* Cambridge, MA: Harvard University Press.

Bronfenbrenner, U. (1989). Ecological systems theory. *Annals of Child Development, 6*, 187–249.

Bush, K., Bohon, S., & Kim, H. (2005). Adaptation among immigrant families. In P. McKenry & S. Price (Eds.), *Families and change* (pp. 307–332). Thousand Oaks, CA: Sage Publications.

Carter, B. (1999). Becoming parents: The family with young children. In B. Carter & M. McGoldrick (Eds.), *The expanded family life cycle* (pp. 249–273). Needham Heights, MA: Allyn & Bacon.

Chang, D. F., & Sue, S. (2003). The effects of race and problem type on teachers' assessments of student behavior. *Journal of Consulting and Clinical Psychology, 71*, 235–242.

Chao, R. (2000). Cultural explanations for the role of parenting in the school success of Asian-American children. In R. D. Taylor & M. C. Wang (Eds.), *Resilience across contexts: Family, work, culture, and community* (pp. 333–363). New Jersey: Lawrence Erlbaum Associates.

Chao, R. K. (1994). Beyond parental control and authoritarian parenting style: Understanding Chinese parenting through the cultural notion of training. *Child Development, 65*, 1111–1119.

Chao, R. K. (2001). Extending research on the consequences of parenting style for Chinese Americans and European Americans. *Child Development, 72*, 1832–1843.

Cheung, M., & Nguyen, S. M. H. (2001). Parent-child relationships in Vietnamese American families. In N. B. Webb (Ed.), *Culturally diverse parent-child and family relationships* (pp. 261–281). New York: Columbia University Press Publishers.

Cho, S. J., Singer, H. S., & Brenner, B. M. (2000). Adaptation and accommodation to young children with disabilities: A comparison of Korean and Korean American parents. *Topics in Early Childhood Special Education, 20*(4), 236–249.

Dacey, J. S., & Travers, J. F. (2006). *Human development: Across the lifespan* (6th ed.). Boston, MA: McGraw Hill.

Hayashino, D. (2003). *A construct development and preliminary validation study of the parenting stress scale for Southeast Asian immigrant and refugee parents.* Unpublished doctoral dissertation, University of Oregon, Eugene.

Hom, T. (1992). Food and mah-jongg. In J. F. J. Lee (Ed.), *Asian Americans* (pp. 152–153). New York: The New Press.

Jain, A., & Belsky, J. (1997). Fathering and acculturation: A study of immigrant Indian families with young children. *Journal of Marriage and the Family, 59*, 873–883.

Jambunathan, S., Burts, D. C., & Pierce, S. (2000). Comparison of parenting attitudes among five ethnic groups in the United States. *Journal of Comparative Family Studies, 31*, 395–406.

Julian, T. W., McKenry, P. C., & McKelvey, M. W. (1994). Cultural variations in parenting: Perceptions of Caucasian, African-American, Hispanic, and Asian American parents. *Family Relations, 43*, 30–37.

Kawamura, K. Y., Frost, R. O., & Harmatz, M. G. (2001). The relationship of perceived parenting styles to perfectionism. *Personality and Individual Differences, 32*, 317–327.

Kelley, M. L., & Tseng, H. (1992). Cultural differences in child rearing: A comparison of immigrant Chinese and Caucasian American mothers. *Journal of Cross-Cultural Psychology, 23*, 444–455.

Kim, B., & Ryu, E. (2005). Korean families. In M. McGoldrick, J. Giordano, & N. Garcia-Preto (Eds.), *Ethnicity and family therapy* (3rd ed., pp. 349–362). New York: Guilford Press.

Kim, B. S. K., & Omizo, M. (2005). Asian and European American cultural values, collective self-esteem, acculturative stress, cognitive flexibility, and general self-efficacy among Asian American college students. *Journal of Counseling Psychology, 52*(3), 412–419.

Kim, S. Y., & Wong, V. Y. (2002). Assessing Asian and Asian American parenting: A review of the literature. In K. S. Kurasaki, S. Okazaki, & S. Sue (Eds.), *Asian American mental health: Assessment theories and methods* (pp. 185–201). New York: Kluwer Academic/Plenum Publishers.

Lai, E., & Arguelles, D. (2003). *The new face of Asian Pacific America: Numbers, diversity, and change in the 21st century.* San Francisco, CA: AsianWeek.

Lee, E., & Mock, M. (2005). Asian families: An overview. In M. McGoldrick, J. Giordano, & N. Garcia-Preto (Eds.), *Ethnicity and family therapy* (3rd ed., pp. 269–289). New York: Guilford Press.

Lee, S. J. (1996). *Unraveling the "model minority stereotype: Listening to Asian American youth.* New York: Teachers College Press.

Lin, K. (1986). Psychopathology and social disruption in refugees. In Williams and Westermeyer (Eds.), *Refugee mental health in resettlement countries* (pp. 61–71). Cambridge, MA: Hemisphere Publishing.

Lum, J. (1998). Family violence. In L. C. Lee & N. Zane (Eds.), *Handbook of Asian American psychology* (pp. 505–525). Thousand Oaks, CA: Sage Publications.

McKown, C. (2004). Age and ethnic variation in children's thinking about the nature of racism. *Journal of Applied Developmental Psychology, 25*, 597–617.

McLoyd, V. (1998). Socioeconomic disadvantage and child development. *American Psychologist, 53*(2), 185–204.

McLoyd, V. C., Cauce, A. M., Takeuchi, D., & Wilson, L. (2000). Marital processes and parental socialization in families of color: A decade review of research. *Journal of Marriage and Family, 62*, 1070–1093.

Mehta, S. (1998). Relationship between acculturation and mental health for Asian Indian immigrants in the United States. *Genetic, Social, and General Psychology Monographs, 1*(1), 61–79.

Min, P. G. (1991). Cultural and economic boundaries of Korean ethnicity. *Ethnic and Racial Studies, 14*, 225–241.

Moritsugu, H. (1992). To be more Japanese. In J. F. J. Lee (Ed.), *Asian Americans* (pp. 99–103). New York: The New Press.

Nagata, D., & Takeshita, Y. (1998). Coping and resilience across generations: Japanese Americans and the World World II internment. *Psychoanalytic Review, 85*(4), 587–613.

Okagaki, L., & Frensch, P. A. (1998). Parenting and children's school achievement: A multiethnic perspective. *American Educational Research Journal, 35*, 123–144.

Parke, R. D. (2004). Development in the family. *Annual Review in Psychology, 55*, 365–399.

Phinney, J. S., & Chavira, V. (1995). Parental ethnic socialization and adolescent coping with problems related to ethnicity. *Journal of Research on Adolescence, 5*, 31–53.

Reid, M. J., Webster-Stratton, C., & Beauchaine, T. P. (2001). Parent training in Head Start: A comparison of program response among African American, Asian American, Caucasian, and Hispanic mothers. *Prevention Science, 2,* 209–227.

Reynolds, J. (2005). Familial and relational transitions across the life span. In D. Comstock (Ed.), *Diversity and development: Critical contexts that shape our lives and relationships* (pp. 269–298). Belmont, CA: Thomson Brooks/Cole.

Serafica, F. C. (1990). Counseling Asian-American parents: A cultural-developmental approach. In F. Serafica, A. Schwebel, R. Russell, P. Isaac & L. Myers (Eds.), *Mental health of ethnic minorities* (pp. 222–244). New York: Praeger Publishers.

Shibusawa, T. (2001). Parenting in Japanese American families. In N. B. Webb (Ed.), *Culturally diverse parent-child and family relationships* (pp. 283–303). New York: Columbia University Press.

Sijuwade, P. O. (2003). A comparative study of family characteristics of Anglo American and Asian American high achievers. *Journal of Applied Social Psychology, 33*, 445–454.

Sluzki, C. (1979). Migration and family conflict. *Family Process, 18*(4), 379–390.

Smith, P. K., & Drew, L. M. (2004). Grandparenting and extended support networks. In M. Hoghughi & N. Long (Eds.), *Handbook of parenting: Theory and research for practice* (pp. 146–159). Thousand Oaks, CA: Sage Publications.

Spickard, P. (1996). *Japanese Americans: The formation and transformation of an ethnic group.* New York: Twayne Publishers.

Tatum, B. D. (1999). *"Why are all the Black kids sitting together in the cafeteria?" and other conversations about race.* New York: Basic Books.

U.S. Bureau of the Census. (2002). *Data highlights.* Available at http://www.census.gov.

U.S. Public Health Service. (2001). *A report of the surgeon general on minority mental health.* Rockville, MD: U.S. Department of Health and Human Services.

Wu, S. (2001). Parenting in Chinese American families. In N. B. Webb (Ed.), *Culturally diverse parent-child and family relationships* (pp. 235–260). New York: Columbia University Press.

Zhou, M., & Bankston, C. (1998). *Growing up American: How Vietnamese children adapt to life in the United States.* New York: Russell Sage Foundation.

18
History and Psychology of
Adoptees in Asian America

RICHARD M. LEE and MATTHEW J. MILLER

OUTLINE OF CHAPTER

Case Synopsis

Mi Kyoung and Mi Young are identical twins born in South Korea. They were adopted into the United States 8 months later by a childless White couple in their early forties who raised them as "American" and renamed them, Sarah and Susan. Although twins, the sisters' current attitudes and experiences as Korean Americans and as adoptees are quite different.

Sarah has begun to publicly use her Korean name, Mi Kyoung, and is actively involved in a Korean adult adoptee group and the local Korean immigrant community. By contrast, Susan feels no meaningful connection to her birth culture. She is quite happy just living her life as a "regular American" without hyphenated identities as a Korean American, Korean adoptee, and Asian American.

Introduction

Sarah and Susan (Mi Kyoung and Mi Young) illustrate the unique and diverse cultural life experiences that distinguish adopted Asian Americans from their non-adopted Asian American peers. Yet we know very little about the history, psychological development, and well-being of Asian adoptees, even though internationally adopted children constitute a sizable proportion of the Asian American population. For the most part, Asian American psychology, like the broader field of ethnic minority psychology, has concentrated on groups of people with more traditional migration patterns, such as immigrants and refugees. **International adoption** does not fit neatly into these discrete categories. Instead, Asian adoptees inhabit the borderlands of race and migration. As a group, they are perceived by society as Asian, but Asian Americans do not necessarily consider adoptees as a part of the larger immigrant community. This oversight of adoptees, by laypeople and scholars alike, is the reason that international adoption is sometimes referred to as the quiet migration (Weil, 1984) and Asian adoptees as the overlooked Asian Americans (Lee, 2006). This chapter provides a thorough review of the history of international adoption, reasons for the popularity of international adoption, and controversies surrounding the practice of international adoption. In addition, we discuss critical racial and cultural issues in international adoption that affect psychological development and review the psychological research on children adopted from Asia and their families.

International Adoption Statistics

Adoption is ubiquitous. It is estimated that about 2.5% of all children in the United States are adopted (U.S. Census, 2003) and approximately 125,000 children are adopted annually (U.S. Department of Health and Human Services, 2004). Six out of 10 people in the United States are affected directly by adoption; a majority of people have placed a child for adoption, been adopted, adopted a child, or had a close family member or friend who was adopted (Evan B. Donaldson Adoption Institute, 1997). Although most adoptions occur domestically through foster care and private/independent adoption, an increasing number of children are adopted internationally. In 1992, international adoption accounted for 5% of all adoptions, but it now accounts for more than 15% of all adoptions (U.S. Department of Health and Human Services, 2004). Consistent with this statistic, it is estimated that 12.5% of all adopted children under the age of 18 years old are considered foreign-born adoptees (U.S. Census, 2003).

Over 225,000 children have been adopted internationally between 1990 and 2005 (U.S. Department of the State, 2006). During this time span, there has been a 300% increase in the annual rate of international adoption to the United States from 7,093 in 1990 to 22,728 in 2005 (see Figure 18.1). Additionally, the demography of internationally adopted children has changed dramatically (see Figure 18.2). Prior to 1995, the top country from which to adopt internationally was South Korea. Today, China, Russia, and Guatemala have since supplanted South Korea. In 2005, it is estimated that 7,906 children were adopted from China, followed by 4,639 from Russia, 3,783 from Guatemala, and 1,630 from South Korea (U.S. Department

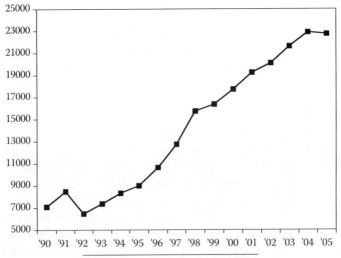

Figure 18.1 International adoption trends.

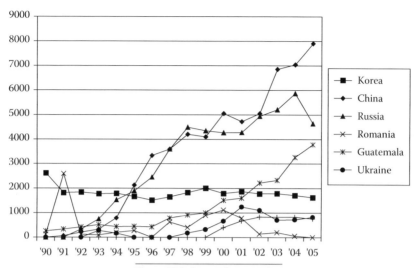

Figure 18.2 Top sending countries.

of State, 2006). Asian adoptees now represent 7.4% of all adopted children under 18 years old, whereas only 3.5% of biological children are of Asian descent (U.S. Census, 2003). Equally impressive, children adopted from China and South Korea represent approximately 15% and 10% of the annual number of legal Chinese and Korean immigrants to the United States (U.S. Department of Homeland Security, 2005).

History of International Adoption

Adoption in its varied forms has occurred throughout the history of humanity as a means to create families, care for children, and pass along lineage, as well as a means to reinforce political alliances, procure indentured labor, and disenfranchise and oppress groups of people (Cole & Donley, 1990; Hübinette, 2006). In the United States, modern adoption as a social and legal practice designed to protect the welfare of children dates back to 1851 when the first adoption law was passed in Massachusetts (Carp, 1998). This landmark law paved the way for domestic adoption to become a way of life for millions of families and children. Subsequent social and legal movements have helped to standardize the practice of adoption and to make it more commonplace in society.

Over the last half century, international adoption has become a popular alternative method to start or enlarge families in the United States and Europe. To understand the rise of international adoption in the United States, it is important to comprehend the world events that precipitated international adoption and the cultural and societal changes that altered people's attitudes toward international adoption. Wars, social upheaval, poverty, oppression, and inadequate social welfare systems in countries have always played a major role in large-scale migration and the international adoption of orphan children is no exception. The first formal instances of international adoption date back to World War II when unaccompanied children from Germany, China, Italy, and Japan, including many fathered by American military personnel, were adopted into American homes (Sokoloff, 1993). These international adoptions were fairly circumscribed and by most accounts did not extend beyond a few years after the war. Aside from some descriptive reports (e.g., Graham, 1957), there is little information about these first cases of internationally adopted children.

Adopted Korean biological sister and brother and their adoptive siblings. (Photo courtesy of Matt Miller.)

The Korean War marked a dramatic shift in the practice and prevalence of international adoption. The initial wave of orphan children adopted during and immediately after the war included many biracial children who were fathered by American military personnel. Soon thereafter, there was a second wave of Korean children from orphanages who were adopted with the assistance and sponsorship of social service agencies, religious organizations, and churches. American families continued to adopt children from South Korea in increasingly larger numbers (up to 7,000–8,000 annually) through the 1980s. However, negative media coverage, particularly during the 1988 Seoul Olympic Games, associated South Korea's economic ascendancy with the export of orphan children. This negative coverage brought about a national shame and embarrassment and eventually resulted in a gradual decrease in the annual rate of international adoptions. Since 1953, it is estimated that the United States has received over 110,000 adopted children from South Korea and there are between 150,000–200,000 Korean adoptees worldwide (Hübinette, 2004). Today, approximately 1,700 children are adopted annually from South Korea to the United States, and Korean adoptees represent more than one-fifth of adopted children in the United States (U.S. Census, 2003).

The Vietnam War was another major turning point in international adoption with Operation Babylift. Operation Babylift began in early April 1975, as American troops were withdrawing from Vietnam, accompanied by over 100,000 Vietnamese refugees fleeing from the North Vietnamese army. During this evacuation, more than 3,000 children were airlifted out of the country and eventually adopted by U.S. families, as well as families in Canada and Europe. Although viewed as a heroic humanitarian act, the operation was controversial

Six Korean War orphans stand outside the Manassas Manor, an orphanage that opened in January 1952. More than 100,000 children became orphans during the war. (Photo courtesy of George Drake. See http://media.collegepublisher. com/media/paper1048/stills/43d6e9828cae0-74-2.jpg and http://media.www.westernfrontonline.com/media/storage/paper1048/news/2006/01/24/Features/Commemorating.Korea-2135994.shtml?sourcedomain=www.westernfrontonline.com&MIIHost=media.collegepublisher.com.)

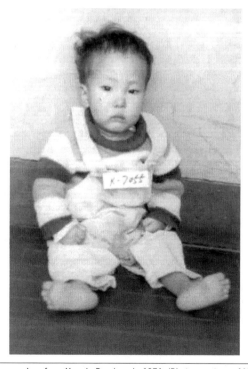

South Korean orphan from Yangju Province in 1974. (Photo courtesy of Matt Miller.)

because some Vietnamese families were unable to locate or be reunited with their children who were airlifted out of the country, and international adoption placements were not always successful (Martin, 2000). For better or worse, Operation Babylift reinforced the notion of international adoption as a noble humanitarian relief effort, especially in the context of a losing war (Melosh, 2002).

Major geopolitical events in the 1990s have helped to reshape the current rise in international adoption of Asian children. Take, for instance, China's family planning policy that promotes only one child per family. As China's one-child policy became more strictly enforced in the late 1980s and early 1990s, families who already had a daughter would sometimes choose to relinquish a second daughter because of the strong cultural preference for boys to carry on family lineage (Johnson, Banghan, & Liyao, 1998). Families often leave these girls in public locations where it is assured that the children will be found and placed in orphanages, because it remains illegal to abandon children. It is now estimated that girls represent more than 95% of international adoptions from China with the remaining children usually special-needs boys. The fall of Communism and the subsequent dissolution of the Soviet Union in the early 1990s also were noteworthy because these historic events led to a dramatic rise in adoptions from former Soviet countries (e.g., Russia and Ukraine). Less mentioned but relevant to the rising influx of Asian adoptees is the steady rate of international adoption from Central Asian countries, such as Kazakhstan and Uzbekistan.

Former President Gerald Ford holding an infant from Operation Babylift. (Photo courtesy of the Gerald R. Ford Library. See http://www.urbanmozaik.com/2001.sept_issue/sept01_film.html.)

Reasons for International Adoption

People choose to adopt internationally for many different reasons. One of the earliest and perhaps most dominant narratives for why people choose international adoption is that individuals and couples are guided by the humanitarian desire to provide children with stable, nurturing families. While humanitarian concern continues to partly explain the continuation of international adoption, the explanation is likely overly simplistic and contrived as an answer for the rising popularity of international adoption. It characterizes adoptees in an essentialized manner as impoverished victims of abandonment and adoptive parents as noble rescuers.

International adoption must be understood within a broader historical, racial, social, and cultural context (Dorow, 2006). For instance, major cultural and technological changes in the United States took place in the mid to late 20th century that contributed to greater public interest in transracial and international adoption. Most notably, the Cold War climate that followed World War II linked together notions of patriotism and citizenship with parenthood and the nuclear family (Klein, 2003). Biological kinship became a paramount force in society and the images of pregnancy, birth, and children were heavily romanticized during this period. Not surprisingly, childless couples began to feel the stigma of infertility, as they were publicly perceived to be deficient or lacking as individuals and as a family unit (Tyler May, 1995). Couples, particularly those with infertility, subsequently sought emotional fulfillment and validation as a family through the adoption of infants and young children.

This sentimental desire to form a nuclear family and raise a young child gradually transformed into a human right among many individuals and couples seeking to adopt. Soon, the demand for adoptable White children, usually born out of wedlock, outpaced their availability (Sokoloff, 1993). By the 1950s, domestic adoption of White children leveled off, as more single parents began to keep their children, while the availability of non-White infants increased. Medical advances, such as more widespread use of birth control and the legalization of abortion in 1973, contributed to the further decreased availability of adoptable children, and led to faster and easier diagnosis of infertility. Other technological advances, such as the introduction of baby formula, made possible the adoption of younger aged infants and children and, shortly thereafter, the preference for adopting infant children was cemented.

It is in this historical context that individuals and couples, including increasingly same-sex couples, started to turn to **transracial adoption** as an alternative means to start or expand families. The civil rights movement in the 1960s and 1970s gradually started to change longstanding racial attitudes held by White couples and adoption agencies. Adoption agencies responded by promoting domestic transracial adoption as a viable option, given the increased difficulty in finding homes for African American children. But by the early 1970s, civil rights activists and organizations, such as the National Association of Black Social Workers, began to protest against the transracial adoption of African Americans, arguing that the children would not develop positive racial identities and consequently be ill prepared to deal with living in a racist society. Similar criticism was levied against the transracial adoption of Native American children (Holt, 2001). These activists and organizations argued that transracial adoption was a form of **cultural genocide**. In the midst of these racial protests, adoption agencies abruptly halted and then avoided the practice of transracial placement until the 1990s when federal legislation was passed to promote domestic transracial adoption.

This social and political backdrop set the stage for international adoption, particularly from Asia, to gain favor by the early 1970s and to expand to its current popularity. For adoption agencies and prospective White parents, international adoption from Asia was viewed as a more viable option that guaranteed the adoption of a child because it entailed less bureaucracy and wait time than private adoption and less controversy than domestic transracial adoption (Bart-holet, 1993). International adoption also satisfied the preference of couples for ostensibly healthy infant children. This preference for healthy infants concurrently reinforced myths about the availability of only older children with special needs in the foster care system. The pressing real-ity is that prospective parents remain less interested in the adoption of Black children—young and older—who constitute one-third of foster care children (U.S. Department of Health and Human Services, 2006). Finally, the geographic and cultural distance between Asia and the United States helped to assure that the children were unlikely to be reclaimed by birth parents—a greater possibility associated with domestic adoption and a persistent fear among adoptive parents.

International Adoption Controversies

International adoption is not without controversy. At the start of the 21st century, adoption scholars posit that Americans today adopt internationally out of convenience and preference (Dorow, 2006). International adoption affords affluent and privileged families an opportunity to adopt with fewer controversies. The Black-White racial dilemma is avoided by adopting a foreign Asian child; questions about birth-parent rights are avoided; and unfounded fears of adopting a foster care baby with serious physical problems are avoided. However, adoption agencies and adoptive parents continue to use humanitarian language and images, such as acting in the best interest of the child, to justify their decisions and actions. Humanitarian language, in turn, serves as a powerful trope to overshadow the reality of familial entitlement, that is, the privi-leged needs of parents to create a nuclear family as taking precedence over the best interest and needs of the child (Lee, 2006).

There also is an increased awareness and concern of infants and children being treated as commodities and not as people with human rights, as well as exploitation of women and fami-lies in developing countries (Park Nelson, 2006). Critics of international adoption argue that prospective parents and adoption agencies from wealthier nations are taking advantage of the abject poverty of developing nations without consideration of the larger geopolitical context (Sarri, Baik, & Bombyk, 1998). The illegal international trafficking of children to satisfy the needs of childless individuals and couples seeking to start a family obviously is an extreme example of such practices, even though illegal adoption practices are not uncommon in some countries (Triseliotis, 2000).

An alternate humanitarian effort, proposed by some activists, is to advocate for and contrib-ute toward greater social welfare infrastructure in these developing countries, while gradually decreasing the rate of international adoption (Lovelock, 2000). Advocates of international adop-tion, by contrast, continue to emphasize the greater immediate need to provide orphans with stable, nurturing families and the role international adoption can play in raising greater aware-ness for the better treatment of orphans. To address some of these legitimate concerns, sending and receiving countries have begun to adopt international rules and regulations, such as those put forth by the Hague Convention on Protection of Children and Cooperation in Respect of Intercountry Adoption of 1993, which prioritizes the welfare of the child.

A more recent, emergent criticism of international adoption is the persistently overlooked transracial experience of children adopted from Asia and elsewhere (Oparah, Shin, & Trenka, 2006). Although there are no official statistics, the vast majority of children from Asia are adopted by White couples and individuals seeking to start or expand their families. A recent epidemiological survey of families with internationally adopted children in Minnesota, for example, reported that over 97% of the parents were White (Lee, Grotevant, Hellerstedt, & Gun-nar, 2006). Yet the transracial aspect of international adoption has received less controversy than in the case of Black-White domestic adoption, possibly because racism continues to be perceived as a Black-White issue and international adoption is still viewed as a humanitarian act. Such reasoning and practices, however, codify Asians as a nonrelevant racial group who can be excluded from racial discourse in the United States (Dorow, 2006).

The Paradox of International Adoption

One of the unique developmental challenges for adopted children is coming to terms with the reality of their adoption (Grotevant, Dunbar, Kohler, & Lash-Esau, 2000). Adoptees must grapple with a myriad of questions surrounding their adoption, such as why did my birth parents relinquish their rights to me; what would it have been like if I were not adopted; do I look like my birth parents; why did my adoptive parents choose to adopt? These questions reflect the inherent contradiction or paradox surrounding adoption. A child must be relinquished by one family to find a home in another family. In the case of international adoptees from Asia, the adoption paradox is further complicated by the transnational and transracial aspects to the experience.

Transnational Adoption Paradox

In contrast to domestic adoption, children like Sarah and Susan who are adopted internationally from Asia are necessarily dislocated from one family, culture, and country and relocated to another family, culture, and country. This experience of dislocation and relocation requires Asian adoptees not only to forgo their roots in the birth family in order to establish a sense of belonging in their adoptive family, but also to experience a loss of birth culture and heritage (Dorow, 2006). It is this loss of birth culture and heritage, while simultaneously acquiring and incorporating the adoptive family's culture and the larger American societal culture, which reflects the heart of the **transnational adoption paradox**. Some adopted individuals, such as Sarah/Mi Kyoung, choose to explore and make sense of this cultural loss, but others like Susan/Mi Young express no interest. Today, there are hundreds of Korean adoptees from the United States and Europe who have chosen to live in South Korea as repatriates in order to reconnect with their lost birth culture and heritage and, thus, make sense of the transnational adoption paradox in their own lives.

Transracial Adoption Paradox

Asian adoptees who are adopted transracially into White families also are exposed to a set of contradictory, racialized experiences that they must learn to navigate and negotiate over the course of a lifetime. Specifically, adoptees receive the benefits and privileges of being raised in a White family, including being perceived and treated by the adoptive family and local community as if they are members of the majority culture. But outside of the family and community, adoptees are perceived and treated by the larger society as racial minorities and therefore subject to prejudice, discrimination, and racism. Lee (2003) described this contradictory set of insider-outsider experiences as the **transracial adoption paradox**. Growing up in the rural Midwest is a striking example of the transracial adoption paradox. Sarah and Susan, for example, knew few other Asian Americans and often were perceived by others in their small community as the token minority. Consequently, they were not fully aware of their minority status and how it has affected them as children. This is a common adoption narrative in which Asian adoptees do not have a racial awakening until they leave home for college in a larger city and find themselves being treated as minorities for the first time in their lives (Meier, 1999).

Importantly, the transnational and transracial adoption paradoxes are not mutually exclusive experiences; they are not necessarily either/or situations. The transnational and transracial experiences may intersect, but they equally may diverge. For example, adoptees might encounter racism, which triggers questions about a person's place in American society and subsequently leads to questions about their birth family. Other times, adoptees might have an interest in their birth family and culture, but not perceive themselves as subjects of racism and discrimination. Asian adoptees independently and concurrently negotiate these cultural sequelae that follow adoption throughout their lifetimes.

The extent to which adoptees try to understand and incorporate birth culture, ethnicity, and race in their everyday lives varies greatly (Lee, 2003). For instance, upon adoption, children acculturate naturally to mainstream White culture within the family and society. The feelings of loss and longing for one's native homeland that are characteristic of the transnational dislocation, however, may not emerge until much later in life and, even then, with varying intensity. Likewise, adoptees may engage in active learning about their ethnic roots and racial group membership as part of their identity development, but others may not. Moreover, not all adoptees are disrupted by these paradoxical experiences. For some adoptees, the need to reconcile with birth family, culture, and race may be less central to their identities and daily lives. Ethnic exploration also may be avoided by adoptees because it makes them feel more different from their predominantly White peers with whom they wish to fit in (Meier, 1999). Clearly, there is a great deal of individual differences in the development and well-being of Asian adoptees when it comes to these paradoxical adoption experiences.

Psychology of International Adoption

One of the most common and pressing questions that arises when psychologists think about internationally adopted children is "How are they doing?" This question about the development and well-being of adoptees seems relatively straightforward, but an underlying assumption is made about adoption when asking this question. Specifically, the adoption of a child is viewed as a natural experiment and, by extension, a natural intervention that aims to address the essential need of a child for a safe, stable, and nurturing home environment in which to develop and grow (Haugaard & Hazan, 2003). An important corollary to this assumption is that a child's life prior to adoption, such as living in foster care, an orphanage, or another form of institution care, is a stressful, deprived situation with adverse short- and long-term consequences on development and well-being. In other words, adoption is conceptualized as an appropriate means to offset the detrimental effects of institutional care and to improve the lives of orphan children. Consequently, asking the question "How are they doing?" reflects a need to know if adoption is working as intended.

In psychology, "How are they doing?" can be answered in a variety of ways. First, it is important to establish the criterion by which to evaluate adoptees. In most cases, adoption researchers are interested in the social (e.g., peer interaction), behavioral (e.g., language and media preference), and emotional (e.g., presence of depressive symptoms) development of the children. More recently, researchers have begun to examine the ethnic, racial, and cultural adjustment of the children. For example, do adopted children identify with being Asian as strongly as Asian immigrant children? Second, it is important to determine the appropriate comparison group when attempting to answer this question. There are three primary ways in which to make this determination: (a) address how Asian adoptees are doing compared to non-adopted peers in their community, (b) address how Asian adoptees are doing compared to children who remain in orphanages and foster care in Asia, and (c) address how Asian adoptees raised transracially in White families are doing compared to Asian adoptees and non-adoptees raised in same-race families. This latter approach would be considered a very strong test of whether growing up in a transracial family had a different effect on a child's development than growing up in an immigrant family.

Most psychological studies of Asian adoptees have focused on the first approach to answering this question; specifically, the comparison of the social, emotional, and behavioral adjustment of adoptees with non-adopted, predominantly White peers in the United States. This comparison is usually made because it is difficult to compare adoptees with orphans and same-race peers due to limited access to these populations. There is no published research that compares children adopted from Asia with children raised in orphanages or foster care families in Asia. There also is limited research on the development and well-being of transracially raised Asian adoptees, compared with either same-race adopted and non-adopted peers. One reason for the lack of comparison studies is that there are few Asian Americans who are adopting children from Asia, although this pattern may change as more Asian Americans delay marriage and pregnancy and are affected by infertility.

Mental Health Outcome

The first empirical studies on transracially adopted children originated largely as a response to the racial and political controversies surrounding transracial adoption in the 1970s (Lee, 2003). Researchers were initially interested in whether the adoption of a minority child (i.e., Black) into a White family would be detrimental to the child's development and well-being. Some **outcome studies** compared transracial adoptees with inracial or same-race adoptees (i.e., Black children raised in Black families), but most early studies compared transracial adoptees with non-adopted children. The line of research eventually expanded to include transnationally adopted children raised transracially in White families.

The bulk of adoption research, which focuses on the behavioral development and mental health outcome of adoptees, generally supports the view that adoptees are doing as well as their non-adopted peers (Lee, 2003). Early studies based on clinical samples of adopted children suggested that adoptees exhibit more behavioral problems, but more recent studies demonstrate that children who are adopted transnationally and transracially are not at higher risk for emotional and behavioral problems. In most cases, roughly 80% to 90% of adoptees have few serious behavioral and emotional problems, a rate comparable to same-race and non-adopted children. Adoptees also tend to have similar levels of self-esteem and social adjustment. A recent meta-analysis of this research over the last 50 years (Juffer & van IJzendoorn, 2005), for example, found that adoptees had more problem behaviors than non-adoptees, but these **effect sizes** were small. Additionally, when Juffer and van IJzendoorn compared domestic and international adoptees, they found that international adoptees had fewer behavioral problems, as well as fewer mental health referrals, than domestic adoptees.

In situations in which adoptees have more serious problems, researchers have identified a variety of pre-adoption mitigating factors, such as age at adoption, length of institutional care, and birth country of origin (Lee, 2003). Notably, Rutter, O'Connor, and the ERA Study Team (2004) have persuasively demonstrated in studies of Romanian orphan children that age at adoption and institutional care likely reflect prenatal and postnatal neglect and abuse which, in turn, have short- and long-term consequences on child development and mental health. In the case of adoptees from South Korea and China, it appears that they have fewer behavioral and emotional problems than children adopted from elsewhere. For example, a national epidemiological study conducted in Sweden found that Asian adoptees, compared to international adoptees from Latin America, had fewer social and emotional adjustment problems (Hjern, Lindblad, & Vinnerljung, 2002). This birth country difference likely reflects better pre-adoption care in Asia.

Although important to our understanding of child development, one major criticism of adoption outcome studies is that it reduces the adoption experience to a methodology to study the more universal experience of resilience in the midst of adversity. What is missing in the research literature is an understanding of the post-adoption experiences of international adoptees and their families. Specifically, the existent literature fails to address the complex and intersecting transracial and transnational issues of international adoption, despite the fact that the first outcome studies began as a response to these concerns. Instead, any group difference found in outcome studies tends to be attributed to pre-adoption adversity, which reinforces the dominant narrative of adoption as a natural intervention for children who were previously raised in stressful and deprived orphanages and institutions. This viewpoint may stem in part from the fact that most studies on adoptees focus on child development and few studies have tracked the lives of adoptees into adolescence and adulthood. What becomes clear, particularly in the lives of adolescent and adult adoptees, is that the post-adoption ethnic and racial experiences of children raised transnationally and transracially in White families are overlooked.

Ethnic Identity Development

Although outcome studies suggest that Asian adoptees adjust well in social, behavioral, and emotional domains, these findings do not address the concern over whether children adopted from Asia experience difficulty in being raised transnationally and transracially in a White family. Research on children of immigrants, for example, find that they generally adapt to American society but can still struggle with acculturative stress and discrimination (Portes & Rumbaut, 2001). Asian adoptees similarly may adjust well to their adoptive families and communities, but this success does not mean that they do not struggle with transnational and transracial issues in their lives. Among the earliest concerns among adoption experts was the extent to which international adoptees would reconcile their ethnicity and race as they grew up in transracial and transnational households, living in predominantly White communities (Benson, Sharma, & Roehlkepartain, 1994; Simon & Altstein, 2000). To address the post-adoption life experiences of adoptees, adoption researchers have begun to examine the racial and ethnic experiences of Asian adopted children.

Research on mainly Korean adoptees suggests that adoptees exhibit a great deal of variability in their ethnic identities, while at the same time easily acculturating and assimilating to American society (Adams, Tessler, & Gamache, 2005; Benson, Sharma, & Roehlkepartain, 1994; Brooks & Barth, 1999; Feigelman & Silverman, 1984; Freundlich & Lieberthal, 2000; Huh & Reid, 2000; Kim, Hong, & Kim, 1979; Lee & Quintana, 2005; Yoon, 2001; Yoon, 2004). Research from the 1970s and 1980s found that earlier generations of Korean adoptees did not identify strongly with their ethnic culture. In a survey of adult Korean adoptees, for example, many adoptees admitted to having identified or viewing themselves as Caucasian or White as children (Freundlich & Lieberthal, 2000). Like children of color growing up in predominantly White environments, most adoptees simply want to fit in with their majority White peers during childhood and adolescence. This desire to assimilate contributes to some adoptees feeling ashamed or embarrassed about their ethnic background as children, particularly in regards to their racial and physical appearance, such as skin color, shape of eyes, and height. Adoptees also may adopt a color-blind position by identifying more strongly with being "just a person" or American. These racial attitudes and feelings often are reinforced by adoptive parents who similarly subscribe to a color-blind racial attitude.

Other studies have found that adoptees identify positively with their ethnic group and do not exhibit ambivalence about their ethnicity and race (Bergquist, Campbell, & Unrau, 2003; Brooks & Barth, 1999). There is some evidence to suggest that the recent generation of adopted children may be even more comfortable with their ethnic group membership than the older generation of adoptees (Westhues & Cohen, 1997). For these younger adoptees, being Korean (or Chinese, Indian, Vietnamese) appears to be more central to their emergent identities. This shift possibly reflects generational changes in familial and societal attitudes about the role and relevance of race and ethnicity in children's lives. More research is needed that examines the development of ethnic identity and specifically what types of life experiences inside and outside of the family contribute to positive and negative ethnic identification.

Similar to children of immigrant parents, research finds that ethnic identity is positively associated with well-being among Asian adoptees. Yoon (2001), for example, found moderate relationships between ethnic identity and well-being, self-esteem, and low psychological distress among Korean adolescent adoptees. However, not all aspects of ethnic identity are necessarily related to greater well-being. For example, adoptees that identify with their culture of origin do not necessarily become interested or invested in Asian culture. In an exploratory study of adult Korean adoptees who were involved in Korean adoption groups, Lee, Yoo, and Roberts (2004b) reported that pride in one's ethnicity was associated with greater well-being; whereas, interest and engagement in one's ethnic culture was associated with lower well-being. This differential effect is contrary to research on non-adopted Asian Americans, which has not found a negative correlation between identity exploration and well-being (Lee & Yoo, 2004a). Other research has found that identity confusion in international adoptees is related to more psychological distress (Cederblad, Hook, Irhammar, & Mercke, 1999). Unlike children of immigrants whose explorations of ethnic culture later in life build upon earlier **cultural socialization** experiences, adult adoptees who are exploring their ethnic culture do not have this foundation. Consequently, they may experience some lowering of well-being as they negotiate the transracial and transnational adoption paradoxes.

Racial Discrimination

Not surprisingly, similar to other minority groups, discrimination and racism can affect the **ethnic identity development** and mental health of Asian adoptees. Adoption narratives are replete with childhood stories of adoptees who were teased, excluded, and assaulted for looking different from their White peers (Kim, 2004; Trenka, Oparah, & Shin, 2006). Adoptees also share stories of being pitied and concurrently discriminated against by members of their own ethnic and racial group, such as by the Korean immigrant community, reinforcing the stigma of adoption. This awareness of racial differences and subsequent discrimination and racism begins early in childhood (Brown & Bigler, 2005). Huh and Reid (2000), for example, documented that Korean adoptees are aware of racial differences and begin to make sense of adoption and race as young as 4 and 5 years old. By early adolescence, these societal experiences of discrimination and racism usually contradict their personal experiences of being raised unconditionally in a White family. Eventually, discrimination and racism cause adoptees to experience ambivalence toward issues of race, culture, and ethnicity (Freundlich & Lieberthal, 2000). Some adoptees attempt to resolve this transracial paradox through further exploration of their ethnic identities; other adoptees tend to minimize these experiences and develop a color-blind racial attitude in an effort to assimilate into White society. This latter coping strategy, in turn, likely leads to a less salient ethnic identity.

Discrimination and racism also affects the mental health and well-being of Asian adoptees. As mentioned earlier, most studies find that international adoptees fare as well as domestic and non-adoptees. The one exception appears to be an elevated risk for suicidal behavior in adolescent and young adult international adoptees, when compared with domestic adoptees, non-adoptees, and immigrants. This epidemiological finding was derived from a series of national cohort studies conducted in Sweden (Hjern et al., 2002; von Brocyskowski, Hjern, Lindblad, & Vinnerljung, 2006), and the researchers suggest racial discrimination against transracial, transnational adoptees as an important post-adoption risk factor that explain this group difference.

However, the findings have yet to be replicated in the United States. Still, a few smaller-scale studies on Asian adoptees in the United States and Europe have confirmed the negative impact of perceived discrimination and racial discomfort on mental health and well-being (Cederblad et al., 1999; Feigelman, 2000; Lee et al. 2004b). There is clearly a need for more research on this topic. There is a particular lack of information about Asian adoptees' experiences with discrimination by members of one's own ethnic and racial group, such as the stigma of adoption within the Asian immigrant community.

Cultural Socialization

Cultural socialization refers to the transmission of ethnic, racial, and cultural information, including culture-specific knowledge, awareness, values, customs, tradition, and behaviors, from adults (primarily parents) to children (Hughes et al., 2006). The intent of cultural socialization is to foster in children the development of a positive ethnic identity, the acquisition of coping strategies to deal with discrimination, and social competence in diverse communities (Lee, 2003). A recent review of the research on minority and immigrant families generally finds that cultural socialization is related to positive ethnic identity development, awareness of discrimination, and greater well-being (Hughes et al., 2006).

Cultural socialization in transracial, transnational adoptive families is unique from same-race minority and immigrant families. In adoptive families, it is not as inherent or natural a process given the racial differences between parents and children. Consequently, it is a wholly extrinsic process for adoptive parents who decide to make an effort to expose their children to the birth culture and to address racial differences. Cultural socialization occurs through explicit instruction, rather than parental modeling of cultural practices. Likewise, it occurs through the provision of opportunities, such as culture camps, rather than in vivo absorption. Adoptive parents also tend to emphasize knowledge and awareness about birth culture but not the values and behaviors of the birth culture. A final distinction is that cultural socialization in adoptive families concurrently places an emphasis on adoption culture, as issues of race, ethnicity, and culture are embedded within the adoption context.

From the start of international adoption, social welfare workers expressed some concern about the transnational and transracial adoption paradoxes and encouraged parents to be sensitive to the cultural transition of the child (Graham, 1957; Valk, 1957). At the same time, the prevailing attitude in society was to ignore or overlook racial and ethnic differences in individuals and families. Asian adoptees subsequently were raised in predominantly White family and community environments that directly and indirectly promoted assimilation to mainstream White America (Meier, 1999). Children's heritages were not always overtly denied or downplayed, but children were encouraged to view themselves "as American as the next child." This color-blind racial attitude toward parenting and child development, however, minimized and invalidated transracial and transnational experiences of children.

By the early 1980s, adoptive families with Korean children began to make greater individual and collective effort to expose their children to Korean culture (e.g., culture camps; language schools) in an effort to help children develop an appreciation for their heritage and a positive ethnic identity. Adoptee narratives and memoirs from the 1990s reveal that adoptees often had ambivalent feelings about such enculturation efforts (Kim, 2000). The experiences raised their curiosity and interest in birth culture, but it also reinforced feelings of differentness during a time when peer acceptance and belonging was paramount. In other instances, adoptees elected to not explore their ethnic heritage because they did not want to upset their adoptive parents and they did not have the awareness, knowledge, and resources to make coherent sense of these experiences.

Today, many adoptive families with children from Korea, China, Vietnam, India, and elsewhere are aware of the importance of incorporating the child's birth culture into family life and are actively involved in the cultural socialization of their children (Lee et al., 2006; Scroggs & Heitfield, 2001; Tessler, Gamache, & Liu, 1999). Adoption agencies also have increased efforts to provide post-adoption services to help facilitate the cultural upbringing of the child, including homeland tours to the birth country, mentorship programs, and sometimes birth parent searches. Culture camps, language schools, and play dates with other adopted children represent common approaches to cultural socialization in transracial and transnational adoptive families. Although these efforts at cultural socialization represent forward progress, critics argue that they often fail to address the geopolitical, economic, and racial politics that underlie transnational and transracial adoption (Dorow, 2006; Trenka et al., 2006).

Cultural socialization can take place independent of parental involvement. The normative developmental process of separation and autonomy from adoptive families allows many adult adoptees to openly negotiate the transracial and transnational adoption paradoxes on their own. Important adult life transitions sometimes facilitate this process, such as the start of college and greater exposure to racial and ethnic diversity (Meier, 1999). Romantic relationships, dating, marriage, pregnancy, and child birth also can lead adoptees to examine the meaning of ethnicity and race in their personal lives. Medical complications are another life change that can motivate an adoptee to search for one's birth family. Whatever the impetus, the extent to which adoptees engage in cultural socialization concurrently reflects their ethnic and **adoptive identity** development.

Cultural socialization research is just beginning to occur. Limited studies find that adoptees who socialize with other Asian children and who participate in cultural activities, such as culture camps and language schools, are more likely to develop positive ethnic identities (Lee & Quintana, 2005). It is equally important for parents to support and participate in cultural activities with their children. White parents who engage their adopted Asian children in discussions regarding ethnicity and race, interact with others who are Asian, and live in an ethnically diverse neighborhood are more likely to facilitate positive ethnic identity development in their children. Yoon (2004), for example, found that Korean adolescent adoptees who perceived their parents as supportive of issues of race and ethnicity had higher ethnic identity scores. However, not all adoptive parents attend to issues of race and ethnicity (Scroggs & Heitfield, 2001). Lee et al. (2006), for example, reported that adoptive parents who are more color-blind in their racial attitudes were less likely to engage in parenting behaviors that promoted cultural socialization in their children.

Adoptive Identity

Surprisingly little research has been conducted on the adoptive identity of Asian adoptees. Most research on this subject has occurred in the context of domestic adoption. Grotevant (1997) and Grotevant et al. (2000) situate adoptive identity in the context of societal attitudes toward kinship and family. Specifically, American society continues to privilege biological kinship over other forms of socially constructed kinship, such as adoptive kinship. It is in this context that adoptees work through the paradox of adoption and "strive to make meaning of their situation while negotiating their differences and similarities from members of their family, including adoptive and birth family members" (Grotevant et al., 2000, p. 381). In his pioneering research on this issue, Grotevant finds that some adoptees may intensely reflect upon their adoption status, while others may give relatively little thought to the issue. As with ethnic identity, the level of interest or preoccupation with adoption is based largely on the salience of adoption to the given individual.

A unique feature of transnational and transracial adoption is that being Asian (or Korean) and being adopted are inextricably connected experiences. An understanding of international adoption requires adoptees to understand the role of race and ethnicity in the adoption process, from pre-placement decisions by parents and agencies to post-adoption life experiences. Conversely, an understanding of race and ethnicity in life requires adoptees to understand the pretext and context for their adoption into a White family in the United States. In this regard, identity development for Asian adoptees reflects a connection with both birth culture and adoption culture. For other adoptees, however, the dual identity as both adoptee and Asian can lead to greater identity confusion. Adoption narratives describe the struggle and stigma adoptees sometimes face from the mainstream White community, including their adoptive families, as well as within the immigrant Asian community, as they negotiate what it means to be adopted and Asian (Trenka et al., 2006).

Hübinette (2004) suggests that Asian adoptees have begun to establish hybrid identities that account for their experiences as both ethnic minorities and adoptees. In other words, Asian adoptees are beginning to define themselves according to salient features of their own lives, rather than trying to force themselves within existing identity paradigms. Adult adoptees, notably Korean Americans who were adopted prior to the 1980s, have begun to organize to give voice to their own concerns and to establish legitimacy within the adoptive community. Adoptees worldwide have formed social and political organizations to strengthen identities, build social bonds and support networks, and establish legitimacy within the larger Asian American and adoption communities. Some adoptees have elected to share their personal journeys through autobiography, poetry, prose, fiction, and documentary to increase public awareness and to educate people inside and outside of the adoption community (Kim, 2000). Other adult adoptees have started to challenge the overall legitimacy and necessity of continued international adoption from South Korea, because the country is now economically capable of internally addressing its social welfare system (e.g., Global Overseas Adoptees Link). These activities reflect the creation of the third space in which adoptees are able to advocate on their own behalf and to identify uniquely as both Asian and adopted, rather than being forced to choose between these two identities and cultural groups (Hübinette, 2004).

In finding their own voices through these adoption-related activities, adult adoptees have begun to contest the color-blind racial attitudes and parenting practices of adoptive families, particularly those from earlier generations, and concurrently have started to advocate on behalf of younger Asian children adopted into White families (Kim, 2004; Oparah et al., 2006). Many adult adoptees are actively engaged with younger adoptees through outreach activities, mentor relationships, and culture camps, thereby serving as role models for the younger generation. They specifically emphasize the need for adoptive families to address ethnic and racial differences within the family and to appropriately incorporate cultural and racial diversity in the lives of their children.

Search and Reunion

At a young age, adoptees begin to inquire about birth family (Brodzinsky, Schechter, & Henig, 1992). As children, they may ask about why they were given up by the birth mother. As children grow older, they become more curious about their pre-adoption life circumstances and may wonder whatever happened to their birth family. The loss and imagining of the birth family, particularly the birth mother, can affect the well-being and complicate the identity development of adoptees (Pavao, 1998). In a study of domestically and internationally adopted children, for example, Smith and Brodzinsky (2002) reported that children with higher levels of negative affect about birth-parent loss had more depressive symptoms and lower self-worth.

As adoptees come to terms with what it means to be adopted transnationally and transracially, they must concurrently come to terms with the ambiguity of their past, including the lack of information about their birth circumstances and their disconnection with the birth family and birth culture (Powell & Afifi, 2005). As evinced in documentaries and narratives (Choy & Choy, 2006), an increasing number of adult adoptees have begun to actively search for their birth families with occasional reunions—some successful and others less so. Adoptive parents also may actively engage in the search process on behalf of their children, although there remains ambivalence on the part of some adoptive families who prefer to not search or not support their child's desire to search. Whether families elect to search for birth family or not, adoption advocates now encourage adoptive parents to begin to address the child's adoption and birth culture at a young age in order to facilitate the resolution of feelings of loss and difference (e.g., Register, 2005; Steinberg & Hall, 2000).

Birth family searches and reunions remain one of the more hotly contested issues in international adoption. In recent years, adoption agencies have made a better effort at educating parents about the importance of addressing these issues in a child's life and many families are open to this issue. However, not all families agree that it is an important issue. In fact, adoptive parents often seek to adopt internationally because they want to avoid situations in which birth parents reclaim parental rights of the child, as sometimes occurs in domestic adoption cases (Tessler et al., 1999). Thus, a fear or worry among some adoptive parents is that they will lose their children when children express interest in and search for the birth family. It is not so much the case that children will reject their adoptive families in favor of the birth families, but parents may fear losing the emotional bond with their children.

Not surprisingly, there also remains a strong belief that the closed adoption process, in which identifying information is not shared and there is no communication between adoptive and birth families, is better for all members of the adoption triad. For a long time, it was believed that open adoption arrangements, which allow identifying information and contact to occur between adoption triad members, would negatively impact the child's identity and development. More recent research contests this longstanding view. Von Korff, Grotevant, and McRoy (2006), for example, reported that adoptees with long-term direct contact with birth parents had lower levels of externalizing problem behaviors than adoptees with no contact. No empirical studies have been conducted to date that examine the psychological correlates of birth family contact and reunions in children adopted internationally from Asia.

Birth Family

Adoption historians, researchers, and advocacy experts (Modell, 2002; Pavao, 1998; Zamostny, O'Brien, Baden, & Wiley, 2003) emphasize the importance of taking into consideration all members of the adoption triad—adoptees, adoptive parents, and birth parents. However, research on internationally adopted children focuses almost exclusively on the adoptee and adoptive family. Overlooked in the research are the life experiences of the birth family, particularly the birth parents, and the role of the birth family in the development and well-being of adoptees.

In most cases of international adoption, information about the birth family is limited because children often are placed anonymously in the care of orphanages. Birth parents may choose to not have contact with the adoptive family for many reasons, including the shame of having relinquished parental rights, not wanting their current family to know about the adoption, and a sincere desire to not want to disturb the child's new adoptive life. In other cases, orphanages and adoption agencies discourage birth parents from seeking or maintaining contact with the child or adoptive family at least until the child reaches adulthood. A great many adoptive parents also choose to not seek more information about the birth family. When adoptive parents or adoptees do seek more information about the birth family, they typically encounter administrative resistance and deception from orphanages and adoption agencies for various reasons, including cultural misunderstanding, concerns over confidentiality, poor record keeping, and the assumption that agencies know what is in the best interest of the adoptee.

The reasons that a birth parent chooses to relinquish a child is complex and not well understood. In China, it is the state's one-child policy and the strong desire for a male heir that contributes to the relinquishment of daughters (Johnson et al., 1998). In South Korea, it is usually the stigma of single motherhood and the lack of resources that motivate teenage girls and young women to place their children for adoption (Dorow, 1999). Regardless of the circumstances that lead to a child's relinquishment, it is important to understand that relinquishment does not mean a birth parent did not love and care for the child. Birth parents often choose to place a child for adoption because they believe it is in the best interest of the child. Other research (e.g., Feast, Marwood, Seabrook, & Webb, 1994; Speirs et al., 2005) suggests that an increasing number of birth parents have been interested in or have initiated searches for the relinquished child. Anecdotal stories of Korean birth mothers also support the desire of some birth mothers for future contact with the child (Dorow, 1999).

There is some conceptual and empirical evidence to suggest that relinquishing a child for adoption is a distressing experience and the most difficult decision for a number of birth parents (Brodzinsky, 1990; Wiley & Baden, 2005). This research is based largely on domestic adoption cases, although Johnson et al. (1998) has documented this finding among Chinese birth families. Wiley and Baden (2005) identified a number of salient issues for birth parents. Among the stressors reported by biological parents of adoptees, issues related to the relinquishment of their child, the nature (voluntary, coerced, or involuntary) of relinquishment, and the period of time post-relinquishment are often associated with a myriad of mixed—and often distressing—emotions and experiences. In spite of these difficulties, the psychological processes and experiences of the biological parents of adoptees receive minimal attention in the literature. There is a need for research that focuses not only on the traumatic aspect of relinquishment but also on factors associated with relinquishment and the post-adoption coping and adjustment of birth parents.

Issues for Consideration

Over the past several decades, international adoption from Asia, mainly China and South Korea but also from Vietnam, India, and the Philippines, has grown exponentially in the United States. Despite the increased prevalence, international adoption continues to have a controversial history—past and present. As described in the chapter, early practices of adoption had social and political agendas that did not necessarily tend to be in the best interests of adoptees. These persistent views on adoption tend to highlight altruistic or humanistic reasons yet remain relatively silent on important geopolitical issues, such as wealth, power, and privilege. In addition, issues related to race, ethnicity, and culture and development continue to be minimized in some adoption circles and sometimes are not addressed at all by some adoption agencies, adoptive families, and other adoption advocates. Although the practice of adoption has not been without controversy, the international adoption of children from Asia will likely continue to be a viable way in which Americans can create or expand families.

Families formed through international adoption typically are portrayed as a new variant of the traditional, nuclear family (Dorow, 2006). However, this romantic dyadic image of the adoptive parent and child is oftentimes predicated on the social construction of family as biologically rooted and consisting of only parents and children (Leon, 2002). It is critical to re-imagine adoptive families as normative and distinctive unto themselves. Adoptive families take on many different shapes. Some families consist of domestically and internationally adopted children. Other families have older biological children and very young adopted children. In a few instances, adoptive families also have incorporated members of the birth families as a part of the larger family. Given the complexity of adoptive family types, it is critically important to understand and study the phenomenological experiences of international adoptees.

In this chapter, we also have highlighted the various psychological processes associated with transnational and transracial adoption. Some are unique to the adoption status (e.g., birth family search) and others are shared with non-adoptees (e.g., exploration of ethnic identity). It is important to note that even for commonly shared experiences such as the exploration of ethnic identity, the adoptee experience of the process may be qualitatively different. Although it is important to reflect on adoptee experiences and development in terms of issues such as ethnic identity, cultural socialization, experiences of discrimination, and adoptive identity, it should also be noted that each of these issues and processes impact the adoptee individually and collectively. That is, these processes do not occur in a vacuum. Experiences of racial discrimination likely impact the ethnic identity development process, which in turn may affect the way in which an adoptee interprets race-related experiences. The processes and outcomes of adoptee experiences are potentially complex and heterogeneous.

There are a number of possible ways in which to improve our understanding of internationally adopted children from Asia. First, our understanding of the psychological processes of transracially and transnationally adopted Asians is built upon a body of cross-sectional research that provides a snapshot of the adoptee experience. There exists a lack of an empirical understanding of international adoption from the perspective of the adoptee, adoptive family, and birth family across the lifespan. Future research employing longitudinal methods may increase our understanding of the Asian adoptee experience and development. Second, as previously mentioned a majority of the adoption research typically associates any adjustment outcome (e.g., mental health) with pre-adoption variables and tends to negate post-adoption experiences. Third, a majority of the research on adoptees compares the adjustment of international adoptees with predominantly White peers in the United States instead of with non-adopted Asian peers. This may reflect a larger tendency in cultural research in the United States, in which members of racial/ethnic minority groups are studied by comparing them to White counterparts or European American culture (Delgado-Romero, Galván, Maschino, & Rowland, 2005; Ponterotto, 1988). It might be advantageous to use more appropriate comparison groups (e.g., non-adopted Asian or Asian American samples). Fourth, research that accounts for the nuanced and complex way in which the myriad psychological processes (e.g., adoptive identity development, ethnic identity development, racial socialization, experiences of racial discrimination) interact and collectively impact the development and adjustment of Asian adoptees will likely advance our knowledge in this area. Lastly, research that operates from a strengths focus (as opposed to a deficit model) and highlights the adaptive coping and strengths of transracially and transnationally adopted Asians will likely add to the current understanding of this population.

Summary

In sum, the history, experience, and presence of Asian adoptees has been overlooked by most scholars, practitioners, and laypeople in this country. However, the continued transnational and transracial adoption of Asian children in the United States has begun to receive attention by some adoption practitioners and researchers. These researchers have highlighted the unique transracial, transnational, and psychological aspects associated with Asian adoption. Although much of this research suggests that the over-all mental health and adjustment of Asian adoptees is approximately equal to that of their non-adopted counterparts, there exist a number of other issues salient to this population. For example, most adoptees must negotiate the transnational and transracial adoption paradoxes. In addition, issues of ethnic identity development, racial discrimination, cultural socialization, adoptive identity, and birth family search and reunion are commonly experienced by Asian adoptees. Given the unique, complex, and heterogeneous experiences of this population, it is critically important for psychologists and mental health professionals to acknowledge the presence of and further explore the life experiences of Asian adoptees.

Discussion Questions

1. Do you think the psychological development of Asian adoptees is substantially different from their non-adopted peers? Give some examples of how the development is similar or different.
2. What do you think are the most salient issues to address when trying to understand the experiences of Asian adoptees? Are there particular developmental periods when certain issues are more likely to arise?
3. Adoptive parents vary in terms of their attention to race/ethnicity and their engagement in cultural socialization. Do you think that there is an "ideal" approach to raising Asian adoptees? Why or why not?
4. In terms of Asian adoptees' ethnic identity (e.g., identifying as Korean, Korean American, or American) and cultural engagement (on a continuum from none to completely engaged in their culture of origin), is there an "ideal" outcome?
5. How might Asian adoptees' experiences as racial/ethnic minorities in the United States potentially differ from those of other non-adopted racial/ethnic minorities?

Case Study

So far this chapter has focused on the history, theory, and research of how adoption affects Asian Americans in their personal lives, daily functioning, and psychological growth and development. The chapter will now shift its focus to the earlier case study of Mi Kyoung and Mi Young to illustrate how Asian Americans who were adopted internationally experience and cope with the issues discussed in this chapter.

Mi Kyoung and Mi Young are identical twins born in South Korea. They were found on the front steps of a hospital in Incheon and placed in a nearby orphanage. A physician estimated that they were 2 months old at the time. They were adopted into the United States 8 months later by a childless White couple in their early forties who raised them as "American" and renamed them, Sarah and Susan. They were completely immersed in U.S. culture and did not engage in any Korean culture or related activities. Sarah and Susan, now 20 years old, grew up in a small, predominantly White community in Nebraska where they were one of only a handful of racial minorities in school and town. Both were actively involved in their school and local community. Sarah now attends college in Chicago; Susan attends college closer to home in Lincoln.

Although twins, the sisters' current attitudes and experiences as Korean Americans and as adoptees are quite different. Sarah never felt that she really fit in growing up and feels strongly that something is missing in her life. She is actively involved in a Korean adult adoptee group and the local Korean immigrant community in Chicago.

She listens to Korean music and watches Korean television dramas. In addition, with the aid of computer software, she is teaching herself to write and speak Korean. She also has begun to publicly use her Korean name, Mi Kyoung, but this name change, along with a desire to search for their birth parents, has strained relations with her adoptive family. By contrast, Susan says that she does not think too much about being adopted and is not interested in learning more about Korean culture or their birth family. She looks back on her childhood as typical and feels that people never made her feel different because of her ethnicity and race. Susan self-identifies as Korean when asked by others but feels no meaningful connection to her birth culture. She is quite happy just living her life as a "regular American" without hyphenated identities as a Korean American, Korean adoptee, and Asian American.

Case Study Discussion

Though identical twins, these sisters have come to strikingly different conclusions regarding the salience or importance of their culture of origin and the meaning associated with being Korean. Initially, it might be confusing as to how identical twins sharing the same environment could develop such different identities. Upon further reflection, it is not difficult to imagine that over the years, Susan and Mi Kyoung may have negotiated aspects of the transracial and transnational adoption paradoxes in different ways. Whereas the *way* in which Susan, Mi Kyoung, and other Asian adoptees negotiate the international adoption paradoxes may vary, there is some consistency with *what* they will negotiate over the course of their life. A majority of adoptees deal with issues related to the centrality of ethnic identification, experiences of racial discrimination and prejudice, reflections on being adopted, varying degrees of exposure to their birth culture, and whether to seek further information about their birth family and how this might impact their relations with their adoptive family. It is clear that the myriad of psychological issues can and likely do shape the developmental trajectory of this population—and that the way in which each of these issues impacts the lives of adoptees can vary significantly. Simply put, there is no norm for transracial and transnational Asian adoptee development and adjustment. Furthermore, the way in which an individual adoptee addresses the transnational and transracial paradoxes may vary across the life span.

In developing an intervention strategy for working with either sister, perhaps the most important component would be to normalize her experience. As previously noted, there are numerous ways in which Asian adoptees negotiate the complex paradoxes and related issues. Therefore, it might be beneficial to highlight the normalcy of her adoptive experiences. It might also be helpful to facilitate a sense of empowerment in the client by constructively raising issues and questions regarding both her status as an adoptee (e.g., "why did my birth parents put me up for adoption?"), her experiences as an adoptee (e.g., "how would my life be different if I wasn't adopted?"), and relationships with her adoptive family (e.g., "if I seek out my birth family, how will my adoptive family feel?"). These questions might seem to touch a taboo topic, but such exploration can be beneficial for the client to explore both cognitively and emotionally. Finally, it might be helpful to connect the client to other adoptees, adoptee networks, or adoption literature. Connecting the client to other Asian adoptees and/or a number of other adoptee resources might allow the client to build a supportive network of individuals and a safe place for the client to explore and share feelings and experiences.

Case Study Discussion Questions

For undergraduate students, please consider the following questions:

1. What are your initial thoughts and feelings regarding the different ways in which Mi Kyoung and Susan have explored and embraced their ethnic heritage?
2. Mi Kyoung's internalization of her ethnic heritage has ultimately resulted in a strained relationship with her adoptive family. Do you think that Mi Kyoung's adoptive parents have the right to be distressed with her desire to find her birth parents? What do you think it would be like to tell your adoptive parents that you are interested in contacting your birth parents?
3. Do you think that Susan will eventually become interested in her birth culture or birth family? Why or why not? Do you think that it is in her best interest to do so?

For graduate students and/or beginning therapists, please consider the following questions:

1. Based on the research with Asian adoptees and your own experience, would you be more concerned for Mi Kyoung or Susan in terms of overall psychological adjustment and well-being? Why?
2. Describe Mi Kyoung and Susan's current development in the context of the transracial adoption paradox and discuss how this might impact your approach to working with each person.
3. Do you think the way in which Mi Kyoung and Susan experience and react to experiences of racism and discrimination differ? Why or why not?

Key Terms

Adoptive identity: An individual's awareness and appreciation of his or her adoption and the extent to which an individual identifies with this group.

Cultural genocide: The destruction and dissolution of an individual's and/or group's cultural heritage.

Cultural socialization: The transmission of ethnic, racial, and cultural information from adults to children.

Effect sizes: Estimates of the strength or magnitude of an intervention effect or association between two variables.

Ethnic identity development: The process by which an individual develops an awareness and appreciation of his or her ethnic group membership status and the extent to which an individual identifies with this group membership.

International adoption: The adoption of a child from one country by a parent(s) who is a citizen and resident of another country; typically, the parent(s) and child have different racial and ethnic backgrounds.

Outcome studies: Medical or psychological research that focuses on the adjustment and adaptation of a particular group or population.

Transnational adoption paradox: The loss of birth culture and heritage while simultaneously acquiring the adoptive family's culture.

Transracial adoption: Adoption occurring across different ethnic and racial groups.

Transracial adoption paradox: A contradictory set of insider-outsider experiences of transracial adoptees in which they are perceived and treated like members of the majority culture by the adoptive family and local community but are viewed as racial minorities and simultaneously experience rejection, prejudice, and racism by the larger society.

For Further Learning and Suggested Readings

The Adoption History Project provides a wealth of original and secondary source data on the history and research of adoption: http://darkwing.uoregon.edu/~adoption/index.html.

The Child Welfare Information Gateway is a U.S. government-sponsored omnibus resource Web site on child welfare, including adoption: http://www.childwelfare.gov/adoption/index.cfm.

The Adoption Ring is one of the oldest and largest online resources for adoption-related issues: http://www.plumsite.com/adoptionring.

The Evan B. Donaldson Adoption Institute is a nonprofit foundation dedicated to advocacy, policy, practice, and research on adoption: http://www.adoptioninstitute.org/index.php.

Annual international adoption statistics can be found at two government Web sites: http://travel.state.gov/family/adoption/stats/stats_451.html and http://www.dhs.gov/ximgtn/statistics.

There are several Asian adoptee-led advocacy organizations, such as Global Adoptees' Overseas Link at http://www.goal.or.kr and International Adoptee Congress at http://www.internationaladopteecongress.org.

Some well-known adoptive parent/family organizations are Families with Children from China at http://www.fwcc.org, Korean American, Adoptee, Adoptive Family Network at http://www.kaanet.com, and Catalyst Foundation at http://www.catalystfoundation.org.

Two powerful documentaries on the Korean and Vietnamese adoptee experiences are *Daughter from Danang* at http://www.daughterfromdanang.com and *First Person Plural* at http://www.pbs.org/pov/pov2000/firstpersonplural.

There are an increasing number of anthologies and memoirs written by transracial and transnational adopted adults. A few noteworthy books include *Outsiders Within* edited by Jane Jeong Trenka, Julia Chinyere Oparah, and Sun Yung Shin (2006, South End Press), *Language of Blood* by Jane Jeong Trenka (2003, Borealis Books), *Seeds from a Silent Tree* edited by Tonya Bishoff and Jo Rankin (1997, Pandal Press), and *A Single Square Picture* by Katy Robinson (2002, Penguin).

Other recommended readings include *I Wish for You a Beautiful Life: Letters from the Korean Birth Mothers of Ae Ran Won to Their Children* edited by Sara Dorow (1999, Yeong & Yeong), *Are Those Kids Yours?* by Cheri Register (1991, Free Press), and *Transnational Adoption: A Cultural Economy of Race, Gender, and Kinship* by Sara Dorow (2006, New York University).

For a review of the psychological research on transracial and transnational adoption, read Lee, R. M. (2003). The transracial adoption paradox: History, research, and counseling implications of cultural socialization. *The Counseling Psychologist, 31,* 711–744 and Juffer, F., & van IJzendoorn, M. H. (2005). Behavior problems and mental health referrals of international adoptees: A meta-analysis. *Journal of the American Medical Association, 293,* 2501–2515.

References
Adams, G., Tessler, R., & Gamache, G. (2005). The development of ethnic identity among Chinese adoptees: Paradoxical effects of school diversity. *Adoption Quarterly, 8,* 25–46.

Bartholet, E. (1993). International adoption: Current status and future prospects. *Adoption, 3,* 89–103.

Benson, P. L., Sharma, A. R., & Roehlkepartain, E. C. (1994). *Growing up adopted: A portrait of adolescents and their families.* Minneapolis, MN: Search Institute.

Bergquist, K. J. S., Campbell, M. E., & Unrau, Y. A. (2003). Caucasian parents and Korean adoptees: A survey of parents' perceptions. *Adoption Quarterly, 6,* 41–58.

Brodzinsky, A. B. (1990). Surrendering an infant for adoption: The birthmother experience. In D. M. Brodzinsky & M. D. Schechter (Eds.), *The psychology of adoption* (pp. 295–315). New York: Oxford University Press.

Brodzinsky, D. M., Schechter, M. D., & Henig, R. M. (1992). *Being adopted: The lifelong search for self.* New York: Anchor Books.

Brooks, D., & Barth, R. P. (1999). "Adult transracial and inracial adoptees: Effects of race, gender, adoptive family structure, and placement history on adjustment outcomes." *American Journal of Orthopsychiatry 69,* 87–99.

Brown, C. S., & Bigler, R. S. (2005). Children's perceptions of discrimination: A developmental model. *Child Development, 76,* 533–553.

Carp, E. W. (1998). *Family matters: Secrecy and disclosure in the history of adoption.* Cambridge, MA: Harvard University Press.

Cederblad, M., Hook, B., Irhammar, M., & Mercke, A. (1999). Mental health in international adoptees as teenagers and young adults: An epidemiological study. *Journal of Child Psychology & Psychiatry & Allied Disciplines, 40,* 1239–1248.

Choy, G. P., & Choy, C. C. (2006). What lies beneath: Reframing daughter from Danang. In J. J. Trenka, J. C. Oparah, & S. Y. Shin (Eds.), *Outsiders within: Writing on transracial adoption* (pp. 221–231). Cambridge, MA: South End Press.

Cole, E. S., & Donley, K. S. (1990). History, values, and placement policy issues in adoption. In D. M. Brodzinsky & M. D. Schechter (Eds.), *The psychology of adoption* (pp. 273–294). New York: Oxford University Press.

Delgado-Romero, E. A., Galván, N., Maschino, P., & Rowland, M. (2005). Race and ethnicity in empirical counseling and counseling psychology research: A 10-year review. *The Counseling Psychologist, 33,* 419–448.

Dorow, S. (Ed.). (1999). *I wish for you a beautiful life: Letters from the Korean birth mothers of Ae Ran Won to their children.* St. Paul, MN: Yeong & Yeong.

Dorow, S. K. (2006). *Transnational adoption: A cultural economy of race, gender, and kinship.* New York: New York University Press.

Evan B. Donaldson Adoption Institute (1997). *Benchmark adoption survey.* Retrieved October 24, 2006, from http://www.adoptioninstitute.org/survey/intro.html

Feast, J., Marwood, M., Seabrook, S., & Webb, E. (1994). *Preparing for reunion: Experiences from the adoption circle.* London: Children's Society.

Feigelman, W. (2000). Adjustment of transracially and inracially adopted young adults. *Child and Adolescent Social Work Journal, 17,* 165–184.

Feigelman, W., and Silverman, A. R. (1984). The long-term effects of transracial adoption. *Social Service Review, 58,* 588–602.

Freundlich, M., & Lieberthal, J. K. (2000). *The gathering of the first generation of adult Korean adoptees: Adoptees' perceptions of international adoption.* Retrieved October 16, 2002, from http://www.adoptioninstitute.org

Graham, L. B. (1957). Children from Japan in American adoptive homes. *Casework Papers,* 130–144.

Grotevant, H. D. (1997). Coming to terms with adoption: The construction of identity from adolescence into adulthood. *Adoption Quarterly, 1,* 3–27.

Grotevant, H. D., Dunbar, N., Kohler, J. K., & Lash-Esau, A. M. (2000). Adoptive identity: How contexts within and beyond the family shape developmental pathways. *Family Relations: Interdisciplinary Journal of Applied Family Studies, 49,* 379–387.

Hague Convention on Protection of Children and Cooperation in Respect of Intercountry Adoption (1993). Retrieved on October 24, 2006, from http://www.hcch.net/index_en.php?act=conventions.text&cid=69

Haugaard, J. J., & Hazan, C. (2003), Adoption as a natural experiment. *Development and Psychopathology, 15,* 909–926.

Hjern, A., Lindblad, F., & Vinnerljung, B. (2002). Suicide, psychiatric illness, and social maladjustment in intercountry adoptees in Sweden: A cohort study. *The Lancet, 360,* 443–448.

Holt, M. I. (2001). *Indian orphanages.* Lawrence, KS: University of Kansas Press.

Hübinette, T. (2004). Adopted Koreans and the development of identity in the 'third space.' *Adoption and Fostering, 28,* 16–24.

Hübinette, T. (2006). From orphan trains to babylifts: Colonial trafficking, empire building, and social engineering. In J. J. Trenka, J. C. Oparah, & S. Y. Shin (Eds.), *Outsiders within: Writing on transracial adoption* (pp. 139–150). Cambridge, MA: South End Press.

Hughes, D., Rodriguez, J., Smith, E. P., Johnson, D. J., Stevenson, H. C., & Spicer, P. (2006). Parents' ethnic-racial socialization practices: A review of research and directions for future study. *Developmental Psychology, 42,* 747–770.

Huh, N. S., & Reid, W. J. (2000). Intercountry, transracial adoption and ethnic identity: A Korean example. *International Social Work, 43,* 75–87.

Johnson, K., Banghan, H., & Liyao, W. (1998). Infant abandonment and adoption in China. *Population and Development Review, 24,* 469–510.

Juffer, F., & van IJzendoorn, M. H. (2005). Behavior problems and mental health referrals of international adoptees: A meta-analysis. *Journal of the American Medical Association, 293,* 2501–2515.

Kim, E. (2000). Korean adoptee auto-ethnography: Refashioning self, family and finding community. *Visual Anthropology Review, 16,* 43–70.

Kim, E. (2004). Gathering "roots" and making history in the Korean adoptee community. In M. Checker and M. Fishman (Eds.), *Local actions: Cultural activism, power and public life* (pp. 208–230). New York: Columbia University Press.

Kim, S. P., Hong, S., & Kim, B. S. (1979). Adoption of Korean children by New York area couples: A preliminary study. *Child Welfare, 58,* 419–427.

Klein, C. (2003). Cold war orientalism: Asia in the middlebrow imagination, 1945–1961. Berkeley, CA: University of California Press.

Lee, D. C., & Quintana, S. M. (2005). Benefits of cultural exposure and development of Korean perspective-taking ability for transracially adopted Korean children. *Cultural Diversity and Ethnic Minority Psychology, 11,* 130–143.

Lee, R. M. (2003). The transracial adoption paradox: History, research, and counseling implications of cultural socialization. *The Counseling Psychologist, 31,* 711–744.

Lee, R. M. (2006). Overlooked Asian Americans: The diaspora of Chinese adoptees. *Asian Journal of Counseling, 13,* 51–61.

Lee, R. M., Grotevant, H. D., Hellerstedt, W. L., Gunnar, M. R., & The International Adoption Project Team. (2006). Cultural socialization in families with internationally adopted children. *Journal of Family Psychology, 20,* 571–580.

Lee, R. M., & Yoo, H. C. (2004a). Structure and measurement of ethnic identity for Asian American college students. *Journal of Counseling Psychology, 51,* 263–269.

Lee, R. M., Yoo, H. C., & Roberts, S. (2004b). The coming of age of Korean adoptees: Ethnic identity development and psychological adjustment. In I. Kim (Ed.), *The Korean Americans: Past, present and future* (pp. 203–224). Elizabeth, NJ: Hollym International.

Leon, I. G. (2002). Adoption losses: Naturally occurring or socially constructed? *Child Development, 73,* 652–663.

Lovelock, K. (2000). Intercountry adoption as a migratory practice: A comparative analysis of intercountry adoption and immigration policy and practice in the United States, Canada and New Zealand in the post WWII period. *International Migration Review, 34,* 907–949.

Martin, A. (2000). *The legacy of Operation Babylift.* Retrieved on October 24, 2006, from http://www.adoptvietnam.org/adoption/babylift.htm

Meier, D. I. (1999). Cultural identity and place in adult Korean-American intercountry adoptees. *Adoption Quarterly, 31,* 15–48.

Melosh, B. (2002). *Strangers and kin: The American way of adoption.* Cambridge, MA: Harvard University Press.

Modell, J. S. (2002). *A sealed and secret kinship: The culture of policies and practices in American adoption.* New York: Berghahn Books.

Oparah, J. C., Shin, S. Y., & Trenka, J. J. (2006). Introduction. In J. J. Trenka, J. C. Oparah, & S. Y. Shin (Eds.), *Outsiders within: Writing on transracial adoption* (pp. 1–15). Cambridge, MA: South End Press.

Park Nelson, K. (2006). Shopping for children in the international marketplace. In J. J. Trenka, J. C. Oparah, & S. Y. Shin (Eds.), *Outsiders within: Writing on transracial adoption* (pp. 89–104). Cambridge, MA: South End Press.

Pavao, J. M. (1998). *The family of adoption.* Boston: Beacon Press.

Ponterotto, J. G. (1988). Racial/ethnic minority research in the Journal of Counseling Psychology: A content analysis and methodological critique. *Journal of Counseling Psychology, 35,* 410–418.

Portes, A., & Rumbaut, R. G. (2001). *Legacies: The story of the immigrant second generation.* Berkeley: University of California Press.

Powell, K. A., & Afifi, T. D. (2005). Uncertainty management and adoptees' ambiguous loss of their birth parents. *Journal of Social and Personal Relationships, 22,* 129–151.

Register, C. (2005). *Beyond good intentions: A mother reflects on raising internationally adopted children.* St. Paul, MN: Yeong & Yeong.

Rutter, M., O'Connor, T. G., & the ERA Study Team. (2004). Are there biological programming effects for psychological development? Findings from a study of Romanian adoptees. *Developmental Psychology, 40,* 81–94.

Sarri, R. C., Baik, Y., & Bombyk, M. (1998). Goal displacement and dependency in South Korean-United States intercountry adoption. *Children and Youth Services Review, 20,* 87–114.

Scroggs, P. H., & Heitfield, H. (2001). International adopters and their children: Birth culture ties. *Gender Issues (Fall),* 3–30.

Simon, R. J., & Altstein, H. (2000). *Adoption across borders: Serving the children in transracial and intercountry adoptions.* Lanham, MD: Rowman & Littlefield.

Smith, D. W., & Brodzinsky, D. M. (2002). Coping with birthparent loss in adopted children. *Journal of Child Psychology and Psychiatry, 43,* 213–223.

Sokoloff, B. Z. (1993). Antecedents of American adoption. *Adoption, 3,* 17–25.

Speirs, C. C., Duder, S., Sullivan, R., Kirstein, S., Propst, & Meade, D. (2005). Mediated reunions in adoption: Findings from an evaluation study. *Child Welfare Journal, 84,* 843–866.

Steinberg, G., & Hall, B. (2000). *Inside transracial adoption.* Indianapolis, IN: Perspectives Press.

Tessler, R., Gamache, G., & Liu, L. (1999). *West meets East: Americans adopt Chinese children.* Westport, CT: Bergin & Garvey.

Trenka, J. J., Oparah, J. C., & Shin, S. Y. (Eds.). (2006). *Outsiders within: Writing on transracial adoption.* Cambridge, MA: South End Press.

Triseliotis, J. (2000). Intercountry adoption: Global trade or global gift? *Adoption and Fostering, 24,* 45–54.

Tyler May, E. (1995). *Barren in the promised land: Childless Americans and the pursuit of happiness.* New York: Basic Books.

U.S. Census. (2003). *Adopted children and stepchildren: 2000.* Retrieved on October 24, 2006, from http://www.census.gov/prod/2003pubs/censr-6.pdf

U.S. Department of Health and Human Services. (2004). *How many children were adopted in 2000 and 2001?* Washington, DC: National Adoption Information Clearinghouse.

U.S. Department of Health and Human Services. (2006). *The AFCARS report: Preliminary FY 2005 estimates as of September 2006 (13).* Retrieved on October 24, 2006, from http://www.acf.hhs.gov/programs/cb/stats_research/afcars/tar/report13.htm

U.S. Department of Homeland Security. (2005). *Yearbook of immigration statistics.* Retrieved on October 24, 2006, from http://www.uscis.gov/graphics/shared/statistics/yearbook/index.htm

U.S. Department of State. (2006). *Immigrant visas issued to orphans coming to the U.S.* Retrieved on October 24, 2006, from http://travel.state.gov/family/adoption/stats/stats_451.html.

Valk, M. A. (1957). Adjustment of Korean-American children in their American adoptive homes. *Casework Papers,* 145–158.

von Brocyskowski, A., Hjern, A., Lindblad, F., & Vinnerljung, B. (2006). Suicidal behaviour in national and international adult adoptees: A Swedish cohort study. *Social Psychiatry and Psychiatric Epidemiology, 41,* 95–102.

Von Korff, L., Grotevant, H. D., & McRoy, R. G. (2006). Openness arrangement and psychological adjustment in adolescent adoptees. *Journal of Family Psychology, 20,* 531–534.

Weil, R. H. (1984). International adoptions: The quiet migration. *International Migration Review, 18,* 276–293.

Westhues, A., & Cohen, J. S. (1997). A comparison of the adjustment of adolescent and young adult intercountry adoptees and their siblings. *The International Journal of Behavioral Development, 20,* 47–65.

Wiley, M. O., & Baden, A. L. (2005). Birth parents in adoption: Research, practice, and counseling psychology. *The Counseling Psychologist, 33,* 13–50.

Yoon, D. P. (2001). Causal modeling predicting psychological adjustment of Korean-born adolescent adoptees. *Journal of Human Behavior in the Social Environment, 3,* 65–82.

Yoon, D. P. (2004). Intercountry adoption: The importance of ethnic socialization and subjective well-being for Korean-born adopted children. *Journal of Ethnic and Cultural Diversity in Social Work, 13,* 71–89.

Zamostny, K. P., O'Brien, K. M., Baden, A. L., & Wiley, M. O. (2003). The practice of adoption: History, trends, and social context. *The Counseling Psychologist, 31,* 651–678.

19
Parachute Kids and Astronaut Families

YUYING TSONG and YULI LIU

OUTLINE OF CHAPTER

Case Synopsis

Andy, a 17-year-old "parachute kid" from Taiwan, was sent to live with his aunt and uncle in California 3 years ago, after his poor academic performance failed to improve. While he initially made friends with some other students in his high school that were in similar situations, he became more socially withdrawn in recent months. He also began to experience conflict with his uncle, who was strict about his grades. Andy struggled to keep up with his homework, especially English. He tried talking to his parents about how he felt, only to be scolded by them for being ungrateful. After turning in a writing assignment that hinted at his feelings of loneliness and despair, Andy was referred to see a school counselor.

Introduction

Children of Asian families are often accompanied by their parents when immigrating to a new country. Recent immigration trends, however, suggest that increasing numbers of children are immigrating alone to live and study abroad in the United States or other countries (Min, 2006). This new trend includes **parachute kids** who are minors from several Asian countries (e.g., Taiwan, Hong Kong, South Korea) immigrating to the United States or other host countries alone. These parachute kids often live alone or with a relative, family friend, or unrelated paid caregiver. A related immigration trend is the **astronaut family**, where one parent immigrates with the children to the host country and the other parent stays in the country of origin. This chapter describes the phenomena of parachute kids and astronaut families that occur most frequently in certain Asian (Taiwanese, Chinese, Korean) communities, including the motivation behind this form of immigration. Furthermore, this chapter describes the social and emotional development of parachute kids and children from astronaut families, and the associated potential risk and protective factors as these children negotiate cultural, developmental, and familial transitions.

Background and Definition

Parachute kids first emerged in the 1980s according to a report by Denise Hamilton (1993a). Parachute kids, different from the adult international students who come to the United States seeking higher education, are much younger children who immigrate to the host country to obtain primary and secondary education without close parental supervision. Parachute kids are defined as underaged foreign students who are sent to live and study in the United States without their parents as early as in the 1st grade. They can be as young as 8 years old, but the majority are between the ages of 13 and 17 years old (Chiang-Hom, 2004). According to government and media reports, most parachute kids come from Taiwan, followed by Korea, Hong Kong, and China. Smaller numbers of parachute kids come from other countries such as Indonesia, Malaysia, and the Philippines (Hamilton, 1993a; Zhou, 1998).

While the term *parachute kids* is used throughout this chapter, it is important to recognize that other terms in English and Chinese are also used interchangeably to describe this population. In Taiwan, these minors are referred to as "little overseas students," or in Mandarin as "Hsiao Liu Hsue Sheng." Other descriptors such as "air-dropped children" have been coined due to the lack of care by parents while attending school abroad. The media has also used other phrases, including "parental dumping," or "child dumping" (Kim, 1998; Leung, 1998; Lin, 1998; Watanabe, 1989). "Unaccompanied minors" is also another common phrase used in academia to describe parachute kids (Kim, 1998; Leung, 1998; Lin, 1998).

Another similar immigration phenomenon is the astronaut family. This refers to families whose head of household (usually the father) is living and working in the country of origin to pursue economic advantages, while the remaining family members settle in the host country. Children in these families are termed satellite children or **satellite kids** (Tsang, Irving, Alaggia, Chau, & Benjamin, 2003). The absent parent or the parent who returns to the home country is termed the astronaut, which is a derivative of the Chinese word *taikongren*, which can mean "a person who spends time in space" (Skeldon, 1994). Individuals studying astronaut families have found that no other type of family is similar to the astronaut family arrangement. Some comparisons have been made and attempt to draw parallels to separated and divorced families; however, such comparisons neglected to take into account the immigration-related issues of the astronaut family (Alaggia, Chau, & Tsang, 2001). Astronaut families are also sometimes referred to as lone-parent families (Tsang et al., 2003), a term which is also not completely accurate, because while the parents are separated by geographical distance, there are regular communications and visitations, and the separation is temporary.

History

Prior to the Immigration Act of 1965, a relatively small number of unaccompanied minors found their way into the United States and were more like goal-directed foreign students who were "protected by a sense of purpose" (Kim, 1998). After the 1965 Immigration Act, the United States saw a rapid growth in many Asian populations and the expansion of Asian communities. In 1990, the U.S. government revised the Immigration of Act of 1965 to raise the number of immigrants and the number of professional immigrants in particular, which has also contributed to a rise in the overall Asian immigration flow (Min, 2006).

Parachute Kids

Among the young overseas students coming from Asian countries, those from Taiwan were the most noticeable and have gained a great deal of media attention in Taiwan (e.g., Cheng, 1991) and also in the United States (e.g., Hamilton, 1993a), due to the larger number of these students compared to those from other countries. From 1983 to 1993, more than 24,000 primary (elementary school children) students and over 13,000 secondary (7th to 12th grade school children) students according to the Taiwanese educational system left Taiwan to attend school in the United States. The majority of these students remained in the United States until the completion of their under-graduate and graduate studies (Government Information Office, 1995). A 1990 study by Helena Hwang and Teri Watanabe estimated that there were 40,000 Taiwanese unaccompanied minors ages 8 to 18 in the United States, with smaller numbers coming from Hong Kong and South Korea (Hamilton, 1993a). Josh Lin (1998) in his review of the literature, estimated there were about 30,000 students from Taiwan studying in the United States, but acknowledged that the data for the number of young Taiwanese overseas students is uncertain due to the lack of official records available and the Taiwan government's policy against sending children abroad for basic education.

Individuals have also estimated that the number of unaccompanied minors has increased significantly since 1991 given the intensified political unrest in Taiwan and Hong Kong (Cheng, 1998). Compared to the number of unaccompanied minors from Taiwan and Hong Kong, the number of students from China paled considerably (Jen, 1998). As for students from Korea, a former employee of the Korean Ministry of Education estimated in 1997 that 7,000 unaccompanied minors were enrolled in elementary and secondary schools in Southern California (c.f. Orellana, Thorne, Chee, & Lam, 2001).

Min Zhou (1998) found that many unaccompanied minors came as foreign students on F-1 visas, and approximately one-third came with their entrepreneurial parents on B-2 visitor visas, which were later adjusted to F-1 status. A similar trend in visa status was also observed in Korean parachute kids (Orellana et al., 2001). Taiwanese children who go abroad for an overseas education are usually between the ages of 6 and 18, and the majority of these students come from upper-middle-class or upper-class socioeconomic families (Lin, 1998).

Astronaut Family

While there is no data on the number of astronauts in the United States, Ramona Alaggia and her colleagues (2001) estimate that 100,000 astronaut immigrants arrived in Canada between 1989 and 1993. The occurrence of such families is common enough for this term to be generally used in the Chinese community and to be noted in mainstream American news (Hudson, 1990).

Purpose of Immigration

Parachute Kids

Most research on parents sending unaccompanied children to the United States found that parents' concern with education was the single most important reason and the main "push" factor in their decision to immigrate. Traditional Asian beliefs have been known to emphasize education as the key for social mobility, success, and distinction (Kim, 1998; Zhou, 1998). In many Asian countries, a college education is a much desired but out of reach goal for most high school graduates, due to the rigorous unified national examinations at both the high school and the college level (Zhou, 1998). For example, in the 18-year-old cohort, only 8% in Taiwan enrolled in college (Forden, 1990), compared to 30% in Japan and 50% in the United States (Shi, 1995). In Hong Kong, the college admissions ratio was only as high as 10% (Leung, 1998). In mainland China, only about 10% or 15% of senior secondary school graduates went to college (Thogersen, 1990). In Korea, in preparing for university entrance, children often submit to a rigorous regime of study that may take them away from home for 15 hours each day (Kim, 1998). The *China Times*, a newspaper in Taiwan, conducted a telephone survey of 1,000 families in Taiwan in August 1991 and found that one out of five families had thoughts of sending their children abroad for education (Cheng, 1991).

In addition to pursuing education abroad, there were also other factors that motivated families to send their children to a new country. The political uncertainty in several Asian countries such as Taiwan, Hong Kong, and South Korea has been a major push factor for parents wanting to send their children to the United States (Kim, 1998; Leung, 1998; Lin, 1992). The fear and anxiety over Taiwan's relationship with China, the uncertainty of post-1997 Hong Kong, and unpredictable government policies in China, have pushed many wealthy families to choose parachuting as a strategy to protect the future of their children (Zhou, 1998). Parents in Taiwan and South Korea may have also wanted their sons to avoid the compulsory military services and for their daughters to take care of their younger brothers in the United States (Kim, 1998; Lin, 1998). Another push factor for Hong Kong parents that Alex Leung (1998) described was their desire to have their children separated from some of the bad influences in Hong Kong, such as the gang known as the "Triad Society." For some families, sending their children abroad to study seemed to be a "status symbol" that was indicative of upper socioeconomic class standing (Leung, 1998). Lastly, Lin (1998) suggests that some Taiwanese parents may have chosen parachuting as part of an already planned immigration process for the family. If the parents needed to stay in Taiwan for family or business reasons, they may have wanted to send their children alone to the United States first to adjust to the language and culture, before the parents were able to join them.

Despite the many factors that prompt parents to send their children abroad, parents of parachute kids decide not to immigrate to the United States with their children due to circumstances that make it more compelling to stay in their countries of origin. Parents of parachute kids may have strong business or professional ties in their countries of origin that provide the financial stability that makes it possible for their children to be in the United States. They may also need to stay and care for other family members. For these parents, parachuting their children is a way to provide them an education that promotes more critical and creative thinking (Rowe, 2006), and prepares them for entrance to U.S. universities, without having to emigrate from the country of origin themselves. They often hope that their children would return to their home countries after being educated in the United States and gaining advantages in the global job market for being able to speak English fluently compared to those who were educated in their countries of origin (Rowe, 2006).

Astronaut Family

Similar to the parents of parachute kids, parents of the astronaut family share many reasons in their decision to have one parent stay in the country of origin while the rest of the family stays in the United States. Such factors included a desire for their children to pursue greater educational opportunities, escaping from a politically uncertain environment, and avoiding compulsory military services. However, more recently, with the booming economics of the East Asian countries, many first-generation immigrants decided that the United States no longer offered as many promising economic opportunities as in their home countries (Zhou, 1998). Additionally, for most of the middle-class or upper-middle-class new immigrants, the employment and financial opportunities in the new country (i.e., United States) were usually less lucrative than in one's home country. Those who were already established in certain professions in their home country (i.e., physician, attorney, architect) found the process of becoming recognized to practice in their respective professions in the host country difficult, in addition to the language barriers. In terms of sustaining lifestyle and financial stability, astronaut families decided that it made sense to have the main income earner (usually the father) stay behind and continue generating a good income as the rest of the family settles in the new country (Tsang et al., 2003). Astronaut families negotiated both the push and pull factors toward immigration by maintaining a presence in both the country of origin and the host country.

Experiences of Parachute Kids in the United States

The living situations of these young parachute kids ranged from having their own house to sharing living spaces with other young students. Lin (1998) classified four types of living arrangements for Taiwanese parachute kids, with (a) minors living by themselves or with siblings in a house or apartment, (b) minors living with legal guardians who are their relatives or parents' friends, (c) minors living with paid legal guardians/caregivers/landlord, or (d) minors living with other students in a boarding school or privately run boarding home. In Christy Chiang-Hom's (2004) study on foreign-born Chinese adolescents, she found that 36% of the unaccompanied minors live with a relative (including 6% with a grandparent), 30% live with a homestay (paid caretakers), 5% with siblings only, 5% with friends of the family, 4% with a cousin, and 3% completely alone.

These different types of living situations give parachute kids greater freedom than they would have had if they lived with their parents. Chiang-Hom's (2004) study suggested that because parachute kids or unaccompanied minors experience a greater level of freedom from their parents' or other adult supervision, they are often less fearful of trying out typically discouraged behaviors such as smoking and drinking. They also have greater access to more spending money than other adolescents due to the large allowances they receive from their parents to cover all of their living expenses. Chiang-Hom (2004) found that, on average, the unaccompanied minors receive approximately $600 a month from their parents and spend about $62 a week (excluding bills), while their immigrant peers report receiving approximately $200 a month and spend $38 a week, which is 39% less a week.

Parachute kids often have to adapt to a new living environment and culture and take on day-to-day living responsibilities. They often not only have to take care of their own needs, but are also in charge of taking care of the needs of their younger sibling(s). The older parachute kids learn on their own how to navigate through different systems, such as school, government agencies (e.g., utilities, DMV), and to deal with the bureaucracy of these systems without adult guidance. At the same time, they are often perceived by school officials, the media, and by some community members as maladjusted foreigners who attend public schools at the expense of American taxpayers with "bad" or "neglectful" parents (Chiang-Hom, 2004; Hamilton, 1993a, 1993b). The San Marino school district in California reported that they had so much trouble with attendance problems among parachute kids that the school district passed a rule in 1991 stating "students must live with relatives no more distant than a first cousin or get a family court in the U.S. to appoint foster parents. Otherwise, they can be expelled or reported to social services or immigration authorities" (Hamilton, 1993a).

Impact of Migration on Parachute Kids and Astronaut Families

The phenomenon of parachute kids and astronaut families has several implications for the psychological, personal, and social development of the children in these situations, as well as for the parent-child relationship. Parachute kids range in age from 6 to 18 upon their arrival to the United States (Lin, 1998; Zhou, 1998). The separation from their parents and a familiar cultural environment for children in this age range is a major adjustment. This early independence is felt in the parachute kids' emotional experience and day-to-day activities, such as being responsible for finances, chores, and grades. At the same time, they are also experiencing other developmental tasks, such as identity formation, engaging in interpersonal and social relationships, and re-negotiating relationships with their parents. The changes associated with immigration and separation from one or both parents make the challenges that come with normative developmental tasks in this age group all the more difficult. Risk factors and protective factors associated with each unique case of parachute kids or astronaut families also shape the impact of this form of migration on these families. Thus, this section will provide an overview of the social-emotional development of these children, including risk factors and protective factors, and the impact on parent-child relationships of these particular forms of immigration.

Social-Emotional Development

The stress of immigration, coping with separation from parents, and having high academic expectations greatly affects the psychological and emotional well-being of parachute children. Whether the children live alone, with relatives, or with a paid caregiver, many of them expressed experiencing loneliness and homesickness. Jeannette Kim recalled her experience at the age of 15 of living with a paid caregiver:

> I tried hard not to cry, but I couldn't help it. . . . My mother kept asking what was wrong, but all I could say was that I felt uncomfortable living in a stranger's house. I didn't want to tell her I was lonely. Not once did I say that word. . . . They're paying for me to study here. . . . I can't tell them I'm lonely. I would feel like such a loser. (Berestein, 1996, p. E01)

Another 14-year-old parachute kid from San Gabriel told a meeting of Chinese American community leaders that "Our living conditions are adequate—the problem is just being lonely. . . . I always think about the past, of festivals like Chinese New Year where everyone was around, my mom, my aunties" (Hamilton, 1993b, p. B3). Leung (1998) also cited anger toward the family as a common feeling, although not an often expressed feeling, among parachute kids. Given that these children were in situations that require them to assume responsibilities beyond their years, Kim (1998) aptly described the development of a "pseudo-adult" role, in which the children suppressed their loneliness in order to be self-sufficient and independent.

Children of astronaut families also reported having similar experiences of premature independence. Alaggia et al.'s (2001) study on astronaut families in Canada from China, Hong Kong, and Taiwan indicated that children from those families assumed greater responsibilities such as translating for family members, paying bills, and taking care of household paperwork. Often the children took on responsibilities left unfulfilled by the absent parent (Aye & Guerin, 2001; Huang, 1998). One of the interviewees in Tracy Huang's (1998) study, Bruce, acknowledged that this increased responsibility promoted maturity: "I didn't get to have a father figure around but, I adjust a little bit, more independent, definitely build a lot of my character. . . It forced me to be mature" (p. 89). On the other hand, there were also negative feelings regarding this premature independence and shortened childhood. Maria stated, "And we had to come to terms with other things, we don't really spend 100% of our free time to play. . . . Back then [in high school], I thought it [father absence] was a setback, because I wasn't able to play" (Huang, 1998, p. 90). Children from astronaut families also experienced the homesickness, loneliness, and frustration that other parachute children face. Although Chien Hung Cheng (1995) found that the accompanied minors were less depressed than unaccompanied minors, one-fourth of accompanied minors in his study met the criteria for clinical depression.

Risk Factors The common feelings of loneliness, sadness, anger, alienation, and homesickness can become precursors for the development of serious psychological and behavioral problems such as depression, anxiety, gambling, or substance abuse. Kim (1998) believes that those who are living without a "warm, caring support system" are at greater risk for developing these problems. As both accompanied and unaccompanied minors report greater degrees of depression than the average American teenager, Cheng's (1995) study suggests that the adjustment process inherent in the immigration experience can be a risk factor in and of itself. Those who live alone or experience conflicts with their caretakers are also likely to be at greater risk (Cheng, 1998). Chiang-Hom (2004) found that the parachute kids in her study indicated more participation in gang fights, more cigarette and alcohol use, and were more sexually active than their immigrant Chinese counterparts who engaged in the same behaviors. Jeannette Kim, who at age 17 moved into her own apartment, spoke of her drinking, truancy, and slipping grades once she lived without supervision: "I would just sit here and watch Korean soap operas and cry. I would cry for the characters, cry for myself, feel sorry for the characters, feel sorry for myself, and wonder what I was doing with my life" (Berestein, 1996, p. E01).

Given the lack of social support and adult supervision that some parachute kids face, joining gangs can also become an attractive option as they provide the emotional company and security typically found in families. Zhou (1998) described that the lengthy amount of free time after school without adult supervision could become a real risk for kids who seek distractions from academic responsibilities. One college student interviewed by Zhou (1998) remembered his parachute kid years:

> Three to ten is a long time to be on one's own. I didn't like it at all. I got bored, turned on the TV, played video games, ate junk food, hung out in cafes with other parachute kids and friends. Good thing that none of my friends were in gangs. (p. 692)

Another potential risk factor for those parachute kids who are left unsupervised and with access to substantial financial resources is the risk of abduction and extortion. While this is a less common occurrence for parachute kids, Josh Winton (1999) and Cathy Lee (1999) reported a case of the kidnapping of a 17-year-old son of a wealthy developer.

Protective Factors Contrary to Cheng's (1995) study, Chiang-Hom (2004) reported that the participants in her study on Chinese immigrant youth indicated that foreign-born Chinese parachute kids have similar rates of depression and loneliness compared to other Chinese youth who reside with their parents. She suggested that there is a self-selection bias in that those parachute kids who came to the United States were selected by their parents due to their potential for a positive adjustment, based on qualities such as their temperament, coping skills, and maturity level. Zhou (1998) provided the following example of a self-selected parachute kid:

> Jane, a college freshman who had been a parachute kid since she was 15, explained, "Not anyone who want to come here can come. Those allowed to come are the ones whose parents believe them to be capable of self-discipline and self-control" (p. 700).

Those parachute kids who took the initiative in deciding to study abroad also seemed to be motivated to do better than those children who were complying with their parents' decisions (Zhou, 1998).

Some parachute kids eventually adjust to the challenge of living without their parents. Hamilton (1993a) described children she interviewed as capable of obtaining high grades, running a household, "paying bills and sometimes cleaning, cooking, or even supervising servants." After a period of adjustment after her arrival, Zoe, one of the children that Hamilton (1993a) interviewed, said that "We really don't know what people run to their parents for, because we've never had them here" (p. A-1). Thus, while loneliness constitutes an inevitable part of the emotional experience of being a parachute kid, the self-selection bias and the eventual adjustment and resilience of these teenagers mitigate the process of coping with the parachute experience.

Chiang-Hom (2004) found that in her study of Chinese parachute kids, forming a social network with a positive peer group who also values education could be a strong protective factor. She noted that most parachute kids associate with other parachute kids or foreign-born youth who share similar values and cultural practices. Zhou (1998) reached similar conclusions in his study, as the parachute kids he interviewed found social support through other parachute kids, church, and other Asian students. Hwang and Watanabe (1990) also found that having a solid support network was important in overseas students' adjustment.

Chiang-Hom (2004) believed that the development of a positive in-group identity and a sense of ethnic solidarity served as another protective factor. However, she noted that this ethnic pride is also coupled with a belief in superiority of Chinese culture over American culture. She asserted that this strong identification and ethnic pride protects against discrimination and prejudice from mainstream society. In addition, she noted that the continued involvement in cultural practices such as language, media, and food allows parachute kids to access resources within the Chinese community, which helped to reduce alienation.

Impact on Parent-Child Relationship

Family units as a whole are also just as impacted as the individual children by these forms of transnational migration. Parents who have made the decision to send their children abroad are faced with unique feelings and challenges in parenting. The separation in distance and different cultures changes the dynamics in the parent-child relationship. For astronaut families, the physical separation between the parents also impacts the marital relationship and relationships with children. The transnational and transcultural living arrangement between parents and children also has many implications for changes in the parent-child relationship, which compound normative developmental issues in the parent-child relationship.

Parachute Kids   Zhou's (1998) study on parachute kids noted that communication between parents and their children became less frequent over time. While phone conversations initially may be filled with a yearning for home and loneliness, the children gradually guarded their feelings in an effort not to worry their parents. One parachute boy stated:

> I call home regularly just so my mom doesn't get worried, but I really don't have much to say. My parents don't live here and don't know what problems and what needs we have here. I don't think they understand what I have to say. (p. 693)

Parents, on the other hand, may feel guilty and worried for being apart from their children. One parent recalled:

> I remember in the first few months, my children called frequently. They cried on the phone saying that they missed home. I was sad but kept saying to them that they were not babies anymore, and that they should act like a big boy or a big girl. But after a while, they didn't call as much. When they did, there were just those simple responses such as "yes" or "no" or "okay." Then I became very worried. (p. 693)

Some parachute kids acknowledged that their parents make up for their guilt by compensating them with material goods, and also expressed bitterness toward their absence. Craig, a parachute kid interviewed by Hamilton (1993a) said, "If they're going to dump me here and not take

care of me, they owe me something. That's my right." (p. A-1) Given the wealthy background of some of the parachute kids' families, several reports (Hamilton, 1993a; Lee, 1999) indicated that the kids receive larger sums of spending money, gifts, luxury cars, and electronic toys as a result of their parents' guilt.

The lack of the parents' presence and direct supervision also calls for other ways of enforcing parental rules. For those parachute kids who are under the watchful supervision of relatives, friends, or paid caretakers, their live-in guardians become their parents' eyes and ears, reporting back their academic progress and behavior. Zhou (1998) calls this alternative type of parenting "remote control." Another method of "remote control" parenting is by controlling the amount of allowance that the kids receive, based on the grades on the report cards the kids typically have to fax to their parents. However, as the children gain more of a sense of independence, they learn ways to work around the "remote control" style of supervision and experience a greater amount of freedom in doing whatever they want to do, simply due to the absence of daily face-to-face contact with parents.

Astronaut Family   Parents and children of astronaut families face a different set of challenges to their relationship due to the absence of one parent. Most notably, children of astronaut families experience role reversal or role redistribution in order to absorb the responsibilities of the absent parent, usually the father (Alaggia et al., 2001; Aye & Guerin, 2001). Along with the increased responsibilities such as managing chores and finances, and watching siblings, children of astronaut families experience a sense of premature independence, but also a feeling of obligation toward taking care of the present parent and the whole family. One youth stated, "My dad said I need to take care of my mother because I am the only person for her" (Alaggia et al., 2001, p. 300). This obligation toward taking care of one's parent also extends across helping the parent navigate a new cultural environment, which may mean helping to translate and interpret matters in the English language, and decode American customs. Given the role reversal between children and parent in astronaut families, power dynamics in the parent-child relationship may also shift. For example, the children may earn their parents' trust by demonstrating their competence in carrying out household tasks and by being responsible, which may allow them to have greater privileges than children of non-astronaut families. Alaggia et al. (2001) found, however, that there were gender differences in the privileges that came with the role reversals, in that the sons in astronaut families had more freedom, such as later curfews and access to cars, than the daughters in these families.

The relationship between the absent parent and their children also changes in a similar fashion to the relationship between parachute kids and their parents. Contact between the parent and the child consists of phone calls, letters, electronic mail, webcams, and visits during the year (Alaggia et al., 2001; Rowe, 2006). Just like for parachute kids (Zhou, 1998), the frequency of communication between the parent and the child also seems to decrease. One youth said, "I dislike that I don't have much communication with my dad. We used to have a little chat after he came back from dinner but now we don't talk much. . . we can only see each other in summer and he needs to work" (Alaggia et al., 2001, p. 301). Huang (1998) also interviewed several children whose fathers reside in Taiwan, and found that those youth who immigrated later and had a close relationship with their father prior to migration were able to have a close relationship after migration. This suggests that the closeness between the absent parent and the child does not automatically decrease after migration, but the relationship will take work to overcome the barriers of distance, immediacy, and eventual gap between parent and child in terms of acculturation and language. One of the participants, Bruce, in Huang's (1998) study said this about the difficulty in communication: "I write in English he [the father] hates it. He likes it when we write, but he complains when we write it in English. He knows we couldn't do any better" (p. 85).

Summary

For a number of reasons, some Asian immigrant families choose to send their children to the United States either with both parents staying in their home country, or with one parent returning to their home country while the other parent stays with the rest of the family in the new host country. Parachute kids are children living alone or with family friends or paid caretakers in the United States. In astronaut families, the financial provider returns back to work in his or her country of origin while frequently visiting family in the United States. The absent parent is termed the *astronaut*, and the children are often termed *satellite children*. Both of these family situations became common in the 1980s and typically exist in middle-class or upper-middle-class families. Some reasons for these families to be geographically apart include the parents' desire for their children to have better educational opportunities and to enjoy the sociopolitical stability in the United States compared to the political climate in their home countries.

Parachute kids and children of astronaut families shoulder many of the emotional and practical consequences of this type of transnational migration. While many of the children interviewed in several of the studies mention that they gain a sense of accelerated independence, feelings of loneliness and homesickness were also prevalent. Without the proper support and supervision, several risk factors exist for the development of depression, substance abuse, gambling, and antisocial behaviors. Those who tend to adjust well are those that make use of available adult supervision and guidance, seek out a network of peers who are similar in background and values, and maintain a connection to their own ethnic identity and community.

Discussion Questions

1. How do you define "a family"?
2. What are the advantages and disadvantages you can think of for a parachute kid?
3. How do you imagine your relationship with your parents and family changing if you were a parachute kid? Or as a child of an astronaut family?
4. What help or resources would you suggest or provide in your community to parachute kids who were having difficulty in adjusting?
5. If you had to develop a manual for parachute kids or an astronaut family manual to assist the kids, what would you include in it?

Case Study

Thus far this chapter has focused on providing the historical background and immigration trend of parachute kids and astronaut families, in addition to discussing the socio-emotional impact on children and their families. This chapter will now shift its focus to illustrating how an Asian American parachute kid experiences and copes with the phenomenon of living in another country apart from his parents. This case study will also provide an example of how a therapist works with the complex issues present for this teenager.

Andy is a 17-year-old high school student living in San Gabriel with his aunt and uncle. He was referred to counseling by one of his teachers after Andy turned in a writing assignment that hinted at recent feelings of despair, loneliness, and sadness. When he came to counseling, he only talked about "feeling tired" and denied his teacher's concerns about his well-being. While he was initially reticent to share his personal feelings with the counselor, he gradually opened up about his experience coming to the United States as a parachute kid at the age of 14. Andy's parents felt that it would be best for him to pursue an education in the United States after his poor scores on the high school entrance exam and his average academic records during junior high school. He was reluctant to leave his friends in Taiwan, but agreed to be sent to live with his aunt and uncle who had moved to San Gabriel 10 years ago. Being apart from his parents and friends was difficult, and Andy also did not get along with his uncle, who was quite strict about his grades and time spent outside of the home. Andy struggled to keep up with all of his coursework in English, when English was one of his worst subjects back in Taiwan. He also felt lonely and isolated, and felt more drawn to other students from Taiwan whom he would converse with during and after classes. However, Andy's uncle did not like for him to spend time with these friends outside of school and wanted him only to focus on school. Andy grew more and more isolated and even began to withdraw from his friends at school. He talked with his parents weekly, and initially told them about how unhappy he was here. After his parents scolded him for being ungrateful, Andy ceased to tell them more about how he was doing and only engaged them in polite conversation about school from then on. He felt happier when his parents visited him once a year, but talked about feeling sad again during holidays when his parents were not here. He was also beginning to lose contact with his junior high school friends from Taiwan, as they were busy with their own high school obligations. Due to the compulsory military service, Andy could not leave the United States to visit family and friends and felt he was growing further and further apart from them. Andy finally admitted that he felt all alone, and that he did not have friends or parents to turn to for help, and he felt guilty for not doing well in school.

Case Study Discussion

The counselor that worked with Andy used an integrated approach to counseling in terms of theoretical orientation and using multiple modalities, and conversed with him in both English and Chinese as Andy felt more comfortable describing his thoughts and feelings in Chinese. The counselor was aware of the possible hesitation Andy may have had in describing his emotional distress due to the stigma of mental health, and also Andy's reservation in appearing "ungrateful" to his family. Therefore they focused first on Andy's symptom of "feeling tired" and possible diagnosis of depression. After discussing possible reasons for Andy's constant fatigue, they were able to start addressing emotional components that were present in his life. The counselor remained empathic, supportive, and nonjudgmental as Andy began sharing more of his feelings of depression. In helping Andy explore the supportive people he had in his life, he identified the aunt that he lived with as being warmer and more caring toward Andy than his uncle. His aunt was asked to join them in a future session so that family members may begin to be incorporated in counseling. Andy also spoke positively about the friends that he made in school, who also came from Taiwan or Hong Kong a few years ago. He was upset that his uncle did not allow him to spend time with these friends outside of school since these friends were focused on school and not into drugs or gangs like his uncle had thought. The counselor worked with Andy's aunt and eventually his uncle to help them understand the emotional struggles that Andy was experiencing, and offered suggestions that would help. His parents were also involved in finding ways to be more available and supportive to Andy, such as more frequent phone calls and lessening their academic expectations. Andy's uncle also started to allow him to socialize with his friends outside of school, and he began to play basketball with them or invited them over occasionally to watch movies. The counselor consistently helped Andy see the broader context of how his relationship to his parents, peers, school, and uncle/aunt have changed due to immigration, rather than to internalize his difficulty in adjustment as his own fault. Throughout the course of counseling, the counselor had to be conscious of her own worldview and beliefs about parent-child relationships, the parachute kid arrangement, and how these beliefs may impact her work with Andy. In addition, the counselor also had to be conscious of the stressors that come with the acculturation process and the different acculturation levels of Andy and his families.

Case Study Discussion Questions

For undergraduate students, please consider the following questions:

1. What are your initial reactions to this vignette?
2. What are your thoughts or reactions when Andy's parents told him that he was "ungrateful" for saying that he was not happy living with his aunt and uncle? How may this relate to your own experiences?
3. What do you think about the counselor's approach in working with Andy?

For graduate students and/or beginning therapists, please consider the following questions:

1. What would be difficult for you in working with Andy as his counselor? What may be some of the transference or countertransference issues?
2. Would the counselor's ethnicity and gender make a difference in his/her relationship and work with Andy? What might be some of those differences?
3. What is your theoretical orientation? Would you use the same orientation in working with Andy?

Key Terms

Astronaut family: Family whose head of household (usually the father) lives and works in the country of origin to pursue economic advantages while the remaining family members reside and try to settle in the host country (e.g., the United States). Children in these families are called satellite children or satellite kids, and the parents are referred to as astronauts.

Parachute kids: Foreign minors, ranging in age from 6 to 18, who are sent to live and study in the United States without their parents as early as in the first grade (also known as air-dropped children).

Satellite kids: Children whose father or mother returns to their country of origin to pursue economic advantages while the other parent stays with them in the host country.

For Further Learning and Suggested Readings

Books

Kuo, B. C. H., & Roysircar, G. (2006). An exploratory study of cross-cultural adaptation of adolescent Taiwanese unaccompanied sojourners in Canada. *International Journal of Intercultural Relations, 30,* 159–183.

Lee, E. (Ed.). (2000). *Working with Asian Americans: A guide for clinicians.* New York: The Guilford Press.

Lin, J. C. H. (Ed.). (1998). *In pursuit of education: Young Asian students in the United States.* El Monte, CA: Pacific Asia Press.

Movies

Better Luck Tomorrow (2003)

Web Sites

http://www.washingtonpost.com/wp-srv/mmedia/photo/080703-3v.htm: A video clip from *Washington Post* (2003) illustrates a community of parachute kids in San Jose, CA, a group of teenagers with access to large amounts of cash and relatively little adult supervision.

References

Alaggia, R., Chau, S., & Tsang, K. T. (2001). Astronaut Asian families: Impact of migration on family structure from the perspectives of the youth. *Journal of Social Work Research, 2*(2), 295–306.

Aye, A., & Guerin, B. (2001). Astronaut families: A review of their characteristics, impact on families and implications for practice in New Zealand. *New Zealand Journal of Psychology, 30*(1), 9–15.

Berestein, L. (1996, June 10). Too young, too soon, youth: "Parachute kids", Asian teens sent here to study, grow up lonely and confused. *The Orange County Register,* p. E01.

Cheng, C. H. (1995). Assessment of depression and risk factors among adolescent Chinese immigrants: A comparative study of accompanied and unaccompanied minors. *Dissertation Abstracts International: Section B: the Sciences & Engineering, 55,* 3581.

Cheng, C. H. (1998). Assessment of depression among young students from Taiwan and Hong Kong: A comparative study of accompanied and unaccompanied minors. In J. C. H. Lin (Ed.), *In pursuit of education: Young Asian students in the United States* (pp. 95–112). El Monte, CA: Pacific Asian Press.

Cheng, K. P. (1991, September 20). Shei chia shau hai e go zen chie liu she [Whose kids go abroad by themselves]. *China Times*, p. 26.

Chiang-Hom, C. (2004). Transnational cultural practices of Chinese immigrant youth and parachute kids. In J. Lee & M. Zhou (Eds.), *Asian American youth: Culture, identity, and ethnicity* (pp. 143–339). New York: Routledge.

Forden, R. W. (1990, February). Taiwan's little overseas students. *NAFSA Newsletter*, p. 7.

Government Information Office (2005). *The Republic of China Yearbook 2005*. Retrieved March 15, 2007, from http://www.gio.gov.tw/taiwan-website/5-gp/yearbook

Hamilton, D. (1993a, June 24). A house, cash and no parents. *Los Angeles Times*, pp. A1, A16.

Hamilton, D. (1993b, July 29). Chinese-American leaders call for action on "parachute kids" immigrants: Taiwan is urged to cut the flow of children sent alone to attend U.S. schools. Programs are proposed to combat isolation of those already here. *Los Angeles Times*, p. B3.

Huang, T. L. (1998). Effects of father absence in Chinese American families. In J. C. H. Lin (Ed.), *In pursuit of education: Young Asian students in the United States* (pp. 76–94). El Monte, CA: Pacific Asian Press.

Hudson, B. (1990, March 25). They juggle business, family ties at jet speed. *Los Angeles Times*, p. B1.

Hwang, H. T., & Watanabe, T. (1990). *Little overseas students from Taiwan: A look at the psychological adjustment issues*. Unpublished master's thesis, University of California at Los Angeles, Los Angeles, CA.

Jen, T. (1998). After the parachute lands: Young students from China. In J. C. H. Lin (Ed.), *In pursuit of education: Young Asian students in the United States* (pp. 62–74). El Monte, CA: Pacific Asian Press.

Kim, S. C. (1998). Young Korean students in the United States. In J. C. H. Lin (Ed.), *In pursuit of education: Young Asian students in the United States* (pp. 44–54). El Monte, CA: Pacific Asian Press.

Lee, C. (1999, July 8). The perils of "parachute kids." *AsianWeek, 20*, 45.

Leung, A. C. N. (1998). "Home alone": The Chinese version—unaccompanied minors from Hong Kong. In J. C. H. Lin (Ed.), *In pursuit of education: Young Asian students in the United States* (pp. 18–26). El Monte, CA: Pacific Asian Press.

Lin, J. C. H. (Ed.). (1992). *Fan yang de hai tze [Children who go abroad]*. Taipei, Taiwan: Teacher Chang Press.

Lin, J. C. H. (1998). Young Taiwanese students in the United States. In J. C. H. Lin (Ed.), *In pursuit of education: Young Asian students in the United States* (pp. 4–17). El Monte, CA: Pacific Asian Press.

Min, P. G. (2006). Asian immigration: History and contemporary trends. In P. G. Min (Ed.), *Asian Americans: Contemporary trends and issues* (pp. 7–31). Thousand Oaks, CA: Sage Publications.

Orellana, M. F., Thorne, B., Chee, A., & Lam, W. S. E. (2001). Transnational childhoods: The participation of children in processes of family migration. *Social Problems, 48*(4), 572–591.

Rowe, J. (2006, March 25). Focus: In Depth—A Taiwanese Diaspora—With patriarchs staying to work in Asia, split families have settled in Irvine with a hope that education will shape their future. *Orange County Register*, p. A3.

Shi, Y. (1995). Returning home? (preface). In L. Zhiping (Ed.), *I want to go home: Voiced from the heart of a parachute kid* (pp. 3–6). Taipei: Yuezhifang.

Skeldon, R. (1994). Reluctant exiles or bold pioneers: An introduction to migration from Hong Kong. In R. Skeldon (Ed.), *Reluctant exiles: Migration from Hong Kong and the new overseas Chinese* (pp. 3–20). London: M. E. Sharpe.

Thogersen, S. (1990). *Secondary education in China after Mao: Reform and social conflict*. Aarhus, Denmark: Aarhus University Press.

Tsang, K. T., Irving, H., Alaggia, R., Chau, S., & Benjamin, M. (2003). Negotiating ethnic identity in Canada: The case of "satellite children." *Youth and Society, 34*(3), 359–384.

Watanabe, T. (1989, March 26). "Child-dumping": Taiwan teens left to struggle in U.S. *San Jose Mercury News*, pp. A1, A10.

Winton, J. (1999, January 6). Authorities fear more abductions of "parachute teens." *Los Angeles Times*, p. B1.

Zhou, M. (1998). "Parachute kids" in Southern California: The educational experience of Chinese children in transnational families. *Educational Policy 12*, 682–704.

20
Multiracial Asian Americans

KAREN L. SUYEMOTO and JOHN TAWA

OUTLINE OF CHAPTER

Case Synopsis

William, a multiracial Chinese American and European American high school senior, was referred to his school counselor following fights with his Asian and White peers. Although William saw himself culturally as Chinese, he felt that he did not fit in with his Chinese or Asian peers because he felt he didn't "look like them." Similarly, he did not fit in with his White peers. William frequently responded to the teasing and rejection from members of both groups by fighting. In therapy, William came to understand his peers' behaviors and his feelings of marginalization as a function of society's rigid racial structure and expectations rather than as an inherent problem within William himself.

Introduction

Have you ever been asked "What are you?" If so, have you considered what the person is asking about? They're not asking about your species ("I'm a human, what are you?"). They are rarely asking about your family ("I'm a mother, a sister, a daughter."). For multiracial people, it is usually understood that they are being asked about their **race**. If you've never been asked this question, people probably think they know what race you are (although they may be wrong!). If you *have* been asked this question a lot, like many multiracial Asian Americans, you probably understand that people generally feel comfortable asking this question because it reflects the importance of racial categorization in U.S. society.

This chapter focuses on the experiences of multiracial Asian Americans. After briefly reviewing a bit of history, we focus particularly on the racial and ethnic identities of multiracial Asian Americans. Racial and ethnic identities are the area most researched in this population: The question "What are you?" challenges one's identification and asks multiracial Asian Americans to place themselves racially within relation to racial categories in the United States. This is not always an easy thing to do, as the identities of multiracial Asian Americans are affected by many

> "What are you?"
> Reflection Activity: *Imagine that you are standing in line at the grocery store. The person behind you looks at you and says "What are you?" What would go through your mind? How would you answer? How would you feel? Imagine that the person appeared to you as White, then imagine them as Asian American, African American or as multiracial or difficult to racially classify. Would the race of the person asking the question affect your experience?*

different influences within the families, social groups and communities, and individuals. This chapter also explores mental health strengths and challenges in multiracial Asian Americans, and connections between mental health and identities. Finally, we return to the case of William and discuss his experience with counseling.

History of Multiracial Asian Americans

The United States has a long history of laws and social attitudes aimed at maintaining racial segregation and White "purity." For over three centuries in the United States, **antimiscegenation** laws created severe legal penalties for people who entered into interracial relationships and marriages, including whipping, loss of citizenship, and jail sentences of up to several years. The earliest of these laws were directed at relationships between African Americans or Native Americans and White European Americans. As Asian immigration increased, concerns about racial purity in relation to Asians also increased. In 1880, California passed an antimiscegenation law prohibiting marriages between Whites and "Negroes, mulattoes, or Mongolians" (Ancheta, 1998, p. 30). Other laws discouraged White Americans from marrying Asians, such as the Cable Act (1922), which declared that any American female marrying an Asian (an "alien ineligible for citizenship") would lose her American citizenship (Ancheta, 1998, p. 24). Other laws such as the law of **hypodescent**—frequently referred to as "the one-drop rule"—also ensured segregation and purity for the White race. The law of hypodescent stated that individuals with as little as 1/16 (and in some cases 1/32) racial minority heritage were considered to be "non-White," regardless of their appearance, experiences, or identities; laws such as this further discouraged Whites from intermarrying for fear of the consequences for their children. Between the years 1630 to 1967, 41 of the current states in the United States passed antimiscegenation laws that restricted interracial relationships. But in 1967, the United States Supreme Court ruled in *Loving v. Virginia* that such laws were a violation of the 14th amendment of the Constitution (http://www.ameasite.org/loving.asp). The *Loving* decision in 1967 reflected changing social attitudes that are evident today in increasing rates of intermarriage. In 1970, there were only 233,000 reported marriages between White and "Other race" (defined by the United States Bureau of the Census as "any race other than White or Black") individuals. In comparison, in 1990, there were 1,173,000 (United States Bureau of the Census, 1999)! And of course, interracial relationships produce multiracial children; multiracial Asian Americans currently make up 14.9% of the entire Asian population in the United States (Williams-Leon, 2003).

Rates of interracial marriage vary considerably among the various Asian American ethnic groups. Consider what you have learned in your history classes about the different Asian ethnic groups in the United States. What do you think might be accounting for these very notable differences? Researchers have found that ethnic groups who have been in the United States longer and who have larger percentages of U.S.-born, later-generation members tend to interracially marry at higher rates (Lee & Fernandez, 1998).

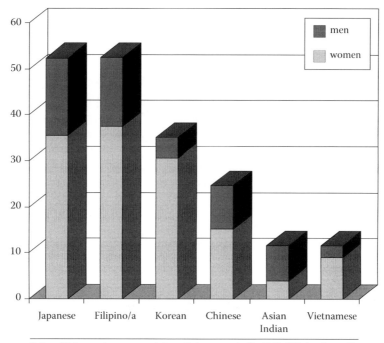

Rates of intermarriage among Asian ethnic groups in the United States (Le, n.d.).

Different racial and ethnic heritages, appearances, and histories within the United States, contribute to very different lived experiences and identities. For example, the experience of a fourth-generation multiracial Japanese American will be quite different from the experience of an immigrant multiracial Vietnamese American. This diversity is important to remember when reviewing research and theory about "the" experience of multiracial Asian Americans.

Although the multiracial Asian American population is growing, the experiences of multiracial Asian Americans are frequently not considered in psychological research, theory, and applied scholarship on Asian Americans. Research that *has* been done on multiracial Asian Americans has focused on issues of identity, the relation of identity to some aspects of mental health (such as self-esteem), and on describing the general mental health picture of multiracial Asian Americans in comparison with other groups. This research, however, is still in its infancy. As you read this chapter, we encourage you to consider how many areas we have not yet explored in relation to multiracial Asian Americans.

Racial and Ethnic Identities of Multiracial Asian Americans[1]

Research exploring multiracial experiences has increased in recent years, often conducted by psychologists who are themselves multiracial Asian Americans (e.g., Christine Iijima Hall, George Kitahara Kich, Maria P. P. Root, Stephen Murphy-Shigematsu). This research, primarily conducted since the 1980s, has been most prolific in the area of racial and ethnic identities.

---

[1] In addition to psychology, several other disciplines, including sociology, nursing, and Asian American Studies, have also contributed significantly to our understanding of racial and ethnic identity formation for multi-racial Asian Americans. Therefore, this discussion will draw on multidisciplinary research and theory about identity development, with a relative emphasis on psychological studies.

Why Is There a Need for Multiracial Identity Models?

Although psychology has differentiated the abstract concepts of race and **ethnicity**, these concepts have generally been confounded as a single construct, particularly in research on identities. Thus, racial and **ethnic identity** models developed for **monoracial** populations frequently assume that racial and ethnic identities will be the same (racial/ethnic identity; Root, 1998; Suyemoto, 2002). However, for many multiracial people, **racial identity** (based on physical appearance and related understandings/experiences with race and racism) and ethnic identity (based on cultural affiliations, traditions, and experiences) may be different. Consider the experience of William in the case synopsis you read earlier. Because he was raised with a strong influence of Chinese culture and tradition, he will likely identify as ethnically Chinese. But because he was rarely seen by others to be Asian, he may be less likely to identify *racially* as Asian. Research on multiracial identity has called for clearer differentiation of racial and ethnic identities (Root, 1998; Suyemoto, 2002; Tashiro, 2002).

In addition, many monoracial models focus within the individual, describing the feelings, thoughts, and choices about race made by an individual. They generally do not focus as much on how feelings, thoughts, and choices are shaped by interactions with *other* people (Root, 1997, 1998; Suyemoto, 2002). However the experiences of multiracial Asian Americans are often those of being not easily identifiable, of "What are you?" encounters, of challenges to their belonging and authenticity from members of their own reference groups, and of racial experiences that change in different contexts.

Models and Theories of Identity for Multiracial Asian Americans

Scholarship on multiracial identity has recognized many of the problematic aspects of monoracial models (e.g., see Root, 1997) and early theorists attempted to develop modifications or new models that better reflected multiracial experience. Kich's (1992) model of biracial identity process was one of the earliest empirically developed models explicitly addressing the developmental process of multiracial identity development. He proposed a three-stage model based on his interviews with Japanese American participants: (1) *awareness of differentness and dissonance,* emphasizing the central experience of feeling different from most or all racial groups; (2) *struggle for acceptance,* where multiracial Asian Americans become more actively aware that their feelings of difference are related to how other people view them and explore possible identities and affiliations, and; (3) *self-acceptance and assertion of an interracial identity,* where multiracial Asian Americans develop a sense of positive identity and self-acceptance and a greater understanding of the meanings of race.

Social Construction of Racial and Ethnic Identities for Multiracial Asian Americans

Social construction of identities means that racial and ethnic identities are created not only by individuals, but also by groups (Suyemoto, 2002). Individuals' identities as Asian American are affected by the Asian American group's meaning of Asian American, by the White European American group's meaning of Asian American, and by other groups' meanings as well; each group's meanings may be different from another group's meanings. For example, White European Americans may see anyone who looks even partly Asian as "Asian American," but the Asian American group might believe that a person has to look monoracial and be familiar with the culture to be truly "Asian American." Almost all of the literature exploring the development of racial and ethnic identities in multiracial Asian Americans describes experiences of exclusion, direct or subtle questioning or rejection of one's claimed identity as Asian American, experiencing discrimination within one's own reference groups due to one's mixed racial heritage, or feeling as if one is expected to not acknowledge some part of one's heritage (e.g., AhnAllen, Suyemoto, & Carter, 2006; Collins, 2000; Hall, 1992;

Herman, 2004; Kich 1992; Mass, 1992; Renn, 2003; Root, 1997, 1998, 2001; Spickard, 1997; Suyemoto, 2004; Valverde, 1992). These experiences of challenge and exclusion come from White European American people and communities, from other people and communities of color, *and* from Asian American and specific Asian ethnic (e.g., Chinese, Cambodian, Indian) people and communities. Thus, different groups' criteria for belonging within the group seem central in the developmental process of racial and ethnic identities for multiracial Asian Americans and emphasize the ways in which racial and ethnic identities are socially constructed.

In the eye of the beholder...
Reflection Activity:

(Photo courtesy of Benjamin Sloat and Steve Aishman.)

Mike is a monoracial Chinese American man who was born in the United States. His father's parents were both immigrants and his mother's family has been in the United States for several generations, having emigrated from China in the 1800s. He speaks fluent Mandarin and fluent English, has friends from many backgrounds, and celebrates both traditional Chinese holidays as well as American holidays.

Martin is a multiracial Chinese White European American man who was also born in the United States. His father's parents were Austrian immigrants and his mother's family has been in the United States for several generations, having emigrated from China in the 1800s. He speaks fluent English, Mandarin, and German, has friends from many backgrounds, celebrates Chinese, Austrian, and American holidays and cultures.

Mark is a multiracial Chinese African American man who was also born in the United States. His father's family descends from Africans brought to the United States as slaves generations ago and his family has been in the United States for several generations, having emigrated from China in the 1800s. Mark speaks fluent Mandarin and English, has friends from many backgrounds, celebrates Chinese and American holidays, and is also connected to African American cultural events and practices.

Imagine that each of them has just moved to a new city. Each of them is attending the Lunar New Year celebration at their local Chinese American Community Center. At the celebration, they each meet a lot of new people. How will the people at the center treat Mike, Martin, and Mark? How would you think about Mike, Martin, and Mark when you met them? What is likely to be the response of others when each man says that he is Asian American or Chinese American? How might Mike, Martin, and Mark be treated differently in other racial or cultural contexts, such as predominantly African American or European American settings?

Note: All names and stories are imaginary and not related to the associated pictures.

Asian White Multiracial Individuals and Group Meanings   Both White European Americans and Asian Americans as a group have historically valued racial purity in relation to their own group (Root, 1998; Spickard, 1997; Suyemoto & Dimas, 2003). Multiracial White Asian individuals frequently do not appear to others to be racially "pure," or to "look Asian" or "look White." This means that they may be viewed by monoracial Asian Americans as "not Asian American," while simultaneously viewed by White European Americans as "not White American." Multiracial Asian White Americans who are asked to choose a single race identity rarely choose White, usually choosing Asian American or a specific Asian ethnic identity (e.g., Japanese American; Herman, 2004; Root, 2001, 2003; Standen, 1996; Suyemoto, 2004; Tashiro, 2002). However, they also describe multiple experiences of exclusion from the Asian American community. They describe simultaneous feelings of belonging and exclusion (AhnAllen et al., 2006) and similarity and difference to both Asian Americans and White European Americans (Suyemoto & Matsumoto, 2001). In cases where Asian White individuals *do* choose White European American identity, the choice seems to be related to isolation from the Asian American family and/or communities (Root, 2003; Suyemoto, 2004).

Asian Black Multiracial Individuals and Group Meanings   Asian Black multiracial individuals have a different experience with their referent groups' meanings. African American communities tend to have less emphasis on racial purity than White or Asian American communities (Suyemoto & Dimas, 2003), as well as greater emphasis on the importance of *claiming* African American identity (Root, 1997; Suyemoto & Dimas, 2003). In addition, Asian American communities have historically accepted the racial hierarchy that places Black Americans below Asians and Whites (Kim, 1999), resulting in greater discrimination against Asian Black multiracial individuals than Asian White multiracial individuals within the Asian American community (Valverde, 1992; Root, 2001). When asked to choose a single racial identity, Asian Black multiracial individuals are more likely to identify as Black than Asian (Hall, 1992; Herman, 2004), suggesting greater acceptance within Black communities or greater exclusion from Asian American communities.

Multiracial Asian White and Asian Black individuals may choose only one identity if given no other choice; however, they may prefer to claim multiple identities. As the multiracial population has grown, researchers are increasingly considering ways of conceptualizing racial and ethnic identities that better encompass multiple and simultaneous identity options.

Resisting Choosing One Box Only: Choosing Multiple Identities

Multiracial individuals have historically been forced to choose a monoracial identity both officially (e.g., on official forms and in research-based questionnaires) and socially (in interpersonal interactions). Research suggests that this forced choice may contribute to psychological distress (Hall, 1992; Root, 1997). More recently, multiracial people have increasingly had the options of choosing a multiracial or mixed identity on official forms (such as the 2000 Census; U.S. Bureau of the Census, 2005) as well as in social interactions. Identity options for multiracial Asian Americans include:

- Monoracial/Monoethnic Identity: Choosing an identity affiliated with a single racial or ethnic group (White, Asian, Black, Native American, Irish, Vietnamese, etc.).
- Mixed Identity: Choosing to acknowledge *both* racial and/or ethnic groups in one's heritage (e.g., Chinese Italian, or Asian White).
- Multiracial Identity: Choosing an identity that emphasizes being multiracial and affiliation with other multiracial people generally (not limited to one's specific racial and ethnic groups), forming a new multiracial group.
- Nonracial Identity: Choosing to opt out of racial identity and deconstructing race categorizations and identities generally.

"A rose by any other name"?
Reflection Activity: *Sometimes not everyone agrees on what a label means or how it should be used. How are the following identity labels similar or different from each other? Would you think differently of someone who used one of these labels rather than another? If you don't know the word, look it up and see what you find.*

Hapa	Multiracial	Biracial	Half-Asian	Double
Mixed race	Amerasian	Eurasian	Asian American	

Research using open-ended questions or offering multiple options for different ways to identify has found that mixed and multiracial identity options are frequently preferred by multiracial Asian Americans (Collins, 2000; Kich, 1992; Renn, 2000 cited in Renn, 2003; Root, 2001, 2003; Spickard, 1997; Standen, 1996). For example, Suyemoto (2004) found that when multiracial Japanese American participants were given a list of possible identities and asked to describe how much they identified themselves as each, participants most highly endorsed multiracial identity, more than Japanese American identity, Asian identity, Japanese identity, and European American identity. When participants were asked to choose one person with whom they most strongly identified, a monoracial White European American, a monoracial Japanese American, or a multiracial African American/Native American, 52% most identified with the Japanese American person but 32% identified with the multiracial person, in spite of the fact that there was no shared racial or cultural heritage. This finding strongly suggests that many multiracial Asian Americans feel that the fact that they are multiracial actively shapes their experiences apart from specific culture or race.

Multiracial Asian Americans may also endorse more than one identity. The mixed-race identity described above is inherently an example of multiple identities at the same time (Collins, 2000; Renn, 2000 cited in Renn, 2003); for example, identifying as Japanese *and* White. Simultaneous multiple identities do not only have to refer to monoracial heritages or identities, but may also include a multiracial identity. Suyemoto (2004) found that her participants endorsed multiracial identity, Japanese American identity, both Japanese and European American (mixed) identity, and American identity simultaneously. Multiracial Asian Americans may also identify differently in different contexts (e.g., in an Asian American church vs. in a primarily White school setting: Tashiro, 2002) or at different developmental stages (e.g., identifying as Asian in high school and multiracial in college).

Dimensions of Racial and Ethnic Identities

Why do multiracial Asian Americans endorse multiple identities simultaneously or at different times and places? What might this teach us about racial and ethnic identities generally? It may be that because of their complex experiences, multiracial Asian Americans are very aware of the multiple meanings of identity. Although psychologists frequently treat identities as a single concept, "identity" is in fact complex and has multiple dimensions. Tashiro (2002) identified five dimensions of mixed-race identity from her interviews with seven African American White and 13 Asian American White multiracial participants:

- *Cultural identity* addressed how the individual internalized cultural core values and worldviews influenced by family and community experiences.
- *Ascribed racial identity* addressed how one was racially identified and labeled by others based on physical appearance or **phenotype**.

- *Racial identification to others* addressed how one labeled oneself publicly, both on official forms and in response to others' social demands for categorization.
- *Racial self-identification* addressed the individual's internal sense of who they were.
- *Situational racialization of feeling* addressed how different contexts could bring out different aspects or "sides" of one's identity or heritage.

The multidimensional approach to multiracial identity supports the differentiation of racial and ethnic identities, and also helps us understand why multiracial individuals might endorse multiple identities. When asked about identities, individuals may consider their internal and personal sense of self or simply a label that is imposed by others. They may evaluate the relational context in which the question is asked, considering whether the questioner is likely to accept, reject, or challenge their claim to a particular identity (e.g., "What do you mean you're Asian? You don't look Asian"). They may consider the political or practical advantage or disadvantage

When I looked "more Asian"…

Reflection Activity: *One possible reason why some multiracial people may identify differently at different developmental ages is because their looks may change and people may respond differently to them because of their changing physical appearance. We think this has been true in our own experiences because people have said we "looked" more Asian at different ages.*

Do you agree? In which pictures do you think we looked most "Asian"? What makes someone "look" Asian? How might our changing looks affect how we might identify?

to claiming a particular identity. They may consider social and group meanings and whether the question being asked is about personal identity or more about group affiliation, identification, and belonging. Thus, the dimension of identity being considered will affect the choice of identity reported. And the different dimensions may or may not be the same.

Influences on Identity Choice and Developmental Process

Not only are there multiple dimensions of identity, but there are numerous factors that influence multiracial Asian Americans' choice of racial and ethnic identities, the strength of these identities, and the ways in which these identities are developed. These factors include: (a) acceptance or exclusion, (b) physical appearance, (c) cultural knowledge, (d) family experiences, (e) historical context, and (f) regional context.

Acceptance or Exclusion   Social experiences of acceptance and exclusion from monoracial communities influence whether multiracial Asian Americans claim monoracial identities (e.g., as White, Asian American, African American, etc.; AhnAllen et al., 2006; Hall, 1992; Herman, 2004; Kich, 1992; Mass, 1992; Renn, 2003; Root, 2001). However, experiences of acceptance and exclusion from monoracial communities don't seem to influence whether multiracial Asian Americans claim a multiracial identity (AhnAllen et al., 2006).

Physical Appearance   How multiracial Asian Americans perceive their own physical appearance and what they believe that others think they look like often affects their racial and ethnic identifications (AhnAllen et al., 2006; Herman, 2004; Khanna, 2004; Mass, 1992; Renn, 2003; Root, 2001; Spickard, 1997; Tashiro, 2002), although phenotype alone does not consistently predict identity (Root, 2001).

Cultural Knowledge   Familiarity, exposure to, and knowledge of ethnic cultures, as well as perceived cultural similarity to cultural groups affect racial and ethnic identifications, although cultural knowledge alone does not consistently predict identity (Hall, 1992; Khanna, 2004; Renn, 2003; Root, 2001; Suyemoto, 2004; Tashiro, 2002).

Family   Parents' and families' guidance, support, communication about race and culture, comfort with multiracial identities/experiences, and familial exposure to cultural heritages also affect the racial and ethnic identities of multiracial Asian Americans (Kich, 1992; Mass, 1992; Renn, 2003; Root, 2001).

Historical Context   The social climate of the particular time in which a multiracial Asian American grew up also affects identity (Root, 2001; Spickard, 1997). The experience of multiracial Asian White Americans who grew up prior to the 1960s (before the *Loving* decision) were characterized by isolation and intense rejection from both Asian and White communities, whereas those who are currently in their teens and early adulthood are experiencing greater acceptance and more identity options (Root, 2001; Spickard, 1997).

Regional Context   Race relations within regional contexts also affect identities (Mass, 1992; Spickard, 1997). For example, multiracial Asian American individuals living in Hawaii have very different experiences from multiracial Asian Americans living in Boston.

Although Root (1998, 2001, 2003) has developed an ecological model that attempts to integrate the multiple influences of inherited influences, traits, and social interactions on both racial and ethnic identities, there has been little research exploring which of these factors affect which dimensions or types of identity (e.g., cultural identity versus racial identity, or self-identification versus identification to others) or whether some influences affect some types of identities more than others.

Judging a book by its cover?

Reflection Activity: *Often it is the perception of physical appearance, and not necessarily appearance itself, that affects identity because not everyone will see "race" in the same way. In our own experiences, some people have said we look racially Asian, while others say we look Latino/a, Native American, or White. Each viewer assumes that his or her perception is "accurate" and related to the characteristics of the person being viewed, not to their own ideas about what it means to be Asian, White, Black, or any other race. Clothes and other aspects can affect how people view race. Look at the following pictures—do the people seem the same in each picture?*

From Steve Aishman and Benjamin Sloat: These pictures are from the "Half-Asian Portrait Series." This project began in 2001 to expose how fluid identity can be for someone who is multiracial Asian. The series has included over 150 half-Asian people across the country creating a visual community of multiracial Asians. Participants presented themselves in "Asian," "Western," and "neutral" guises with specific colored backgrounds associated with each guise. When the three backgrounds are shown together in a triptych, they are red, white, and blue, a reference to how this situation of mixed races and cultures is inherently an American one. Participants adjusted their appearances in ways they thought would visually emphasize one trait over another to create the different guises, changing clothes, changing how they looked at the camera, or changing expression. Thus, participants "performed" identity with an awareness that they would be viewed by others. The meanings of being multiracial Asian are often imposed by others, and this project serves to question not only what multiracial Asians consider to be "Asian" or "Western" about themselves and their appearance, but also how the viewer sees these things. People who see these photos frequently say things like "That person doesn't look Asian (or Western)." Our question to all viewers is "What does Asian (or Western) look like to you?" (Photos courtesy of Benjamin Sloat and Steve Aishman.)

Although the vast majority of the research examining multiracial Asian Americans has focused on racial and ethnic identities, some studies have examined mental health issues. This research suggests that the mental health issues faced by multiracial Asian Americans are related to their social experiences and other influences that are described above. However, the lack of research that has been conducted on mental health and challenges in multiracial Asian Americans means that we actually know very little about these experiences or how best to help multiracial individuals facing psychological difficulties.

Mental Health and Multiracial Asian Americans

Although more research is needed, the mental health of multiracial individuals has been of interest to psychologists for close to 80 years. Unfortunately, the social sciences have a history of **pathologizing** multiracial people by not attending sufficiently to their contextual experiences. Early theories based in racist attempts to prove the biological importance of racial purity and white racial superiority framed the multiracial experience as both physically and mentally degenerating the positive characteristics of both races (Tucker, 2004). This paradigm and later related theory, which viewed multiracial individuals as caught between two conflicting cultures, confused, and psychologically unhealthy (e.g. Stonequist, 1937), has resulted in blaming multiracial individuals for their own distress related to racial experiences. These theories have not generally considered how social structures promoting rigid racial categorizations may be what is problematic. More recent research challenges the idea of multiracial people as inherently unhealthy, demonstrating positive aspects of the multiracial psychological experience while at the same time recognizing their specific challenging circumstances (e.g., Collins, 2000; Hall, 1992; Root, 1998; Suyemoto, 2004).

Positive Experiences Related to Being Multiracial

Although experiences of social isolation and marginalization from monoracial groups may be common for multiracial Asian Americans, it seems that these experiences may also foster cognitive, affective, and social experiences that are positive and should therefore be viewed as strengths. Research conducted with multiracial Japanese American participants indicated that many experiences most strongly attributed to being multiracial were positive (see Table 20.1).

Table 20.1 Experiences Associated With Being Multiracial

Most common cognitive and affective experiences	Quotes supporting these experiences
1. Being sensitive to or aware of cultural cues	"I think it [being multiracial] has made me expertly cued to cultural cues….I'm always trying to learn… how does one act here and what are the cultural norms.'"
2. Appreciating multiple views	"I can look at the issues from a number of different views, not only one or the other, but three or four."
3. Understanding the importance of tolerance and the acceptance of difference	"… being mixed, I can see two different perspectives and I can understand the importance of tolerance and everything along that line."
4. Disliking excluding others	"Whenever I start feeling like lines are being drawn to shut other people out, then I start backing away."
5. Feeling different	"There's always a consciousness of being different. I always knew I was different."

From Suyemoto (2004).

Additional studies with multiracial Asian Americans support these findings and suggest that both Japanese Black and Japanese White multiracial individuals feel they are able to move easily within and among different racial settings (Collins, 2000; Hall, 1992). Multiracial Asian Americans have also been found to experience lower levels of intergroup anxiety and xenophobia (Stephan & Stephan, 1991) and higher levels of trust and communication with peers in general, compared to monoracial participants (Cauce et al., 1992).

This research calls into question the assumption that socially marginalizing experiences are necessarily related to negative mental health outcomes and suggests that many multiracial people are able to respond to negative social experiences in ways that are positive and healthy.

Research on Mental Health in Multiracial Asian Americans

Some research has examined more traditional measures of mental health such as self-esteem, depression, and anxiety. In relation to self-esteem, many comparative studies have indicated that multiracial Asian Americans' self-esteem is similar to or higher than monoracial Asian Americans' self-esteem (e.g., Bracey, Bámaca, & Umana-Taylor, 2004; Stephan & Stephan, 1989), although in some cases lower than monoracial White European Americans (Stephan & Stephan, 1991). In relation to depression and anxiety, although some studies have found no differences or even significantly *less* depression among multiracial samples when compared to monoracial samples (e.g., Cauce et al., 1992) a few studies have found specific populations of multiracial Asian Americans to experience more depression (McKelvey & Webb, 1996; Yamaguchi-Williams et al., 2005) and anxiety (Yamaguchi-Williams et al., 2002) than monoracial Asian Americans.

Relations of Multiracial Racial and Ethnic Identities to Mental Health

The limited research examining mental health in multiracial Asian Americans frequently considers the relations between racial and ethnic identities and mental health and has used samples primarily consisting of Asian White biracial individuals. This research suggests that multiracial Asian Americans who identify most strongly as Asian or Asian American (i.e., minority monoracial identification) or who identify strongly with *both* their Asian and their non-Asian heritage (i.e., mixed race identification) tend to have more positive outcomes than those who do not identify with their Asian heritage (Bracey et al., 2004; Suzuki-Crumly & Hyers, 2004; Yamaguchi-Williams et al., 2002; Yamaguchi-Williams et al., 2005). This includes findings of higher self-esteem (Bracey et al., 2004) and less intergroup anxiety and depression (Suzuki-Crumly & Hyers, 2004).

Models for understanding how multiracial identity choices potentially affect well-being may be particularly important for clinicians. As you read about William in the "Case Study" section on p. 394, try to use some of the theory that you have encountered in this chapter to develop your own ideas about what he might be experiencing.

Summary

More research is clearly needed to increase psychologists' understanding of the experiences of multiracial Asian Americans. This chapter reviews the growing body of scholarship related to racial and ethnic identities in multiracial Asian Americans. It is clear from this research that the development of racial and ethnic identities for multiracial Asian Americans is a complex process affected by social attitudes and interactions within multiple racial communities in the United States, including the dominant White European American group and the Asian American group. Racial and ethnic identities are multidimensional and influenced by many factors. This chapter also reviews the limited research on mental health, which suggests that (a) multiracial Asian Americans experience strengths as well as challenges related to being multiracial and (b) racial and ethnic identities are frequently related to mental health.

Although our understanding of multiracial Asian Americans is growing, there is much that we have not yet explored about this population, particularly in relation to mental health, but also in relation to the many other experiences more fully explored within monoracial Asian Americans as described in this text, including issues of acculturation, religion and spirituality, family issues and experiences, gender differences and similarities, sexuality, peer relationships, and experiences of racism and prejudice. This research will need to attend to differences within multiracial Asian Americans due to different ethnic, racial, and generational statuses.

As the multiracial Asian American population increases, the meaning of "Asian American" has been challenged. To contribute to inclusivity, positive mental health, and social justice within our own communities, we must examine our understandings and shape new meanings. Spickard states:

> [T]he task for the dominant group in America is to rearrange its understandings to accommodate the reality of biracial identity. Asian Americans must also rearrange their understandings. This means redefining in more inclusive terms what it means to be an Asian American. (p. 55)

Discussion Questions

1. The *Loving* decision in 1967 contributed to an increase in interracial relationships and a corresponding increase in multiracial people. Consider what you have learned from this chapter as well as the earlier chapter on relationships. Would you ever date or marry someone from a different racial background? What are your thoughts and feelings about possibly having multiracial children?

2. Review the sections of this chapter on multiple identities. How do you identify in relation to race and ethnicity? Do you have one identity or several? Has your identity (or identities) changed over time or in different circumstances?

3. In relation to the dimensions of identity: Consider the dimensions of your own identity. What is your cultural identity? What is your ascribed racial identity? How do you racially identify to others? What is your racial identification? In terms of "situational racialization of feeling," do your feelings about your identity change in different situations? Are the different dimensions of your identity similar or different?

4. Consider the section on influences on identity. Do you think that these variables affect your racial and ethnic identities? Which influences are most important in your life?

5. Imagine that you look racially different: How would this affect your relationships and your identity? What if you had (or didn't have) different types of cultural knowledge? What if other people refused your identity or told you that you couldn't identify the way that you do or that you weren't really part of that group? How would that affect you?

6. Consider what you have learned from the many other chapters in this book. How might multiracial Asian Americans' experiences be similar to or different from the experiences of monoracial Asian Americans described in these other chapters?

7. Wikipedia is a Web site similar to an encyclopedia but created by users who can update and add to information. When this chapter was written, the entry on multiracial people (http://en.wikipedia.org/wiki/Multiracial) was very broad, with little specific discussion of any racial group's experience. There was no entry for "multiracial identity," or

"multiracial Asian Americans," although there was an entry on Amerasians (http:// en.wikipedia.org/wiki/Amerasian). Check out Wikipedia and consider what information is missing and what could be added to better incorporate the experiences of Asian American multiracial people.

8. If you were a counselor seeing a multiracial Asian American client, what kinds of questions would you ask about experiences that might be related to evaluating his or her mental health or to figuring out how to counsel this client effectively?

Case Study

William is a multiracial Asian and White 17-year-old high school senior. He was raised by his mother, who is an immigrant from China. He has had little contact with his European American father for the last 15 years. William was recently referred to his school counselor—a White European American male—following a fistfight he was involved in with a White peer during the lunch period. Only 1 month ago, William had been suspended from school for a similar incident with an Asian American peer. Prior to meeting with William, the school counselor met with his mother, Lien, who said she began to notice changes in William's friends and behavior about 1 year ago. Lien felt that William's girlfriend and new friends, whom she described pejoratively as "Spanish people" have been negatively influencing his behavior.

Over the remainder of his senior year, William and his therapist discussed his thoughts and feelings about his fighting, as well as about his current peer and romantic relationships. His therapist was careful to always consider these experiences within William's multiple cultural and racial environments, his school setting, peer groups, and other relevant contexts. Although ambivalent at first about exploring his racial and cultural experiences, William began to express a sense of frustration at the rejection he experienced from the Asian American community, which included some of his Chinese family members, as well as from the Asian American and White European American youth at school. William stated that at school he felt most comfortable around his Latino/a friends because when he was with them he felt that he did not "stand out" as much and felt accepted. William's therapist was aware of racial tensions between the Latino and Asian communities within the public high school. Because William's therapist initially perceived William to be Latino, he imagined that William's relationships with his White and Asian peers may be discouraged by others who similarly saw William as Latino.

William's therapist understood William's peer choices to result from the teasing and rejection from both his Asian and White peers. Rather than responding to these issues by seeing William as problematic because he was associating with peers who were not members of his racial groups (i.e., Latinos rather than Asian or White peers), William's therapist appreciated William's *ability to relate* cross-racially and to develop a meaningful partnership and friendships with his Latino/a peers, despite significant cultural gaps in experience. Emphasizing this personal strength, the therapist helped William develop more appropriate ways of responding to his Asian and White peers' teasing by fostering an understanding of the social issues involved.

Additionally, the therapist provided William with new language and understandings derived from the multiracial literature, which he felt would facilitate William's understanding of his complex racial and cultural experiences. For instance, the therapist helped William differentiate his *racial experience* from his *ethnic and cultural experience*, and considered with him his *ascribed identity* as a Latino and the *situational context* demanding monoracial partnerships. These new understandings eventually helped William develop greater self-acceptance and situate his difficulties externally, rather than interpreting his relational difficulties as an internal problem or deficit. This knowledge also helped William communicate with his mother, and specifically helped him increase her awareness of her own anti-Latino/a racism, which was increasingly becoming a source of family conflict as his relationship with his Latina partner was becoming more and more serious.

William's therapist also understood that change needed to occur within the school. He initiated teacher trainings about multiracial students and how to incorporate multiracial literature, history, and social experiences within school curricula. Additionally, the therapist encouraged William to himself become an advocate of social change, contributing to changing the negative racial relations between students. With the therapist's guidance, William facilitated the creation of a multiracial student club, which helped other multiracial students normalize their experience of being "outside the box." William's therapist knew that groups such as I-Pride, Hapa Issues Forum, Swirl and SwirlBoston, and numerous college groups have helped multiracial individuals by affirming their experiences of exclusion and challenge from their monoracial peer groups, creating a new multiracial social group, and validating the choice of a multiracial identity (Renn, 2003). With some of his Latino and developing Asian American friends, William also participated in a new social club that focused on positive race relations and understandings between different groups. William used his new understandings about race and race relations to emerge as a leader in both groups.

Case Study Discussion Questions

For undergraduate students, please consider the following questions:

1. How are William's experiences with racial categorization similar to or different from your own?
2. How would you have reacted to your peers if you were William?
3. Given your own experiences with racial categorizations and peer relations and your current understandings of the experiences of multiracial Asian Americans, what should high school counselors and teachers do to contribute to positive educational and social experiences?
4. If you had been William's counselor, what would you have done similarly or different?

For graduate students and/or beginning therapists, please consider the following questions:

1. How would *you* conceptualize William's anger and how would you approach your treatment together?
2. How would your race and ethnicity and related experiences influence your decisions, understandings, and interactions with William as his therapist?
3. How did you feel about his therapist's focus on creating change within the school in addition to creating change in William? How did this approach reflect your idea of what it means to be a therapist?

Key Terms

Ethnicity: A grouping of individuals based on shared cultural values, meanings, and behaviors, frequently related to a shared geographical history. Examples of Asian ethnic groups include Chinese, Hmong, Malaysian, Pakistani, Thai, or Vietnamese.

Ethnic identity: A sense of connection to or recognition of one's ethnic heritage or heritages, created interdependently between one's own meanings of their ethnicity and a socially agreed upon meaning of one's ethnic group boundaries.

Hypodescent: Law instituted as early as the 18th century stating that anyone with greater than 1/16 non-White ancestry is *not* considered a White person (also known as the "one-drop" rule).

Miscegenation: Historical term meaning marriage or intimate relations between people who are identified to be of different races. Until 1967, some states in the United States had laws aimed at preventing such unions.

Monoracial: Of or related to a single racial group; for example, a person with parents who are both racially identified as Asian may be described as monoracial Asian.

Pathologizing: Unnecessarily or inaccurately deeming an individual or a particular group of individuals sick, unhealthy, or non-normative.

Phenotype: External, physical appearance of a person or a group of people (contrast with genotype). In the United States, each racial group's phenotype is comprised of a socially (not biologically) defined set of morphological characteristics (e.g. African Americans; coarse hair texture, brown skin color).

Race: A socially constructed categorization system with no biological or genetic basis that attempts to group the people of the world into broad categories (e.g. Asian, Black, Latino/a, Native American, White), primarily on the basis of phenotype (see above).

Racial identity: The lens through which one interprets her or his own racial experience that may involve a sense of affinity and connection to their racial reference group or groups, as well as an explicit understanding of the socially constructed idea of race.

For Further Learning and Suggested Readings

Books

Edited Scholarly

Root, M. P. P. (Ed.). (1992). *Racially mixed people in America*. Newbury Park, CA: Sage.

Williams-Leon, T., & Nakashima, C. L. (Eds.). (2001). *The sum of our parts: Mixed heritage Asian Americans*. Philadelphia: Temple University Press.

Fiction and Narratives About Multiracial Asian Americans and Other Multiracial People

Arboleda, T. (1998). *In the shadow of race: Growing up as a multiethnic, multicultural, and "multiracial" American*. Mahwah, NJ: Lawrence Erlbaum.

Camper, C. (Ed.) (1994). *Miscegenation blues: Voices of mixed race women*. Toronto: Sister Vision.

Gaskins, P. F. (Ed.) (1999). *What are you?: Voices of mixed race young people*. New York: Henry Holt.

Web Sites

Eurasian Nation: http://www.eurasiannation.com/index.htm

Half Asian Photo Project (Benjamin Sloat and Steve Aishman): http://www.halfasian.net

The Hapa Project (Kip Fulbeck): http://www.seaweedproductions.com/hapa

References

AhnAllen, J. M., Suyemoto, K. L., & Carter, A. S. (2006). Relationship between physical appearance, sense of belonging and exclusion, and racial/ethnic self-identification among multiracial Japanese-European Americans. *Cultural Diversity and Ethnic Minority Psychology*.

Ancheta, A. N. (1998). *Race, rights, and the Asian American experience*. New Brunswick, NJ: Rutgers University Press.

Bracey, J. R., Bámaca, M. Y., & Umana-Taylor, A. J. (2004). Examining ethnic identity and self esteem among biracial and monoracial adolescents. *Journal of Youth and Adolescents, 33*(2), 123–132.

Cauce, A. M., Hiraga, Y., Mason, C., Aguilar, T., Ordonez, N., & Gonzales, N. (1992). Between a rock and a hard place: Social adjustment of biracial youth. In M. P. P. Root (Ed.), *Racially mixed people in America* (pp. 207–222). Newbury Park, CA: Sage Publications.

Collins, J. F. (2000). Biracial Japanese American identity: An evolving process. *Cultural Diversity and Ethnic Minority Psychology, 6*, 115–133.

Hall, C. C. I. (1992). Please choose one: Ethnic identity choices for biracial individuals. In M. P. P. Root (Ed.), *Racially mixed people in America* (pp. 250–264). Newbury Park, CA: Sage Publications.

Herman, M. (2004). Forced to choose: Some determinants of racial identification in multiracial adolescents. *Child Development, 75*, 730–748.

Khanna, N. (2004). The role of reflected appraisals in racial identity: The case of multiracial Asians. *Social Psychology Quarterly, 67*(2), 115–131.

Kich, G. (1992). The developmental process of asserting a biracial, bicultural identity. In M. P. P. Root (Ed.), *Racially mixed people in America* (pp. 304–321). Newbury Park, CA: Sage Publications.

Kim, C. J. (1999). Racial triangulation of Asian Americans. *Politics and Society, 27*(1), 105–138.

Le, C. N. (n.d.). *By the numbers: Dating, marriage, and race in Asian America*. Retrieved February 15, 2006, from http://www.imdiversity.com/villages/asian/family_lifestyle_traditions/le_interracial_dating.asp

Lee, S. M., & Fernandez, M. (1998). Trends in Asian American racial/ethnic intermarriage: A comparison of 1980 and 1990 census data. *Sociological Perspectives, 41*(2), 323–342.

Mass, A. I. (1992). Interracial Japanese Americans: The best of both worlds or the end of the Japanese American community? In M. P. P. Root (Ed.), *Racially mixed people in America* (pp. 265–279). Newbury Park, CA: Sage Publications.

McKelvey, R. S., & Webb, J. A. (1996). A comparative study of Vietnamese Amerasians, their non-Amerasian siblings, and unrelated, like-aged Vietnamese immigrants. *American Journal of Psychiatry, 153*(4), 561–563.

Renn, K. A. (2000). Patterns of situational identity among biracial and multiracial college students. *The Review of Higher Education, 23*(4), 399–420.

Renn, K. A. (2003). Understanding the identities of mixed-race college students through a developmental ecology lens. *Journal of College Student Development, 44*, 383–403.

Root, M. P. P. (1997). Multiracial Asians: Models of ethnic identity. *Amerasia Journal, 23*(1), 29–41.

Root, M. P. P. (1998). Reconstructing race, rethinking ethnicity. In A. S. Bellack & M. Hersen (Eds.), *Comprehensive clinical psychology* (pp. 141–160). New York: Pergamon.

Root, M. P. P. (2001). Factors influencing the variation in racial and ethnic identity of mixed-heritage persons of Asian ancestry. In T. Williams-Leon & C. L. Nakashima (Eds.), *The sum of our parts: Mixed heritage Asian Americans* (pp. 62–70). Philadelphia: Temple University Press.

Root, M. P. P. (2003). Five mixed-race identities: From relic to revolution. In L. I. Winters & H. L. DeBose (Eds.), *New faces in a changing America: Multiracial identity in the 21st century* (pp. 3–20). Thousand Oaks, CA: Sage Publications.

Spickard, P. R. (1997). What must I be? Asian Americans and the question of multiethnic identity. *Amerasia Journal, 23*(1), 43–60.

Standen, B. C. S. (1996). Without a template: The Korean/White experience. In M. P. P. Root (Ed.), *The multiracial experience: Racial borders as the new frontier* (pp. 245–259). Thousand Oaks, CA: Sage Publications.

Stephan, C. W., & Stephan, W. G. (1989). After intermarriage: Ethnic identity among mixed-heritage Japanese-Americans and Hispanics. *Journal of Marriage and the Family, 51*, 507–519.

Stephan, W. G., & Stephan, C. W. (1991). Intermarriage: Effects on personality, adjustment, and intergroup relations in two samples of students. *Journal of Marriage and the Family, 53*, 241–250.

Stonequist, E. V. (1937). *The marginal man: A study in personality and culture conflict*. New York: Russell & Russell.

Suyemoto, K. L. (2002). Redefining "Asian American" identity: Reflections on differentiating ethnic and racial identities for Asian American individuals and communities. In L. Zhan (Ed.), *Asian Americans: Vulnerable populations, model interventions, and clarifying agendas* (pp. 195–231). Boston: Jones and Bartlett.

Suyemoto, K. L. (2004). Racial/ethnic identities and related attributed experiences of multiracial Japanese Americans. *Journal of Multicultural Counseling and Development, 32*, 206–221.

Suyemoto, K. L., & Dimas, J. M. (2003). To be included in the multicultural discussion: Check one box only. In J. S. Mio & G. Y. Iwamasa (Eds.), *Culturally diverse mental health: The challenges of research and resistance* (pp. 55–81). New York: Brunner-Routledge.

Suyemoto, K. L., & Matsumoto, A. (2001). *Concurrent identification and similarity/difference feelings in multiracial Japanese Americans.* Poster presented at the 2001 annual convention of the American Psychological Association, San Francisco, CA.

Suzuki-Crumly, J., & Hyers, L. L. (2004). The relationship among ethnic identity, psychological well-being, and intergroup competence: An investigation of two biracial groups. *Cultural Diversity and Ethnic Minority Psychology, 10*(2), 137–150.

Tashiro, C. J. (2002). Considering the significance of ancestry through the prism of mixed-race identity. *Advances in Nursing Science, 25*(2), 1–21.

Tucker, W. H. (2004). "Inharmoniously adapted to each other": Science and racial crosses. In A. S. Winston (Ed.), *Defining difference: Race and racism in the history of psychology* (pp. 109–133). Washington DC: American Psychological Association.

United States Bureau of the Census. (1999). *Interracial married couples: 1960 to present.* Retrieved January 7, 1999, from the United States Census at http://www.census.gov/population/socdemo/ms-la/tabms-3.txt

United States Bureau of the Census (2005). *We the people of more than one race in the United States.* Retrieved April 5, 2008 from the United States Census at http://www.census.gov/prod/2005pubs/censr-22.pdf

Valverde, K. C. (1992). From dust to gold: The Vietnamese Amerasian experience. In M. P. P. Root (Ed.), *Racially mixed people in America* (pp. 144–161). Thousand Oaks, CA: Sage Publications.

Williams-Leon, T. (2003). Census, consensus? APAs and multiracial identity. In E. Lai & D. Arguelles (Eds.), *The new face of Asian Pacific America: Numbers, diversity, & changes in the 21st century* (pp. 17–21). San Francisco: Asian Week.

Yamaguchi-Williams, J. K., Else, I. R. N., Hishinuma, E. S., Goebert, D. A., Chang, J. Y., Andrade, N. N., et al. (2005). A confirmatory model for depression among Japanese American and part-Japanese American adolescents. *Cultural Diversity and Ethnic Minority Psychology, 11*(1), 41–56.

Yamaguchi-Williams, J. K., Goebert, D., Hishinuma, E., Miyamoto, R., Anzai, N., Izutsu, S., et al. (2002). A conceptual model of the cultural predictors of anxiety among Japanese American and part-Japanese American adolescents. *Cultural Diversity and Ethnic Minority Psychology, 8*(4), 320–333.

21

Racism: "It Isn't Fair"

ALVIN N. ALVAREZ

OUTLINE OF CHAPTER

Case Synopsis
Introduction
Racism Defined
Asian Americans and Racism: Past to Present
Psychology and Racism
Case Study
References

Case Synopsis

Brian was sitting in the overcrowded subway car, tightly wedged in, when the older White man shuffled his way through in search of a seat. Finding none, the old grizzled man simply sat on the floor. As people shifted at the next stop and created some space, Brian managed to get up and offer the old man his seat. The old man whipped his head around, glared at Brian, and yelled at the top of his lungs, "What kind of a man are you?" Brian was stunned for a bit but the older man continued. "Where I was raised, a man don't give no seat to another man! Where were you raised? Maybe you should go the f@%# back where you came from!!! We shoulda took care of all you Japs when we had the chance. . . . " Even as he sat with his therapist, recounting the incident, Brian could still feel a whirlpool of fury, embarrassment, and helplessness clouded by a resigned sense that it just never stops.

Introduction

The irony didn't escape Brian. Going back to where he was from meant that he would be going back to Los Angeles. But he was fairly sure that wasn't what the man meant. And to add to that, Brian wasn't even Japanese—he was Filipino and his grandfather fought Japanese soldiers during the war. Not that it mattered to the older man who probably thought all those Asian people looked alike. But Brian had seen it before—whether it was him, his friends, his *Titas* with their accents, his parents who worked so hard to make it here, or even watching TV or flipping through a magazine, the **racism** that they experienced was both pervasive and exhausting. To place Brian's racial experiences and perhaps the experiences of you, your friends, and your family into perspective, the current chapter will address the role of racism in the lives of Asian Americans from a psychological perspective. Specifically, the chapter begins with a discussion of how psychologists have defined racism and the various types of racism that one may encounter. The chapter will then examine historical and contemporary experiences of Asian Americans with racism. This section will be followed by an overview of the current psychological research on racism against Asian Americans, which sheds light on issues such as the **prevalence** of racism, the consequences of racism, and how individuals cope with such experiences. Lastly, the chapter returns to Brian's story and the role of counseling in addressing Asian Americans' experiences with racism, and then provides resources and activities to expand upon this chapter.

Racism Defined

Racism. The word conjures powerful images from men with hoods and burning crosses to swastikas. But what exactly is racism? Does racism only appear on horseback with men in hoods? Can a school be racist or is racism something only between individuals? Is racism the same as prejudice? To clarify these key questions and to provide a foundation for the current chapter, a conceptual understanding of racism may be helpful. While numerous scholars have wrestled with definitions of racism (Jones, 1997), for the purposes of the current chapter, Jones's (1972) definition effectively illustrates key aspects of racism. According to Jones, "racism results from the transformation of race prejudice and/or ethnocentrism through the exercise of power against a racial group defined as inferior, by individuals and institutions with the intentional and unintentional support of the entire culture" (p. 172). Whereas **racial prejudice** refers to a negative attitude toward individuals and groups on the basis of race, racism consists of behaviors and actions that are based on racially prejudicial attitudes and supported by the larger dominant culture. Hence, the support of the larger culture points to a key aspect of racism—the element of power. In other words, the racial hierarchies inherent in racism are formalized and given legitimacy or power by a system of cultural values and beliefs and manifested in institutional and individual actions that are sanctioned by those beliefs. Although racial prejudice is an attitude that anyone can endorse, racism occurs when that prejudice is given institutional and cultural legitimacy. Given that racism is embedded into a culture, acting upon those beliefs becomes a normative and acceptable form of behavior. As a result, racism can be both intentional and unintentional, as Jones points out. In other words, individuals and institutions are not necessarily conscious of the racial beliefs that motivate their actions because their underlying beliefs are engrained in the culture and regarded as the norm. A final aspect of racism is that it is a systemic phenomenon. In effect, the cultural, institutional, and individual elements of racism each reinforce one another and therefore perpetuate a larger social system. So, while Brian's encounter with the old man on the subway is clearly an encounter between two individuals, the old man has most likely been socialized in a larger culture and by institutions that give legitimacy to the racial stereotype of Asians as foreigners, as not belonging here, and, at times, as the "enemy." In effect, the old man is not simply an individual acting, intentionally or not, on his racist beliefs; he is also a product of a larger social system that has supported and perpetuated these beliefs.

Building upon his definition of racism, Jones (1997) has further differentiated between three different types of racism: (a) individual, (b) institutional, and (c) cultural. According to Jones, **individual racism** occurs when individuals act upon their belief in their own racial superiority and the inferiority of other racial groups. Examples of individual racism may be found in acts of bullying, theft, verbal harassment, assault, and at times homicide. As an extension of individual racial beliefs, **institutional racism** refers to laws, regulations, policies, and practices that serve to restrict the rights, choices, and mobility of a racial group in systems such as business, housing, justice, health, education, and so forth. In effect, institutional racism occurs when social systems reinforce and reflect the racial prejudices of the members of the dominant racial group. Lastly, **cultural racism** is reflected in the pattern of underlying values, beliefs, traditions, and assumptions that promote the dominance of one racial group over another. For instance, cultural racism can be found in how a society defines and values standards of beauty, forms of communication, normative family dynamics, religious standards and so forth. So, cultural racism can be found just by opening a magazine and observing both the individuals who are included

Table 21.1 Types of Racism

Type	Definition	Examples
Individual	Individuals acting upon their belief in their own racial superiority and the inferiority of other races	Bullying, verbal harassment, physical assault, theft, vandalism
Institutional	Laws, regulations, policies, and practices that serve to restrict the rights, choices, and mobility of a race	Chinese Exclusion Act, Japanese American internment, English-only initiatives, glass-ceiling effects, income-to-education disparities
Cultural	Values, beliefs, traditions, and assumptions that promote the dominance of one race over another	Beauty defined as tall, blond, fair skin; normative communication defined as direct and assertive; value placed on individualism and independence
Vicarious	Witnessing racism against others	Observing or witnessing an incident without being directly targeted
Microaggression (or daily racism)	Subtle insults and differential treatment that may be covert or overt	Being ignored in a line; receiving poorer service; exclusion from events
Collective	Perceptions of the extent to which one's racial group is affected by and the target of racism	Understanding of Asian American history; awareness of anti-Asian violence and hate crimes

and those who are not. In effect, cultural racism can be regarded as the implicit and explicit beliefs and values that fuel racism and are expressed through individual and institutional acts.

Building upon Jones's work, other scholars have argued that racism can also take additional forms (Essed, 1991; Harrell, 2000). For instance, Harrell has argued that racism does not have to be experienced directly by an individual and that **vicarious racism** (i.e., incidents that are witnessed by an individual), can be an equally powerful psychological experience. Moreover, Harrell refers to **daily racism** microstressors or microaggressions as subtle slights, insults, and differential treatment that result in a gradual sense of denigration and being devalued. These microaggressions may include being treated rudely or disrespectfully, receiving poor service at stores, or perhaps simply being invisible or dismissed by others on the basis of race. Lastly, Harrell has argued that communities may experience what she refers to as **collective racism** or perceptions of the extent to which one's entire racial group is affected by and the target of racism. Thus, despite the popular conceptualization of racism as strictly an event between individuals, such as the encounter that Brian had, social scientists have argued that racism is a multidimensional phenomenon that is manifested in a variety of forms.

Asian Americans and Racism: Past to Present

"Go the f@%# back where you came from!!!" In recalling Brian's experience on the subway, the focus shifts from racism in general to the experiences of Asian Americans in particular. As you recall the potent images of Brian's encounter, think about what comes to mind when you think about Asian Americans and racism. What images, events, and stories emerge for you? To assist readers with this exploration and to provide them with a historical context, it may be helpful to review Asian Americans' historical experiences with racism. For a more thorough review, readers may want to refer to Chan's (1991) authoritative *Asian Americans: An Interpretive History* or Mio, Nagata, Tsai, and Tewari's (2007) chapter on racism in the *Handbook of Asian American Psychology*.

Since their arrival on the sugar plantations of Hawaii, the mines of California, and the canneries of Alaska, racism and discrimination have been consistent themes in the life experiences of Asian Americans regardless of their port of entry. Although actively recruited and initially well received as a source of cheap labor in various industries, Asian American immigrants were eventually treated with discrimination, suspicion, and fear. Chan (1991) writes that the early Chinese immigrants were perceived as "nothing more than starving masses, beasts of burden, depraved heathens and opium addicts" (p. 45). In regard to individual racism, she found that upon their arrival in the United States, the Chinese became targets of violence, murder, vandalism, and mass expulsions from their homes—a pattern that was repeated with subsequent Asian immigrants. Beginning with the 1871 Los Angeles Chinese Massacre and the death of 20 Chinese immigrants (the first documented anti-Asian incident of its kind), various Asian ethnic communities have experienced similar levels of violence and murder (Chan, 1991). For instance, Asian Indian laborers had their campsites burned and were expelled from Live Oak, California, in 1908; a mob attacked Japanese workers and forcibly expelled them from Turlock, California, in 1921; and the 1930 Watsonville riots involved mobs of disgruntled White workers who formed "hunting parties" against Filipinos (Chan, 1991).

Parallel to individual racism, Asian Americans also experienced institutional racism in the form of regulations and laws designed to restrict their economic, social, educational, and civil rights in this country. The most striking example of the intersection of racism and institutional power came with the internment of 120,000 Japanese Americans during World War II, the majority of whom were U.S. citizens at the time. Without a trial or formal charges placed against them, Executive Order 9066 forced an entire racial community—from babies to the elderly—to sell and relinquish their homes, businesses, and anything else that couldn't fit into a suitcase on short notice, move into assembly areas such as race tracks, and then be shipped off to desolate camps under armed guard (Chan, 1991). Imagine that this happened to you, your family, and everyone else you knew simply because of your race and the assumption that you were guilty. How might you react to this treatment?

Japanese American family awaiting evacuation and internment. (Photo courtesy of National Archives.)

Institutional racism, however, was also manifested in other aspects of daily life. For instance, Asian Americans have been the target of ethnic-specific business taxes, residential segregation codes, as well as prohibitions from owning property, receiving an education, intermarrying across racial groups (i.e., **anti-miscegenation laws**), and becoming U.S. citizens (i.e., **anti-naturalization laws**) (Chan, 1991). Indeed, Chinese Americans became the first ethnic group in the history of the United States to be specifically banned from immigration with the passage of the Chinese Exclusion Act of 1882. With these exclusionary laws enacted against the Chinese, the need for cheap labor resulted in the recruitment and immigration of other Asian ethnic groups, such as the Japanese, Filipinos, and Asian Indians. However, consistent with the experiences of the Chinese, subsequent exclusionary laws and policies fueled by anti-Asian sentiments effectively banned these ethnic groups as well. For instance, the Gentlemen's Agreement of 1907 restricted Japanese immigration and the Immigration Act of 1917 created the Asiatic Barred Zone that prevented immigrations by the remaining Asian ethnic groups from South Asia, Southeast Asia, and the Pacific Islands—thereby effectively halting Asian immigration. An initial exception to these laws was Filipino laborers who had unrestricted access to the United States since the Philippines was a U.S. colony and they were considered U.S. nationals. However, as with other Asian ethnic groups, the passage of the Tydings-McDuffie Act in 1934 closed this ethnic loophole. While ostensibly designed to grant independence to the Philippines, the act also resulted in the reclassification of all Filipinos already living the United States as aliens and limited future Filipino immigration to 50 individuals per year (Chan, 1991).

Apart from exclusionary immigration laws, naturalization policies also illustrated the extent to which Asian Americans were the targets of institutional racism. In a famous case, Takao

"Welcome to America."

"Positively No Filipinos Allowed," Stockton Hotel, circa 1930s. (From Stegner, Wallace (1945). *One Nation.* New York: Houghton Mifflin. Photo by Sprague Talbott.)

Ozawa petitioned for citizenship under the argument that one's beliefs and behaviors rather than race should be the criteria for citizenship and by that standard, his assimilation into White society should qualify him to be White—one of the racial groups eligible for citizenship (Wu, 2003). However, in 1922, the U.S. Supreme Court essentially argued that White referred to Caucasians alone and that Ozawa was ineligible. Following Ozawa's case, Dr. Bhagat Thind who was a Punjabi immigrant and U.S. Army veteran initially granted U.S. citizenship since Indians were considered by anthropologists as Caucasians, presented his case for citizenship. However, the same U.S. Supreme Court that tried the Ozawa case, eventually revoked Thind's citizenship in 1923 by ruling that citizenship was reserved for "White persons" which was not synonymous with "Caucasians" (Chan, 1991; Wu, 2003). In effect, these two cases illustrate the extent to which institutional racism defies logic while maintaining privilege. The exact same Supreme Court essentially ruled that Ozawa was not eligible for citizenship because he was "White" but not "Caucasian" whereas Thind was not eligible because he was "Caucasian" but not "White."

Although events such as the Chinese Exclusion Act and the internment of Japanese Americans are historical in nature, they established and underscored a pattern of racism and discrimination against Asian Americans that continues to this day. Longstanding Asian American stereotypes, such as "heathens," "devious," "exotic," and "perpetual foreigners" (see Aoki and Mio's chapter on stereotypes in this text for more on this topic) continue to influence how Asian Americans are treated. Parallel to the experiences of the earliest immigrants, the National Asian Pacific American Legal Consortium (NAPALC; 2003) has found that Asian Americans continue to be the target of hate crimes that span the range from vandalism and robbery to physical attacks, rape, and murder. Indeed, the murder of Vincent Chin in Detroit in 1982 by two disgruntled autoworkers has become a watershed moment in the history of Asian America. As Chin was celebrating his bachelor's party, Ron Ebens and Michael Nitz began taunting Chin with racial slurs under the assumption that he was Japanese. At one point Ebens was reported to have said, "It's because of you little motherf*%kers that we're out of work," when in fact Ebens was working full time. The slurs escalated to fighting, which ended when Ebens and Nitz chased down and caught Chin and proceeded to hit him repeatedly with a baseball bat until Chin lost consciousness. As he lost consciousness, Chin said, "It isn't fair." Four days later, Vincent Chin died on June 23, 1982, from his injuries, only 5 days before his wedding day. Ebens and Nitz were tried and sentenced to 3 years in probation and $3,780 in fines for the murder of Vincent Chin. Subsequent hearings and appeals cleared both Nitz and Ebens of all charges and neither served any time in jail for their actions ("It Isn't Fair," 1983). Imagine Nitz holding Chin down while Ebens hits him on the head with a bat and then imagine them being acquitted of all charges. As you try to reconcile those images, what are your reactions? To explore more about this incident and the resulting trial, viewing Choy and Tajima's classic and moving film *Who Killed Vincent Chin? (1987)*.

Following the murder of Vincent Chin and the acquittal of his killers, Asian American communities across the country mobilized and formed advocacy and civil rights groups to respond to similar incidents and violations against Asian Americans. Unfortunately, while Chin's murder was clearly the most publicized, numerous murders and attacks of Asian Americans have occurred since that time. In particular, readers are referred to the Asian American Justice Center's (see Suggested Readings below) *Annual Audit of Anti-Asian Violence Against Asian Pacific Americans,* which reviews the sobering murders of Joseph Ileto in 1999, Thien Minh Ly in 1997, Mijanur Rahman in 2002, Mohammed Hossain in 2002, as well as other anti-Asian hate crimes. Strikingly, NAPALC (2003) has reported that there has been an increasing incidence of anti-Asian hate crimes and that following the September 11 attacks on the East Coast, members of the South Asian community in particular became targets of numerous hate crimes. Moreover, NAPALC has documented that an increasing number of these hate crimes have occurred at both high schools and colleges.

Vincent Chin. (Photo courtesy of *Asian Week*.)

Contemporary racism against Asian Americans, however, is not limited to such individual and overt acts of violence. Institutional racism in the form of policies, regulations, and practices continue to affect Asian Americans. For instance, Ancheta (1998) observed that initiatives to make English an official language have generally been located in areas with large Asian and/ or Latino populations. In numerous cities, initiatives have been created to limit the number of public and business signs from being written in a non-English language. Moreover, Asian Americans have been denied jobs and fired from positions due to their accents and have been prohibited from speaking their language of origin in their workplace (Ancheta, 1998). In the workplace, Asian Americans, despite the stereotype as economically successful "model minorities" (see Lee, Wong, & Alvarez's chapter in this text), continue to earn less than their White colleagues.

According to Woo (2000), Asian Americans in the workplace have bumped up against the **glass ceiling**, which refers to attitudes and organizational barriers that prevent qualified individuals from career advancement. Examples of the glass ceiling are evidenced by disparities in income, despite equivalent educational degrees, disproportionately lower representation of Asian Americans at the managerial and executive level, longer times until promotion, as well as denials of promotions (Woo, 2000). Institutional barriers against Asian Americans can also be found in the educational system (Chan, 1991). Since the 1990s elite universities such as Harvard, UC Berkeley, Stanford, and Princeton have been accused of differential acceptance of Asian Americans despite similar or higher levels of academic achievement. Consequently, regardless of ethnic group, gender, geographic region, or socioeconomic status, the contemporary evidence indicates that racism continues to affect the lives of Asian Americans.

Psychology and Racism

Given both this historical and contemporary evidence, what role does psychology play in all of this? How does psychology help either Brian, his therapist, or people in general, make sense of these racial experiences? As one step toward answering this question, a review of the psychological research on Asian Americans and racism may be helpful. The research on Asian Americans and racism has been a relatively recent, yet rapidly growing, area of interest for social scientists. Prior to the 1990s, much of the research on racism focused on the development of racial attitudes rather than on the psychological experience of being the target of racism (Burkard, Medler, & Boticki, 2001). Moreover, when social scientists examined the impact of racism on people of color, they generally focused on the experiences of African Americans (Williams, Neighbors, & Jackson, 2003) and devoted minimal attention to Asian Americans. Nevertheless, despite such delays, a growing body of research since 2000 has provided social scientists with a foundation for investigating key questions about Asian Americans' experiences with racism and its psychological implications. Therefore, the following sections will examine the current literature on Asian Americans and racism as it relates to issues of (a) prevalence, (b) awareness of racism, (c) psychological consequences, and (d) coping.

Prevalence

A key element for consideration is the prevalence of Asian Americans' experiences with racism (i.e., the frequency of its occurrence). For instance, how typical is Brian's experience on the subway? Is racism a daily event? Does racial discrimination happen only occasionally? Although basic and seemingly simple questions, the variations in research designs have made answering them a challenge for researchers. For instance, there may be differences in prevalence based on the type of racism that one is examining. The experience of losing a job or perhaps being denied housing due to one's race may be far less prevalent (but no less salient) than being treated rudely or verbally harassed due to one's race. Additionally, prevalence may vary according to the timeframe being investigated (i.e., lifetime prevalence, past year, past month). Nevertheless, a number of studies are able to provide some insights into this issue.

In terms of large-scale studies, Gee, Spencer, Chen, Yip, and Takeuchi (2007) examined the responses of the first nationally representative sample of Asian Americans in the National Latino and Asian American Study. Gee et al. found that Asian Americans described racism (e.g., treated with less respect, being called names) as a relatively infrequent event, occurring less than once a year, a rate that is comparable to that found in other communities of color. Indeed, in additional studies, comparable lifetime prevalence rates have been found among Chinese Americans (Goto, Gee, & Takeuchi, 2002) and Filipino Americans (Mossakowski, 2003). Specifically, Goto et al. (2002) found that 21% of Chinese Americans reported being discriminated against due to their race or language at one point in their life and 15% of Filipinos reported having experienced at least one incident of racism in their lifetime (Mossakowski, 2003). However, a focus on lifetime prevalence rates of discrimination may underestimate the prevalence of racism since it may be difficult for people to recall precisely the number of events that have occurred over their entire lives and given the covert nature of racism, people may reappraise or minimize such events over time (Gee et al., 2007; Mossakowski, 2003).

Indeed, when researchers have investigated specific types of racism within specific periods of time, a more complex picture of prevalence begins to emerge. For instance, when examining the prevalence of racism in the last month, Mossakowski found that 34% of Filipinos reported that people acted as though they were inferior, 31% were treated disrespectfully or with less courtesy, and 26% received poor service. Additionally, Noh and Kaspar (2003) found that 40% of Korean Canadians reported being verbally harassed whereas 24% reported being threatened, and 7% reported being hit due to their race. Similarly, Alvarez, Juang, and Liang (2006) also found that in the past year, 98% of Asian American students reported experiencing a microaggression at least once and that over the last 5 years, 99% witnessed at least one incident of vicarious racism.

Additionally, given the heterogeneity within the Asian American community, the prevalence of racism may also vary according to a number of different factors such as ethnicity, geography, generational status, and gender. For example, the frequency of one's encounters with racism may also differ by ethnic group. Various studies have found that Filipinos experience racism with greater frequency than other Asian groups (Alvarez et al., 2006; Gee et al., 2007; Kuo, 1995). In regard to gender, men have been found to report greater incidence of racism than women (Alvarez et al., 2006; Kuo, 1995; Lee, 2005). With respect to region, individuals in San Francisco report a higher incidence of racism than individuals in either Maryland (Liang, Alvarez, Juang, & Liang, 2007) or Honolulu (Gee et al., 2006). Lastly, the perception of racism appears to increase as the length of residency in this country increases (Goto et al., 2002).

With the variety of results that have been found, a number of conclusions can be made about the complexity of determining the prevalence of racism against Asian Americans. First, the interpretation of these results must take into account both the type of racism and the time period that is being examined. Second, experiences with racism may vary according to the type being examined with incidents such as verbal harassment and differential treatment potentially having a higher frequency than incidents such as physical harassment and threats. Lastly, there is evidence to suggest that the experience of racism is not the same for all segments of the Asian American community and that one must be cautious about broad generalizations.

Awareness of Racism

As Brian faced the barrage of hostility from the older man, his perception of the event as a racist event is key to how he will respond, how he will cope, and perhaps the outcomes of the encounter. To the extent that Brian did not think of this event as a form of racism, it is likely that he will respond to the situation in a very different way than if he regarded this as a racial incident. Nevertheless, Brian's frustration and sense that "*it just never stops*" suggests that Brian has previously encountered and is aware of racism against Asian Americans. Thus, a central question for social scientists is, "*What contributes to Brian's and other Asian Americans' awareness of racism?*" Although such a question is clearly a critical one to address, empirical examinations of this issue have been minimal and more research is needed in this area.

Nevertheless, psychology suggests that racial identity theory (Helms, 1990) may provide a useful conceptual framework for understanding how Asian Americans may perceive racism (Alvarez & Helms, 2001). In brief, according to Helms and Cook (1999), racial identity theories "explain individuals' intrapsychic and interpersonal reactions to societal racism" (p. 81). Theoretically, racial identity theories propose that individuals progress through statuses of identity ranging from a color-blind status, in which one minimizes or trivializes racism, to later statuses in which they are conscious of and actively addressing racism. Given his awareness of racism, Brian appears to be at a relatively well-developed status of racial identity development. Thus, the use of racial identity theories may provide Asian Americans with a framework for assessing their own understanding of race and racism. For a more thorough review of racial identity theory, please see Chang and Kwan's chapter on racial identity in this text.

In support of this, Alvarez and Helms (2001) found that racial identity was related to one's awareness of racism among Asian Americans. Specifically, they found that when Asian Americans primarily operate from a developmental status in which they are immersed in their culture, hostile toward White Americans, and hypervigilant against racism, then they are more likely to perceive racism. In contrast, individuals who operate from a status in which they are ambivalent about racism and only have a beginning awareness of racism are less likely to perceive racism. Expanding on these findings, Alvarez, Juang, and Liang (2006) found that **racial socialization** experiences also influenced Asian Americans' awareness of racism and their racial identity development. According to Alvarez et al., racial socialization experiences such as talking explicitly with parents, friends, and family about race and racism contribute to whether

Asian Americans are aware of racism. Conversely, individuals without such experiences may find it more difficult to recognize racism as it occurs. It stands to reason that the more one is exposed to role models who are open about and freely discuss racism and their experiences, the more likely it is that such individuals are prepared to recognize and deal with racism.

Nevertheless, opportunities to receive such racial socialization experiences may also present a challenge for Asian Americans. Despite their historical roots in the United States, the majority of Asian Americans (i.e., 69%) are first-generation immigrants with a large percentage having immigrated within the last 20 years (Reeves & Bennett, 2004). Given this demographic reality, Alvarez and Chen (in press) have argued that large segments of the Asian American community may be new to the racial hierarchies and racial dynamics in this country. Coming from relatively homogeneous racial environments in their own countries, race and racism as experienced in the United States may be quite unfamiliar. In contrast to African American communities in which there is a greater likelihood of finding elders who have longstanding experiences with and family histories of racism, Asian Americans may find it more challenging to find and learn from such elders within their community. Look within your own network of family and friends. How many of these individuals are second generation or higher? How often did your elders talk to you about race and racism?

Additionally, while Asian American immigration is often portrayed as waves of immigration, it is important to recognize that each wave may not be connected or be aware of the experiences of prior waves. For instance, although Chinese American immigration began with farm laborers and miners in the mid-1800s, newly arrived immigrants from Taiwan, Hong Kong, and Shanghai may be unfamiliar with the history and experiences of these earlier immigrants. In effect, the community's collective memory or sense of collective racism may lack continuity from one immigration wave to another (Alvarez & Yeh, 1999). Consider your own family—are your elders aware of the experiences of earlier immigrants within your own community? If not, then it may be difficult for new Asian American immigrants to obtain a shared, historical appreciation of the racial experiences of the immigrants who came before them. To the extent that one lacks this historical foundation, then it may be challenging to understand one's current experiences with racism in a larger social context. As you reflect on your understanding of Asian American history, think about when and how you learned about the experiences of the miners, laborers, and plantation workers who came before you. Who taught you about these experiences and how did it shift your understanding about race and racism?

In light of these challenges to obtaining an awareness of racism, the role of education and social support becomes critical. Alvarez (2002) has argued that higher education in particular is a critical period of development for Asian Americans' racial consciousness. With Asian American students being exposed to lectures, guest speakers, and formal courses such as Asian American psychology, history, literature, and so forth, college may be an opportunity to learn about oneself and one's community in a manner that may not have been previously available. However, the avenues to awakening an individual's racial consciousness do not have to be rooted in Asian American issues. Learning about the histories and experiences of other oppressed groups through courses in African American studies, La Raza studies, women's studies, Native American studies, and LGBTQ studies may be equally transformative for individuals. Moreover, Asian American students' understanding of race and racism may be further expanded by their exposure to vital learning experiences outside of the classroom. For instance involvement in Asian American student advocacy groups, protests on Asian American related issues from immigration reform to sweatshops to Asian American studies, attendance at Asian American student and academic conferences, as well as contact with Asian American faculty and staff can be potent opportunities for consciousness raising. Indeed, as suggested by Alvarez et al.'s (2006) study, mentors and the opportunity to openly discuss issues of race may be vital catalysts for Asian Americans. Thus, students may want to consider what opportunities are available to them at their institution, both inside and outside of the classroom, that may provide them with the space to explore, discuss and expand their understanding of race, racism, and Asian American issues.

Psychological Consequences

Returning to Brian's encounter, another critical issue for psychologists is whether his experience has any adverse effects. What are the consequences not only of his experience on the subway but also his accumulated experiences as an Asian American over the course of his lifetime? Are these experiences harmful, or are they simply instances of verbal harassment he should shrug off? In response to these key questions and in contrast to the range of results found in studies on the prevalence and awareness of racism, studies on the consequences of racism against Asian Americans have been uniformly consistent. Specifically, numerous studies have found that racism has an adverse impact on the psychological and physical well-being of Asian Americans (Beiser & Hou, 2006; Fisher, Wallace, & Fenton, 2000; Gee et al., 2007; Noh & Kaspar, 2003). For instance, in the National Latino and Asian American Study (NLAAS), Gee et al. (2007) found that racial discrimination increased the likelihood that Asian Americans would experience a psychological disorder, even after controlling for other stressors such as poverty, family conflict, and physical health concerns. Even more strikingly, Gee et al. found that the probability of experiencing a psychological disorder more than doubled among those individuals who reported the highest levels of discrimination. Gee et al. also reported that the discrimination was particularly associated with higher levels of depression and anxiety, as found in other studies (Beiser & Hou, 2006; Greene, Way, & Pahl, 2006). Additionally, despite fewer studies on the topic, discrimination against Asian Americans has also been linked to chronic health conditions. Using data from NLAAS, Gee, Spencer, Chen, and Takeuchi (in press) found that the experience of discrimination was associated with an increased incidence of cardiovascular disease, pain, and respiratory illnesses among Asian Americans.

In another compelling study, Loo and her colleagues (2001) examined the racial experiences of Asian American Vietnam veterans. With North Vietnamese soldiers as the enemy, Loo theorized that Asian American veterans would be exposed to a racially stigmatizing and therefore stressful

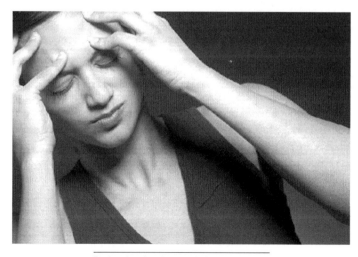

Racism is related to psychological distress.

environment. The stress for Asian American veterans therefore comes from a military environment that Loo referred to as the "gook syndrome" in which people are conditioned to define, fight, and dehumanize an enemy who looks like you. Additionally, the sense of cultural identification with a community identified as the enemy may also contribute to the stress of this environment. Living in such an environment, Loo found that Asian American veterans' race-related stressors and exposure to racial prejudice in this environment was related to post-traumatic stress order and psychological distress more so than exposure to actual combat! In other words, the experience of racism, more so than combat exposure, was a robust predictor of psychological disorders.

Additional studies have provided further evidence of the range of damaging effects that racism has on Asian Americans' psychological well-being. For instance, a number of studies have found that the experience of racial discrimination is related to lower levels of self esteem (Fisher, Wallace, & Fenton, 2000; Greene, Way, & Pahl, 2006). It stands to reason that as Asian Americans encounter racial experiences that convey a sense of being devalued, then they may be more likely to internalize these experiences and devalue themselves. Similarly, Iyer and Haslam (2003) found in their study of South Asian women that racial teasing was associated with disturbed eating behavior and a distorted body image. They speculated that since racial teasing denigrates one's race, Asian American women may be more apt to place greater value on White standards of beauty and be more likely to evaluate themselves and their bodies more negatively. Being the target of racism has also been found to be associated with substance abuse. Gee, Delva, and Takeuchi (2004) found that racial discrimination was related to alcohol dependence, as well as the use of both prescription medications and illegal substance among Filipino Americans. Gee et al. speculated that the use of these various substances may be one method that Asian Americans use to cope with their experiences with racism.

Given that one of the current stereotypes of Asian Americans is the model minority, the impact of this stereotype on Asian Americans has yet to be empirically examined in depth. After all, in contrast to negative stereotypes, it would seem that such a seemingly positive stereotype should be relatively harmless. Right? However, preliminary findings suggest that the model minority myth, innocuous as it seems, may have significant consequences. For instance, Rosenbloom and Way (2004) found that Asian American youth face discrimination from their peers more so than other students of color. In other words, they are more likely to be teased, harassed, socially isolated, and at times physically attacked and robbed by their peers. As one African American youth pointed out, "The teachers think the Chinese kids can do everything....Kids bother the Chinese kids in the hallway" (p. 420). In effect, the perception of Asian Americans' academic success (i.e., the model minority myth) is racially divisive and makes Asian Americans a target for other racial groups. Moreover, Cheryan and Bodenhausen (2000) found that the model minority myth may also elicit what they called a "choke under pressure" phenomenon. Cheryan and Bodenhausen found that when ethnic identity was made salient for Asian American women, they had difficulty concentrating and their math performance subsequently diminished. The researchers concluded that the high expectations associated with their race (e.g., "Asians do well in math") may have increased the pressure they felt and diminished the academic performance of these women. Reflect a moment on the model minority myth. How does it impact you? Hence, from seemingly positive stereotypes to subtle racial microaggressions, the psychological literature has consistently found that racism has detrimental effects for Asian Americans.

Coping

As Brian recounts his encounter to his therapist, the natural question arises, How do Asian Americans cope with their experiences with racism? Do they talk to people about it? When you had an experience with racism, what did you do? While such questions are clearly valuable, the psychological research on Asian Americans' racism-related coping strategies remains scant. Conceptually, psychologists (Lazarus & Folkman, 1984) have broadly categorized coping into two primary strategies: (a) **problem-focused coping**, such as planning or taking action to modify or minimize a stressor, and (b) **emotion-focused coping**, such as regulating or moderating the emotional impact of a stressor. In terms of racism, problem-focused coping may be reflected in deciding to report the incident to the authorities or perhaps even confronting a perpetrator. In contrast, emotion-focused coping may involve talking with friends and family, seeking the advice of others, or simply venting.

In the earliest study on how Asian Americans cope with racism, Kuo (1995) found that Asian Americans adopted what he referred to as a strategy of accommodation. Specifically, he found that Asian Americans preferred to use strategies that focused on restructuring their cognitions about racism. For instance, Kuo found that 53% "told themselves that discrimination was not really important and that 54 percent often or sometimes just tried to ignore discrimination" (p. 119). In contrast, fewer than half of the participants were willing to talk with friends or family or report the incident with a civil rights or ethnic-based organization. Moreover, Kuo found that the choice of coping strategy may be influenced by a variety of factors. First, Kuo found that gender was related to the choice of coping strategy such that men were more likely to use accommodation strategies and women were more likely to turn to friends and family for support. Second, Kuo found differences in the choice of coping strategy according to ethnicity. Specifically, he found that Filipinos and Japanese were more likely than Chinese and Koreans to take action by turning to friends, family, and ethnic organizations whereas Koreans and Japanese were more likely than Filipinos and Chinese to use accommodation strategies. Lastly, Kuo found that education was negatively related to the use of accommodation strategies. In other words, Asian Americans who were more educated were less likely to dismiss or ignore their experiences with racism. Kuo theorized that education may be one indicator of an individual's access to or familiarity with social resources and that with greater education comes a greater likelihood that an individual will utilize these resources. In effect, Kuo suggests that the nature of how Asian Americans cope with racism may be a complex phenomenon that is reflective of the heterogeneity within the community.

To echo Kuo's work, the work of Noh and his colleagues (Noh et al., 1999; Noh & Kaspar, 2003) underscores the complexity of how one chooses to cope with racism and the resources that are available to a community. In their large-scale study of Korean Canadian adults, Noh and Kaspar (2003) found that the use of problem-focused strategies was associated with lower levels of depression and that the use of emotion-focused strategies was associated with higher levels of depression. However, in contrast, when Noh et al. (1999) studied Southeast Asian refugees in Canada, they found just the opposite. Within their sample of refugees, emotion-focused coping strategies were related to lower levels of depression. Forbearance or an attitude of acceptance about racism was particularly effective in reducing depression. According to Noh and Kaspar (2003), the differences in the effectiveness of various coping strategies may illustrate the diversity of Asian American communities. For instance, their sample of Korean Canadians consisted of relatively well-educated and economically stable individuals who lived in Canada for 20 years on average. In contrast, their study with refugees consisted of individuals with lower levels of economic, educational, and social capital. So, imagine how you might react to racism if you were newly arrived into this country and had a relatively minimal understanding of both the resources and rights available to you. What would you do? How might your responses be different if you were an immigrant with a doctorate and lived a relatively upper-middle-class lifestyle? The manner in which one copes with racism may be indicative of an individual's relative power, familiarity with the racial dynamics of this country, and an ability to access appropriate resources.

Researchers (Kuo, 1995; Noh et al., 1999) have also suggested that the manner in which one copes with racism may be reflective of one's culture. For example, in Noh et al.'s study of South-east Asian refugees, the authors argued that the use of forbearance may be an effective means of coping because it is consistent with cultural expectations that place a value on maintaining interpersonal relationships and minimizing conflicts. Similarly, Kuo (1995) found that endorse-ment of traditional Asian values was related to higher utilization of accommodation strategies of coping. In support of this line of reasoning, Yoo and Lee (2005) found that cognitive restruc-turing techniques effectively reduced the negative impact that racism had on Asian Americans' psychological well-being but only when they were strongly identified with their ethnic group. In other words, the choice and effectiveness of Asian Americans' coping strategies may depend on the extent to which they identify with their race and ethnicity.

Given the relatively minimal amount of research in this area, it would be premature to con-clude that one type of coping is universally more effective than another. Additionally, as Kuo (1995) observed, the current state of the literature does not allow us to determine definitively why Asian Americans choose one coping strategy over another, whether it be for socioeconomic rea-sons, cultural reasons, or reasons that have yet to be determined. The challenge of understanding how Asian Americans cope with racism is twofold. First, as the research clearly indicates, the various segments of the Asian American community differ on a variety of dimensions—such as socioeconomic status, educational level, and generational status—all of which may influence how they cope with racial discrimination and the resources available to them. Second, as Liang, Alva-rez, Juang, and Liang (2007) observed, racism itself is a multifaceted experience that may vary from encounter to encounter. For instance, how one copes with a verbal harassment from a pro-fessor may be quite different from how one copes with verbal harassment from a group of strang-ers in an unfamiliar neighborhood. Hence, it may be difficult to determine which type of coping is effective for a specific type of racism, given that both racism and the style of coping may depend a great deal on the situational context as well as psychological variations in the individual.

Until continued research in this area can provide more consistent trends, the critical issue for psychologists and educators will be to equip and expand Asian Americans' repertoire of coping strategies and facilitate their ability to choose the strategy that is most appropriate to the situation. While at times, silence and acceptance of a specific incident may be the only feasible options in terms of political or perhaps physical safety, it is equally important to help Asian Americans recognize that there may be additional options such as talking with friends and fam-ily, discussing racial incidents in support groups, or perhaps learning more about Asian Ameri-can issues as a form of empowerment. For instance, on a campus or a corporation, there may be policies and procedures for dealing with incidents of racism and discrimination or perhaps an ombudsperson who can act as a mediator. Similarly, there may be cultural community centers, advocacy groups, or civil rights organizations to provide an individual with some guidance. Additionally, counseling centers, community mental health centers, cross-cultural centers, and women's centers may have resources or support groups that provide a forum for discussing one's experiences in a safe environment. Given the subtleties, complexities, and persistence of racism, psychologists can play a pivotal role in breaking the silence by providing support, resources, and most importantly, validation for the racial experiences of Asian Americans.

Summary

This chapter provides an overview of Asian Americans' experiences with racism from a psychological perspective. The chapter begins with definitions of racism and prejudice that serve as the foundation for the chapter. To provide a rationale for the current chapter, historical and contemporary examples of racism against Asian Americans are provided. The chapter segues into an overview of the existing psychological research into racism against Asian Americans, with an emphasis on (a) prevalence rates, (b) awareness of racism, (c) consequences, and (d) coping. To engage the reader with the issues raised in this chapter, discussion questions, learning activities, a case study, and resources are provided below. In particular, the chapter returns to an in-depth discussion of Brian's experiences to illustrate how psychologists may work with clients to cope with racism. While the chapter raises the issue of racism from a historical, empirical, and conceptual perspective, the underlying objective of the current chapter was to challenge readers to reflect upon their own personal experiences with racism and its impact on them as individuals as well as the community as a whole.

Discussion Questions

1. What experiences have you had with racism?
   a. Which experiences stand out to you?
   b. How did these experiences affect you?
   c. How did you cope with them? What worked? What didn't?
2. What do you know about Asian American history?
   a. How does this affect you?
   b. Where and when did you learn about this?
   c. What are you curious to know more about?
3. What have your parents, family, friends, and significant others taught you about racism?
   a. What was the impact of this on you?
   b. Why do you think they did or did not tell you about this?
4. When you think of racism, what comes to mind?
   a. What is racism to you?
   b. Where does it occur?
   c. Who causes it?
5. Refer back to the types of racism discussed in the chapter—institutional, cultural, and individual.
   a. Provide an example of each in your own life.
   b. Provide an example of each within your campus.
   c. Provide an example of each at your workplace.
6. What can Asian Americans do about racism?
   a. What can you do as an individual?
   b. What can you do as a group or a community?
   c. What role do other communities of color play in this?
   d. What role do White Americans play in this?

Case Study

Brian is a 20-year-old, first-generation, Filipino American man. He comes from an intact family, with three siblings and his parents. His parents immigrated to the United States when Brian was 5 years old and moved to predominantly White neighborhoods in Lansing, Michigan. His father and mother both work for the city as an accountant and chemist, respectively. Brian is the oldest child and he was the only one born in the Philippines. Brian is in his third year of college, and he is majoring in biology with the hope of becoming a physician. He has worked very hard toward this goal, having volunteered in nursing homes and city clinics for the last 3 years and starting his training as an EMT. Although he likes the work, he has been worried that he wouldn't make it to medical school, especially after getting C's in chemistry. He has been experiencing a great deal of stress since he realizes that the clock is ticking and as a last resort, he went to see a therapist at the counseling center to help him "get his mind off things."

The incident on the subway happened just as Brian was headed back to campus for his appointment with his therapist. It was his fourth time seeing her and he had found her to be helpful with managing his stress and helping him to consider some options about school and work. By the time he arrived, he was furious and he couldn't shake the image of the old man taunting him, over and over again. All he could do was think of all the things he had wanted to say to the man . . . but that got him even more frustrated with himself since he didn't say any of it. At the time he was stunned. As he sat down and his therapist noticed his agitation, his story poured out of him in a torrent and all he wanted to do was wring the old man's neck. But even as he was telling his story, he wasn't quite sure how his therapist was handling all of this, especially since she was White.

Case Study Discussion

The therapist approaches her work from a multicultural, feminist, and developmental perspective. In other words, she recognizes that individuals, institutions, and relationships exist within a cultural framework that influences their assumptions and worldviews. Additionally, she recognizes that systems of oppression across dimensions such as race, gender, sexual orientation, and so forth maintain positions of both privilege and oppression, which affect one's psychological well-being. Her developmental worldview has also taught her that negotiating and coming to an awareness of oppression is a developmental process and that one's identity is shaped by this process. Within this framework, she recognizes and continually wrestles with her privileges as a White, heterosexual, well-educated individual and attempts to reconcile these aspects of herself with her lifelong experiences as the target of sexism.

As the therapist focuses her attention onto Brian, it is clear that he is emotionally upset and that the incident on the subway is quite raw and traumatic. With this awareness in mind, she simply allows Brian to vent the emotions he was unable to express on the subway and she validates the anger and the pain of the encounter. Recognizing herself as a White woman and that this may make Brian feel somewhat awkward in talking about this, she gently inserts the comment, "It's this type of incident that reminds me of why people of color can be angry with White folks, like me." In so doing, she hoped to validate any feelings that Brian may have had toward Whites as a result of this encounter while also conveying to him her own awareness of herself as a White woman.

When Brian heard her say this, he was shocked. He had never heard a White person acknowledge their Whiteness. Although he was wondering how she would take all of this, he knew he couldn't bring that up and he was relieved yet curious that she did so. Brian and his therapist discuss what it is like for him to talk about race and racism given their interracial differences. They also discuss areas in which their experiences converge such as their respective experiences with different forms of oppression (i.e., racism and sexism). The therapist invites Brian to reflect on what he would need from her as a White therapist in order to hear his experiences with racism as well as any of his concerns about the fact that she is a White woman. She pointed out that although talking about race is often treated as a taboo topic, she believed that it would be easier if they could first be open about the racial experiences that they both bring to therapy.

As Brian feels increasingly comfortable with his therapist's racial understanding and openness, he begins to deepen his sense of trust in their relationship and decides to continue with therapy and focus on discussions about race and racism. Over multiple sessions, they discuss the scope of Brian's experiences and reactions to racism—both overt and covert—as well as being the target of discrimination from White people and other people of color as well. To get a baseline understanding of Brian's racial socialization, the therapist explores what Brian has been taught about racism as well as how he has coped with these incidents in the past. For the most part, he reported that he would just get "pissed off and move on" and that "it's just the way it is. . . . " The counselor explores the effectiveness of these coping strategies and invites him to consider if an exploration of alternative ways of coping might be helpful. Throughout the course of counseling, Brian and his therapist begin exploring additional forms of coping to see if these would be feasible to him. Over time, they also discuss Brian's involvement with and exposure to other Asian American individuals and student groups, the role of his family in addressing issues of racism, his understanding of Asian American issues and history, as well as his knowledge of Asian American resources both on and off campus.

Case Study Discussion Questions

For undergraduate students, please consider the following questions:

1. How similar or different are your racial experiences from Brian's?
   a. How would react to this situation?
   b. How might you cope with this situation?
2. If Brian came to you about this incident, how would you help him?
3. If you talked about race or culture with a therapist, what would you need from her or him in order to do so?

For graduate students and/or beginning therapists, please consider the following questions:

1. How would you respond initially to Brian as he came into the session?
2. What in your own experiences would
   a. Make it easy to work with Brian on this?
   b. Make it challenging to work with Brian on this?
3. How do you raise race, culture, and ethnicity in your own work? Be specific and explicit.

Key Terms

Anti-miscegenation laws: Laws prohibiting marriage or cohabitation across racial groups.

Anti-naturalization laws: Laws prohibiting individuals from becoming citizens.

Collective racism: Perceptions of the extent to which racism is experienced by one's racial group.

Cultural racism: Values, beliefs, traditions, and assumptions that promote the superiority of one racial group over another.

Daily racism: Racial microaggressions, such as insults, disrespect, etc., that denigrate and dehumanize individuals.

Emotion-focused coping: Regulating or moderating the emotional impact of a stressor.

Glass ceiling: Attitudes and organizational barriers that prevent qualified individuals from career advancement.

Individual racism: Individual actions based on a belief in the racial superiority of one's own group and the inferiority of other racial groups.

Institutional racism: Laws, regulations, policies, and practices that restrict the rights, choices, and mobility of a racial group.

Prevalence: Rate or frequency of occurrence.

Problem-focused coping: Planning or taking action to modify or minimize a stressor.

Racial prejudice: Negative attitude toward individuals and groups on the basis of race.

Racial socialization: Experiences that educate an individual about race and racism.

Racism: Transformation of race prejudice and/or ethnocentrism through the exercise of power against a racial group defined as inferior, by individuals and institutions with the intentional and unintentional support of the entire culture.

Vicarious racism: Incidents of racism that are witnessed by or reported to an individual.

For Further Learning and Suggested Reading

1. Family Interview: Conduct an interview with your family about their experiences with racism and discrimination. Develop a list of questions that intrigue you such as their understanding of racism, the way the cope, and its impact on them. Be aware of your reactions to what they report and take note of what resonates with you, what surprised you, and perhaps what angered or saddened you.

2. Interracial Interview: Conduct an interview with a Person of Color, who is not Asian American, about their experiences with racism. In what ways are their experiences and their understanding of racism similar to or different from your own?

3. Biographies: Prepare or read biographies on notable Asian Americans and focus on how they experienced and dealt with racism. To start you off, consider individuals such as Bhagat Singh Thind, Yuri Kochiyama, Sammy Lee, Fred Korematsu, Gordon Hirabayashi, Philip Vera Cruz, Frank Wu, Helen Zia, Haing Ngor, Norman Mineta, Angela Oh, Patsy Mink, Gordon Locke.

4. Chin Case Study: Do an in-depth case study of the murder of Vincent Chin. Review information related to Mr. Chin's life, Ron Ebens, Michael Nitz, and the attack in 1982. Investigate the details of the trial, its outcome and the role of the larger Asian American community. Reflect on what your reactions are to this incident and how it influences your own understanding of racism and your identity as an Asian American.

5. Life Histories: Read the life histories of Japanese Americans online at the Japanese American National Museum. Go to http://www.janm.org/nrc and click on the Life History Transcripts Online Link-Regenerations Project.

6. Web Sites: Explore the Asian American Justice Center's website. In particular, download and review the Annual Audits of Violence Against Asian Pacific Americans which can be found under Publications in the Anti-Asian Violence and Race Relations section. Additionally, explore any of the civil rights websites listed in this chapter.

7. Debates: Arrange a debate on an Asian American issue such as college quotas, glass ceilings in the workplace, affirmative action, or English-only initiatives. Divide a group into a pro-group and a con-group. Conduct the research needed for the debate and have a judge to determine who makes the most effective arguments.

8. Films: Watch any of the films listed below, such *American Sons, Letters to Thien, Punjabi Cab,* etc. Or go to the Center for Asian American Media (http://asianamericanmedia.

org) and pick additional films. Take note of your reactions and those aspects of the film that affected you the most.

9. Issues: Identify an issue that you believe is discriminatory against Asian Americans. It can be a policy, an action, a norm, a publication, an event and so forth. Think about what you may do to address this issue and the steps required. How might you involve others? What do you need to learn? What is a reasonable goal for you?

10. Advocacy: Develop a plan for how you might address anti-Asian racism at your campus. Think about what the issues are, who your target audience is, what they need to learn and be aware of, and how you might facilitate that learning.

Books and Readings

Alvarez, A. N., & Kimura, E. F. (2001). Asian Americans and racial identity: Dealing with racism and snowballs. *Journal of Mental Health Counseling, 23*(3), 192–206.

Ancheta, A. N. (1998). *Race, rights and the Asian American experience.* New Brunswick, NJ: Rutgers University Press.

Chan, S. (1991). *Asian Americans: An interpretive history.* Boston: Twayne.

Hall, P. W., & Hwang, V. M. (2001). *Anti-Asian violence in North America.* Walnut Creek, CA: AltaMira Press.

Mio, J. S., Nagata, D. K., Tsai, A. H., & Tewari, N. (2007). Racism against Asian Pacific Islander Americans. In F. T. L. Leong, A. G. Inman, A. Ebreo, L. H. Yang, L. Kinoshita & M. Fu (Eds.), *Handbook of Asian American psychology* (2nd ed.). Thousand Oaks, CA: Sage Publications.

National Asian Pacific American Legal Consortium. (2003). *Remembering: A ten year retrospective.* Washington, DC.

U. S. Commission on Civil Rights. (1992). *Civil rights issues facing Asian Americans in the 1990s.* Washington, DC.

Wu, F. H. (2002). *Yellow: Race in America beyond Black and White.* New York: Basic Books.

Civil Rights Groups

Asian American Justice Center: http://www.advancingequality.org
Japanese American Citizens League: http://www.jacl.org
National Alliance of Vietnamese American Service Agencies: http://www.navasa.org
National Federation of Filipino American Associations: http://www.naffaa.org
National Korean American Service & Education Consortium: http://www.nakasec.org
Organization of Chinese Americans: http://www.ocanational.org
Sikh American Legal & Defense Education Fund: http://www.saldef.org

Movies

American Sons (1995): docudrama about Asian American men's experiences
Blue Collar and Buddha (1988): clash between Laotian refugees and a blue-collar town in Illinois
Color of Honor (1988): story of Japanese Americans in the military during World War II
Letters to Thien (1997): murder of Thien Minh Ly
A Personal Matter: Gordon Hirabayashi vs. the United States (1992): Hirabayashi's stand against Japanese internment
Punjabi Cab (2004): experiences of Sikh cab drivers post-9/11
Sa-I-Gu (1993): Korean American women's perspectives on the LA riots
Separate Lives: Broken Dreams (1994): impact of the Chinese Exclusion Act of 1882
Shot Heard 'Round the World (1997): murder of Yoshi Hattori
Who Killed Vincent Chin (1987): murder of Vincent Chin in Detroit

Web Sites

Angry Asian Man: http://www.angryasianman.com
Asian Nation—Asian American History, Demographics, and Issues: http://www.asiannation.org
Model Minority—A Guide to Asian American Empowerment: http://www.modelminority.com

References

Alvarez, A. N. (2002). Racial identity and Asian Americans: Supports and challenges. In M. K. McEwen, C. M. Kodama, A. N. Alvarez, C. Liang, & S. Lee (Eds.), *Working with Asian American students: New directions for student services* (pp. 33–44). San Francisco: Jossey-Bass.

Alvarez, A. N., & Chen, G. A. (in press). Organizational applications of racial identity theory: An Asian American perspective. In C. Thompson & R. Carter (Eds.), *Racial identity theory: Applications to individual, group, and organizational intervention* (2nd ed.). New York: John Wiley & Sons.

Alvarez, A. N., & Helms, J. E. (2001). Racial identity and reflected appraisals as influences on Asian Americans' racial adjustment. *Cultural Diversity and Ethnic Minority, 7,* 217–231.

Alvarez, A. N., Juang, L., & Liang, C. T. H. (2006). Asian Americans and racism: When bad things happen to "Model Minorities." *Cultural Diversity and Ethnic Minority Psychology, 12*(3), 477–492.

Alvarez, A. N., & Yeh, T. L. (1999). Asian Americans in college: A racial identity perspective. In D. Sandhu (Ed.), *Asian and Pacific Islander Americans: Issues and concerns for counseling and psychotherapy* (pp. 105–119). Commack, NY: Nova Science Publishers.

Ancheta, A. N. (1998). *Race, rights and the Asian American experience.* New Brunswick, NJ: Rutgers University Press.

Beiser, M. N. M., & Hou, F. (2006). Ethnic identity, resettlement stress and depressive affect among Southeast Asian refugees in Canada. *Social Science and Medicine, 63,* 137–150.

Burkard, A. W., Medler, B. R., & Boticki, M. A. (2001). Prejudice and racism: Challenges and progress in measurement. In J. G. Ponterotto, J. M. Casas, L. A. Suzuki, & C. M. Alexander (Eds.), *Handbook of multicultural counseling* (2nd ed., pp. 457–481). Thousand Oaks, CA: Sage Publications.

Chan, S. (1991). *Asian Americans: An interpretive history.* Boston: Twayne.

Cheryan, S., & Bodenhausen, G. V. (2000). When positive stereotypes threaten intellectual performance: The psychological hazards of "Model Minority" status. *Psychological Science, 11*(5), 399–402.

Essed, P. (1991). *Understanding everyday racism: An interdisciplinary theory.* Thousand Oaks, CA: Sage Publications.

Fisher, C. B., Wallace, S. A., & Fenton, R. E. (2000). Discrimination distress during adolescence. *Journal of Youth and Adolescence, 29,* 679–695.

Gee, G. C., Chen, J., Spencer, M. S., See, S., Kuester, O. A., Tran, D., et al. (2006). Social support as a buffer for perceived unfair treatment among Filipino Americans: Differences between San Francisco and Honolulu. *American Journal of Public Health, 96,* 677–684.

Gee, G. C., Delva, J., & Takeuchi, D. T. (2006). Relationships between self-reported unfair treatment and prescription medication use, illicit drug use, and alcohol dependence among Filipino Americans. *American Journal of Public Health, 96*(8), 1–8.

Gee, G. C., Spencer, M., Chen, J., & Takeuchi, D. T. (in press). A nationwide study of discrimination and chronic health conditions among Asian Americans. *American Journal of Public Health.*

Gee, G. C., Spencer, M., Chen, J., Yip, T., & Takeuchi, D. T. (2007). The association between self-reported racial discrimination and 12-month DSM-IV mental disorders among Asian Americans nationwide. *Social Science and Medicine, 64,* 1984–1996.

Goto, S. G., Gee, G. C., & Takeuchi, D. T. (2002). Strangers still? The experience of discrimination among Chinese-Americans. *Journal of Community Psychology, 30*(2), 211–224.

Greene, M. L., Way, N., & Pahl, K. (2006). Trajectories of perceived adult and peer discrimination among Black, Latino, and Asian American adolescents: Patterns and psychological correlates. *Developmental Psychology, 42,* 218–238.

Harrell, S. P. (2000). A multidimensional conceptualization of racism-related stress: Implications for the well-being of people of color. *American Journal of Orthopsychiatry, 70,* 42–57.

Helms, J. E. (1990). *Black and White racial identity: Theory, research, and practice.* Westport, CT: Greenwood Press.

Helms, J. E., & Cook, D. A. (1999). *Using race and culture in counseling and psychotherapy: Theory and process.* Needham Heights, MA: Allyn & Bacon.

It isn't Fair (1983, November 14) [Electronic version]. *Time.* Retrieved from http://www.time.com/time/magazine/article/0,9171,952248,00.html

Iyer, D. S., & Haslam, N. (2003). Body image and eating disturbance among South Asian American women. *International Journal of Eating Disorders, 34,* 142–147.

Jones, J. M. (1972). *Prejudice and racism.* New York: McGraw Hill.

Jones, J. M. (1997). *Prejudice and racism* (2nd ed.). New York: McGraw Hill.

Kuo, W. H. (1995). Coping with racial discrimination: The case of Asian Americans. *Ethnic and Racial Studies, 18,* 109–127.

Lazarus, R. S., & Folkman, S. (1984). *Stress, appraisal, and coping.* New York: Springer Publishing.

Lee, R. M. (2005). Resilience against discrimination: Ethnic identity and Other-group orientation as protective factors for Korean Americans. *Journal of Counseling Psychology, 52,* 36–44.

Liang, C. T., Alvarez, A. N., Juang, L. J., & Liang, M. X. (2007). The role of coping in the relationship between perceived racism and racism-related stress for Asian Americans: Gender differences. *Journal of Counseling Psychology, 54,* 132–141.

Loo, C. M., Fairbank, J. A., Scurfield, R. M., Ruch, L. O., King, D. W., Adams, L. J, & Chemtob, C. M. (2001). Measuring exposure to racism: Development and validation of a race-related stressor scale (RRSS) for Asian American Vietnam veterans. *Psychological Assessment, 13*(4), 503–520.

Mio, J. S., Nagata, D. K., Tsai, A. H., & Tewari, N. (2007). Racism against Asian Pacific Islander Americans. In F. T. L. Leong, A. G. Inman, A. Ebreo, L. H. Yang, L. Kinoshita & M. Fu (Eds.), *Handbook of Asian American psychology* (2nd ed.). Thousand Oaks, CA: Sage Publications.

Mossakowski, K. N. (2003). Coping with perceived discrimination: Does ethnic identity protect mental health? *Journal of Health and Social Behavior, 44*(3), 318–331.

National Asian Pacific American Legal Consortium. (2003). *Remembering: A ten year retrospective.* Washington, DC.

Noh, S., Beiser, M., Kaspar, V., Hou, F., & Rummens A. (1999). Perceived racial discrimination, coping, and depression among Asian refugees in Canada. *Journal of Health Social Behavior, 40,* 193–207.

Noh, S., & Kaspar, V. (2003). Perceived discrimination and depression: Moderating effects of coping, acculturation, and ethnic support. *American Journal of Public Health, 93,* 232–238.

Reeves, T. J., & Bennett, C. E. (2004). *We the people: Asians in the United States, Census 2000 special reports CENSR-17.* Washington, DC: U.S. Department of Commerce.

Rosenbloom, S. R., & Way, N. (2004). Experiences of discrimination among African American, Asian American and Latino adolescents in an urban high school. *Youth and Society, 35*(4), 420–451.

U. S. Commission on Civil Rights. (1992). *Civil rights issues facing Asian Americans in the 1990s.* Washington, DC.

Williams, D. R., Neighbors, H. W., & Jackson, J. S. (2003). Racial/ethnic discrimination and health: Findings from community studies. *American Journal of Public Health, 93*(2), 200–208.

Woo, D. (2000). *Glass ceilings and Asian Americans: The new face of workplace barriers.* Walnut Creek, CA: AltaMira Press.

Wu, F. H. (2003). *Yellow: Race in America beyond Black and White.* New York: Basic Books.

Yoo, H. C., & *Lee, R. M.* (2005). Ethnic identity and approach-type coping as moderators of the racial discrimination/well-being relation in Asian Americans. *Journal of Counseling Psychology, 52,* 497–506.

22
Stereotypes and Media Images

GUY AOKI and JEFFERY SCOTT MIO

OUTLINE OF CHAPTER

Case Synopsis

Justin Lin, the director of *Better Luck Tomorrow* and *Annapolis* among other films, was selected to direct *The Fast and the Furious: Tokyo Drift*. This film was to be the third installment of this popular street car racing franchise. Thus, while this was a big budget film entrusted in the hands of a relatively young film director, Lin had the credentials to do a good job. He wanted an **Asian American** actor who worked with him before (Sung Kang) to be the lead character, but the studios wanted a White actor to be the lead character despite the fact that the setting was in Japan, and Lin was supposed to call the shots on the movie.

Michelle Kwan, one of the world's most famous ice figure skaters, was one of the favorites to win a gold medal in the 1998 Winter Olympics in Nagano, Japan, for the United States. When she was leading the competition after the short program for her event, anticipation grew that she would win the Olympic Gold for the United States. However, after Kwan made an unfortunate stumble in her long program, Tara Lipinski of the United States won the gold medal, with Kwan taking the silver medal. Incredibly, the headline on the MSNBC Web site after this event read: "American beats out Michelle Kwan."

Four years later, Kwan was again favored for the Olympic gold medal in the 2002 Winter Olympics in Salt Lake City, Utah. Again, she led the field after the short program. However, as she had done in 1998, Kwan stumbled in her long program. Sarah Hughes won the Olympic gold medal and Kwan had to settle for the bronze medal. The headline in the *Seattle Times* read: "Hughes Good as Gold: American beats out Kwan, Slutzkaya."

Introduction

The examples presented epitomize problems faced by Asian Americans in the United States media machine, today. In the case of Justin Lin, although a proven movie director, the studios did not feel that an Asian American actor should play the lead of a franchise film genre, and they vetoed Lin's choice. Asian Americans—particularly males—are thought of as supporting actors if even cast at all.

As Kwan's case indicates, the headlines about her imply that Asian Americans are not "real" Americans but perpetual foreigners. Michelle Kwan was born in Torrance, California, and had she won the gold medal, it would have been for the United States (of course, her silver medal was added to the total medal count for this country). Even more outrageous was that 4 years later, the *Seattle Times* made the same mistake, despite the fact that Seattle has one of the largest percentages of Asians in the United States, and the governor of the State of Washington was Gary Locke, a third-generation Chinese American who served on Seattle's City Council for years before becoming Washington's top elected official.

This chapter will discuss several ways in which Asian Americans are misrepresented in the media. As many have indicated in the past, the media can have a profound effect in making people believe the stereotypes they see. Indeed, there is evidence that Asian American children have no Asian heroes, as they reported admiring Black figures the most and White figures next; they did not identify *any* Asian or Latino figures as being admirable (Children Now, 1998; Cortés, 2000). There are at least five significant ways that the media have portrayed Asians and Asian Americans. Asians are seen as being: (a) perpetual foreigners; (b) **mysterious**; (c) **exotic**; (d) "arm candy" for White males; and (e) **invisible**. The fifth point may seem contradictory, but you will see how it is relevant to the stereotyping of Asians and Asian Americans.

Quite often, people use the terms **stereotype, prejudice, discrimination**, and **racism** interchangeably. In the psychological literature, these terms are distinct from one another (Mio, Barker-Hackett, & Tumambing, 2006; Mio, Nagata, Tsai, & Tewari, 2007; Myers, 2005). While we will be focusing on stereotypes of Asians and Asian Americans in this chapter, we will briefly discuss the differences among these four forms of categorization.

Stereotypes are cognitions about people based on their categorization into an identifiable group. These cognitions can be based upon fact, fiction, or a grain of fact that is exaggerated. For example, to say that Asians tend to be shorter than Whites is a statement of fact. However, even with this fact, one must appreciate a wide variation within each group, as there are some tall Asians (e.g., the basketball player Yao Ming, who is 7′6″ tall) and some short Whites (e.g., former Secretary of Labor Robert Reich, who would joke about how he used to be over 6 feet tall before he got beaten down to his current height of 4′8″). A stereotype about Asians based upon fiction is that one cannot tell Asians apart. It is interesting that Asians have no problem telling themselves apart, but when Whites cannot tell Asians apart, they attribute this to Asian characteristics as opposed to their own failure in being able to distinguish one person from another. In movies and television programs, therefore, Asians are interchangeable, with actors of Chinese descent playing Japanese parts, actors of Japanese descent playing Korean parts, actors of Korean descent playing Vietnamese parts, etc. A more serious problem is when *issues and customs* of one country are mixed up with issues and customs of another country, such as "Chinese-sounding" words being spoken by a supposedly Japanese character, or ritualistic Japanese suicide (*hara kiri*) being done by a supposedly Vietnamese character.[1] Finally, stereotypes based upon a grain of fact that is exaggerated means that sometimes people notice small differences but then exaggerate these differences. For example, a professor may be accurate to say that in general, Asian/Asian American students tend to be quieter than their White colleagues. However, it would be inaccurate to say that Asian/Asian American students never talk, whereas White students always talk. Another example of this process is that Asian/Asian

---

[1] Because there are so few actors of Asian descent in Hollywood and because there are so few parts written for Asians/Asian Americans, we are *not* advocating that every single character is matched with the ethnic heritage of the actor. Again, the more serious problem is that of mixing up issues and customs of the cultures.

American students tend to do better in academics than other students. In comedy shows, this has led to all other students groaning when a student of Asian descent is in their classes in comedy shows. The Asian student is only used as a stimulus for the "main" characters to talk to one another and express their concern about the Asian student, whereas the Asian student rarely has any lines in the scene except to give sophisticated answers to teachers' questions, thus reinforcing the stereotype.

Prejudice is a bias against or in favor of a group of people based upon that group's categorization. Typically, prejudice is a negative evaluation of members in the target group. For example, a professor can be neutral about students who talk more or talk less, but if a professor had negative evaluations of Asian/Asian American students because they did not talk as much as their non-Asian/Asian American counterparts, that becomes a prejudice against the students. Even positive biases can have negative evaluations. For example, Asian/Asian American students are seen to be good in mathematics. Implicitly, this can mean that professors may not think that these students can excel in subjects other than mathematics. Another implication of this positive bias is that when an Asian/Asian American student does not excel in mathematics, a professor may feel that the student is either lazy or is not trying very hard. We are aware of an actual case involving this exact issue, as a Vietnamese student in the 1980s lamented that a mathematics professor thought he was not trying very hard in his mathematics course. The student said that he was from a poor farming family who fled Vietnam after the fall of Saigon. In Vietnam, he had very little formal schooling, yet his mathematics professor accused him of not trying very hard in the course and reprimanded him. In the previous scenario about other students groaning about being in the same class as an Asian/Asian American student, the positive attribute of being intelligent is actually turned into a negative attribute, as it is the source of derision among the other students who feel burdened by having to compete with an Asian student—intelligent or not.

Discrimination is behavior toward people based upon their categorization. While stereotypes and prejudice occur entirely within the mind and do not directly affect others, discrimination does. This negative behavior can occur without intentional malice of the one performing the negative behavior, but typically it is intentional. An example of discrimination without intentional malice is when one behaves negatively based upon norms developed by tradition, such as if someone were to cast a Shakespearean part to a White actor merely because White actors have always been used for these parts. The director may not have any enmity toward an Asian American actor but may simply not think of this actor as playing a Shakespearean lead. An example of discrimination based on intentional malice is when a director believes that Asian American actors are not good enough to portray a Shakespearean character so does not even consider casting such actors in these parts. In the example above where actors of Asian descent tend to only portray smart students who are the target of derision by other actors, they typically do not have any dialogue. Where Asian students do have dialogue, it is typically to show that they are "nerds" and that the goal of the other students is to get the Asian student to either act in undesirable manners or for the other students to finally outperform this overachieving student.

Racism is the institutionalized mistreatment of people based upon their classification in a racial/ethnic group on the downside of power. It is one thing for someone to discriminate against another person; it is quite another thing for this person to have the institutional power to discriminate. For example, it is one thing for individual Americans to hate people of Japanese descent during World War II after the bombing of Pearl Harbor; it is quite another thing for the U.S. government to declare that American citizens of Japanese descent were enemies of the country and to incarcerate them for the duration of the war unless they were willing to join the U.S. Armed Forces for the war effort. With respect to **media images**, Asians are typically completely left out of consideration, particularly when the movies are dealing with racial issues.

Aoki (2005) pointed out that the critically acclaimed movie *Crash* (Haggis, 2005) dealt with issues of race in the Los Angeles area. However, this movie primarily dealt with how Whites and Blacks felt about one another, and these two groups had four and five major characters, respectively, representing their points of view. There was also an in-depth examination of how Latinos with shaved heads and tattoos are viewed as gangsters or criminals, and there was a sensitive scene with such a Latino man and his daughter to counter that stereotype. There was also an examination of an Iranian family and how an older Iranian man felt victimized by the American culture while his daughter was trying to mediate between her two cultures. However, every major Asian in the film was foreign born, continuing the stereotype of Asians as the perpetual foreigner. Second, Asians were only used as "comic relief," as the movie begins with the tired old stereotype of Asians being bad drivers when a Korean immigrant woman gets into a car accident, and three-quarters of the way through the movie two Black characters run over an Asian man who gets stuck under their vehicle ("There's a Chinaman under the car. What do we do?"). At the end of the movie, there is another car accident in the middle of Chinatown, and it is discovered that the Korean immigrant man who was run over had illegal immigrants locked up in his van.

Asian American Stereotypes in the Media

Asians Seen as Perpetual Foreigners

Throughout the history of television and motion pictures, Asian American and Asian characters have spoken with Asian accents. While the majority of Asian American actors grew up in the United States and therefore do not have Asian accents, Hollywood writers, producers, and directors usually ask them to use them. As a result, the viewing audience gets the impression that the Asian face = foreigner. And not usually a sympathetic foreigner, either. In many cases, the Asian character is made foreign in order to use him as a joke—a bewildered immigrant who does not know what is going on around him—or a victim to feel sorry for.

In his acceptance speech for receiving a Media Achievement Award by the **Media Action Network for Asian Americans** (MANAA; see http://www.manaa.org), noted playwright David Henry Hwang said that while growing up in the 1950s, when he saw an Asian on television, he would instinctively turn the channel because he knew that the characterization would probably be an embarrassing reflection of him. Hwang most likely represented thousands of other Asian Americans who felt unwanted and ridiculed by their own country—the United States of America.

For example, *Breakfast at Tiffany's* (Edwards, 1961) was marred by Mickey Rooney's yellow-faced, buck-teethed portrayal of the befuddled Japanese man, Mr. Yunioshi. In *Sixteen Candles* (Hughes, 1984), the name and character of Long Duk Dong, a foreign exchange student, is played for laughs. He speaks in halting English as members of the host White family try, uncomfortably, to adjust to him (especially in conversation around the dinner table).

There is some basis for the belief that most Asians in the United States are foreigners: 62% of them are immigrants. However, the media rarely depicts Asian American characters who are assimilated to Western society and hold mainstream jobs. Instead, they are usually seen in ethnic-specific occupations like martial artists, ninjas, laundry owners, grocers, businessmen, geishas, prostitutes, gangsters, and Chinese restaurant workers. This fails to acknowledge their roles as lawyers, doctors, educators, psychologists, policemen, teachers, etc.

Judge Lance Ito gained notoriety during the O. J. Simpson trial in 1995.

Even within the narrow definition of what Asian characters can be, they are almost always trumped by their White counterparts. For instance, in movies like *Showdown in Little Tokyo* (Lester, 1991), and *The Karate Kid II* (Avildsen, 1986), seemingly all of the Asian male adversaries know martial arts, but the White hero is more skilled in it and uses the Asian-born art form to defeat them with it.

Even when presented with real-life examples of assimilated Asian Americans—or those who were born and raised in the United States—radio disc jockeys and public figures have still felt comfortable portraying them as foreigners. Judge Lance Ito, who presided over the O. J. Simpson trial, was mocked by New York Senator Alfonse D'Amato on the Don Imus radio show (April 4, 1995), saying in a faux Japanese accent, "Judge Ito loves the limelight. He's making a disgrace of the judicial system." In order to further demean the jurist, D'Amato also referred to him as "Little Judge Ito."

John London's morning show on Los Angeles radio KKBT-FM parodied an interview local TV anchor Tritia Toyota (another Japanese American who does not speak with an Asian accent) conducted with Ito by having both speak with accents and Toyota asking the judge about the kind of rice he likes to eat. London's main competition, the Bakka Boys of Power 106, also aired skits mocking well-known assimilated Asian Americans. When the media watchdog group MANAA met with the station's management to discuss the matter, the music director responded by asking, "Well, if you're so proud of being Asian American, then why aren't you speaking with accents? 'Cause you're imitating White people."

This woman believed that, in order to be true to themselves, people of Asian descent had to speak with Asian accents—that it was not natural for assimilated or American-born Asians to speak non-accented English. Are European immigrants from non-English speaking countries and their American-born children also selling out by speaking English and not retaining a European accent for generations to come? Or is this only expected of Asian Americans and other minorities because their facial features do not fit the White/Black racial paradigm that has defined this country for most of its existence and are therefore thought of as Other?

On January 24, 2006, on his syndicated morning radio show, Adam Carolla mocked the Asian Excellence Awards, a mainstream event that acknowledged Asian American talent and attracted White and Black celebrities like Quentin Tarantino and Magic Johnson. In the supposed recording of the category of "Best Male Actor in a TV Series," three or four men and a woman said nothing but variations of "ching chong" and "chong chong" for 52 seconds. As we will see in the Contemporary Issues section of this chapter, it is not inherently negative to portray Asian Americans with accents or as foreigners as long as they are well-balanced characters relatable to the audience. However, when the mainstream media is dominated by portrayals of Asians speaking with heavy accents, the broader public acquires those stereotypic expectations. How many times have Asian Americans been approached by non-Asians with questions such as "Where did you learn to speak English so well?" or "Where are you from?" Such questions only serve to make Asian Americans feel like strangers in their own land.

Asians as Mysterious

Because Asian people and their cultures seem so different from that of White America, writers have often exploited the unknown aspects of the community to paint them as mysterious beings—sometimes with strange, unexplained powers. One of the archetypal villains dates back to Sax Rohmer's 1913 novel, *The Insidious Dr. Fu Manchu*. In films, the title character could hypnotize people, and his mean-slanted eyebrows and features—thin, long mustache, and long fingernails—conveyed someone definitely from another land with secrets we could only guess at. The fact that he was often played by White men (Boris Karloff, Warner Oland) underscores this was what White men thought villainous Asian men to be like. Even good guy detective Charlie Chan, who, more often than not, was played by White actors (including Sidney Toler and Oland, again), spoke in fortune cookie one-liners, bowed, and talked in halting English, which distinguished himself from his White colleagues. In *Charlie Chan at the Opera* (Humberstone, 1936), a police sergeant complimented Chan, saying, "You're all right. Just like chop suey. A mystery, but a swell dish."

Other examples of Asians being mysterious throughout the years were presented in *The Black Widow* (Bennett & Brannon, 1947), *Remo Williams: The Adventure Begins* (Hamilton, 1985), and *My Life* (Rubin, 1993).

But in most films, the mystery of Asian men was promoted as a negative trait. In *Thoroughly Modern Millie* (Hill, 1967), the character, Tea, wears silk robes and a white Fu Manchu mustache. Whenever he appears on screen, it is marked by gongs. In the end, he proves himself to be a trusted servant, but according to Kashiwabara (1996), the stereotype of this character and the mystery surrounding him clearly made the heroine of the film (Julie Andrews) uncomfortable even after his proven trustworthiness.

Kashiwabara describes "inscrutable" as "a total lack of emotion. An inscrutable Asian never smiles, laughs, or grimaces. The face instead is left completely impassive and unmoving." However, there is nothing inherently threatening about such a lack of facial emotion. The British, for example, are credited with a "stiff upper lip," a form of impassivity. But the British version lacks the threat inherent in inscrutability. Since the facial expression is the same, the difference must come from the context. In the case of the Asian man, the context of the expression is his Asian face. So the threatening aspect of his impassivity comes not so much from his expression, but from his features. We have learned to assign certain characteristics such as duplicity to an impassive Asian face by seeing such characters act treacherously in film after film.

Even the beloved Mr. Miyagi, the *sensei* (teacher) played by Noriyuki "Pat" Morita in the *Karate Kid* films, was mysterious in how he withheld information from his student, Daniel (Ralph Macchio), who wanted to learn how to defend himself against school bullies: The martial artist had the teenager "waxing on" and "waxing off" his car to the point of frustration. Finally, the method to the *sensei*'s madness was made clear when he started throwing blows at Daniel, telling him to "wax on" and "wax off." By this point, those deeply ingrained hand movements instinctively went up to block Miyagi's fists, implicitly explaining that the martial arts teacher had been training his young charge how to defend himself all along.

Nowadays, when several Asian Americans are featured in a television show, it is usually for the typical *Chinatown* episode seen on countless police dramas: White cops investigate a murder and get pulled into the underground seediness of a Chinatown or Little Tokyo where buildings are mere facades for what lurks behind them or literally underground beneath street level. This perception of Asian communities had roots in such films as *Chinatown after Dark* (Paton, 1931), *Secrets of Wu Sin* (Thorpe, 1932), *The Hatchet Man* (Wellman, 1932), and *The Black Widow* (serials). Rogin (1992) says that "the outside world saw [Chinatowns] as tourist attractions at best, and as islands of crime and violence at worst." Marchetti further asserts, "Old San Francisco from 1927 made it look like prostitution is the main business of Chinatown, 'the modern Sodom and Gomorrah'" (p. 207). Everson (1964) wrote that like a deceptive character, "underneath a picturesque veneer, Chinatown hides its violence and corruption" (p. 38).

The stereotype of Asians as mysterious has at least two psychological effects upon both the majority society and Asians themselves. First, if Asians are mysterious, they are essentially unknowable. The unknown is thought to be dangerous, so this stereotype serves to keep the two communities apart. The second effect is that if Asians are mysterious and unknowable, why *try* to get to know them?

Asians as Exotic

The American Heritage Dictionary (Morris, 1979) defines exotic as "1. From another part of the world; not indigenous; foreigner. 2. Having the charm of the unfamiliar; strikingly and intriguingly unusual or beautiful" (p. 461). This has usually applied to the portrayal of Asian women and has become part of their allure most notably in movies like *Teahouse of the August Moon* (Mann, 1956), *Sayonara* (Logan, 1957), *The World of Suzie Wong* (Quine, 1960), and *My Geisha* (Cardiff, 1962). Many were patterned after the *Madame Butterfly* (Belasco, 1928) story where an Asian woman, denied love with her White lover, commits suicide (the lead character in the Broadway musical *Miss Saigon* [Hytner, 1991] also kills herself, but, "nobly," so her Amerasian son will have a better life in the United States). Kashiwabara asserted that Asian women had opportunities to play lead roles as geishas, but Asian men were relegated to small parts as servants.

Marchetti (1993) wrote:

> The geisha became such a popular character that "it appeared as if the geisha was Hollywood's chief emblem of postwar reconciliation." . . . Many specifically compare Asian and White women, only to find the White women lacking. *Sayonara* (1957/Logan), for example, "holds Katsumi up as a paragon of female virtue. Later, she is shown performing her domestic tasks, cooking, serving guests, bathing her husband, cheerfully and quietly. Direct descendant of the geisha, the submissive Asian woman, became an icon" (p. 134).

Today, the inherently "exotic" nature of Asian women is used to sell them as sex objects in adult videos (a Google search for "Asian exotic" elicits four full pages of nothing but porn videos/DVDs featuring Asian women). Yet the supposed mysterious, unusual, yet attractive qualities of Asian women are not usually applied to Asian men nor valued in the same way (White men will say they like Asian women because they are so exotic; how many White women say the same about Asian men?).

That which is foreign or unfamiliar can also become a negative. This is seen in the **dragon lady** stereotype introduced in the comic strip *Terry and the Pirates* on December 16, 1934. The character, whose name was actually Dragon Lady, was a conniving woman who used her powers of seduction to entice men then backstab them to reach her own gains. This stereotype was reinforced in *Chinatown after Dark* (Paton, 1931), the daughter of the Fu Manchu character in many books and films (beginning with Corrigan's 1931 *The Daughter of Fu Manchu*), along with *Shadow of Chinatown* (Hill, 1936). In the *Black Widow* serial (Bennett & Brannon, 1947), Madame Sombra, in helping her father to become emperor of Earth, disguises herself as a fortune-teller and kills enemies by injecting them with deadly spider venom.

The psychological effect of the exotic stereotype renders Asian women as desirable only for the sexual pleasures to be enjoyed by White men or as potential seductresses only to lead to betrayal. Therefore, when Asian women express their desire to be taken seriously in areas such as employment or finances, they are dismissed as not knowing what they are talking about or they are thought to be less desirable because they are not acting like the passive sexual object that originally attracted their partner, thus leading to a subtle threat of the partner leaving the relationship. However, for Asian men, the exotic traits are translated into mysteriousness, which is almost always a negative characteristic, as discussed before.

Asian Women as the Property of White Men

Whereas the majority of Asian Americans marry Asian Americans (Sailer, 2003), the media has gone out of its way to encourage the Asian female/White male model of romance. It has been seen in films like the aforementioned *The World of Suzie Wong* and in *Come See the Paradise* (Parker, 1990) and *Double Happiness* (Shum, 1994) where Asian women fall in love with White men for no given reason, leading to the conclusion that they are attractive merely because they are White.

Indeed, in *Come See the Paradise*, after a Japanese American boy approaches Tamlyn Tomita's character in 1936, one of her Japanese American girlfriends takes delight in pointing out, "She just blew you off, Jack!" Soon, Tomita meets a real "Jack" (Dennis Quaid), a friend of her brother's. They go to a restaurant in Little Tokyo and within minutes are kissing.

According to Kashiwabara, the marked contrast between the desirability of White men over Asian men was made clear at least as far back as 1924's *The Thief of Baghdad* (Walsh), the Asian princess in this film is courted by an array of Asian princes, all of whom she rejects. However, she immediately falls in love with Douglas Fairbanks, the White lead actor of the film.

An example that illustrates the extremes to which some writers will go to establish the preference of White men was seen in 1985's *Year of the Dragon* (Cimino): Reporter Tracy Tsu (Ariane) is devastated when Asian thugs break into her apartment and rape her. Yet she does not mind it when White hero Lt. Stanley White (Mickey Rourke) does.

In general, Asian women are paired romantically with White men (and sometimes Black men) and Asian men are paired with no one. This phenomenon was so prevalent that in 1994, Kip Fulbeck produced his video, *Some Questions for 28 Kisses*, which featured historic examples of Asian women kissing White men. The Asian female/White male archetype has continued to been seen in more contemporary films as *Rambo: First Blood Part II* (Cosmatos, 1985), *Heaven and Earth* (Stone, 1993), *Pillow Book* (Greenaway, 1996), and *Double Happiness* (Shum, 1994). Asian female/Black male pairings are seen in *Mississippi Masala* (Nair, 1992), *One Night Stand* (Figgis, 1997), and on TV's *Grey's Anatomy* (2005–present). The only Asian couples we see tend to be "harmless, asexual" grandparents. It is as if seeing two Asian young people together would make a movie or television episode "too Asian" for the comfort of executives.

As a matter of fact, in the rare instances where Asian men have been paired romantically with someone, it has been with a White female and usually in movies that were based on real-life stories: *The Lover* (Annaud, 1992), *Dragon: The Bruce Lee Story* (Cohen, 1993), and *Bridge to the Sun* (Perier, 1961). With only a few notable exceptions (*Crimson Kimono*, Fuller, 1959; *Hiroshima Mon Amour*, Resnais, 1959; and *The English Patient*, Minghella, 1990), Asian men are almost never romantically paired with White women in fictional stories.

In most action features, the leading man (Sylvester Stallone, etc.) almost always ends up in bed with the lead female. But even in *The Replacement Killers* (Fuqua, 1998), which paired Chow Yun Fat and Mira Sorvino, nothing romantic happened. Astonishingly, Jet Li, the supposed Romeo in *Romeo Must Die* (Bartkowiak, 2000) and Aaliyah, the female Black lead actress, did not even share a kiss.

The effects of this stereotype are clear. First, Asian and Asian American men are never presented as a desirable option. Quite often Asian women are heard to say, "I don't date Asian men because it is like dating my brother." Clearly, White women rarely say this about dating White men. Second, such media portrayals serve to suggest that non-Asian men *should* pursue Asian women and that Asian women *should* date/marry White and other non-Asian men.

Asians as Invisible

Whereas Asians are very visible as villains, they are rarely given the chance to play heroes even in occupations or places where they thrive. Consider the fact that about one of every six physicians in the United States is of Asian descent yet Asian American doctors are infrequently seen on network television. As a matter of fact, it was not until the fifth season of *ER* (1994–present) that an Asian American regular—Ming-Na Wen—was added (incredulously, we got a Croatian doctor, played by Goran Visnjic, first).

With the exception of Ling Woo (Lucy Liu) on TV's *Ally McBeal*, there has not been a regular Asian American lawyer on *any* popular television legal drama (*L.A. Law*, *Picket Fences*, and *The Practice*). Even in *Girls Club* (2002), which featured 20-something women lawyers in San Francisco—a city with a 33% Asian population—all the stars were White.

Consider that the 2000 census told us that 58% of Hawaii is of Asian/Pacific Islander descent. No television show in history set in Hawaii has ever starred an Asian/Pacific Islander. The main hero has always been played by White or, in the case of NBC's *Hawaii* (2004), even Black men (Blacks make up only 3% of the 50th state). In reality, in 1997, the governor of Hawaii was Filipino American and the chief of Honolulu police was Japanese American. Yet CBS was ready to shoot a pilot for a new *Hawaii Five-O* series with all of those jobs played by Whites. Producer/writer Kim LeMasters admitted he was only looking for White men to play the top three roles. When asked why none of them could be Asian, he explained that in order to accommodate the change in race, he would have to change the characters' backgrounds which he was unwilling to do because he wanted to shoot the pilot in two weeks.

Upon examination of the shooting script, the descriptions for those three roles were as follows: (a) Man who headed the D.C. office of the FBI and becomes head of the FBI in Hawaii. When Steve McGarrett is murdered, he is asked to take over Five-O. (b) Man who was born in California but came to Hawaii as a youth and has come to be trusted and accepted by the locals. (c) 20-something-year-old who looks like he stepped out of a *GQ* magazine. None of the descriptions would have prevented Asian men from playing them—except in the mind of the writer himself (after pressure upon CBS, Russell Wong was eventually cast in the lead).

Even when movies take place in environments where Asians are prevalent, they are usually relegated to the background and the story focuses on a White male who is injected into the plot. *Go For Broke!* (Pirosh, 1951), named after the rallying cry of the segregated Japanese American

100th/442nd Battalion, focused on White star Van Johnson. *Come See the Paradise* (Parker, 1990), with the Japanese American interment camp as a backdrop, concentrated on the uninteresting (and unmotivated) romance between Quaid and Tomita at the expense of the more gripping drama of those in camp who lost everything and men who had to decide whether or not to fight for their country.

Although Asian Americans were primarily responsible for developing the import-car culture, when *The Fast and the Furious* (Cohen, 2001) made the big screen, the protagonists were White and Black and the main Asian was a villain (Rick Yune). Even in the well-intentioned *The Last Samurai* (Zwick, 2003), which demonstrated a respect for Japanese culture, we saw the story through the eyes of a Westerner played by Tom Cruise (ironically, in the end, it was supporting actor Ken Watanabe who received an Oscar nomination for his work, not Cruise).

In order to accommodate White actors, Asian roles are sometimes changed to make their casting possible. In the controversial Broadway musical, *Miss Saigon* (Hytner, 1991), the part of the engineer—arguably the most popular character in the production—was made Eurasian so British White actor Jonathan Pryce could play him—and with yellow-faced prosthetics.

Even when viewers think they are watching an Asian person, they may not be: The Chinese couple in *The Good Earth* (Franklin, 1937) was played by Paul Muni and Luise Rainer, Kwai-Chang Caine in *Kung Fu* (1972–75, 1993–97) was performed by David Carradine, Billy Kwan in *The Year of Living Dangerously* (Weir, 1982) was portrayed by Linda Hunt, and the mysterious Ciun in *Remo Williams* (Hamilton, 1985) was played, with the aid of heavy makeup, by Joel Grey, who is Jewish.

Again, the invisibility stereotype marginalizes Asians and Asian Americans. This leads to both the general public *and* Asians themselves believing that they are not capable of being central to films or even in everyday organizations. Consequently, we see in the academic world that while there are more PhDs per capita in the Asian community, Asians have the lowest top administrator position of any racial group (Suzuki, 1997).

The Changing Images of Asians

While Asians and Asian Americans have been continually stereotyped by the broader media, many have ignored these images and have become trailblazers in areas not typically associated with their racial/ethnic groups. These areas include performing arts, film, television, athletics, and other professions.

Performing Arts

Jin Au-Yeung is the son of Chinese immigrants. Known simply as Jin, he was born in Miami and developed his talents as a rap performer (http://en.wikipedia.org/wiki/Jin_(rapper), 2006), cut three albums, and made an appearance in the movie *2 Fast 2 Furious* (one of his songs made its soundtrack). Jin also recorded a blistering rap against Hot 97 New York disc jockeys who mocked victims of the horrific tsunami that destroyed parts of Thailand, Indonesia, Sri Lanka, and India in December 2004. Other rap artists/singers of Asian descent are Foxy Brown and Amerie, who are half Filipino and half Korean, respectively, Hugo, a Filipino American writer/producer of The Neptunes, and pop singer Jocelyn Enriquez, a Filipino American, who gained some success in the 1990s. Moreover, many Asian Americans have been successful on so-called reality contest shows: Harlemm Lee (of Chinese/Filipino descent) won the singing/dancing competition on *Fame* in 2003, Dat Phan (of Vietnamese descent) was named *The Last Comic Standing* in its inaugural 2004 season, and Jasmine Trias (of Filipino/Spanish/Chinese descent) placed third on *American Idol* in 2004.

However, stereotypes run deep and strong, as neither Lee nor Phan were able to capitalize on their prizes (Lee's album was released without any promotion and his manager supposedly said he did not know how to market an Asian performer; Phan's development contract with NBC did not result in any special or series despite such prizes/opportunities being promised the winner). Trias released a CD in Hawaii that did not get much distribution nationwide.

Film

While Asians and Asian Americans have been in movies throughout the years, there had never been a widely distributed film whose main actors were exclusively of Asian descent until Justin Lin's (2003) *Better Luck Tomorrow*. Although this groundbreaking movie featured stereotypes— Asian American straight-A students who indulge in criminal behavior and ultimately murder (but see Wayne Wang, below)—it was seen from their point-of-view. Another filmmaker, Chris Tashima, has been making shorts with predominantly Asian American casts. His first movie, *Visas and Virtue* (1997), won an Academy Award for short films, and dealt with the little-known story of Chiune Sugihara. Sugihara was the Japanese diplomat in Nazi-occupied territories who wrote visas for thousands of Jews, saving up to three times as many Jews as did the better known Oskar Schindler. Tashima's second movie, *Day of Independence* (2003), told the story of the Japanese American internment during World War II.

The above films have Asian American content, but other Asian and Asian American movie-makers have gained much more notoriety producing "mainstream" films. M. Night Shyamalan (of Indian descent but reared in the United States) made popular motion pictures such as *The Sixth Sense* (1999), *Unbreakable* (2000), *Signs* (2002), and *The Village* (2004). While Ang Lee (of Taiwanese descent) directed many films concentrating on Asian characters and themes earlier in his career, he is more widely known for his mainstream movies: *Sense and Sensibility* (1995), *The Ice Storm* (1997), *The Hulk* (2003), and *Brokeback Mountain* (2005) for which he won the 2006 Academy Award for Best Director, the first Asian director (and first of any ethnic minority group) to win this award (his Asian film, *Crouching Tiger, Hidden Dragon* [2000] also became widely known). After his success with *Better Luck Tomorrow,* the aforementioned Justin Lin gained credibility with larger Hollywood studios and directed *Annapolis* (2006) and also did the honors on *The Fast and the Furious: Tokyo Drift* (2006). Finally, Wayne Wang, a Chinese American director, has been making low-budget but critically acclaimed films for a while (e.g., *Chan Is Missing,* 1982; *Dim Sum,* 1989), but his big break came when he directed *The Joy Luck Club* (1993). After these Asian-focused movies, he has made mainstream films such as *Maid in America* (2002) and *Last Holiday* (2006).

Harold and Kumar Go to White Castle (2004), while written and directed by non-Asians, was the first "buddy" movie to feature Asian American leads (Korean American John Cho and South Asian American Kal Penn). Many action flicks have starred Asian men (Jackie Chan, Chow Yun Fat, Jet Li), but the actors have usually been from foreign countries, have limited English-speaking ability, and have been paired with non-Asian accomplices.

Television

The first attempt to present an Asian American family on television was *All American Girl* with Margaret Cho in 1994. Although this series failed, it was an acknowledgment that the Asian/ Pacific Island community was worthy of seeing itself reflected on a weekly television show.

There has not been any television series that focused exclusively on Asian Americans since then. However, there have been attempts to include more Asian and Asian American regulars on popular shows, for example Lucy Liu's abrasive Ling Woo on *Ally McBeal* (1998–2002). While some saw her character as yet another dragon lady, she actually betrayed no one. And as her character evolved, Ling revealed a kind, sensitive heart, making her even more intriguing.

One popular television genre is the hospital drama. As stated earlier, one out of every six medical doctors in the United States is of Asian descent. Yet, these hospital shows usually do not include *any* Asian doctors as regular cast members. A hospital series in the 1980s was *St. Elsewhere* (1982–1988), and two of the original interns were played by Japanese American Kim Miyori and Kavi Raz (of Indian descent). Yet, Miyori's character was named "Wendy Armstrong." She was single, so Armstrong was not a married name, and there was no discussion of her being adopted, so her last name was a mystery to the audience. Unfortunately, in the second season, Miyori's Armstrong character died from an eating disorder, and Raz's character was dropped after the second season with hardly any interesting story lines ever developed for him (France Nuyen—who is French/Vietnamese—became a regular in the show's last two seasons).

Perhaps the most unbelievable of "coincidences" was in 1994 when both *ER* (1994–present) and *Chicago Hope* (1994–2000) debuted with great fanfare: Both of these hospital programs were set in Chicago and used ensemble casts, yet neither featured *any* Asian doctors or nurses as regulars. After protests from Asian groups such as MANAA in 1999, *ER* finally added a regular Asian doctor (Ming-Na Wen of Chinese descent) to its line-up. Wen was later fired, but NBC West Coast President Scott Sassa, probably fearing MANAA's reaction, reinstated her (Aoki, 2002). By the time Wen left the show by her own choice in 2004, Parminder Nagra, a woman of Indian descent, had joined the cast in 2003. Most recently, *Grey's Anatomy* (2005–present) cast Korean Canadian Sandra Oh as one of its lead characters.

Usually, when Asians are portrayed as foreigners, they are one-dimensional victims or as irritating immigrants who do not speak English. An exception to this is found in *Lost* (2004–present), a hit series with an ensemble cast whose plane, on its way to Los Angeles, crashes on a mysterious island. It includes Korean nationals (played by Yunjin Kim, an actress from Korea, and Daniel Dae Kim, a Korean American actor) and Sayid (Naveen Andrews, a White/Indian British actor), a former Iraqi Republican Guard soldier who beds another regular, an attractive blonde. (Unfortunately, the blond actress was killed near the end of the second season, so her relationship with Sayid could not be explored more deeply.) These characters are written with enough depth that the audience can empathize more easily with them despite their foreign roots.

Other Asian American regulars currently seen on television include B. D. Wong, a Chinese American actor, who portrays a forensic psychologist on *Law and Order: SVU*. While Wong's character is a regular on this program, it is clearly a supporting role, as no episodes center around him, and he rarely is on screen for more than a few scenes.

Athletics

Asians have been traditionally thought of as small in stature. Men were stereotyped as bookish and nerdy, women as small and demure. Because Asians and Asian Americans had not achieved prominence in athletics, these stereotypes remained unchallenged. To the extent that children and adolescents see athletes as role models, Asians and Asian Americans have not served in this capacity in this country. However, in recent years, Asian descent athletes have begun to emerge.

The first major sports figure in recent years was Michael Chang, a Chinese American. In the 1970s and 1980s, U.S. stars such as Stan Smith, Jimmy Connors, and John McEnroe dominated men's tennis. But none of them ever won the French Open. In 1989, Chang became the first American to accomplish that in 35 years.

Asian athletes such as Yao Ming are beginning to change public opinion of Asians.

Other Asian American champions have been Greg Louganis (who is half Samoan), who won four gold diving medals at the 1984 and 1988 Olympics; Japanese American Kristi Yamaguchi, who took home the Winter Olympics gold medal in 1992 for figure skating; Chinese American Michelle Kwan who was the six-time world champion in figure skating and whose 1998 and 2002 Winter Olympics performances were discussed in the opening of this chapter; Apolo Anton Ohno, of Japanese and White descent, won individual gold medals in both the 2002 and 2006 Winter Olympics (with five medals overall); Samoan American Junior Seau, who became one of the best linebackers in professional football and led his San Diego Chargers team to the 1995 Super Bowl; Samoan American Troy Polamalu, who was a Super Bowl winning linebacker with the Pittsburgh Steelers in 2006; Korean American Michelle Wie, who became a professional golfer at the age of 16 and who has already played in several professional men's golf tournaments; and professional golfer Tiger Woods, who is actually more Asian (his mother is Thai; his father, half Chinese) than any other ethnicity.

Incidentally, when Kwan had to pull out of the 2006 Winter Olympics due to an injury, NBC acknowledged her as the most recognizable athlete at the games and feared its television ratings would suffer due to her absence. Ironically, while an Asian American (Kwan) was predicted to win the gold medal in figure skating, an Asian (Japan's Shizuka Arakawa) ended up winning it, and the ratings did not suffer appreciably with Kwan's absence.

Since Hideo Nomo broke into professional baseball in 1995, a number of Japanese national baseball players have played in the major leagues, including Ichiro Suzuki, Hideki Matsui, Shigetosi Hasegawa, and Kazuo Matsui. Other Asian baseball players, particularly from Korea, have followed, including Chan Ho Park, Jae Seo, and Byun Young Kim. Teams from Japan and Korea were among the best baseball teams in the first-ever World Baseball classic in 2006, as the Korean team defeated the United States and had the best overall record, and Japan won the championship. Moreover, China's 7'6" Yao Ming, currently the tallest player in the National Basketball Association (wikipedia), has put to rest the belief that all Asians are diminutive.

Summary

Asian Americans are seen as perpetual foreigners, mysterious, exotic, "arm candy," or they are simply invisible, at least as far as the mainstream media is concerned. The media has a profound effect in making people believe the stereotypes they see. Indeed, there is evidence that Asian American children have no Asian heroes (Cortés, 2000). As we have documented, the media perpetuates the stereotypes they created years ago through commissions and omissions even in modern-day films and television programs. These stereotypes have negative effects for Asians and non-Asians alike. Asians and Asian Americans may adopt the stereotypes that they can only be nerdy bookworms who cannot be leaders in their field, and Asian women may reject Asian men in favor of White men as mates because of the constant media barrage portraying this combination as commonplace or even expected. Whites and other non-Asians similarly see those of Asian descent as nerds to make fun of, exotic and passive female companions, or foreigners who can never be part of mainstream America.

Partly due to media watchdog organizations such as MANAA, media portrayals of individuals of Asian descent have been slowly changing in recent years. As Asians and Asian Americans gain more footing in the entertainment industry and in athletics, they have the potential to challenge misinformation that has come before, helping the youth of today develop a more positive sense of self and a more realistic reflection of their own images.

Discussion Questions

1. If you were a casting agent, what would be your primary reasons to choose a particular race or ethnicity of an actor/actress?
2. What images have you most frequently seen of Asian Americans as represented in the media?
3. What areas of the media have you found Asian Americans to be lacking in the most?
4. If you were to direct and/or produce a show or film, what do you think you might be up against if you chose an all Asian American cast?
5. We all have a potential role to play in negating offensive Asian American images in the media and elsewhere. Next time you see Asian Americans presented negatively, what actions can you take? Who will you contact?
6. If you were asked to be in a commercial, TV show, or film and your character was a stereotyped image of an Asian immigrant with no other characters to balance out your stereotyped character, what would you do?
7. In the case study below, what do you think of how Justin Lin handled the problem of stereotypes by the producers of *The Fast and the Furious: Tokyo Drift*?
8. How do you think that Justin Lin and other Asian/Asian American filmmakers can change the minds of studio executives about actors of Asian descent?

Case Study

Justin Lin, the director of *The Fast and the Furious: Tokyo Drift*, found a way to overcome the stereotypes and racism in Hollywood (Chung, 2006). Below is how Lin ultimately was able to incorporate Sung Kang into the film in a major role that was able to showcase his talent and demonstrate to the viewing public that Asian Americans can play significant roles in the movies and society. Lin also changed the script to portray how Tokyo is, today, instead of the stereotyped images that the producers originally had in mind.

Justin Lin originally asked Sung Kang to read for the main character in *The Fast and the Furious: Tokyo Drift*. However, the studio wanted the main character to be portrayed by a White actor. Lin then asked Kang to read for a "cool" character that was written for an African American actor that the producers already had in mind. Because Kang did such a good job reading for this character, the producers were impressed with him and allowed Lin to create a new character for Kang. This new character ended up being the Tokyo mentor for the fish-out-of-water main character. Because Kang's character played a Korean American who had to adapt to Japan, he could mentor the White American actor from his own experience as an outsider.

Lin also changed the whole feel of the movie. The original script had Tokyo depicted as being old-world, with Buddhas and kimonos and other kinds of stereotypic images that Americans have of Japan. In reality, Tokyo is a modern city, and the central theme of the movie was drifting—a modern technique of street car racing that allows cars to slide through sharp turns ("drifting") while maintaining the speed of the car. Thus, the film would have been a ridiculous juxtaposition of stereotyped images with an ultra-modern racing technique. What Lin did in the movie was to depict modern touches of Tokyo like "lazy Susan" parking structures, playing soccer on rooftops, and high-intensity neon signs throughout the city. Thus, Lin's movie broke two stereotypes: Asian American male actors cannot be main characters, and Japan is an old-world spiritual and passive environment.

Case Study Discussion Questions

1. In thinking of the case study of Justin Lin and *The Fast and the Furious: Tokyo Drift*, how would you apply notions of direct and indirect communication?
2. Would Justin Lin have been more effective using different forms of communication when dealing with the studio executives? Why or why not?
3. What types of stereotypes were applied by the studio executives when conceptualizing the movie? Discuss these stereotypes as they apply to the case.

Key Terms

Asian American: Individual whose heritage is from East Asia, including China, Japan, and Korea; Southeast Asia, including Vietnam, Cambodia, and Thailand; South Asia, including India, Pakistan, Bangladesh, Afghanistan, and Sri Lanka; and the Pacific Islands, including Hawaii, the Philippines, Tahiti, Guam, Indonesia, and Malaysia. More recently, individual whose heritage is from the Middle East has sometimes been included, including Saudi Arabia, Iraq, Iran, Syria, Yemen, Jordan, Qatar, Lebanon, Palestine, and the United Arab Emirates, particularly because of their confusion with Sikhs in India.

Discrimination: Behavior, typically negative, toward an individual or an identifiable group based upon the classification of the individual or group.

Dragon lady: The characterization of Asian women as manipulative sexual beings who seduce White men, then betray them.

Exotic: The characterization of Asians as being foreign and out of the ordinary. This is typically seen as positive or desirable for Asian women and negative or undesirable for Asian men.

Invisible: Stereotype that marginalizes Asians and Asian Americans. This leads to both the general public *and* Asians themselves believing that they are not capable of being central to films or even everyday organizations.

Media Action Network for Asian Americans: Organization whose mission is to create an environment free of racism through the accurate, balanced, and sensitive Asian American images. Dedicated to monitoring and advocating balanced, sensitive, and positive coverage and portrayal of Asian Americans. Please see http://www.manaa.org for further information.

Media images: The images of Asians and Asian Americans portrayed by the media, typically in stereotypic manners. However, these images may be changing.

Mysterious: The characterization of Asians as being unknowable or strange.

Prejudice: A prejudging, typically negative belief of individuals or groups based upon their classification, such as race.

Racism: Typically applied to institutionalized practices, a routine mistreatment of individuals or groups based upon their racial classification.

Stereotype: The belief that an individual or group of individuals should behave in certain common and predictable manners based upon their classification, such as race.

For Further Learning and Suggested Readings

Media and Movies Portraying Asian Americans

Asian Excellence Awards
Better Luck Tomorrow
The Black Widow (serials)
Breakfast at Tiffany's
Bridge to the Sun
Chan Is Missing
Charlie Chan at the Opera
Chinatown after Dark
Come See the Paradise
Crash
Crimson Kimono
Crouching Tiger, Hidden Dragon
The Daughter of Fu Manchu
Day of Independence
Dim Sum
Double Happiness
Dragon: The Bruce Lee Story
The English Patient
ER
Fast and the Furious
Go For Broke!
Grey's Anatomy
Harold and Kumar Go to White Castle
The Hatchet Man
Heaven and Earth
Hiroshima Mon Amour
The Joy Luck Club
Karate Kid films
The Last Samurai
Lost
The Lover
Madame Butterfly

Miss Saigon
Mississippi Masala
My Geisha
My Life
One Night Stand
Pillow Book
Rambo: First Blood Part II
Remo Williams: The Adventure Begins
The Replacement Killers
Romeo Must Die
Sayonara
Secrets of Wu Sin
Shadow of Chinatown
Showdown in Little Tokyo
16 Candles
Some Questions for 28 Kisses
Teahouse of the August Moon
The Thief of Baghdad
Thoroughly Modern Millie
Visas and Virtue
The World of Suzie Wong
Year of the Dragon

Reading

Asian Week
Audrey magazine
The Insidious Dr. Fu Manchu (novel)
Rafu Shimpo newspaper
Years of Infamy (memoir)

Web Sites

Asian Week: http://news.asianweek.com/news
MANAA: http://www.manaa.org

References

Ally McBeal (1998–2002). Fox [TV series].
Annaud, J-J. (Director). (1992). *The Lover* [motion picture].
Aoki, G. (Director). (2002). *The MANAA Story* [video].
Aoki, G. (2005, May 14). Hard to look away from this "Crash." *Rafu Shimpo, 5.*
Avildsen, J. (Director). (1984). *The Karate Kid* [motion picture].
Avildsen, J. (Director). (1986). *The Karate Kid II* [motion picture].
Bartkowiak, A. (Director). (2000). *Romeo Must Die* [motion picture].
Belasco, D. (1928). *Madame Butterfly.* Boston: Little, Brown, & Co.
Bennett, S., & Brannon, F. (Directors). (1947). *The Black Widow* [film serials].
Cardiff, J. (Director). (1962). *My Geisha* [motion picture].
Children Now. (1998). *A different world: Children's perceptions of race and class in the media.* Oakland, CA.
Chung, P. W. (2006, June 16). The Fast and the Furious: Tokyo Drift. *AsianWeek.* Retrieved August 13, 2006, from http://news.asianweek.com/news/view_article.html?article_id=6acd58fded0cb2bb0c6325
Cimino, M. (Director). (1985). *Year of the Dragon* [motion picture].
Cohen, R. (Director). (1993). *Dragon: The Bruce Lee Story* [motion picture].
Cohen, R. (Director). (2001). *The Fast and the Furious* [motion picture].
Corrigan, L. (Director). (2001). *The Daughter of Fu Manchu* [motion picture].

Cortés, C. E. (2000). *The children are watching: How the media teach about diversity.* New York: Teachers College Press.

Cosmatos, G. (Director). (1985). *Rambo: First Blood Part II* [motion picture].

Edwards, B. (Director). (1961). *Breakfast at Tiffany's* [motion picture].

ER (1994–present). [NBC television series].

Everson, W. (1964). *The bad guys: A pictorial history of the movie villain.* New York: Citadel.

Figgis, M. (Director). (1997). *One Night Stand* [motion picture].

Franklin, S. (Director). (1937). *The Good Earth* [motion picture].

Fulbeck, K. (Director). (1994). *Some Questions for 28 Kisses* [video].

Fuller, S. (Director). (1959). *The Crimson Kimono* [motion picture].

Fuqua, A. (Director). (1998). *The Replacement Killers* [motion picture].

Girls Club (2002). [Fox television series].

Greenaway, P. (Director). (1996). *The Pillow Book* [motion picture].

Grey's Anatomy (2005–present). [ABC television series].

Haggis, P. (Director). (2005). *Crash* [motion picture].

Hamilton, G. (Director). (1985). *Remo Williams: The Adventure Begins* [motion picture].

Hawaii (2004). [NBC television series].

Hill, G. R. (Director). (1967). *Thoroughly Modern Millie* [motion picture].

Hill, R. F. (Director). (1936). *Shadow of Chinatown* [motion picture].

Hughes, J. (Director). (1984). *16 Candles* [motion picture].

Humberstone, B. (Director). (1936). *Charlie Chan at the Opera* [motion picture].

Hytner, N. (Director). (1991). *Miss Saigon* [play].

Kashiwabara, A. (1996). *Vanishing son: The appearance, disappearance, and assimilation of the Asian-American man in American mainstream media.*

Kung Fu (1972–1975). [TV series].

Kung Fu: The Legend Continues (1993–1997). [TV series]

Lee, A. (Director). (1995). *Sense and Sensibility* [motion picture].

Lee, A. (Director). (1997). *The Ice Storm* [motion picture].

Lee, A. (Director). (2000). *Crouching Tiger, Hidden Dragon* [motion picture].

Lee, A. (Director). (2003). *The Hulk* [motion picture].

Lee, A. (Director). (2005). *Brokeback Mountain* [motion picture].

Lester, M. (Director). (1991). *Showdown in Little Tokyo* [motion picture].

Lin, J. (Director). (2003). *Better Luck Tomorrow* [motion picture].

Lin, J. (Director). (2006). *Annapolis* [motion picture].

Lin, J. (Director). (2006). *The Fast and the Furious: Tokyo Drift* [motion picture].

Logan, J. (Director). (1957). *Sayonara* [motion picture].

Mann, D. (Director). (1956). *Teahouse of the August Moon* [motion picture].

Marchetti, G. (1993). *Romance and the "yellow peril": Race, sex, and discursive strategies in Hollywood fiction.* Berkeley: University of California Press.

Minghella, A. (Director). (1990). *The English Patient* [motion picture].

Mio, J. S., Barker-Hackett, L., & Tumambing, J. S. (2006). *Multicultural psychology: Understanding our diverse communities.* Boston: McGraw-Hill.

Mio, J. S., Nagata, D. K., Tsai, A. H., & Tewari, N. (2007). Racism against Asian/Pacific Americans. In F. Leong, A. G. Inman, A. Ebreo, L. Yang, L. M. Kinoshita, & M. Fu (Eds.), *Handbook of Asian American psychology* (2nd ed., pp. 341–361). Thousand Oaks, CA: Sage Publishers.

Morris, W. (Ed.). (1979). *The American heritage dictionary of the English language.* Boston: Houghton Mifflin Company.

Myers, D. G. (2005). *Social psychology* (8th ed.). Boston: McGraw-Hill.

Nair, M. (Director). (1992). *Mississippi Masala.* [motion picture].

Parker, A. (Director). (1990). *Come See the Paradise* [motion picture].

Paton, S. (Director). (1931). *Chinatown After Dark* [motion picture].

Perier, E. (Director). (1961). *Bridge to the Sun* [motion picture].

Pirosh, R. (Director). (1951). *Go for Broke* [motion picture].

Quine, R. (Director). (1960). *The World of Suzie Wong* [motion picture].

Resnais, A. (Director) (1959). *Hiroshima Mon Amour* [motion picture].

Rogin, M. (1992). Making America home: Racial masquerade and ethnic assimilation in the transition to talking pictures. *The Journal of American History, 79*(3), 1050.

Rohmer, S. (1913). *The insidious Dr. Fu Manchu.* New York: McBride, Nast, & Co.

Rubin, B. J. (Director). (1993). *My Life* [motion picture].

Sailer, S. (2003, March 16). The myth of interracial marriage. Retrieved from Vdare.com.

Shum, M. (Director). (1994). *Double Happiness* [motion picture].

Shyamalan, M. N. (Director). (1999). *The Sixth Sense* [motion picture].

Shyamalan, M. N. (Director). (2000). *Unbreakable* [motion picture].

Shyamalan, M. N. (Director). (2002). *Signs* [motion picture].

Shyamalan, M. N. (Director). (2004). *The Village* [motion picture].

St. Elsewhere (1982–1988). [NBC TV series].

Stone, O. (Director). (1993). *Heaven and Earth* [motion picture].

Suzuki, B. H. (1997, June). Introductory remarks. *Leadership in Education for Asian/Pacifics (LEAP) workshop*, California State Polytechnic University, Pomona.

Tashima, C. (Director). (1997). *Visas and Virtue* [motion picture].

Tashima, C. (Director). (2003). *Day of Independence* [motion picture].

Thorpe, R. (Director). (1932). *Secrets of Wu Sin* [motion picture].

Walsh, R. (Director). (1924). *The Thief of Baghdad* [motion picture].

Wang, W. (Director). (1982). *Chan is Missing* [motion picture].

Wang, W. (Director). (1989). *Dim Sum* [motion picture].

Wang, W. (Director). (1993). *The Joy Luck Club* [motion picture].

Wang, W. (Director). (2002). *Maid in America* [motion picture].

Wang, W. (Director). (2006). *Last Holiday* [motion picture].

Weir, P. (Director). (1982). *The Year of Living Dangerously* [motion picture].

Wellman, W. (Director). (1932). *The Hatchet Man* [motion picture].

Zwick, E. (Director). (2003). *The Last Samurai* [motion picture].

23
Stress, Refugees, and Trauma

EUNICE C. WONG, J. DAVID KINZIE, and J. MARK KINZIE

OUTLINE OF CHAPTER

Case Synopsis

Phat is a 33-year-old Cambodian woman who appeared almost expressionless, but with barely concealed sadness in the first interview. Her chief complaint was "I have lost everything," but her multiple symptoms included poor sleep, irritability, lack of enjoyment, fatigue, and depressed mood. On further questioning she mentioned she had nightmares two times a week of bloody, gory scenes that had been real events during her 4 years of Pol Pot concentration camp experience.

Introduction

War, political upheaval, and widespread violence led to a mass influx of refugees from Southeast Asia to the United States, beginning in 1975. Recent estimates indicate that over a million refugees from Cambodia, Laos, and Vietnam have sought haven in the United States (Niedzwiecki, Duong, & Center, 2004). Many experienced significant trauma including torture, witnessed killings, and starvation (Chan, 2004; Uba, 1994). Thus, the circumstances surrounding the evacuation and eventual resettlement of scores of Southeast Asian refugees are distinct from many of the immigration experiences of other Asian American groups. Even though Southeast Asian refugees within the United States are decades removed from the tribulations that caused them to flee from their homeland, the impact of trauma and its associated stressors are still evident today. In this chapter, key aspects related to the adjustment of Southeast Asian refugees in the United States will be discussed. Specifically, the chapter will provide an overview of the following: (a) the historical events that led to the creation of numerous refugees from Southeast Asia; (b) the stressors associated with immigrating to and resettling within the United States; (c) the impact of trauma on refugee well-being; and (d) the provision of mental health services.

Historical Events

In 1975, a series of Communist takeovers in Southeast Asia marked the beginning of what would result in the largest group of refugees to resettle in the United States within recent history. Prior to this period, there had been no real substantial history of immigration from Southeast Asia to the United States.

Vietnam

On April 30, 1975, the Northern Vietnamese Communist Army captured Saigon, the capital city of South Vietnam, establishing the end of the Vietnam War and the beginning of Communist rule in the region. In the days preceding the fall of Saigon, masses of South Vietnamese, many who had worked closely with the Americans or the U.S.-backed Republic of Vietnam government, fled Vietnam fearing retribution by the Communists. Approximately 125,000 were granted refugee status and resettled in the United States, constituting the first large wave of refugees from Vietnam. Most were highly educated, skilled, and urbanized (Haines, 1996). Starting in 1978, a second wave of refugees—often referred to as the "boat people"—escaped Vietnam largely on overcrowded, treacherous boats that were vulnerable to pirates who pillaged, raped, murdered, and assaulted passengers. The majority of "boat people" were either South Vietnamese who were imprisoned and tortured in "reeducation" camps or ethnic Chinese Vietnamese facing increasing persecution by the Communist Socialist Republic of Vietnam. It is estimated that over 80% of the voyages were attacked by pirates and that 200,000 Vietnamese refugees died while making the voyage (Lee & Lu, 1989). Before gaining admission to the United States, refugees often spent extended periods of time in temporary refugee camps, where further experiences of abuse and harsh conditions were reported. Unlike the first wave of Vietnamese refugees, the second wave of refugees experienced an immigration pathway marked by multiple instances of trauma exposure in Vietnam, overseas, and in refugee camps, before finally arriving in the United States. Further, this second wave of refugees, who tended to be less educated and from agrarian backgrounds, arrived during a time when government policies toward resettlement were less supportive, which made transitioning and successful adaptation to U.S. life even more challenging. Increased international attention to the plight of the "boat people" resulted in the establishment of the Orderly Departure Program in 1979, which allowed for direct immigration from Vietnam to the United States for the South Vietnamese with ties to the U.S. government or those with relatives of Vietnamese refugees already in the United States. The program later extended eligibility to Vietnamese who had been detained in reeducation camps, were former political prisoners, or were the Vietnamese children of U.S. servicemen. From 1979 to 1999, it is estimated that more than 500,000 Vietnamese gained entry to the U.S. under this program (United Nations High Commissioner for Refugees, 2001). The latest estimates indicate that 759,482 Vietnamese refugees have been admitted to the United States since 1975 (Niedzwiecki et al., 2004).

Cambodia

On April 17, 1975, less than 2 weeks before the fall of Saigon, the Pol Pot–led radical Communist group *Khmer Rouge* overtook the capital city Phnom Penh, ending Cambodia's first civil war by defeating the U.S.-backed Khmer Republic (Chan, 2004). Days before the siege of Phnom Penh, thousands of Cambodians were airlifted out of the country with the assistance of the U.S. government. Under the leadership of Pol Pot, the Khmer Rouge isolated Cambodia from the outside world and began a 4-year reign of terror. In an attempt to remove all traces of Western and traditional influence, teachers, Buddhist monks, businessmen, military leaders, and doctors were killed. Hundreds of thousands were executed in forced labor camps; most died of starvation and

	1975 Communist takeovers	1975 Refugee arrivals in U.S.	1976-1978 More arrivals	1979 Orderly Departure Program	1979-1985 More arrivals	1986-1990 More arrivals	1991-1995 More arrivals	1996-2002 Latest arrivals
Vietnam	Socialist Republic of Vietnam	First wave 125,000	Second wave "boat people" 16,200		305,272	108,648	152,952	51,410
Cambodia	Khmer Rouge	Escaped with U.S. aid 4,600	More arrivals 2,700		118,383	19,019	426	44
Laos	Pathet Lao	Escaped with U.S. aid 800	More arrivals 18,600		124,413	61,579	33,354	3,250

Figure 23.1 Timeline of historical events and immigration waves.

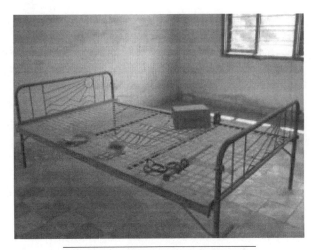

Khmer Rouge prison in Phnom Penh, Cambodia.

disease. These crude camps attempted rigid indoctrination by disassembling all traces of family life through the separation of husbands, wives, and children. The basic context of Cambodian culture, traditional values, religion, educational systems, and family life was destroyed. Nearly 2 million of the 7 million Cambodians died during this time (Chan, 2004). Eventually, the intense scrutiny and brutality of the Khmer Rouge amassed a growing resistance, which with the support of the Communist Socialist Republic of Vietnam, drove Pol Pot and his Khmer Rouge leaders out of power. Cambodia then plunged into its second civil war beginning in 1979. During this period, over half a million Cambodians fled to refugee camps established along the Cambodia-Thailand border, where further abuses and traumas were experienced. After spending years in the squalid and insidious conditions of the refugee camps, many were granted admission into other countries for resettlement.

For nearly 150,000 Cambodians, the United States became a place of refuge and offered the opportunity to rebuild lives after enormous suffering and tragedy. The large majority of Cambodian refugees granted admission in the United States arrived between 1981 and 1985. It was not until the end of 1991 that the civil war ended when the United Nations enforced a cease-fire. Cambodian refugees resettled throughout the 50 states of America with the largest communities established in California, Massachusetts, and Washington. As Sucheng Chan (2004) notes the Khmer Rouge killed an estimated 90% of the educated population residing in Cambodia in an attempt to eradicate all traces of Western influence. Consequently, the Cambodian refugee population that resettled in the United States came with limited human capital.

Laos

Within months of the Communist takeovers in Vietnam and Cambodia, Laos too came under Communist rule by the Pathet Lao in December 1975. The Pathet Lao was a Communist group backed by North Vietnam that played a vital role in the Vietnam War. With the assistance of the Pathet Lao, North Vietnam set up the Ho Chi Minh trail that ran along the Laos border, which provided a strategic passageway for troops and military supplies to be transported from North Vietnam to South Vietnam. In response to and to protect U.S. interests in the region, the United States recruited and trained tens of thousands of Laotians, mostly of Hmong descent, to counteract their military operations. They were promised that if Laos fell to the Pathet Lao and North Vietnam, the United States would give them shelter and provide for their needs. It is estimated that over 30,000 Hmong soldiers were recruited into war and that their death rates were

10 times as high as American soldiers serving in Vietnam (Fadiman, 1998). With the withdrawal of U.S. support at the end of the Vietnam War, the Pathet Lao took over the country and began a Marxist government sparking a mass departure from Laos that consisted of Laotians from the lowlands and Hmong and Mien from the highlands. The thousands who fled across the Mekong River into Thailand were set up in the refugee camps along the Thailand border, and many of these refugees were resettled in the United States. Among the Hmong who remained in Laos, thousands were sent to reeducation camps where they experienced harsh conditions and hard labor, often leading to their deaths. Others retreated to the high mountainous areas and continued to stage counterattacks. Even today, many continue to escape from the mountains and the jungle area and report continued attacks against them from both the Lao and Vietnamese military forces. The last major resettlement of about 15,000 from the Thai refugee camp occurred in 2004 (U.S. Department of State, 2004). As recently as 2005, thousands of Hmong fled from the jungles of Laos to refugee camps in Thailand (United Nations News Centre, 2007). Although the Thai government has forcibly repatriated Hmong refugees to Laos, they have agreed to halt deportation as plans are being made to resettle them in other countries. Recent estimates indicate that there are nearly a quarter million refugees from Laos now resettled in the United States (Niedzwiecki et al., 2004).

Trauma Exposure

According to the *Diagnostic Statistical Manual for Mental Disorders,* Fourth Edition (DSM-IV; American Psychiatric Association, 1994), traumatic stressors consist of witnessed or directly experienced events that involve either the threat of or actual death or serious injury to oneself or others. Direct experiences of traumatic events include military combat, violent personal assault (e.g., sexual assault, physical attack, robbery), kidnapping, torture, incarceration as a prisoner of war or in a concentration camp, as well as severe automobile accidents, natural or manmade disasters, and being diagnosed with life-threatening illness. Witnessed events that are considered traumatic stressors include serious injury or death of another person due to violent assault, accident, war, or disaster or unexpectedly seeing a dead body or body parts. Learning about life-threatening events experienced by others is also considered to be a traumatic stressor.

By this definition, numerous accounts, in terms of personal, clinical, and research reports, have documented high levels of trauma exposure among many Southeast Asian refugees. In a clinic sample of Southeast Asian refugees, one study found that patients were exposed to an average of 10 traumatic events including starvation, torture, sexual abuse, and solitary confinement (Mollica, Wyshak, & Lavelle, 1987). A statewide survey of Southeast Asian refugees residing in California reported that over half had experienced either death or separation from family members and about a third experienced multiple losses or separations (Gong-Guy, 1987). Only about a third of those who had been separated from family members experienced reunification. Among the Southeast Asian refugee groups, Cambodians have been reported to experience the most severe levels of trauma exposure under the Khmer Rouge's reign of terror, which attempted to scourge the country of all traces of Western and Cambodian traditional influences that stood in the way of establishing a classless utopian society (Chung & Kagawa-Singer, 1993). One study conducted with a probability sample of Cambodian refugees residing in Long Beach, California, home to the largest Cambodian refugee community in the United States, indicated that almost all had experienced near-death due to starvation (99%) (Marshall, Schell, Elliott, Berthold, & Chun, 2005). In addition, a large majority had experienced a combat situation (98%), forced labor like an animal or slave (96%), and the murder of a family member or friend (90%). Out of 35 different trauma types assessed, Cambodian refugees reported an average of 15 different kinds of traumatic experiences before immigrating to the United States.

The high level of trauma exposure found among Southeast Asian refugees is emblematic of a markedly different immigration pathway from many other Asian American immigrant groups. The Communist takeovers in Vietnam, Cambodia, and Laos were preceded by a mass and abrupt exodus of thousands of refugees. Often refugees had from a few weeks to a few hours to prepare for their escape. Fleeing from persecution and danger, many were separated from family members. As described by Kunz (1973) refugees are often "pushed out" and forced to leave their homelands. In contrast, the immigration process for non-refugees is often an extended, orderly, and safe process in which the destination of the new resettlement country is known and preparations can be arranged. For refugees, the flight from one's home was often filled with fear and further exposure to traumatic events. Already exposed to bombings, fighting, and persecution while residing in their war-torn countries, many refugees had to endure being hunted by militia, jungles filled with land mines, or treacherous boat rides. The journey often entailed witnessing the death or remains of other refugees who did not survive their flight from home. For those who were unable to leave shortly after the Communist takeovers, many faced years of brutal conditions in reeducation camps before escaping to follow the same hazardous plight. According to Uba (1994), approximately 40% of refugees reported that a family member had died while attempting to leave Southeast Asia.

Unlike many immigrants, refugees often encounter an intermediary step before permanent resettlement in a new country. Many reside in temporary refugee camps established along the borders of neighboring countries. Refugees from Cambodia and Laos reported the lengthiest

Photo from *New Year Baby* (2006). United States: Broken English Productions LLC.

stays, with an average of 3 years spent in refugee camps before being relocated to the United States, in contrast to an average of a year and half for those from Vietnam (Gong-Guy, 1987). For many, the refugee camps offered no reprieve from the emotional travails so far endured. Reports of squalid conditions, food shortages, and abuses by camp officers revealed yet another phase of the immigration process that was marked by traumatic experiences (Mollica, Cui, McInnes, & Massagli, 2002). Further, refugees were often faced with a fate that was uncertain and largely out of their control. Refugees could be denied admittance to host countries and repatriated to their native country. If granted admission, refugees often had no control over which country they would be resettled to and whether they would be resettled in the same country with family members. Understandably, pre-migration trauma, including the degree of refugee camp experience, has been significantly linked to the adjustment of Southeast Asian refugees in the United States and other resettlement countries (Boehnlein, Kinzie, Ben, & Fleck, 1985; Marshall et al., 2005).

Resettlement Stress in the United States

Southeast Asian refugees arriving in the United States faced the dual challenge of dealing with the stresses related to adapting to a new culture, while simultaneously coping with the aftermath of trauma. Among a group of Southeast Asian refugees who had resettled in the United States for over 5 years, 81% continued to express concerns about being separated from missing family members, 67% had painful memories of the war and their departure, and 58% worried about difficulties in communicating with those in their home country (Stein, 1980). Many Southeast Asian refugees may be emotionally burdened with feelings of anger, loneliness, grief, and guilt for having survived atrocities (Abe, Zane, & Chun, 1994; Eisenbruch, 1991; Gong-Guy, 1987; Uba, 1994). As will be discussed in a subsequent portion of the chapter, the emotional and psychological consequences of exposure to multiple traumas can persist even after a significant time after resettlement in the United States and may result in psychiatric clinical conditions such as **post-traumatic stress disorder** (PTSD) and **major depressive disorder**.

Several studies have indicated that the adjustment and well-being of Southeast Asian refugees is related not only to pre-migration trauma experiences (Blair, 2000; Rumbaut, 1985), but to the post-migration conditions of the resettlement country (Chun, Eastman, Wang, & Sue, 1998; Chan, 2004; Westermeyer, Vang, & Neider, 1983). Often national as well as local government policy can play a large role in buffering the stresses associated with immigration. As Chan (2004) documents, U.S. receptivity to the plight of Southeast Asian refugees waxed and waned,

Locals in the Mekong Delta's (Vietnam) floating market.

but with the passage of time support eventually dwindled. As a result, Southeast Asian refugees arriving in the latter waves of immigration often faced more restrictive refugee assistance policies such as limited opportunities for English language classes and job skills training as well as stricter criteria for and shortened periods of financial assistance. The availability of resources, government assistance, and economic opportunities also varied from state to state causing secondary migration movements among many Southeast Asian refugees (Chan, 2004; Desbarats, 1985).

Existing studies on immigrant-related stressors for other Asian American groups have informed much of the knowledge on Southeast Asian refugee adjustment. Immigrants and refugees are often exposed to a similar set of stressors associated with having to adapt to life in a new country. Such stressors can heighten the risk for mental health and adjustment-related problems (Blair, 2000; Chun et al., 1998). A brief review of major stressors commonly experienced by immigrants and refugees upon resettlement in the United States is provided below.

Acculturative Stress

Having to navigate an entirely new set of surroundings and customs can be stressful. The road toward adjusting to a new resettlement country is filled with challenges. Tasks that were once simple in one's native country such as grocery shopping or paying bills may be difficult and erode one's sense of self-efficacy. Some of the major acculturative stressors experienced by refugees are having to learn a new language, customs, and values. In a study with Cambodian, Laotian, Hmong, and Vietnamese refugees, difficulty with English was cited as one of the top four pressing problems (Uba, 1994). Lack of English proficiency often resulted in a significant downward shift in social status especially for refugees with highly educated and skilled backgrounds (Chung, 2001). With limited opportunities for English language learning many refugees were forced to take menial labor jobs with little prospects of future advancement. Lin, Tazuma, and Masuda (1979) found that high levels of stress were exhibited by Vietnamese refugee men who had experienced a change in social status because of nontransferable job skills. Similarly, in a study examining the relationship between pre-migration and post-migration factors to psychological distress, Westermeyer, Vang, and Neider (1983) found that Hmong refugees who had the most developed role identities in their native countries had the highest risk for depression. In a stratified sample of community residents of Cambodian, Vietnamese, Laotian, and Hmong ethnicity, acculturative stress related to learning a new language, finding employment, reestablishing social networks, and redefining roles was the strongest predictor of mental health, even after accounting for pre-migration factors (e.g., trauma exposure) (Nicholson, 1997).

Financial Stress

Financial stress is a significant post-migration factor that has been linked to the adjustment and well-being of refugees (Blair, 2000; Chung, 2001; Marshall et al., 2005). The degree of education and transferable job skills obtained before immigrating to the United States often influenced refugees' ability to become economically self-sufficient after resettlement. On average, refugees from Vietnam were more highly educated than Laotians and Cambodians. For example, Vietnamese refugees reported an average of 10 years of education compared to an average of 3 years among Hmong refugees (Gong-Guy, 1987). In terms of literacy in the native language, over 95% of Vietnamese reported fair or better literacy in their native language compared to over 35% of Hmong. Further, 1 out of every 10 Vietnamese refugees had a professional or technical job in their home country, compared to other Southeast Asian refugee groups who had half as many skilled professionals. After an average of 5 years post-resettlement in the United States, nearly half of Vietnamese refugees were participating in the labor force compared to only a fifth of

A Lao market trader, just set up for the night market in Luang Praband.

Cambodians and Hmong residing in California (Gong-Guy, 1987). However, a substantial proportion of all Southeast Asian refugee groups were fully dependent on public assistance. Nearly 80% of Cambodians, 80% Hmong, and 50% Vietnamese were receiving welfare payments for economic subsistence. More recent estimates indicate that the financial status of Southeast Asian Americans is improving; however, a significant proportion continue to live below the poverty line. In 1999, approximately 30% Cambodian Americans, 37% Hmong Americans, and 16% Vietnamese Americans were below the poverty line compared to 12% of the overall U.S. population (Niedzwiecki et al., 2004).

Family Stress and Loss of Social Support

Many Southeast Asian refugees faced significant family losses. Family members and friends were often lost through war-related deaths or separations that occurred during the flight from their homelands. Some refugees were resettled in regions in the United States with limited avenues for social support (Uba, 1994). Many studies have established that the greatest casualties in family loss occurred among Cambodian refugees due to the atrocities committed by the Khmer Rouge (Rumbaut, 1985; Gong-Guy, 1987). A disproportionate number of Cambodian male deaths occurred during the Khmer Rouge era leaving many fatherless families. Approximately 20% of Cambodian households are estimated to be female-headed households (U.S. Census Bureau, 1990). Among dual parent households, significant sources of family conflict were also engendered by circumstances that created role reversals within the family. For example, many Southeast Asian women were pushed into the workforce for the economic survival of the family. Having not worked in their native countries, this newfound role can challenge traditional norms that emphasize patriarchal authority (Ascher, 1985; Uba, 1994). Role reversals between parents and children have also been noted as significant sources of post-migration family stress

Floating market in Cambodia. (Charles Vogl, 2005. United States: Broken English Productions LLC.)

(Ida & Yang, 2003). Often refugee children acculturate at a faster rate than their parents, acquiring English language skills and familiarity with American culture. As a result, many children take on the role as translators and are given many family responsibilities, which may disrupt the traditional authoritative role of parents. Boehnlein et al. (1995) found that Vietnamese and Cambodian refugees reported that their relationships with their adolescent children were significant sources of concern.

Post-Migration Trauma

Many Southeast Asian refugees were relocated to highly dense, unsafe, crime-ridden urban areas (Chan, 2004; Uba, 1994). Two systematic studies have examined post-migration exposure to trauma. In Marshall et al.'s (2005) study with Cambodian refugees residing in Long Beach, California, substantial rates of exposure to community violence were found. Specifically, after resettling in the United States, nearly a third of Cambodian residents had seen a dead body in the neighborhood (34%), experienced a robbery (28%), had been chased by people trying to hurt them (22%), or had been verbally threatened with serious physical harm (22%). Similarly high rates of violence exposure were found in an earlier study conducted with Cambodian refugee parents and their adolescent children residing in the same community (Berthold, 1999).

Disaggregating Asian American Immigrant and Refugee Groups

Although Asian American immigrants and refugees may experience similar stressors as they adapt to life in the United States, important differences have been documented. For example, when examined as a group, about a quarter of Asian Americans live in linguistically isolated households (i.e., households in which no family member 14 years old or older is English language proficient). However, relatively higher rates are found when Southeast Asian groups are examined individually; more than a third of Cambodian, Laotian, Hmong, and Vietnamese families were designated as linguistically isolated households (see Figure 23.2). Comparable differences between examining Asian Americans in the aggregate versus individual subgroups can be seen on household size and dependence on public assistance.

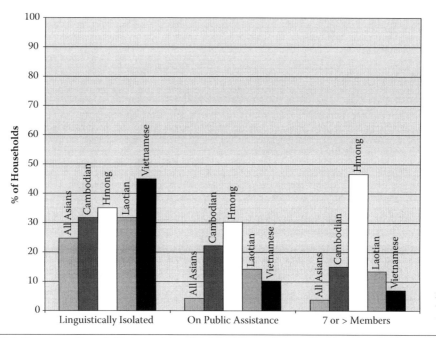

Figure 23.2 Percentage of households designated as linguistically isolated, on public assistance, and with seven or more family members. Data from Niedzwiecki et al. (2004).

Important differences may also be masked when the heterogeneity of Asian Americans is not considered in comparison to other ethnic groups. For example, a higher proportion of Cambodian and Laotian Americans live below the poverty line compared to Hispanic and African Americans; however, such differences would not be observable if Asian Americans were

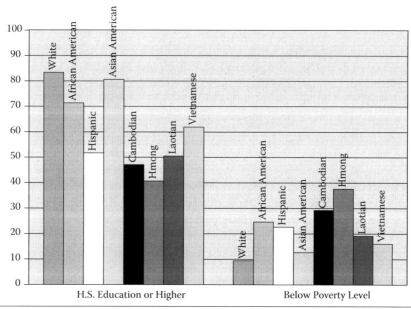

Figure 23.3 Percentage with a high school education or higher and percentage living below the poverty level. Data from Niedzwiecki et al. (2004).

examined in the aggregate (see Figure 23.3). Similarly, a smaller proportion of Cambodian and Hmong Americans have obtained a high school education or higher than African, Hispanic, and White Americans.

Health Outcomes

Much attention has been paid to the emotional and psychological impact of traumatic life events. It has been well-established that survivors of traumatic, life-threatening experiences are at increased risk for mental health problems (Breslau et al., 1998; Kessler, Sonnega, Bromet, Hughes, & Nelson, 1995). In terms of specific psychiatric disorders, a substantial proportion of trauma survivors have been shown to develop PTSD and major depression. According to the DSM-IV (American Psychological Association, 1994), the symptoms of PTSD include re-experiencing the event through distressing recollections, nightmares, and flashbacks; avoidance of reminders and feeling numb; and increased vigilance and arousal. Symptoms of major depression include depressed mood, hopelessness, guilt, lack of pleasure from formerly pleasurable activities, poor concentration and memory, and suicidal thoughts. A brief review of studies on PTSD and depression among Southeast Asian refugees is provided below.

Mental Health

Although varying rates of PTSD and depression have been found among Southeast Asian refugee populations, studies consistently demonstrate that a substantial proportion meet diagnostic criteria for at least one of the two psychiatric disorders. Studies on mental health disorders among Southeast Asian refugee populations have been conducted with clinic and community samples, which may account for some of the observed variation in prevalence rates of PTSD and depression. Among psychiatric clinic patient samples, rates of PTSD and depression have ranged between 50% to 70% and 71% to 82%, respectively (Kinzie et al., 1990; Mollica et al., 1987). Slightly lower rates of depression (between 20% and 50%) have also been documented among Vietnamese refugees in primary care settings (Buchwald, Manson, Dinges, Keane, & Kinzie, 1993; Lin, Ihle, & Tazuma, 1985).

Among a stratified sample of Southeast Asian community residents, Nicholson (1997) found the following prevalence rates: 40% depression, 35% anxiety, and 14% PTSD. Sack et al. (1994) examined rates of PTSD among a random sample of Cambodian adolescents and their parents residing in Portland, Oregon, and Salt Lake City, Utah. Substantial rates of PTSD were found among adolescents (20%), their mothers (58%), and their fathers (33%). Blair (2001) conducted a study with Cambodian refugees who had resettled in Utah for an average of 8 years. High rates of PTSD (45%) and depression (51%) were also documented. In a recent study conducted with a probability sample of Cambodian refugees living in Long Beach, California—home to the largest Cambodian community in the United States—findings indicated that even though almost two decades had elapsed since resettlement in the United States, over 60% met criteria for PTSD and over 50% for depression (Marshall et al., 2005). These findings are congruent with many clinic studies that have shown that a substantial proportion of Southeast Asian refugee patients continue to experience PTSD and depression-related problems even after a significant duration of time has passed since resettling (Boehnlein et al., 2004; Kinzie, 1989).

Numerous studies have documented a dose-response relationship between trauma exposure and risk for PTSD and depression (Blair, 2000; Marshall et al., 2005; Mollica, McInnes, Poole, & Tor, 1998). Namely, trauma exposure is positively associated with vulnerability to PTSD and depression. Studies have also found differential effects of pre-migration trauma and post-migration stressors on risk for psychiatric problems. Among Cambodian adolescents residing in temporary refugee camps, Savin, Sack, Clarke, Meas, and Richart (1996) found that earlier war trauma had a stronger association with PTSD, whereas more recent stressors (e.g., threat of repatriation) were more strongly linked to depression. In a study conducted with 170 Cambodian youth and 80 of their mothers who resettled in the United States, Sack, Clarke, and Seeley (1996) found that PTSD was related to both pre-migration trauma exposure and resettlement-related stressors. However, depression was much more strongly tied to recent stressors. In the Blair (2000) study of Cambodian adult refugees residing in Utah, risk for PTSD and depression was positively associated with both number of war traumas and resettlement stressors (Blair, 2000). Findings indicate that both pre-migration trauma and post-migration stressors are significantly tied to subsequent distress levels in the resettlement country.

Physical Health

Although Southeast Asian refugees were subjected to traumas that may have had physiological as well as emotional consequences (e.g., starvation, torture), relatively few studies have focused on the physical health status of refugees. In Gong-Guy's (1987) California needs assessment survey, only a small proportion of Southeast Asian refugees reported having excellent health. Trauma exposure as well as the stresses associated with resettling in a new country have been posited as contributing factors to poor health among Southeast Asian refugees (Uba, 1994). Uba and Chung (1991) found that pre-migration trauma exposure was associated with poor physical health among Cambodian refugees who had been resettled for a number of years in the United States. In one of the few studies examining the long-term physical health outcomes of refugees, Wong et al. (2007) compared the physical health status of Cambodian refugees to a sample of California residents that was matched on gender, age, income, ethnicity, urbanicity, and immigrant status. High rates of disability (69%) and self-reported fair or poor health status (89%) were found among Cambodian refugees compared to the matched California sample (26% and 46%, respectively). Addressing the physical health needs of Southeast Asian refugees are vital given that poor physical health has been associated with poor mental health in refugee (Mollica et al., 1999; Weine et al., 2000) and non-refugee populations (Litz, Keane, Fisher, Marx, & Monaco, 1992; Wolfe, Schnurr, Brown, & Furey, 1994).

Mental Health Services

Barriers to Care

Many have posited that Southeast Asian refugees encounter numerous barriers to obtaining mental health care (Gong-Guy et al, 1991; Kinzie, 1985; Uba, 1994). In a California statewide needs assessment survey of Southeast Asian refugees, Gong-Guy (1987) revealed major gaps in mental health service delivery. At the time of the study, Southeast Asian refugees had been resettled in the United States for an average of 5 years. Gong-Guy (1987) noted a serious shortage of bilingual and bicultural mental health providers. For example, in a survey of mental health professionals working at public institutions servicing Southeast Asian refugees, not one professionally trained Cambodian service provider was found (Gong-Guy et al., 1991). Long treatment delays were also noted with some refugee groups having to wait 3 to 12 months before obtaining services.

In addition to the aforementioned structural barriers, many have also noted that Southeast Asian refugees may experience significant cultural barriers to mental health services. Professional mental health services have been characterized as a last resort when all other sources of care, such as community resources, family, and traditional healers have been exhausted (Kinzie, 1985; Mollica et al., 1987; Nguyen & Anderson, 2005). Unfamiliarity and discomfort with Western mental health treatment, which often involves open communication of personal problems and distress, have also been cited as major barriers to care (Mollica et al., 1987; Kinzie et al., 1988). Other commonly cited culturally based barriers to mental health care include lack of confidence in Western psychological services, family prohibitions against seeking professional help, and fears of shame and stigma (Leong & Lau, 2001; Sue & Sue, 1999). Although considered a universal barrier, the stigma of mental illness is frequently cited as a barrier that may be especially salient for Asian Americans (Leong & Lau, 2001; Uba, 1994).

Much of the knowledge on barriers to care for Southeast Asian refugees share the same limitations as in studies conducted with other Asian American immigrant groups. Limitations include a predominant reliance on expert opinion, clinical anecdotes, and convenience samples. In contrast to using a convenience-based sample, Wong et al. (2006) examined mental health service barriers among a probability sample of 490 Cambodian refugees residing in Long Beach, California. Surprisingly, a relatively small proportion endorsed commonly cited cultural barriers such as distrust of Western care (4%), greater confidence in indigenous treatment (5%), stigma (5%), family reluctance (<1%), or feared discrimination (15%). Instead, most endorsed structural barriers such as high cost (80%) and language (66%). A similar pattern was found among those with a probable diagnosis of PTSD or depression. Findings suggest that structural, not cultural, barriers are the most critical obstacles to care in this U.S. Cambodian refugee community. Although findings run counter to the relative emphasis that has been placed on cultural barriers to care, a few recent studies have yielded consistent findings with respect to attitudes toward mental health service utilization. Daley (2005) interviewed a small sample of Cambodian refugee parents and their children and found generally positive endorsements toward the use of mental health services. Nguyen and Anderson (2005) assessed attitudes toward seeking mental health services among Vietnamese Americans who had resided in the United States for at least 8 years. Findings revealed rather favorable attitudes toward mental health services; moreover, comparable help-seeking preferences for professional mental health resources (i.e., psychiatrist, psychologist, physician) and family/community resources (i.e., relative, immediate family member, grandparent, close friend, religious leader) were found.

Utilization Rates

Few studies have examined Southeast Asian refugees' utilization of mental health services. Gong-Guy (1987) noted that each of the Southeast Asian groups had been differentially exposed to Western medicine before immigrating to the United States. The Vietnamese were described as those most likely to have been exposed to Western medicine and the Hmong the least likely. Upon arrival in the United States, all of the Southeast Asian refugee groups significantly increased their use of Western medicine, while simultaneously relying on traditional forms of medicine. It is unclear, however, whether this shift included an increased receptivity to Western mental health care. In a study of outpatient mental health services, Ying and Hu (1994) found that Southeast Asian Americans were overrepresented in the mental health service system relative to their proportion within the Los Angeles general population. Further, relative to other Asian American groups, Southeast Asian Americans had higher utilization rates, but exhibited worse outcomes. In Blair's (2001) study with Cambodian refugees in Utah, only 9% had sought any type of mental health treatment even though 45% qualified for a diagnosis of PTSD.

In contrast, Marshall et al. (2006) found high rates of mental health service utilization among their large probability sample of Cambodian refugees in Long Beach, California. Among a subsample of 339 Cambodian refugees who met past 12-month criteria for PTSD, depression, or alcohol use disorder, 70% had sought care from medical care providers (e.g., family or primary care doctor) and 46% from mental health providers (e.g., psychologists, counselor), within the past year for emotional and psychological problems. A recent study conducted with a nationally representative sample of Asian Americans found that among Vietnamese Americans who met past 12-month criteria for a DSM-IV disorder, almost 50% had sought mental health–related services in the past year (Abe-Kim et al., 2007). These rates of mental health service utilization exceed those found for the general U.S. population. Data from the National Comorbidity Survey Replication Study reported that approximately 41% of U.S. population with a documented mental health need (i.e., past 12-month DSM-IV disorder) had obtained mental health–related services (Wang et al., 2005). Such findings counter widely held notions that Asians, including Southeast Asian refugees, seldom seek Western mental health services (Uba, 1994; Hsu, Davies, & Hansen, 2004). Marshall et al. (2006) offer several possible explanations to account for their study's findings including a greater burden of mental health need relative to other Asian Americans, increased opportunities for contact with mental health professionals via refugee social services networks, and the availability of health insurance coverage due to poverty and disability.

In a corresponding study using data from Marshall et al. (2006), utilization rates of complementary and alternative providers were compared to use of Western health providers for emotional and psychological problems (Berthold et al., 2007). Complementary and alternative providers included monk or religious person, fortune teller, traditional Asian doctor (e.g., herbalist, acupuncturist, masseuse), and Kruu Khmer (i.e., traditional Cambodian healer). Among the subsample of Cambodian refugees who had established mental health need (i.e., past year DSM diagnosis), over a third had sought complementary and alternative services compared to 70% who had seen a Western health professional. Additional analyses were conducted given that some have suggested that the use of complementary and alternative services may inhibit Western mental health services among Asian Americans (Ito & Maramba, 2002; Lin, Inui, Kleinman, & Womack, 1982). For example, the U.S. Surgeon General's Report *Mental Health: Culture, Race, and Ethnicity* concluded that reliance on alternative resources is a contributing factor to Asian American underutilization of Western mental health services (USDHHS, 2001). Findings indicated that only a small proportion of Cambodian refugees (5%) relied exclusively on complementary and alternative medicine. Further, a significant positive association was found between utilization of complementary and alternative services and Western mental health services. Such findings run counter to prevailing beliefs regarding complementary and alternative services acting as a barrier to Western mental health services. However, little empirical research has been conducted on mental health service utilization patterns among Southeast Asian refugees. Additional research is needed to better understand the treatment seeking process, including whether complementary and alternative care versus Western care is sought first, the degree to which utilization of one type of treatment may delay treatment seeking of another, and satisfaction with both types of services.

PTSD Practice Guidelines

Guidelines for the provision of PTSD treatment have been issued by several expert consensus panels (Ballenger et al., 2000; Ursano et al., 2004). Recommended interventions include pharmacological treatment, psychotherapy interventions, education, and adjunctive support services. In terms of pharmacological treatment, selective serotonin reuptake inhibitors (SSRIs), especially sertraline, are generally recommended as first-line choices. With respect to psychotherapeutic interventions, the guidelines identify several evidence-based practices including exposure therapy and cognitive behavioral therapy (CBT). Though there are no known studies that have examined the extent to which Southeast Asian refugees are receiving evidence-based PTSD treatment, a few studies have examined the effects of CBT-based interventions and medication on PTSD symptoms with small clinic samples of Southeast Asian refugees. Otto et al. (2003) randomly assigned 10 Cambodian refugee women with PTSD to either a treatment of sertraline alone or combined treatments. The combined treatment consisted of psychoeducation, exposure, cognitive-restructuring, and sertraline, which resulted in medium to large effects sizes in PTSD symptom reduction. In a similar study, Hinton et al. (2004) examined the therapeutic efficacy of a culturally adapted CBT for 12 Vietnamese refugees with treatment-resistant PTSD and comorbid panic attacks. Large effect sizes were also found for the reduction of anxiety, depression, and PTSD symptoms over the course of 11 sessions.

The Next Generation

The significant and enduring effects of trauma exposure on the physical and mental health well-being of Southeast Asian refugees have been well documented. However, few investigations have examined the adjustment of the U.S.-born children of Southeast Asian refugees. Most studies have focused on the adjustment of U.S.-born children of immigrants without separate attention to the unique status of U.S.-born children of refugees. Little is known about the effects of trauma exposure and acculturative-related stresses on the parenting capacities of refugees and the subsequent impact on their children. Further study is needed to understand the extent to which the effects of trauma are being transmitted to the second generation, even though the U.S.-born children of refugees may not have been directly exposed to the traumas experienced by many of their parents. Additional study is needed to understand factors that promote or impede the well-being of the next generation of U.S.-born children of Southeast Asian refugees.

Summary

In a recent report, the U.S. Surgeon General identified Southeast Asian refugees as a high-need population (U.S. Department of Health and Human Services, 2001). Studies show that many Southeast Asian refugees continue to experience serious mental health problems even after a significant duration of time has passed since resettling in the United States. Further research is needed to better understand the factors that underlie these high levels of psychiatric problems. Only a limited number of studies have focused on mental health service utilization, barriers to care, and evidence-based practices within Southeast Asian refugee populations. Thus, it is unknown whether the mental health need documented in this population is due to inadequate access to treatment, the unavailability of quality mental health treatment, or the enduring, pernicious effects of trauma. Findings suggest that the current process of resettling refugees, while addressing their immediate material and security needs, may not adequately address their long-term health problems. Additional efforts are needed to fulfill the United Nations High Commissioner for Refugees' vision of resettlement as providing a lasting end to the suffering of refugees.

Discussion Questions

1. Imagine leaving your home in the next 2 days. What would that be like? What would you leave? What would you take?
2. Imagine being forced to leave your country in the next month and going to a country where you don't speak the language. What would that be like?
3. Imagine that you have been beaten with a stick. What might be your reaction be to seeing a similar type of stick again?
4. Imagine that you have spent most of your life in one culture, but you were forced to leave. You have settled in a new country with very different expectations on how to live.

Your children have adopted this new way of living and seem to be forgetting where they came from. How might you feel and act?

Case Study

Phat had a complicated history and clinical course. She was born in the rural area of Cambodia, the third of eight children, and she had attended school for 3 years. At the age of 20, Pol Pot came to power and she was separated from her family for 4 years and endured these 4 years in forced labor. She was starved and beaten on the legs many times. After hearing shooting at night, she saw many corpses the next day. Her brother was killed by Pol Pot cadres. She was forced to marry in 1976 and had her first child a year later. She was separated from her husband and they were finally united as refugees in Thailand in 1979. During the time in Thailand, the husband had multiple affairs that continued even after they came to the United States in 1982. The couple separated formally in 1987 and the patient's symptoms worsened. The patient was involved in a new relationship that was also abusive and caused her much grief. This is when she came to the clinic and said she "had lost everything." A petite, quiet, and sad Asian woman who spoke appropriately with depressed affect without psychotic symptoms; she had good insight about current stresses but minimized the past trauma.

She has been seen in the clinic for 14 years with a complicated course. After she improved on medicine, group, and individual therapy, her daughter developed a brain disease and was in a coma for several months. Following this, the daughter had a long period of rehabilitation in which her personality was characterized by irritability and confusion. During this time the patient had an increase in both depressive and PTSD symptoms.

A second problem occurred later when the oldest son stopped going to high school and became "disrespectful." A third crisis involved her current husband's alcoholism, antisocial and abusive behavior. Subsequently, he spent several years in jail and upon his release his behavior did not improve. After much ambivalence, she finally was able to separate. She said, "I have been a loser again." She developed multiple medical problems including hypertension and a bleeding disorder, both of which required ongoing medical treatment.

For a person like Phat, it is important to consider that there are social, psychological, and biological factors involved, all at the same time. During different times in her life, different factors will have greater or lesser importance. Phat's problems will not be solved all at once, but with supportive counseling she can be encouraged to maximize her resources and improve her quality of life. Social factors relevant to Phat include the stress of acculturation into American society and poor education. The deaths of family members limited her familial support, a key element of coping in her culture. Her husbands' own difficulties appeared to even complicate matters even more. Phat was exposed to horrific trauma that involved grief over the loss of close family members. New stressors, like the difficulties with her husband and the medical illness of her daughter, made her feel like she lost everything. It is very common for someone who has been exposed to trauma to be very sensitive to new stressors. It is as if the new stress reminds them of past times they have been alone and afraid. It has been useful for Phat to gently and compassionately help her gain insight into this. From a biological point of view, Phat suffers from the symptoms of PTSD and major depression; the symptoms of both wax and wane over time. Medications, including antidepressants, have been very helpful for her.

The general approach advocated by cross-cultural psychiatrists is to address the social, psychological, and biological factors in a highly supportive and safe environment. It is important to have an understanding about the patient's background and the trauma the patient endured; it is useful to consult with others who have similar backgrounds. Clinics will often utilize counselors and interpreters who act as cultural ambassadors interpreting the culture as well as the language. The initial step in approaching this patient is to establish a feeling of safety. Only when it is clear that the interviews are confidential and respectful should you go on. If at any time the patient feels unsafe or appears frightened, it is important to slow down and reestablish safety. It is important to listen to the trauma story and allow the patient to go into the amount of depth she feels safe giving. Often patients' lives were difficult even before the identified trauma, and it is important to elicit this history. Patients complaints and comments need to be taken seriously, even if they are physical complaints, rather than psychological. Often physical complaints are based on psychological pain. Patients may have found that discussing their suffering in physical terms may be more comforting; or they may be unaware of a connection. Currently Phat's life has settled down with reduced symptoms. She keeps regular group and individual clinic appointments and continues to take medicine for depression and PTSD. She says the clinic and treatment has "saved my life."

Case Study Discussion Questions

For undergraduate students, please consider the following questions:

1. What are your initial reactions to this vignette?
2. What are your thoughts and reactions to Phat's second husband also being abusive?
3. Are there other important cultural, social, psychological, or biological factors in Phat's case?

For graduate students and/or beginning therapists, please consider the following questions:

1. What is your theoretical orientation regarding work with trauma victims? Is it necessary to confront a patient's trauma as a method of exposure work?
2. What may be the transference and countertransference issues in a long-term therapeutic relationship with Phat?
3. Do you think that psychiatric medications are truly necessary in cases of severe PTSD such as Phat's?

Key Terms

Major depressive disorder: A mood disorder. As defined by the American Psychiatric Association, the symptoms include depressed mood, lack of pleasure from formerly pleasurable activities, and problems with sleep and appetite. Memory and concentration are impaired as well.

Post-traumatic stress disorder: An anxiety disorder that results from a very stressful experience (typically the event often involves the witnessed death of others or threatened loss of life to self or others). As defined by the American Psychiatric Association, the symptoms include re-experiencing symptoms (such as distressing memories, nightmares, and feeling as if the traumatic event is recurring); avoidance symptoms (avoiding thoughts and feelings about the trauma and feelings of detachment); and persistent symptoms of increased arousal.

For Further Learning and Suggested Readings

Books

Ngor, H. (1987). *A Cambodian odyssey.* New York: Macmillan Publishing Company.

Tseng, W.-S., & Streltzer, J. (Eds.). (1997). *Culture and psychopathology: A guide to clinical assessment.* Philadelphia: Brunner/Mazel.

Tseng, W.-S., & Streltzer, J. (Eds.). (2001). *Culture and psychotherapy: A guide to clinical practice.* Washington, DC: American Psychiatric Press.

Movies

The Killing Fields
New Year Baby

Web Sites

The Cambodian Genocide Program at Yale University: http://www.yale.edu/cgp

References

Abe, J., Zane, N., & Chun, K. (1994). Differential responses to trauma: Migration-related discriminants of post-traumatic stress disorder among Southeast Asian refugees. *Journal of Community Psychology. Special Issue: Asian-American mental health, 22*(2), 121–135.

Abe-Kim, J., Takeuchi, D. T., Hong, S., Zane, N., Sue, S., Spencer, M. S., et al. (2007). Use of mental health-related services among immigrant and U.S.-born Asian Americans: Results from the National Latino and Asian American Study. *American Journal of Public Health, 97*(1), 91.

American Psychological Association. (1994). *Diagnostic and statistical manual of mental disorders* (4th ed.). Washington, DC.

Ascher, C. (1985). The social and psychological adjustment of Southeast Asian refugees. *The Urban Review, 17*(2), 147–152.

Ballenger, J. C., Davidson, J. R., Lecrubier, Y., Nutt, D. J., Foa, E. B., Kessler, R. C., et al. (2000). Consensus statement on posttraumatic stress disorder from the International Consensus Group on Depression and Anxiety. *Journal of Clinical Psychiatry, 61*(5), 60–66.

Berthold, S. M. (1999). The effects of exposure to community violence on Khmer Refugee adolescents. *Journal of Traumatic Stress, 12*(3), 455–471.

Berthold, S. M., Wong, E. C., Schell, T. L., Marshall, G. N., Elliot, M. N., Takeuchi, D., Hambarsoomians, K. (2007). Patterns of complementary alternative medicine and conventional mental health care among U.S. Cambodian refugees. *Psychiatric Services, 58*, 1212–1218.

Blair, R. B. (2001). Mental health needs among Cambodian refugees in Utah. *International Social Work, 44*(2), 179.

Blair, R. G. (2000). Risk factors associated with PTSD and major depression among Cambodian refugees in Utah. *Health and Social Work, 25*(1), 23–30.

Boehnlein, J., Tran, H., Riley, C. M. A., Vu, K., Tan, S. M. D., & Leung, P. (1995). A comparative study of family functioning among Vietnamese and Cambodian refugees. *Journal of Nervous & Mental Disease, 183*(12), 768–773.

Boehnlein, J. K., Kinzie, J. D., Ben, R., & Fleck, J. (1985). One-year follow-up study of posttraumatic stress disorder among survivors of Cambodian concentration camps. *American Journal of Psychiatry, 142*(8), 956–959.

Boehnlein, J. K., Kinzie, J. D., Sekiya, U., Riley, C., Pou, K., & Rosborough, B. (2004). A ten-year treatment outcome study of traumatized Cambodian refugees. *Journal of Nervous & Mental Disease, 192*(10), 658–663.

Breslau, N., Kessler, R. C., Chilcoat, H. D., Schultz, L. R., Davis, G. C., & Andreski, P. (1998). Trauma and posttraumatic stress disorder in the community: The 1996 Detroit area survey of trauma. *Archives of General Psychiatry, 55*(7), 626–632.

Buchwald, D., Manson, S. M., Dinges, N. G., Keane, E. M., & Kinzie, J. D. (1993). Prevalence of depressive symptoms among established Vietnamese refugees in the United States: Detection in a primary care setting. *Journal of General Internal Medicine, 8*(2), 76–81.

Chan, S. (2004). *Survivors: Cambodian refugees in the United States*. Urbana, IL: University of Illinois Press.

Chun, K. M., Eastman, K. L., Wang, G. C. S., & Sue, S. (1998). Psychopathology. In L. C. Lee & N. W. S. Zane (Eds.), *Handbook of Asian American psychology* (pp. 457–483). Thousand Oaks, CA: Sage Publications.

Chung, R. C., & Kagawa-Singer, M. (1993). Predictors of psychological distress among Southeast Asian refugees. *Social Science & Medicine, 36*(5), 631–639.

Chung, R. C. Y. (2001). Psychosocial adjustment of Cambodian refugee women: Implications for mental health counseling. *Journal of Mental Health Counseling, 23*(2), 115–126.

Daley, T. C. (2005). Beliefs about treatment of mental health problems among Cambodian American children and parents. *Social Science & Medicine, 61*(11), 2384–2395.

Desbarats, J. (1985). Indochinese resettlement in the United States. *Annals of the Association of American Geographers, 75*(4), 522–538.

Eisenbruch, M. (1991). From post-traumatic stress disorder to cultural bereavement: Diagnosis of Southeast Asian refugees. *Social Science & Medicine, 33*(6), 673–680.

Fadiman, A. (1998). *The spirit catches you and you fall down*. New York: Farrar, Straus and Giroux.

Gong-Guy, E. (1987). *California Southeast Asian mental health needs assessment*. Oakland, CA: Asian Community Mental Health Services.

Gong-Guy, E. (1991). Clinical issues in mental health service delivery to refugees. *American Psychologist, 46*(6), 642–648.

Haines, D. W. (1996). *Refugees in America in the 1990s: A reference handbook*. Westport, CT: Greenwood Press.

Hinton, D. E., Pham, T., Tran, M., Safren, S. A., Otto, M. W., & Pollack, M. H. (2004). CBT for Vietnamese refugees with treatment-resistant PTSD and panic attacks: A pilot study. *Journal of Traumatic Stress, 17*(5), 429–433.

Hsu, E., Davies, C. A., & Hansen, D. J. (2004). Understanding mental health needs of Southeast Asian refugees: Historical, cultural, and contextual challenges. *Clinical Psychology Review, 24*(2), 193–213.

Ida, D. J., & Yang, P. (2003). Southeast Asian children and adolescents. In J. T. Gibbs & L. N. Huang (Eds.), *Children of color: Psychological interventions with culturally diverse youth* (pp. 265–296). San Francisco: John Wiley & Sons.

Ito, K. L., & Maramba, G. G. (2002). Therapeutic beliefs of Asian American therapists: Views from an ethnic-specific clinic. *Transcultural Psychiatry, 39*(1), 33.

Kessler, R. C., Sonnega, A., Bromet, E., Hughes, M., & Nelson, C. B. (1995). Posttraumatic stress disorder in the National Comorbidity Survey. *Archives of General Psychiatry, 52*(12), 1048–1060.

Kinzie, J. D. (1985). Cultural aspects of psychiatric treatment with Indochinese refugees. *American Journal of Social Psychiatry, 5*(1), 47–53.

Kinzie, J. D. (1989). Therapeutic approaches to traumatized Cambodian refugees. *Journal of Traumatic Stress, 2*(1), 75–91.

Kinzie, J. D., Boehnlein, J. K., Leung, P. K., Moore, L. J., Riley, C., & Smith, D. (1990). The prevalence of posttraumatic stress disorder and its clinical significance among Southeast Asian refugees. *American Journal of Psychiatry, 147*(7), 913–917.

Kinzie, J. D., Leung, P., Bui, A., Ben, R., Keopraseuth, K. O., Riley, C., et al. (1988). Group therapy with Southeast Asian refugees. *Community Mental Health Journal, 24*(2), 157–166.

Kunz, E. F. (1973). The refugee in flight: Kinetic models and forms of adjustment. *International Migration Review, 7*, 126–146.

Lee, E., & Lu, F. (1989). Assessment and treatment of Asian-American survivors of mass violence. *Journal of Traumatic Stress, 2*(1), 93–120.

Leong, F. T. L., & Lau, A. S. L. (2001). Barriers to providing effective mental health services to Asian Americans. *Mental Health Services Research, 3*(4), 201–214.

Lin, E. H., Ihle, L. J., & Tazuma, L. (1985). Depression among Vietnamese refugees in a primary care clinic. *American Journal of Medicine, 78*(1), 41–44.

Lin, K. M., Inui, T. S., Kleinman, A. M., & Womack, W. M. (1982). Sociocultural determinants of the help-seeking behavior of patients with mental illness. *Journal of Nervous & Mental Disease, 170*(2), 78–85.

Lin, K. M., Tazuma, L., & Masuda, M. (1979). Adaptational problems of Vietnamese refugees. *Archives of General Psychiatry, 36*, 955–961.

Litz, B. T., Keane, T. M., Fisher, L., Marx, B., & Monaco, V. (1992). Physical health complaints in combat-related post-traumatic stress disorder: A preliminary report. *Journal of Traumatic Stress, 5*(1), 131–141.

Marshall, G. N., Berthold, S. M., Schell, T. L., Elliott, M. N., Chun, C. A., & Hambarsoomians, K. (2006). Rates and correlates of seeking mental health services among Cambodian refugees. *American Journal of Public Health, 96*(10), 1829.

Marshall, G. N., Schell, T. L., Elliott, M. N., Berthold, S. M., & Chun, C. A. (2005). Mental health of Cambodian refugees 2 decades after resettlement in the United States. *Journal of the American Medical Association, 294*, 571–579.

Mollica, R. F., Cui, X., McInnes, K., & Massagli, M. P. (2002). Science-based policy for psychosocial interventions in refugee camps: A Cambodian example. *Journal of Nervous & Mental Disease, 190*(3), 158–166.

Mollica, R. F., McInnes, K., Poole, C., & Tor, S. (1998). Dose-effect relationships of trauma to symptoms of depression and post-traumatic stress disorder among Cambodian survivors of mass violence. *British Journal of Psychiatry, 173*, 482–488.

Mollica, R. F., McInnes, K., Sarajlic, N., Lavelle, J., Sarajlic, I., & Massagli, M. P. (1999). Disability associated with psychiatric comorbidity and health status in Bosnian refugees living in Croatia. *Journal of American Medical Association, 282*, 433–439.

Mollica, R. F., Wyshak, G., & Lavelle, J. (1987). The psychosocial impact of war trauma and torture on Southeast Asian refugees. *American Journal of Psychiatry, 144*(12), 1567–1572.

Nguyen, Q. C. X., & Anderson, L. P. (2005). Vietnamese Americans' attitudes toward seeking mental health services: Relation to cultural variables. *Journal of Community Psychology, 33*(2), 213–231.

Nicholson, B. L. (1997). The influence of pre-emigration and postemigration stressors on mental health: A study of Southeast Asian refugees. *Social Work Research, 21*(1), 19–31.

Niedzwiecki, M., Duong, T. C., & Center, D. (2004). *Southeast Asian American statistical profile.* Washington, DC: Southeast Asia Resource Action Center (SEARAC).

Otto, M. W., Hinton, D., Korbly, N. B., Chea, A., Ba, P., Gershuny, B. S., et al. (2003). Treatment of pharmacotherapy-refractory posttraumatic stress disorder among Cambodian refugees: A pilot study of combination treatment with cognitive-behavior therapy vs sertraline alone. *Behavior Research and Therapy, 41*(11), 1271–1276.

Rumbaut, R. G. (1985). Mental health and the refugee experience: A comparative study of Southeast Asian refugees. In T. C. Owan (Ed.), *Southeast Asian mental health: Treatment, prevention, services, training, and research* (pp. 433–486). Rockville, MD: National Institute of Mental Health.

Sack, W. H., Clarke, G. N., & Seeley, J. (1996). Multiple forms of stress in Cambodian adolescent refugees. *Child Development, 67*(1), 107–116.

Sack, W. H., McSharry, S., Clarke, G. N., Kinney, R., Seeley, J., & Lewinsohn, P. (1994). The Khmer adolescent project. I. Epidemiologic findings in two generations of Cambodian refugees. *Journal of Nervous & Mental Disease, 182*(7), 387–395.

Savin, D., Sack, W. H., Clarke, G. N., Meas, N., & Richart, I. (1996). The Khmer adolescent project: III. A study of trauma from Thailand's Site II refugee camp. *Journal of the American Academy of Child & Adolescent Psychiatry, 35*(3), 384–391.

Stein, B. (1980). *Refugee resettlement programs and techniques: A research report submitted to the Select Committee on Immigration and Refugee Policy.* East Lansing, MI: Michigan State University Resource Center for Refugee Resettlement.

Sue, D. S., & Sue, D. (1999). *Counseling the culturally different* (3rd ed.). New York: John Wiley & Sons.

Uba, L. (1994). Asian Americans: Personality patterns, identity, and mental health. New York: Guilford Press.

Uba, L., & Chung, R. C. (1991). The relationship between trauma and financial and physical well-being among Cambodians in the United States. *Journal of General Psychology, 118*(3), 215–225.

United Nations High Commissioner for Refugees. (2001). *The state of the world's refugees 2000: Fifty years of humanitarian action.* New York: Oxford University Press.

United Nations News Centre. (2007). *UN agency concerned as Thailand deports Lao Hmong to Laos, reiterates offer to help.* Accessed May 30, 2007, from http://www.un.org/apps/news/story.asp?NewsID= 21376&Cr=thailand&Cr1=#

Ursano, R. J., Bell, C., Eth, S., Friedman, M., Norwood, A., Pfefferbaum, B., et al. (2004). Practice guideline for the treatment of patients with acute stress disorder and posttraumatic stress disorder. *American Journal of Psychiatry, 161*(11 suppl), 3–31.

U.S. Department of Health and Human Services. (2001). *Mental health: Culture, race, and ethnicity. A supplement to mental health: A report of the Surgeon General.* Rockville, MD.

U.S. Department of State. (2004). Hmong refugee resettlement interviews underway at Wat. *U.S. Refugee Admissions Program News, 2,* 1–4.

U.S. Surgeon General (2001). *Mental health: culture, race, ethnicity. Supplement to mental health: a report of the Surgeon General.* Washington, DC: Government Printing Office.

Wang, P. S., Lane, M., Olfson, M., Pincus, H. A., Wells, K. B., & Kessler, R. C. (2005). Twelve-month use of mental health services in the United States results from the National Comorbidity Survey replication. *Journal of the American Medical Association, 62*(6), 590–592.

Weine, S. M., Razzano, L., Brkic, N., Ramic, A., Miller, K., Smajkic, A., et al. (2000). Profiling the trauma related symptoms of Bosnian refugees who have not sought mental health services. *Journal of Nervous & Mental Disease, 188*(7), 416–421.

Westermeyer, J., Vang, T. F., & Neider, J. (1983). Migration and mental health among Hmong refugees. Association of pre-and postmigration factors with self-rating scales. *Journal of Nervous & Mental Disease, 171*(2), 92–96.

Wolfe, J., Schnurr, P. P., Brown, P. J., & Furey, J. (1994). Posttraumatic stress disorder and war-zone exposure as correlates of perceived health in female vietnam War veterans. *Journal of Consulting and Clinical Psychology, 62*(6), 1235–1240.

Wong, E. C., Marshall, G. N., Schell, T. L., Elliott, M. N., Hambarsoomians, K., Chun, C. A., et al. (2006). Barriers to mental health care utilization for U.S. Cambodian refugees. *Journal of Consulting and Clinical Psychology, 74*(6), 1116–1120.

Wong, E. C., Schell, T. L., Marshall, G. N., Elliott, M. N., Babey, S. H., & Hambarsoomians, K. (2007). The legacy of violence exposure: The relative physical health status of Cambodian refugees 2 decades after resettlement. Manuscript submitted for publication.

Ying, Y. W., & Hu, L. T. (1994). Public outpatient mental health services: Use and outcome among Asian Americans. *American Journal of Orthopsychiatry, 64*(3), 448–455.

24

A Frank Discussion on Asian Americans and Their Academic and Career Development

SUSANA M. LOWE

OUTLINE OF CHAPTER

Case Synopsis

A second-generation Filipina American, female undergraduate named Alicia is referred to the counseling center after revealing to her advisor that she is thinking about suicide. The student is on academic probation and tells the counselor she doesn't see any way out. She has been studying engineering, but her grades in that major have been consistently poor. She says to the counselor her family will never understand who she really is and that's why she feels hopeless.

Introduction

This chapter is designed for readers who are interested in Asian American academic and career development, with a special emphasis on concepts that would apply to those interested in becoming counselors. There is an introduction to two career assessment strategies and tools, followed by discussion of relevant sociocultural concepts. The role of **collectivism** as a value orientation that can both expand upon or at times conflict with predominant views on career development is discussed. Academic achievement and the impact of Asian Americans being seen as a **model** minority are also addressed. To encourage active learning, there are reflection exercises and activities referred to throughout the chapter. There are two clinical case studies toward the end of the chapter (with names and circumstances modified to protect client confidentiality) to challenge readers on how to apply the concepts that are discussed to professional counseling with Asian Americans. Woven throughout are anecdotes from the author's experience as a counseling psychologist who provided academic, personal, and career counseling to college students for a number of years.

Why focus a chapter on Asian American academic and career development? The educational and career development process for Asian Americans may frequently parallel that of another American who is not of Asian descent. However, it is important to examine how the experience for Asian Americans is informed by a variety of specific factors such as race, culture, and socio-economic status. In addition, one should take caution not to assume a simple one-size-fits-all approach when assessing for the importance of cultural versus other kinds of factors in describing someone's career or academic situation.

Sometimes people think dichotomously about their career and the rest of life. Doing so can be problematic because it implies people aren't living while they work, and it assumes that one's life at work doesn't influence life outside of work and vice versa. There is an assumption that unpaid work, such as volunteer or reproductive work, doesn't qualify as real work. (Reproductive work is unpaid work related to child-rearing, homemaking, and running a household.) In a professional counseling context, if a counselor doesn't consider the kind of life and lifestyle clients wish to have or feel they must achieve, the counselor could mistakenly guide clients toward a career that hinders their goals for life outside the paid work environment. For example, suppose a client expresses a desire to become a neurosurgeon at a brain trauma center, but tells the counselor that their highest priority is to spend time with the children; to focus on how to achieve just the professional goal is to obscure a major priority in the client's life. In some cases, the client might be the caretaker of aging parents and depending on the cultural and family dynamics, there might be some boundaries in the type of paid work or location of work the client seeks. In essence career and life are interwoven and if one is to be a counselor it is beneficial to look at life/career development in a holistic manner.

College students grapple with a lot of life questions, such as relationships, academics, family, and career issues. Many Asian Americans are raised to view higher education as the main path to success (Leong & Hardin, 2002). Anecdotally, common academic concerns that Asian American college students report to their counselors include parental expectations that they will excel academically. When taken to extremes, students can feel as if whatever they do is not enough or they feel stress and anxiety that they are underperforming, disappointing not only their parents but also themselves. Many Asian Americans have reported struggling to find a path consonant

"Take the opportunity now to explore. Don't feel locked in due to parental pressures or the urge to decide about the future. Get to know yourself; explore personal and work options." —Rick Low, Ph.D., Counseling Psychologist, UC Berkeley.

with their family's goals for them, but also something they feel is a good fit with their personality (Kim, 1993). Some have talked about how stressful it is when getting family financial support for college is made contingent upon parents approval of their field of study.

Another area to pay attention to when thinking about Asian Americans and academic/career issues is race. While there are no longer laws prohibiting Asian Americans from pursuing certain careers or preventing them from attending certain schools, stereotyping and racism have not disappeared. Students have said instructors still make assumptions that Asian Americans will excel in math and science, and when they don't they often fall through the cracks (i.e., don't receive the academic support they need). College students may also contend with fears of shame or loss of face to their families for not excelling in the manner that is expected. In addition, students are very aware of the role of race as a barrier to pursuing some careers, such as acting. Young people are taught very early on about how they do or do not fit the facial features and body image of those who are successful.

The next section introduces some widely used career development theories and tools. Although these were designed with a mainstream American audience in mind, they are useful resources when utilized with strategies that address culture and other factors related to Asian American clients.

Holland's Theory of Types

Some of the most helpful career development theories are those that make intuitive sense and are also fairly easy to apply. John **Holland's theory of types** is based on the idea that if the work environment is a good match for someone's personality, they are more likely to be happy and

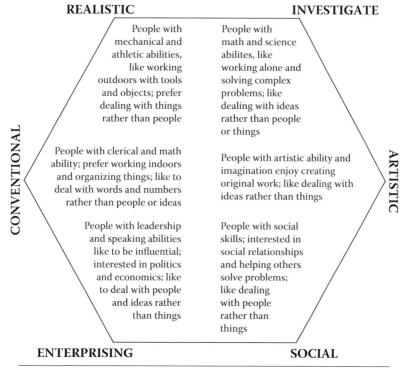

Holland Hexagon. From http://departments.oxy.edu/career/studentinfo/RIASEChexagon.htm.

satisfied with their job. This is just one cluster of factors to consider when exploring college majors and careers. In the counseling field, being open to examining issues from many different angles is wise. According to Holland (1985), there are six personality types or preferences in the world. He would describe most people as having a preference for a combination of two to three of these types. These are: (a) realistic (people who are drawn to the outdoors, using tools and machines, building things, being very mechanical); (b) investigative (analytical, mathematically or scientifically inclined, interested in researching problems or issues); (c) artistic (creative, unconventional, enjoy opportunities to express self, value originality); (d) social (cooperative, interested in helping people, altruistic, highly verbal); (e) enterprising (enjoy managing, persuading, especially in an atmosphere of financial reward, appreciate power, status, wealth); and (f) conventional (engage in organizing and planning, value dependability, follow rules and regulations, often work in financial institutions).

The Strong Interest Inventory is a widely used career assessment tool that helps identify which of the six Holland codes are most descriptive of a person's style. Using the principle of "congruence," the inventory can narrow the field of choices to those that offer a likely fit between personality preferences and the personality preferences prevalent in a variety of work environments. For example, rather than focusing on skills required for a specific career, this theory emphasizes finding people of like mind. Imagine being at a social gathering, and how you might gravitate toward certain people over others. This might be due to having more in common with those folks; the theory of types extends that idea to the workplace. There is a good deal of evidence to suggest that congruence is a factor in satisfaction at the workplace. The Skills Confidence Inventory is an instrument that is frequently offered as an accompaniment to the Strong Interest Inventory in order to compare interests to one's perception of competency in the same six personality preference areas. There is some research that suggests the 1994 Strong Interest Inventory is as valid an instrument to use with Asian Americans as with Caucasian Americans (Lattimore & Borgen, 1999).

Myers–Briggs Typology

The **Myers–Briggs typology** theory and indicator is also highly utilized in career counseling at colleges and universities (Leong, 1991). Katharine Briggs was intrigued by the work of Carl Gustav Jung on archetypes, and with her daughter Isabel Myers developed a typology and a method of measuring four bipolar dimensions of personality, the Myers–Briggs Type Indicator (MBTI). The distribution of these dimensions is then employed as part of a counseling discussion of how the client's personality style might fit with certain tasks on the job as well as different personalities and work environments. The theory of career decision making that Myers–Briggs best fits is trait-factor theory (Parsons, 1909), which is essentially the idea that having a clear understanding of the self, one's attitudes, and abilities as well as knowledge of the requirements and conditions of success in different lines of work can then help a person find an appropriate career.

The four dimensions measured include: (a) extroversion-introversion E-I (extroverts are energized by being in and interacting in the interpersonal world, whereas introverts are energized by time they spend alone or engaged in activities with a few people); (b) sensing-intuition S-N (sensing types use their five senses to perceive the world and value what is concretely perceivable whereas intuitive types perceive what is possible in the world and tend to prefer abstract thinking); (c) thinking-feeling T-F (thinking types prefer to make decisions based on logical rational thought whereas feeling types make decisions utilizing an analysis of impact on relationships); and (d) judging-perceiving J-P (judging types prefer to plan, make decisions, and have situations set whereas perceiving types like to be spontaneous, leave things open ended, and prefer to not to close off options). The theory posits that each person has a dominant, auxiliary, tertiary, and least preferred dimension. A person is expected to grow and develop their less developed sides as they mature, and learn to appreciate opposite types and how they contribute to relationships and the workplace (Sharf, 1997; Myers, 1962).

One reason why the MBTI might be popular is that it helps people think about how they are in the world, both in terms of how they perceive their environment and people as well as the way they make decisions. Students have reported that it's easy to remember the four letter codes and bring the profile back to their family and friends for further discussion. Anecdotally this has had the effect of stimulating conversation about what works in relationships, the causes of conflict, as well as encouraging further research into careers using a wealth of resources that tie MBTI profiles to workplace profiles.

Please turn to Activity 1 at the end of the chapter for an exercise related to these career inventories (for interest or possibly for credit). Most college and university counseling centers offer these career assessment inventories for free or for a nominal fee. College alumni are frequently eligible to get assessment at a fee lower than that available in the community.

The above assessments are utilized in helping clients choose an academic major and explore careers, but there is much more to deciding what to do with one's life. For many Asian Americans, cultural value orientation is likely to play a role as well.

The Role of Collectivism in Asian American Career Development

People acquire many cultural attitudes and beliefs through tacit learning, not always through explicit dogma. Most bicultural Asian American children become aware at some point that their families are different to some extent from White American families, as often indicated by language, food, and custom differences, especially for those Asian Americans who grew up in predominantly White American neighborhoods. One of the most noticeable issues raised by Asian American college student counseling clients has been the lack of parents saying "I love you" or talking about feelings. Students, especially those with immigrant parents, sometimes feel sad about not being able to communicate fully who they are, what they study at school, or what their extracurricular and community activities are about in such a way that parents understand. Cultural constructs, such as collectivism and **individualism** help to frame these phenomena.

A number of authors (Leong, 1991; Lowe, 2005) have discussed the roles of two value orientations, collectivism and individualism, in shaping the career development experiences of Asian Americans. It can be argued that cultural transmission of both orientations occurs for Asian Americans who are both strongly influenced by their families of origin as well as socialized and educated in the United States. It has been well documented that individualism is a predominant value system in the United States and western Europe, and that collectivism is predominant in a number of Asian nations (Markus & Kitayama, 1991; Triandis, 1995). What does this mean? Well, individualism is a system of thought whereby the self is defined as the basic unit of survival, where development includes individuating from one's family of origin, and personal goals take priority over the goals of those with whom one has relationships (Hui, 1988; Triandis, 1995). Collectivism presupposes that the group or collective is the basic unit of survival, that development involves seeking and maintaining interdependent relationships, and the needs of the collective supersede the needs of the individual. Collectivists value the success of the intimate group (i.e., frequently this is the family and other people with whom the individual has a close bond); a collectivist gains satisfaction by attending to and having needs attended to by the collective.

How does this pertain to academic and career development for Asian Americans? To the extent that Asian American families still adhere to collectivist values, and there is much variation in this due to time of immigration, socioeconomic status, acculturation, and so on, Asian American youth may feel strongly obligated to achieve not only for themselves but for their families. For example, a highly collectivist family is likely to have parents who invest a lot of resources and time emphasizing the importance of school for their child. They may convey, not necessarily in an explicit manner, that their child should focus on school achievement and not other things (well, perhaps honoring the family and older siblings and helping younger ones, but not dating before college!). There may be an understanding that parents made sacrifices for the child to have the ability to attend school in the United States or to afford the music lessons they are taking, for example. In turn, there is an implicit expectation that the child will work hard to be successful and that the achievement will be shared by their parents and family members. Asian American college student clients have recounted times when they were embarrassed or irritated by their parents boasting about their achievements to friends and relatives. Conversely, many students have expressed sadness and anxiety that if they did not meet the high standards expected of them by their parents and themselves that they would bring shame upon their families; that they would be a disgrace. From an individualist perspective, this interdependence between parents and children, especially during the college years when adolescents transition to adulthood, seems problematic. Asian American college students who seek counseling help for issues related to academic pressure often encounter counselors who were trained in a western individualist tradition whereby the counselor would suggest that parents are enmeshed with their children, and would encourage the student to individuate from their parents in order to focus on what they want for themselves (Lowe, 2005). This may indeed be the process the client chooses, but it is important to note when the counselor's guidance is actually stemming from a cultural bias that presumes individualism is better than collectivism.

In addition to involvement in their children's academics, some Asian Americans find their parents have strong wishes and desires for their children to pursue certain careers and have strong influence over career choice (Leong, Kao, & Lee, 2004). Tang (2002) found evidence that Asian American college students were more likely than Caucasian American students to have their career choices be influenced by family. Castro and Rice (2003) found evidence that Asian Americans do indeed have strong concerns about meeting high parental expectations. Moreover, some Asian American college student clients say that parents value careers with prestige and status, such as medicine, engineering, and law. For immigrant families who have experienced relative poverty in their countries of origin, some pursue the American dream in terms of climbing the socioeconomic ladder, accumulating wealth via the aforementioned types of careers. These careers are also fitting from a Confucian perspective, an influence on many East Asian Americans, in that they require many years of the noble pursuit of education. Castelino (2004) reported that less acculturated South Asian Americans felt greater interest and self-efficacy in pursuing the stereotypic jobs, whereas more acculturated South Asian Americans felt greater comfort breaking away from the expected paths. This finding seems to speak to the phenomenon that as Asian Americans acculturate, they and perhaps their families as well may be more willing to accept a wider variety of ways to define success in career.

In terms of counseling, several authors have suggested that counselors take into consideration the validity of collectivist perspectives on the relationships between Asian American children and their parents regarding academic achievement and career choice (Leong, 1991; Lowe, 2005). Bicultural Asian Americans are often caught between two worlds. If most of their education has been completed in the United States, they are very likely to have been taught that they can choose to be whatever they wish to be when they grow up, that when they become adults their lives are their own, and that the natural course of things is to become more like friends or equals with parents as they grow and mature. In contrast, within a more collectivist frame, the roles of children and parents remain ostensibly the same throughout life; grown children, even as they reach middle age, do not become more equal with parents as in the individualist frame. Parents likely continue to assume an important role in academic/career/life decision making, and there is a sharing of not only accomplishments but of material goods and time with one another. Lowe (2005) found that counselors who addressed collectivist issues with clients seeking career counseling were found to be more culturally sensitive than those who took a more individualist approach. A counselor who is well versed in both value orientations who can help a client negotiate potential conflicts between polar opposite influences is likely to be more culturally competent than someone who assumes either a rigidly individualistic or collectivistic viewpoint. For example, a counselor could explore the academic interests of their college student client in terms of what majors fit his personality style, as well as discuss to what extent, if any, there are expectations from parents for him to pursue a certain kind of academic field or career. From there, the counselor would assess if both personal and collective interests converge or diverge, and help the client figure out if there is the possibility of fulfilling expectations and desires on both sides. For example, the author earned a doctoral degree, which made her parents proud of her, satisfying their value of high achievement in education, but it was in a field that she felt very passionate about—psychology (not exactly the type of career her parents dreamed of)!

In conclusion, the career exploration process can be enhanced by utilizing person-environment as well as trait-factor approaches in conjunction with a discussion of cultural values and potential bicultural conflict between collectivist versus individualist perspectives. Because these values are often lived rather than explicitly learned or understood, well-informed counselors can help clients articulate the roots of their worldview. Where do their desires, wishes, hopes, and dreams come from, and what influences their family to wish or want what they want for them? Are their experiences idiosyncratic or perhaps related to historical and cultural worldviews? Counselors can also help their clients negotiate the varying influences in hopes of arriving at a way of being that makes sense in their identity, interpersonal, familial, and cultural context.

"Your life and career rarely follow the plan you intend or expect. My advice: Keep your road map in your glovebox, but know on the way to your destination, there will be detours and scenic routes that you think are slowing you down, but are actually really important to this journey called 'Your Life.'" —Amy G. Lam (far right), Ph.D., Research Director, California Young Women's Collaborative–National Asian Pacific Women's Forum (NAPAWF), and women from NAPAWF.

Please turn to Activity 2 at the end of the chapter for a reflection exercise on collectivism and individualism. The next section covers issues of academic achievement and risk for Asian Americans, shifting the focus from personality and cultural factors motivating academic and career development to examining some of the social forces that factor into the academic experiences of Asian Americans.

Asian Americans and Academics: A Model Minority?

According to the 2000 Census, Asian Americans graduated from college at a rate of 42.9% and earned advanced degrees at a rate of 6.5% (http://www.asian-nation.org, 2006). These rates of educational attainment are higher than for any other racial group in the 2000 Census. There are numerous theories on why Asian Americans excel at such high rates, most of which focus on cultural values within Asian families, such as those mentioned earlier in the chapter, as key factors in promoting high achievement in education. How Asian American families transmit these values and what effect they have on students has been the subject of much research. Asakawa and Csikszentmihalyi (1998) found that Asian parental practices structure their children's lives to facilitate academic success, including high involvement in college decision making, limiting time for nonacademic activities, and also requiring fewer chores (freeing time for homework) than European American families. At the same time, they found that Asian parents were less likely to be involved in actual academic activities, possibly due to language and educational gaps between immigrant parents and children. There is some evidence to suggest that families with East Asian origins "invest more aggressively in financial, human, and within-family social capital"; in other words keeping with a collectivist worldview, Asian families who value educational attainment tend to put more resources into their children's academic programs, regardless of whether economic resources are abundant (Kim & Chun, 1994; Sun, 1998). Others have examined Asian American motivation, and found that compared to Anglo American students, Asian Americans displayed higher levels of fear of failure, and that this in turn served as a motivating factor for achievement; avoiding failure (i.e., achieving academic excellence) would help prevent a son or daughter from a loss of face for the family or collective (Eaton & Dembo, 1997; Zusho, Pintrich, & Cortina, 2005).

However, Sue and Okazaki (1990) broke away from relying solely upon cultural values explanations and reported that Asian Americans may pursue education as the only viable means of upward mobility in the United States context, due to limitations and restrictions in other achievement pathways that don't rely on education, such as professional sports. They challenged the assumptions that there is something inherently academically superior about Asians or that cultural values explain the achievement phenomenon. Some researchers have also reported that Asian American peer support for academic excellence can compensate for the "negative consequences of authoritarian parenting" or other adverse factors impeding academic achievement (Gloria & Ho, 2003; Steinberg, Dornbusch, & Brown, 1992).

In U.S. society, Asian Americans are frequently viewed as a homogeneous group and characterized as having high academic achievement. Even though a high proportion of Asian Americans have earned college degrees, there is still a substantial proportion with less than a high school education (Gloria & Ho, 2003). When considering academic achievement among Asian Americans, it is important to disaggregate the data to examine the academic experiences of different groups within Asian America. For example, Filipinos, Pacific Islanders, and Southeast Asians appear to have lower levels of educational achievement compared to Chinese, Japanese, and Korean Americans (NEA, 2005). Teranishi (2002) reported that Southeast Asian Americans are not achieving at rates consistent with the model minority image: "In 1998, 64 percent of Southeast Asian adults were without a high school diploma [and] in 1990, 64 percent of

Hmongs, 43 percent of Cambodians, and 35 percent of Laotians lived in poverty, in contrast to 30 percent of African Americans and 28 percent of Latinos" (p. 19). A report by the National Education Association of the United States (2005) stated that 53.3% of Cambodians, 59.6% of Hmong, 49.6% of Laotians, and 38.1% of Vietnamese over the age of 25 had less than a college education. The report, which drew from the 2000 U.S. Census and nationwide educational research, stated that a major determination in level of educational attainment among various Asian American groups is social class.

Asian Americans raised in the U.S. context represent a much smaller percentage of these achievement statistics than those who are foreign born and raised. In 2001, "32 percent of doctorates conferred in the United States were to Asians, 86 percent of the degrees were actually conferred to international students from Asia" (Teranishi, 2002). This is an important point, as some people pit Asian Americans up against other ethnic Americans by saying that Asians as a racial minority can achieve—why can't others? Yet the fact that foreign-born and -raised Asians are advancing at far greater rates than those raised in American society challenges the assumption that Asian Americans educated in this society enjoy guaranteed upward mobility.

Because they have been treated as a homogeneous group always at the pinnacle of academic achievement, Asian Americans who are at risk for academic failure may not get the help or resources they need. Most of the literature on students at risk in the educational system focuses on other ethnic minority children, rendering Asian American youth in need of academic intervention invisible (Yeh, 2002). The fact that 58.4 percent of Indian and Pakistani Americans have completed college, but only 2.9 percent of Hmong Americans have college degrees is a prime example of why it is misleading to generalize about Asian American academic achievement. Immigration history and status are also pertinent factors. Asian Americans who came to the United States as refugees from war-torn countries, under dire circumstances tend to be more academically at risk than those who immigrated voluntarily or whose adjustment was facilitated by the U.S. government (e.g., the first wave of Vietnamese refugees received far more resources in resettlement than subsequent refugees from Southeast Asia). During a community dialogue with Cambodian leaders in Lowell, Massachusetts in 2000, people told stories that illustrated how war trauma affects everyone in a community. One leader said his mother would hide under the bed whenever she heard fireworks on the Fourth of July; he would often have to leave work to attend to her symptoms of post-traumatic stress. The same leader reported that Cambodian youth in his community feel anger and rage at the older generation for always going on about their own trauma from the past, and minimizing the challenges youth face in terms of gun violence and gang activity in their community now. He said he felt caught in the middle with no shortage of challenges he was facing himself!

Chang and Le (2005) found that delinquent peer affiliations among Chinese and Southeast Asian youth were related to negative school attitudes and decreased academic achievement. They suggested that Southeast Asian youth encounter a lot of adjustment problems, including discrimination. Even if some Asian Americans excel in education, academic achievement does not automatically translate into "effective functioning in life" (Ying, 2001). In fact, one report about Asian gangs in the Los Angeles area during the 1990s noted that despite high academic achievement, youth were involved in violent and criminal behavior, and that because of the achievement at school some of their high-risk behaviors were being overlooked and left untreated (Sweeney, 2002).

Additional stressors that may put Asian Americans at risk in education include English as a second language as well as economic pressures. Yeh (2002) reported that many low-income Asian American families feel obligated to take care of extended family members, and

"The hardest part of the work (antiracism/anti-oppression) is working within ourselves to unlearn the internalized oppression that we do onto ourselves and others and to learn to live life beyond survival, thriving to be whole in who we are."
—Truc Nguyen, anti-oppression trainer and community activist.

college-age Asian Americans may have responsibilities to care for their younger siblings or use their college financial aid to help support their families.

In conclusion, it is important to examine not only the reasons that contribute to academic success for some Asian Americans, but also to recognize that there is tremendous diversity within Asian America. Educational and social interventions are needed to mitigate the adverse effects of a variety of factors hindering Asian American academic mobility, such as refugee trauma, social class, language barriers, and so on. Furthermore, academic achievement does not necessarily equate to social adjustment or success. Please turn to the end of the chapter to do Activity 3.

The Glass Ceiling

According to the U.S. Glass Ceiling Commission (1995), Asian Americans were found to encounter an "impenetrable" **glass ceiling**. The glass ceiling refers to the barrier Asian Americans hit when it comes to being promoted to top management despite relatively high success in all other respects at the workplace. While Asian Americans are seen as a whole group to be high achieving in education, there are other racial stereotypes, such as being passive and having a philosophy of "don't rock the boat." Le (2006) also noted that highly educated Asian Americans are often institutionally tracked and confined to technical positions within companies because their supervisors assume they are not interested in managerial or executive positions. Le goes on to report that Asian Americans have trouble penetrating the old boys network, because they are persistently seen as outsiders and foreigners. Right after the 1998 Winter Olympics figure skating final, MSNBC's headline read, "American Beats Out Kwan," a rude reminder of how even while skating for the American team, representing her country, Asian American figure skater Michelle Kwan was still labeled a foreigner (Astudillo, 2002).

One invaluable resource on the glass ceiling effect on Asian Americans is Deborah Woo's (2000) book, "Glass ceilings and Asian Americans: The new face of workplace barriers." In it she reviews the three types of barriers to advancement that were articulated by the U.S. Glass Ceiling Commission and how they relate to Asian Americans. These include: (a) societal barriers; (b) internal structural barriers ; and (c) governmental barriers. For example, a societal barrier is the stereotype that Asian Americans are not interested in leadership positions. If managers in institutions generalize this stereotype to all Asian Americans that work for them, then the result is they will not identify, track, or mentor Asian American employees for advancement to leadership roles. An internal structural barrier might manifest in the form of not being able to penetrate the old boys network. Asian Americans are often blocked from important informal networks, which can impede an Asian American's ability to climb the corporate ladder. Finally, governmental barriers include inadequate dissemination of information about the glass ceiling as well as tendencies to lump Asian Americans into one interchangeable ethnic/racial group. For more information, refer to Woo (2000). Another resource for Asian Americans, especially those who wish to advance in the corporate world, is Jane Hyun's (2005) "Breaking the Bamboo Ceiling: Career strategies for Asians." Hyun's work is based on her experiences as an executive coach and diversity strategist to Fortune 500 companies and universities. It is often useful to hear from nonacademics about career strategies, and Hyun uses a variety of real-life examples to illustrate how Asian Americans can understand themselves individually and culturally in the workplace, as well as navigate challenging waters in the corporate world on the way to advancement. Please turn to the end of the chapter for Activity 4.

Thus far in this chapter, theories and concepts have been reviewed to help the reader conceptualize personality, cultural, racial, and socioeconomic issues in relation to Asian Americans and academic or career development. The next section contains a clinical case study to help illustrate how a professional counselor might work with an Asian American client who is grappling with issues regarding academics and career.

Case Study of Alicia

Alicia is a second-generation Filipina female client who came to counseling because she was feeling depressed and suicidal. She was an engineering major on academic probation. She stated that when she entered college, she felt strongly about the major, as she had always liked working with mechanical things, taking things apart and putting them back together. As she approached her second year, she began to feel disillusioned by the field and at the same time as if her skills were not up to par. In session she appeared emotionally shut down, stated she didn't care about life anymore. Upon further exploration, Alicia revealed that what she always wanted to do was serve her community. She grew up in a neighborhood that was plagued by joblessness and juvenile crime. She shared that she wanted to join the police force, but her mother dismissed the idea out of hand. The client said her mom didn't care about her wishes, that she just wanted the prestige of someone in the family becoming an engineer so that she could tell all the relatives about it.

The counselor's orientation toward counseling was integrative, incorporating interpersonal process theory and also helping the client to negotiate cultural and intergenerational differences between herself and her mom. The counselor made an effort to validate the client's sad and hopeless mood because she was feeling that her needs didn't matter to her mother. The counselor also tried to share that Asian parents often promote the value of careers that lead to a stable financial future over higher risk careers, especially when parents have immigrated from places/situations in which there was financial struggle. And in this student's case, her mom could no longer practice the profession she had in the Philippines because of different certification requirements as well as the cost and time of having to complete additional education while raising a family. By discussing her predicament within the context of being Asian American, her mom's immigration experiences, and socioeconomic issues, the counselor hoped to convey to the client that she is not alone in her struggle, that there have been other Asian Americans who experienced quandaries choosing a career that would please their parents when it so happens such a career is not what the individual wants.

This was a seemingly no-win situation in that the client cared about her family and didn't want to disappoint them (in fact already felt quite a bit of shame about being on academic probation), but at the same time was resistant to letting go of her own dream to serve her community in the justice arena. Often, when Asian Americans experience conflict with parents, they attribute the conflict to their parents' idiosyncrasies or personalities, even though frequently there is some cross-cultural miscommunication. The counselor said to her that sometimes Asian parents promote certain careers because that is the only way they believe their children can secure for themselves a happy and prosperous future. Sometimes, the counselor told Alicia, parents need to be educated about the possibilities of having success through channels other than those they'd heard about. The counselor said that Asian parents may not verbally express their love for their children; they might try to show it by their actions in supporting their children through school, guiding them the best way they know how. She explained it could be the case that her mom wants her to have a good life. The counselor asked Alicia if she had told her mom how difficult a time she was having with the engineering degree. She even went so far as to nudge the client to talk about her depression with her mom.

In the next session, the client reported that she had a conversation with her mom in which she expressed how she was feeling, why she didn't want to continue with engineering, and why she felt so strongly about wanting to be a police officer. To the client's surprise, her mom responded by saying it didn't matter to her that she stick to engineering, that she wanted her daughter to be happy with what she did. Her main concern was that her daughter follow through and finish what she started. Mom apparently felt she needed to nag her daughter to finish what she started and the engineering issue was in large part about trying to teach responsibility. In this session the client seemed more energized, even smiled a little, but then began to express irritation at mom's controlling behavior. In a few more sessions' time, the client managed to complete her application to the police force, reported that her mom had begun talking to her friends about her daughter's commitment to helping the community, and the client reported she was no longer having suicidal thoughts. She said she was beginning to tolerate her mom's fussiness over her; that although she was annoyed her mom reviewed her application and insisted on delivering it to the police academy herself, she did feel her mom cared and that she could make her proud of her after all.

Case Study of Alicia Discussion Questions

For undergraduate students, please consider the following questions:

1. Have you ever known an Asian American who got really stressed out, anxious, depressed, or suicidal because of fear of not living up to their parents' expectations academically? What about career expectations?

2. Have you ever known an Asian American who pursued a "stable" career but at the same time had a burning passion to do something else? What was that something else and did the person plan to fulfill that passion somehow? How?

3. Write a paragraph on your thoughts and reactions to reading the case study. How did the theories and ideas from the chapter inform your reading of the case?

For graduate students and/or beginning therapists, please consider the following questions:

1. Prior to reading this chapter, how might you have approached working with Alicia yourself? How about after you read the chapter?

2. What additional ideas do you have for working with a student with Alicia's presenting concern?

3. How would you have worked with Alicia if her mom refused to give her consent and approval to her daughter pursuing a career in law enforcement?

Case Study of Rex: The Importance of Considering Life Transitions

When students go to their college counseling center to do career exploration during a time when life, family, and friends are in a stable place, it seems feasible to fall back into looking at interest inventories, personality inventories, exploring job/internship opportunities, lifestyle choices, cultural influences, and so on. However, life has a way of changing dramatically and unpredictably at times. It is important to discuss

"Career paths are full of curves and side routes that allow you to explore new ideas and most importantly shape a career that is tailored to your unique talents and strengths. A lot of times, people who have taken less traditional career paths or have had more than one career are innovative, flexible, and willing to take risks—key qualities needed to stand out as a leader in your field." —ManChui Leung, Director, HIV Program, Asian and Pacific Islander American Health Forum.

some of the ways dealing with life can be a surprise and actually change the way one approaches career or academic development. For example, the death of a family member or otherwise significant person in one's life can often make time seem like it is standing still. Financial hardships, responsibility for caretaking of elders or younger siblings, demands to be near home to help with the family business, are all examples of life issues that can significantly impact academic life and the way a person approaches developing a career. Here is another case illustration described initially without the counselor's conceptualization.

Rex was a Korean American junior who came to counseling after finding out that his father was diagnosed with a terminal illness. At first he was in shock, just talking about the treatments and needing to make trips home. As the weeks went by, and his father's condition worsened, Rex started to have trouble concentrating on schoolwork. He started to show signs of depression, specifically anhedonia (lack of taking pleasure in things he usually enjoyed), irritability, hopelessness, self-loathing, sadness, desire to retreat from friends. He consented to a medication evaluation and was prescribed antidepressants. Rex's dad didn't speak much English, and Rex felt as if he could not communicate well with him, that his dad didn't really know him or understand him. This was a profound sorrow for him. Secondly, Rex was convinced that he was not a good son, that he had been impatient with his dad, rebelled often, and now that he was dying, there was no way to make up for that. Within a few months' time, Rex's father passed away and Rex continued to feel aimless, hopeless, and sad. He had no interest in school, but felt he had to finish for his dad.

After his father's death, Rex floundered. He could not articulate any meaning in his life. He thought that he might try to have a better relationship with his mom. He decided to pursue a graduate education, although he persisted in his belief that he was a bad son, and nothing could change that.

Case Study of Rex Discussion Questions

1. What are your initial thoughts about Rex's condition and situation?
2. What are your ideas, or how do you conceptualize the main issues to work on in counseling?
3. What are some of the personal, familial, and cultural themes in his life?
4. How would you approach counseling him?

Assuming the reader has reflected on the case, here are some thoughts from a professional counselor's point of view. First, it is important to realize that sudden changes in life can and do happen, and this can throw off a person's plans or take them on a different path than what had been envisioned. When someone is anticipating or grieving the loss of a loved one, bearing witness to their experience and listening to their story is paramount. Counselors do not have the ability to take the person's pain away or change the situation, and so sitting with the person and showing them that someone cares, that someone can tolerate the intensity of the emotions can matter to the client a great deal. There are themes of loss, not only of Rex's parent, but of his ability to ever fulfill his sense of obligation to be a good son. Because of the language barrier between him and his parents (a frequent phenomenon in second-generation Asian Americans due at least in part to the fact that American K-12 schools rarely offer Asian language programs), Rex is left feeling permanently disconnected from his dad. Rex felt as if his dad would want him to finish school and go to graduate school, but since his passing, Rex has just been going through the motions. The challenge in counseling might be to help Rex find meaning in life again, perhaps for him to show some intention in getting to know the parent who is still living. What will Rex do with the limitations in that relationship, and now that he realizes that life can end rather suddenly, what experiences does he want to have with his mom, for himself? Can Rex overcome his self-loathing and feel as if he deserves to live and thrive even if he might never feel he was a good son?

Putting Something Into Practice

Readers are encouraged to interview an Asian American who loves what he or she does, whether it is paid or unpaid work or a combination of both. Sample questions include: What do you do? How did you get into it? Were there experiences or people in your past that influenced you to do this work? What's rewarding about it? What's challenging? Do you have any advice for me? Does your paid work afford you the ability to have time for the kinds of hobbies, passions, family life, and so on, that you want? Is there something missing? What's next for you?

Summary

This chapter provided an overview of several theories on career development that college students are likely to encounter. The reader was invited to consider a variety of contextual factors, such as race, culture, and socioeconomic status in formulating ideas about Asian Americans and their academic and career development. Areas highlighted were the role of collectivism and individualism, model minority stereotypes, an examination of Asian Americans who are at risk academically, and the glass ceiling. The chapter provided a variety of reflection exercises and two case studies to deepen the understanding of readers who are potentially interested in entering the counseling profession.

"Looking back, I wish I knew about other career options! I have always loved fashion and design, but thought that career options in this field were impractical and difficult to achieve. As an Asian American woman who grew up in Nebraska, I wish I had more role models in college. From an early age, I felt I was 'stereotyped' by peers and teachers regarding my career choices. People often *assumed* I was going to be a physician or a doctor of some sort. Throughout my early educational experience I believe I internalized these values, and did not realize the value of exploring other career options until recently." —Juli Fraga, Psy.D., psychologist and entrepreneur.

Key Terms

Collectivism: A value orientation that presupposes the group or collective is the basic unit of survival, that development involves seeking and maintaining interdependent relationships, and the needs of the collective supersede the needs of the individual. Collectivists value the success of the intimate group; a collectivist gains satisfaction by attending to and having needs attended to by the collective.

Glass ceiling: The relatively high success of Asian Americans, and yet the seeming wall they hit when it comes to being promoted to top management.

Holland's Theory of Types: A career development theory positing that matching the person's personality preferences to the work environment may lead to work satisfaction.

Individualism: A system of thought whereby the self is defined as the basic unit of survival, where development includes individuating from one's family of origin, and personal goals take priority over the goals of those with whom one has relationships.

Model minority: The perception that Asian Americans excel in areas of academic, economic, and career success where other ethnic minorities in the United States do not. This tends to be an overgeneralization that assumes Asian Americans are a homogeneous group.

Myers–Briggs typology: A method of measuring four bipolar dimensions of personality; the distribution of these dimensions describes how personality style might fit with certain tasks on the job as well as how this style interacts with different personalities and work environments.

For Further Learning and Suggested Readings

Activity 24.1: Make an appointment at your campus counseling and career center. Ask to take the Strong Interest Inventory (and Skills Confidence Inventory if available) and the MBTI. See if you can guess your RIASEC code (two to three top preference types for you) and your MBTI code (four letters: E or I, S or N, T or F, J or P) before you receive your results. Look at the top 10 careers listed on your summary sheet and see whether any of those careers are ones that you have considered, whether or not you think you are capable of getting into those careers. Are there any careers you are interested in, but hesitate to pursue? Why? Take your MBTI results and interview some friends to determine whether some of your similarities and differences hinge on the bipolar dimensions. For example, as a "P," I prefer to leave my weekends open but one of my best friends likes to plan far in advance; sometimes that causes conflict! Next, do some research at your career resource center or library to see what kinds of careers people with your Holland and MBTI codes frequently choose. Make a list of careers that are still in the running for you, whether you think you might pursue them directly out of college or if it is something you might like to do later in life.

Activity 24.2: Do you know any Asian Americans, including yourself if applicable, whose parents: (a) expect high academic achievement; (b) prefer that their children choose careers requiring higher education and providing stable financial futures; or (c) discourage pursuit of any activities that might detract from academic success? For extra credit, read the Markus and Kitayama (1991) article or the Hui (1988) article. Make a list of the kinds of values and communication styles that seem familiar to you or to an Asian American friend. Which values and communication styles don't resonate with you? To what extent do you think the differences might be due to family/individual acculturation and adoption of individualist values?

Activity 24.3: Thinking about your academic history, who was central in helping you get to college? What were the barriers you had to overcome? What, if any, are current barriers to your academic success? Have you ever assumed that all—or the vast majority of—Asian Americans excel in school? Do you know an Asian American who struggled in school? Who, if anyone, offered support and assistance to that person? What was the outcome for that person?

Activity 24.4: Have you ever wondered what people assume about you upon first meeting you? Make a list. If you are Asian American, how many of these characteristics relate to racial stereotypes? Get into a small group of peers in your class. Discuss the similarities and differences on your list. Ask someone who is not Asian American and someone who is Asian American outside of class what they would assume about you, particularly regarding your academic capabilities, interests, career goals, and likelihood of future success. Reflect on how these discussions felt, and write a paragraph (perhaps for extra credit) about whether and to what extent thinking about racial stereotypes affects your thoughts about your future career. How might barriers defined by the U.S. Glass Ceiling Commission inform your thoughts about career advancement?

Students today are fortunate to have books, the Web, and increasingly (slowly) more media that create visibility for Asian Americans in diverse careers, in addition to those "stable" careers (not that there is anything wrong with those!). Here are some resources for you to check out.

Books

APAs in the New Millennium. (2000). *Asian American policy review, IX.* Cambridge: J. F. K. School of Government. A compendium of current social and political issues for Asian Americans in the 21st century. [*S.M.L.: Look up the members of the executive advisory board and academic advisory board for examples of prominent Asian Americans (and for inspiration).*]

Garcia, R. (Ed.). (2001). *Out of the shadows: Asians in American cinema.* New York: Asian CineVision.

Ling, A. (Ed.). (1999). *Yellow light: The flowering of Asian American arts.* Philadelphia: Temple University Press. Biographies of Asian-American artists, writers, poets. [*S.M.L.: Check out Arthur Sze's poetry!*]

Moon, K. R. (2005). *Yellowface: Creating the Chinese in American popular music and performance, 1850s-1920s.* New Brunswick, NJ: Rutgers University Press. [*S.M.L.: Historical analysis of Chinese performance, race, and the imaging of Chinese Americans through music and stage performance.*]

Poon, I. (2001). *Leading the way: Asian American artists of the older generation.* Wenham, MA: Gordon College.

Wong, D. (2004). *Speak it louder: Asian Americans making music.* New York: Routledge. [*S.M.L.: Ethnomusicology text that explores Asian Americans creating music in historical and contemporary contexts.*]

Web Sites[1]

Online Resources for Occupational Information

America's CareerInfonet—career exploration: http://www.acinet.org/acinet/library.asp?category=1.4

Career Exploration—occupational information: http://www.khake.com/page2.html

Career Library Web site—occupational information: http://www.uhs.berkeley.edu/students/careerlibrary/index.shtml

Careers in Business: http://www.careers-in-business.com

CollegeGrad—career information: http://www.collegegrad.com/careers/all.shtml

Jobstar—guides for specific careers: http://www.jobstar.org/tools/career/spec-car.cfm

---

[1] Courtesy of the Career Library and stellar librarian/manager Kathleen Cassidy, M.A., at UC Berkeley.

Occupational Outlook Handbook—U.S. Department of Labor: http://www.bls.gov/oco
Onet Online—occupational information: http://online.onetcenter.org
Princeton Review: http://princetonreview.com/cte
Salary.com—search for nationwide job salaries: http://www.salary.com
Wetfeet Press—industry professionals; career and industry profiles: http://www.wetfeet.com
UC Berkeley Career Center—career fields: http://www.career.berkeley.edu/Infolab/CareerFields.stm
Vault Reports—industry information: http://www.vault.com/hubs/industrylist.jsp

Majors and Career Information
Careers for You Major—University of Kansas: http://www.ku.edu/%7Euces/major/index.shtml
College Majors and Career Information—Rutgers University: http://careerservices.rutgers.edu/Career
    Handouts.html
Kaleidoscope of Careers—College of Mount St. Joseph: http://www.msj.edu/career/guide/kaleidoscope.
    htm
Majors and Careers—Indiana University: http://www.indiana.edu/%7Eudiv/majors/alphahome.html
What Can I Do With a Major In...?—University of North Carolina at Wilmington: http://www.uncwil.
    edu/stuaff/career/majors

Graduate School Information
Career Library Web site—graduate school information: http://uhs.berkeley.edu/students/careerlibrary/
    index.shtml
Gradschools.com: http://www.gradschools.com
Petersons—graduate program search: http://www.petersons.com
PhD.org—grad school rankings: http://www.phds.org/rankings
UC Berkeley Career Center—graduate school: http://career.berkeley.edu/Grad/Grad.stm

Google Searches
Becoming a _____
Career Information _____
Professional Association for _____

References

Asakawa, K., & Csikszentmihalyi, M. (1998). The quality of experience of Asian American adolescents in activities related to future goals. *Journal of Youth and Adolescence, 27*(2), 141–163.

Astudillo, R. (2002). *Michelle Kwan controversy still haunts us.* AsianWeek.com, March 1–March 7.

Castelino, P. (2004). *Factors influencing career choices of South Asian Americans: A path analysis.* Unpublished doctoral dissertation, Loyola University Chicago.

Castro, J. R., & Rice, K. G. (2003). Perfectionism and ethnicity: Implications for depressive symptoms and self-reported academic achievement. *Cultural Diversity and Ethnic Minority Psychology, 9*(1), 64–78.

Chang, J., & Le, T. N. (2005). The influence of parents, peer delinquency, and school attitudes on academic achievement in Chinese, Cambodian, Laotian, or Mien, and Vietnamese youth. *Crime & Delinquency, 51*(2), 238–264.

Eaton, M. J., & Dembo, M. H. (1997). Differences in the motivational beliefs of Asian American and non-Asian students. *Journal of Educational Psychology, 89*(3), 433–440.

Gloria, A. M., & Ho, T. A. (2003). Environmental, social, and psychological experiences of Asian American undergraduates: Examining issues of academic persistence. *Journal of Counseling & Development, 81,* 93–105.

Holland, J. (1985). Making vocational choices: A theory of vocational personalities and work environments. Englewood Cliffs, NJ: Prentice Hall.

Hui, C. H. (1988). Measurement of individualism-collectivism. *Journal of Research in Personality, 22,* 17–36.

Hyun, J. (2005). *Breaking the bamboo ceiling: Career strategies for Asians.* New York: Harper Collins.

Kim, E. Y. (1993). Career choice among second-generation Korean-Americans: Reflections of a cultural model of success. *Anthropology and Education Quarterly, 24,* 224–248.

Kim, U., & Chun, M. B. J. (1994). Educational "success" of Asian Americans: An indigenous perspective. *Journal of Applied Developmental Psychology, 15,* 329–343.

Lattimore, R. R., & Borgen, F. H. (1999). Validity of the 1994 Strong Interest Inventory with racial and ethnic groups in the United States. *Journal of Counseling Psychology, 46*(2), 185–195.

Le, C. N. (2006). Employment & occupational patterns of APAs. *Asian Nation: The Landscape of Asian America.* Retrieved from IMDiversity.com

Leong, F. T. L. (1991). Career development attributes and occupational values of Asian American and White American college students. *The Career Development Quarterly, 39,* 221–230.

Leong, F. T. L., & Hardin, E. (2002). Career psychology of Asian Americans: Cultural validity and cultural specificity. In G. Hall & S. Okazaki (Eds.), *Asian American psychology: Scientific innovations for the 21st century* (pp. 131–152). Washington, DC: American Psychological Association.

Leong, F. T. L., Kao, E. M, & Lee, S. (2004). The relationship between family dynamics and career interests among Chinese Americans and European Americans. *Journal of Career Assessment, 12*(1), 65–84.

Lowe, S. M. (2005). Integrating collectivist values into career counseling with Asian Americans: A test of cultural responsiveness. *Journal of Multicultural Counseling and Development, 33*(3), 134–145.

Markus, H. R., & Kitayama, S. (1991). Culture and self: Implications for cognition, emotion, and motivation. *Psychological Review, 98,* 224–253.

Myers, I. B. (1962). *The Myers-Briggs type indicator.* Palo Alto, CA: Consulting Psychologists Press.

National Education Association of the United States. (2005). *Status of Asian Americans & Pacific Islanders in Education.* Washington, DC.

Parsons, F. (1909). *Choosing a vocation.* Boston: Houghton Mifflin.

Sharf, R. S. (1997). *Applying career development theory to counseling* (2nd ed.). Pacific Grove: Brooks/Cole.

Steinberg, L., Dornbusch, S., & Brown, B. B. (1992). Ethnic differences in adolescent achievement: An ecological perspective. *American Psychologist, 47,* 723–729.

Sue, S., & Okazaki, S. (1990). Asian American educational achievement: A phenomenon in search of an explanation. *American Psychologist, 45,* 913–920.

Sun, Y. (1998). The academic success of East-Asian-American students – An investment model. *Social Science Research, 27,* 432–456.

Sweeney, N. (2002). Conditions favorable for increase in Asian gang activity. *Milwaukee Journal Sentinel,* p. 01B.

Tang, M. (2002). A comparison of Asian American, Caucasian American, and Chinese College Students: An initial report. *Journal of Multicultural Counseling and Development, 30,* 124–134.

Teranishi, R. (2002). The myth of the super minority: Misconceptions about Asian Americans. *The College Board Review, 195,* 17–21.

Triandis, H. C. (1995). *Individualism and collectivism.* Boulder, CO: Westview Press.

U.S. Glass Ceiling Commission. (1995). *A solid investment: Making full use of the nation's human capital* (final report of the commission). Washington, DC: U.S. Government Printing Office.

Woo, D. (2000). *Glass ceilings and Asian Americans: The new face of workplace barriers.* Walnut Creek, CA: AltaMira Press.

Yeh, T. L. (2002). Asian American college students who are educationally at risk. *New Directions for Student Services, 97,* 61–71.

Ying, Y. (2001). Asian American college students as model minorities: An examination of their overall competence. *Cultural Diversity and Ethnic Minority Psychology, 7*(1), 59–74.

Zusho, A., Pintrich, P. R., & Cortina, K. S. (2005). Motives, goals, and adaptive patterns of performance in Asian American and Anglo American students. *Learning and Individual Differences, 15,* 141–158.

25

Asian American Activism, Advocacy, and Public Policy

KAREN Y. CHEN and CHERI L. PHILIP

OUTLINE OF CHAPTER

Case Synopsis

Teresa was one of the thousands of Vietnamese immigrants affected by Hurricane Katrina in New Orleans, Louisiana, in 2005. During the hurricane, she and her family decided to flee to Houston, Texas, because it is known to have a large Vietnamese community. However, she and her family have no friends and family in the city, and had difficulty finding help. They found out that their home was completely destroyed during the natural disaster, and they ended up taking refuge in the Chinese shopping mall along with innumerable other Vietnamese immigrants displaced by the hurricane. In the aftermath, Teresa started to feel sad and hopeless about her situation. She was referred to a therapist to help deal with her problems, but unfortunately, centers in Houston offering mental health services for Vietnamese Americans and Asian Americans, in general, were severely understaffed in the wake of the hurricane. It took a very long time for Teresa to find a therapist to treat her. Asian American activists brought local, state, and national attention to this growing problem of limited culturally and linguistically appropriate mental health services. While their efforts were met with some success, there continues to be a shortage of mental health providers trained to meet the needs of an increasingly diverse country.

Introduction

The history of Asian American **activism**, **advocacy**, and **public policy** is varied and complex. Teresa's case illustrates this complexity by highlighting the multiple domains in which Asian Americans can play a role in better serving the needs of the Asian American community at large. This chapter provides historical and contemporary perspectives on the role of Asian Americans and their engagement with the American sociocultural, legal, and political systems. The first section provides an overview of the history of Asian Americans and their involvement with the American system on issues related to U.S. citizenship, racial equality, and educational structures and curriculum. While Asian Americans are often considered to be the model minority, this is a very limited and one-sided characterization. This perception overshadows the collective social issues and struggles that this group faces as the 21st century American landscape shifts.

The following section highlights some of the citizens, activists, and politicians who forced the public to take notice of the role of Asian Americans in the various social, educational, and political domains. The final section of the chapter is devoted to discussing the arenas in which Asian Americans have been active in critiquing the American educational, legal, and political system and the role that psychologists can play in connecting communities, advocacy organizations, and governmental structures to affect change at the local, state, and national levels.

Who Are Asian Americans?

Asian Americans' role in public policy and advocacy has been somewhat ambiguous because Asian Americans are so heterogeneous (representing over 20 nationalities), and there has been an ongoing debate about what it means to be Asian American. The Asian American population has been through a number of changes since the earliest recorded immigrants from Asia reached America's shores in 1820 (as reported by the Immigration Commission: Leung, 1989). Among these changes have been a reclassification of racial status (see *Takao Ozawa and Bhagat Singh Thind vs. the United States Supreme Court*: Takaki, 1998) and an incorporation of newer Asian immigrants (post-1960s) into the larger Asian American racial label. In fact, according to new estimates recently released by the U.S. Census Bureau, the nation's population of Asian ancestry continues to grow at a much faster rate than the population as a whole.

According to the 2000 Census, the largest proportions of Asian Americans in the United States in 2000 were of Chinese ancestry (2.7 million), followed by 2.4 million Filipinos, 1.9 million Asian Indians, 1.2 Vietnamese, and 1.1 million Koreans. These five groups represent 80% of the Asian American population and are primarily foreign-born, with continued ties to their native countries (U.S. Census Bureau, 2002). Because Asian Americans have not historically been very cohesive due to the vast cultural and linguistic differences among the Asian ethnic groups, advocacy among the group hasn't been as united when compared with other racial groups. However, with the growing number of U.S.-born Asian Americans, this group is now starting to identify more with the racial label, *Asian American*, and we are seeing more advocacy efforts among Asian Americans as a group rather than as separate Asian ethnic entities. Despite a somewhat fractured engagement in public policy and advocacy, Asian Americans have been involved in American public life during many critical points of U.S. history related to civil rights, and in recent years have become increasingly more engaged in public policy development and advocacy.

History of Asian American Advocacy and Activism

Scholars note that Asian Americans have been at the front lines of some of the major social justice movements related to foreign policy (e.g., protesting Vietnam War) as well as education reform (e.g., establishment of racial and ethnic studies departments) and racial discrimination (e.g., mobilizing to protest hate crimes perpetrated against Asian Americans: Fong, 1998; Takaki, 1998; Lien, 2001).

Educational Protest

In the late 1960s, students at San Francisco State College (now San Francisco State University: SFSU) became disgruntled after the university fired a Black faculty member (George Murray) and showed a lack of support for their Black studies program. They were also frustrated with the lack of support for the formation of other ethnic studies programs (e.g., Asian American, American Indian studies, etc.), leading to the decision to mobilize, strike, and protest college decisions. The students collectively protested across racial lines to pressure the university to

Asian American activism.

provide a curriculum that reflected their social experiences and interests. This resulted in the longest student strike in history (approximately 5 months) and many university-level changes, including the formation of Black, Asian American, and Native American studies programs and the appointment and reinstatement of faculty members of color (Whitson, 1977).

As a result, Asian American studies programs have sprouted in colleges and universities around the country since the late 1960s, reflecting the interest in understanding the Asian American experience and discourse. However, there has been some disconnect within the departments regarding who is really Asian American, and areas of collaboration and coalition have been a challenge. There has been fractious tension within Asian American studies programs regarding the criteria by which one qualifies as an authentic or representative Asian American (Kibria, 1998; Prashad, 1998; Shankar & Srikanth, 1998). Some scholars argue that it is necessary to reconsider the ways in which Asian Americans are defined as some groups have been left out of the dialogue regarding curriculum development (Shankar & Srikanth, 1998). However, it has been noted that there are others in the field that have been content to focus largely on issues pertinent to the Chinese and Japanese American experience (Mazumdar, 1989). Since the initial definition of the Asian racial group referred primarily to those with roots in East Asian countries, those from Southeast or South Asia have at times been left out of the dialogue (Shankar & Srikanth, 1998). However there has been a reshifting of who is actually included in the Asian American racial category because the demographics of Asian Americans has changed significantly post-1965. In fact, the five fastest-growing Asian ethnic groups are Bangladeshi, East Indian, Pakistani, Hmong, and Sri Lankan (U. S. Census Bureau, 2002). Thus, scholars have come to recognize that Asian Americans have become a much more broad and diverse group.

Mobilization Against Anti-Asian American Discrimination

When looking historically at the immigration patterns of Asian ethnic groups to the United States, there were several critical points that contributed to present-day advocacy around issues that have implications for the Asian American community today. First, with the onset of hard economic times in the 1870s, other immigrants and European Americans began to compete for

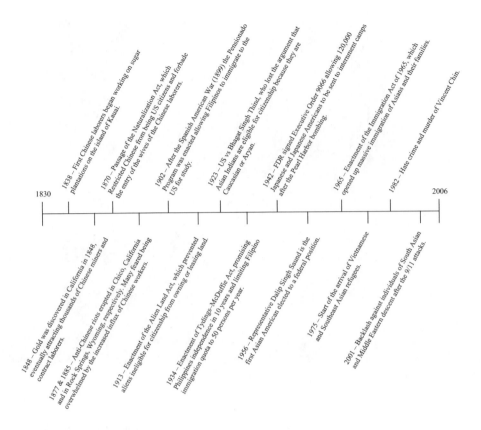

the jobs traditionally performed by Chinese immigrants. Along with economic competition came racial suspicion, which led to anti-Chinese riots and pressure for the exclusion of Chinese immigrants from the United States. The result of this pressure was the Chinese Exclusion Act, passed by Congress in 1882 (Takaki, 1998). This act also applied to several Asian ethnic groups (Japanese, East Indians, Filipinos) and made it difficult for them to gain entry into the United States or to be able to obtain U.S. citizenship.

The Asian American population does have a history of experience with racial discrimination. Most Asian American experts would argue that one of the greatest affronts to the Asian American community in U.S. history is the internment of Japanese Americans following the bombing of Pearl Harbor. Unfortunately during the internment, the Japanese American community, and even the greater Asian American community, was not well coordinated or equipped to fight against this gross social injustice. Many Asian Americans responded by showing their patriotism to this country. Specifically, Japanese Americans were more likely to emphasize their American identity rather than their Japanese identity, and Korean and Chinese individuals were often quick to disassociate themselves from their Japanese peers (Daniels & Kitano, 1970; Daniels, Taylor, & Kitano, 1986; Fong, 1998; Nagata, 1990; Takaki, 1998).

Interestingly, analogous patriotic behavior was found among individuals of Middle Eastern and South Asian descents after the 9/11 attacks on September 11, 2001. Specifically, these individuals prominently displayed American flags on their cars and in and around their homes to emphasize their American identity. Examples of violations of the civil liberties of several Asian ethnic groups abounded during this time and may have produced an elevated sense of patriotism by these groups to avoid overt (as well as subtle) backlash (Jayadev, 2002; Mak, 2002).

In the decades following the Japanese internment, Japanese Americans unified as a community and persistently sought reparations from the U.S. government for the loss of physical property and physical and emotional damage caused by the internment. As a result of their efforts, Congress passed the Civil Liberties Act of 1988, which became known as the Japanese American Redress Bill. The act acknowledged the injustice of the internment and mandated Congress to pay each victim of internment in reparations totaling $1.2 billion (about $20,000 per individual) and an additional $400 million in benefits. The reparations were sent with a signed apology from President Clinton on behalf of the American people (Nagata, 1993; Takaki, 1998).

More recently, the American public has witnessed the unification of Asian Americans around hate crimes directed at their community. Asian Americans have brought to light violent attacks of hate directed at their community members and advocated for justice against these hate crimes. One of the more well-known acts of racial discrimination against Asian Americans is the murder of Vincent Chin. During the national economic recession of 1982, two white autoworkers upset about their recent layoff from their jobs at Ford Motor Company (due to competition from Japanese automakers) took out their aggressions on an Asian American male (of Chinese origin) whom they mistook for Japanese. The perpetrators beat the young Chinese American engineer, Vincent Chin, to death with a baseball bat. During the beating, one held Chin down while the other swung the bat repeatedly at his head. The injuries from the beating resulted in a broken skull and shortly after, Chin died from these injuries. For this heinous crime the two men each received probation and a mere $3,780 fine (see American Citizens for Justice, 1983, for a review).

The Asian American community was outraged by this clearly violent racial hate crime and the perpetrators' light punishment. The community mobilized and led mass protest and advocacy efforts to seek justice against Chin's unwarranted death. While the perpetrators never received a harsher sentence then what was described above, Asian Americans were able to bring national attention to this case, and the American public became more cognizant of Asian American hate crimes. The community's united efforts around this cause paved the way for more successful advocacy against racial discrimination of Asian Americans in the future.

Racial discrimination against Asian Americans has also manifested in other ways. Recent trends toward outsourcing historically middle-class jobs to countries such as India and China have resulted in negative sentiments toward these countries and their citizens. Due to the perpetual foreigner status that Asian Americans still cope with today (see Goto, Gee, & Takeuchi, 2002, for a review), this sentiment influences how East Indian and Chinese Americans are perceived in this country. As anti-immigrant sentiments continue to grow and persist, many Asian American advocacy organizations have worked tirelessly to fight injustice directed at Asian immigrants.

Major Events Related to Advocacy in Asian American History

The Model Minority Myth and Coalition Building

When the term *model minority* was first coined in *New York Times Magazine* and *US News & World Report*, it largely applied to a belief that Japanese and Chinese immigrant individuals were self-sufficient and their children were able to succeed because of close family ties and a strong work ethic (Petersen, 1966). However, as time has passed there have been additional beliefs associated with the model minority conceptualization, including the notion that all Asians are good at math and are high academic achievers. While the model minority stereotype is seemingly positive, not all Asian Americans share this view because the stereotype carries great pressure to live up to extremely high standards (Wu, 2002).

Frank Wu, legal scholar, dean and professor of law at Wayne State University in Detroit, Michigan, describes the conundrum of Asian Americans as model minorities. A former professor of law at Howard University (1995–2004), Wu discusses his role as the first Asian American faculty member in a predominantly African American academic context and what is required for Asian Americans to be fully engaged in a coalition with other groups of color when it comes to petitioning for minority issues in his book, *Yellow: Race in America beyond Black and White*. A central

Grace Lee Boggs. (Courtesy of Grace Lee Boggs and Amy Gerber.)

issue that Wu uses to preface his argument hinges on the notion that "Asian Americans are made, not born" (Wu, 2002, p. 360). The statement, "being made," refers to the notion that the naming and creation of the term Asian American initially derived from a need to develop the group for political reasons, particularly after the civil rights movement (Espiritu, 1992). While this label can serve to unify the Asian American community, that was not its original intention when the racialization of the Asian racial group began (Lee, 2004). Wu noted from personal experience that he felt obliged to be Asian American and join Asian American organizations to deal with the issues that affected a broad range of individuals of different ethnicities.

Beyond the ability to work with individuals of varying Asian ethnicities, Asian Americans can also work with other racial and ethnic minority groups. Wu noted that the categorizations used to define races are artificial and can serve to either divide or unite communities of color. Scholars have argued that the racialization of Asian Americans as a model minority (suggesting superiority over other groups and a perceived advantage in terms of socioeconomic status) has limited their ability to partner with other non-White groups when dealing with issues around oppression and racism (Lien, 2001; Omi & Winant, 1994). However, oppression and racism does exist in the Asian American community. Wu (2002) stressed that not only must Asian Americans be united, but they must also join others from a variety of racial backgrounds in the pursuit of racial equity and justice.

Grace Lee Boggs and Yuri Kochiyama are two Asian American activists who have dedicated their lives to cross such racial boundaries in coalition building. Both women have worked with African Americans and Latino/as on a range of social justice issues from civil rights and racial discrimination to environmental justice.

Activists to Know

Grace Lee Boggs was born in Providence, Rhode Island, to Chinese immigrant parents in 1915. Boggs received her BA from Barnard College in 1935 and her PhD in philosophy from Bryn

Mawr College in 1940. In 1953 she moved to Detroit where she married James Boggs, an African American labor activist, writer, and strategist. Working together in grassroots groups and projects, they were partners for over 40 years until Mr. Boggs's death in July 1993. In 1992, with her husband and other community organizers, Boggs founded Detroit Summer: a multicultural, intergenerational youth program that has been focused on rebuilding Detroit. Boggs has been an activist, writer, and speaker for over 60 years. Her political involvement encompasses major American social movements in labor, civil rights, Black power, Asian American, women's, and environmental justice. Her autobiography, *Living for Change*, published by the University of Minnesota Press in March 1998, is widely used in university classes on social movements (Boggscenter.org, 2006).

During the 1960s, Yuri Kochiyama was among the many Asian Americans who embraced the Black Power movement (Wei, 1993). She and other Asian Americans were inspired by the teachings of Malcolm X, which focused on developing a nationalistic ideology and feelings of pride in one's ethnicity (Lien, 2001). She became an active member of the Black Power movement and was even one of Malcolm X's confidantes. Kochiyama, a resident of Harlem, was instrumental in taking the lead on many issues affecting the Asian American community. Her work over the years has involved issues such as international political prisoner rights, nuclear disarmament, and Japanese redress for World War II internment (Fujino, 2005).

Current Advocacy Efforts Among Asian Americans

So far, this chapter has highlighted some of the key social justice issues that Asian Americans have participated in and described some of the influential Asian Americans leaders who engaged

Yuri Kochiyama. (Courtesy Associated Press/Mike Wintroath, photographer.)

and challenged the American public about the role of Asian Americans in this country. This section discusses ways in which Asian Americans more recently have been involved in advocacy and public policy. Asian Americans increasingly realize that to effectively influence policies and programs that directly affect them, they need to become an integral part of the political process. In the past few decades, an increasing number of Asian Americans are engaged in civic participation, with many taking on leadership positions and playing a significant role in local, state, and national politics (Chang, 2001).

Much of Asian Americans' increased involvement in public advocacy can be linked to a strong commitment by national Asian American organizations to educate and involve its members and the broader Asian American community in public policy and advocacy. For example, the Japanese American Citizens League (JACL) has been a leader within the Asian American community since the early part of the twentieth century. JACL, as the oldest and largest Japanese American civil rights organization, was founded in 1929 to address issues of discrimination targeted specifically at individuals of Japanese ancestry residing in the United States. Their mission continues to be securing and maintaining the civil rights of Japanese Americans and all others who are victimized by injustice and prejudice.

The Organization of Chinese Americans (OCA) has also been a prominent figure within the Asian American community in numerous advocacy initiatives. Its members were among the first Asian American groups to advocate to their Congressional representatives on relevant Asian American issues during the mid-1970s. Some of its early accomplishments included a House Resolution for an Asian/Pacific American Heritage Week, to include Chinese Americans and other Asian Americans federal minority opportunity programs advocating for expanding, and collaborating with the National Council of La Raza, the largest national Latino civil rights and advocacy organization, to defeat a proposed reduction to a bilingual education program in a federal education legislation. Even though the mission of OCA, which has 80 chapters and college affiliates, is to serve primarily Chinese Americans, it has and continues to work with the entire Asian American community. For example in 1996, OCA established the Asian and Pacific Islander American Vote project (APIAVote). The APIAVote, as a national coalition of nonpartisan and nonprofit organizations, developed and implemented the first ever nationwide Asian American voter education and registration program. During the 2004 election year, APIAVote conducted 28 community voter outreach training sessions, registered over 45,000 new Asian American voters, and made "Getting Out the Vote" calls in seven different Asian ethnic languages in key locations.

More recently, the Asian American community has witnessed a strong network of Asian American–oriented civil rights organizations serving as tireless advocates of social justice issues for its community. This network includes the Asian American Justice Center (AAJC) of Washington, DC, the Asian American Institute of Chicago, Asian Pacific American Legal Center (APALC) of Southern California in Los Angeles and the Asian Law Caucus in San Francisco. These organizations have been instrumental in advancing the civil rights of Asian Americans in issues related to affirmative action, anti-Asian violence prevention/race relations, U.S. census, immigrant rights, language access, and voting rights.

Each of these Asian American organizations is committed to increasing community education and participation on public policy and civil rights issues affecting all Asian Americans. For example, AAJC supported University of Michigan during their affirmative action lawsuits and filed amicus curiae briefs in the U.S. Court of Appeals and in the U.S. Supreme Court arguing the benefits of diversity for all Americans, including Asian Americans. AAJC, which produces an annual audit of hate crimes against Asian Americans for the past 10 years, has also been a leader among civil rights organizations in the fight against anti-Asian American biased crimes.

The Asian American Institute created a Voting Rights program to monitor voting polls in the Chicago area to ensure that the availability of bilingual voting assistance, as mandated by the Department of Justice. APALC, as the nation's largest legal organization serving the Asian and Pacific Islander (API) communities, has improved immigrant rights in numerous settings. For example, they increased public awareness about poor labor practices in the garment industry, which disproportionately affects Asian immigrant women, and won several cases against institutions for language discrimination. Asian Law Caucus is the nation's oldest legal and civil rights organization serving low-income Asian American communities. Not only did they litigate the well-known Asian American case *Korematsu v. United States* (a controversial 1944 Supreme Court case ruling that the United States government's decision to send Japanese Americans to the internment camps was not unconstitutional), but they have also provided free legal service to hundreds of low-income clients in areas related to housing, employment, immigration, government benefits, and senior rights for over 30 years.

Asian American Activism on School Campuses

Advocacy of Asian American issues is not just limited to changing local, state, and federal legislation. Many Asian American grassroots efforts started on college and university campuses. In fact, many Asian Americans first became activists for their communities when they were undergraduates.

As described earlier, Asian American students, alongside other racial and ethnic minority students, actively advocated for the establishment of ethnic studies programs at San Francisco State College. To this day, Asian American students continue to fight for Asian American studies programs in their colleges and universities. However, Asian American activism extends beyond their push for an Asian American studies department. Asian American students have been getting college officials to take notice of the many challenges that Asian American students *and* faculty face. For example, Southeast Asians and Pacific Islanders are underrepresented in colleges and universities and benefit from affirmative action initiatives and programs that promote campus diversity. Thus, when racial preference programs were under attack, such as through California's Proposition 209 in 1996 and the affirmative action lawsuits against the University of Michigan in the early 2000s, many Asian American students were in the front lines and rallied their support for affirmative action and campus diversity. Their actions ranged from holding educational workshops about these issues to lobbying for the defeat of Proposition 209 and protesting in front of the Supreme Court. Asian American students have also advocated for other important issues, including increasing the number of tenured, Asian American faculty; providing financial aid to Asian Americans with economic hardships; establishing Asian American resource centers and instituting more culturally inclusive college curriculum; and developing tighter partnerships between Asian American students and their communities and between Asian American students and other racial and ethnic minority groups.

Many Asian American organizations, both volunteer-based and professional nonprofits, have been working with undergraduate and graduate students to develop their advocacy and leadership skills to effectively mobilize and champion issues affecting their community. For example, the OCA has developed a unique training program for Asian American student leaders and activists, called the Asian/Pacific Islander American College Leadership Training. These 2-day trainings, which are held at different universities across the country each year, hone students' leadership and organizational skills within the context of understanding the viewpoints and experiences of Asian Americans and other students of color. This program has been an invaluable experience for innumerable young Asian Americans. Several national and regional-based student organizations, including the Midwest Asian American Student Union (MAASU), the

East Coast Asian American Student Union (ECAASU), and the National Asian American Student Conference (NAASCON), have also held annual conferences with a similar goal to educate Asian American students about issues affecting their community and to develop the necessary skills to address them.

There is clearly no shortage of issues for Asian American students to advocate for. Many Asian American undergraduates embraced their college years because they gained greater knowledge about issues affecting themselves and their community. Subsequently they were spurned into action to improve the lives of fellow Asian Americans. The college environment has been a feeding ground for young Asian Americans to learn and cultivate their advocacy skills. Many Asian Americans have continued to hone those abilities in their future endeavors, whether it was through their volunteer efforts or actually working in the policy field.

Asian Americans in Politics

The first Asian American who was elected into a federal political position as a Congressperson was Dalip Singh Saund in 1956. Since then, many more Asian Americans have been represented in federally elected and appointed positions. In 2006, Asian Americans were represented in 2 Senate seats, 6 House of Representatives seats, and 2 U.S. Cabinet positions. Despite the increasing number of Asian Americans in public policy at the local, state, and national level, Asian Americans are still underrepresented in policymaking positions.

During the early 1990s, several national Asian American political figures realized they needed to find a mechanism to effectively mobilize the few Asian Americans in office and become a united voice for the Asian American community. Thus the Congressional Asian Pacific American Caucus (CAPAC) was formed in 1994. It was established by then Congressman Norman Mineta as a **bipartisan** and **bicameral** Congressional caucus to promote Asian American issues and advocate for the concerns of this community. The Caucus includes members of different Asian ethnicities and members with a high concentration of Asian Americans in their district or who have an interest in Asian American issues.

During its early days, CAPAC was led by four prominent Asian American members of Congress: Congressman Norman Mineta, Congresswoman Patsy Mink, Congressman Robert A. Underwood, and Congressman David Wu. CAPAC has grown substantially since its inception. In 2006, CAPAC was chaired by Congressman Mike Honda, with 11 members serving on the executive board and over 100 associate members. Since its establishment, the Caucus has worked on a multitude of legislative initiatives supporting Asian Americans, including promoting the visibility of Asian Americans in political and civic processes, advocating for refugee and immigrant issues related to their legal protection and economic opportunities, and supporting health and education initiatives that affect Asian Americans.

Even with the creation of CAPAC, the Asian American policy community still felt that Asian Americans needed a better understanding of public policy and advocacy. Thus, Asian Pacific American members of Congress and other APA community leaders founded the Asian Pacific American Institute for Congressional Studies (APAICS) in 1995 as an organization to build the political pipeline of Asian Americans at all levels—local, state, and national. As a nonprofit, nonpartisan, educational organization, APAICS has and continues to support, promote, and conduct education and informational activities, research and programs designed to enhance and increase the participation of the Asian American community in the political process within all facets of the government.

Role of Asian American Psychologists in Public Policy

As mentioned above, Asian Americans, in general, are becoming more engaged in politics. The same holds true for Asian American psychologists. Both in Washington, DC, and many

regions heavily populated with Asian Americans, Asian American psychologists have represented themselves in various aspects of civic participation. For example, they have testified
in hearings for local, state, and federal legislatures on a range of issues pertinent to Asian
Americans and other racial and ethnic minority groups, including the need for culturally and
linguistically appropriate mental health services and immigrant rights related to social and
health care. Asian Americans have also been invited by the White House and different federal
agencies to serve on nationally recognized committees. For example, Dr. Larke Huang was
appointed by President George W. Bush to serve on the President's New Freedom Commission
on Mental Health (http://www.mentalhealthcommission.gov, 2002), and in April 2006 she was
appointed the Senior Advisor on Children, Office of the Administrator, in the Substance Abuse
and Mental Health Services Administration (SAMHSA) at the U.S. Department of Health and
Human Services. Angela Oh, a renowned Asian American activist, was appointed by President William Clinton to serve on the President's Initiative on Race (http://clinton5.nara.gov/
Initiatives/OneAmerica/america_onrace.html).

However, compared to the general public and even to other racial and ethnic groups, Asian
American psychologists can still be more politically active. Asian American psychologists, as
both a racial and ethnic minority and a mental/behavioral health provider, have a unique voice
to contribute to various hot topics currently being debated. Some of these issues include availability and accessibility of linguistically and culturally appropriate behavioral and mental health
services and the effects of hate crimes on society and its victims.

Use of mental health services is slowly becoming more accepted in the general public. There
are an increasing number of mental health providers in this country. However, the Surgeon
General's 2001 report, *Mental Health: Culture, Race and Ethnicity*, found that there is a lack of
behavioral and mental health providers and services targeting the Asian American community
and other communities of color (http://mentalhealth.samhsa.gov/cre/default.asp). This was particularly apparent during the aftermath of Hurricane Katrina, when there was a clear lack of
culturally and linguistically competent health and social services for communities of color was
clearly apparent. While this issue received massive national attention, it was mostly presented
as a Black-White conflict and it overshadowed the problem within the Asian American community affected by the hurricane. Specifically, a significant number of Southeast Asian immigrants,
particularly of Vietnamese descent, in Louisiana were displaced from their home, and many
experienced trauma and other mental health problems as a result of the natural disaster. However, there was an extreme shortage of mental health providers who were bilingual in English
and Vietnamese or even had experience working with the Vietnamese American community.
Thus, many hurricane survivors of Vietnamese descent did not receive proper or rapid treatment for their psychosocial problems.

During these types of situations, Asian American psychologists can be great advocates on
behalf of the Vietnamese and other Asian American communities about the need for culturally and linguistically appropriate mental and behavioral health services for the greater Asian
American population. They understand and recognize the role of cultural sensitivity in quality
mental health services. Their activism can be exhibited in multiple domains beyond just working towards changing local, state, and federal legislation. Efforts can include: advocating for
translators within the agency; leading outreach efforts in their own communities and other
communities of color; working with professional organizations, such as the American Psychological Association and American Counseling Association, to promote policies and programs
supporting more culturally and linguistically appropriate mental health services; and helping
clients recognize how systemic and institutional racism affects their behavior.

Asian American psychologists can also participate in advocacy efforts on other pertinent
issues, such as the need to eliminate racial hate crimes. The Asian American community has

witnessed their share of racial hatred toward their community members since the first Asian immigrants came to this country. Biased crimes against Asian Americans persist at high levels. In fact after the 9/11 attacks, there was a spike in hate crimes and racial discrimination targeting South Asians (National Asian Pacific American Legal Consortium, 2002). The Asian American community worked swiftly to condemn these acts of violence and hold the government accountable for investigating and prosecuting the perpetrators. Asian American psychologists can provide a unique perspective in these advocacy efforts. Specifically, there is a significant body of psychological research focused on different aspects of racial discrimination, from examining the effect of racial discrimination on victims and their family and community to understanding the causes of racial hatred and discrimination (Clark, Anderson, Clark, & Williams, 1999; Rumbaut, 1994). The literature provides convincing support for why there needs to be concerted efforts to eliminate racial hate crimes and prevent future acts of racial discrimination. This scientific research is a distinct source of data that highlights the ways in which the Asian American psychology community can continue to fight against racial hatred.

How to Become Involved in Advocacy and Public Policy

Even though people may be civic-minded or concerned about a particular social issue, sometimes they do not know how to become engaged in advocacy efforts. Fortunately, there are now a lot more opportunities available to introduce young and more advanced scholars to the world of public policy.

For individuals interested in engaging in the political process at the federal level, the ideal place to experience the political process is in Washington, DC, working in either the legislative or executive branch. Many universities offer internships or study abroad opportunities for their students to spend a semester in the nation's capital. To increase the pipeline of Asian Americans in the political process, several Asian American organizations, including the OCA and JACL, also offer policy internships and postgraduate fellowships for young Asian Americans in the District of Columbia. In fact, the Conference on Asian Pacific American Leadership (CAPAL) offers a Washington Leadership Program, a free summer educational and leadership development workshop series for any Asian American student interning in Washington, DC. Established over two decades ago, the Washington Leadership Program informs young Asian Americans about issues concerning their community and their role in public policy.

Individuals can also easily participate in public policy at the federal level in their hometown. Each House of Representatives member has an office in their district, and each senator has offices in the major cities of their state. These offices always welcome students to volunteer or intern in their office. This would be a great opportunity to understand the political process without having to reside in the nation's capital.

Public policy also operates at the local and state level. It would be opportune to take advantage of understanding regional politics since in some ways it is easier to influence local policies and programs than federal policies and programs. Similar to working at the district offices of your federal congresspersons, internship and volunteer opportunities are also always available with the state legislators and local elected officials.

As described earlier, activism for many Asian Americans began on college campuses. Many college campuses have Asian American organizations whose mission is to educate fellow students about issues affecting their community or actively advocate for issues pertinent to Asian Americans in their colleges or in the larger community. Asian American students can become involved with these organizations. Or for colleges and universities with a smaller Asian American population, Asian American students can connect to other Asian Americans and become activists for their community through participation in regional or national Asian American student organizations. These are just a few examples of how Asian Americans can be involved in public policy and advocacy.

Summary

This chapter provided a snapshot of Asian Americans' experience with advocacy and public policy, from identifying pivotal moments in U.S. history that spurred the Asian American community to mobilize and advocate for their rights as human beings and as U.S. citizens to describing important individuals and organizations who led the community in their fight for social justice. While Asian Americans have made significant progress in improving their situation in the United States, Asian Americans still struggle to be seen as equals to their mainstream counterparts. Continued engagement in the policy arena, whether it is at the grassroots level or working within the government, is one necessary component toward addressing those challenges and breaking down those barriers.

Discussion Questions

1. What are some major milestones that characterize the history of Asian Americans in their struggle for racial and political equality?
2. What are the different capacities (e.g., as a mental health provider, psychology student or faculty, behavioral health researcher, an Asian American) through which you can get involved in advocacy activities pertinent to the Asian American community?
3. How would you compare Asian Americans' involvement in public policy and advocacy to that of other groups of color, such as African Americans and Latino/as?
4. How can psychology programs improve their curricula and policies to better serve the needs of their Asian American student and faculty?
5. What are some of the key issues that Asian Americans can become more politically engaged in?

Case Study

Thus far, this chapter has focused on providing the historical background and current trends of Asian Americans, including Asian American psychologists, and their role in public policy. As described above, there are many issues that Asian Americans can be politically engaged in, such as supporting education reform that benefit Asian Americans and combating hate crimes against Asian Americans. This case study will provide an example of how Asian American psychologists and even any psychologists working with a diverse population can advocate for the concerns and needs of their Asian American clients.

Teresa is a Vietnamese immigrant who began showing signs of depression in the aftermath of Hurricane Katrina. She was referred to a therapist to seek help for her psychological problems, but there were no psychologists who were fluent in Vietnamese or even culturally sensitive to Vietnamese issues immediately available to see her. Teresa's situation is unique in that her condition was exacerbated by the natural disaster, and the series of events following the natural disaster. Specifically, Houston was overwhelmed in the ability to adequately accommodate and address all of the concerns and needs of the Vietnamese individuals displaced by the hurricane. Culturally and linguistically appropriate mental health providers were few and far between. Unfortunately, this problem is not unique just to the Houston area following the hurricane.

The lack of culturally and linguistically appropriate mental health providers is a national problem.

Even though the number of racial and ethnic minorities is growing in this country, there are not enough mental health providers trained to serve the increasingly diverse community. Prevalence of mental health problems is relatively consistent across racial groups, although rates of certain types of psychological problems might vary across groups. However, people of color are less likely to seek help for mental health problems compared to Whites. The main reasons include: the shortage of mental health providers culturally trained to work with racial and ethnic minority groups; the limited number of mental health centers with bilingual therapists; and the lack of able translators to work with individuals who have low English fluency.

Many local, state, federal legislators, government officials, and psychology graduate programs realize the need to address this problem of accessible and available, culturally and linguistically appropriate mental health services. A 2004 report from the President's New Freedom Commission on Mental Health confirmed the growing mental health needs of racial and ethnic minorities, including limited capabilities of mental health providers to provide culturally sensitive services. In response to this problem, more psychology graduate programs are incorporating cultural competency training into their core curriculum. Furthermore, some laws have attempted to rectify this problem to make mental health services more accessible to racial and ethnic minorities. However there is not widespread consensus about the best way to solve this problem. Advocates of this issue have tried to rally the Asian American community and mental health providers around this issue, but they continue to face an uphill battle. One major obstacle is that many key legislators and policymakers do not see this as a primarily local, state, or federal problem. Until they do, very little progress will be made.

Case Study Discussion Questions

For undergraduate students, please consider the following questions:

1. What are your initial reactions to this vignette?
2. What are some ways that you can get involved within your college or within your community to help groups who face issues that are similar to Teresa's?
3. What are other issues that the Asian American community can mobilize and rally around? What kind of tools and skills does the Asian American community need to effectively advocate around these issues?

For graduate students and/or beginning therapists, please consider the following questions:

1. Do you believe that there is a lack of culturally and linguistically appropriate mental health services available for racial and ethnic minorities? If so, as a mental health professional, what do you think your role is in addressing this problem both at the systematic and client level?
2. What are some ways that you could advocate for clients whom you feel are not getting adequate mental health services?
3. How can mental health practitioners connect with policy makers to make mental health services more accessible for the racial/ethnic minority clientele that they serve?
4. How can your research serve as a form of intellectual advocacy that provides empirical and theoretical support to this issue and other problems affecting communities of color?

5. What are some ways that psychology graduate programs can better prepare their students to serve the needs of the Asian American community and other communities of color?

Key Terms

Activism: Intentional action to bring about social or political change and is in support of, or opposition to, one side of an often controversial argument.

Advocacy: Acting on behalf of an individual or group of individuals in order to give them a voice against systems of oppression and educating individuals, communities, and government on social justice and human rights issues.

Bicameral: The characteristic of having two branches, chambers, or houses, such as the United States Congress, which is composed of the Senate and the House of Representatives.

Bipartisan: An effort endorsed by both political parties (i.e., Democrats and Republicans) or a group composed of members of both political parties.

Public policy: Working with institutions to change or create laws and practices, which are in accord with the needs of the public or a given population.

For Further Learning and Suggested Readings

Asian American Organizations

American Citizens for Justice: http://www.americancitizensforjustice.org/index.htm
Asian American Justice Center: http://www.advancingequality.org
Japanese American Citizens League: http://www.jacl.org
Japanese Internment: http://www.pbs.org/childofcamp/resources/books.html
Organization of Chinese Americans: http://www.ocanatl.org

To learn more about the featured activists (Grace Lee Boggs and Yuri Kochiyama, respectively) in this chapter visit:
http://www.boggscenter.org
http://www.learntoquestion.com/seevak/groups/2004/sites/kochiyama/main.html

To learn more about Asian Americans in politics check out:
Dalip Singh Saund: http://www.aaa-fund.org/history/dalip_saund.asp
Elaine Chao: http://www.whitehouse.gov/government/chao-bio.html
Norman Mineta: http://www.whitehouse.gov/government/mineta-bio.html
Patsy Mink: http://bioguide.congress.gov/scripts/biodisplay.pl?index=M000797

Movies

The Grace Lee Project
Who Killed Vincent Chin?
Yuri Kochiyama: Passion for Justice

References

American Citizens for Justice. (1983). Retrieved March 4, 2006, from http://www.aamovement.net/history/acj1.html

Chang, G. (2001). *Asian Americans and politics: Perspectives, experiences, and prospects.* Palo Alto, CA: Stanford University Press.

Clark, R., Anderson, N. B., Clark, V. R., & Williams, D. R. (1999). Racism as a stressor for African Americans: A biopsychosocial model. *American Psychologist, 54*(10), 805–816.

Daniels, R., & Kitano, H. L. (1970). *American racism: Exploration of the nature of prejudice.* Englewood Cliffs, NJ: Prentice Hall.

Daniels, R., Taylor, S. C., & Kitano, H. L. (1986). *Japanese Americans, from relocation to redress.* Salt Lake City, UT: University of Utah Press.

Espiritu, Y. L. (1992). *Asian American panethnicity: Bridging institutions and identities.* Philadelphia: Temple University Press.

Fong, T. P. (1998). *The contemporary Asian American experience: Beyond the model minority.* Upper Saddle River, NJ: Prentice-Hall.

Fujino, D. C. (2005). *Heartbeat of struggle: The revolutionary life of Yuri Kochiyama.* Minneapolis, MN: University of Minnesota Press.

Goto, S., Gee, G. C., & Takeuchi, D. (2002). Strangers still? The experience of discrimination among Chinese Americans. *Journal of Community Psychology, 30*(2), 211–224.

Jayadev, R. (2002). *DOD plan would restrict immigrants in computer industry.* Independent Media Institute, CA. Retrieved March 4, 2005, from http://www.alternet.org/911oneyearlater/12735

Kibria, N. (1998). The racial gap: South Asian American racial identity and the Asian American movement. In L. D. Shankar & R. Srikanth (Eds.), *A part yet apart: South Asians in Asian America* (pp. 69–78). Philadelphia: Temple University Press.

Lee, E. (2004). American gatekeeping: Race and immigration law in the twentieth century. In N. Foner & G. M. Fredrickson (Eds.), *Not just black and white: Historical and contemporary perspectives on immigration, race and ethnicity in the United States* (pp. 119–144). New York: Russell Sage Foundation.

Leung, G. (1989). Timeline of Asian immigration. *Asian American reader.* Unpublished manuscript. Retrieved February 6, 2005, from http://www.cis.umassd.edu/~gleung/nacaf/Timeline.htm

Lien, P. (2001). *The making of Asian America through political participation.* Philadelphia: Temple University Press.

Mak, K. (2002). The Asian Pacific American Legal Center (APALC) Remembers 9/11.

Mazumdar, S. (1989). General introduction: A woman-centered perspective on Asian American history. In Asian Women United of California (Eds.). Making waves: An anthology of writings by and about Asian American women (pp. 1–22). Boston: Beacon Press.

Nagata, D. (1990). The Japanese American internment: Impact upon the children of the internees. *Journal of Traumatic Stress, 3*(1), 47–69.

Nagata, D. (1993). *Legacy of injustice: Exploring the cross-generational impact of the Japanese American internment.* New York: Plenum Press.

National Asian Pacific American Legal Consortium. (2002). *Backlash, Final Report: 2001 Audit of Violence against Asian Pacific Americans.* Retrieved January 6, 2007, from http://www.advancing equality.org/files/2001_Audit.pdf

Omi, M., & Winant, H. A. (1994). *Racial formation in the United States: From the 1960s to the 1990s.* London: Routledge.

Petersen, W. (1966). Success story, Japanese-American style. *New York Times Magazine,* 20–43.

Prashad, V. (1998). Crafting solidarities. In L. D. Shankar & R. Srikanth (Eds.), *A part yet apart: South Asians in Asian America* (pp. 105–126). Philadelphia: Temple University Press.

Rumbaut, R. G. (1994). The crucible within: Ethnic identity, self-esteem, and segmented assimilation among children of immigrants. *International Migration Review, 28,* 748–794.

Shankar, L. D., & Srikanth, R. (1998). Closing the gap: South Asians challenge Asian American studies. In L. D. Shankar & R. Srikanth (Eds.), *A part yet apart: South Asians in Asian America* (pp. 1–24). Philadelphia: Temple University Press.

Surgeon General. (2001). *Mental health: Culture, race, ethnicity.* Retrieved January 6, 2007, from http://mentalhealth.samhsa.gov/cre/default.asp

Takaki, R. (1998). *Strangers from a different shore.* Boston: Little, Brown.

U. S. Census Bureau. (2002). *The Asian population: 2000.* Census 2000 Brief No. C2KBR/01-16. Retrieved April 26, 2003, from http://www.census.gov/population/www/cen2000/briefs.html.

Wei, W. (1993). *The Asian American movement.* Philadelphia: Temple University Press.

Whitson, H. (1977). *Strike! A chronology, bibliography, and list of archival materials concerning the 1968-1969 strike at San Francisco State College.* Washington, DC: Educational Resources Information Center. Retrieved October 15, 2006, from http://www.library.sfsu.edu/strike

Wu, F. (2002). *Yellow: Race in America beyond black and white.* New York: Basic Books.

26
Physical Health and Wellness

SHAMIN LADHANI and SZU-HUI LEE

OUTLINE OF CHAPTER

Case Synopsis

Meet Salma, a 21-year-old, first-generation, Pakistani American female. Salma has been seeking counseling for depression for 6 months. Recently, she reports to her psychologist that she has been experiencing cramps in her abdomen in addition to her depressed mood symptoms. Salma shared that her cramps become so painful it debilitates her. She has been skipping classes and canceling social engagements as result. Salma is too embarrassed to let her family and friends know she is in therapy let alone letting them know about her physical pain. Salma was shocked when her psychologist suggested that Salma consults with her gynecologist. How could her psychologist suggest something that only a married woman should worry about? Salma comes from a culture where female reproductive health is not openly discussed. She is taught that gynecological visits were only necessary if one is sexually active, which based on her upbringing, also means someone who was married. Therefore, Salma has not been receiving annual Pap smears and has not taken preventative steps for diagnoses of cervical or ovarian cancer. Upon the strong recommendation of the psychologist, she was referred to a physician for her abdomen pains. After some testing, Salma was informed that she has developed large cysts in her ovaries and has developed cancer in her uterus and will not be able to have children. The news was devastating to Salma and her family.

Introduction

This chapter will present research and discuss the physical and medical health concerns pertaining to Asian American populations. Thus far, several chapters in this book have discussed the psychological and mental health of Asian American and Pacific Islander (AAPI) populations. Physicians and mental health professionals have found that physical, medical, and mental health are dynamically related to one another. Especially within the majority of Eastern cultures it is impossible to talk about mental health without including physical health. For Asian Americans in particular the physical and mental aspects of a person are well intertwined. Eastern philosophy has long subscribed to the idea of mind and body as an interconnected entity with reciprocal

effects on both. Therefore, specific physical health concerns relevant to AAPI populations are important to highlight along with the relevant mental health issues. Given the vast diversity of this group, the concepts presented here will provide a general overview of health issues across the life span. The chapter will begin with discussing the major health concerns impacting Asian Americans (i.e., heart disease, diabetes) and will survey issues faced by infants, children, and the elderly of this population. Following that, the chapter will explore the Asian cultural context and worldview in relation to illness understanding and expression. For example, what do **Taoism** and the **yin-yang principle** have to do with how Asian Americans understand their physical health? Continuing with the exploration of the Asian worldview, the chapter will turn the focus to issues of death and dying to provide a more holistic understanding of how Asians approach physical health on the continuum. Finally, the chapter will conclude with issues of health disparity and provide recommendations for health prevention and wellness.

Major Health Issues

You might be surprised to know that when assessed as a whole, Asian Americans appear to be one of the healthiest groups in the United States but when Asian ethnic subgroups (e.g., Chinese, Korean, Vietnamese) are examined individually, great disparities exist (Esperat, Inouye, Gonzalez, Owen, & Feng, 2004). It is difficult to fully and accurately capture the status of health in Asian Americans and its ethnic subgroups because Asian Americans are often lumped together in one large sample group in research studies. Unfortunately, the broad scope of available data can limit the awareness of the true health status of Asian Americans and mask the health disparities that exist within this population. Furthermore, health disparities are often ignored due to the model minority myth discussed in earlier chapters. This myth portrays Asian Americans as excelling above the dominant majority in socioeconomic and educational attainment but is

deceptive as it leads people to ignore the real health issues faced by this population (Esperat et al., 2004). In this section, prominent health issues within the Asian American communities will be surveyed. Whenever the data are available, health status of specific Asian ethnic subgroups will be incorporated.

The American Heart Association reported the leading causes of death among Asian American men and women to be cancer and heart disease (see Figure 26.1), with heart disease as the leading cause of death for Asian Americans (American Heart Association, 2004). Heart disease

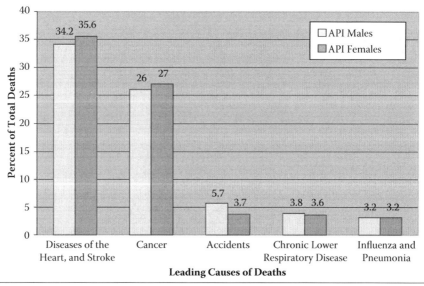

Figure 26.1 Statistics on Asian/Pacific Islanders and cardiovascular diseases. (American Heart Association: http://americanheart.org.)

leads to many other medical disorders such as high blood pressure, stroke, and coronary artery disease. Asian American males have higher mortality rates than European Americans males due to stroke. Among Asian Indians in the United States, the number of individuals with coronary artery disease is four times higher than European Americans. A study of Cambodian, Hmong, Laotian, and Vietnamese boys ages 10–15 found a greater mean systolic blood pressure with Hmong boys having a greater propensity for high blood pressure, which may lead to potential risks for heart disease (Asian and Pacific Islander American Health Forum, 2003b). National differences in the incidence of heart disease and stroke can be found. For example, the United States has a significantly high incidence of heart disease compared to incidence of heart disease reported in Japan. Interestingly, when comparing Asians living in the United States with those living in their native Asian countries, significant differences can be found. For example, Japanese men in the United States had higher mortality rates due to heart disease than Japanese men living in Japan, suggesting that lifestyle changes through Westernization may have an influence on one's heart health (Esperat et al., 2004). Immigration to the United States tends to show this trend for increased incidence of heart disease and has been cited as the reason for the high rates in Asian Indians and other immigrant groups.

Many cancers afflict Asian Americans in general, and several Asian American communities have higher incidences of cancers than European Americans. Liver cancer, while fairly uncommon in the general U.S. population is among the top three cancers among Asian Americans. The high incidence of liver cancer can be accounted for by the high rates of Hepatitis B in the Asian population. Although the incidence of Hepatitis B is 0.3% of the U.S. population, over half of those individuals are Asian Americans. Southeast Asian immigrants' rates of lung cancer are 18% higher than European Americans. Among Korean Americans stomach cancer has high prevalence and has been found to be five times greater than that of European Americans. In Japanese Americans the rate of cancers are at or below the incidence in the United States.

Table 26.1 Cancer Health Disparities: Summary Fact Sheet

Group	Cancer incidence rates (no. of new cases each year)	Cancer death rates (no. of new cases each year)	Breast cancer—female incidence	Breast cancer—female death	Cervix cancer—incidence	Cervix cancer—death	Liver and bile duct—incidence	Stomach—incidence	Lung and bronchus—female incidence	Colon and rectum—female incidence
African American	512.3[a]	248.1[a]	34.7[a]	119.4	11.1	5.3[a]	14	15.9[a]	55.2[a]	56[a]
White	479.7	195.3	25.9	141.1[a]	8.7	2.5	6.7	12	51.1	45.3
Asian/Pacific Islander	335.6	119.9	12.7	96.6	8.9	2.7	9.7[a]	13	28.3	39.7
Hispanic/Latino	352.4	135.2	16.7	89.9	15.8[a]	3.5	7.3	12.9	23.6	32.3
American Indian/ Alaska Native	233.6	132.4	13.8	54.8	4.9	2.6	5	7.4	23.3	32.2

Source: National Cancer Institute and the National Center for Health Statistics (http://www.cancer.gov/newscenter/healthdisparities).
Statistics are for 1998–2002, are adjusted to the 2000 U.S. standard million population, and represent the number of new cases of invasive cancer per year per 100,000 population or the number of deaths per year per 100,000 population.
[a] Highest of all groups.

As with the general population, breast cancer is the leading cancer diagnosis among Asian American women, and Asian American women have the third highest incidence rate after Caucasians and African Americans (see Table 26.1). Among Asian American women, high rates of cervical cancer coincide with low incidence of Pap test screening and it is the leading cancer diagnosis of Vietnamese women (U.S. Department of Health and Human Services, 2003; Yi, Gor, & Hoang, 2004). Invasive cervical cancer has higher rates in Southeast Asian American women than for European Americans. Most studies find that diagnosis of cancers occur more frequently at the advanced or end-stage level due to less access to health care, less participation in screening measures, and avoidance of Western medicine altogether (Esperat et al., 2004). For example, how many of your Asian American mothers or fathers discussed preventative Pap smear examinations and the importance of annual gynecologic exams? Due to the taboo of seeing a gynecologist and fear of breaking one's hymen during an exam, young Asian women are often discouraged from taking the preventative measures of a health screening. Due to the disparities in cancer screening among Asian American women demonstrated in national survey findings, efforts are placed on finding ways to increase preventive care. So far, research has found that factors associated with increased likelihood of obtaining cancer screens include having a regular doctor, having a female physician, and receiving care at community, hospital, or multi-specialty clinics rather than private clinics (Taylor et al., 2004). However, it is also clear that ways to account for the cultural taboos and stigmas would be critical to helping Asian American women, for example, seek the services they might need.

Diabetes has become of interest recently among Asian American populations. Part of this reason is that as immigrants acculturate and change diet, obesity rates begin to climb, putting individuals at risk for Type 2 diabetes. A study in Seattle found that diabetes among Japanese

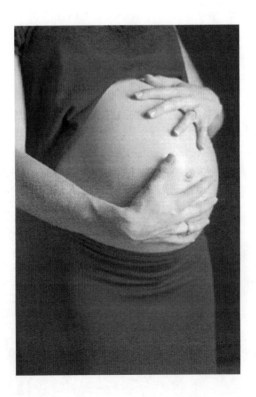

Americans was two to three times higher than for European Americans (McNeely & Boyko, 2004). For Asian Indians, one study found that they were seven times more likely to suffer from Type 2 diabetes than the general population (Asian and Pacific Islander American Health Forum, 2003b). As mentioned before, Western lifestyle may be leading to changes in diet and activity among Asian American immigrants. These results coincide with the high risk for heart disease among Asian Americans as diabetes can lead to cardiac problems.

Major Health Issues Impacting Asian American Infants and Children

Asian American women are less likely to receive prenatal care than are European Americans. It is thought that Asian American women may seek help from family members during pregnancy rather than receive care from an obstetric physician. Another reason is that historically in Asian countries prenatal care is not common and is primarily a Western phenomenon, not seen as necessary for childbirth. Further, Asian Indian and Japanese women in the United States tend to give birth to low-weight babies (Vu, 1996). This may be related to lack of or late prenatal care. If there are cultural taboos about seeking help from professionals during childbirth or about women being examined by male physicians, Asian American women are far less likely to seek prenatal care. This could have implications on nutrition for mother and baby and may result in late diagnosis of fetus problems, leading to increased incidence of low-weight babies.

Few studies have looked at health issues among Asian American children. The studies that have examined these issues show positive results. Although Asian American children are at risk for chronic conditions (persistent, longstanding, or recurrent disease), this risk is below that for the general U.S. population. They had lower incidence of congenital disease and chronic conditions. However, in a study by Yu, Huang, and Singh (2004), health status and health service utilization was examined among Asian American children and found that Asian American children were more likely than European Americans to be without health insurance and less likely to have had a checkup within the last 12 months. This may contribute to an increased incidence of chronic conditions in children as it has been demonstrated that less access to health care leads to later diagnoses of preventable conditions.

One disease among Asian American children that has been recognized in the United States is Kawasaki Disease, an acute disease of unknown cause affecting especially infants and children

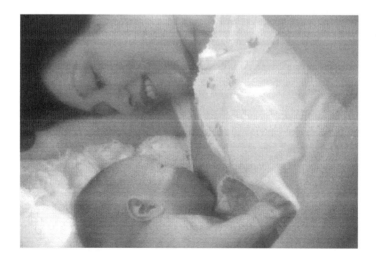

that is characterized by symptoms such as a fever, reddish macular rash (discoloration of the skin) especially on the trunk, conjunctivitis (pink eye), inflammation of mucous membranes (as of the tongue), and swollen lymph nodes in the neck. It affects 19 out of 100,000 children typically of Korean or Japanese descent. This disease usually afflicts children under the age of 5 and is not preventable. This disease has particular implications for health disparities among Asian Americans because if it is caught and treated within 10 days of onset it does not lead to long-term health problems. However, if treated anytime beyond that point, it can lead to serious complications and long-term heart problems. Another disease that afflicts Asian American children is Sudden Infant Death Syndrome or SIDS. Rates of SIDS were shown to be highest among Chinese Americans with a rate of 1.3 per 1,000 in California (Dhooper, 2003). According to the American Lung Association rates of SIDS in the Asian American population are lower than for any other racial/ethnic group. Although reasons are not known it may be related to relatively low incidence of smoking in Asian American women.

Major Health Issues Impacting Asian American Elderly

Among Asian Americans, the elderly are the most at-risk group for chronic health issues. Elderly Chinese Americans have a higher incidence of liver, nasopharyngeal, stomach, and rectal cancers. Conditions such as cancers and heart disease tend to be the leading causes of death among the elderly. Interface with Western medicine has been the primary reason that disparities exist. Chronic conditions affecting the Asian American elderly population appear to be at or slightly below that of European Americans although this may be related to underreporting. In a study by Torsch and Ma (2000), Chinese elders often rated their health positively despite the presence of a chronic condition. The elders would seek treatment for health issues that were alterable and would accept ones that they found to be a part of normal aging. Elderly Asian Americans might perceive that some suffering and pain is an acceptable and expected part of the aging process, which leads to underreporting and late diagnoses of preventable or curable conditions. The limited ability to speak English and lack of culturally sensitive practices also impact the help-seeking behaviors of the elderly.

The collectivistic nature of Asian American communities may serve as a safeguard to health problems as perceived social support leads to physical and psychological well-being. The concept

of **filial piety** is an important concept in Asian American families, which means one is to care for elders in the family. It is expected that children will respect and honor their elders by taking care of them as they get older. When individuals reach end of life, children are often faced with the dilemma of placing elders in nursing homes or caring for them in the home. This is often associated with much guilt in second and subsequent generations of Asian Americans as filial piety dictates the need to respect elders. Although this concept remains strong in Asian Americans, demands placed on them by Western society has made it increasingly difficult to care for elders while maintaining career and family life.

Understanding Illness Within the Asian Cultural Context

Differences in illness expression, treatment, and conceptualization influence how Asian Americans present during time of sickness. Treatment is expected to be comprehensive, encompassing the mind, body, and spirit, paying special attention to the interaction of the three. Taoism, a belief system that has origins in China and Vietnam, directs the use of medicine and underlying causes of the disease process. This belief describes a system of forces that balance one another. A disease process would be described as an imbalance between these forces. Treatment would involve attempting to balance these forces, which is often done through herbal remedies using hot and cold properties. Additionally, remedies that would attend to psychological issues such as meditation and imagery would be recommended as well as massage and **acupuncture** to treat physical symptoms. Taoism has often been referred to as the yin-yang balance principle and is reflected in all aspects of life.

> The yin-yang principle states that every object contains both yin and yang—two elements that are the unity of opposites, for example, sky and earth, hot and cold, and growth and decline. (Torsch & Ma, 2000, p. 474)

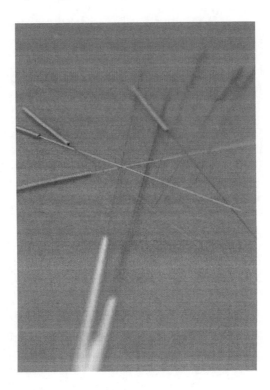

Balance and harmony are actively sought for optimal life functioning. The Traditional Chinese Medicine approach is also in line with the mind-body connection and deems that psychological disorders are often the cause of physical problems. If an aspect of homeostasis is impacted, it will inevitably impact other aspects that maintain the individual's balance. Thus, chronic distress and emotional upset will lead to dysfunction of the physical aspects (i.e., blood, oxygen, heart function) and lead to disease. Taoism has implications for the expression of illness in Asian Americans. Those individuals that live by this belief system may express illness in ways uncommon to Western medicine as imbalances of hot or cold or somatic complaints, which may be manifestations of psychological issues.

For individuals of Hmong descent, disease is viewed as a disturbance in the balance of the dynamic interaction of souls, spirits, and persons which, will have implications in the expression of illness in this population (Plotnikoff, Numrich, Wu, Yang, & Xiong, 2002). A **shaman** is utilized to restore this balance by navigating and negotiating with the spiritual world for the person's lost or captured soul. Traditional Hmong beliefs are animistic, meaning that life is seen as the spiritual and physical worlds coexisting, side by side. Souls are believed to provide health to the individual and to keep the balance of the spiritual, the mental, and the physical. When souls are taken or lost, then the body becomes ill. A study done in Minnesota on Hmong Shamanism found that care performed by shamans was effective and was primarily used as a complement to Western medicine (Plotnikoff et al., 2002). Given the principle of mind-body connection, Asian Americans often find Western medicine confusing with the specialty of mental health being separated from physical health. The idea of seeing a "specialist" is particularly problematic as it is believed that health issues should be treated holistically. The concept of a physician focused solely on one aspect of the body does not fit well with an Eastern view of

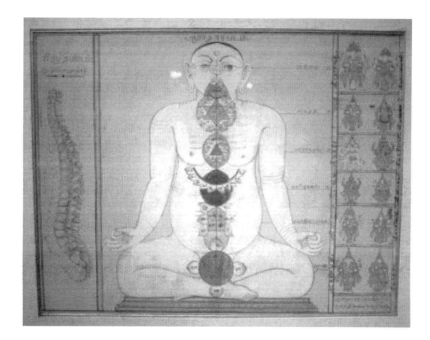

integrated and comprehensive treatment. Additionally, thinking this way may be a function of age, time since immigration, and level of **acculturation**. How do you approach medical issues compared to what your parents or elders do?

Of particular concern in Asian Americans is the high incidence of **somatization**. An individual who complains of physical symptoms due to psychological distress with no medical explanation characterizes somatization. Expression of symptoms often occurs unconsciously and transfers emotional issues into specific somatic complaints. Somatization was initially thought of as denial or repression of psychological symptoms. This tendency to present primarily with somatic complaints has made it challenging for clinicians working with Asian Americans. Some theories have made assumptions about the psychological-mindedness of Asian Americans and the lack of psychological terminology in Asian languages (Lin & Cheung, 1999). Emotional language may be referred to in symbols or metaphors, which may be related to the stigma associated with mental illness in Asian American cultures (Parker, Cheah, & Roy, 2001). However, recent research has proven these theories about somatization to be unfounded. East Asian medicine explains distress in terms of balancing and is believed to have the result of physical manifestations (Pang, 2000). This may lead to the overpresentation of somatic complaints including the feeling that somatic suffering is what is appropriate to present in a health care setting. Several research studies have come out suggesting that symptom expression of psychological distress may be culturally sanctioned (Parker, Cheah, & Roy, 2001). Due to Asian traditions of viewing the body and mind as unitary rather than dualistic, patients tend to focus more on physical discomforts than emotional symptoms, leading to an overrepresentation of somatic complaints. Many mental health issues are not properly treated due to oversights or inappropriate referrals made by primary care physicians, leading to diagnostic errors, delays, and inaccessibility to treatment (Bhugra & Flick, 2005).

Studies have found that, although Asian Americans present with physical symptoms, they often are fully aware of the emotional and psychological aspects of their illness but may perceive the medical setting as appropriate only for presenting physical symptomatology. Other studies conducted with several Asian American populations found that *directly asking* patients led to report of psychological symptoms. Seeing illness as an imbalance, Asian Americans may see psychological distress as private and an expected part of their illness and focus on the physical aspects of their care when seeing a physician. Additionally, underreporting of psychological distress has also been linked to a belief that anxiety and depression are a normal part of a response to life's stresses and not clear signs of a disease process. A study by Angel and Thoits (in Pang, 2000) suggested that, "The more traditional the culture the less differentiation between physical illness and psychological disturbance" (p. 200).

Asian Worldview on Death and Dying

To further the understanding of how the Asian worldview directs Asian Americans' understanding of physical health, this section will explore the concepts of death and dying by first examining traditional practices involving end-of-life and then discuss how acculturation affects those traditions. Traditionally, Asian Americans may prefer not to talk about death, especially when a family member is imminently dying. Family members may decide to keep knowledge of death from a loved one, not to cause emotional stress and preserve the ability of the soul to obtain liberation. In one study on Japanese Americans it was found that more acculturated individuals preferred disclosure of a terminal illness (Cheung, Alden, & Wheeler, 1998). In a review article of Chinese Americans it was found that most individuals would want to be notified of a terminal illness at the same time as the family (Payne, Chapman, Holloway, Seymour, & Chau, 2005). In Hmong culture it is thought that talk of death may lead to worsening health and loss of soul. Alerting the individual of their impending death may also precipitate or hasten death. This is a particularly controversial issue that comes into conflict with Western medicine as the idea of keeping a terminal diagnosis from a patient is uncomfortable.

Asian American rituals, beliefs, and practices differ across cultures. Most beliefs have roots in religion and spirituality. **Confucianism, Buddhism,** and Taoism have influenced Chinese culture. Each one places significant importance on different aspects that affect the dying process. Confucianism puts emphasis on worship of ancestors and preserving the body to respect one's elders. As a result, the body is kept as close to its original state upon burial. The belief systems dictate that one's body was a gift from ancestors and should not be defaced upon death. This is important in the case of organ donation, as some Asian Americans feel that by donating an organ an ancestor may be born into another life missing that organ. One conflict with that theory is that in Buddhist belief it is thought that only the soul is reborn and organ donation should not have an impact on rebirth.

In Buddhism, it is believed that to be reincarnated one must live a good and honest life to achieve a higher level of **reincarnation**. Any acts that are thought to be negative could lead to one being reborn as an animal and premature death is thought to be the result of punishment from doing wrong in another life. This punishment could be passed on to extended family members if the person who does something bad is not punished in this life. For example, if one is living a particularly difficult life or is plagued with chronic illness it is believed that the family may be being punished for wrongdoings in this life or a previous life. In Taoism, there is an emphasis on eating the right balance of foods and maintaining good health to promote longevity of life. Among Asian Indians beliefs about life come from Hinduism and the laws of **Karma**. Each life is linked to previous lives and actions taken in those past lives. The process of being born, moving through life stages and development and death are all a part of the life cycle and that the accumulation of good Karmas will lead to liberation of the soul or "jivanmukta" (Braun & Nichols, 1997). Think of your own traditions or rituals practiced in your family; some may have roots in your ethnic heritage.

In several Asian American communities the deceased are not forgotten once they pass and are often celebrated. Chinese celebrate *Chug Ming* and make offerings in respect of the dead. Vietnamese remember their loved ones in the third and seventh lunar months. The third lunar month is called *Thanh Minh* and is the time the family goes to the cemetery to tend to the grave. The seventh month is called *Vu Lan* and is the time when the family goes to the temple to pray for the deceased soul. To celebrate the lives of those who have died, Japanese Buddhists perform traditional dances at the temple during the *Obon* season. To honor the deceased, Asian Americans often keep altars or memorials representative or symbolic of their ancestors in their homes to allow for prayer and blessings for good fortune and rebirth. The celebrations allow families to join together during these times and celebrate individuals that have passed and they serve as support and protection from prolonged grief. In Buddhist and Hindu belief, death is a part of the natural cycle of life. If a person has lived his or her life, there should be no grief. So often in the Western world, death is approached with fear or not approached at all. How different might it be for you if death was conceptualized as a natural part of the life cycle and that discussions about death were not uncomfortable?

Acculturation has an impact on how rituals and traditions about death and dying are carried out in the United States. For example wearing black to funerals has been increasingly accepted in some Asian American communities even though white is the color most commonly worn to Asian/Asian American funerals. Cremation has also become more acceptable as Asian Americans adopt Western and Christian values. It is also believed that acculturation may influence shortening and abbreviated rituals and practices as they relate to the death and dying process. Although several Asian American communities traditionally hold continuous memorial services days after the death of a loved one, this has been increasingly difficult in today's society with family members spread throughout the globe and unable to stay for the continuous rituals.

Shortening of rituals and ceremonies and meeting less often with family may have an impact on grief and bereavement.

Health Disparity

By reflecting on what has already been presented in this chapter, one might begin to understand and appreciate how Asian Americans experience physical illnesses and prefer to cope with them within their cultural context. For example, why didn't Salma consider a gynecologist visit to be an option for her? Perhaps Salma didn't want to bring unnecessary negative attention to her family for having an unmarried daughter visit a gynecologist. Wanting to maintain harmony and to honor one's family, problems are often kept hidden from the public eye. Asian American communities are often reluctant to access help from mainstream services due to cultural beliefs, stigma, and real as well as anticipated shame (Sue & Sue, 1994). Therefore, public services are inevitably not viewed as an appropriate option.

Health disparity is not always referring to the differences in health care services, needs, and access. Issues of health disparity actually exist in the broader context of social and economic inequality, prejudice, and bias. Despite the availability of effective treatments, many physical health issues go untreated due to cultural, personal, medical, financial, and legal/governmental barriers. In 2001, the Commonwealth Fund supported the Health Care Quality Survey, which examined a wide range of health care quality measures comparing minority Americans (i.e., Asian Americans, African Americans, and Hispanics) with European Americans (Johnson, Saha, Arbelaez, Beach, & Cooper, 2004). Overall, the survey results indicated that minority Americans do not fare as well as European Americans. Less than half of the Asian Americans in the sample reported their doctors listened to everything they had to say compared to nearly 70% of the European American patients reported being listened to. While nearly 80% of the European American patients indicated that their physicians involved them in health care decisions as much as they wanted, less than 60% of Asian Americans reported this. Compared with 62% of the overall population, only 45% of Asian Americans indicated being very satisfied with their health care. Across all racial and ethnic groups surveyed, the respondents perceived that their doctors did not understand their background and cultural values. Traditional practices and healing methods are frequently used to alleviate distress both before and after patients and their family members approach the conventional health care system.

The Commonwealth Fund 2001 Health Care Quality Survey (Ngo-Metzger, Legedza, & Phillips, 2004) found that Asian Americans were twice as likely as European Americans in general to use acupuncture and the services of traditional healers. Among the Asian Americans surveyed, more than a third of Vietnamese (38%) and Japanese (36%) use herbal medicines, 24% of Koreans use acupuncture, and 14% of Chinese consult with traditional healers. However, often such traditional practices and healing methods are not reported to physicians voluntarily. Increased risk of adverse interaction with Western treatments and misdiagnosis can result from the nondisclosure. If health services are to be seen as effective and credible resources, it is important for health service providers to evaluate how their services are perceived within the cultural context of those who seek the services. Health care professionals' ability to recognize and respond to their own and their patients' cultures would signify cultural competency of the health care professionals.

Health Prevention and Wellness

How well do you know your family's medical history? What health risk factors might you need to know about? Asian Americans are less likely to seek preventive care than other Americans. For example, the Commonwealth Fund 2001 Health Care Quality Survey indicated that Asian

Americans are less likely to receive physician counseling about smoking cessation (68% of Asian smokers vs. 79% of total U.S. smokers), healthy diet and weight (35% vs. 49% overall), exercise (45% vs. 50% overall), and mental health (14% vs. 19% overall). The same survey also revealed that Asian Americans were less likely than any other groups to report their doctors discussed with them issues surrounding lifestyle choices (e.g., nutrition, exercise) and mental health issues (e.g., depression). This is concerning because without proper preventive measures the health status of Asian Americans will continue to be compromised. As discussed earlier, there are systemic issues that make health service utilization difficult for Asian Americans. However, there are also culturally relevant barriers that might decrease the likelihood of Asian Americans seeking professional attention (e.g., stigma, shame). To decrease the health disparity that exists, the solution must be multi-pronged. While continuous effort on making systematic changes are warranted, public education and health risk awareness would also be instrumental in helping more Asian Americans utilize health services and/or make lifestyle choices that would protect their health.

Based on the recommendation of health organizations such as the Office of Minority Health, there are many things patients, service providers, and the government can do to promote a healthy lifestyle and to address the health disparities that exist. At the individual level, lifestyle changes such as healthy diet and regular exercise help to promote one's overall health. To that extent, incorporation of meditation, yoga, and other physical activities that are familiar within the Asian cultural context may increase likelihood of engaging in these activities. Preventive care might include regular health screens, yearly physicals, immunizations, and refraining from tobacco and alcohol. At the service providers' level, culturally and linguistically appropriate services should be provided. Cultural competency training is important for individual providers to assure that cultural misunderstandings do not impede on appropriate services being provided. At the governmental level, funding for research and clinical efforts should be allocated. Standards for culturally and linguistically appropriate services should be established and enforced nationwide.

The role of a **clinical health psychologist** is of importance in addressing the complex nature of physical and mental health needs in Asian Americans. Clinical health psychologists often work in medical centers and are trained to focus on the psychological impact of medical disorders. Areas of expertise include: promoting prevention and wellness, addressing health

disparities and health behavior change, coping with chronic illness, adjusting to new diagnosis, and treatment of the psychiatric aspects of disease processes. Clinical health psychologists can play a unique role in advocating for an interdisciplinary approach to treatment in the case of Asian Americans. By suggesting that Asian American patients' illness is conceptualized holistically and providing complementary therapies such as meditation or herbal remedies, health psychologists can optimize care, educate other health professionals, and take a step toward addressing the disparity. As this chapter highlighted, the intersections of culture and health issues cannot be ignored.

Summary

The following statement summarizes the points raised in this chapter: "Every man is in certain respects: (a) like all other men, (b) like some other men, and (c) like no other man" (Kluckhohn & Murray, 1948, p. 35). It is clear that the prevalence of physical health problems among Asian Americans is noteworthy despite the stereotype of being the model minority. Like everyone else, Asian Americans are not immune to health concerns. As a group, there are cultural factors that speak directly to their experiences and expressions of health issues that are different from other racial/ethnic groups. Of course, while universal and group aspects of a person should be of focus, it is important to also consider elements of each person's own individuality. In order to promote understanding of the existing disparities between health care needs, actual service utilization, and availability of culturally appropriate services, we must take into account the complex nature of people.

The ultimate aim of this chapter is to use the current knowledge base from research as a foundation and move toward a deeper appreciation of how culture intersects with physical health and well-being of Asian Americans. Consistent with the other chapters in this text, this chapter presented issues of physical health and wellness pertaining to Asian American populations using a culture-specific approach. This approach, known as the **emic perspective**, takes into account culturally relevant factors such as values and worldviews, which influence the lives, experiences, thoughts, and behaviors of the individuals of a cultural group (Sue & Sue, 2003). While a cultural universal approach, known as the **etic perspective**, could highlight the uniting commonalities among people, to truly appreciate the experiences of Asian Americans, one must begin by understanding the cultural context of Asian Americans. Using the emic perspective, one is reminded that losing sight of the cultural context could lead to cultural misunderstandings and particularly to our interest, unmet physical and mental health needs, inappropriate services provided, and a silenced community.

Discussion Questions

1. Given that somatic symptoms tend to dominate the clinical presentation of Asian Americans what would be important for a clinician to ask during a clinical interview?
2. What are the health risk factors prevalent in Asian American communities?
3. What ideas do you have to promote service utilization by Asian Americans? How would you overcome the cultural and linguistic barriers?
4. Do you think all physicians should be informed of alternative healing methods such as herbal medicine and acupuncture? Should it be part of their medical training?
5. How might a clinical health psychologist be helpful in a case of a terminally ill Asian American patient? What information would be important for the psychologist to communicate to the medical team? To the family? To the patient?

Case Study

Unfortunately, the clinical synopsis of Salma is not far from what is frequently seen by physical and mental health care providers. Due to Salma's cultural background and her upbringing, she had not been receiving annual Pap smears nor taken any preventative steps for diagnoses of cervical or ovarian cancer. From a cultural perspective, reasons for her hesitation to see a gynecologist are understandable though very concerning. If you are a woman reading this, have you had your annual Pap test? If not, take some time to reflect the potential reasons behind this. As discussed earlier, Asian American women exhibit high rates of cervical cancer and this rate coincides with low incidence of Pap test screening. Due to the taboo of seeing a gynecologist and a fear of breaking one's hymen during an exam, young Asian women are often discouraged from taking the preventative measures of a health screening. However, while keeping to the value of saving one's virginity until marriage, one's life and ability to bear children might be placed at risk as a result. This issue is not only relevant to women, it also calls to the attention of men because they will have wives and daughters who would benefit from knowing the implications of not taking these preventative steps. If you are a man reading this, how might you talk to your daughter or sister about preventive health examinations?

When working with Asian American clients, a culturally competent psychologist would need to know the cultural context of this client to fully appreciate how illnesses are understood, expressed, and approached by the client. For example, just as Salma had experienced, there is often the desire to keep the family honor and maintain harmony within the family by withholding information. This might account for the reluctance or avoidance of getting professional help. A culturally competent psychologist could help the client work through the emotions of guilt and shame by helping the client reframe the belief that seeking appropriate help automatically equates dishonoring the family. Psychologists and physicians should be particularly sensitive to the dynamic relationship between physical, medical, and mental health found within Asian American communities. Collaboration across disciplines would certainly facilitate this.

Case Study Discussion Questions

For undergraduate students, please consider the following questions:

1. What are your thoughts about Salma's reaction when her psychologist suggested that Salma consults with a gynecologist? How might you react if a similar recommendation was made to you? How would your culture and upbringing influence your reaction?
2. Salma is too embarrassed to tell her family and friends what she is going through. What are some reasons as to why she is feeling this way? How might this relate to your own experiences?
3. Salma's situation took a devastating turn. Given her case what might be done to encourage other young Asian American women to get regular health screenings?

For graduate students and/or beginning therapists, please consider the following questions:

1. As a clinician, how might you present the recommendation for Salma to consult with a gynecologist? What would you do if she adamantly refuses to follow your recommendation?
2. Although Salma's family is devastated over the news of cancer and her inability to bear children, they also have become preoccupied with the possibility they may not find a man to marry her. As a clinician, how might you work with Salma's family to help them support Salma through this difficult time? What recommendations would you make to the family?
3. Considering conceptualizing the case from alternative theoretical modalities, what framework appears to make most sense? How will you proceed if Salma continues treatment? What interventions would be most appropriate?

Key Terms

Acculturation: The modification of the culture of a group or individual as a result of contact with a different culture.

Acupuncture: A procedure used in or adapted from Chinese medical practice in which specific body areas are pierced with fine needles for therapeutic purposes or to relieve pain or produce regional anesthesia.

Buddhism: The religion represented by the many groups, especially numerous in Asia, that profess varying forms of this doctrine and that venerate Buddha.

Clinical health psychologist: Applies scientific knowledge of the interrelationships among behavioral, emotional, cognitive, social, and biological components in health and disease to the promotion and maintenance of health; the prevention, treatment, and rehabilitation of illness and disability; and the improvement of the health care system.

Confucianism: Relating to, or characteristic of, Confucius, his teachings, or his followers.

Emic perspective: A cultural-specific approach taking into account culturally relevant factors such as values and worldviews, which influence the lives, experiences, thoughts, and behaviors of the individuals of a cultural group.

Etic perspective: Cultural universal approach that highlights the uniting commonalities among people.

Filial piety: In Confucian thought, one of the virtues to be cultivated, a love and respect for one's parents and ancestors.

Karma: The total effect of a person's actions and conduct during the successive phases of the person's existence, regarded as determining the person's destiny.

Reincarnation: Rebirth of the soul in another body.

Shaman: A member of certain tribal societies who acts as a medium between the visible world and an invisible spirit world and who practices magic or sorcery for purposes of healing, divination, and control over natural events.

Somatization: Expression of psychological distress by physical symptoms without medical explanation

Taoism: A principal philosophy and system of religion of China based on the teachings of Lao-tzu in the sixth century B.C. and on subsequent revelations. It advocates preserving and restoring the Tao in the body and the cosmos.

Yin-Yang principle: In Chinese philosophy, the two cosmic forces of creative energy, yin being feminine/negative and yang being masculine/positive, from which everything originates and depends upon the interaction of the opposite and complementary principles.

For Further Learning and Suggested Readings

Asian and Pacific Islander American Health Forum: http://www.apiahf.org
Centers for Disease Control and Prevention: http://www.cdc.gov
National Asian American Pacific Islander Mental Health Association: http://www.naapimha.org
National Library of Medicine—Asian American Health: http://asianamericanhealth.nlm.nih.gov
The Office of Minority Health: http://www.omhrc.gov

References

American Heart Association. (2004). *Asian/Pacific Islanders and cardiovascular diseases-statistics.* Retrieved November 17, 2005, from www.americanheart.org.

Asian and Pacific Islander American Health Forum. (2003a). *Health brief series: Asian Americans and Pacific Islanders and HIV/AIDS.* Retrieved November 17, 2005 from www.apiahf.org.

Asian and Pacific Islander American Health Forum. (2003b). *Health briefs series: Cambodians, Chinese, Hmong, Japanese, Koreans, South Asians, and Vietnamese in the United States.* Retrieved November 17, 2005, from www.apiahf.org.

Bhugra, B., & Flick, G. R. (2005). Pathways to care for patients with bipolar disorder. *Bipolar Disorders, 7*(3), 236–245.

Braun, K. L., & Nichols, R. (1997). Death and dying in four Asian American cultures: A descriptive study. *Death Studies, 21*(4), 327–359.

Cheung, A. H., Alden, D. L., & Wheeler, M. S. (1998). Cultural attitudes of Asian-Americans toward death adversely impact organ donation. *Transplantation Proceedings, 30*(7), 3609–3610.

Dhooper, S. S. (2003). Health care needs of foreign-born Asian Americans: An overview. *Health & Social Work, 28*(1), 63–73.

Esperat, M. C., Inouye, J., Gonzalez, E. W., Owen, D. C., & Feng, D. (2004). Health disparities among Asian Americans and Pacific Islanders. *Annual Review of Nursing Research, 22,* 135–159.

Johnson, R. L., Saha, S., Arbelaez, J. J., Beach, M. C., & Cooper, L. A. (2004). Racial and ethnic differences in patient perceptions of bias and cultural competence in health care. *Journal of General Internal Medicine, 19*(2), 101–110.

Kluckhohn, C., & Murray, H. A. (1948). *Personality in nature, society, and culture.* New York: Knopf.

Lee, S. K., Sobal, J., & Frongillo, E.A. Jr. (2000). Acculturation and health in Korean Americans. *Social Science & Medicine, 51*(2), 159–173.

Lin, K. M., & Cheung, F. (1999). Mental health issues for Asian Americans. *Psychiatric Services, 50*(6), 774–780.

McNeely, M. J., & Boyko, E. J. (2004). Type 2 diabetes prevalence in Asian Americans: Results of a national health survey. *Diabetes Care, 27*(1), 66–69.

Ngo-Metzger, Q., Legedza, A. T. R., & Phillips, R. S. (2004). Asian Americans' reports of their health care experiences. *Journal of General Internal Medicine, 19*(2), 111–119.

Pang, K. Y. C. (2000). Symptom and somatization among elderly Korean immigrants. *Journal of Clinical Geropsychology, 6*(3), 199–212.

Parker, G., Cheah, Y., & Roy, K. (2001). Do the Chinese somatize depression? A cross-cultural study. *Social Psychiatry and Psychiatric Epidemiology, 36*(6), 287–293.

Payne, S., Chapman, A., Holloway, M., Seymour, J.E., & Chau, R. (2005). Chinese community views: Promoting cultural competence in palliative care. *Journal of Palliative Care, 21*(2), 111–116.

Plotnikoff, G. A., Numrich, C., Wu, C., Yang, D., & Xiong, P. (2002). Hmong shamanism: Animist healing in Minnesota. *Minnesota Medicine, 85*(6), 29–34.

Taylor, V. M., Schwartz, S. M., Yasui, Y., Burke, N., Shu, J., Lam, et al. (2004). Pap testing among Vietnamese women: Health care system and physician factors. *Journal of Community Health: The Publication for Health Promotion and Disease Prevention, 29*(6), 437–450.

Torsch, V. L., & Ma, G. X. (2000). Cross-cultural comparison of health perceptions, concerns, and coping strategies among Asian and Pacific Islander elders. *Qualitative Health Research, 10*(4), 471–489.

U.S. Department of Health and Human Services. (2001). *Mental health: Culture, race, and ethnicity, a Supplement to mental health: A report of the Surgeon General.* Rockville, MD.

U.S. Department of Health and Human Services. (2003). *Health problems in Asian American/Pacific Islander and Native Hawaiian women.* Retrieved November 17, 2005, from http://www.womenshealth.gov/faq/Asian_Pacific.htm.

Vu, H. H. (1996). Cultural barriers between obstetric-gynecologists and Vietnamese/Chinese immigrant women. *Texas Medicine, 92*(10), 47–52.

Yi, J. K., Gor, B., & Hoang, T. (2004). What we know and don't know about Asian American health in Texas. *Texas Medicine, 100*(11), 64–70.

Yu, S. M., Huang, Z. J., & Singh, G. K. (2004). Health status and health services utilization among US Chinese, Asian Indian, Filipino, and other Asian/Pacific Islander children. *Pediatrics, 113*(1), 101–107.

27
Psychopathology and Clinical Issues With Asian American Populations

OANH MEYER, MANVEEN DHINDSA,
CARMEL GABRIEL, and STANLEY SUE

OUTLINE OF CHAPTER

Case Synopsis
Introduction
Cultural Issues
Minority Status
Protective Factors
Prevalence of Mental Disorders
Mental Health Services
Case Study
References

Case Synopsis

Mae was a 24-year-old, recently married immigrant from Hong Kong. Also from Hong Kong, her husband worked as an electrical engineer in an aerospace company. Both lived in a small house with his parents. Mae seemed always in conflict with her parents-in-law, who constantly criticized whatever she did. Yet they expected her to be a dutiful daughter-in-law who would serve them without complaints. Her relationship deteriorated to the point where she was feeling anxious, depressed, and angry. She felt she could not turn to her husband because he often defended his parents and their criticisms of her. Mae started to exhibit bodily aches and pains as well as **psychological** symptoms and believed that her only option was to seek a divorce from her husband.

Introduction

In this chapter, we discuss the mental health of Asian Americans. Mental health includes issues of psychological well-being, rates of mental disorders, services to treat mental disorders, and factors that influence mental health. Many factors obviously affect mental health. The biopsychosocial model of mental health proposes that **biological**, psychological, and **social** phenomena affect well-being, such as **genetic** and biological predispositions, environmental conditions (e.g., stress), and the adaptive capacity and resiliency of individuals. Our focus is primarily on the psychological and social influences on mental health rather than hereditary and biological factors. Furthermore, as illustrated in Figure 27.1, mental health can be examined on three different levels (Kluckhohn & Murray, 1950). First, the universal level includes the factors that impinge on all human beings. For example, all human beings have a survival instinct and need air to breathe. Second, the individual level includes the very unique experiences that one has and that others may not have. For example, each person has a unique set of experiences involving family

Three Levels of Analysis

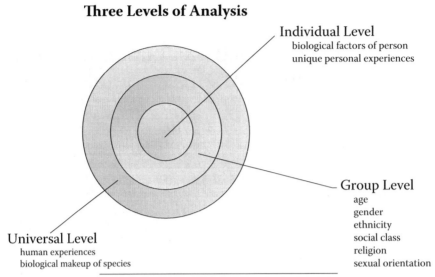

Individual Level
biological factors of person
unique personal experiences

Group Level
age
gender
ethnicity
social class
religion
sexual orientation

Universal Level
human experiences
biological makeup of species

Understanding mental health from three levels of analysis.

and community that no other person has. Third, at the group level, human beings share experiences with some but not all others. The basis for this shared experience could be ethnic, cultural, demographic, or situational similarity. In our discussion of Asian Americans, we are specifically focused on the group level—namely, the shared experiences that people have as Asians in the United States.

Some of the major shared experiences associated with being Asian American are cultural background, immigration, and minority status. While much heterogeneity exists within and between the different Asian groups, we try to identify those conditions that affect mental health and that are applicable to many Asians in the United States. The shared experiences include learning cultural values unique to being Asian, dealing with culture conflicts that develop partly due to the **acculturation** process, and being a member of a minority group in the United States. Many questions and issues are raised in this chapter. For example, does becoming acculturated to American society improve mental health? Do prejudice and discrimination negatively impact one's mental health? What is the prevalence of mental disorders among Asian Americans? Do Asian Americans use mental health services? How can services be more effective?

Cultural Issues

Acculturation and Mental Health

Cultural values are important because they help determine how one evaluates mental health and mental disorders, what kinds of symptoms are displayed when one has a mental disorder, what kind of help and remedies are sought to alleviate mental distress, and what kinds of cultural resources are available in the promotion of mental health. Before illustrating how culture is important in all of these processes, we must first identify Asian cultural values and the process of acculturation.

As a population, Asian Americans tend to have certain values that reflect Asian cultures. These values include a hierarchical family structure, an extended family orientation, emotional restraint, emphasis on conformity, a collectivist orientation, obedience to parents, gender-specific roles, deference to authority figures, modesty, shame/guilt orientation, and respect for elders

(Sue & Sue, 1999; Uba, 1994). Obviously, not all Asian Americans have these values and specific Asian American subgroups may differ. The Asian cultural value of conformity, for example, is enforced in many aspects of life, as children are socialized to conform to the group in order to increase group harmony and minimize "sticking out" (Markus & Kitayama, 1991). Values like conformity are a part of many Asian cultures.

When individuals have contact with a new host society, they face many challenges, such as adjusting to a new language, different customs and norms for social interactions, unfamiliar rules and laws, and in some cases extreme lifestyle changes (e.g., rural to urban). Acculturation is a process by which members of one cultural group adopt the beliefs and behaviors of another group. It involves the acquisition of language, attitudes, values, and roles of the dominant society, and the process of adjusting to these changes (Organista, Organista, & Kurasaki, 2003). Adapting to a new host society successfully can strengthen the individual, as he or she develops bicultural skills and effectively reconciles or integrates the two cultures. However, the demands of adaptation can often lead to increased stress, what Berry and Kim (1988) refer to as **acculturative stress**. Acculturative stress tends to be at its peak during the initial months of contact with the new culture (Zheng & Berry, 1991) and may contribute to poorer mental health status. Difficulties that may increase acculturative stress include learning a new language and problems seeking employment. Several studies indicate that premigration trauma, time of migration, acceptance from the dominant host society, cultural orientation, and prejudice may be involved in determining levels of acculturative stress and mental health status (Organista et al., 2003).

Acculturation introduces challenges that can be associated with a number of problems during the life span, including depression, anxiety, exposure to and use of alcohol and drugs, behavioral problems at home and school, perceived discrimination, and negative expectations

Many Asian cultures emphasize conformity, especially early on in life.

for the future (Vega & Alegria, 2001). While some findings suggest that some acculturated Asian Americans have a greater prevalence of mental disorders (Takeuchi et al., 2006), most studies reveal that Asian Americans' length of stay in America is negatively correlated with rates of mental disorders, as opposed to other ethnic minority groups, such as Mexican Americans. That is, the longer Asian Americans stay in America, the less likely they are to have mental disorders or emotional problems (Sue, Keefe, Enomoto, Durvasula, & Chao, 1996). Indeed, Kuo and Tsai (1986) found that among Asian American immigrants, those who moved to the United States at an earlier age exhibited fewer adjustment difficulties. These findings are consistent with those from other studies that suggest that foreign-born Asian Americans report greater levels of interpersonal distress than non-Hispanic Whites, even after controlling for other demographic differences (Abe & Zane, 1990). Therefore, acculturation may play a role in the decreased rates of mental disorders or distress in the Asian American population over time. Mexican Americans, on the other hand, show the opposite trend. The longer they stay in America, the more mental disorders they exhibit. The reasons for this increase are not known. Perhaps many have high initial expectations for upward mobility but then face the reality of prejudice and discrimination over time; many may experience a loss of cultural ties (and associated protective factors) or loss of family support, or perhaps conditions in the United States (rugged individualism, competition, etc.) place individuals under conditions of stress. At this point, the precise reasons for the positive relationship between acculturation and increased mental disorders among Mexican Americans are unknown. The expectations of Asian immigrants in the United States may differ from those of Mexican Americans. For Asian Americans, stressors include the lack of English language proficiency, knowledge of resources, etc. As Asian Americans become acclimated to the customs, language, and social structure of their host society, acculturative stress may decrease, causing a reduction in rates of psychological problems.

Mediating and Moderating Variables

As acculturation increases, however, qualifying factors (mediators and moderators) such as **intergenerational conflict**, stigma, and prejudice can negatively influence mental health in Asian Americans. Therefore, it is important to examine other factors as well, such as the context of family. Nguyen and Peterson (1993) found that among Vietnamese American college students, there was a positive correlation between acculturation and depression. Because the sample was comprised of younger individuals, Organista et al. (2003) speculated that measuring acculturation of college students may not tell the whole story. For example, if the students are acculturating more rapidly than their parents, there may be growing value differences, and thus tensions between them and their less acculturated parents. This can, in turn, lead to greater distress and mental health problems. Asian values emphasize filial piety (respect, reverence, and devotion to family and family goals) and the children's obedience toward their parents. However, as Asian children become more acclimated to American society, they often seek more independence than their parents are willing to give. Thus, the clash that is caused by the parents' demand for obedience and the children's struggle for independence may result in high tensions between Asian parents and their children, a struggle referred to as *intergenerational conflict*.

Differences in how a group migrates to the host society may also influence acculturative stress and the onset and duration of mental disorders. These variables include the nature of migration (e.g., forced vs. voluntary, refugee status, etc.), the receptiveness of the host society, and the degree of similarity between the culture of origin and the new culture (Berry, 1997; Berry & Annis, 1974; Berry & Kim, 1988; Berry, Kim, Minde, & Mok, 1987). Moreover, premigration trauma can have a large effect on rates of long-term mental disorders in immigrants, irrespective of the acculturation process. Many Southeast Asian refugees experienced various traumas, including starvation, torture, death of loved ones, and forced labor in their homelands prior to coming to the United States. These experiences have resulted in high rates of mental disorders including post-traumatic stress disorder and depression (Marshall, Schell, Elliott, Berthold, & Chun, 2005).

Research has shown that those immigrants who have persistent problems in cultural adaptation are more at risk for developing long-term mental disorders, such as chronic depression (Westermeyer, Neider, & Vang, 1984). These persistent problems include, but are not limited to, difficulty acquiring English language proficiency and problems due to premigration trauma. One of the problems with having limited English proficiency in the United States is that it affects functioning in important daily domains such as employment (Westermeyer & Her, 1996); in turn, employment status can influence well-being. For example, employers may be more inclined to hire someone who speaks English fluently over a less fluent but equally qualified Asian American immigrant, who may then be unable to support the family financially. This could increase the risk of individuals developing certain mental disorders, such as depression or anxiety.

Postmigration factors also contribute to long-term mental health outcomes. That is, important life changes that often result from immigration, such as loss of one's previous social role or vocation, the need to rebuild one's social network, and separation from family are related to poorer mental health outcomes (Organista et al., 2003). Moreover, it could be that those who have persistent, higher expectations of America (such as imagined financial success based on the belief that America is the "Land of Opportunity") may often develop long-term mental health problems if their expectations or beliefs about America are unfulfilled.

Successful psychological adjustment during the acculturation process may also depend on the cultural orientation the individual chooses to adopt. Berry and Kim (1988) have identified four distinct cultural orientations that immigrants adopt as a result of the acculturation process: assimilated, separatist, bicultural, and marginal. Individuals who are assimilated completely adopt the behaviors and thinking of the dominant host culture. In contrast, individuals who are separatists remain completely immersed in the language, activities, and beliefs of their culture of origin. Bicultural individuals are those who move fluidly between both their culture of origin and the new host culture. Finally, marginalists are isolated from their culture of origin as well as the dominant society (Organista et al., 2003). To examine which of these four groups were more psychologically well-adjusted, Ying (1995) conducted a study with Chinese Americans and showed that a bicultural orientation predicted lower depression (compared with all other cultural orientations), more positive and less negative affect (compared with separatist orientation), and better life satisfaction (compared with separatist and marginalist orientations). From these results, it seems as though biculturalists fare better mentally than others.

Minority Status

Over the course of time, Asian Americans have experienced various forms of discrimination and have been the targets of numerous stereotypes. In the past, discrimination was overt and stereotypes were primarily negative; more recently, Asian Americans have been stereotyped as law-abiding, intelligent, and hardworking individuals (Leong, 2000). Statistics collected by the U.S. Census and other agencies seem to support this image. In the 2000 Census, 28.7% of Asian Americans held a bachelor's degree compared to 18.6% of non-Hispanic Whites (U.S. Bureau of the Census, 2000). The U.S. Census also revealed that a greater number of Asian Americans than Whites reported obtaining an advanced degree. Moreover, Asian Americans' divorce rates were much lower than those found among Whites. Asian Americans also tended to engage in criminal activities at a far lower rate than Whites and African Americans. The Department of Justice Federal Bureau of Investigation (n.d.) 2004 crime report indicated that Asian Pacific

Islanders comprised only 1.2% out of the total arrested for violent crimes (murder, forcible rape, robbery, and aggravated assault), whereas Whites and African Americans comprised 57.8% and 40.1%, respectively. Additionally, Asian Pacific Islanders were also arrested for property crimes (burglary, larceny-theft, motor vehicle theft, and arson) at a rate far lower than their White and African American counterparts. Asian Pacific Islanders also had lower drug abuse violations and a lower incidence of vandalism. These data depict them as the model minority, who are nonproblematic, good citizens, and impervious to the troubles of the greater society such as prejudice and intercultural conflict (Liang, Li, & Kim, 2004). Such an image, however, implies that Asian Americans are homogeneous and overlooks the subtle forms of discrimination that are experienced by individual members of this racial group.

Furthermore, the model minority image presents serious consequences for Asian Americans at the workplace. This image portrays Asian Americans as compliant, diligent, and successful and overlooks the subtle forms of discrimination Asian Americans may experience. While on the surface these positive characteristics appear innocuous, they actually depict Asian Americans as lacking leadership qualities and, consequently, reduce their chances of obtaining high-level positions (Chan, 2003). For example, an Asian American man who has completed the same level of education as a White man may face a glass ceiling due to his ethnicity and characteristics associated with his ethnic group; he may not be promoted to higher managerial positions. Such situations are not isolated incidents; rather they are commonplace and corroborated in research. Leong (1998) found that when comparing Asian Americans, African Americans, and White Americans, Asian American men had the lowest wages when variables such as education and occupation were held constant. Such inequities at the workplace have received modest attention due to the fact that they are primarily masked by the model minority image. Thus, members of this minority group may be treated differently, have different opportunities for social mobility, and possess less power, resources, and incomes. In a study examining Asian Americans' perceptions of discrimination, Goto, Gee, and Takeuchi (2002) found that 21% of Chinese Americans in their sample reported feeling discriminated against due to their race, ethnicity, language, or accent. Moreover, 43% reported experiencing discrimination within the past year.

Minority status does not result only in negative social consequences, but more importantly, it can result in increased risk for psychopathology among Asian Americans (Alegria et al., 2004). One outcome of occupying a minority status in society may be experiencing discrimination and increased levels of stress and dissatisfaction. One's position in society may determine a trajectory for social mobility and when such a trajectory is limited due to an individual's race or ethnicity, an individual may experience feelings of worthlessness and a reduced sense of control (Chun, Eastman, Wang, & Sue, 1998). This psychosocial explanation may offer fruitful information for therapists working with Asian American clients suffering from psychological distress. The point is that Asian Americans do suffer considerable stress from migration, culture conflict, and minority status.

Protective Factors

It should be noted that cultural factors as well as experiences as a minority group member can *increase or decrease* the risk of developing mental disorders. While racism and minority group status may affect the nature of mental health services received and the level of stress experienced, ethnic minority groups may also have cultural resources that enhance mental health or mitigate the effects of certain stressors (Sue & Chu, 2003). Cultural and family bonds can sometimes buffer individuals from experiencing the negative effects associated with acculturative stress, particularly if they place a great deal of value on the support received from their family, cultural reference group, and so on. These buffers can reduce the mental health problems that might arise as a result of acculturative stress. For example, many ethnic minority college

Many Asian families have strict gender and role relationships, as can be seen in this family photograph.

students take shelter from the harsh realities of perceived discrimination and acculturative stress by joining clubs, organizations, and events catered toward their particular ethnic group, such as the Asian Student Association. These organizations often meet monthly or weekly and sponsor events such as dances and fundraisers. Asian American clubs and organizations offer an outlet for those of a specific Asian or pan-Asian ethnicity to join together, discuss problems, share ideas, network, and encourage one another. Sharing common troubles may help alleviate acculturative stress by making Asian Americans feel as though there are others who understand their troubles and are willing to help. Not only can immigrants relate to and rely on members of their own ethnic group for social support, but the Asian family structure can provide a buffer for negative events that occur outside of the home. For example, George DeVos (1978, 1982) argued that highly structured role relationships in Japanese families can protect family members from stressors outside the family. These role relationships and gender relationships are evident in all aspects of family life. They provide stability and predictability. For example, if a father is humiliated and degraded by prejudice and discrimination from the outside community, he can still return home and demand respect and obedience because of his roles as father and husband.

Likewise, Francis Hsu (1971) believed that Chinese culture emphasizes kinship ties from birth to death, so that affective or emotional needs tend to be fulfilled within the family, but at the price of conformity to family and elders. This family security enhances mental health and functioning. The Surgeon General's report stated that cultural resilience, community resources, and culturally based faith and spirituality have been proposed as enhancing mental health for ethnic minority groups (U.S. Department of Health and Human Services, 2001).

Prevalence of Mental Disorders

What is the actual extent of mental disorders among Asian Americans? Because of the relatively small population in the United States (5%), even when Asian Americans are included as part of the sample of large-scale studies, it is often not possible to estimate the prevalence of mental disorders for this population. While estimates have been made using the Epidemiologic Catchment Area (ECA) data, English-speaking Asian Americans comprised less than 2% ($n = 242$) of the total sample and were sampled primarily from the Los Angeles site (Sue & Chu, 2003; Zhang et al., 1998).

The ECA indicated that nearly 20% of the American population either had experienced a mental disorder within the past 6 months or currently were experiencing one, but prevalence rates for the Asian American community were not established because of inadequate sampling. While the ECA sampled respondents from five U.S. cities, the National Comorbidity Survey (NCS) (Kessler et al., 1994) attempted to estimate prevalence rates on the basis of a representative sample of the entire U.S. population. Again, because of the small sample of English-speaking Asian Americans and the fact that the group of respondents overall was small, extremely diverse, and not representative of any particular Asian American subgroup, no prevalence estimate could be established with any confidence.

The Chinese American Psychiatric Epidemiological Study (CAPES), conducted in 1993–1994, examined rates of depression among more than 1,700 Chinese Americans in Los Angeles County (Takeuchi et al., 1998). The study attempted to estimate the prevalence rates of selected mental disorders among Chinese Americans and to identify the factors associated with mental health problems in that population, which was composed primarily of Chinese immigrants. Results showed that Chinese Americans had low-to-moderate levels of depressive disorders. About 7% reported experiencing depression in their lifetime, and a little over 3% had been depressed during the past year. These rates were lower than those found for the general population in the NCS, but similar to those for the Los Angeles site of the ECA.

In another large-scale study, the National Surveys on Drug Use and Health used a subsample of 134,875 adults aged 18 and older (Harris, Edlund, & Larson, 2005). This study examined racial and ethnic differences in mental health problems, the use of mental health care, and the self-reported need for mental health care using nationally representative data. Results from this study suggested relatively low rates of self-reported mental health problems and service use among Asians compared with Whites.

One complication in trying to estimate the prevalence of mental disorders is the possibility that Asian Americans may exhibit **culture-bound** syndromes. A culture-bound syndrome denotes recurrent, locality-specific patterns of aberrant behavior and troubled experiences. They do not fit into contemporary diagnostic and classification systems such as the *Diagnostic and Statistical Manual* of the American Psychiatric Association. Thus Asians may have specific disorders that are recognized in their cultures or societies and not in other cultures. One example of such a disorder is **neurasthenia**, which is characterized by fatigue, weakness, poor concentration, diffuse aches and pains, sleep disturbances, and gastrointestinal problems. In the CAPES study of Chinese in Los Angeles, about 7% were found to exhibit neurasthenia (Zheng et al., 1997). In estimating the prevalence of disorders, one must consider not only widely recognized disorders, but also those that are unique to particular cultural groups.

Other problems have hindered the study of mental disorders among Asian Americans such as the lack of funding for research on Asian Americans, problems in the ability to compare groups; conceptual, linguistic, and scalar validity of measures of disorders; cultural bias in diagnostic and conceptual schemes; existence of **culture-bound** syndromes; the role of racism

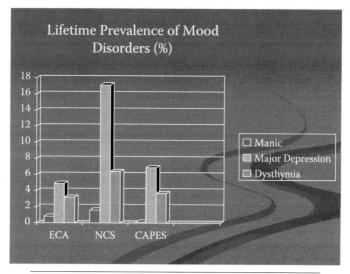

Lifetime prevalence of mood disorders in three epidemiological studies.

and acculturation in estimating prevalence rates; resilience because of cultural factors; and premigration status and reasons for entering the United States among immigrant or refugee groups (Sue & Chu, 2003).

Most of the available investigations of Asian Americans are small-scale studies, often based on selected groups or on selected disorders; some are not true prevalence studies. This means that the findings from these studies should be viewed with a great deal of caution because they may have methodological weaknesses. Nevertheless, they offer some insight into possible mental health problems among Asian Americans. Investigations by Kuo and colleagues (1984; Kuo & Tsai, 1986) examined community samples of four different Asian American groups: Chinese, Japanese, Filipino, and Korean. Asian Americans were found to have higher average scores on a measure of depression than did Whites. About 19% of the Asian Americans were identified as having potential cases of depression. The rates may be even higher among Southeast Asian refugees, a group identified to be at high risk for mental disorders (Marshall et al., 2005). Kinzie, Boehnlein, Leung, and Moore (1990) reported that 70% of their Southeast Asian refugee patients met the criteria for a diagnosis of post-traumatic stress disorder. Westermeyer (1988) also reported that 43% of adult Hmong refugees met the criteria for mental disorders such as adjustment disorder, major depression, and paranoia—twice the expected rate of the general U.S. population. Other studies (Hurh & Kim, 1990; Loo, Tong, & True, 1989; Ying, 1988) also suggest that the rates of emotional disturbance among Asian Americans are not extraordinarily low.

Personality studies over the past 30 years point to adjustment problems of Asian Americans. D. Sue and his colleagues (Sue, 1973; Sue & Frank, 1973; Sue & Kirk, 1973) found evidence that Japanese and Chinese American college students, compared with non-Asian students, tended to experience greater feelings of anxiety, loneliness, and discomfort. Such problems encountered by students were also found by Sue and Zane (1985). Chinese American students were found to experience anxiety, and this was especially common among recent immigrants. While the academic achievement levels (i.e., grades) of the Chinese students exceeded those of the general student body, these students still experienced high levels of anxiety. Other studies have found similar patterns. Okazaki (1997) found that Asian American college students reported higher levels of anxiety and depression compared to White college students. Also, Abe and Zane (1990) found that Asian American foreign-born students reported greater levels of interpersonal distress than their White counterparts, even after residing an average of 10 years in the United States.

In conclusion, prevalence rates for Asian Americans are difficult to determine; available evidence indicates that rates are low, but in the same general range as rates for Whites. There also appears to be a discrepancy between symptom findings and prevalence of disorders. In contrast to prevalence rates for mental disorders, studies of mental health symptoms suggest that Asian Americans tend to describe themselves with more numerous and more serious symptoms than non-Hispanic Whites. Finally, contrary to the hypothesis that cultural factors may enhance mental health, acculturation appears to be related to improved mental health at least for some Asian Americans. Data from the National Latino and Asian American Study (NLAAS), the first national epidemiological survey on Asian Americans in the United States, examined life-time and 12-month prevalence rates of psychiatric disorders. Results from this study showed that immigration factors were associated with mental disorders, but in varying ways for Asian men and women. Among women, those who were foreign born were less likely than U.S.-born women to have a lifetime case of mental health disorders. That is, women born in another country were less likely to have any lifetime depressive, anxiety, substance abuse, and psychiatric disorder compared to U.S.-born women. For 12-month disorders, nativity was strongly associated with an anxiety disorder. In addition, second-generation women were particularly at risk for lifetime and 12-month disorders. For Asian men, however, those who spoke English proficiently tended to have lower rates of lifetime and 12-month disorders compared to nonproficient speakers (Takeuchi et al., 2006). That is, men who spoke English well were less likely to have any lifetime depressive, anxiety, and psychiatric disorder compared to men who were less proficient in English.

Mental Health Services

Service Utilization

Almost all of the past studies of utilization rates of mental health services have demonstrated low rates of utilization among Asian Americans. Studies (Brown, Huang, Harris, & Stein, 1973; Cheung, 1989; Los Angeles County Department of Mental Health, 1984; Snowden & Cheung, 1990; Sue, 1977; Sue, Fujino, Hu, & Takeuchi, 1991) consistently demonstrate that Asian Americans tend to be underrepresented in psychiatric clinics and hospitals compared to their proportion in the population. The underrepresentation occurs whether student or nonstudent populations, inpatients or outpatients, or different Asian American groups are considered. In a utilization and therapy effectiveness study of ethnic minority college students, White Americans reported the greatest number of sessions attended, whereas Latinos attended the fewest number of sessions. African Americans and Asian Americans attended significantly fewer sessions than White students. Not only did Whites attend the most sessions during their treatment, but they also consistently reported the least distress (Kearney, Draper, & Baron, 2005). In one of the most comprehensive analyses, Matsuoka, Breaux, and Ryujin (1997) examined Asian Americans' use of services at state and county mental hospitals, private psychiatric hospitals, Veterans Administration psychiatric services, residential treatment centers for emotionally disturbed children, nonfederal psychiatric services in general hospitals, outpatient psychiatric clinics, multi-service mental health programs, psychiatric day/night services, and other residential programs in the United States. In general, it was found that utilization of services by Asian populations was low, regardless of their population density in various states of the United States. These findings are consistent with a report by Zhang, Snowden, and Sue (1998). Asian Americans were unlikely to seek services of any kind for mental health problems, including help from friends and family members. Every population underutilizes in the sense that not all individuals with psychological disturbances seek help from the mental health system. However, considerable evidence suggests that Asian Americans are more likely than the general population to underutilize services.

Severity of Disturbance

Studies consistently demonstrate that in addition to low utilization of services, those Asian Americans who do use services are more severely disturbed (Brown et al., 1973; Lee, Lei, & Sue, 2001; Sue & Sue, 1974). Durvasula and Sue (1996) concluded that the level of disturbance is high among Asian American outpatients using multiple indicators of disturbance. These indicators included a higher proportion of severe diagnosis, lower level of functioning scores, and a higher proportion of psychotic features among those diagnosed with mood disorders.

The evidence is quite convergent that few Asian Americans use the mental health service system. The alternative explanation that low utilization of services is caused by the low rate of mental disturbance is weakened by findings that Asian Americans who do seek treatment are more severely disturbed than White Americans. These findings suggest that underutilization of services does not imply a lower need for services. Lin, Inui, Kleinman, and Womack (1982) found that Asian Americans were more likely than Whites to have a delay in the recognition of mental health symptoms and a delay in participation in a treatment program.

A number of factors affect utilization and effectiveness of mental health services. Some of the factors involve accessibility (e.g., including ease of using services, financial cost of services, and location of services), availability (e.g., existence of services), cultural and linguistic appropriateness of services, knowledge of available services, and willingness to use services (DHHS, 2001). Obviously, the nature of one's problems influences utilization. Culturally based factors are also important to consider, such as shame and stigma, conceptions of mental health, and alternative services. These have all been implicated as factors that account for low utilization among Asian Americans (Kim, 1978; Sue & Morishima, 1982; Tracey, Leong, & Glidden, 1986).

Improving Health Services

What kinds of services should be established? Three suggestions are important to consider. First, in mainstream mental health facilities where there are few Asian American personnel, service providers should receive multicultural training to work with Asian American clients. This can be particularly effective, since Asian American clients attribute more credibility to culturally sensitive mental health professionals (Gim, Atkinson, & Kim, 1991). The training should cover assessment, psychotherapy, and case management and include issues such as cultural values and behaviors, pre- and postmigration experiences, and so on. Asian American consultants should also be available to service providers. Second, mainstream mental health programs should employ more Asian American personnel, who are bilingual and bicultural. Such personnel can be of immense benefit in providing effective services. Third, ethnic-specific or nonmainstream services should be created. Ethnic specific services (ESS) are those that may be similar to mainstream ones (e.g., a clinic or hospital) but are specifically designed to service an ethnic population. For example, a specific ward at San Francisco General Hospital and the Asian Pacific Counseling and Treatment Center in Los Angeles were created to serve Asian Pacific Americans. They typically employ bilingual and bicultural personnel, post notices in English and Asian languages, serve Asian foods or drinks, and so on—all in an attempt to respond to the cultural needs of Asian Pacific Americans.

Ethnic-specific mental health services have been found to reduce service inequities (i.e., differential premature termination rates and treatment outcome) for Asian Americans (Flaskerud

& Hu, 1994; Lau & Zane, 2000; Yeh, Takeuchi, & Sue, 1994), while not creating any such inequities for White clients (Zane, Hatanaka, Park, & Akutsu, 1994). Furthermore, ethnic clients who attended ethnic-specific programs had a higher return rate and stayed in treatment longer than those using mainstream services (Takeuchi, Sue, & Yeh, 1995).

Utilization can be increased by making services more culturally competent, as noted by Brach and Fraser (2000). Culturally competent strategies include: interpreter services, recruitment and retention of minority staff, cultural competency training programs, coordination with traditional healers, use of community health workers (liaisons in the community), culturally competent health promotion, including family and/or community members, immersion into another culture, and administrative and organizational accommodations (e.g., location, hours of operation, written materials). The delay between onset of symptoms and seeking help through the mental health system can be reduced with the availability of such services (Lin & Cheung, 1999). These culturally relevant services should be strengthened, and new ethnic-specific programs should be established. Local, state, and federal governments should place these services and programs as a high priority in terms of funding and development.

Treatment Considerations

Because of the shame and stigma over mental health problems, Asian Americans are more likely to seek help at counseling or educational rather than psychiatric services. Those who use services may express somatic complaints instead of emotional problems (headaches, stomachaches, inability to concentrate or sleep, fatigue, etc.).

Mental health professionals treating Asian American clients should be aware of this and other unique factors (which will be discussed in another chapter) specific to Asian Americans. One important consideration is that some Asian Americans combine Western and traditional medicine (Chung & Lin, 1994). This can result in adverse consequences, with many herbs interacting with psychotropic medications (Lin & Cheung, 1999). Additionally, Lin and Cheung noted that Asian clients require less dosage for the same psychotropic medication as White clients and that the side effects of psychotropic medication can be more severe for Asians.

Summary

Certain factors are particularly important in understanding the mental health of Asian Americans. They include culture and assimilation, minority group status, and immigration status. Research suggests that these factors influence mental health. While the prevalence of mental disorders and psychological disturbance among Asian Americans are difficult to ascertain, the available evidence suggests that the rates are somewhat low but within the range found for other Americans. What is clear is that Asian Americans tend not to use mental health services because of shame and stigma, cultural differences in help-seeking, and the cultural mismatch between mainstream mental health services and Asian cultural values and practices. Many Asian Americans delay using services until symptoms become very severe. In order to improve the cultural responsiveness of services, several recommendations should be considered. They include the enhancement of cultural knowledge and competency among providers and changing aspects of treatment to be more compatible with clients' cultures.

Practice Exercises

1. Locate a mental health care center in your area and interview a mental health care provider about issues of client diversity and cultural competency.

2. Reflect on your relationship with your parents and list areas of conflict between your-self and your parents. What are the major differences that arise? What are the major causes of such differences?

3. With another person, act out the role of a therapist and client, addressing important issues when working with ethnically diverse populations.

Discussion Questions

1. Who would you go to first if you had life challenges?

2. Would you ever seek therapy? Why or why not?

3. What is your understanding of mental illness? What have you observed? How have you reacted?

4. Compare and contrast the stereotypes of Asian Americans earlier in history and more recently. What do you attribute the changes to and why have some old stereo-types remained the same? What are the implications of such stereotypes on mental well-being?

5. When troubled or lonely, does it help to be around others of your same ethnicity? How about others who share similar problems?

6. Do you feel as though your friends who share your same ethnicity understand you bet-ter than others who do not share your ethnicity?

Case Study

This chapter has presented research and theory concerning mental health among Asian Americans. To further illustrate the issues of emotional distress, family con-flicts, cultural considerations, and treatment, the case of Mae (see Sue & Morishima, 1982), who was introduced at the beginning of this chapter, is discussed in more detail. The case involved a young Chinese woman, Mae C., who sought treatment at a mental health center. She was extremely distraught and stated that she would have to seek a divorce. Tearfully, she related her dilemma. Mae was a recent immi-grant from Hong Kong who met and married her husband (also a recent immi-grant from Hong Kong) in the United States. Their marriage was going fairly well. Then about 6 months ago, her husband succeeded in bringing over his parents from Hong Kong who intended to live with Mae and her husband. While she was not enthusiastic about having her in-laws live with her, Mae realized that her husband wanted them to live together. Mae realized that both of them were obligated to help his parents. However, after his parents arrived, Mae increasingly felt that her relationship with her in-laws was unbearable. Mae was expected to dutifully serve them. The mother-in-law expected Mae to cook and serve dinner, to do laundry, and to do other chores. At the same time, her mother-in-law would constantly complain that Mae did not cook the dinner right, that the house was always messy, and that Mae should wash certain clothes separately. It was also apparent that her husband's parents felt that Mae was not of the same social class as their son. The parents-in-law soon displaced Mae and her husband from the master bedroom. The guest room was located in the basement, and the parents refused to sleep in the basement because it reminded them of a tomb.

Mae would complain to her husband about his parents. Her husband would excuse his parents' demands by referring to the fact that his parents were getting old. Most times, he avoided any potential conflict; after all, he was the eldest son and wanted to be obedient. He also tended to stay at work for long hours, perhaps avoiding the conflicts at home. Although Mae realized that she had an obligation to his parents, the situation was becoming intolerable to her.

What kind of solution can be found in Mae's case? After discussing the matter at a case conference, a number of suggestions were made. We could have encouraged Mae to confront her in-laws. Some suggestions included marital counseling or extended family therapy involving Mae, her husband, and her in-laws. However, in Mae's particular case, such tactics would have been difficult for her or her husband to carry out. Feelings of guilt and shame would have been extensive, and family relationships would have been seriously jeopardized. The in-laws would have felt betrayed if they found out that Mae was seeing a therapist about family problems. In other words, a number of cultural considerations seemed to hinder the use of traditional psychotherapeutic treatment approaches such as marital counseling and family therapy. The cultural considerations involved cultural obligations between parents and children, guilt and shame, and keeping family problems within the family.

It is worth noting that Chinese often experience in-law or family generational conflicts. In such circumstances, Chinese often use intermediaries or people who have credibility or authority with each conflicting party. We did find that Mae considered one relative, her uncle (the older brother of the mother-in-law), to be quite understanding and sensitive. We asked Mae to contact the uncle, who lived in a city about 50 miles from Mae. The uncle seemed to realize the gravity of the situation and visited Mae and her family. After having dinner with the family, he took his sister (Mae's mother-in-law) aside and told her that Mae looked very unhappy, that possibly she was working too hard, and that she needed a little more praise for the work that she was doing in taking care of everyone. The mother-in-law expressed surprise over Mae's unhappiness and agreed that Mae was doing a fine job. Without directly confronting each other, Mae's uncle and mother-in-law understood the subtle messages each conveyed. Her older brother was indirectly criticizing his sister about her treatment of Mae. After this interaction, Mae reported that her mother-in-law's criticisms did noticeably diminish and that she had even begun to help Mae with the chores.

The case illustrates how Chinese cultural role relationships can create problems. While in-law problems are not unique to Chinese, role expectations (daughter-in-law should be obedient and dutiful; parents take precedence over sons) can be a source of conflict. Furthermore, in our discussion of treatment, cultural considerations were weighed. Rather than using typical psychotherapeutic strategies between client and therapist, a third-party intermediary was utilized.

Case Study Discussion Questions

For undergraduate students, please consider the following questions:

1. Do you think conflicts between parents (or parents-in-law) and children are common? What kinds of problems are fairly common?
2. What are expectations that parents have regarding the obedience of their children or the younger generation?
3. How should adolescents and young adults handle problems with their parents and come to a successful resolution?

For graduate students and/or beginning therapists, please consider the following questions:

1. What can help to alleviate the guilt and shame that Asian Americans often have over seeking mental health treatment for personal or family problems?
2. How can therapists develop credibility and rapport when working with Asian American families in psychotherapy?
3. What can be done to integrate cultural considerations or cultural features into current mental health treatment practices?

Key Terms

Acculturation: The outcome of new knowledge about the host culture and exchange of cultural features and patterns from sustained contact with this culture.

Acculturative stress: Reduction in physical and mental well-being due to the stress accompanied from the acculturation process.

Social: An effect produced by environmental factors.

For Further Learning and Suggested Readings

Movies

Better Luck Tomorrow
The Killing Fields
The Wedding Banquet

Readings

Tan, A. (1989). *The joy luck club*. United States: New York: Putnam Adult.
U.S. Department of Health and Human Services. (2001). *Mental health: Culture, race, and ethnicity—a supplement to mental health: A report of the Surgeon General*. Rockville, MD: U.S. Department of Health and Human Services, Public Health Service, Office of the Surgeon General.

References

Abe, J. S., & Zane, N. W. (1990). Psychological maladjustment among Asian and White American college students: Controlling for confounds. *Journal of Counseling Psychology, 37*, 437–444.

Alegria, M., Takeuchi, D., Canino, G., Duan, N., Shrout, P., Meng, X. L., et al. (2004). Considering context, place and culture: The National Latino and Asian American Study. *International Journal of Methods in Psychiatric Research, 13*, 208–220.

Berry, J. W. (1997). Immigration, acculturation and adaptation. *Applied Psychology: An International Review, 46*, 5–68.

Berry, J. W., & Annis, R. C. (1974). Acculturation stress: The role of ecology, culture and differentiation. *Journal of Cross-Cultural Psychology, 5*, 382–406.

Berry, J. W., & Kim, U. (1988). Acculturation and mental health. In P. Dasen, J. W. Berry, & N. Sartorius (Eds.), *Health and cross-cultural psychology: Towards applications* (pp. 207–236). Beverly Hills: Sage.

Berry, J. W., Kim, U., Minde, T., & Mok, D. (1987). Comparative studies of acculturative stress. *International Migration Review, 21*, 491–511.

Brach, C., & Fraser, I. (2000). Can cultural competency reduce racial and ethnic health disparities? A review and conceptual model. *Medical Care Research and Review, 57*, 181–217.

Brown, T. R., Huang, K., Harris, D. E., & Stein, K. M. (1973). Mental illness and the role of mental health facilities in Chinatown. In S. Sue & N. Wagner (Eds.), *Asian-Americans: Psychological perspectives* (pp. 212–231). Palo Alto, CA: Science and Behavior Books.

Chan, C. S. (2003). Psychological issues of Asian Americans. In P. Bronstein & K. Quina (Eds.), *Teaching gender and multicultural awareness: Resources for the psychology classroom* (pp. 179–193). Washington, DC: American Psychological Association.

Cheung, F. K. (1989). *Culture and mental health care for Asian Americans in the United States.* Paper presented at the annual meeting of the American Psychiatric Association, San Francisco, CA.

Chun, K. M., Eastman, K. L., Wang, G. C. S., & Sue, S. (1998). Psychopathology. In L. Lee & N. Zane (Eds.), *Handbook of Asian American psychology* (pp. 457–483). Thousand Oaks, CA: Sage Publications.

Chung, R. C. Y., & Lin, K. M. (1994). Help-seeking behavior among Southeast Asian refugees. *Journal of Community Psychology, 22,* 109–120.

Department of Justice Federal Bureau of Investigation. (n.d.). *2004 persons arrested report.* Retrieved April 26, 2006, from http://www.fbi.gov/ucr/cius_04/persons_arrested/table_46-49.html

DeVos, G. (1978). *Selective permeability and reference group sanctioning: Psychological continuities in role degradation.* Paper presented at Seminar on Comparative Studies in Ethnicity and Nationality, University of Washington, Seattle.

DeVos, G. (1982). Adaptive strategies in U.S. minorities. In E. E. Jones & S. J. Korchin (Eds.), *Minority mental health* (pp. 74–117). New York: Praeger.

Durvasula, R., & Sue, S. (1996). Severity of disturbance among Asian American outpatients. *Cultural Diversity and Mental Health, 2,* 43–51.

Flaskerud, J. H., & Hu, L. (1994). Participation in and outcome of treatment for major depression among low income Asian Americans. *Psychiatry Research, 53,* 289–300.

Gim, R. H., Atkinson, D. R., & Kim, S. J. (1991). Asian-American acculturation, counselor ethnicity and cultural sensitivity, and ratings of counselors. *Journal of Counseling Psychology, 38,* 57–62.

Goto, S. G., Gee, G. C., & Takeuchi, D. T. (2002). Strangers still? The experience of discrimination among Chinese Americans. *Journal of Community Psychology, 30,* 211–224.

Hall, G. C. N. (2003). The self in context: Implications for psychopathology and psychotherapy. *Journal of Psychotherapy Integration, 13,* 66–82.

Harris, K. M, Edlund, M. J., & Larson, S. (2005). Racial and ethnic differences in mental health problems and use of mental health care. *Medical Care, 43,* 775–784.

Hsu, F. L. K. (1971). Psychosocial homeostasis and Jen: Conceptual tools for advancing psychological anthropology. *American Anthropologist, 73,* 23–44.

Hurh, W. M., & Kim, K. C. (1990). Correlates of Korean immigrants' mental health. *Journal of Nervous and Mental Disease, 178,* 703–711.

Kearney, L. K., Draper, M., & Baron, A. (2005). Counseling utilization by ethnic minority college students. *Cultural Diversity and Ethnic Minority Psychology, 11,* 272–285.

Kessler, R.C., McGonagle, K.A., Zhao, S., Nelson, C.B., Hughes, M., & Eshleman, S., et al. (1994). Lifetime and 12-month prevalence of DSM-III-R psychiatric disorders in the United States: Results from the National Comorbidity Survey. *Archives of General Psychiatry, 51,* 8–19.

Kim, B. L. C. (1978). *The Asian Americans, changing patterns, changing needs.* Montclair, NJ: Association of Korean Christian Scholars in North America.

Kinzie, J. D., Boehnlein, J. K., Leung, P. K., & Moore, L. J. (1990). The prevalence of posttraumatic stress disorder and its clinical significance among Southeast Asian refugees. *American Journal of Psychiatry, 147,* 913–917.

Kluckhohn, C., & Murray, H. A. (1950). Personality formation: The determinants. In C. Kluckhohn & H. A. Murray (Eds.), *Personality in nature, society and culture* (pp. 35–48). New York: Alfred A. Knopf.

Kuo, W. H. (1984). Prevalence of depression among Asian-Americans. *Journal of Nervous and Mental Disease, 172,* 449–457.

Kuo, W. H., & Tsai, Y. (1986). Social networking, hardiness, and immigrant's mental health. *Journal of Health and Social Behavior, 27,* 133–149.

Lau, A., & Zane, N. (2000). Examining the effects of ethnic-specific services: An analysis of cost-utilization and treatment outcome for Asian American clients. *Journal of Community Psychology, 28,* 63–77.

Lee, J., Lei, A., & Sue, S. (2001). The current state of mental health research on Asian Americans. *Journal of Human Behavior in the Social Environment, 3,* 159–178.

Leong, F. T. L. (1998). Career development and vocational behaviors. In L. Lee & N. Zane (Eds.), *Handbook of Asian American psychology* (pp. 359–398). Thousand Oaks, CA: Sage Publications.

Leong, F. T. L. (2000). Asian American psychology. In A. E. Kazdin (Ed.), *Encyclopedia of psychology* (Vol. 1, pp. 259–264). New York: Oxford University Press.

Liang, C. T. H., Li, L. C., & Kim, B. S K. (2004). The Asian American Racism-Related Stress Inventory: Development, factor analysis, reliability, and validity. *Journal of Counseling Psychology, 51,* 103–114.

Lin, K. M., & Cheung, F. (1999). Mental health issues for Asian Americans. *Psychiatric Services, 50,* 774–780.

Lin, K. M., Inui, T. S., Kleinman, A. M., & Womack, W. M. (1982). Sociocultural determinants of the help-seeking behavior of patients with mental illness. *Journal of Nervous and Mental Disease, 170,* 78–85.

Loo, C., Tong, B., & True, R. (1989). A bitter bean: Mental health status and attitudes in Chinatown. *Journal of Community Psychology, 17,* 283–296.

Los Angeles County Department of Mental Health. (1984). *Report on ethnic utilization of mental health services.* Los Angeles: Department of Health.

Markus, H. R., & Kitayama, S. (1991). Culture and the self: Implications for cognition, emotion, and motivation. *Psychological Review, 98,* 224–253.

Marshall, G. N., Schell, T. L., Elliott, M. N., Berthold, S. M., & Chun, C. A. (2005). Mental health of Cambodian refugees two decades after resettlement in the United States. *Journal of the American Medical Association, 294,* 571–579.

Matsuoka, J. K., Breaux, C., & Ryujin, D. H. (1997). National utilization of mental health services by Asian Americans/Pacific Islanders. *Journal of Community Psychology, 25,* 141–145.

Nguyen, L., & Peterson, C. (1993). Depressive symptoms among Vietnamese-American college students. *Journal of Social Psychology, 133,* 65–71.

Okazaki, S. (1997). Sources of ethnic differences between Asian American and White American college students on measures of depression and social anxiety. *Journal of Abnormal Psychology, 106,* 52–60.

Organista, P. B., Organista, K. C., & Kurasaki, K. (2003). The relation between acculturation and ethnic minority mental health. In K. M. Chun, P. Balls Organista, & G. Marin (Eds.), *Acculturation: Advances in theory, measurement, and applied research* (pp. 139–161). Washington, DC: American Psychological Association.

Snowden, L. R., & Cheung, F. K. (1990). Use of inpatient mental health services by members of ethnic minority groups. *American Psychologist, 45,* 347–355.

Sue, D. W. (1973). Ethnic identity: The impact of two cultures on the psychological development of Asians in American. In S. Sue & N. Wagner (Eds.), *Asian-Americans: Psychological perspectives* (pp. 140–149). Palo Alto, CA: Science and Behavior Books.

Sue, D. W., & Frank, A. C. (1973). A typological approach to the psychological study of Chinese and Japanese American college males. *Journal of Social Issues, 29,* 129–148.

Sue, D. W., & Kirk, B. A. (1973). Differential characteristics of Japanese-American and Chinese-American college students. *Journal of Counseling Psychology, 20,* 142–148.

Sue, D. W., & Sue, D. (1999). *Counseling the culturally different: Theory and practice.* New York: Wiley and Sons.

Sue, S. (1977). Community mental health services to minority groups: Some optimism, some pessimism. *American Psychologist, 32,* 616–624.

Sue, S., & Chu, J. Y. (2003). The mental health of ethnic minority groups: Challenges posed by the supplement to the Surgeon General's report on mental health. *Culture, Medicine and Psychiatry. Special Issue: The Politics of Science: Culture, Race, Ethnicity, and the Supplement to the Surgeon General's Report on Mental Health, 27,* 447–465.

Sue, S., Fujino, D. C., Hu, L. T., & Takeuchi, D. T. (1991). Community mental health services for ethnic minority groups: A test of the cultural responsiveness hypothesis. *Journal of Consulting and Clinical Psychology, 59,* 533–540.

Sue, S., Keefe, K., Enomoto, K., Durvasula, R., & Chao, R. (1996). Asian American and White college students' performance on the MMPI-2. In J. N. Butcher (Ed.), *International adaptations of the MMPI: Research and clinical applications* (pp. 206–220). Minneapolis, MN: University of Minnesota Press.

Sue, S., & Morishima, J. K. (1982). *The mental health of Asian Americans* (1st ed.). San Francisco: Jossey-Bass.

Sue, S., & Sue, D. W. (1974). MMPI comparisons between Asian-American and non-Asian students utilizing a student health psychiatric clinic. *Journal of Counseling Psychology, 21*, 423–427.

Sue, S., & Zane, N. W. (1985). Academic achievement and socioemotional adjustment among Chinese university students. *Journal of Counseling Psychology, 32*, 570–579.

Takeuchi, D. T., Chung, R. C., Lin, K. M., Shen, H., Kurasaki, K., & Chun, C., et al. (1998). Lifetime and twelve-month prevalence rates of major depressive episodes and dysthymia among Chinese Americans in Los Angeles. *American Journal of Psychiatry, 155*, 1407–1414.

Takeuchi, D. T., Sue, S., & Yeh, M. (1995). Return rates and outcomes from ethnicity-specific mental health programs in Los Angeles. *American Journal of Public Health, 85*, 638–643.

Takeuchi, D. T., Zane, N., Hong, S., Chae, D. H., Gong, F., & Gee, G. C., et al. (2006). Immigration and mental disorders among Asian Americans. Manuscript submitted for publication.

Tracey, T. J., Leong, F. T., & Glidden, C. (1986). Help seeking and problem perception among Asian Americans. *Journal of Counseling Psychology, 33*, 331–336.

Uba, L. (1994). *Asian Americans: Personality patterns, identity, and mental health.* New York: Guilford Press.

U.S. Bureau of the Census. (2000). *Educational attainment of the population 25 years and over by sex, race, and Hispanic origin: March 2000* (Current Population Reports).

U.S. Bureau of the Census. (2000). *Marital status of the population 15 years and over by sex, race, and Hispanic origin: March 2000* (Current Population Reports).

U.S. Department of Health and Human Services. (2001). *Mental health: Culture, race, and ethnicity—a supplement to mental health: A report of the Surgeon General.* Rockville, MD: U.S. Department of Health and Human Services, Public Health Service, Office of the Surgeon General.

Vega, W. A., & Alegria, M. (2001). Latino mental health and treatment in the United States. In C. W. Aguirre-Molina & R. E Zambrana (Eds.), *Health issues in the Latino community.* San Francisco: Jossey-Bass.

Westermeyer, J. (1988). DSM-III psychiatric disorders among Hmong refugees in the United States: A point prevalence study. *American Journal of Psychiatry, 145*, 197–202.

Westermeyer, J., & Her, C. (1996). English fluency and social adjustment among Hmong refugees in Minnesota. *Journal of Nervous and Mental Disease, 184*, 130–132.

Westermeyer, J., Neider, J., & Vang, T. F. (1984). Acculturation and mental health: A study of Hmong refugees at 1.5 and 3.5 years postmigration. *Social Sciences Medicine, 18*, 87–93.

Yeh, M., Takeuchi, D. T., & Sue, S. (1994). Asian American children in the mental health system: A comparison of parallel and mainstream outpatient service centers. *Journal of Clinical Child Psychology, 23*, 5–12.

Ying, Y. W. (1988). Depressive symptomatology among Chinese-Americans as measured by the CES-D. *Journal of Clinical Psychology, 44*, 739–746.

Ying, Y. W. (1995). Cultural orientation and psychological well-being in Chinese Americans. *American Journal of Community Psychology, 23*, 893–911.

Zane, N., Hatanaka, H., Park, S., & Akutsu, P. (1994). Ethnic-specific mental health services: Evaluation of the parallel approach for Asian American clients. *Journal of Community Psychology, 22*, 68–81.

Zane, N., Sue, S., Chang, J., Huang, L., Huang, J., Lowe, S., et al. (2005). Beyond ethnic match: Effects of client–therapist cognitive match in problem perception, coping orientation, and therapy goals on treatment outcomes. *Journal of Community Psychology, 33*, 569–585.

Zhang, A. Y., Snowden, L. R., & Sue, S. (1998). Differences between Asian and White Americans' help seeking and utilization patterns in the Los Angeles area. *Journal of Community Psychology, 26*, 317–326.

Zheng, X., & Berry, J. W. (1991). Psychological adaptations of Chinese sojourners in Canada. *International Journal of Psychology, 26*, 451–470.

Zheng, Y. P., Lin, K. M., Takeuchi, D., Kurasaki, K. S., Wang, Y. X., & Cheung, F. (1997). An epidemiological study of neurasthenia in Chinese-Americans in Los Angeles. *Comprehensive Psychiatry, 38*, 249–259.

28
Body Image Among Asian Americans

KATHLEEN KAWAMURA and TIFFANY RICE

OUTLINE OF CHAPTER

Case Synopsis
Introduction
Influences on Asian American Body Images
Impact of Body Image Dissatisfaction
Facilitating a Healthy Body Image
Case Study
References

Case Synopsis

Soon is a 19-year-old, Korean American woman attending a 4-year university in Southern California. Over the past year, Soon has become increasingly preoccupied with her physical appearance. She had been self-conscious of her "single eyelids" since she was a young child, but more recently she began considering "Asian eyelid surgery." In addition, despite her petite figure, she counted calories, skipped breakfast, and avoided eating out with friends for fear that she would be tempted to overeat. Soon was convinced that a prettier face and a thinner body would help her feel more confident. Her roommate Kimi became concerned when she noticed that Soon seemed sad much of the time and was withdrawing from her friends. Kimi decided to speak to Soon about meeting with a therapist at their university counseling center before Soon became more depressed or took any drastic measures to change her appearance.

Introduction

Body image refers to thoughts, attitudes, and beliefs about one's own physical appearance. Research on body image has focused on dissatisfaction with body size and has been conducted primarily with European American women. Though the number of studies conducted with ethnic minority groups has steadily been increasing, there remains a distinct paucity of research conducted with Asian Americans as compared to African Americans and Hispanic Americans. Researchers may have assumed that because of their smaller body size, Asian American women are protected from body size dissatisfaction or that as the "model minority," Asian Americans have few psychological problems, including body image dissatisfaction (model minority issues are further discussed elsewhere in the book).

Recent research has shown that Asian Americans are in fact susceptible to body size dissatisfaction, and that for Asian Americans, both men and women may be vulnerable to body image dissatisfaction. General findings regarding Asian American body images have shown that Asian American women desire to be smaller whereas Asian American men desire to be heavier. In addition, body size may not be the only physical attribute that is salient for Asian Americans. As a visibly distinct ethnic minority group, Asian American men and women may become self-conscious of physical characteristics that set them apart from people of other racial

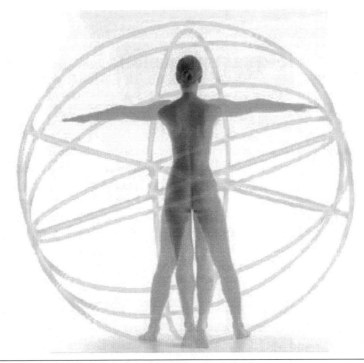

Body image attitudes can be influenced by a myriad of factors, including the media, cultural values, peers, parents, and personality.

backgrounds, such as their facial features and skin color. This chapter will explore the various influences on the development of body image dissatisfaction in Asian American women and men and will describe ways in which individuals may react to body image dissatisfaction. Lastly, factors that facilitate a positive body image will also be discussed.

Influences on Asian American Body Images

An individual's body image is shaped by macro-level sociocultural influences, micro-level interpersonal experiences, and individual, intrapersonal characteristics. Greater sociocultural influences include culturally determined beauty ideals and cultural values regarding the importance placed on physical appearance. Asian Americans are often exposed to sociocultural messages originating from both the United States and Asia, and thus their body image satisfaction may depend on which cultural values they adhere to. Though messages about specific beauty ideals can have a strong impact on the development of Asian American body images, general sociocultural factors such as collectivistic orientation and religious practice can also influence the body image of Asian Americans. Interpersonal experiences that shape Asian American body images can include childhood interactions with parents and peers, while individual characteristics can include perfectionism, self-consciousness, and ethnic identity. The following section will describe in more detail these various factors that can influence the development of Asian American body images.

Sociocultural Factors

Beliefs Regarding Body Size   Though some Asian cultures have traditionally valued obesity as a sign of beauty, prosperity, or good health, cultural values in modern Asian countries seem to

Many women in both the U.S. and Asia experience intense pressure to achieve an ideal of thinness that is difficult to attain.

have shifted toward thinness as the desired ideal for women. This is similar to Western societies, where the mass media has generally endorsed an increasingly thinner body size as the ideal physique for women, and thinness has long been equated with beauty, success, and happiness. In many Asian countries, the women are already thin by Western standards but appear to be striving to become even thinner. For example, in Japan, an advertisement shows how a 5′3″ woman was able to drop from 116 to 96 pounds through the use of diet pills, which based on medical standards is a change from "normal weight" before the diet to "under weight" afterwards (Graham, n.d.). The idealization of an extremely thin body may contribute to body size dissatisfaction in Asian and Asian American women despite a relatively small body size.

Theorists hypothesize that globalization and the resulting spread of Western ideals may be partially responsible for the shift in Asian beauty standards from the idealization of more endowed bodies to that of thinness bordering on emaciation. Dr. Anne Becker and her colleagues (Becker, Burwell, Gilman, Herzog, & Hamburg, 2002) conducted an empirical investigation on the influence of Western media on body size dissatisfaction. Teenage girls in Fiji were surveyed right after the introduction of television in 1995 and then again 3 years later. After exposure to Western television, with shows such as Melrose Place and Beverly Hills 90210, there was a sharp increase in eating disorder symptoms, and the girls who watched more television were more vulnerable to body size dissatisfaction. Traditionally, the Fijian culture valued a more robust body figure, and in fact, "going thin" was seen as a condition to be treated, but this no longer seemed to be the case, especially with the younger generations. The researchers posit that the changes were due not just to exposure to Western television but to societal modernization, which was occurring at the same time as the introduction of television.

With modernization come increased educational and occupational opportunities for women, and physical attractiveness may be seen as an influential factor in obtaining positions in more professional occupations. For example, researchers in the United States found that for women, increased body mass was related to decreased job prestige and there existed a bias against hiring overweight women (Conley & Glauber, 2005; Pingitore, Dugoni, Tindale, & Spring, 1994).

For women, physical attractiveness, specifically a thin body, may be seen as an important factor in achieving social and occupational success.

Researchers in China hypothesize that this may be why women in more modernized provinces of China exhibit elevated symptoms of eating disordered symptoms as compared to women in more rural provinces (Lee & Lee, 2000). As Asian American women also gain greater access to professional opportunities, they too may become vulnerable to the belief that a thinner body will lead to occupational success. In their chapter on body image issues among girls and women, Ruth Striegal-Moore and Debra Franko (2002) describe how the pursuit of thinness is driven by the **myth of transformation**, where losing weight is believed to be the ticket to positive changes in both economic and interpersonal social status.

In general, much more importance is placed on physical appearances for women than for men, but this is not to say that men are immune to body size dissatisfaction. Men in modern, Western societies are described as suffering from the **Adonis complex**, referring to the half-man, half-god character of Greek mythology whose muscular, moderately sized, V-shaped body is seen as the ideal masculine image (Olivardia, 2002).

In the United States, the ideal physical shape has become increasingly muscular. For example, GI Joe action figures have become larger and more muscular (Corson & Andersen, 2002), and the average Playgirl centerfold has lost 12 pounds of fat and gained 27 pounds of muscle over the last 25 years (Olivardia, 2002). Fitness and health magazines displaying images of muscular men have also become common in the United States.

In comparison to the United States, many countries in Asia appear to promote images of a more slender physique for men with less emphasis on muscularity. This may be due to the tendency for Asian men to be less bulky and smaller in stature than European American men

Asian American men may be influenced by societal norms in the U.S. that idealize a muscular build for men.

but may also be due to Asian sociocultural influences. Harvard researchers Chi-Fu Yang, Peter Gray, and Harrison Pope (2005) hypothesized that Taiwanese men in their study were less concerned with their muscularity than were European American men because in Taiwan, intellect, rather than muscularity and fitness, is valued as a more important measure of masculinity. In addition, traditional male roles are still more common in Taiwan, while in Westernized countries, women have begun to challenge traditional roles by competing for occupations that had previously been held only by men. Consequently, Western societies may have elevated the importance of the male body, rather than male roles, as the primary measure of masculinity. The Harvard researchers also found that there are fewer media images of undressed men in Taiwan, reflecting the lack of societal pressure in Asia on men to be conscious of their bodies.

There may be less of an emphasis on the male body in Asia, but Asian American men are still exposed to the body consciousness of American society. Thus, Asian American men may still experience societal pressures to be well built, but perhaps the physical ideal for Asian American men takes into account the difficulty for many Asian American men to achieve the same body type as GI Joe. In an online magazine geared toward Asian Americans, H.Y. Nahm (n.d.) encourages Asian American men to recognize the value of a boxer's "balance, stamina and vitality" over a football player's "bulk, stopping power and visual intimidation." He also describes how the physiques of actors such as Bruce Lee, Jet Li, and Jackie Chan can be commendable ideals in that they embody the "old physical traditions of Asian cultures" that also promote the ethics and aesthetics of martial arts. Therefore, for Asian American men, emphases on body size differ between Western, Asian, and Asian American communities, whereas for Asian American women, thinness appears to have become a universal ideal.

Activity 1: Examining the Impact of Media Messages
In the space below, write the names of magazines or other publications, and who they are marketed toward (i.e., women, singles, Asian Americans). Then list whether you feel this publication has a positive, negative, or neutral effect on a person's body image. Next, write the ways in which you feel your body image might be affected by this publication.

Beliefs Regarding Facial Features   Research studies have found that Chinese, Japanese, and Asian Indians report greater dissatisfaction with facial features as compared to European Americans, and that Asian Americans are particularly self-conscious about their eyes (Mintz & Kashubeck, 1999). "Double eyelids" and a narrower nose are rated by some Asian Americans as being attractive physical features (Choe, Sclafani, Litner, Yu, & Romo, 2004). The "double eyelid" typical of

Name of publication	Who marketed toward?	Positive, negative, or neutral effect on body image?	In what ways might your body image have been affecgted by this publication?

European Americans consists of a well-defined eyelid crease and fold, whereas the single "eye-lid," or epicanthic eye fold, is an eyelid without a crease. As many as 50% to 70% of Asian Pacific populations may be born with single eyelids (Ohmori, 1990).

Theorists appear to be split regarding the factors that contribute to the idealization of physical features such as the double eyelid or the narrower nose. Some theorists argue that larger, rounder eyes with double eyelids and a narrow, sculpted nose reflect universal ideals of beauty, whereas other theorists assert that the idealization of these features reflect Western influence. The fact that a Japanese surgeon introduced a non-incision technique to create a double eye-lid as early as 1868 is often cited as evidence that this feature reflects a universal standard of beauty. On the other hand, the artwork of 19th-century Japan often portrays the *bijin*, or beautiful woman, as having small, slanted eyes, which suggests that even though eyelid surgery was available, beauty ideals at that time were still more in line with Asian features. In his article on Asian eyelid surgery, Todd Inouye (1996) explains how it was not until World War II with the spread of European and American cultures into Asian countries that demands for this procedure increased dramatically. Therefore, European American features may seem universal only

Portrayals of women in traditional Asian artwork suggest that in the past, small slanted eyes were associated with beauty.

because European images and ideals have been disseminated throughout Asian countries and communities over the last hundred years.

European American physical features are not only the established aesthetic ideal but are also associated with upward social mobility, respect, acceptance, and self-esteem (Root, 1990). In comparison, Asian Americans may be vulnerable to discriminatory practices based on their physical features, and even third- or fourth-generation Asian Americans may be perceived as foreigners. In a qualitative study on the self-image of Asian American adolescents, Stacey Lee and Sabina Vaught (2003) describe how Hmong adolescent girls expressed a belief that "not being White prevented them from being accepted as authentic Americans." A young Asian American woman describes how her self-esteem was impacted by images in fashion magazines: There was always, especially in like *Teen* magazine, you're supposed to be thin and beautiful, and look just like everybody else. They were all thin and they had blond hair and blue eyes and white skin. I never really thought I could look like them" (Lee & Vaught, 2003, p. 462).

For Asian American women, one way to achieve acceptance and recognition in Western cultures is to fit into an ultra-feminine, exotic, and hypersexual ideal. A young Asian American woman explains that "Somehow, I thought that if I changed my hair color and changed my appearance to be more Americanized and more Westernized that would be good . . . I might look exotic, but not foreign" (Lee & Vaught, 2003, p. 463). Thus, the achievement of "Americanization" may be seen by some Asian American women as being possible only through "exoticization." For Asian American women, this contributes to the added struggle of dealing with sexism in that the stereotypical physical features "admired" in Asian women are also submissive and sexualized characteristics (Hall, 1995).

Beliefs Regarding Skin Color Though theorists debate whether the idealization of European American eyes and noses is due to Western influence or not, most agree that the idealization of white skin is not solely a reflection of Western ideals. For centuries, some Asian cultures have viewed white skin as a sign of femininity, purity, and upper social class while darker skin was seen as a result of outdoor labor by lower-class farm workers. Historical artwork from Japan portrays geishas with skin whitened with makeup, and in China, pearl powder was either ingested or applied topically to help induce whiteness of the skin. For some Asian countries, colonization by European and Central Asian countries may have further encouraged the association between white skin and both beauty and power.

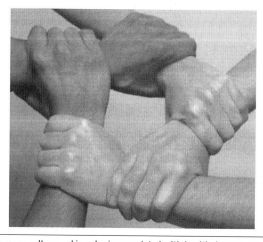

In many cultures, skin color is associated with health, beauty, or power.

There is evidence that the idealization of light skin continues to be prevalent throughout modern Asia. Asian models and actresses are often light skinned, and women dressed with clothes to protect the skin and wielding umbrellas to block out the sun continue to be familiar sights in Asia. In Hong Kong, Malaysia, the Philippines, South Korea, and Taiwan, 4 out of 10 women report using skin-whitening creams, and in Thailand, "dam tap pet" (black like duck's liver), referring to dark skin coloring, is used as a degrading term (Fuller, 2006). A worldwide matchmaking site for South Asians, Shaadi.com, includes a description of skin complexion ranging from fair to wheatish to dark along with other "basic" information such as age, marital status, and height. This reflects the value placed on skin color.

Though lighter skin seems to be favored in most Asian communities, Asian Americans are also exposed to messages from the United States that promote golden tans as signs of beauty and health. Tanning salons and the sight of people sun bathing are not uncommon in the United States, and self-tanners, bronzing makeup, and tinted lotions are being marketed as safe ways to achieve a tanned appearance without exposing oneself to the damaging rays of the sun. Therefore, Asian Americans are exposed to multiple messages regarding skin color with *light* skin being valued as a sign of beauty in many Asian countries, *white* skin being valued as a sign of social power and acceptance in many Western countries, and *tan* skin being valued as a sign of health and vitality in the United States. With skin color, as with body size and facial features, the complex interaction of beliefs originating from both the United States and Asia needs to be taken into account to fully understand the impact of sociocultural influence on the body image of Asian Americans.

Other Body Ideals   In studies on satisfaction with breast size, Asian American women reported as much or more dissatisfaction as compared to European American women (Koff & Benavage, 1998; Mintz & Kashubeck, 1999). Koff and Benavage found that similar to European American women, Asian American women appear to associate larger breast size with being more popular, assertive, confident, and desired by men while smaller breast size was associated with negative attributes such as being lonely and depressed. The researchers also asked participants to report actual breast size and ideal breast size and found that Asian American and European American women evidenced similar levels of actual-ideal discrepancy.

Research has also found that Asian Americans compared to European Americans are more dissatisfied with their height (Kawamura, 2001; Kennedy, Templeton, Gandhi, & Gorzalka, 2004). In Kawamura's study, dissatisfaction with height was assessed using multiple methods. First, participants reported their actual height and their ideal height, and actual-ideal discrepancies were calculated. Secondly, participants were asked to rate how satisfied they were with their heights. In both measures of body evaluation, Asian American men and women expressed more dissatisfaction than did European American men and women. Lastly, in the same study, 19% of Asian American women and 16% of Asian American men indicated that their height was the physical feature they were most dissatisfied with. This is compared to 2% of European American women and 7% of European American men who indicated that their height was the physical feature they were most dissatisfied with. Similarly, Kennedy found that Chinese Canadians were most likely to feel they were too short, followed by Indo Asian Canadians, and then European Canadians.

Activity 2: Understanding the Influence of Traditional Beauty Ideals
In small groups, discuss the traditional beauty ideals in your culture. Do these ideals vary from the elder to the younger members of your family? In what ways were these ideals communicated to you? How do these ideals affect your body image attitudes?

Cultural Values   Sociocultural messages about physical features may have a strong impact on an individual's appraisal of those specific features (e.g., body size, eye shape, skin color), while general sociocultural influences, such as collectivistic values in many Asian cultures, may influence feelings about one's general appearance. Asians from collectivistic cultures often develop a heightened awareness of the effects of their behaviors on the group, and to preserve harmony there is often pressure to act in a manner that does not reflect poorly on the group. This collectivistic demand may also lead to an expectation, especially for women, to maintain perfect physical appearance so as to not bring shame on the group. Collectivistic cultures also value modesty and the restraint of strong emotions, and thus when asked about their body image satisfaction, Asian Americans may seem neutral in their evaluation. Interestingly, though modesty is valued in collectivistic cultures, boasting about one's child seems to be a socially appropriate manner in which to express pride. Children may thus feel pressure to maintain their physical appearance in order to project a positive image of their family. Asian Americans may feel pressure not only as a representative of their families but of the larger Asian American community, especially if they are one of only a few Asian Americans in their community.

For some Asian Americans, religious practice or orientation may be another general sociocultural factor that influences body image attitudes. For example, certain religious practices associated with religious observances in the Muslim culture, such as fasting during the day during Ramadan, may be related to the development of eating disorder symptoms. In one study on a group of school children in Britain, Muslim Asians reported higher levels of bulimic symptoms than Hindu Asian children (Ahmad & Waller, 1994). In another study, eating disorder symptoms in Muslim women worsened over Ramadan (Bhadrinath, 1990). For women who are vulnerable to body image dissatisfaction, temporary restrictions on eating may trigger a pattern of dieting and weight loss that can then progress into an eating disorder. In comparison, some religious orientations may work to buffer against body image dissatisfaction. Religions more common in Asia, such as Islam, Buddhism, and Hinduism eschew materialism, and this may include viewing physical appearance as a type of external materialistic good that detracts from spiritual growth. Therefore, those individuals who ascribe to religions that focus on internal versus external beauty may be less likely to focus on their own physical appearance.

Interpersonal Experiences

As compared to sociocultural beliefs about physical appearance, interpersonal experiences with parents and peers are more tangible factors that can influence the development of body image

Being teased about racial characteristics in childhood can contribute to body image dissatisfaction that continues into adulthood.

attitudes. Body image theorists have hypothesized that over-intrusive parenting can lead to the development of body image dissatisfaction. The restrictive dieting in anorexia is often described as a reaction against parental intrusiveness and an attempt to assert internal control over perceived loss of external controls. Because Asian parents tend to use food provision as a sign of love and because outward rebellion against parents may not be possible, refusal to eat may be an effective yet indirect way of rebelling against intrusive parents. Empirical studies with Asian Indian British women found that perceived overprotectiveness of parents and conflict with parents about socializing and choice of friends were indeed associated with symptoms of eating disorders (Furnham & Husain, 1999; Mujtaba & Furnham, 2001).

Parental criticism has also been identified as a factor that may contribute to the development of body image dissatisfaction (Kearney-Cooke, 2002). Asian American parents often use critical and authoritarian parenting techniques, referred to as "shaming," to help motivate their children to succeed. For some Asian American parents, the success of a daughter is evaluated by her beauty and marital status. Thus, some parents may be hypercritical of their daughter's physical appearance because they are trying to motivate her to achieve a beautiful appearance and because beauty may be vital in attracting a marriage partner. Unfortunately, for some children, the intense focus on physical appearance can contribute to the development of perfectionism and self-consciousness, which are both related to harsh self-criticism.

Parents are often an influential factor in the development of the self-image of children, but with regard to body image dissatisfaction, interactions with peers can have just as strong or stronger impact. In fact, teasing by peers has been identified as one of the most commonly reported precipitants of body image dissatisfaction (Smolak, 2002).

Many Asian Americans report being teased during their childhood about their racial features. Compared to other ethnic groups, Asian American youth report being more likely to prefer being European American if they could choose to do so (Lee & Zhan, 1998). For Asian American youth, being teased about racial features may lead to dissatisfaction with racially identifying features. Experiences with more serious prejudice, stereotyping, and discrimination may lead to not only dissatisfaction but internalized racism, or self-loathing of racially identifying features.

Activity 3: Understanding Body Image Rituals
Get into small groups with both men and women in each group. Discuss body image rituals for both genders (e.g., shaving, applying makeup). Talk about how American societal expectations impact each gender's desire to engage in these rituals. How have these rituals affected you personally? How do these rituals affect your body image? Where were these rituals learned?

Individual Characteristics

In the general population, perfectionism and self-consciousness are characteristics that can lead to higher levels of body image dissatisfaction (Cash & Szymanski, 1995; Davis, 1997). Perfectionism is defined as having excessively high standards with harsh self-criticism when those standards are not met. For body image perfectionists, intense body image dissatisfaction frequently occurs because of the difficulty of attaining perfect physical appearance. Therefore, perfectionism is strongly correlated with eating disorders. Research has found that Asian Americans as compared to European Americans report higher levels of perfectionism (Kawamura, Frost, & Harmatz, 2002), which may lead to the higher levels of body image dissatisfaction found in some Asian American groups (Cummins et al., 2005). Self-consciousness is another individual characteristic that has been found to be related to higher levels of body image dissatisfaction in the general population. As previously described, collectivistic pressure may contribute to higher levels of self-consciousness, and research has shown that for Asian Americans, this elevated self-consciousness is related to higher levels of body image dissatisfaction (Koff, Benavage, & Wong, 2001).

Though perfectionism and self-consciousness are individual factors studied in the general populations, ethnic identity level is an important individual characteristic for Asian Americans that may be associated with differences in body image attitudes. Individuals with an unexamined ethnic identity are unlikely to have strong personal feelings about their racial characteristics and may be more focused on other body features. Individuals whose ethnic identity involves actively rejecting their traditional culture are likely to denigrate or be embarrassed of racial characteristics indicative of their Asian heritage. This particular stage of ethnic identity development would be most vulnerable to low self-esteem and negative physical self-concept due to the inability to change one's racial features. Individuals whose ethnic identity involves strongly identifying with their ethnic culture would be expected to greatly value their racial characteristics that make them unique and set them apart from other ethnic groups. Lastly, individuals with an achieved ethnic identity would likely have the most stable body images as this stage of ethnic identity achievement is associated with a global acceptance of the self. These individuals would be expected to have an appreciation of the physical features they like balanced with an acceptance of the physical features they do not.

Both Kawamura (2002) and Hall (1995) have similarly hypothesized about the role of ethnic identity on body image satisfaction, but the empirical research has been mixed. Tsai, Curbow, and Heinberg (2003) found that an achieved ethnic identity was related to a lower incidence of body image disturbance and eating-disordered symptoms among Taiwanese American women, whereas both Iyer and Haslam (2003) and Phan and Tylka (2006) found that ethnic identity did not predict body image disturbance. Phan and Tylka hypothesized that ethnic identity only influences body preoccupation and internalization of the thin ideal through its relationship to self-esteem, and that self-esteem is the primary predictor of body image dissatisfaction. Therefore, regardless of stage of ethnic identity, it may be that a strong sense of self will protect against body image dissatisfaction.

Activity 4*: Increasing Awareness of Negative Messages*
In the space below, list any part of your body with which you feel dissatisfied and then write out typical negative thoughts associated with this part of your body. Then, list what influences may have contributed to your dissatisfaction with this part of your body.

Body part dissatisfied with	Typical negative thoughts about this part of your body	What contributes to your dissatisfaction with this part of your body

Impact of Body Image Dissatisfaction

Body size dissatisfaction may be met with attempts to change body size with women seeking ways to lose weight and men seeking ways to gain muscle. Dissatisfaction with facial features or skin color can result in a wide range of fixing behaviors ranging from the use of cosmetics to plastic surgery. The following section will describe findings in Asia and the United States regarding behavioral responses to body image dissatisfaction.

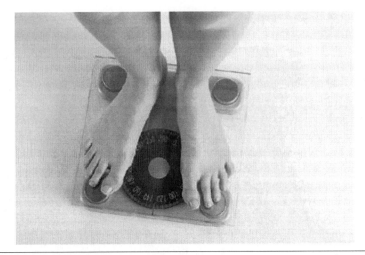

Dissatisfaction with body size can lead to constant dieting or to dangerous eating disorders.

Body Size

For most women, the ideal body size is difficult to attain, which can lead to frantic efforts to lose weight or prevent weight gain. Eating disorder symptoms such as dieting, binging, or purging are the most studied behaviors associated with body image dissatisfaction. A review of recent studies in the United States and Britain found that women of Chinese, Korean, Japanese, Pakistani, and Asian Indian descent report similar or higher levels of body size dissatisfaction when compared to European American women but have lower levels of disordered eating behaviors (Cummins, Simmons, & Zane, 2005). However, it is not clear whether Asian American women are less

Dissatisfaction with facial features can lead to harmless behaviors such as using makeup in an attempt to alter appearances or to more extreme behaviors such as plastic surgery for more permanent changes.

likely to report eating disorder symptomatology or whether they do in fact have lower levels of eating disorder pathology.

While women try to lose weight, men are often trying to gain weight, specifically through increasing muscle mass. The concern with body size dissatisfaction with men is that extreme dissatisfaction may lead to increased risk of using steroids to gain muscle mass (Corson & Andersen, 2002). Researchers have wondered whether the smaller size of Asian American men would leave them more vulnerable to body size dissatisfaction and resulting steroid use. Studies directly comparing Asian American and European American men have produced conflicting findings with some showing similar levels of dissatisfaction and others showing Asian American men as being more dissatisfied (Barnett, Keel, & Conoscenti, 2001; Mintz & Kashubeck, 1999). Further studies are needed to explore the body images of Asian American men and its relationship to steroid use.

Facial Features

Behaviors associated with dissatisfaction with facial attributes can range from temporary procedures to enhance or hide physical features to more drastic and permanent changes.

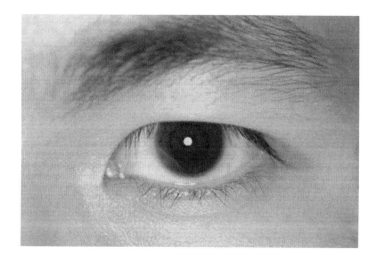

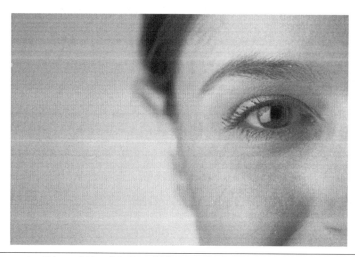

Some Asians with an epicanthic eye fold, or "single eyelid," pursue plastic surgery to create a crease, or "double eyelid."

For Asian American women dissatisfied with their eyes, makeup and colored contacts are convenient ways to change the appearance of eyes. A more labor-intensive method of changing the look and shape of eyes is through the use of tapes and glues to hold the eyelid crease in place to create a double eyelid. Koji Honpo, a Tokyo-based company, sells a series of eye glues called "Eye Talk" including glue with rosemary extract to soften the eyelids, glue that can be applied using a pencil applicator, and glue that resists perspiration. The company Web site even provides a video to demonstrate the application of the eye glue (http://www.koji-honpo.co.jp).

The most drastic and permanent means of changing one's physical appearance is through the use of plastic surgery. In countries such as China, Taiwan, Japan, and especially South Korea, plastic surgery appears to be on the rise and can be described as commonplace by some accounts. Though official statistics from Asian countries are unavailable, an article by the BBC reported that "by conservative estimates, 50% of South Korean women in their 20s living in Seoul have had some form of cosmetic surgery" (Scanlon, 2005). Eyelid surgery appears to be the most commonly requested cosmetic surgery procedure in Asia. *Time Magazine Asia* describes how plastic surgery in Taiwan has doubled to 1 million procedures a year in the last 5 years. Thailand has started to develop plastic surgery tours for Asians from other countries seeking affordable cosmetic surgery. Another indicator of the prevalence of plastic surgery is the 200,000 malpractice lawsuits that have been filed against unqualified cosmetic surgery practitioners in China (Cullen, 2002).

In the United States, Asian Americans comprised 3% of all cosmetic patients, which was the smallest percentage out of European Americans (84%), Hispanic Americans (6%), and African Americans (5%). The most commonly requested surgical procedures by Asian Americans were nose reshaping, eyelid surgery, and breast augmentation (American Society of Plastic Surgeons, 2005). Nose reshaping surgery, or rhinoplasty, for Asian Americans typically involves a narrowing and elevating of the nose. Eyelid surgery, or blepharoplasty, requested by European Americans typically consists of removal of fat from the upper and lower eyelids. In comparison, **Asian cosmetic eye surgery** or double eyelid surgery involves stitching a permanent crease into the eyelid to produce a double eyelid or rearranging the internal structures. Eugenia Kaw (1993) uses the term **medicalization** of racism to describe the way in which medical textbooks use scientific terminology to describe typical Asian features as abnormal and unattractive features to be corrected, thus using science to legitimize racist notions that the European American ideal is the only beauty ideal.

Skin Color

Behaviors associated with dissatisfaction with skin color may initially appear less complicated than those associated with dissatisfaction with facial features. Certainly, using sun block or wearing protective clothing to block out the harmful rays of the sun or applying makeup powder are all quite harmless measures. Less known to the general public are the possible dangers involved in unregulated skin-whitening products. In 2002, a health scare occurred in Hong Kong after two whitening creams were found to have 9,000 and 65,000 times the recommended doses of mercury (Bray, 2002); mercury has a whitening effect on the skin but can also lead to nerve damage, coma, and death. Another common whitening agent, hydroquinone, is restricted in the United States but can be found with higher potencies in illegally produced whitening creams from developing countries (Fuller, 2006). Hydroquinone may be cancerous in large doses and can also lead to redness and itching, the appearance of dark patches of skin, and permanent inhibition of the skin's ability to produce pigment. Though Asian American women may be protected by Federal Drug and Administration guidelines in the United States, purchases made from companies overseas need to be made with caution.

Facilitating a Healthy Body Image

While negative body image is a frequent topic of discussion, less attention is typically paid to positive body image. Research on positive body image has indicated that being cognizant of sociocultural messages about weight and shape can protect women against a negative body image and can contribute to body pride (Henderson-King, Henderson-King, & Hoffman, 2001). Once aware of sociocultural messages, detracting from the narrow focus on physical appearance and focusing on a sense of holistic wellness and balance can further facilitate a positive body image. Both yoga and tai chi focus on bodily sensations, agility, and general health and have been practiced in Asia for thousands of years. Research has shown that these exercises are in fact associated with greater satisfaction with physical appearance and increased body acceptance (Daubenmier, 2005; Li, Harmer, Chaimeton, Duncan, & Duncan, 2002). Both yoga and tai chi, as traditional Asian exercises, may be especially helpful in promoting positive body image among Asian Americans because participating in a traditional form of exercise can be a way for them to connect not only with their body but with their traditional culture on a simultaneous physical and mental level.

Various athletic pursuits have also been found to impact a person's body image. Research from Jaffee and Lutter (1995) found that there was a positive association between levels of sports participation and body satisfaction. However, certain sports can have different effects on body image. Some athletic pursuits, such as soccer and tennis, encourage a focus on coordination and power. In general populations, this decreased focus on body type may encourage athletes of these sports to feel more positively about their bodies. Other sports, such as gymnastics, running, and figure skating, are often more focused on body leanness, and consequently, may foster more negative body images. Therefore, Asian Americans who engage in sports, especially those that focus on body function versus appearance, may be more likely to have positive body image attitudes.

Activity 5: *Developing a Positive Body Image*
In small groups, discuss any negative ideas men and women of your age typically hold about their bodies. Brainstorm ways in which more people can be encouraged to develop more positive body images attitudes. Consider how changes can be made on the level of the individual, the family, the community, and the culture.

For Asian American, participating in physical activities such as tai chi or yoga can help promote a positive connection with not only the body but also to cultured conditions.

Shifting the focus of attention from physical appearance to body function and physical and emotional health can help facilitate the development of a more positive body image.

Summary

Asian American men and women appear to be vulnerable to body image dissatisfaction with their body size, facial features, and skin color. Various sociocultural influences such as cultural ideals regarding beauty and collectivistic values of preserving group harmony, modesty, and restraint of strong emotions can impact the development of Asian American body images. On a more interpersonal level, intrusive parenting styles and parental pressure to maintain a perfect appearance can lead to body image dissatisfaction. Childhood experiences with teasing or racism are also likely to lead to a negative body image. On a more individual level, characteristics such as perfectionism, self-consciousness, and ethnic identity level can influence Asian American body images.

Asian Americans may react to body image dissatisfaction by engaging in relatively harmless behaviors such as dieting and wearing makeup to change body size and facial features, respectively, and eating disorders and plastic surgery can be viewed as the more extreme versions of these behaviors. Changing skin color can usually be done through harmless means such as avoiding the sun or using self-tanning lotions, but there are dangers in using unregulated whitening creams. Rather than changing the disliked physical features, another approach to alleviate body image distress is to develop a more positive body image. This can be done through focusing on health and body function rather than physical appearance. Yoga, tai-chi, and certain sports can all help facilitate the development of positive body images.

Discussion Questions

1. What are some of your typical negative thoughts associated with your body? What might have contributed to your dissatisfaction with these parts of your body?
2. What are ways in which more people can be encouraged to develop more positive body images attitudes? How can changes be made on the level of the individual, the family, the community, and the culture?
3. What are the traditional beauty ideals in your culture? Do these ideals vary from the elder to the younger members of your family? How were these ideals communicated to you? How do these ideals affect your body image attitudes?

4. What are some body image rituals for both genders (shaving, applying makeup)? How do these rituals affect your body image?

5. Think of some of the magazines and/or publications you read. In what ways do you feel your body image might be affected by these publications?

Case Study

Thus far this chapter has focused on providing information on the influences on the development of body image dissatisfaction in Asian American women and men, reactions to body image dissatisfaction, and ways to facilitate a positive body image. This chapter will now shift its focus to illustrating how an Asian American woman experiences and copes with her body image. This case study will also provide an example of how a therapist works with the complex issues present for this teenager.

Soon is a 19-year-old, Korean American woman who moved to the United States with her family from Seoul, Korea, when she was 9 years old. She spent her childhood and adolescence living in a middle-class suburb of Boston, Massachusetts, and last year she moved to Southern California to attend a 4-year university. Soon's roommate gets frustrated because Soon takes almost 2 hours getting ready in the mornings. In comparison, her roommate Kimi, a Japanese American woman born and raised in Hawaii, spends many of her mornings surfing or jogging before hopping into the shower and going to her classes. Kimi often becomes annoyed because she thinks Soon is too obsessed with her own appearance.

Soon is especially self-conscious of her eyes. She was born with "single eyelids," or eyelids without folds, and has been self-conscious of this trait since she was a young child. A few months ago, Soon came across a Web site for a plastic surgeon's office that specialized in "Asian eyelid surgery" to make Asian women look more "alive" and "awake." Many of the Asian actresses that she idolizes have undergone eyelid surgery, and several of her cousins in Seoul have gotten eyelid surgeries when they were in their teens. Soon is adamant that these surgeries would help her fit in with her peers and feel more attractive. Kimi does not understand her roommate's decision. She too was born with "single eyelids" but feels that her eyes reflect her ethnic heritage of which she feels proud. Kimi thinks that Soon is "selling out" in an attempt to look more European American. Soon and Kimi often have heated disagreements regarding physical appearance and body image.

Since coming to college, Soon has also become increasingly self-conscious of her figure. At 5′3″, she weighs 100 pounds, and despite her petite figure, she keeps a log of the food she eats, skips breakfast, and declines invitations to go out to eat with friends. In comparison, Kimi is 5′2″ and weighs 125 pounds. She is aware of being heavier set than many of the other Asian American women on campus but feels comfortable with her body type and tries to focus more on her fitness and strength than on her physical appearance. Kimi became worried when she noticed that Soon was becoming more sad and withdrawn and often talked about losing more weight or getting plastic surgery as a way to help herself feel better. Kimi decided to talk to Soon about seeking help from a counselor. Soon reluctantly walked over to the college counseling center with Kimi.

Case Study Discussion

The counselor that worked with Soon used a culturally integrated cognitive behavioral approach. The counselor developed a strong therapeutic alliance with Soon by allowing Soon to discuss topics that were initially less threatening and by validating Soon's emotional concerns. Within a few sessions, Soon began to disclose her concerns regarding her weight and body image, and the counselor then assessed Soon's body image dissatisfaction. The situations that triggered Soon's body image distress were stressful events, looking in the mirror, and eating. Typical thoughts were related to disliking her eyelids, feeling overweight, and fearing that she was unattractive to others, especially men. A core assumption was that her physical appearance would prevent her from ever being happy with herself, feeling accepted, or having a boyfriend. Feelings associated with her body image distress were sadness, guilt, frustration, and fear. Her typical coping behaviors were to avoid friends, smoke cigarettes, and either avoid mirrors or stare at herself in the mirror for up to 30 minutes.

Soon and her counselor then discussed ways in which childhood and family experiences may have led to the development of a negative body image. Soon talked about being one of few Asian Americans in her elementary school and being teased by the other children. Soon also described how at home, she was teased by her sister who had double eyelids, and her sister was often referred to by aunts and uncles as "the pretty sister." She realized that these early experiences contributed to her fears of rejection by others and of never finding a man who would find her attractive. Soon found it especially helpful to learn about various ethnic identity levels and how her early interpersonal experiences may have led to her rejecting her traditional culture and her Asian features. Soon and her counselor also explored family beliefs regarding physical attractiveness. Soon realized that her family highly valued a slender physique and double eyelids and that these beliefs were consistent to cultural ideals in South Korea. Soon began to recognize ways in which sociocultural factors and interpersonal experiences shaped her body image and also began to see her body image dissatisfaction as being more reflective of her desire to be accepted by others.

After fully understanding Soon's body image dissatisfaction, the counselor began to teach Soon a technique called "cognitive restructuring." Cognitive restructuring involved identifying automatic judgmental thoughts Soon had about her body such as, "My single eyelids make me look ugly," and shifting her perspective to a more compassionate and accepting perspective, such as "I'm learning to become comfortable with my eyelids. They're at least okay. There are other parts of my body that I really like, like my feet." Soon and her counselor also used a strategy called "examining the evidence" where she sought out evidence that was contrary to her fear that others would reject her such as the fact that Soon had made many close friends in college and had male friends who seemed friendly with her. To help Soon better tolerate uncomfortable emotions and to help her be less reactive to her distressing thoughts, the counselor also taught Soon relaxation methods, such as deep breathing and progressive muscle relaxation. Soon was also given "homework assignments" between therapy sessions such as practicing yoga and journaling about body parts she liked or appreciated to help her make a healthy and positive connection with her body. Eventually, Soon's mood and self-esteem improved, and she began to use a strategy called "exposure" where she exposed herself to situations she had previously avoided such as going out with her friends for dinner.

Case Study Discussion Questions

For undergraduate students, please consider the following questions:

1. What do you think about Soon's initial behaviors regarding both dieting and seeking plastic surgery?

2. Identify some of the factors that may have contributed to Soon's dissatisfaction with her face and body. Identify some of the factors that may have contributed to Kimi's satisfaction with her face and body.
3. What do you think of the counselor's approach in working with Soon?

For graduate students and/or beginning therapists, please consider the following questions:

1. How might the counselor's own body type and body image impact the counseling process with Soon?
2. How might the counselor's ethnicity and gender impact work with Soon?
3. What are the strengths and weaknesses of the theoretical approach used in the counselor's work with Soon? Compare this with your own theoretical orientation.

Key Terms

Adonis complex: Ideal in modern, Western societies where a moderately sized, V-shaped body is seen as the ideal masculine image.

Asian cosmetic eye surgery: Also called double eyelid surgery. Involves stitching a permanent crease into the eyelid or rearranging the internal structures to produce a double eyelid.

Body image: Thoughts, attitudes, and beliefs about one's own physical appearance.

Medicalization of racism: Term to describe how science is used as a means to legitimize racist notions that the European American ideal is the only beauty ideal.

Myth of transformation: Idea that a thinner body will lead to occupational success and social acceptance.

For Further Learning and Suggested Readings

Cash, T. F. (1997). *The body image workbook: An 8-step program for learning to like your looks.* Oakland: New Harbinger Publications.

Cash, T. F., & Pruzinsky, T. (2002). *Body image: A handbook of theory research and clinical practice.* New York: Guilford Press.

Hall, C. C. (1995). Asian eyes: Body image and eating disorders of Asian and Asian American women. *Eating Disorders,* 3, 8–19.

Kaw, E. (1993). Medicalization of racial features: Asian American women and cosmetic surgery. *Medical Anthropology Quarterly,* 7, 74–89.

Root, M. P. (1990). Disordered eating in women of color. *Sex Roles,* 22, 525–536.

References

Ahmad, S., & Waller, G. (1994). Eating attitudes and body satisfaction among Asian and Caucasian adolescents. *Journal of Adolescence,* 17, 461–470.

American Society of Plastic Surgeons. (2005). *National Clearinghouse of Plastic Surgery Statistics procedural statistics: 2005 cosmetic demographics.* Retrieved May 20, 2006, from http://www.plastic-surgery.org/public_education/loader.cfm?url=/commonspot/security/getfile.cfm&PageID=17860

Barnett, H. L., Keel, P. K., & Conoscenti, L. M. (2001). Body type preferences in Asian and Caucasian college students. *Sex Roles,* 45, 867–879.

Becker, A. E., Burwell, A. E., Gilman, S. E., Herzog, D. B., & Hamburg, P. (2002). Eating behaviors and attitudes following prolonged television exposure among ethnic Fijian adolescent women. *British Journal of Psychiatry,* 180, 509–514.

Bhadrinath, B. R. (1990). Anorexia nervosa in adolescents of Asian extraction. *British Journal of Psychiatry,* 156, 565–568.

Bray, M. (2002). Skin deep: Dying to be White. CNN.com/World. Retrieved January 28, 2006, from http://edition.cnn.com/2002/WORLD/asiapcf/east/05/13/asia.whitening

Cash, T. F., & Szymanski, M. L. (1995). The development and validation of the Body-Image Ideals Questionnaire. *Journal of Personality Assessment,* 64, 466–477.

Choe, K. S., Sclafani, A. P., Litner, J. A., Yu, G., & Romo, T. (2004). The Korean American Woman's Face: Anthropometric measurements and quantitative analysis of facial aesthetics. *Archives of Facial Plastic Surgery, 6,* 244–252.

Conley, D., & Glauber, R. (2005). *Working paper No. 11343: Gender, body mass, and economic status.* National Bureau of Economic Research. Retrieved on May 20, 2006, from http://papers.nber.org/papers/w11343.pdf

Corson, P. W., & Andersen, A. E. (2002). Body image issues among boys and men. In T. F. Cash & T. Pruzinsky (Eds.), *Body image: A handbook of theory, research, and clinical practice* (pp. 192–199). New York: Guilford Press.

Cullen, L. T. (2002). Changing faces. *TIME Asia Magazine, 160*(4). Retrieved January 28, 2006, from http://www.time.com/time/asia/covers/1101020805/story.html

Cummins, L. H., Simmons, A. M., & Zane, N. W. S. (2005). Eating disorders in Asian populations: A critique of current approaches to the study of culture, ethnicity, and eating disorders. *American Journal of Orthopsychiatry, 75,* 553–574.

Daubenmier, J. (2005). The relationship of yoga, body awareness, and body responsiveness to self-objectification and disordered eating. *Psychology of Women Quarterly, 29,* 207–219.

Davis, C. (1997). Normal and neurotic perfectionism in eating disorders: An interactive model. *International Journal of Eating Disorders, 22,* 421–426.

Fuller, T. (2006). Glamour at a price in Asia: Use of skin whiteners raises safety concerns. *International Herald Tribune.* Retrieved June 12, 2006, from http://www.iht.com/articles/2006/05/01/news/skin.php.

Furnham, A., & Husain, K. (1999). The role of conflict with parents in disordered eating among British Asian females. *Social Psychiatry and Psychiatric Epidemiology, 34,* 498–505.

Graham, E. (n.d.). *The slim get slimmer: Secrets of losing weight Japan style.* My Nippon. Retrieved May 31, 2006, from http://www.mynippon.com/dreamland/fukulove3.htm

Hall, C. C. (1995). Asian eyes: Body image and eating disorders of Asian and Asian American women. *Eating Disorders, 3,* 8–19.

Henderson-King, D., Henderson-King, E., & Hoffman, L. (2001). Media images and women's self-evaluations: Social context and importance of attractiveness and moderators. *Personality and Social Psychology Bulletin, 27,* 1407–1416.

Inouye, T. (1996). Roundabout looks. *Metroactive.* Retrieved January 28, 2006, from http://www.metroactive.com/papers/metro/06.27.96/asian-eyes-9626.html

Iyer, D. S., & Haslam, N. (2003). Body image and eating disturbance among South Asian American women: The role of racial teasing. *International Journal of Eating Disorders, 34,* 142–147.

Jaffee, L., & Lutter, J. M. (1995). Adolescent girls: Factors influencing low and high body image. *Melpomene: A Journal for Women's Health Research, 14*(2), 14–22.

Kaw, E. (1993). Medicalization of racial features: Asian American women and cosmetic surgery. *Medical Anthropology Quarterly, 7,* 74–89.

Kawamura, K. Y. (2001). Body image attitudes of Asian American and Caucasian American women and men. *Dissertation Abstracts International: Section B: The Sciences and Engineering, Vol. 62*(4-B).

Kawamura, K. Y. (2002). Asian American body image. In T. F. Cash & T. Pruzinsky (Eds.), *Body Image: A handbook of theory, research, and clinical practice* (pp. 243–249). New York: Guilford Press.

Kawamura, K. Y., Frost, R. O., & Harmatz, M. G. (2002). The relationship of perceived parenting styles to perfectionism. *Personality and Individual Differences, 32,* 317–327.

Kearney-Cooke, A. (2002) Familial influences on body image development. In T. F. Cash & T. Pruzinsky (Eds.), *Body image: A handbook of theory, research, and clinical practice* (pp. 99–107). New York: Guilford Press.

Kennedy, M. A., Templeton, L., Gandhi, A., & Gorzalka, B. B. (2004). Asian body image satisfaction: Ethnic and gender differences across Chinese, Indo-Asian and European descent students. *Eating Disorders: The Journal of Treatment and Prevention, 12,* 321–336.

Koff, E., & Benavage, A. (1998). Breast size perception and satisfaction, body image, and psychological functioning in Caucasian and Asian American college women. *Sex Roles, 38,* 655–673.

Koff, E., Benavage, A., & Wong, B. (2001). Body-image attitudes and psychosocial functioning in Euro-American and Asian-American college women. *Psychological Reports, 88,* 917–928.

Lee, C. L., & Zhan, G. (1998). Psychosocial status of children and youths. In L. C. Lee & N. W. S. Zane (Eds.), *Handbook of Asian American Psychology* (pp. 137–163). Thousand Oaks, CA: Sage Publications.

Lee, S., & Lee, A. M. (2000). Disordered eating in three communities of China: A comparative study of female high school students in Hong Kong, Shenzhen, and rural Hunan. *International Journal of Eating Disorders, 27,* 317–327.

Lee, S. J., & Vaught, S. (2003). You can never be too rich or too thin: Popular and consumer culture and the Americanization of Asian American girls and young women. *Journal of Negro Education, 4,* 457–467.

Li, F., Harmer, P., Chaimeton, N. R., Duncan, T. E., & Duncan, S. C. (2002). Tai Chi as a means to enhance self-esteem: A randomized controlled trial. *Journal of Applied Gerontology, 21*(1), 70–89.

Mintz, L. B., & Kashubeck, S. (1999). Body image and disordered eating among Asian American and Caucasian college students. *Psychology of Women Quarterly, 23,* 781–796.

Mujtaba, T., & Furnham, A. (2001). A cross-cultural study of parental conflict and eating disorders in a non-clinical sample. *International Journal of Social Psychiatry, 47,* 24–35.

Nahm, H. Y. (n.d.). Politics of the Asian male physique: Building good physiques carries more significance for Asian American men than for any other men on earth. *Gold Sea: Asian American Body Works.* Retrieved May 20, 2006, from http://goldsea.com/Body/AM/am.html

Ohmori, K. (1990). Esthetic surgery in the Asian patient. In J. D. McCarthy (Ed.), *Plastic surgery* (pp. 2415–2435). Philadelphia: Saunders.

Olivardia, R. (2002). Body image and muscularity. In T. F. Cash & T. Pruzinsky (Eds.), *Body Image: A Handbook of Theory, Research, and Clinical Practice* (pp. 210–218). New York: Guilford Press.

Phan, T., & Tylka, T. L. (2006). Exploring a model and moderators of disordered eating with Asian American college women. *Journal of Counseling Psychology, 53*(1), 36–47.

Pingitore, R., Dugoni, B. L., Tindale, R. S., & Spring, B. (1994). Bias against overweight job applicants in a simulated employment interview. *Journal of Applied Psychology, 79*(6), 909–917.

Root, M. P. (1990). Disordered eating in women of color. *Sex Roles, 22,* 525–536.

Scanlon, C. (2005). The price of beauty in South Korea. BBC News. Retrieved January 28, 2006, from http://news.bbc.co.uk/2/hi/programmes/from_our_own_correspondent/4229995.stm

Smolak, L. (2002) Body image development in children. In T. F. Cash & T. Pruzinsky (Eds.), *Body image: A handbook of theory, research, and clinical practice* (pp. 65–73). New York: Guilford Press.

Striegal-Moore, R., & Franko, D. (2002). Body image issues among girls and women. In T. F. Cash & T. Pruzinsky (Eds.), *Body image: A handbook of theory, research, and clinical practice* (pp. 183–191). New York: Guilford Press.

Tsai, D., Curbow, B., & Heinberg, L. (2003). Sociocultural and developmental influences on body dissatisfaction and disordered eating attitudes and behaviors of Asian women. *Journal of Nervous and Mental Disease, 191,* 309–318.

Yang, C. J., Gray, P., & Pope, H. G. (2005). Male body image in Taiwan versus the West: Yanggang Zhiqi meets the Adonis Complex. *American Journal of Psychiatry, 162,* 263–269.

29

Asian American Indigenous Healing and Coping

CHRISTINE J. YEH and AGNES KWONG

OUTLINE OF CHAPTER

Case Synopsis
Introduction
Theory and Research
Facts and Figures
Case Study
References

Case Synopsis

Nina is a Hindu, 20-year-old college student who emigrated from India. She comes to the university health clinic for help with a variety of physical problems and is then referred to a counselor. The counselor soon learns that Nina has experienced discrimination and harassment associated with her cultural background. Nina is embarrassed to share with the counselor that she typically seeks help from an Astrologer and practices Hatha yoga with other Hindu friends. The counselor must find ways to connect with Nina that are culturally sensitive and incorporate indigenous perspectives of health and healing.

What do you do when you are stressed? How do you tend to cope with bigger problems or small daily stressors? Some people talk to friends and family, others seek professional help, while many others want the help of a healer. In this chapter the authors define and discuss **indigenous healing**, coping, and culturally based syndromes from an Asian American perspective.

Introduction

Indigenous healing, also referred to as traditional or alternative medicine, describes the numerous healing systems used by various cultural and ethnic populations for thousands of years, well before modern medicine practices were established ("Traditional and Indigenous Healing Systems," n.d.). In particular, indigenous healing practices were created from the culture's nature, worldview, history, beliefs, and accessibility of resources in various parts of the world. Such practices refer to beliefs and customs that are designed to treat the members of a given group (Helms & Cook, 1999). While counseling and psychotherapy are viewed as the primary methods of psychological healing in the United States (Sue & Sue, 1999), the strong reliance on emotional expression, autonomy, and individual verbalization contradict Asian American cultural values emphasizing emotional restraint, social harmony, and familial privacy.

Indigenous healing methods originating from Asian countries reflect the cultural values and beliefs of Asians, which are often incongruent with seeking help through counseling or psychotherapy, the primary methods of psychological healing in the United States (Sue & Sue, 1999). Indeed, this incongruence may contribute to the consistent findings that Asian Americans do not use mental health services as much as would be expected based on their population size in the United States (Leong, 1986; Uba, 1994). Rather than seeking emotional and psychological help from mental health professionals, many Asians and Asian Americans may prefer to turn to organizations or healers indigenous to their ethnic community (i.e., indigenous healers), such as churches, physicians, elders, and family members (Sue & Morishima, 1982; Yeh & Wang, 2000).

This chapter aims to highlight indigenous healing methods from an Asian perspective. In doing so, an interdependent perspective of healing and Asian **culture-bound syndromes** will be presented and contrasted to Western principles of traditional counseling and psychotherapy. Furthermore, **collectivistic coping**, which includes strategies such as **family support, respect for authority figures**, intracultural coping, **relational universality, forbearance, social activity**, and **fatalism** will be provided as a culturally congruent model from which to conceptualize coping from an Asian perspective. A case study will be presented to highlight some of the key issues relating to indigenous healing and some compelling facts and figures will be offered, as well as key references in the field.

Theory and Research

Mental Health Underuse Among Asians and Asian Americans

In the United States, Asian Americans and Pacific Islanders have some of the lowest rates of utilization of mental health services among all the ethnic populations even though they demonstrate mental illness at a similar rate to other ethnic groups (Leong, Wagner, & Tata, 1995). For the small group of Asian Americans who seek mental health treatment, they are less satisfied with the care and have poorer short-term outcomes than White Americans (Zane, Enomoto, & Chun, 1994). A number of authors have argued that the barriers to use of mental health services among Asians and Asian Americans may be the cultural incongruence or inappropriateness of psychotherapy as a way of dealing with problems (e.g., Sue & Sue, 2004; Uba, 1994; Yeh & Hwang, 2000). In order to better understand this cultural incongruence, it is important to consider how one's cultural orientation influences approaches to mental health and to recognize some of the fundamental differences between Western and Asian approaches to healing and coping.

Cultural Orientation and Indigenous Healing

The indigenous healing and coping methods used by Asians and Asian Americans are largely influenced by cultural values, beliefs, and **self-construal** (i.e., the way in which one sees oneself). Generally speaking, while western European cultures have been associated with **individualism** or a more **individualistic orientation** and have been found to emphasize an **independent self-construal**, Asian cultures and members from these cultural groups have been associated with **collectivism** or a more **collectivistic orientation** and **interdependent self-construal**, respectively (Markus & Kitayama, 1991; Triandis, Bontempo, & Villareal, 1988).

Having an interdependent view of the self includes seeing the self as connected to and less differentiated from others and the social context. Individuals with an interdependent self-construal are motivated to fit in with important others and to fulfill and create obligations. Furthermore, they value the ability to control behaviors, thoughts, emotions, and motivations since self-restraint is required to put others' needs and desires first. For example, for the Penan in Malaysia, there is only one word for the terms *he, she,* and *I* combined and six different terms for *we*, emphasizing the importance of the group. Also for the Penan, sharing is a cultural norm deemphasizing individual ownership. Thus there is no word for "thank you" since receiving is never considered anything special. Everything belongs to the group (Lillard, 1997).

Another example of interdependence is reflected in the term *kejime*. According to Bachnik (1986), kejime is a central concern in Japanese elementary education where good classroom behavior is evaluated not by one's ability to work independently but by one's ability to shift from formality and informality across different relationship contexts. The influence of interdependence extends beyond the realm of relationships and includes one's connections with the mind and body, spiritual world, and nature (Yeh, Hunter, Madan-Bahel, Chiang, & Arora, 2004).

On the other hand, individuals with an independent concept of self see the self as stable and separate from the social context. They tend to engage with others by expressing their own thoughts, feelings, and actions and value self-promotion, autonomy, assertiveness, and uniqueness (Markus & Kitayama, 1991; Singelis, 1994). For example, when you look at the definition of *self* in the dictionary it reads, "The total being of one person, the individual, individuality. One's own interests or advantage. One's uniqueness" (American Heritage Dictionary, 2006).

There are a number of important differences between Western versus interdependent perspectives of healing that shape the help-seeking patterns of many Asians and Asian Americans. According to Yeh et al. (2004), these differences include the distinction between (a) a linear versus a circular perspective; (b) a cognitive/affective basis versus a spiritual basis of well-being, and (c) an active versus a passive helping role.

Western conceptualizations of helping originate from a discrete cause-and-effect framework that implies a unidirectional approach, whereas interdependent notions of helping and healing emphasize intuitive reasoning and qualitative understanding, extending beyond mere objectivity and deductive reasoning (Lee & Armstrong, 1995; Ornstein, 1972; Yeh et al., 2004). Thus, an interdependent perspective of healing places behaviors and their consequences within a multidimensional and circular context (Lee & Armstrong, 1995). For example, Yeh (2001) along with her research group interviewed a number of indigenous healers about their understanding of being an effective or "competent" healer. Quotes from these interviews highlight cultural discrepancies in the meaning of competency between Western medical views and beliefs from indigenous healers. For example, a **Buddhist monk**, who practices monasticism, adopting a strict religious and ascetic lifestyle in the traditions of Buddhism, was asked how he knew when he had helped someone. He replied, "When balance is achieved. When patients can be with one another and become one another and there is a sense of social harmony. It is then we know that things are well" (Yeh, 2001; Hunter, Arora, Madan-Bahel, Chiang, & Yeh, 2002).

Western psychological healing perspectives remain in the mental and physical realms of existence, often neglecting or minimizing the spiritual realm (Lee & Armstrong, 1995; Yeh et al., 2004). On the other hand, healing from an interdependent perspective assumes the interconnectedness between the mental, physical, and spiritual. From this point of view, spiritual health is considered as important as psychological, emotional, and physical well-being. For example, in an interview with an Indian **Pranic healer** (a person who uses energy-based healing techniques that utilizes the life-force or *prana* to balance, harmonize and transform the body's energy processes ["What Is **Pranic Healing?**," n.d.]), the healer stated that he realized when someone had been helped "when the energy of your physical existence (Brahma), your emotional existence (Vishnu), and the higher consciousness (Mahesh) is balanced" (Yeh, 2001; Hunter et al., 2002).

Finally, helpers working from a Western perspective tend to take on a more passive role during the intervention process than helpers who work from a more interdependent perspective (Yeh et al., 2004). Rather than acting as mere facilitators of client change, indigenous healers generally assume that clients have problems or issues that are beyond their control and that it is their responsibility to bring about client change. From this point of view, clients are often given direct and specific solution-oriented advice by the healer (Yeh et al., 2004). In an interview, a **Reiki healer** (someone who channels the universal life energy to stimulate the body's natural healing process ["What Is **Reiki?**," n.d.]) described his role as someone who "teach(es) a gentle

Tai Chi.

form of comforting family and friends which will offer a path for healing all humanity as one. Opening the heart and cleansing the mind" (Yeh, 2001; Hunter et al., 2002).

Underlying the aforementioned key differences between Western versus interdependent perspectives of healing is the emphasis on interconnectedness between the elements of human existence. Whereas traditional Western psychological healing methods have generally approached physical, mental, and spiritual as separate entities (Sue & Sue, 2003) and cognitive, affective and behavioral functioning as a reflection of intrapsychic forces, interdependent perspectives emphasize a more holistic approach, integrating the mind, body, and spirit and their interconnectedness with the environment (Yeh et al., 2004). Reflective of a holistic perspective, a Chinese **Qigong healer** (someone who can direct or emit external life energy or *Qi* for the purpose of healing others ["Welcome to the Qigong Institute!," n.d.]) shared her view of the origins of her patients' problems and her role as a healer using **Qigong healing**: "When patients have emotional problems there will be some parts in their bodies where the flow of chi (energy) is stuck or blocked. By connecting my chi with theirs, I help them be more balanced" (Yeh, 2001; Hunter et al., 2002).

Indigenous Healing and Culture-Bound Syndromes

There are many cultural factors that influence Asian Americans' use of indigenous healers: cultural orientation, ethnic identity, acculturation, cultural explanations for illness, and specific cultural factors (such as available social support systems, religion, kin networks, etc.). In particular, a critical problem with the Western medical model of psychology and psychiatry is that many cultural groups do not share this conceptualization of mental health and disease and in fact have a considerably unique and shared cultural view of health. It follows that perspectives of healing should be consonant with indigenous perceptions and beliefs about disease and health.

Culture-Bound Syndromes It is very likely that at some point you or someone you know will experience a psychological problem. Some of these problems are experienced emotionally, while others are experienced physically (chest pains, trouble sleeping, etc.). Not all psychological disorders are translatable in other cultures. In fact, most cultures have their own specific understandings of psychiatric disorders. Culture-bound syndromes (also known as culture-specific syndromes) are a combination of somatic and psychiatric symptoms that are recognized in a particular cultural setting (American Psychiatric Association, 2000). The *Diagnostic and Statistical Manual of Mental Disorders-IV-TR* (DSM-IV-TR) also includes a description of the most common culture-bound syndromes. The notion of culture-bound syndromes is critical to consider in relation to indigenous healing since methods of healing are often linked to particular symptoms as well as beliefs about somatic components. There are many well-known culture-bound syndromes that are specific to Asian countries that may impact the Asian American and Asian immigrant communities in the United States.

As seen in indigenous healing approaches, Asian culture-bound syndromes often represent a strong mind-body connection. For example, dhat, which originates from India, refers to "severe anxiety and hypochondriacal concerns with the discharge of semen, whitish discoloration of the urine, and feelings of weakness and exhaustion" (American Psychiatric Association, 2000). This syndrome is very similar to rok-joo in Thailand, jiryan in India, sukra prameha in Sri Lanka, and shenkui in China, where the anxiety stems from the malfunction of the penis or genitalia. It is also similar to koro in Malaysia, which is "an episode of sudden and intense anxiety that the penis (or in the rare female cases, the vulva and nipples) will recede into the body and possibly cause death" (Glossary of Culture-Bound Syndromes, 2001, p. 2). Other Asian culture-bound syndromes underscore somatization over emotional expressions. For example, neurasthenia (also known as shenjing shuairuo) is viewed as a Chinese version of major depressive disorder but the emphasis is on the physical rather than psychological symptoms such as weakness or fatigue, chest pain, intense heartbeat that may be irregular (palpitations, tachycardia); cold, clammy hands and feet; abnormally rapid breathing (hyperventilating); dizziness or faintness; periodic sighing; and/or sweating for no apparent reason, yet it is triggered by anxiety and depression (Kleinman & Mechanic, 1981).

Other examples of Asian culture-bound syndromes also highlight the cultural emphasis on emotional restraint. For example, hwa-byung or wool-hwa-bung in Korea, also known as anger syndrome is hypothesized to stem from the suppression of anger. Symptoms include insomnia, panic, fear of impending death, indigestion, palpitations, generalized aches and pains, and a feeling of a mass in the epigastrium (Glossary of Culture-Bound Syndromes, 2001). In addition to the emphasis on physical and psychological symptoms, Asian culture-bound syndromes also often highlight connections to the spiritual and ancestral world. For example, hsieh-ping in Taiwan is a short period of being in a daze during which one is overcome by an ancestral ghost, who tries to communicate to one's family members. Symptoms of hsieh-ping include disorientation, tremors, and visual or auditory hallucinations. Similarly, in Korea, shin-byung syndrome is exemplified by anxiety and a series of somatic problems such as dizziness, appetite loss, insomnia, and gastrointestinal problems. Individuals also experience dissociation and possession by ancestral spirits. If you were to meet someone who claimed to be possessed by a spirit or ancestral ghost, how would you react? What would your assumptions be about that person?

Many Asian culture-bound syndromes also highlight the cultural emphasis on interdependence and are associated with intense social reactions and feelings. What would you do if someone you loved suddenly locked himself in a room and refused to come out? How would you deal with this problem? Perhaps one of the most interesting culture-bound syndromes from Japan is hikikomori, a phenomenon of youth and young adults who suddenly withdraw from society by shutting themselves in a room in their home for a minimum of 6 months (Jones, 2006). Such confinement and isolation often results from social pressures, relationships, family conflicts, and a disinterest in relationships. Most of the hikikomori are male and a Japanese psychologist, Dr. Saito Tamaki estimates there are 1 million hikikomori in Japan (roughly 20% of all male youth in Japan). Most cases are the oldest son in the family, perhaps because of the strong familial pressure they receive to succeed (Jones, 2006). There have also been cases reported in South Korea, Taiwan, Hong Kong, and among Asian immigrants in the United States.

Perhaps what is most interesting about this culture-bound syndrome is not just the description of the phenomenon, but how it is dealt with in Japan as well. Specifically, most families who have hikikomori leave them alone in hopes that they will grow out of it. Many do not share this syndrome with anyone, including close friends and family, and they create stories to hide the secret. While there are different programs emerging in Japan to address hikikomori, families are slow to respond. These responses to such a prevalent problem must be understood in the context of Asian cultural values. While from an American perspective, many parents may assertively respond to the social confinement, in Japan, such an approach may be harmful to social harmony. Moreover, many Japanese families may wish to keep the hikikomori a secret in order to save face and maintain social relations (Jones, 2006).

The typical Japanese responses for dealing with hikikomori reflect important cultural orientations and values that exist for other culture-bound syndromes as well. For example, in treating various syndromes such as neurasthenia, the most common method is to treat the physical symptoms only with herbal remedies, acupuncture, or other forms of traditional Chinese medicine. Similarly, when treating syndromes that have a spiritual component, it is common to use prayer, ancestral worship, and communication with spirits (Inman, Yeh, Madan-Bahel, & Nath, 2007). Hence, indigenous healing methods must be considered in the context of a culture's understanding and conceptualization of disease and health, in addition to cultural orientation and self-construal. Cultural-specific responses to disease or stress may not always involve a designated indigenous healer and may also refer to an individual's culturally responsive coping strategies (Yeh, Arora, & Wu, 2005).

Collectivistic Coping   The emphasis of collectivistic cultures on group cohesion and interdependent selves on interconnectedness, the maintenance of harmony, and conformity influence the help-seeking patterns of individuals with interdependent selves (Yeh et al., 2005). Specifically,

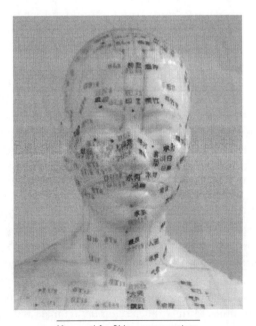

Map used for Chinese acupuncture.

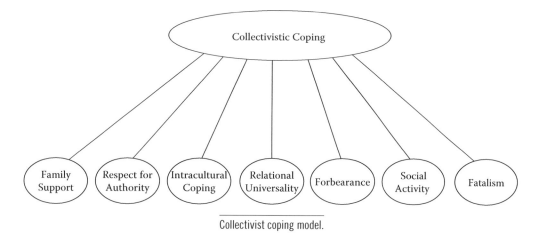

Collectivist coping model.

Asians with a more interdependent sense of self may cope with problems using methods that focus on changing the self rather than changing the situation (Cross, 1995; Yang, 1986; Yeh et al., 2005). When you have a psychological problem, do you always seek comfort from your family? Why or why not? When do you seek help from friends or authority figures like a teacher? It has been demonstrated that people from collectivistic, and especially Asian, cultures tend to cope in ways that involve important relationships and a belief in fate. Accordingly, Yeh et al. (2005) proposed a new theoretical model for collectivistic coping, which includes the following coping strategies: family support, respect for authority, intracultural coping, relational universality, forbearance, social activity, and fatalism.

Family Support   The family has been found to play a central role in supporting and caring for each other in numerous Asian cultures including Chinese, Korean, Japanese, Taiwanese, and Thai (Yeh et al., 2005). In fact, previous research indicates that Asians and Asian Americans tend to seek support and help from family members rather than mental health professionals as a way of coping (Yeh, Inose, Kobori, & Chang, 2001; Yeh, Inman, Kim, & Okubo, 2006; Yeh & Wang, 2000). These findings are consistent with the idea of the interdependent self being intertwined with and inseparable from in-group members and important others (Markus & Kitayama, 1991). Additionally, disclosing personal problems to the family may be preferred over talking to others since revealing problems to people outside of the family is believed to bring shame and guilt to the entire family (Sue, 1994).

Respect for Authority   Based on Confucian values, the Asian American family structure is hierarchical so that older members of the family, including even siblings who are slightly older, command respect from those who are younger (Uba, 1994). Accordingly, Asian Americans have also been found to cope with problems by seeking advice from authority figures in the community such as elders (Atkinson, Ponterotto, & Sanchez, 1984) and seeking help from parents (Suan & Tyler, 1990; Yeh et al., 2001).

Intracultural Coping   Intracultural coping refers to "the use of supportive networks comprised of racially similar individuals, such as one's family network or community-based social groups" (Yeh et al., 2005). Similar to intracultural coping, is relational universality. There is a fundamental sense of interconnectedness between interdependent individuals, others, and their environment that makes seeking support, advice, and guidance from people who are experiencing similar problems an important coping strategy. We refer to this as relational universality. This strategy may be particularly helpful for Asians and Asian Americans because interdependent individuals seek to closely connect with others around common factors and experiences (Yeh et al., 2005). For example, Yeh et al. (2004) found that Asian Americans tended to cope with the death of a family member by seeking support and connection with other families who also lost a close relative.

Forbearance   Forbearance refers to the withholding of one's opinions and emotions or the restraint shown in the face of provocation, as a means to maintain social harmony (Yeh et al., 2005). Forbearance is important in Asian cultures where suppression of conflict (Fugita, Ito, Abe, & Takeuchi, 1991) and withholding the free expression of feelings (Tashima & Ito, 1982) are valued and the desire to achieve or strive for personal gain is deemphasized (Lee, 1997) in order to promote interpersonal harmony. The tendency to keep problems to themselves in order not to disturb social harmony has been found among Japanese students (Fukuhara, 1989) and other Asian students (Yeh & Inose, 2002).

Social Activity   The use of social supports is an important coping strategy for interdependent individuals due to their inherent sense of connectedness with others (Liu, 1986; Mau & Jepsen, 1988; Yeh & Inose, 2002; Yeh & Wang, 2000). The tendency to use social relations as a source of support has been found among Asian Americans (Yeh & Wang, 2000), Japanese college students (Yeh et al., 2001), and Chinese, Japanese, and Korean immigrant adolescents (Yeh & Inose, 2002).

Fatalism   Fatalism as a coping mechanism refers to the tendency to merge with contextual, social, or spiritual forces and to accept certain outcomes rather than trying to change one's surroundings in order to cope with problems. While independent selves attempt to control one's environment, individuals from collectivistic cultures may have a tendency to believe that control lies in contextual or external forces and endorse a sense of **harmony control**. Morling and Fiske (1999) describe harmony control as "an active, intentional endeavor in which people recognize the agency in contextual, social, or spiritual forces and attempt to merge with these forces" (p. 382). Hence, harmony control involves an external locus of control and acceptance that forces outside one's control may dictate the outcome.

This model of collectivistic coping was supported by the results of a qualitative study conducted by Yeh, Inman, Kim, and Okubo (2006). In this study, Asian Americans who lost a member of their family in the World Trade Center attacks were found to use a number of collectivistic coping methods such as familial coping, intracultural coping, relational universality, forbearance, fatalism/spirituality, and indigenous healing methods. These participants tended to turn to more traditional and culturally congruent ways of healing and coping with their loss than to use mental health services.

Facts and Figures

At present, there is very little information on the prevalence of indigenous healers in the United States, and in particular with Asian American populations. There are a few reasons for this lack of information: (a) There is limited systematic research on the use of indigenous healers; (b) many indigenous healers are not formally registered with any official mental health service organization or hospital; (c) many indigenous healers work in a private practice, in a religious organization or community setting, or out of their own home and are difficult to locate; and (d) many indigenous healers are immigrants and do not speak English fluently so research on this group can be especially challenging.

Woman practicing yoga.

The World Health Organization (WHO) has projected that between 65% and 85% of the world's population uses indigenous healing or traditional medicine as their principal form of care for physical and psychological problems, and in parts of Asia, this percent is close to 80%. For example, in China, the use of traditional herbs accounts for 30% to 50% of the total consumption of traditional medicine. In the United States, it is estimated that 158 million adults have used some form of alternative remedies or indigenous healing (World Health Organization, 2003).

Summary

In this chapter, we provide a conceptual framework for understanding the roles of indigenous healers and indigenous healing approaches from an Asian American cultural orientation and view of self. In particular, the importance of interdependence is underscored and indigenous healing methods are contrasted with Western notions of talk therapy in various ways. According to Yeh et al. (2004), these differences include the distinction between: (a) a linear versus a circular perspective; (b) a cognitive/affective basis versus a spiritual basis of well-being; and (c) an active versus a passive helping role. Quotes from interviews with specific indigenous healers are used to highlight these important characteristics of indigenous healers.

In addition, this chapter emphasizes the importance of culture-bound syndromes and collectivistic methods of coping as they relate to indigenous approaches to healing. Namely, in Asian cultures, methods of healing are inextricably linked with perceptions of disease and health as well as the mind-body relationship. Such beliefs about the world and one's interrelationship among others, the body, and the spiritual and natural world are reflected in coping methods and the manifestation and presentation of culture-bound syndromes. The authors provide specific descriptions of various syndromes, indigenous healers, and collectivistic coping methods. Relevant references and resources are also presented along with a case study and description of a culturally responsive intervention for the case.

Discussion Questions

1. Think about your last visit to a doctor. What questions did the doctor ask you? What did he or she focus on? How did he or she relate to you? In thinking about your experience with medical doctors and/or mental health professionals, what cultural values and beliefs do you think their approach to healing reflects? How does this differ with the cultural values and beliefs that Asian indigenous healing methods reflect?

2. Look up one of the Web sites on indigenous healing mentioned in the chapter. In what ways does this healing method resonate with your cultural orientation? In what ways does it differ? Would you ever consider seeing this particular type of healer? Why or why not? Which indigenous healing methods are most appealing to you or someone you know? Explain why.

3. Visit one of the kinds of indigenous healers discussed in this chapter (e.g., Reiki healer, Qigong healer). How was his or her approach to healing different or similar to other Western medical and mental health professionals?

4. Look up a specific disorder in the DSM-IV-TR (for example, Narcissistic Personality Disorder, Dependent Personality Disorder, Schizophrenia, Anorexia Nervosa, etc.). In what ways is this disorder a culture-bound syndrome? What cultural biases are apparent in the specific criteria? Would this be considered a mental disorder in an Asian cultural context? Why or why not?

5. Think about a recent stressful situation that you encountered. How did you cope with the situation? Did you seek professional psychological help (i.e., see a psychiatrist or psychologist, etc.)? Or did you cope in a way that was collectivistic (i.e., intracultural coping, relational universality, etc.)?

Case Study

Nina is a 20-year-old, single, heterosexual, Hindu college student who emigrated from India to pursue a college degree in the United States. She was referred to the health clinic for chest pains, faintness, and fatigue. The medical clinic was unable to identify any physical roots for her symptoms and suspected they were related to her experiences with culture shock and then referred her to a counselor. At the intake session, Nina was quiet, withdrawn, and anxious. She described feeling worried about what her peers and teachers think of her and she also described having trouble sleeping. Nina stated that a few months ago, she was walking down the street and a group of White students started harassing her, telling her to "go home" and "you don't belong here." They continued to yell at her for several minutes and follow her and no one stopped to help her. Since that experience, she has been nervous about being harassed again for her background. She believed that her dark skin color and Indian background made her especially vulnerable to the stereotype of a terrorist. She has not shared her experience with anyone except for her roommate who dismissed the encounter as a rare event. Nina has never been to counseling and does not know what to expect. She is also very self-conscious about what the counselor may think about her as well. The counselor asked Nina how she typically copes with difficult or stressful situations. Nina was embarrassed to share with the counselor that she has turned to a Vedic astrologer common among Hindus. She has also practiced Hatha yoga with other Hindu friends. After the incident, she began to feel ambivalent about these practices because she was worried about getting harassed if she identified too strongly with other South Asians.

Intervention

The intervention for the case study incorporates multicultural and postmodern perspectives (see Corey, 2005, for overview). For example, social constructionism contends that realities are socially and contextually informed and clients' worldviews and realities are accepted. Moreover, social constructivists emphasize how stories create meanings for individuals and are embedded in social relationships (Gergen, 1999). Hence, the counselor should spend time listening to Nina's story and trying to understand her worldview and perspective. The counselor should not interpret her experiences as irrational.

In the intake meeting, it is critical for the counselor to make a strong connection with Nina so that she returns to counseling in the future and commits herself to the process. The high priority that Asian Americans place on collectivism and relational harmony (Markus & Kitayama, 1991; Yeh & Hwang, 2000) helps to provide a framework for the initial sessions. Specifically, since Nina is not familiar with counseling, she may also be embarrassed to ask questions about the counselor's role. To save face for the client, it is important to normalize the counseling process while explaining how counseling may be beneficial to Nina's presenting concerns. It is important for the counselor to be flexible in providing culturally meaningful counseling.

Since Nina feels cultural stigmas around expressing her harassment, a possible way to build rapport and trust is to establish achieved credibility (Sue & Zane, 1987). Sue and Zane (1987) contend that a client's perception of low achieved credibility may in part explain premature termination. Achieved credibility may be accomplished by conceptualizing the client's concern in a way that is congruent with her cultural orientation and by offering a "gift" to the client in the first session (Sue & Zane, 1987). Gift giving, or offering a direct and immediate benefit from counseling, symbolically underscores the value of a relationship in Asian culture. A gift to Nina may involve offering a clear explanation for her symptoms and past experience (Sue & Zane, 1987). It should also involve a belief in the physical distress (stomach pains, fatigue, dizziness) she is experiencing.

Moreover, when working with someone like Nina, it is important to recognize the strong mind and body connection present in Asian American culture. The mind, body, and spirit are not viewed as separate, but as interconnected systems. It follows that intervention with Nina should incorporate an appreciation for this holistic perspective. Hence, it would be important for the counselor to validate her physical symptoms and treat them as real. In the beginning, the counselor should treat physical symptoms and ask about them ("How are you sleeping?" "How does your stomach feel?" "When do you feel dizzy?"). Some counselors may be tempted to "explain" the physical symptoms as merely somatic expressions that are not "real," but such an explanation is culturally biased and will only alienate Nina from the counseling experience and will alienate her feelings.

A culturally responsive intervention must incorporate relevant indigenous healing practices and aspects of the client's naturalistic collectivistic coping strategies. Specifically, it is very common for South Asian Hindus to consult an astrologer for important events and guidance (Inman, Yeh, Madan-Bahel, & Nath, unpublished manuscript). The counselor may try to work collaboratively with an astrologer to offer direction and faith as Nina heals from the racist encounter. In considering Nina's intracultural coping styles, the counselor may help Nina connect with other Hindu students who may have a shared experience with discrimination. Such a connection would help validate Nina's feelings and also provide her with some social support. Finally, the counselor should consider consulting with members of the Hindu community and college campus about providing a safe environment for South Asian students. This may involve offering workshops and training to foster cultural sensitivity.

Case Study Discussion Questions

For undergraduate students, please consider the following questions:

1. What are your personal reactions to Nina seeking help from an astrologer? Is this something you would ever feel comfortable doing?
2. To what extent do you believe in fate?
3. To what extent do you believe you have control of your destiny?
4. How does your worldview impact how you cope with stress? Do these beliefs differ depending on the situation? Give an example of how.

For graduate students and/or beginning therapists, please consider the following questions:

1. In thinking about the case study, how would you work with Nina?
2. How would you work with the university to deal with the larger systemic issues of discrimination?

Key Terms

Buddhist monk: A person who practices monasticism, adopting a strict religious and ascetic lifestyle, in the traditions of Buddhism.

Collectivism/collectivistic orientation: A cultural orientation associated with the subordination of personal goals to the goals of some collective, which is usually a stable in-group, and life satisfaction is derived from carrying out social roles and obligations to this stable in-group (Markus & Kitayama, 1991). Asian countries have been described as more collectivistic where as western countries have been described as more individualistic.

Collectivistic coping: Coping strategies and methods that reflect the collectivistic cultural values, beliefs, and behaviors of interdependent individuals. Collectivistic coping strategies include family support, respect for authority figures, intracultural coping, relational universality, forbearance, social activity, and fatalism (Yeh, Arora, & Wu, 2005).

Culture-bound syndromes: Combination of somatic and psychiatric symptoms that are recognized in a particular cultural setting (American Psychiatric Association, 2000 Diagnostic and Statistical Manual of Mental Disorders-IV-TR).

Family support: A dimension of collectivistic coping that refers to the tendency to seek support and help from family members in order to cope with problems (Yeh, Arora, & Wu, 2005).

Fatalism: A dimension of collectivistic coping that refers to the tendency to merge with contextual, social, or spiritual forces and to accept certain outcomes rather than trying to change one's surroundings in order to cope with problems (Yeh, Arora, & Wu, 2005).

Forbearance: A dimension of collectivistic coping that refers to the tendency to seek support, advice, and guidance from people who are experiencing similar problems (Yeh, Arora, & Wu, 2005).

Harmony control: An active, intentional endeavor in which people recognize the agency in contextual, social, or spiritual forces and attempt to merge with these forces (Morling & Fiske, 1999).

Indigenous healing: Also referred to as traditional or alternative medicine, the numerous healing systems used by various cultural and ethnic populations for thousands of years, well before modern medicine practices were established ("Traditional and Indigenous Healing Systems," n.d.).

Individualism/individualistic orientation: A cultural orientation associated with the attainment of personal goals (Markus & Kitayama, 1991). Western countries have been described as more individualistic whereas Asian countries have been described as more collectivistic.

Independent self-construal: Interdependent and independent self-construals refer to the way individuals view themselves. The independent self-construal emphasizes the separateness, internal attributes, and uniqueness of individuals (Singelis, 1994).

Interdependent self-construal: Interdependent and independent self-construals refer to the way individuals view themselves. The interdependent self-construal emphasizes connectedness, social context, and relationships (Singelis, 1994).

Pranic healer: A person who uses energy-based healing techniques that utilizes the life-force or *prana* to balance, harmonize and transform the body's energy processes.

Pranic healing: A form of energy healing that removes diseased energies from the patient's invisible energy body and by transferring fresh vital energy or *prana* to the affected areas with the use of the hands.

Qigong healer: A person who can direct or emit external life energy or *Qi* for the purpose of healing others.

Qigong healing: A method of healing originating from China that refers to the art of managing the breath or *Qi* to achieve and maintain good health to enhance the leverage and stamina of the body in coordination with the physical process of respiration.

Reiki: A form of energy healing and method of natural healing based on application of universal life energy with the use of hands and is used in the treatment of physical, emotional, spiritual or mental disease.

Reiki healer: A person who channels the universal life energy to stimulate the body's natural healing process.

Self-construal: The way in which one sees oneself (Singelis, 1994).

Relational universality: A dimension of collectivistic coping that refers to the tendency to seek support, advice, and guidance from people who are experiencing similar problems in order to cope with problems (Yeh, Arora, & Wu, 2005).

Respect for authority: A dimension of collectivistic coping that refers to the tendency to cope with problems by seeking advice from authority figures in the community (Yeh, Arora, & Wu, 2005).

Social activity: A dimension of collectivistic coping that refers to the tendency to use social supports in order to cope with problems (Yeh, Arora, & Wu, 2005).

For Further Learning and Suggested Reading

The journal *Culture, Medicine, and Psychiatry* has numerous articles that offer in-depth case studies of culture bound syndromes and indigenous and traditional medicine approaches to healing.

Books

Kleinman, A., & Lin, T-Y. (Eds.). (1981). *Normal and abnormal behavior in Chinese culture.* Dordrecht, The Netherlands: D. Reidel Publishing Company.

Lee, C. C., & Armstrong, K. L. (1995). Indigenous models of mental health interventions: Lessons from traditional healers. In J. G. Ponterottos, J. M. Casas, L. A. Suzuki, & C. M. Alexander (Eds.), *Handbook of multicultural counseling* (pp. 441–456). Thousand Oaks, CA: Sage Publications.

Simons, R. C., & Hughes, C. C. (Eds.). (1985). *The Culture-bound syndromes: Folk illnesses of psychiatric and anthropological interest.* Dordrecht, The Netherlands: D. Reidel Publishing Company.

Yeh, C. J., Hunter, C. D., Madan-Bahel, A., Chiang, L., & Arora, A. K. (2004). Indigenous and interdependent perspectives of healing: Implications for counseling and research. *Journal of Counseling & Development, 82,* 410–419.

Movies

Below are documentaries and movies that focus on Asian indigenous healing, healers, and mental health issues:

Fool's Dance (1983): mysterious patient offers proof that there is method to his madness.

The Laughing Club of India (2000): documentary about a variety of laughing clubs in India and how they are used to serve various purposes.

The Split Horn (2001): role of a Shaman in a Hmong immigrant community in Wisconsin.

Web Sites

The following is a list of key Web sites for key terms discussed in this chapter:

Acupuncture: http://www.acupuncture.com, http://www.acupuncturetoday.com

Chakra or aura healing: http://www.chioshealing.com

Culture-bound syndromes: http://weber.ucsd.edu/~thall/cbs_intro.html, http://www.healthandhealingny.org/tradition_healing/index_trad.html, http://www.psychiatrictimes.com/p011163.html

Culture-specific diseases: http://anthro.palomar.edu/medical/med_4.htm

Pranic healing: http://www.pranichealing.com

Qigong healing: http://www.qigong.com, http://www.qi.org

Reiki healing: http://www.reiki.org

References

The American Heritage Dictionary of the English language, 4th ed. (2006). Boston: Houghton Mifflin Company.

American Psychiatric Association. (2000). *Diagnostic and statistical manual of mental disorders* (4th ed., pp. 897–904). Washington, DC.

Atkinson, D. R., Ponterotto, J. G., & Sanchez, A. R. (1984). Attitudes of Vietnamese and Anglo-American students toward counseling. *Journal of College Student Personnel, 25,* 448–452.

Bachnik, J. M. (1986). Time, space, and person in Japanese relationships. In J. Hendry & J. Webber (Eds.), *Interpreting Japanese society: Anthropological approaches* (pp. 49–75). Oxford: JASO.

Corey, G. (2005). *Theory and practice of counseling and psychotherapy* (7th ed.). Belmont, CA: Brooks/Cole.

Cross, S. E. (1995). Self-construals, coping, and stress in cross-cultural adaptation. *Journal of Cross-Cultural Psychology, 26,* 673–697.

Fugita, S., Ito, K., Abe, J., & Takeuchi, D. (1991). Japanese Americans. In N. Mokuau (Ed.), *Handbook of social services for Asian and Pacific Islanders* (pp. 61–77). New York: Greenwood Press.

Fukuhara, M. (1989). Counseling psychology in Japan. *Applied Psychology: An International Review, 38,* 409–422.

Gergen, K. (1999). *An invitation to social construction.* Thousand Oaks, CA: Sage Publications.

Glossary of Culture-Bound Syndromes. (2001). Retrieved May 7, 2006, from http://weber.ucsd.edu/~thall/cbs_glos.html

Helms, J. E., & Cook, D. A. (1999). *Using race and culture in counseling and psychotherapy: Theory and process.* Needham Heights, MA: Allyn & Bacon.

Hunter, C. D., Arora, A. K., Madan-Bahel, A., Chiang, L., & Yeh, C. J. (2002, August). *Indigenous and interdependent perspectives of healing: Implications for counseling and research.* Poster session presented at the annual meeting of the American Psychological Association, Chicago, IL.

Inman, A. G., Yeh, C. J., Madan-Bahel, A., & Nath, S. (2007). Bereavement and coping of South Asian families post 9/11. *Journal of Multicultural Counseling and Development, 35,* 101–115.

Jones, M. (2006, January 15). Shutting themselves in. *New York Times.*

Kleinman, A., & Mechanic, D. (1981). Mental illness and psychosocial aspects of medical problems in China. In A. Kleinman & L. Tsung-Yi (Eds.), *Normal and abnormal behavior in Chinese culture.* Dordrecht, The Netherlands: D. Reidel.

Lee, C. C., & Armstrong, K. L. (1995). Indigenous models of mental health interventions: Lessons from traditional healers. In J. G. Ponterottos, J. M. Casas, L. A. Suzuki, & C. M. Alexander (Eds.), *Handbook of multicultural counseling* (pp. 441–456). Thousand Oaks, CA: Sage Publications.

Lee, E. (1997). Chinese American families. In E. Lee (Eds.), *Working with Asian Americans: A guide for clinicians* (pp. 46–78). New York: Guilford Press.

Leong, F. (1986). Counseling and psychotherapy with Asian-Americans: Review of the literature. *Journal of Counseling Psychology, 44,* 196–206.

Leong, F. T. L., Wagner, N. S., & Tata, S. P. (1995). Racial and ethnic variations in help-seeking attitudes. In J. G. Ponterroto, J. M. Cases, L. A. Alexander (Eds.), *Handbook of multicultural counseling.* Thousand Oaks, CA: Sage Publications.

Lillard, A. S. (1997). Other folks' theories of mind and behavior. *Psychological Science, 8*(4), 268–274.

Liu, W. T. (1986). Culture and social support. *Research on Aging, 8,* 57–83.

Markus, H. R., & Kitayama, S. (1991). Culture and the self: Implications for cognition, emotion, and motivation. *Psychological Review, 98,* 224–253.

Mau, W-C., & Jepsen, D. A. (1988). Attitudes toward counselors and counseling processes: A comparison of Chinese and American graduate students. *Journal of Counseling and Development, 67,* 189–192.

Morling, B., & Fiske, S. T. (1999). Defining and measuring harmony control. *Journal of Research in Personality, 33,* 379–414.

Ornstein, R. E. (1972). *The psychology of consciousness.* San Francisco: Freeman.

Singelis, T. M. (1994). The measurement of independent and interdependent self-construals. *Personality and Social Psychology Bulletin, 20,* 580–591.

Suan, L. V., & Tyler, J. D. (1990). Mental health values and preferences for mental health resources of Japanese-American and Caucasian-American students. *Professional Psychology: Research and Practice, 21,* 291–296.

Sue, D. W. (1994). Asian-American mental health and help-seeking behavior: Comment on Solberg et al. (1994), Tata and Leong (1994), and Lin (1994). *Journal of Counseling Psychology, 41,* 292–295.

Sue, D. W., & Sue, D. (1999). *Counseling the culturally diverse: Theory and practice* (3rd ed.). New York: Wiley.

Sue, S., & Morishima, J. (1982). *The mental health of Asian Americans.* San Francisco: Jossey-Bass.

Sue, S., & Zane, N. (1987). The role of culture and cultural techniques in psychotherapy. *American Psychologist, 42,* 37–45.

Tashima, E., & Ito, K. (1982). *Asian American self-concept: Preliminary thoughts on illness express and the role of women.* Los Angeles: UCLA Asian American Studies Center.

Traditional and Indigenous Healing Systems. (n.d.). Retrieved May 7, 2006, from http://www.healthandhealingny.org/tradition_healing/index_trad.html

Triandis, H. C., Bontempo, R., Villareal, M. (1988). Individualism and collectivism: Cross-cultural perspectives on self-ingroup relationships. *Journal of Personality and Social Psychology, 54,* 323–338.

Uba, L. (1994). *Asian Americans: Personality patterns, identity, and mental health.* New York: The Guildford Press.

Welcome to the Qigong Institute! (n.d.). Retrieved May 15, 2008, from http://www.qigonginstitute.org.

What is Pranic healing? (n.d.). Retrieved May 15, 2008, from http://www.lifepositive.com/pranic-healing.html.

What is Reiki? (n.d.). Retrieved May 15, 2008, from http://www.reiki.org/faq/WhatisReiki.html.

World Health Organization. (2003, May). Traditional medicine fact sheet N# 134. Retrieved May 7, 2006, from http://www.who.int/mediacentre/factsheets/fs134/en/print.html

Yang, K. S. (1986). Chinese personality and its change. In M. H. Bind (Ed.), *Psychology of the Chinese people* (pp. 107–170). Hong Kong: Oxford University Press.

Yeh, C. J. (2001). *Indigenous ideas about cultural competence.* Invited symposium panel speaker at the National Multicultural Counseling Summit, Santa Barbara, CA.

Yeh, C. J., Arora, A. K., & Wu, K. (2005). A new theoretical model of collectivistic coping. In P. T. P. Wong & C. J. Wong (Eds.), *Handbook of multicultural perspectives on stress and coping.* New York: Springer.

Yeh, C. J., Hunter, C. D., Madan-Bahel, A., Chiang, L., & Arora, A. K. (2004). Indigenous and interdependent perspectives of healing: Implications for counseling and research. *Journal of Counseling & Development, 82,* 410–419.

Yeh, C. J., & Hwang, M. (2000). Interdependence in ethnic identity and self: Implications for theory and practice. *Journal of Counseling and Development, 78,* 420–429.

Yeh, C. J., Inman, A., Kim, A. B., & Okubo, Y. (2006). Asian American collectivistic coping in response to 9/11. *Cultural Diversity and Ethnic Minority Psychology, 12,* 134–147.

Yeh, C. J., & Inose, M. (2002). Difficulties and coping strategies of Chinese, Japanese and Korean immigrant students. *Adolescence, 37,* 69–82.

Yeh, C. J., Inose, M., Kobori, A., & Chang, T. (2001). Self and coping among college students in Japan. *Journal of College Student Development, 42,* 242–256.

Yeh, C. J., & Wang, Y-W. (2000). Asian American coping attitudes, sources, and practices: Implications for indigenous counseling strategies. *Journal of College Student Development, 41,* 94–103.

Zane, N., Enomoto, K., & Chun, C. (1994). Treatment outcomes of Asian- and White-American clients in outpatient therapy. *Journal of Community Psychology, 22,* 177–191.

30

Seeking, Receiving, and Providing Culturally Competent Mental Health Services

A Focus on Asian Americans

NITA TEWARI

OUTLINE OF CHAPTER

Case Synopsis

Keith: "Hey, what's been happening with you lately Mike? Every time we go out, you don't wanna go—we get together at Josh's house, mix drinks, play videogames, then go out to eat. But you stay home. What's up with you, man?"

Mike: "Not feelin' it; don't wanna be around people right now. Life's not feelin' good. Tired of my parents fightin', my bro's in a gang, my parents don't know cuz they're workin' all the time and my sis is too busy with her own family."
Keith: "Yeah, so nothin's changed; same family you always had. Why aren't you goin' out with us now?"

Mike: "It's different. I'm just really tired of the family stuff and I need my family to change, I want life to be different. I think about it all the time, and just can't deal with it anymore."

Keith: "So, why don't you go see a counselor or somethin'? We're gettin' tired of asking you to hang out and sometimes we don't even ask, cuz' we know you're gonna say no."

Mike: "I'm not seein' a counselor or some head doctor. Chicks and crazy folks go to counseling centers. No way am I waitin' in the lobby with those crazies. And I'm Asian. Asians don't go to counseling."

Keith: "See this is what I'm talkin' about. You got issues and you're not dealin' with them. You know you need to talk about what's happenin' with you and all your family crap, but you're not goin'."

As you read this, the 30th chapter in *Asian American Psychology: Current Perspectives*—the last chapter in the book, you have a basic understanding of the field of Asian American psychology, but not all that it encompasses. The topics in the book merely introduce readers to core concepts and evolving areas that have emerged from the field over the past 40 years. Each chapter contains some combination of history, theory, research, practice, and application with some chapters leaning heavier on one or the other. No chapter in the book has focused entirely on what therapy is about for Asian Americans, who the mental health professionals are, and how diversity plays a role in the service and delivery of mental health services. Therefore, this chapter will discuss the topic of seeking, receiving, and providing mental health services with a focus on Asian Americans. Given that readers of this textbook include a combination of students and clinicians, the chapter will shift between presenting information from the perspective of clients seeking therapy to providing information for clinicians thinking about servicing Asian American populations.

Introduction

Let's be realistic. Seeing a **psychologist** remains a bit of a mystery for many people and certainly there are Asian Americans unfamiliar with the therapy process. While the opening case synopsis may seem exaggerated or stereotypical for some audiences, there are still many Asian Americans who maintain the perspective that mental health services are only for those who are severely disturbed or "crazy." However, mental health services are also utilized by individuals coping with everyday life adjustment, transitions, and challenges in addition to those struggling with severe psychiatric concerns. Take a moment to sit back, reflect, and consider what some of the psychological concerns might be for Asian Americans—perhaps acculturation conflicts, cultural clashes, pressure to succeed, academic achievement, and family duty might come to mind. Quite often when people think of Asian Americans, they don't think of the unique psychological differences between a Southeast Asian American trauma survivor, a fourth-generation Japanese American in an interracial relationship, an Indian arranged-marriage newlywed couple adjusting to life in America, or even the multiple identities of a lesbian Filipina female. Frequently, Asian Americans are perceived as being of East Asian descent, such as Chinese, Japanese, or Korean, and are lumped together as having the "same issues" regardless of their individual or ethnic differences. The above-mentioned examples barely touch the surface of Asian American psychology, a psychology comprised of one of the fastest-growing, vastly rich, and complex ethnic groups living in this country today (Leong et al., 2007).

Most Asian Americans in the United States were born abroad and represent over 25 Asian group identities and linguistic diversity of over 100 languages and dialects (U.S. Census Bureau, 2000; U.S. Department of Mental Health and Human Services, 2001). The near 11 million mono-, bi-, and multiracial Asian Americans (U.S. Census Bureau, 2000) share similarities, yet, have psychological journeys and differences unlike other major ethnic groups due to their immigration histories, cultural, racial, and ethnic characteristics. So, chances are an Asian American supervisor, coworker, student, or client has already walked through your door, or will soon with Asian Americans representing close to 4% of the national population with higher percentages in states such as California, New York, Hawaii, and others following close behind (U.S. Census Bureau, 2000). In 2007, diversity is no longer an issue of Black and White, but also Asian American and everything else in between.

So, what happens when Asian American clients walk into counseling centers? What will therapists do? What kind of services will they provide? What kind of services will clients receive? Who will provide the mental health services? These are all questions asked and studied by scholars and practitioners in Asian American psychology over the past several decades as there is clinical and research evidence on the psychological concerns and mental health service needs of the Asian American community. This chapter will specifically focus on introducing students and clients to the provisions of seeking and receiving mental health services while also providing information to students and clinicians serving Asian American populations. The goals of the chapter are: (a) to discuss the mental health utilization rates of Asian Americans and the barriers to seeking mental health services; (b) to discuss where Asian Americans go when they have family struggles or personal problems; (c) to demystify the counseling process and to educate readers on what counseling means for Asian Americans; and (d) to discuss what is needed in providing culturally competent mental health services to Asian Americans. The last part of the chapter will expand on the opening case synopsis with Mike as the client in a case study with discussion, followed by discussion questions, activities, and suggested readings and resources for further learning.

Asian American Mental Health: Seeking Services

So, *why should we study Asian American psychology and focus on Asian Americans as a different racial/ethnic group?* In psychology, don't students learn how individuals think, feel, and relate? Students are taught that behaviors are influenced by biology, genetics, nervous system, and body chemistry and that emotions range on a continuum of abnormal or normal, disordered or typical (Myers, 2006). However, what students have not been taught as frequently or rigorously is that traditional theories of psychology have historically been based and normed on European and Western paradigms typically applicable to upper-middle-class European and White Americans. After several decades of negative conceptions of minority individuals' cultures, inaccurate psychiatric diagnoses, and failure to take into account racial and ethnic backgrounds when conducting psychological assessments of diverse individuals, mental health researchers and practitioners recognized the limitations of employing only traditional European and Western theories of psychology when working clinically with diverse populations (Guthrie, 1998; Parham, White, & Ajamu, 1999).

As diversity in America increased, disparities in providing mental health services to people of color, including Asian Americans, result from attitudes toward seeking therapy, barriers to receiving treatment, and prematurely terminating counseling (Uba, 1997). Disparities and inequalities in health care facing racial and ethnic minorities exist today as concluded by the Department of Health and Human Services (Sue & Zane, 2006). Community agencies, public mental health clinics, and professionals throughout the United States have been unprepared and challenged in providing adequate psychological services to specific populations due to a lack of appropriate multicultural training. As a result, approaches and psychologies geared toward understanding, assessing, and conceptualizing ethnically and culturally specific populations developed in an effort to provide the best possible mental health services (Atkinson, Morten, & Sue, 1989; Sue & Sue, 1999). The next several sections will discuss some of the challenges facing Asian American populations who seek and receive mental health services.

Utilization Rates

Do Asian Americans go to counseling? Yes, they do, but less frequently than other cultural groups. Several studies have been conducted on the utilization rates of mental health services by Asian American populations since 1977 (U.S. Department of Mental Health and Human Services, 2001; Yang & WonPat-Borja, 2007). The majority of large-scale studies have taken place in public county mental health systems, community agencies, and university counseling center settings and included adolescents and adults in their sample sizes. Many of the classic studies on Asian American mental health services utilization rates were conducted in the 1970s, 1980s and 1990s, such as those conducted by Sue (1977), Loo, Tong, and True (1989), O'Sullivan, Peterson, Cox, and Kirekby (1989), Snowden and Cheung (1990), Leong (1994), Matsuoka, Breaux, and Ryujin (1997), Zhang, Snowden, and Sue (1998), and others. The studies consistently found that Asian Americans tend to underutilize mental health services in relation to their representation in the population. Furthermore, findings reflected that the numbers of Asian Americans using mental health services were less than other ethnic groups including European Americans. Recently, Kearney, Draper and Baron (2005) examined counseling utilization rates among ethnic minority college students and found that Asian Americans utilized counseling services less than their African American, Latino American, and Caucasian American counterparts. Kearney et al. (2005) also found that Asian Americans presented at **intake** with the greatest distress in comparison to other racial groups. Again, research showed that Asian Americans are less likely to utilize mental health services in comparison to others.

Currently, data from National Latino and Asian American Study (NLAAS) are being examined nationally by researchers on mental health–related services, and new developments are emerging in preliminary analyses and published results (Meyers, 2006; Takeuchi, 2007). In the latest research published by Abe-Kim et al. (2007) on the use of mental health–related services (general medical and specialty mental health services) among immigrant and U.S.-born Asian Americans, findings indicate that the rates of mental health use, subjective satisfaction, and perceived helpfulness of mental health–related services varied by an individual's birthplace (nativity status) and by their generational status. Abe-Kim et al. (2007) found that U.S.-born Asian Americans had higher rates of service use than did their immigrant counterparts. Intuitively, these findings makes sense since U.S.-born Asian Americans are more likely to be acculturated and accustomed to the idea of using psychological services if and when needed. Results from the NLAAS mental health study also indicated that third-generation or later individuals with a likely diagnosis had high rates (62.6%) of service use in the last 12 months (Abe-Kim et al., 2007), further supporting the finding that more acculturated individuals were likely to use services if and when needed. Among the population represented, 8.6% of Asian Americans sought treatment compared to 17.9% of the general population and 34% with a diagnosable illness sought treatment compared with 41% of the general population. The overall underrepresentation of Asian Americans and Pacific Islanders using the mental health care systems occurs regardless of the individual's age, gender, or geographic location (U.S. Department of Mental Health and Human Services, 2001). Previous and current studies clearly highlight the differences between ethnic groups in regard to mental health service utilization rates, but also the differences within the Asian American ethnic groups with regard to nativity (where one was born) status and generation status (Abe-Kim et al., 2007).

Barriers to Seeking Help

What does this mean? What are barriers to seeking help? Any Asian American can go to counseling, can't they? Research and clinical studies have identified common barriers over the years that have prevented Asian Americans from taking advantage of mental health services (Atkinson, 2004; Leong, Wagner, & Tata, 1995; Uba, 1997). Leong et al. (1995) describe cultural barriers as factors influencing the utilization of mental health services. First, financial limitations act as a barrier. There are Asian Americans unable to go to counseling, simply because they can not afford it. In the 2006 Report of the American Psychological Association (APA) Task Force on Socioeconomic Status, socioeconomic factors and social class are noted as fundamental determinants of mental health functioning with education, income, and occupation being important dimensions of socioeconomic status. Income is related to access to goods and services, and if people can afford mental health care, then individuals have greater chances in achieving better health and adjustment (APA Task Force on Socioeconomic Status, 2006). Abe-Kim, Takeuchi, and Hwang (2002) reported that subjects in their Chinese American Epidemiological Study (CAPES) had a greater probability of seeking out mental health care if they had insurance coverage at the time they sought help even though they found that income was not predictive of mental health help seeking in their study. Given the diversity in the Asian American community, it is important to note that poverty rates vary considerably. For example, Filipinos have the lowest poverty rates of 6.3%

among Asian Americans, followed by Japanese with a 9.7% poverty rate and Asian Indians with a 9.8% poverty rate (Reeves & Bennett, 2004). On the considerably lower end, 37.8% of Hmongs are living in poverty, 29.3% of Cambodians are living in poverty, Laotians are at 18.5%, Pakistanis at 16.5%, and 16% of Vietnamese are living in poverty (Le, 2007; Reeves & Bennett, 2004). Asian American groups with lower poverty rates are less likely to face barriers due to their financial and other resources, but groups such as the Hmongs and Cambodians who have the highest individual poverty rates of all Asian groups may face the greatest challenges in obtaining needed mental health care. Thus, a lack of financial resources and affordability are considered barriers to help seeking (Atkinson, 2004; U.S. Department of Mental Health and Human Services, 2001).

The second barrier in seeking and receiving mental health services that has been identified in the literature is the lack of available mental health services. For example, simple proximity can serve as an inhibitor to accessing mental health services (Atkinson, 2004). If an Asian individual recently migrated to America and has not obtained a license, is unable to drive, is without public transportation, or lives at a great distance from a mental health clinic, then chances are this person will forego seeking the care or help when needed. Thus, lack of nearby mental health services and geographic inaccessibility are considered barriers to seeking treatment (Uba, 1997).

A third barrier that Uba (1997) and others have discussed is client suspiciousness toward therapy. Clients are often unfamiliar with the role of mental health professionals and unaware of the patient-therapist confidentiality. The lack of knowledge as to what happens upon entering treatment and what happens if personal issues are discussed leaves many Asian Americans feeling fearful and suspicious. Earlier publications also suggested that some Asian American clients may fear that European American therapists may force them to adapt to their standards and ways of living or inaccurately assess and conceptualize their problems (Sue, 1973). Suspiciousness of mental health services among Asian Americans may also stem from a reaction to having possibly been victims of historical, institutional, and personal discrimination by clinics run by European Americans (Nagata, 1989a as cited in Uba, 1997; Sue, 1973). If an individual is unfamiliar with the services available, and outreach on mental health services is not occurring in translated languages, or in Asian communities, parts of the population will remain unfamiliar with the types of help available.

The fourth and perhaps most relevant barrier is the lack of available culturally sensitive and multiculturally competent mental health providers. The lack of culturally competent mental health providers has received considerable attention in the literature as to why ethnic minorities do not seek or receive mental health treatment (Atkinson, 2004; Inman, Yeh, Madan-Bahel, & Nath, 2007; Yeh, Inman, Kim, & Okubo, 2006). For some Asian Americans, it may be difficult to develop a relationship with a therapist when the therapist has no experience, understanding, or training specific to serving Asian Americans. Language barriers are considered factors in the underutilization of services because if agencies only employ English-speaking personnel, then non-English-speaking individuals who are seeking services may not receive the care they need. As a provision to eliminating this barrier, interpreters or bilingual practitioners have been recommended to increase minority mental health utilization rates (U.S. Department of Mental Health and Human Services, 2001). A counselor effectively trained in cultural competencies would be the next logical step in order for counselors of any ethnicity to understand and empathize with their clients (Kim & Omizo, 2003; Tarn et al., 2005). Although ethnic matching may be important, it is not always an option for clients. Tarn et al. (2005) notes that cultural competency training may enhance patient trust by "promoting understanding and acceptance of different cultural norms" (p. 345) and being trained in such therapeutic guidelines can prevent mistakes in the counseling session such as overgeneralizing, assumption of cultural expertise, and so on (Kim & Omizo, 2003). Overall, an absence of culturally sensitive, ethnically or racially similar personnel and a scarcity of practitioners untrained in language-specific services are believed to contribute to the overall low rates of mental health service utilization for Asian Americans (Uba, 1997).

Client-Counselor Ethnic Match

In keeping with the theme of the lack of available culturally sensitive and competent mental health practitioners, scholars and clinicians have also discussed the role of **client-counselor ethnic match** in therapy (Brinson & Kottler, 1995; Kim, Ng, & Ahn, 2005; Trimble, 2007). This is a broad area that has produced mixed results and discussions on whether an Asian American or other minority client should see a counselor of the same background, race, or ethnicity. In the psychological literature, two threads in this line of client-counselor ethnic match research have emerged. One focuses simply on matching people based on phenotype or genotype, and the other basically focuses on match by one's **worldviews** and other such psychological variables. With regard to the first thread of matching clients and counselors solely on ethnicity, the recent literature (2000–2006) regards client-counselor ethnic matching as relevant, but not critical to positive therapeutic outcomes. Gamst, Dana, Der-Karabetian, and Kramer (2001) concluded that ethnically matching Asian American counselors to clients had positive effects on clients' Global Assessment of Functioning (GAF) scores and retention. Such results indicate ethnic matching should remain an important factor to consider when counseling Asian Americans in community mental health centers. Gamst further emphasized that ethnic match is not the only underlying factor that may yield positive results in therapy. Maramba and Hall's (2002) meta-analysis of previous findings found that ethnic matching was a poor predictor of clinical outcome in general. Therefore, in considering the opening case, Mike's friend Keith should not assume that referring his friend Mike to a psychologist of the same ethnicity will produce the best clinical and therapeutic outcomes simply based on this similarity.

Worldview

In the second thread in this client-counselor ethnic match research, a review of the literature clearly shows that counselor-client match in worldview is equally if not more important than just an ethnic match (Kim, Ng, & Ahn, 2005; Tarn et al., 2005; Zane et al., 2005). Worldviews are characterized as personal assumptions, beliefs, and philosophies that affect how we think about the world, one's attitudes, values, and beliefs and what it means to you (Ibrahim, 1985; Ivey, Ivey, & Simek-Morgan, 1997; Sue & Sue, 1999). Worldviews typically differ between minority and majority individuals from the dominant culture and are believed to be important to clinical conceptualizations and positive or negative mental health treatment outcomes. The assumption is if a client and counselor share the same worldview orientation, there is less chance for prejudice, bias, discrimination, and **premature termination**, and greater chances for optimal therapeutic outcomes (Ibrahim, 1985; Ivey et al., 1997; Sue & Sue, 1999). Kim et al. (2005) notes that "having a shared worldview among clients and counselors . . . is important in establishing a good working relationship and helping clients feel understood by the counselors" (p. 73). Trust building can take place after individual worldviews are firmly established between client and counselor. Additionally, Zane et al. (2005) argued that a client-therapist cognitive match with regard to problem perception, coping orientation, and therapy goals may explain why clients matched based on ethnicity tend to stay longer and do better in treatment, assuming that an ethnic match is composed of cognitive matching and other factors. In using the opening case example again, if Keith were to refer Mike to a psychologist who shared a similar worldview, Mike would likely be matched with someone who had similar ways of thinking, believing, and feeling about the world. Such a match would decrease the chances of premature termination, and increase the potential of Mike remaining in therapy with a positive experience.

Ethnic and Racial Identity

Concepts such as client-counselor ethnic match and worldviews have been considered important to seeking, receiving, and providing effective mental health services. Other psychological variables falling into the second thread in the line of research on client-counselor ethnic match are ethnic and **racial identity**. Ethnic and racial identity variables have also been studied as factors related to counseling and treating clients (Gurung & Mehta, 2001). Thus, in respecting these concepts as notable to the role of receiving therapy as client and providing therapy as clinician, the concepts will briefly be defined. Cokley (2007), in his recent article, defined **ethnic identity** as the subjective sense of ethnic group membership that involves self-labeling, sense of belonging, preference for the group, positive evaluation of the ethnic group, ethnic knowledge, and involvement in ethnic group activities. Cokley defined racial identity as the collective identity of any group of people socialized to think of themselves as a racial group. Several researchers have conducted research and written in this area (Alvarez & Kimura, 2001; Helms & Cook, 1999; Inman, 2006; Phinney, 1996), examining the roles and relationships of ethnic/racial identity levels to counseling, racism, and other variables. The assumption has been that differing ethnic and racial identities between clients and counselors are likely to negatively impact mental health outcomes and service utilization rates—however there continues to be debate on these constructs and their role in positive mental health and counseling. Chang and Kwan discuss ethnic and racial identity in greater detail earlier in the text.

The Stigma of Seeking Mental Health Services

Now, let's go back to the opening case example. What are the chances that Mike, an Asian American young adult, would hear his parents say something like: "*Honey, why don't you go to counseling? It's a great option for handling stress. As parents we've been challenged in raising you given your father's Bipolar I diagnosis and my own Adult Child of Alcoholic (ACOA) issues. I know your Dad has manic episodes and his spending sprees, alcoholism, depression, and anger have been hard to deal with combined with my perfectionism and high expectations placed upon you. You could use some effective coping and stress management skills in dealing with us. Go to therapy.*" Chances of hearing this from any parent are highly unlikely, but perhaps more unlikely if the parent is a first-generation Asian immigrant parent! Culturally speaking, scholars have talked about the stigma, shame, and **loss of face** associated with going to counseling within Asian American communities (Leong et al., 1995; Yeh & Huang, 1996; Zane & Yeh, 2002).

The study of Asian values is extremely important and relevant because adherence to Asian values has been found to be related to one's positive or negative attitudes toward seeking professional psychological help (Kim & Omizo, 2003). In Kim and Omizo's (2003) study, findings indicated that those who were highly enculturated (held traditional Asian values) had less positive attitudes toward seeking psychological help—in other words, they are less likely to see a counselor. Asian cultural values, acculturation, and enculturation play important roles in the attitudes and behaviors of Asian Americans (Kim, Atkinson, & Yang, 1999) and Kim discusses these in further detail in his chapter on Acculturation and Enculturation. Briefly, Asian values examined have included: (a) collectivism, (b) conformity to norms, (c) emotional self-control, (d) family recognition through achievement, (e) humility, (f) avoidance of family shame, (g) deference to authority, and (h) filial piety (Kim, Li, & Ng, 2005; Kim et al, 1999). Loss of face, another commonly used term in the Asian American psychological literature, is defined as the importance of one's moral reputation and social integrity that is gained and maintained by the performance of specific roles recognized in interpersonal dynamics between family members and society (Kim, 2007; Zane & Yeh, 2002). Generally, Asian Americans further removed from migration will adhere to U.S. mainstream cultural norms more strongly than Asian Americans who are recent migrants; recent immigrants or those less acculturated, are believed to possess values and traits most consistent with traditional Asian values (Chang, Chang, & Chu, 2007; Kim, Atkinson, & Umemoto, 2001).

So, if the reader assumes that Mike, the Asian American individual presented at the beginning of the chapter, strongly adheres to the Asian value of wishing to avoid shaming his family, even in his time of distress, Mike is unlikely to seek therapy given his concern with how his family may "look" to the counselor or others in the Asian community. Behaviorally, Mike has non-Asian American friends, is very involved in his ethnic community, but worries that people may "talk" if they found out he was going to counseling. What if his aunts and uncles think that his parents are doing something wrong in parenting him? What if he feels "bad and guilty" when he starts talking about his experiences with his family? Such thoughts are present among Asian Americans and often prevent individuals from talking freely and openly about family issues with an "outsider" versus a trusted, close family member or friend in their ethnic community. Mike is already concerned with being perceived as "crazy," as many Americans are (Vogel, Wade, & Haake, 2006), plus his "Asian side" further prevents him from getting the help he needs.

The stigma of seeking services has gained much press, especially during the coverage of the Virginia Tech shooting by gunman Cho in 2007. Dr. Wei-Chin Hwang, a columnist for the *Seattle Times*, discussed the tragedy of the Virginia school shooting and highlighted that, unfortunately, families are also victims of stigma. He wrote how public embarrassment, loss of face, and fear of community reactions may inhibit families and individuals from taking the necessary steps to deal with mental illness, and that there is a stigma toward mental illness that is also a societal value. Whether the feelings, beliefs, or values toward seeking mental health services are traditional Asian or societal, he writes that such "feelings are real and until societal values can be changed, those suffering from mental illness will continue to delay seeking help until their problems get intolerably worse—or will not get any help at all" (Hwang, 2007). Thus, the stigma of seeking mental health services can not be underestimated as a factor in the underutilization of psychological and psychiatric services (U.S. Department of Mental Health and Human Services, 2001; Sue & Sue, 1999).

Now, think back to the opening response to Mike regarding seeking services, what are other possible responses he may hear from his parents, his counselor, or the community with regard to his distress? The chapter began with a dialogue between Mike and his friend Keith who encouraged Mike to seek counseling. However, Mike had some preconceived ideas about counseling, and he also feared the reaction he may receive from parents, counselors, and his community.

When and Where Asian Americans Seek Psychological Support

If Asian Americans decide to go to counseling, where do they go for treatment? How do they get help when needed? Values in the Asian American community can be viewed as a double-edged sword. On one hand, there can be the fear of shaming the family and the emphasis on maintaining emotional self-control among those who adhere to traditional Asian values; yet, on the other hand, adhering to such values and relying on one's family and the extended network in the community can serve as huge source of emotional support, especially for recent immigrants. For instance, Abe-Kim et al. (2002) examined predictors of help seeking for emotional distress among 1,503 Chinese Americans who completed interviews through the CAPES study. Interestingly, she and her colleagues found that a lack of family support was not associated with seeking help from any health provider, but that the presence of family conflict was what precipitated seeking help when using both formal and informal types of mental health services. Based on these results, when family conflict is present, individuals are likely to use formal services and see a health care professional such as a primary care physician with physical symptoms; or see a mental health professional with psychiatric symptoms and/or use informal services. With regard to the use of informal services, Abe-Kim et al. (2002) found that 39% sought services from ministers and priests. Many times there is an emphasis on turning to the community for support rather than professionals or outsiders since the community network is revered as having the potential to provide religious, spiritual, and ethnic resources congruent to one's cultural orientation. Such information illuminates the relevance of informal services for individuals in distress regardless of their knowledge of the availability of formal mental health services.

Similar themes in using both formal and informal mental health support have been found by Inman et al. (2007) in their research on South Asians, and by Yeh et al. (2006) in their study on Asian Americans impacted by the tragedy of 9/11. These authors examined the types of services that South Asian and Asian Americans sought when faced with the tragedy of a loss of a family member. Participants in these studies generally found counseling to be unhelpful for the following reasons: (a) They felt that the services received were not culturally relevant; (b) they feared being perceived as crazy; and (c) they believed in the importance of keeping family problems within the bounds of close ones and solving them on their own. The loss of someone in the 9/11 attack would precisely be a situation where if someone was to seek therapy it would be "understandable" and perhaps even encouraged.

What these authors found is that South Asians and Asian Americans utilized **collectivistic** coping methods to deal with their losses. For example, participants sought support from family and extended members (i.e., familial coping), comfort from within their own ethnic groups (i.e., intracultural coping) and reassurance from those who experienced a similar loss (i.e., relational universality). Additionally, participants felt the need to avoid burdening their families and friends and chose to rely on themselves by bearing or suppressing their worries (i.e., forbearance). Fatalistic notions of a belief in a higher order (destiny, meant to happen) were also used as coping methods in these studies. Individuals also used **individualistic** coping methods such as exercising or cooking to distract themselves with both communities perceiving counseling as going against their cultural values. The diversity of coping techniques among Asian Americans, East Asians, and Filipinos include healing methods such as fortune-telling, meditation, Chinese medicine, attending church, seeing a priest, going to temple, and seeking other resources for support (Yeh et al., 2006). South Asian participants turned to palm readers, read from scriptures, sought support from swami's, pandits, astrologers; they lit lamps and incense, went to temples, mandirs, or other spiritual centers (Inman et al., 2007). See Yeh and Kwong's chapter for more detail on the above concepts, indigenous healing, and additional methods of psychological support.

Given the differences among groups, Asian Americans seek the resources most culturally congruent, acceptable, and nonstigmatizing to their belief system and values. Also, community outreach programs, classes, workshops, books, and other such resources provide psychoeducational information on topics commonly prevalent in Asian American communities. For those not seeking support or treatment anywhere, research has indicated that *when* Asian Americans finally decide to seek therapy and present at community mental health centers, or university counseling centers, they present with worse symptoms than other ethnic groups, meaning their level of distress has been found to be greater than European Americans and other ethnic groups (Abe-Kim et al., 2002; Abe-Kim et al., 2007; Kearney et al., 2005; U.S. Department of Mental Health and Human Services, 2001).

Clearly, Asian Americans seek support from both formal and informal services such as medical professionals, mental health service providers, and religious leaders (Abe-Kim et al., 2002). Also, Asian Americans *do* face psychiatric issues and psychological complications as do other groups even though utilization of mental health services is lower in comparison. There are also Asian Americans who use mental health services readily and have positive attitudes toward seeking help as well as those who prefer to use informal methods of seeking psychological support.

Demystifying Mental Health Services: Receiving Services

Identifying Types of Mental Health Professionals and Therapy Modalities

What kind of professionals should Asian Americans see? What's the difference between a clinician, a therapist, a psychologist, a social worker, or a **marriage and family therapist** *(MFT) and a* **psychiatrist**? *What do people talk about in therapy?* This section is written with the purpose of demystifying what mental health services are all about. A discussion of who mental health professionals are, what types of therapy are available, and what therapy entails will follow. Few resources describe information on utilizing formal mental health services for Asian Americans. Who are the mental health professionals? Terms such as *psychologist, clinician, psychotherapist,* and *counselor* are often used interchangeably. A psychologist typically has the longest amount of training, attends a graduate or professional school, and has the title of Doctor as a result of having earned a PhD (Doctor of Philosophy) or PsyD (Doctor of Psychology). Psychologists spend an average of 7.2 years, in addition to their undergraduate college degree, in education and training and may see clients in private practice or any number of mental health settings. Psychologists must also be licensed by the Board of Psychology in their state and uphold the Standards and Practices of the **American Psychological Association** and are most likely to be a **clinical psychologist** or **counseling psychologist**. Clinical and counseling psychologists may also refer to themselves as psychotherapists.

A social worker, who is another type of mental health service provider, has a degree in social work from a college or university program accredited by the Council on Social Work Education and usually has 2 years of training post-bachelor's degrees and a Licensed Clinical Social Worker is one who has obtained their license to practice. The undergraduate degree is a Bachelor of Social Work (BSW) and graduate degrees include the Master of Social Work (MSW) and the Doctorate in Social Work (DSW). Some type of credentialing or licensing is also required for **social workers** providing therapy. A licensed professional counselor, LPC, is the most common master's level licensed mental health professional outside of California. A marriage and family therapist completes 2 years of training and accrues a set number of clinical hours to obtain licensure (AAMFT, 2007). Finally, psychiatrists have MD degrees, have received medical training, are licensed to prescribe medication to patients and may also provide psychotherapy depending on their training and interests.

The literature has also discussed that Asian Americans find it less stigmatizing to see a primary care physician, thus it is not uncommon for certain Asian Americans to manifest psychological symptoms as physical symptoms or to somatize, when seeing their doctor (U.S. Department of Mental Health and Human Services, 2001). Somatization refers to an expression of distress that is manifested as general or vague physical complaints (Chun, Eastman, Wang, & Sue, 1998), and although somatization is common across all cultures, significant cultural variations in prevalence are believed to exist (Yang & Wonpat-Borja, 2007). Overall, seeing a medical doctor is much more culturally acceptable than seeing a psychologist or mental health professional among Asians and Asian Americans, thus one can not dismiss the role of primary care physicians as well in providing psychological support. Asian American individuals may see any of the aforementioned mental health professionals in settings such as hospitals, county mental health agencies, private practices, community centers, or doctors' offices when and if needed. Given the brief overview of the types of professionals, the next section will discuss the range of therapy modalities used in providing mental health services to Asian Americans.

Utilizing Mental Health Services: Therapy Modalities

Now that readers are familiar with who provides therapy, what types of counseling services will Asian Americans encounter? Asian Americans have options to seek the following types of counseling services—individual, couples, family, or **group therapy**. Content that is discussed in these types of counseling service are kept confidential, unless there is a risk of harming oneself or another person; in this case, professionals are mandated to breach confidentiality in order to safeguard individuals. **Individual psychotherapy** is one-on-one counseling between the counselor and the client in which a learning process occurs. For example, Asian Americans may seek individual counseling for grief, loss, alcohol or substance abuse, divorce, sexual or physical abuse, job or career changes, difficulty in adjusting to American culture, racism, parenting, or coping with challenging family members. Individual psychotherapy is intended to change people cognitively, affectively, and behaviorally through a process whereby something new is learned, relearned, or unlearned (Corsini & Wedding, 1989). The goal is to produce change at the individual's level of experience or at the level of the individual's environment depending on each client's case (Prochaska, 1984). In conducting therapy, therapists typically incorporate elements from several theoretical frameworks and provide therapy with an eclectic or integrative orientation rather than choosing one approach in working with all clients (Cynkar, 2007). See Figure 30.1.

Figure 30.1 Individual psychotherapy and counseling. Ninety-five percent of women say they are likely to consult a mental health professional or recommend a family member do so versus 87% of men (APA Survey, 2004). Here a second-generation Chinese American woman discusses the traditional hierarchy in her family and the role of elders in raising her children. She views herself as an American who wishes to teach her children Chinese cultural values and the skills needed to succeed in America. In this case, the client comes from an educated, financially stable, and highly acculturated background and therefore sees counseling as an option for support and learning.

Couples therapy is an option for couples experiencing psychological or physical challenges in their relationship. Problems in one's relationships can stem from communication difficulties, marital dissatisfaction, unhappiness between partners, disagreements in raising children, job changes, and other such life situations which create stress among a partnership and family. The goal for couple's counseling is to improve the relationships between partners or to help with the dissolution of a difficult relationship with minimum harm to all involved. Marital satisfaction has been found to be affected by both spouses' mental health, and greater individual mental health is important for maintaining a satisfying marriage (Atkins et al., 2005). Therefore, depending upon what a person's mental health may be, partners can influence the other's marital happiness. Asian Americans may seek relationship counseling related to cultural differences within a partnership, for intergenerational conflicts between parents or in-laws, gender role differences, and concerns regarding the mental health of their significant other (Tewari, 2000; Tewari, Inman & Sandhu, 2003). Co-therapists may also be used in couples therapy to minimize counselor bias, avoid siding with a partner, and maintaining impartiality. See Figure 30.2.

Family therapy may also be utilized by Asian Americans in cases where intergenerational conflict is occurring between parents and their children. Challenges between generations or within the family may revolve around education or marriage pressure, autonomy issues versus family obligation, differences in cultural expectations, family members experiencing severe psychiatric or psychological symptoms. Reasons for seeking family therapy could also include

Figure 30.2 Asian American couples in therapy. Couples counseling may be used by a couple as the primary mode of therapy or in conjunction with individual counseling. The couple may be interviewed or assessed independently or together as a couple depending on the mental health professional's theoretical orientation or approach to working with couples. Couples therapy may be led by one or two therapists, also known as conjoint therapy. In this example, the couple who is in an interracial relationship (Korean and Chinese American) are experiencing increased tension between each other due to their family's expectations of which type of marital partner to choose and desiring that they marry someone with similar ethnic backgrounds.

family issues of role reversal resulting from adaptation to the United States, thereby creating changes in the hierarchy or family system based on gender roles, financial income, or occupation (Inman & Tewari, 2003). The goal of family therapy is to provide support and direction to individuals and families within the context of the family system experiencing conflict. A family is believed to be a natural social system, with its own rules, roles, power structure, forms of communication, negotiation, and problem solving (Goldenberg & Goldenberg, 1985).

In some Asian American families, there is a likelihood that emotional attachments and loyalties may fluctuate as changes in the family's system occur, such as with the birth of a child, adoption, divorce, marriage, or death of family members. Additional stressors that could potentially lead Asian Americans to seek family therapy could include developmental and life adjustment issues, moving, job changes, or retirement—essentially, a number of issues can lead to dysfunction within the family unit (Horne & Ohlsen, 1982). Family therapy approaches can include two therapists, also known as co-therapists, who could either be male or female. Co-therapy was developed to prevent a single therapist from becoming entangled in a family system and may also be used to complement a therapist lacking in culturally specific knowledge and skills.

Group therapy is a mode of counseling in which six to eight people meet face-to-face with one or more trained leaders to talk about what is troubling them. Group members give feedback to each other by expressing their own feelings about what others say and do. This interaction gives group members an opportunity to try out new behaviors and to learn more about the ways they interact with others with guidance and facilitation by a leader or co-leaders. In group counseling, people tend to behave in the same way they do in their own environment (Yalom, 1985), thus, re-enacting their behaviors in the presence of other groups members in a trusting and supportive environment, which allows each individual to confront themselves and others in a constructive manner that facilitates change (see Figure 30.3). Individuals may join groups based on similarities of challenges such as an Asian American women's support group, an alcoholics anonymous group, a sexual assault survivor's group, grief groups, or even health support groups such as those diagnosed with cancer support groups (Tewari, Inman, & Sandhu, 2003). Any one of the above-mentioned therapy modalities can be joined based on self-interest, referral by a psychologist, friend, doctor, or the clergy.

An understanding of the types of mental health professionals and kinds of therapy modalities is the first step in educating Asian American communities about mental health care and utilization. Familiarity and knowledge regarding psychological care and support can increase rates of mental health service use, therefore this next section will lay out and demystify the process of what occurs in individual therapy, a common modality of mental health care.

The Counseling Process: From Intake to Termination

This section serves as an education to the "mystery" of counseling and explores what happens in therapy between a psychologist and a client. For someone like Mike, fear of the unknown may add yet another barrier to seeking help from a counselor. Once a decision is made to see a counselor, an initial intake session and first meeting is scheduled. Prior to the first meeting, the client may be asked to fill out intake paperwork. The goal of an intake form and first session is to gather demographic and background information on clients. Confidentiality is always discussed in the first session regardless of the information gathered. Thus, in the initial sessions of therapy and on the intake forms, clients can expect to discuss the following: (a) identifying information (age, gender, ethnicity, relationship status, academic level, referral source); (b) presenting problem (stated or identified reason(s) for appointment); (c) history of the presenting problem (development, course, duration, severity, exacerbating issues, meaning of problem to client); (d) pertinent family history (brief description of family or other factors that are relevant

Figure 30.3 Asian American women's group in a university counseling center. Several university counseling centers, community mental health agencies, and private practices have offered psychoeducational support and psychotherapy groups for women of mono-, bi-, and/or multiracial Asian descent sharing similar experiences and concerns as Asian American women. Issues discussed in such groups may include topics such as Asian versus American cultural values, maintaining cultural traditions, gender roles, relationship/arranged marriage concerns, life/career planning, self-confidence building, assertiveness training, family responsibility, autonomy and independence, family dynamics, increasing interpersonal communication skills, and other such life challenges. Groups such as these may have one or two group leaders who screen clients entering the group to ensure a good fit between the clients' expectations/needs of the group and the group's purpose and goals of the members. This particular group was comprised of several Asian American women of differing ethnicities and religions (i.e., Korean, Indian, and Chinese Americans; and Muslim, Hindu, and Christian religions), ages (18–27), and socioeconomic backgrounds (low to high); however, they shared similarities in experiencing and responding to people and their world and were thus able to share and give feedback through facilitation by the group leaders.

such as substance abuse, physical or emotional abuse, medical/psychiatric issues, acculturation level, racial/ethnic identity, immigration status, socioeconomic status, supportive/unsupportive family members); (e) social history (kind of support, positive or negative, spiritual/religious faith); (f) academic or career functioning (grades, class attendance, probation status, academic pressure, job/occupational changes, promotion challenges, retirement); (g) psychotherapy history (all prior psychotherapy and/or psychiatric hospitalizations, any psychotropic medications, responses or lack of responses to treatment); (h) medical history (any significant past/current medical conditions that might impact client's functioning or condition; listing medications currently taken, any head trauma, seizures, diabetes or thyroid disorder); (i) substance use (level of past and current use and listing of substances, client's perception of use); (j) mental status exam (presentation, mood, orientation, thought process—perceptual disturbance, impulse control, judgment, reliability, and insight); (k) suicidality/dangerousness (past or current suicidal or homicidal ideation/attempts); (l) legal/emergency risk factors (any reasons for decisions regarding unusual interventions or reporting); (m) assessment (brief conceptual statement of the problem and its meaning to the client, DSM-IV-R diagnoses, whether testing is needed); and (n) disposition/plan (treatment plan, modality, issues to be addressed, goals, status at end of session, scheduling issues, etc.). While Mike, and others who are unfamiliar with counseling, may find this list of topics to be intimidating, there is a purpose to all of this. The scope and depth of these questions enables the counselor to have a clearer understanding of what is troubling a client, which in turn results in a more effective plan for treatment.

In a study on prioritized assignment to intake appointments for Asian Americans at an ethnic-specific mental program, intake appointments, decisions, and assignments were found to be especially critical among Asian American groups due to their being the least likely ethnic group to seek mental health care (Akutsu, Tsuru, & Chu, 2006). Delays for intake assignment were believed to potentially increase the risk of nonattendance for reluctant clients, therefore making timing very important for first-time users of mental health services (Akutsu et al., 2006). Akutsu and his colleagues (2006) found that language preference, ethnicity, suicidality, violent behavior, physical and sexual abuse, and psychotic symptoms increased the likelihood of being prioritized for the earliest intake appointment. Interestingly, they also found that being female, being of an older age, and having somatic complaints decreased the likelihood of a prioritized assignment. Therefore, clinical, demographic, and ethnically related factors are important in making decisions about intake assignment with the goals of improving intake attendance by Asian Americans.

Once the initial information is gathered (more than one session may be needed to gather information about a client's history), the counselor can then determine if she or he is able to work with the client or whether the client wishes to work with another counselor. At this point, the client or counselor may determine whether one is culturally competent to provide the services needed. People often assume that once a meeting occurs, one needs to stick with that particular therapist—this is not the case. Clients and counselors have the prerogative to choose whether to continue the professional relationship pending the accessibility, resources, and availability of other mental health providers. Once it has been determined that the client and counselor are a good match, an effective and culturally competent therapist will reevaluate initial goals and treatment plans as the therapy progresses. As mentioned earlier, counselors may employ various theoretical orientations and therapeutic strategies tailored to the client's cultural value system, acculturation/enculturation levels, racial or ethnic identity, and psychological or psychiatric needs.

In working with Asian Americans unfamiliar with the therapy process, a competent therapist typically spends some time discussing what therapy is about, what his or her role is, and how it works. When the client is comfortable with therapy and is no longer ambivalent about the process, the psychologist may then reconsider whether a directive or collaborative style, or combination of the two, would best facilitate the growth and change of their client. Essentially, the client and counselor are to work together and the counselor's job is not to give advice solely, but to assist the client in determining what is in the client's best interest in facilitating their growth, healing, and change. As mentioned earlier, treatment interventions may vary as a function of acculturation (Hall & Eap, 2007; Kim et al., 2005); however, a culturally competent mental health professional will consider the importance of assessing what is best for each individual client.

The number of sessions that a person may see a professional is dependent upon several factors such as insurance, financial resources, scope of the problem, session limits of the practice or center, and the client's readiness to resolve their presenting problem and the readiness to terminate. Psychotherapy guidelines also state that clinicians must prepare the client for ending therapy, or terminating. In this case, a culturally competent therapist serving Asian Americans would begin discussing and reviewing the initial goals, emotional growth, changes in one's attitudes and behaviors prior to the last session. Preparing for the last session allows for adequate closure, continued change, and a plan in case future challenges arise. In small communities where Asian Americans may run into their Asian American mental health providers, therapists often prepare their clients for those occasions in which "they may run into one another," and how to handle the situation given the confidentiality and nature of the relationship.

In an ideal world, it would be wise for clients to assess whether their particular mental health professional has the skills and experience in providing therapy with one's ethnic/cultural group and is knowledgeable in the presenting problem area. Since the reasons for seeking counseling are varied among Asian Americans and counselors typically employ their own counseling strategies when working with clients, it is best for the client to simply ask whether their counselor is familiar with the cultural norms, traditions, customs, and values and one's racial and ethnic group. Depending on a person's language skills, knowledge of counseling and assertiveness abilities, a question such as "Have you worked with clients experiencing X or Y with Z?" may be helpful. The response to this question can serve as a basis for a good match and effective therapeutic relationship.

Additionally, it is important that Asian Americans begin to see themselves as consumers with the right to have a full understanding of both the therapist and therapy process. Assessing a good mental health professional and one who is culturally competent is not an easy task for the majority of individuals in need of mental health services. A therapeutic relationship may not work out, or the match may just not feel right despite the good intentions of both the client and the counselor. Regardless, it is important for the client to shop around and find the right fit and connection and not to remain with someone due to feeling that there is no one else who can help or that all therapists "suck." Overall, guidelines and characteristics exist for those believed to be effective in providing multicultural counseling and therapy and those who are believed to work toward cultural competency. The next section will briefly touch upon examples of treatment interventions and clinical strategies considered in working with Asian American populations. This section is in no way comprehensive—an entire chapter can be devoted to treatment interventions and clinical strategies alone!

Treatment Considerations and Clinical Strategies

Readers are now familiar with treatment strategies and characteristic of culturally competent mental health professionals and the types of services available. A discussion of treatment interventions and clinical strategies can follow. Psychological intervention is not necessarily limited to formal or informal therapy services. Intervention can also take place through workshops, classes, online support groups, and community outreach and may be just as transformative, powerful, and facilitative of change and healing. Asian American psychology courses have been helpful in increasing personal reflection, self-understanding, and identifying when one needs interventions. Workshops at conferences on Asian American values, acculturation, enculturation, and racial/ethnic identity have been known to facilitate awareness and self-empowerment through knowledge. Even online support groups have the potential to provide support, guidance, and information (Chang & Yeh, 2003).

Given the broad spectrum of how interventions and strategies can take place, some scholars have discussed specific empirically supported treatments and strategies in working with Asian American populations. For example, Hall and Eap (2007) discussed cognitive-behavioral interventions and pharmacotherapy (therapy involving a combination of medication and cognitive therapy) as helpful in reducing depression among Asian Americans, and acupuncture and meditation as helpful in reducing anxiety among certain groups of Asian Americans. Inman and Tewari (2003) have found that using cultural genograms, stories or narratives, self-disclosure, bibliotherapy, and psychoeducation to be useful strategies in working with specific

Figure 30.4 Asian American client journaling. Journaling is an effective strategy for clients learning to track their emotions, reactions, and coping strategies. It is also used to facilitate expressiveness between sessions and to prepare clients for future therapy sessions. Some clients also write in their journal for self-care and relaxation. For clients who tend to be less talkative in session, this is often a way to bridge communication between more reserved Asian American clients and their therapists. In this case, an international student finds journaling to be effective in expressing her feelings of adjusting to a new a country.

Asian American populations. Journaling is also an effective strategy for clients to express their thoughts and feelings in-between sessions. Many counselors will encourage clients to write in their journals so clients can begin to track patterns in their responses, actions, and behaviors to particular events. For clients who have difficulty expressing their feelings in sessions, journaling is helpful in allowing the client to focus on their emotions in private and in preparation for therapy sessions when needed (see Figure 30.4).

Essentially, the objectives of several treatment goals, interventions, and strategies include ways of educating, providing objectivity, and normalizing what may be seen as shameful or stigmatizing throughout the healing and change process. Strategies and interventions including connecting with clients, proper assessment, facilitating awareness, setting goals, taking action/ instigating change on the part of the counselor, as well as appropriate feedback and accountability can serve as a framework to guide and inform clinicians about the possibilities that exist when working with Asian American clients (Gallardo, Yeh, Parham, & Trimble, in progress). Other chapters in this text also touch upon treatment considerations and various methods in treating culture-bound syndromes and culturally specific issues. The next section will focus on effective and culturally sensitive strategies for serving Asian Americans.

Culturally Competent Mental Health Services: Providing Services

Multicultural Counseling and Cultural Competency

The words in this title have been huge buzzwords in the field of psychology and the mental health world for decades now (Ponterotto & Mallinckrodt, 2007), and standards for multicultural competency have been developed across several mental health professions. **Multiculturalism** and diversity are no longer just politically correct concepts, but an everyday reality for most students, clinicians, supervisors, administrators, employers, and educators in the United States. Multiculturalism has been labeled the fourth force in psychology after psychodynamic psychology (Freud, Jung, and Adler), cognitive-behavioral (Watson, Thorndike, Skinner, etc.), and existential-humanistic (Rogers, May, and others). Multicultural counseling and therapy, the fourth force began in the 1970s (Ivey, Ivey, & Simek-Morgan, 1997; Ponterotto & Mallincrokdt, 2007). The movement began as a challenge to traditional psychological theories and techniques that were developed by European Americans. Not only were the traditional theories developed primarily by European American individuals, normed for people of Western culture, but most of the case studies and samples were also based on White or European American populations. As psychology advanced in the 21st century mental health professionals, theorists, and scientists realized that they could not apply European American standards, frames of reference in psychology, or White models to individuals not of European descent. Certain traditional theories of psychology have been used by scholars and clinicians to theorize, conceptualize, and diagnose ethnically, racially, and culturally diverse individuals over time. When using traditional theories of psychology normed for European Americans and Westeners, minority individuals were often being viewed by some individuals as culturally, psychologically, or psychiatrically deficient, NOT different (White & Parham, 1990).

Multicultural Guidelines and Evidence-Based Practice in Psychology

Multiculturalism is a term that emerged out of cross-cultural and ethnic minority psychology and is defined as the examination of cultural identities and differences, understanding worldviews and stating that multiple belief systems exists across people and cultures (Hoshmand, 2006; Ponterotto, Casas, Suzuki, & Alexander, 1995). In 1990, APA published the first *Guidelines for Providers of Psychological Services to Ethnic, Linguistic, and Culturally Diverse Populations* to set the stage for mental health workers with such populations. In 1992 the guidelines were revised to further reflect that: "Psychologists are aware of cultural, individual, and role differences, including those related to age, gender, race, ethnicity, national origin . . . etc." under Principle D: Respect of People's Rights and Dignity (p. 1598). Currently, psychologists refer to the 2002 **Guidelines on Multicultural Education, Training, Research Practice, and Organizational Change for Psychologists** published by APA and adopted as the official policy by the APA Council of Representatives. In 2002, the guidelines defined multiculturalism and diversity as terms being used interchangeably to include aspects of identity stemming from gender, sexual orientation, disability, socioeconomic status or age. Multiculturalism, in an absolute sense, recognizes the broad scope of dimensions of race, ethnicity, language, sexual orientation, gender, age disability, class status, education, religious/spiritual orientation and other cultural dimensions ("Guidelines," 2002, pp. 9–10).

The guidelines are meant to reflect the study of psychology, current society, the needs of particular individuals and groups historically marginalized within and by psychology based on their ethnic/racial heritage, social group identity and membership. They are also reflective of the knowledge and skills needed for the profession by taking into account the historical and sociopolitical factors that influence the psychological well-being of clients and constituencies in America—all areas that mental health professionals need to be cognizant of. The Asian American population is a perfect example of individuals representing varied sociopolitical, historical, and immigration histories in America, thus reinforcing the importance of psychologists referring to the guidelines when engaging in multicultural practice. Cultural competency, another commonly used term, is the cultural knowledge or skills to deliver effective interventions to members of a particular culture (Sue & Zane, 2006). Scholars and practitioners have spent a considerable amount of time operationalizing cultural competency and developing guidelines to ensure the best possible service to diverse populations.

Additionally, in terms of other latest developments, the American Psychological Association has also emphasized **evidence-based practice in psychology** (EBP). Although there has been debate over the helpfulness of EBPs in reducing mental health disparities with clients from ethnic minority groups (Sue & Zane, 2006; Sue, Zane, & Hall, 2006), the APA Task Force has encouraged taking into account the full range of evidence psychologists and policymakers must consider in working with patients and clients (APA Task Force, 2006). The 2005 APA Task Report defined EBP in psychology as being the integration of the best available research with clinical expertise in the context of patient characteristics, culture, and preferences and has been a notable current topic in psychology. Ideally, in considering cultural perspectives while providing psychotherapy, an integration of EBP and the *Multicultural Guidelines* makes sense in considering patient values to ensure public access to quality mental health. An incorporation of both may inform and position psychologists to work with diverse populations such as Asian Americans. See Table 30.1 for the **Guidelines on Multicultural Education, Training, Research, Practice, and Organizational Change for Psychologists.**

Table 30.1 Guidelines on Multicultural Education, Training, Research, Practice, and Organizational Change for Psychologists

Commitment to Cultural Awareness and Knowledge of Self and Others

Guideline #1: Psychologists are encouraged to recognize that, as cultural beings, they may hold attitudes and beliefs that can detrimentally influence their perceptions of and interactions with individuals who are ethnically and racially different from themselves.

Guideline #2: Psychologists are encouraged to recognize the importance of multicultural sensitivity/responsiveness, knowledge, and understanding about ethnically and racially different individuals.

Education

Guideline #3: As educators, psychologists are encouraged to employ the constructs of multiculturalism and diversity in psychological education.

Research

Guideline #4: Culturally sensitive psychological researchers are encouraged to recognize the importance of conducting culture-centered and ethical psychological research among persons from ethnic, linguistic, and racial minority backgrounds.

Practice

Guideline #5: Psychologists strive to apply culturally appropriate skills in clinical and other applied psychological practices.

Organizational Change and Policy Development

Guideline #6: Psychologists are encouraged to use organizational change processes to support culturally informed organizational (policy) development and practices.

Source: Guidelines on multicultural education, training, research, practice, and organizational change for psychologists. Washington, DC: American Psychological Association, 2002.

Multicultural competence is a professional standard in which a mental health professional makes an ongoing commitment to achieve change in their awareness, knowledge, and skills (Sue & Sue, 1999). The process of changing one's awareness level, knowledge base and, skill acquisition as a therapist is not something that a mental health professional accomplishes overnight when working with diverse populations and striving to become culturally competent. Sue and Sue (1999) believe it is an active process, and that one does not reach an end point—learning is lifelong in becoming a multiculturally competent counselor. Multicultural researchers and clinicians in psychology have spent a significant amount of time studying mental health services and how to best provide them to Asian Americans. Asian Americans would be best served in seeing a mental health care professional who was familiar with the culture, had similar client/counselor values, worldviews, and had similarity in race or ethnicity (though this last element is controversial; see earlier discussion), in providing the most effective culturally competent mental health services. Mike would definitely benefit from having a culturally competent provider.

Social Justice and Advocacy

Finally, another critical and relevant area in providing and receiving mental health services is social justice and advocacy in counseling. Many mental health professionals go beyond facilitating growth and producing change on the individual level; many "work to change social institutions, political and economic systems, and governmental structures that perpetuate unfair practices, structures, and policies in terms of accessibility, resource distributions, and human rights" (Fouad, Gerstein, & Toporek, 2006, p. 1). This means that competent professionals maintain an ethical practice, and are willing to work cooperatively with other agencies, providers, and researchers to best address the client's or community's needs in considering goals (Toporek & Williams, 2006). Mike may need his counselor to advocate for him in the case of his parents. Hypothetically, if Mike's mother or father were being discriminated against in the workplace due to mental illness, a counselor committed to social justice and advocacy may educate Mike on the policies and procedures in the workplace, walk him through the steps needed to take action, and identify any additional sources of support. In other cases, mental health professionals may act as a social change agent at the systemic level, for example in civil rights, ameliorating abuse, partaking in legislative efforts, and other areas of interest and need. Socioeconomic and social class should be assessed when moderating and considering interventions (Liu, 2002). Resources for socioeconomically advantaged and privileged clients that are available through their environment may relate to treatment outcomes; therefore, sociostructural factors should also be assessed (Liu, 2002; Liu & Ali, 2005). Either way, counselors should be educated in providing culturally competent mental health services, have the knowledge to assist clients with limited knowledge and access to resources, and be prepared to consider social justice and advocacy as needed.

Summary

Throughout this book, chapter authors have discussed in great detail the factors impacting the psychology, growth, and development of Asian subgroups in the United States. Almost every chapter has emphasized that Asian Americans represent diverse populations in terms of ethnicity, language, culture, education, income level, English proficiency, and sociopolitical experiences. Although cultural ties exist among the different Asian American communities, recognizing the differences among groups has been crucial. Therefore, it is only fitting to end with this as well. With regard to mental health services, acculturation level, generational status, immigration history, cultural values, racial and ethnic identity, and religion—these all impact and influence one's likelihood and decision to seek therapy. Readers should now be familiar with the process of seeking, providing, and receiving culturally competent mental health services for Asian Americans. The purpose of this chapter is to introduce readers to the process of seeking, receiving, and providing culturally competent mental health services. The first section of the chapter covers several areas of Asian American mental health including the barriers and factors that influence Asian Americans seeking help. The second section, followed by demystifying the therapy process, discusses who provides therapy and what counseling entails for those unfamiliar with mental health services. The last section highlights recent guidelines in providing culturally relevant treatment and presents recent developments in the provisions of mental health care. Throughout the chapter, readers are challenged to think about why and how Asian Americans may or may not use mental health services. The chapter ends with discussion questions, an in-depth case study of Mike in counseling, and a list of resources including readings, Web sites, and film suggestions for further learning. Key terms are also listed to highlight relevant topic areas and content throughout the chapter.

Discussion Questions

1. Consider who you may turn to when you face problems or crises. Who do you turn to? How would your answer be different if you were or were not Asian American? Would your answer be different?
2. What may be challenging for you about seeking counseling? What might prevent you from seeking counseling?
3. Where do your friends and family seek support when they have a problem? How might your answer be different if you or your family members are Asian American? Who are your/their primary sources of support?
4. How might your family react if they found out you were seeing a counselor? Might your parents react differently if they were Asian immigrants? Or fourth-generation Asian Americans?
5. If you have been to counseling, what counseling strategies have been helpful and unhelpful? What qualities or skills would you look for in your counselor?
6. Should multicultural guidelines and competencies be mandated for all counselors? How should they be enforced?
7. Visit a community mental health center that primarily serves Asian Pacific American populations.
8. Choose a particular mental health disorder and determine whether particular Asian American subgroups would handle the illness differently.
9. If you or a friend has an Asian ethnic heritage or background, develop a family genogram and identify who are the transmitters of Asian culture, traditions and heritage or whether other cultural values are emphasized within the family.
10. Imagine you are a psychologist. List variables and factors important to you in your assessment of an Asian American client. What would you want to know first in your work with your Asian American client?

Case Study

So far this chapter has focused on the theory and research of how Asian American clients learn about the therapeutic process. The chapter will now shift its focus to a case study that illustrates how Asian Americans experience counseling and cope with personal issues.

Beginning Phase of Therapy

Mike is a single, 22-year-old, heterosexual, Thai American, 1.5-generation male majoring in political science and is a graduating senior at a major West Coast university. He is the youngest of two siblings. His parents have been married for 25 years, work full-time, and had immigrated to America 15 years ago when Mike was 7 years old. Mike reports wanting to withdraw from college and exhibits a decreased interest in social activities. Although Mike's friend Keith mentioned the idea of seeing a counselor, as an Asian male, Mike is ambivalent about going to counseling and is unsure of how "being seen in the waiting room" and "talking to a stranger" might reflect on him. Mike is not sure if he needs counseling, does not know of any friends who might have used the university counseling center, and is too shy to ask. A month has passed by and his friends have stopped calling him and offering him invitations. Mike finally decides to go online to read about the counseling center at his university. He reads some blogs and finds that counseling is helpful for some, but not for others. Mike remains apprehensive for weeks and finds that he further alienates himself. Mike, finally, makes a decision, calls the counseling center, schedules an appointment, and "plans" to talk about his career plans and graduation instead of his family life and social situation.

Mike's heart races, and his palms are sweaty as he fills out the intake paperwork in the waiting room. He avoids eye contact with other students hoping that others would not "see" him or recognize him. The counselor arrives, she is Indian American, appears friendly, and walks with him back to her office. The counselor looks over the paperwork, recognizes Mike's nervousness, and states: "It's not easy walking into the counseling center, filling out paperwork and talking to a complete stranger is it?" Mike replied "No" and felt a little more at ease. The counselor then proceeds to talk with him about confidentiality, the cultural stigma associated with seeking counseling, what counselors talk about in the first meetings, discussed the counseling process and how counseling works. The counselor also gave Mike the opportunity to ask questions and share his expectations of what he hopes to gain from counseling.

Initial time spent in educating the client regarding the therapy process was imperative for establishing trust, rapport, and credibility with Mike as an Asian American who was unfamiliar with any type of mental health service. The discussion of the counseling process was a relief to Mike since he was too embarrassed or nervous to talk about why he was there. The counselor also acknowledged the cultural stigma, articulated a flexible treatment plan, thus enabling Mike to feel more at ease about the counseling process and what to expect. The counselor's decision to educate and teach Mike about what they were going to discuss was key in increasing his comfort level.

By the fourth session, Mike began to open up regarding his social alienation and "not wanting to do things with his friends because he felt different." The counselor acknowledged how difficult this must be and asked him about his cultural identity. Mike was surprised that she was aware of these issues and felt validated that she addressed them. As the counselor assessed Mike's level of ethnic identity, she was aware of not generalizing his experiences and constantly reflected upon her knowledge, skills, and expertise in working with Thai American individuals. Upon further discussion of what it meant for Mike to be different, the counselor also self-disclosed her college experiences of being "different" from her peers who were primarily White and other ethnicities. As a result of her self-disclosure, Mike felt "normal" that he was not the "only one" to experience ethnic and racial identity concerns as an Asian American. Such a strategy was evidence for Mike that his counselor was aware, culturally sensitive, had skills, knowledge, and experience in working with Asian American clients. In discussing culturally relevant topics, Mike felt his counselor "understood him."

Middle Phase of Therapy

As Mike continued to feel more comfortable and safe, Mike began to be more honest and share other reasons he felt "different" such as his feeling that his parents weren't "normal." He described that his parents primarily worked full-time, that they had financial struggles and that his father "got drunk a lot and got mad a lot" when he was growing up. As therapy progressed, Mike discussed more personal matters. The counselor was considerate in talking about his parents in a respectful manner as to not "shame" him or his parents to "an outsider or stranger." Instead, the counselor addressed acculturation, enculturation, and values in the context of Mike's wanting to individuate from his parents, but knowing he couldn't given his values of filial piety (duty to his parents).

Although the counselor was aware, had appropriate skills and knowledge to work with Asian Americans, she continued to ask Mike a number of questions regarding his culture, identity, and the role that his ethnic background played so that she would not make assumptions, and could check any potential biases or preconceived notions that she had regarding Thai American males. The counselor spent a great deal at the beginning of therapy exploring his history, family dynamics (including generational conflict), important values, and various identities. As the counselor continued to assess Mike, it was clear that Mike had both individualistic and collectivist qualities regarding his cultural identity and how to cope with his parents. The counselor helped Mike identify the strategies he has used in the past in dealing with his father and helped Mike to develop new coping skills with each session. Had the counselor not established trust, credibility, and exhibited cultural competence, Mike would have likely dropped out of counseling, or prematurely terminated in the initial stages of therapy.

By the eighth session, Mike had become accustomed to coming to counseling, although he continued to feel discomfort when he shared new personal information for the first time since talking about "stuff" was "so out of character for him." As the counselor continued to gather further family history, she found that the mental illness of Mike's father was more than his alcoholism. Mike's father had been diagnosed with Bipolar I disorder 5 years before. In their work together, she facilitated his self-awareness and decision making, and created avenues for Mike to empower himself by providing him with reading materials (bibliotherapy) on bipolar disorder as a mental illness. Given his trust toward the counselor, she was able to challenge him in thinking about future problems and how he would handle various life situations if they arose regarding his family and friends. As a result of therapy, Mike realized that he was worried about discussing his career plans with his parents and had withdrawn from them over the years because of his "on and off" relationship with his father. However, Mike still wanted his parents to see him as a "good son" and wondered if they viewed him in that manner. He feared embarrassing them as a result of his past actions and constantly worried about being different from his friends.

Last Phase of Therapy

Although a solid therapeutic alliance and good working relationship had been established, there were a few times when the counselor noticed that Mike did not agree with some of the suggestions offered by the counselor. However, Mike did not openly discuss his disagreements at first. The counselor gently confronted him, knowing that he was unlikely to disagree with her as an elder authority figure. Therefore, she checked in with him occasionally about any potential disagreement in continuing to strengthen their working relationship and maintain an effective therapeutic process. Finally, after much encouragement, Mike let her know if he was upset about something they discussed, yet still did not initiate such a conversation on his own; he only provided feedback when asked. The counselor did not pressure him about this matter further and accepted this as part of Mike's cultural identity and values.

Mike continued to see his therapist until he graduated. Mike had slowly begun to socialize again. He took steps toward rebuilding his relationship with his parents through role playing and brainstorming various approaches of handling his parents with his counselor, his weekly journaling, and "homework assignments" throughout therapy. The assigned weekly homework kept the process structured for Mike and this appealed to him greatly. **Termination** of therapy was difficult after all they had been through together. They discussed the termination process for a few sessions before they actually terminated. At termination they discussed their work together and his future goals. Mike stated that he finally understood his bicultural identity, meaning that he views himself as both "Thai" and "American." Over his counseling sessions, he has come to realize that he needs to manage his multiple social identities in balancing the pressure from his family to remain as "Thai" as possible and his desires to acculturate to his multicultural environment and social circle. Mike brought his counselor a thank you card and a drawing that he made. The counselor also wrote him a card indicating all that she had learned from him, highlighting his strengths. By the end of therapy, at the 14th session, Mike had worked through his disappointment in himself, found strength in being true to himself and became closer to his family as a result. He also experienced what counseling was like for the first time in his life as a 22-year-old Asian American male.

Case Study Discussion Questions

For undergraduate students, please consider the following questions:

1. What are your initial reactions to this case regarding Mike?
2. What role do you believe his ethnic identity and culture played in his relationship with his friends?
3. What do you think about the counselor's approach in working with Mike? What were the strategies employed by the counselor in working with Mike?
4. How are your attitudes about seeing a counselor similar to and different from Mike's? What would help you to see a counselor?

For graduate students, please consider the following questions:

1. If you are a beginning therapist, would you feel equipped to address Mike's presenting concerns? If yes, describe the skills and strategies you would employ. If no, describe what you think you might need to know in effectively working with Mike.
2. How would you conceptualize Mike's case? What aspects would you pay more or less attention to?
3. How would you apply your theoretical orientation in Mike's case? What theoretical orientations do you think would be best in working with someone like Mike?
4. Have you had clients similar to Mike? What did or did not prove to be effective in your work?

Key Terms

American Psychological Association: Located in Washington DC, the APA is the largest scientific and professional organization representing psychology in the United States. Its membership includes more than 150,000 researchers, educators, clinicians, consultants, and students. APA works to advance psychology as a science and profession and as a means of promoting health, education, and human welfare.

Client-counselor ethnic match: A match between clients and counselors based on similar ethnicities. Decisions to pair clients and counselors may be based on phenotype and genotype matching. Research in the past has supported the notion of pairing individuals based on similar ethnicities to decrease premature termination, and increase the effectiveness of therapy.

Clinical psychologist: Typical training lasts 5–7 years ending with a doctor in philosophy, a PhD, or PsyD degree in clinical psychology. They adhere to the standards and ethics established by the APA. They are educated and trained to generate and integrate scientific and professional knowledge and skills so as to further psychological science, the professional practice of psychology, and human welfare. Clinical psychologists are involved in research, teaching, and supervision, program development and evaluation, consultation, public policy, professional practice, and other activities that promote psychological health in individuals, families, groups, and organizations. Their work can range from prevention and early intervention of minor problems of adjustment to dealing with the adjustment and maladjustment of individuals whose disturbance requires them to be institutionalized (Society of Clinical Psychology, Division 12, 2007).

Collectivistic: A value orientation with an emphasis on an inextricable connectedness to each other.

Counseling psychologist: Typical training lasts 5–7 years ending with a doctor in philosophy, a PhD degree in counseling psychology. Counseling psychologists adhere to the standards and ethics established by the APA. They participate in a range of activities including teaching, research, psychotherapeutic and counseling practice, career development, assessment, supervision, and consultation. They employ a variety of methods closely tied to theory and research to help individuals, groups, and organizations function optimally as well as to mediate dysfunction. Interventions may be either brief or long-term; they are often problem-specific and goal-directed. These activities are guided by a philosophy that values individual differences and diversity and a focus on prevention, development, and adjustment across the life span, which includes vocational concerns (Society of Counseling Psychology Division 17, 2007).

Couples therapy: An option for couples experiencing psychological or physical challenges in their relationships. Problems in one's relationships can stem from communication difficulties, marital dissatisfaction, unhappiness between partners, disagreements in raising children, job changes, and other such life situations that create stress among a partnership and family. Essentially, such counseling includes premarital counseling, child counseling, divorce or separation counseling, and other relationship counseling. The goal for relationship counseling is to improve the relationships between partners or to help with the dissolution of a difficult relationship with minimum harm to all involved.

Ethnic identity: The subjective sense of ethnic group membership that involves self-labeling, sense of belonging, preference for the group, positive evaluation of the ethnic group, ethnic knowledge, and involvement in ethnic group activities.

Evidence-based practice in psychology: In 2005, the APA Task Report defined evidence-based practice in psychology as being the integration of the best available research with clinical expertise in the context of patient characteristics, culture, and preferences. For further information on evidenced-based practice in psychology, view http://www.apa.org/practice/ebpstatement.pdf.

Family therapy: An intervention orientation intended to help a family system restore its previous level of functioning and a therapeutic effort to enhance a family's environment to improve overall family functioning.

Group therapy: A mode of counseling where six to eight people meet with one or more trained leaders to talk about what is troubling them. Group members give feedback to each other by expressing their own feelings about what others say and do. This interaction gives group members an opportunity to try out new behaviors and to learn more about the ways they interact with others with guidance and facilitation by one or two group leaders. Content in the group therapy sessions is kept confidential, and sessions may be open or closed depending on the type of group.

Guidelines on Multicultural Education, Training, Research, Practice, and Organizational Change for Psychologists: Developed by APA with four primary goals: (a) rational and needs for addressing multiculturalism and diversity in education, training, research, practice, and organizational change; (b) basic information, relevant terminology, current empirical research from psychology and related disciplines; (c) references to enhance ongoing education, training, research, practice, and organizational change methodologies; and (d) paradigms that broaden psychology as a profession.

Individual psychotherapy: One-on-one counseling between the counselor and the client in which a learning process occurs. Individual psychotherapy is intended to change people cognitively, affectively, and behaviorally and a process whereby something new is learned, relearned, or unlearned with the goal being producing change at the individual's level of experience or at the level of the individual's environment depending on each client's case.

Individualistic: A value orientation referring to separateness or independence from each other.

Intake: Usually the first session of counseling in which background and relevant information is obtained. Usually during the intake, the client and counselor discuss goals, a treatment plan, or referral.

Loss of face: The importance of one's moral reputation and social integrity that is gained and maintained by the performance of specific roles recognized in interpersonal dynamics between family members and society.

Marriage and family therapist: Therapist that treats a wide range of serious clinical problems, including depression, marital problems, anxiety, individual psychological problems, and child-parent problems. MFTs are a group of practitioners who evaluate and treat mental and emotional disorders, other health and behavioral problems, and address a wide array of relationship issues within the context of the family system. MFTs have graduate training (a master's or doctoral degree) in marriage and family therapy and at least 2 years of clinical experience. Marriage and family therapists are recognized as a "core" mental health professional along with psychiatry, psychology, social work, and psychiatric nursing (American Association for Marriage and Family Therapy, 2007).

Multiculturalism: The psychology of examining cultural identities, differences, understanding worldviews and stating that multiple belief systems exist across people and cultures.

Psychologist: A psychologist is a scientist and/or clinician who studies psychology, the systematic investigation of the human mind, including behavior, and cognition. Psychologists are trained to help people cope effectively with life problems using techniques based on research, their clinical skills and experience while taking into account the person's unique values, goals, and circumstances. Psychologists work in many settings including research institutions, private practices, universities, community mental health centers, hospitals, government agencies, schools, military organizations, in corporations and other workplaces.

Premature termination: When an individual drops out of counseling or treatment prior to achieving needs and goals.

Psychiatrist: Psychiatrists are doctors of medicine (MDs) or osteopathy (DOs) and are certified in treating mental illness using the biomedical approach to mental disorders. Psychiatrists may also go through significant training to conduct psychotherapy (for example psychoanalysis or cognitive-behavioral therapy), but it is their medical training that differentiates them from other mental health professionals. In their evaluation of the patient, psychiatrists may prescribe psychiatric medications, conduct physical exams, order/interpret laboratory tests, and/or brain imaging, scans and order other medically necessary tests.

Racial identity: The collective identity of any group of people socialized to think of themselves as a racial group.

Social workers: Social workers are found in public agencies, private businesses, hospitals, clinics, schools, nursing homes, private practices, police departments, courts, and other workplaces. Social workers serve individuals, families, and communities and have degrees in social work from a college or university program accredited by the Council on Social Work Education. The undergraduate degree is the Bachelor of Social Work (BSW). Graduate degrees include the Master of Social Work (MSW) and the Doctorate in Social Work (DSW) or PhD. An MSW is required to provide therapy and most states require practicing social workers to be licensed, certified, or registered.

Termination: The process in which a client ends therapy. Typically the counselor and client come to an agreement on the completion of therapy. Termination of therapy generally occurs over a few counseling sessions prior to completion.

Worldviews: Often defined by how a person perceives his or her relationships with the world (nature, time orientation, social relationships, etc.). Worldviews can also be characterized as personal assumptions, beliefs, and philosophies that affects how one thinks about the world and what it means to the individual.

For Further Learning and Suggested Readings

Books and Readings

Hall, G. C., & Okazaki, S. (Eds.). (2002). *Asian American psychology: The science of lives in context.* Washington, DC: American Psychological Association.

Hong, G. K., & Ham, M. D. (2001). *Psychotherapy and counseling with Asian American clients: A practical guide.* Thousand Oaks, CA: Sage Publications.

Lee, E. (Ed.). (2000). *Working with Asian Americans.* New York: Guilford Press.

Leong, F. T. L., Inman, A., Ebreo, A., Yang, L. H., Kinoshita, L., & Fu, M. (Eds.). (2007). *Handbook of Asian American psychology* (2nd ed.). Thousand Oaks, CA: Sage Publications.

Min, P. G., & Kim, R. (Eds.). (2006). *Asian Americans: Contemporary trends and issues* (2nd ed.). Thousand Oaks, CA: Pine Forge Press.

Mahalingam, R. (Ed.) (2006). *Cultural psychology of immigrants.* New Jersey: Lawrence Erlbaum and Associates.

Mio, J. S., & Iwamasa, G. Y. (Eds.). (2003). *Culturally diverse mental health: The challenges of research and resistance.* New York: Brunner-Routledge.

Roysircar, G., Sandhu, D. S., & Bibbins, V. E. (Eds.). (2003). *Multicultural competencies: A guidebook of practices.* Virginia: Association of Multicultural Counseling and Development.

Surgeon General's Report—Mental Health Report: Culture, Race and Ethnicity (2001).

Uba, L. (2002). *A postmodern psychology of Asian Americans: Creating knowledge of a racial ethnic minority.* Albany, NY: State University of New York Press.

Movies

American Chai (2001)

APA videos at http://www.apa.org/videos. (2005 Fall). Working with Asian American clients with Jean Lau Chin. *Series V: Multicultural Counseling.*

Daughter from Danang (2002)

The Debut (2000)

Double Happiness (1994)

The Joy Luck Club (1993)

First Person Plural (2000)

Namesake (2007)

The Way Home (2003)

Web sites on Multicultural Psychology, Mental Health, and General Health

American Psychological Association: http://www.aapaonline.org

South Asian Psychological Networking Association: http://www.oursapna.org

Mental health educational materials in English, but in video format: http://anxietybc.com/parent/

A variety of mental health and health information in 20 different languages by GlaxoSmithKline: http://www.programstogo.com/zones/multilangconsumer/default.jsp

A variety of mental health and health-related topics in English only, but some are also in video format. Most are sponsored by unrestricted funds from pharmaceutical companies: http://www.healthology.com/main/condition_centers.aspx:

Early child care information in five different languages by the International Child Resource Institute: http://www.globalhealthychildcare.org

Cross cultural resources for primary health care by the School of Medicine at UCSF: http://medicine.ucsf.edu/resources/guidelines/culture.html

Hogg Foundation for Mental Health—The University of Texas at Austin: Services, Research, Policy, and Education—Cultural adaptation: Providing evidence-based practices to populations of color: http://www.hogg.utexas.edu/programs_cc.html

References

Abe-Kim, J., Takeuchi, D. T., Hong, S., Zane, N., Sue, S., Spencer, M.S., et al. (2007). Use of mental health-related services among immigrant and US-born Asian Americans: Results from the National Latino and Asian American Study. *American Journal of Public Health, 97*(1), 91–98.

Abe-Kim, J., Takeuchi, D., & Hwang, W. (2002). Predictors of help seeking for emotional distress among Chinese Americans: Family matters. *Journal of Consulting and Clinical Psychology, 70*(5), 1186–1190.

Akutsu, P. D., Tsuru, G. K., & Chu, J.C. (2006). Prioritized assignment to intake appointments for Asian Americans at an ethnic-specific mental health program. *Journal of Consulting and Clinical Psychology, 74*(6), 1108–1115.

Alvarez, A. N., & Kimura, E. F. (2001). Asian Americans and racial identity: Dealing with racism and snowballs. *Journal of Mental Health Counseling, 23*(3), 192–206.

American Association for Marriage and Family Therapy. (2007). *FAQ's on MFT's.* Retrieved July 12, 2007, from http://www.aamft.org/faqs/index_nm.asp#

APA Policy by the APA Council of Representatives. (2002). *Guidelines on multicultural education, training, research, practice, and organizational change for psychologists.* Washington, DC: American Psychological Association.

APA Presidential Task Force on Evidence-Based Practice. (2006). Evidence-based practice in psychology. *American Psychologist, 61,* 271–285. Washington, DC: American Psychological Association.

APA Task Force on Socioeconomic Status. (2006). *Report of the APA task force on socioeconomic status.* Washington, DC: American Psychological Association.

Atkins, D. C., Berns, S. B., George, W. H., Doss, B. D., Gattis, K., & Christensen, A. (2005). Prediction of response to treatment in a randomized clinical trial of marital therapy. *Journal of Consulting and Clinical Psychology, 73*(5), 893–903.

Atkinson, D. R. (2004). *Counseling American minorities.* New York: McGraw Hill.

Atkinson, D. R., Morten, G., & Sue, D. S. (1989). *Counseling American minorities: A cross cultural perspective.* Dubuque, IA: Wm. C. Brown Publishers.

Brinson, J. A., & Kottler, J. A. (1995). Minorities underutilization of counseling centers' mental health services: A case for outreach and consultation. *Journal of Mental Health Counseling, 371–385.*

Chang, E. C., Chang, R. & Chu, J. C. (2007). In search of personality in Asian Americans: What we know and what we don't know. In F. T. L. Leong, A. Inman, A. Ebreo, L. H. Yang, L. Kinoshita, & M. Fu (Eds.). *Handbook of Asian American psychology* (2nd ed., pp. 265–282). Thousand Oaks, CA: Sage Publications.

Chang, T., & Yeh, C. J. (2003). Using online groups to provide support to Asian American men: Racial, cultural, gender and treatment issues. *Professional Psychology, Research and Practice, 34*(6), 634–643.

Chun, K. M., Eastman, K. L., Wang, G. C. S., & Sue, S. (1998). Psychopathology. In L. C. Lee & N. W. S. Zane (Eds.), *Handbook of Asian American psychology* (pp. 457–483). Thousand Oaks, CA: Sage Publications.

Cokley, K. (2007). Critical issues in the measurement of ethnic and racial identity: A referendum on the state of the field. *Journal of Counseling Psychology, 54*(3), 224–234.

Corsini, R. J., & Wedding, D. (1989). *Current psychotherapies* (4th ed). Itasca, IL: F. E. Peacock Publishers.

Cynkar, A. (2007). Demand a seat. *The Monitor.* Washington, DC: American Psychological Association.

Division 29, Division of Psychotherapy. (2007). *Approaches to psychotherapy.* Retrieved on July 12, 2007, from http://www.divisionofpsychotherapy.org/student/Approaches.htm

Fouad, N. A., Gerstein, L. H., Toporek, R. L. (2006). Social justice and counseling psychology in context. In R. L. Toporek, L. H. Gerstein, N. A. Fouad, G. Roysircar, & T. Israel (Eds.). (2006). *Handbook for social justice in counseling psychology: Leadership, vision, and action* (pp. 1–16). Thousand Oaks, CA: Sage Publications.

Gallardo, M. E., Yeh, C. J., Parham, T. A., Trimble, J. (in preparation). Working culturally and competently with persons of African, Asian, Latino and Native descent: The culturally (adaptive) responsive model of counseling.

Gamst, G., Dana, R. H., Der-Karabetian, A., & Kramer, T. (2001). Asian American mental health clients: Effects of client match and age on global assessment and visitation. *Journal of Mental Health Counseling, 23,* 57–71.

Goldenberg, I., & Goldenberg, H. (1985). *Family therapy: An overview* (2nd ed.). California: Brooks/Cole Publishing.

Gurung, R. A. R., & Mehta, V. (2001). Relating ethnic identity, acculturation, and attitudes toward treating minority clients. *Cultural Diversity and Ethnic Minority Psychology, 7*(2), 139–151.

Guthrie, R. V. (1998). *Even the rat was white: A historical view of psychology* (2nd ed.). Needham Heights, MA: Allyn & Bacon.

Hall, G. N., & Eap, S. (2007). Empirically supported therapies for Asian Americans. In F. T. L. Leong, A. Inman, A. Ebreo, L. H. Yang, L. Kinoshita, & M. Fu (Eds.), *Handbook of Asian American psychology* (2nd ed., pp. 449–468). Thousand Oaks, CA: Sage Publications.

Helms, J. E., & Cook, D. A. (1999). *Using race and culture in counseling and psychotherapy: Theory and process.* Needham Heights, MA: Allyn & Bacon.

Horne, A., & Ohlsen, M. (1982). *Family counseling and therapy.* Illinois: F. E. Peacock Publishers.

Hoshmand, L. T. (Ed.). (2006). Culture and the field of psychotherapy and counseling. In L. T. Hoshmand (Ed.), *Culture, psychotherapy and counseling: Critical and integrative perspectives* (pp. 25–46). Thousand Oaks, CA: Sage Publications.

Hwang, W. C. (2007, May 18). Mental illness, racial identity and the Virginia Tech shooting. *Seattle Times.* Retrieved on July 30, 2007 from http://archives.seattletimes.nwsource.com/cgi-bin/texis.cgi/web/vortex/display?slug=asian18&date=20070518

Ibrahim, F. A. (1985). Effective cross-cultural counseling and psychotherapy: A framework. *The Counseling Psychologist, 13,* 625–638.

Inman, A. G. (2006). South Asian women: Identities and conflicts. *Cultural Diversity and Ethnic Minority Psychology, 12,* 306–319.

Inman, A. G., & Tewari, N. (2003). The power of context: Multicultural issues in marriage and family counseling with South Asian families. In G. Roysircar-Sodowsky, D. S. Sandhu, & V. S. Bibbins (Eds.), *A guidebook: Practices of multicultural competencies (MCC Guidebook).* Virginia: American Counseling Association Publishers.

Inman, A. G., Yeh, C. J, Madan-Bahel A., & Nath, S. (2007). Bereavement and Coping of South Asian Families post 9/11. *Journal of Multicultural Counseling and Development, 35,* 101–115.

Ivey, A. E., Ivey, M. B., & Simek-Morgan, L. (1997). *Counseling and psychotherapy: A multicultural perspective.* Needham Heights: Allyn & Bacon.

Kearney, L. K., Draper, M., & Baron, A. (2005). Counseling utilization by ethnic minority college students. *Cultural Diversity and Ethnic Minority Psychology, 11*(3), 272–285.

Kim, B. S. K. (2007). Acculturation and enculturation. In F. T. L. Leong, A. Inman, A. Ebreo, L. H. Yang, L. Kinoshita, & M. Fu (Eds.). *Handbook of Asian American psychology* (2nd ed., pp. 141–158). Thousand Oaks, CA: Sage Publications.

Kim, B. S. K., Atkinson, D. R., & Umemoto, D. (2001). Asian cultural values and the counseling process: Current knowledge and directions for future research. *Counseling Psychologist, 29,* 570–603.

Kim, B. S. K., Atkinson, D. R., & Yang, P. H. (1999). The Asian Values Scale: Development, factor analysis, validation and reliability. *Journal of Counseling Psychology, 46,* 342–352.

Kim, B. S. K., & Li, L. C., & Ng, G. F. (2005a). The Asian Values Scale—Multidimensional: Development, reliability and validity. *Cultural Diversity & Ethnic Minority Psychology, 11,* 187–201.

Kim, B. S. K., Ng, G. F., & Ahn, A. J. (2005b). Effects of client expectation for counseling success, client-counselor worldview match, and client adherence to Asian and European American cultural values on the counseling process with Asian Americans. *Journal of Counseling Psychology, 52*(1), 67–76.

Kim, B. S. K., & Omizo, M. M. (2003). Asian cultural values, attitudes toward seeking professional psychological help, and willingness to see a counselor. *The Counseling Psychologist, 31,* 343–361.

Le, C. N. (2007). Socioeconomic statistics & demographics. *Asian-Nation: The Landscape of Asian America.* Retrieved July 25, 2007, from http://www.asian-nation.org/demographics.shtml

Leong, F. T. L. (1994). Asian-Americans' differential patterns of utilization of inpatient and outpatient public mental health services in Hawaii. *Journal of Community Psychology, 22,* 82–89.

Leong, F. T. L., Inman, A., Ebreo, A., Yang, L. H., Kinoshita, L., & Fu, M. (Eds.). (2007). Introduction and overview. In F. T. L. Leong, A. Inman, A. Ebreo, L. H. Yang, L. Kinoshita, & M. Fu (Eds.). *Handbook of Asian American psychology* (2nd ed., pp. 1–8). Thousand Oaks, CA: Sage Publications.

Leong, F. T. L., Wagner, N. S., & Tata, S. P. (1995). Racial and ethnic variations in help-seeking attitudes. In J. G. Ponterotto, J. M., Casas, L. A., Suzuki, & C. M. Alexander (Eds.), *Handbook of multicultural counseling* (pp. 415–438). Thousand Oaks, CA: Sage Publications.

Liu, W. M. (2002). The social class-related experiences of men: Integrating theory and practice. *Professional Psychology: Research and Practice, 33,* 355–360.

Liu, W. M., & Ali, S. R. (2005). Addressing social class and classism in vocational theory and practice: Extending the emancipatory communitarian approach. *Counseling Psychologist, 33,* 189–196.

Loo, C., Tong, B., & True, R. (1989). A bitter bean: Mental health status and attitudes in Chinatown. *Journal of Community Psychology, 17,* 283–296.

Maramba, G. G., & Hall, G. N. (2002). Meta-analysis of ethnic match as a predictor of dropout, utilization, and level of functioning. *Cultural Diversity and Ethnic Minority Psychology, 8,* 290–297.

Matsuoka, J. K., Breaux, C., & Ryujin, D. H. (1997). National utilization of mental health services by Asian Americans/Pacific Islanders. *Journal of Community Psychology, 25*(2), 141–145.

Meyers, L. (2006). Asian-American mental health. *Monitor on Psychology, 37*(2), 44–46.

Myers, D. G. (2006). *Psychology.* New York: W.H. Freeman and Company.

Nagata, D. (1989a). Japanese American children and adolescents. In Jewelle T. Gibbs, Larke N. Huang, and Associates (Eds.), *Children of color: Psychological interventions with minority children* (pp. 67–113). San Francisco: Jossey-Bass.

O'Sullivan, M. J., Peterson, P. D., Cox, G. B., & Kirekby, J. (1989). Ethnic populations: Community mental health services ten years later. *Journal of Community Psychology, 17*(1), 17–30.

Parham, T. A., White, J. L., & Ajamu, A. (1999). *The psychology of Blacks: An African-American perspective,* 3rd ed. New Jersey: Prentice Hall.

Phinney, J. S. (1996). When we talk about ethnic groups, what do we mean? *American Psychologist, 51,* 918–927.

Ponterotto, J. G., Casas, J. M., Suzuki, L. A., & Alexander, C. M. (Eds.). (1995). *Handbook of multicultural counseling.* Thousand Oaks, CA: Sage Publications.

Ponterotto, J. G., & Mallinckrodt, B. (2007). Introduction to the special section on racial and ethnic identity in counseling psychology: Conceptual and methodological challenges and proposed solutions. *Journal of Counseling Psychology, 54*(3), 219–223.

Prochaska, J. O. (1984). *Systems of psychotherapy: A transtheoretical analyses* (2nd ed.). Pacific Grove, CA: Brooks/Cole.

Reeves, T. J., & Bennett, C. E. (2004). *We the people: Asians in the United States, Census 2000 Special Reports.* Washington, DC: U. S. Census Bureau.

Snowden, L. R., & Cheung, F. K. (1990). Use of inpatient mental health services by members of ethnic minority groups. *American Psychologist, 45*(3), 347–355.

Society of Clinical Psychology, Division 12, A Division of the American Psychological Association. (2007). *About clinical psychology.* Retrieved July 12, 2007, from http://www.apa.org/divisions/div12/aboutcp.html

Society of Counseling Psychology, Division 17, A Division of the American Psychological Association. (2007). *About counseling psychologists.* Retrieved July 12, 2007, from http://www.div17.org/students_defining.html

Sue, D. W., & Sue, D. (1999). *Counseling the culturally different: Theory and practice* (3rd ed.). New York: Wiley and Sons.

Sue, S. (1973). Training of "third world" students to function as counselors. *Journal of Counseling Psychology, 20,* 73–78. Community mental health services to minority groups.

Sue, S., (1977). Community mental health services to minority groups. Some optimism, some pessimism. *American Psychologist, 32*(8), 616–624.

Sue, S., & Zane, N. W. (2006). Ethnic minority populations have been neglected by evidence-based practices. In J. C. Norcross, L. E. Beutler, & R. F. Levant (Eds.), *Evidence-based practices in mental health: Debate and dialogue in the fundamental questions* (pp. 338–345, 359–361). Washington, DC: American Psychological Association.

Sue, S., Zane, N. W., & Hall, G. (2006). *Generating a movement within a movement: Evidence based practices in psychology and cultural competence.* Paper presentation at the Asian American Psychological Association Convention, New Orleans, LA.

Takeuchi, D. (2007, January). *Developmental context and mental disorders among Asian Americans.* Paper presentation in the symposium, Asian American Immigrant Families and Mental Health in Developmental Context, National Multicultural Conference and Summit, Seattle, WA.

Tarn, D. M., Meredith, L. S., Kagawa-Singer, M., Matsumura, S., Bito, S., Oye, R. K., & et al. (2005). Trust in one's physician: The role of ethnic match, autonomy, acculturation, and religiosity among Japanese and Japanese Americans. *Annals of Family Medicine, 3,* 339–347.

Tewari, N. (2000). *Asian Indian Americans clients presenting at a university counseling center: An exploration of their concerns and a comparison to other groups.* Unpublished doctoral dissertation, Southern Illinois University, Carbondale.

Tewari, N., Inman, A. G., & Sandhu, D. S. (2003). South Asian Americans: Culture, concerns and therapeutic strategies. In J. Mio & G. Iwamasa (Eds.), *Culturally diverse mental health: The challenges of research and resistance* (pp. 191–209). New York: Brunner-Routledge.

Toporek, R. L., & Williams, R. A. (2006). Ethics and professional issues related to the practice of social justice in counseling psychology. In R. L. Toporek, L. H. Gerstein, N. A. Fouad, G. Roysircar, & T. Israel (Eds.). (2006). *Handbook for social justice in counseling psychology: Leadership, vision, and action* (pp. 17–34). Thousand Oaks, CA: Sage Publications.

Trimble, J. E. (2007). Prolegomena for the connotation of construct use in the measurement of ethnic and racial identity. *Journal of Counseling Psychology, 54*(3), 247–258.

Uba, L. (1997). *Asian Americans: Personality patterns, identity, and mental health.* New York: Guilford Press.

U.S. Census Bureau. (2000). *Census 2000.* Washington, DC.

U.S. Department of Mental Health and Human Services. (2001). *Mental health: Culture, race and ethnicity—A supplement to mental health: A report of the Surgeon General—Executive Summary.* Rockville, MD: U.S. Department of Health and Human Services.

Vogel, D. L., Wade, N. G., & Haake, S. (2006). Measuring the self-stigma associated with seeking psychological help. *Journal of Counseling Psychology, 53*(3), 325–337.

White, J. L., & Parham, T. A. (1990). *The psychology of Blacks: An African-American perspective*, 2nd ed. New Jersey: Prentice-Hall.

Yalom, I. D. (1985). *The theory and practice of group psychotherapy.* United States: Basic Books.

Yang, L. H., & WonPat-Borja, A. J. (2007). Psychopathology among Asian Americans. In F. T. L. Leong, A. Inman, A. Ebreo, L. H. Yang, L. Kinoshita, M. Fu (Eds.), *Handbook of Asian American psychology* (2nd ed., pp. 379–405). Thousand Oaks, CA: Sage Publications.

Yeh, C. J., & Huang, L. K. (1996). The collectivistic nature of ethnic identity development among Asian-American college students. *Adolescence, 31,* 645–661.

Yeh, C. J., Inman, A. G., Kim, A. B., & Okubo, Y. (2006). Asian American families collectivistic coping strategies in response to 9/11. *Cultural Diversity and Ethnic Minority Psychology, 12*(1), 134–148.

Zane, N. W., Sue, S., Chang, J., Huang, L., Huang, J., Lowe, S., & et al. (2005). Beyond ethnic match: Effects of client-therapist cognitive match in problem perception, coping orientation, and therapy goals on treatment outcomes. *Journal of Community Psychology, 33* (5), 569–585.

Zane, N. W. S., & Yeh, M. (2002). The use of culturally-based variables in assessment: Studies on loss of face. In K. S. Kurasaki & S. Okazaki (Eds.), *Asian American mental health: Assessment theories and methods* (pp. 123–138). New York: Kluwer Academic/Plenum.

Zhang, A. Y., Snowden, L. R., & Sue, S. (1998). Differences between Asian- and White – Americans' help-seeking and utilization patterns in the Los Angeles area. *Journal of Community Psychology, 26,* 317–326.

Author Index

Subject Index

Page numbers followed by f indicate figures; those followed by t indicate tables.

impact on counseling process, 107–108
indigenous healing and, 560–562
masculinity and, 219–220
parenting and, 301, 319, 321
passing down to children, 327–328
patriarchy, 196–197, 198, 203, 217, 304, 321
relational orientation, 298, 304, 305, 307, 310
religion and, 145–146
Culture-bound syndromes, 526, 560, 562–564, 567, 570
Culture shock, 196

D

Daily racism, 401, 401t, 415
D'Amato, Alfonse, 425
Das Bagai, Vaisho, 12
Dating, 201, 216–217, 225, 252, 273–274, 303–304.
    See also Marriage; Relationships
  abuse and, 286–287
  acculturation and, 279
  attractiveness and media influences on, 280
  case study of, 273
  community influences on, 281
  ethnic identity and, 279–280
  experiences with interdating and friendships, 280
  family influences on, 280–281
  influence of density and propinquity on, 281
  sexuality and, 250, 255–257
Daughter of Fu Manchu, The, 428
David, E. J. R., 60–61
Day of Independence, 431
Death and dying, 510–512
  acculturation and rituals of, 511–512
  honoring the dead, 511
  religious beliefs and, 510
Deconstruction, 90–92, 95
Depression, 75, 76, 519, 527–528
  acculturation and, 522
  among caregivers, 307
  among children, 299, 300
  definition of, 458
  of parachute kids, 371, 372
  parenting style and, 300
  physical health and, 499
  physical symptoms of, 563
  racism and, 409
  related to strategies for coping with racism, 411
  among Southeast Asian refugees, 447, 452–453, 523
Des Jardins, Kunya, 43
Details, 215–216
Detroit Summer, 489
Dharma, 137, 138

Dhat, 563
DHP (Digital History Project), 42, 47
Diabetes, 204, 504–505
Diagnostic and Statistical Manual of Mental Disorders (DSM-IV), 237, 445, 452, 526, 563
Diet, 513
Digital History Project (DHP), 42, 47
Dim Sum, 431
Discrimination, 124, 212, 422
  against Asian adoptees, 349–350
  colonial mentality and, 163
  definition of, 423, 435
  glass ceiling and, 12, 24, 25, 213, 405, 416, 472–473, 478, 524
  health effects of, 409
  against lesbian, gay, bisexual, and transgender persons, 233, 237–239
  mental health effects of, 524
  mobilization against, 485–487
  model minority image and, 523–524
  parenting and, 328–329
  peer, 74, 82
  perpetual foreigner stereotype and, 76, 487
  racism, 399–416
  reverse, 73
  against war brides, 195–196
  in workplace, 213, 405
Dissonance status of racial identity, 117–118, 130, 221, 228
Diversity of Asian Americans and Pacific Islanders, 71–73, 72t, 115, 295, 576
  family demographic profiles, 296–297, 297t, 319, 319t
  immigration history, 98
  salience of various social identities, 175–176
  socioeconomic status, 71–73
  within-group differences, 174, 191
Division of South Asian Americans (DoSAA), 43, 46, 47
Division of Students (DoS), 43, 46, 47
Division of Women (DoW), 31, 41, 43–44, 46, 47
Divorce, 276, 277t, 278, 287–288, 523
Domestic violence, 202–203, 262, 304
DoSAA (Division of South Asian Americans), 43, 46, 47
DoS (Division of Students), 43, 46, 47
"Dotbusters," 13
"Double eyelid," 541–542, 549f, 550
Double Happiness, 428
DoW (Division of Women), 31, 41, 43–44, 46, 47, 204, 205
Drag culture, 238
Drag kings, 234, 236f
Dragon: The Bruce Lee Story, 429